PERSONNEL MANAGEMENT

McGRAW-HILL SERIES IN MANAGEMENT

Keith Davis and Fred Luthans, Consulting Editors

LEE AND DOBLER   Purchasing and Materials Management: Text and Cases
LEVIN, McLAUGHLIN, LAMONE, AND KOTTAS   Production/Operations Management:
    Contemporary Policy for Managing Operating Systems
LUTHANS   Introduction to Management: A Contingency Approach
LUTHANS   Organizational Behavior
LUTHANS AND THOMPSON   Contemporary Readings in Organizational Behavior
McNICHOLS   Executive Policy and Strategic Planning
McNICHOLS   Policymaking and Executive Action
MAIER   Problem-Solving Discussions and Conferences: Leadership Methods and Skills
MARGULIES AND RAIA   Conceptual Foundations of Organizational Development
MAYER   Production and Operations Management
MILES   Theories of Management: Implications for Organizational Behavior
    and Development
MILES AND SNOW   Organizational Strategy, Structure, and Process
MILLS   Labor-Management Relations
MITCHELL   People in Organizations: An Introduction to Organizational Behavior
MOLANDER   Responsive Capitalism: Case Studies in Corporate Social Conduct
MONKS   Operations Management: Theory and Problems
NEWSTROM, REIF, AND MONCZKA   A Contingency Approach to Management: Readings
PETIT   The Moral Crisis in Management
PETROF, CARUSONE, AND McDAVID   Small Business Management: Concepts and
    Techniques for Improving Decisions
PORTER, LAWLER, AND HACKMAN   Behavior in Organizations
PRASOW AND PETERS   Arbitration and Collective Bargaining: Conflict Resolution
    in Labor Relations
QUICK AND QUICK   Organizational Stress and Preventive Management
REDDIN   Managerial Effectiveness
SARTAIN AND BAKER   The Supervisor and the Job
SAYLES   Leadership: What Effective Managers Really Do ... and How They Do It
SCHLESINGER, ECCLES, AND GABARRO   Managing Behavior in Organizations:
    Text, Cases, Readings
SCHROEDER   Operations Management: Decision Making in the Operations Function
SHORE   Operations Management
SHULL, DELBECQ, AND CUMMINGS   Organizational Decision Making
STEERS AND PORTER   Motivation and Work Behavior
STEINHOFF   Small Business Management Fundamentals
SUTERMEISTER   People and Productivity
TANNENBAUM, WESCHLER, AND MASSARIK   Leadership and Organization
VANCE   Corporate Leadership: Boards, Directors, and Strategy
WALKER   Human Resource Planning
WERTHER AND DAVIS   Personnel Management and Human Resources
WOFFORD, GERLOFF, AND CUMMINS   Organizational Communications: The Keystone to
    Managerial Effectiveness

Edwin B. Flippo

Professor of Management
University of Arizona

PERSONNEL MANAGEMENT

Sixth Edition

McGraw-Hill Book Company

New York • St. Louis • San Francisco • Auckland •
Bogotá • Hamburg • London •
Madrid • Mexico • Montreal • New Delhi •
Panama • Paris • São Paulo • Singapore • Sydney •
Tokyo • Toronto

PERSONNEL MANAGEMENT

67890DOCDOC898

ISBN 0-07-021321-6

This book was set in Times Roman by Waldman Graphics, Inc.
The editors were Kathi A. Benson and John R. Meyer;
the designer was Merrill Haber; the production supervisor
was Leroy A. Young. Project supervision was done by
The Total Book.
R. R. Donnelley & Sons Company was printer and binder.

Library of Congress Cataloging in Publication Data

Flippo, Edwin B.
    Personnel management.

    (McGraw-Hill series in management)
    Bibliography: p.
    Includes bibliographies and indexes.
    1. Personnel management. I. Title. II. Series.
HF5549.F583 1984   658.3   83-11286
ISBN 0-07-021321-6

Contents

PART ONE   INTRODUCTION

PART TWO   PROCUREMENT

PART FIVE   INTEGRATION

PART SIX   MAINTENANCE

x
Contents

List of Exercises and Cases

Preface

Though updated, this text continues to rely upon the basic framework that has characterized it from its first edition in 1961. It has proved to be sufficiently flexible and comprehensive to absorb the many changes occurring in the field during the last two decades. The basic framework consists of the following sequence of functions:

1. *Procurement* of personnel
2. *Development* through training and education
3. *Compensation* to insure equity and incentive
4. *Integration* to align interests of employees, management, and the union
5. *Maintenance* to insure continuation of this able and willing workforce
6. *Separation* to return personnel to society when no longer required

The text can be summarized in one somewhat lengthy sentence: *Personnel management is the planning, organizing, directing, and controlling of the procurement, development, compensation, integration, maintenance, and separation of human resources, to the end that individual, organizational, and societal objectives are accomplished.*

Major new features of the current edition include a new chapter on Quality of Work Life and Quality Circles, as well as a new half-chapter on human resources planning. In addition, new emphasis is provided on the following subjects: sexual harassment, pregnant employees, Supreme Court decisions concerning Affirmative Action, behavior modeling in training, behavioral expectancy and observation scales in performance appraisal, dual career families, plateaued careers, comparable value in compensation, new services such as vanpooling and child care, attribution theory, path-goal leadership theory, concessionary bargaining with unions, grievance processing in nonunion firms, OSHA rule changes and Supreme Court decisions dealing with economics versus safety, and predictions for the coming decade.

A special attempt has been made to add more figures and tables, with over fifty new ones included. All supplementary readings have been changed and updated. Another feature is the addition of a brief case for each chapter as discussion starters. With respect to the longer cases and exercises, two new exercises have been added (weighted application blanks and promotion) and one new case (The New Engineer). A final additional feature is the insertion of major excerpts from popular business magazines and newspapers, particularly *Business Week, Fortune,* and *The Wall Street Journal.* Twenty of the twenty-four chapters have boxes for material from these sources.

I continue to recognize the impact and contributions of former colleagues such as Ralph Davis, Ohio State University; Keith Davis, Arizona State University; Michael Jucius, Ohio State and Arizona Universities; and William Voris, The American Graduate School of International Management. I acknowledge and welcome the comments of reviewers including: Professor George Beason, Wichita State University; Professor Joseph Crowley, Community College of Philadelphia; Professor Keith Davis, Arizona State University; Professor Thomas W. Faranda, Faranda and Associates; Professor Robert Howard, Loyola University of Chicago; Professor Richard J. Melucci, Adelphi University; Professor Leonard Rico, University of Pennsylvania; Professor Foster C. Rinefort, Eastern Illinois University; Dr. Nathaniel Stewart, Stewart and Associates Consultants; and Professor Jerry Wofford, The University of Texas at Arlington. I am indebted to many professors, managers, and students throughout the nation and the world who have submitted comments and suggestions. It is my continued hope that the framework for understanding the human resources field presented in this book will prove to be of value to students, teachers, and practitioners.

Edwin B. Flippo

PERSONNEL
MANAGEMENT

PART ONE

INTRODUCTION

The history of personnel management is short in one sense, but long in another. Modern personnel management dates back only to the 1940s; personnel problems requiring managerial attention date back to the time of the industrial revolution. In this part of the text we shall examine the managerial and operative functions of personnel. The status of the field will be analyzed in the light of its past as well as with reference to such modern challenges as are posed by changes in human values, technical demands of large corporations, increasing governmental controls, changes in the work force skill mix, and pressures toward social responsibility. It concludes with a look at the specialized unit, the personnel department, that is primarily responsible for dealing with these issues.

chapter 1

The Nature and Challenge of Personnel Management

At one time in our history, ''liking people'' appeared to be sufficient for choosing to work in the field known as personnel management. Preferring to work with humans rather than objects is still important, but it is grossly insufficient in these modern times. Personnel management is one of our most complex and challenging fields of endeavor. Not only must the firm's requirements for an effective work force be met, the personnel manager must be greatly concerned with the expectations of both employees and society in general. Society at large has proclaimed its human resources to have vital needs that move beyond a ''work force'' status. The employee is simultaneously an instrument of the firm, a human being, and a citizen.

The role of the personnel manager has thus changed through time. At first, the dominant role was to satisfy top management in procuring and maintaining a work force that would be instrumental to organizational productivity. As knowledge expanded in executing this role, the manager began to understand the necessity for ascertaining and accommodating to the needs of the human beings who constituted that work force. He or she constantly searched for that program which would support the accomplishment of *both* organizational and individual objectives. The job was made more difficult by such factors as the rise of the modern labor union, the increasing educational level of societal members, the increasing size and complexity of the organization and its technology, and the insistent and sometimes violent demands of less privileged segments of our society. This last-named factor has led to the final major alteration of the personnel manager's role. Though society ''permits'' and encourages the use of its citizens as means to organizational ends, the fact that they constitute an instrumental work force in no way detracts from the fact that they are (1) human beings with certain inalienable rights, and (2) society's citizens with assigned rights and privileges. In this newly expanded role, the personnel manager will at worst act as the organization's social conscience, and at best will work as an informed specialist, with all members of the organization in determining and meeting the demands of this social role.

The modern personnel manager therefore requires a broad background in such fields as psychology, sociology, philosophy, economics, and management. He or she must

3

deal with issues and problems that often do not have "right answers" obvious to all. There will be required an ability to understand that which is not logical, a capacity to project oneself into other positions without losing perspective, and a skill in predicting human and organizational behavior. Reading or studying a text such as this will not magically change one into an effective personnel executive. Study should be of material assistance, however, in giving a perspective from which to view the field, in suggesting possible answers to current problems, and helping to define the way toward further improvement and research. Certainly, in this text the technical content of the field will be thoroughly discussed. The personnel manager who does not meet the demands of this initially assigned role may not be around to worry about the other two. We shall also emphasize and attempt to define the nature of the forces brought to bear by individuals and society. As suggested in Figure 1-1, the personnel manager needs to keep his or her head above water while moving ahead in the confluence of these three major streams of influence.

DEFINITION OF PERSONNEL MANAGEMENT

It is appropriate and helpful to offer, at the beginning of the discussion, a definition of the subject to be covered. In the following definition we are presenting an outline of this entire text. In the first place, we are dealing with two categories of functions, managerial and operative. A manager is one who exercises authority and leadership over other personnel; the president of a firm is certainly a manager, and so also is the department head or supervisor. On the other hand, an operative is one who has no authority over others but has been given a specific task or duty to perform under managerial supervision. Thus, the personnel manager is a manager and as such must perform the basic functions of management. This is true no matter what the nature of the operative function. Yet a comprehensive definition of personnel management must include also the operative functions in the field. In outline form, the definition would appear as follows:[1]

1 Management functions
   a Planning
   b Organizing
   c Directing
   d Controlling

2 Operative functions
   a Procurement
   b Development
   c Compensation
   d Integration

[1]The listing of major management functions varies with the experts. Perhaps the original listing was that of Henri Fayol in *General and Industrial Management*. He proposed a sequence of planning, organizing, commanding, coordinating, and controlling. Others suggest (1) planning, organizing, and controlling, (2) planning, organizing, staffing, directing, controlling, innovating, and representing, and (3) just planning and controlling. The differences are in emphasis rather than in content.

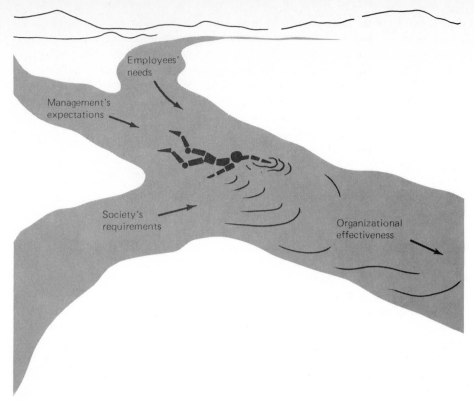

Figure 1-1   Confluence of forces on personnel manager.

  e Maintenance
  f Separation

  It is therefore possible, as mentioned in the preface, to summarize this entire text into one sentence: *Personnel management is the planning, organizing, directing, and controlling of the procurement, development, compensation, integration, maintenance, and separation of human resources to the end that individual, organizational, and societal objectives are accomplished.* A brief elaboration of the component parts of this definition follows.

  Planning Effective managers realize that a substantial portion of their time should be devoted to planning. For the personnel manager, planning means the *determination in advance of a personnel program that will contribute to goals established for the enterprise.* Presumably, the process of goal establishment will involve the active and enlightened participation of the personnel manager, with his or her expertise in the area of human resources.

  Organizing After a course of action has been determined, an organization must be established to carry it out. An organization is a means to an end. Once it has been determined that certain personnel functions contribute toward the firm's objectives, the personnel manager must form an organization by *designing the structure of relationships among jobs, personnel, and physical factors*. One must be aware of the complex relationships that exist between the specialized unit and the rest of the organization. Because of increasing expertise in this function, many top managements are looking to the personnel manager for advice in the general organization of the enterprise.

Directing At least in theory, we now have a plan and an organization to execute that plan. It might appear that the next logical function would be that of operation, doing the job. But it has been found that a ''starter'' function is becoming increasingly necessary. In our above definition, this function was labeled ''direction,'' but it may be called by other names, such as ''motivation,'' ''actuation,'' or ''command.'' At any rate, a considerable number of difficulties are involved in *getting people to go to work willingly and effectively*.

Controlling Now, at last, the personnel functions are being performed. But what is the management duty at this point? It is logical that its function should be that of control, that is, the observation of action and its comparison with plans and the correction of any deviations that may occur, or, at times, the realignment of plans and their adjustment to unchangeable deviations. Control is the managerial function concerned with *regulating activities in accordance with the personnel plan, which in turn was formulated on the basis of an analysis of fundamental organization goals*.

It is believed that the four above-named functions are basic and common to all managers. In Chapter 3, the personnel manager's responsibilities for planning, organizing, and controlling will be discussed. The essence of the fourth function, direction, is so closely allied with the operative function of integration that its discussion will be delayed until later in this text. Though all managers must unavoidably direct their subordinates, the personnel manager should possess exceptional expertise.

There is a skill in managing that can be transferred to various operative areas, but no one will deny that an effective manager must know what it is that he or she is managing. The greater portion of this text is devoted to these personnel operative functions.

Procurement This first operative function of personnel management is concerned with the *obtaining of the proper kind and number of personnel necessary to accomplish organization goals*. It deals specifically with such subjects as the determination of human resources requirements and their recruitment, selection, and placement. The determination of human resources required must rest upon a prior design of job duties, a decision that is increasingly being affected by the personnel manager's objective of meeting human needs. Some jobs are better left to robots than human beings. The objective of meeting society's requirements often affects procurement programs in the forms of affirmative action and equal opportunity. The actual hiring process entails a multitude of activities designed to screen personnel, such as reviewing application forms, psychological testing, checking references, and conducting interviews. These activities are presented and analyzed in Chapters 4 to 8.

Development After personnel have been obtained, they must be to some degree developed. Development has to do with the *increase of skill, through training, that is necessary for proper job performance*. This is an activity of very great importance and will continue to grow because of the changes in technology, the realignment of jobs, and the increasing complexity of the managerial task. Discussion of operative, managerial, and organization development will be presented in Chapter 9, to be followed by performance appraisal and career development in Chapters 10 and 11.

Compensation   This function is defined as the *adequate and equitable remuneration of personnel for their contributions to organization objectives*. Though some recent morale surveys have tended to minimize the importance of monetary income to employees, we nevertheless contend that compensation is one of the most important functions of personnel management. In dealing with this subject, we shall consider only economic compensation. Psychic income is classified elsewhere. The basic elements of a compensation program are presented in Chapters 12 to 14, with an emphasis upon such subjects as job evaluation, wage policies, wage systems, and some of the recently devised extra-compensation plans.

Integration   With the employee procured, developed, and reasonably compensated, there follows one of the most difficult and frustrating challenges to management. The definition labels this problem ''integration.'' It is concerned with the attempt to *effect a reasonable reconciliation of individual, societal, and organizational interests*. It rests upon a foundation of belief that significant overlappings of interests do exist in our society. Consequently, we must deal with the feelings and attitudes of personnel in conjunction with the principles and policies of organizations. This broad problem, as well as the narrower related problems, such as grievances, disciplinary action, and labor unions, will be covered in Chapters 15 to 20.

Maintenance   If we have executed the foregoing functions well, we now have a willing and able work force. Maintenance is concerned with the perpetuation of this state. The maintenance of willingness is heavily affected by communications with employees, a subject discussed in Chapter 21. The physical condition of the employee should be maintained, and health and safety will be the subject of Chapter 22.

Separation   If the first function of personnel management is to secure the employee, it is logical that the last should be the separation and return of that person to society. Most people do not die on the job. The organization is responsible for meeting certain requirements of due process in separation, as well as assuring that the returned citizen is in as good shape as possible. In Chapter 23, we shall discuss such types of separations as retirement, layoff, out-placement, and discharge. The final chapter is devoted to the subject of research in all personnel functions, and some consideration of the processes of introducing change should research findings demand it.

The purpose of all the activity outlined above, both managerial and operative, is to assist in the accomplishment of basic objectives. Consequently, the starting point of personnel management, as of all management, must be a specification of those objectives and a determination of the subobjectives of the personnel function. The expenditure of all funds in the personnel area can be justified only insofar as there is a net contribution toward basic goals. For the most part these are goals of the particular organization concerned. But as suggested earlier, society is tending to impose human goals upon the private business enterprise, goals that may or may not make an immediate contribution to an organization's particular objectives.

THE ROLE OF THE PERSONNEL MANAGER

Every organization has a personnel function whether or not a specific personnel manager has been so designated. Every organization must hire, train, pay, motivate, maintain, and ultimately separate employees. If a specialized personnel manager exists, he or she

FIGURE 1-2
Activities Handled by Personnel Departments

Activity	% of All Companies (503)			
	Extent of Personnel Department's Responsibility			No Such Activity at Company/Facility
	All	Some	None	
Personnel records/reports	94	5	*	—
Personnel research	85	3	*	11
Insurance benefits administration	84	13	3	—
Unemployment compensation administration	83	12	4	1
EEO compliance/affirmative action	78	20	1	*
Wage/salary administration	76	22	*	*
Workers' compensation administration	73	19	8	*
Tuition aid/scholarships	70	12	8	11
Job evaluation	66	29	2	3
Health/medical services	65	14	9	12
Retirement preparation programs	64	15	4	17
Pre-employment testing	64	10	1	25
Vacation/leave processing	62	29	8	*
Induction/orientation	59	39	2	—
Promotion/transfer/separation processing	57	41	2	—
Counseling/employee assistance programs	57	26	2	15
Pension/profit-sharing plan administration	55	30	8	7
College recruiting	54	17	2	26
Recreation/social/recognition programs	53	32	8	7
Recruiting/interviewing/hiring	52	47	*	*
Attitude surveys	52	12	2	34
Union/labor relations	50	17	2	31
Complaint/disciplinary procedures	48	50	1	*

can contribute much to greater organizational effectiveness. In the past, assignment to this function often constituted a one-way ticket to oblivion. But today, the increasingly critical nature of problems and challenges in the more effective utilization of human resources has greatly elevated the status of the field. It is estimated that human resources subjects now consume about 20 percent of the total attention of top management; predictions have been made that this will soon rise to 30 percent. In the past, it has been typical to pay the personnel manager about 70 percent of what his or her peers receive in the fields of marketing and finance. But recently the percentage salary increases have

FIGURE 1-2
Activities Handled by Personnel Departments (*Continued*)

9

The Nature and
Challenge of
Personnel
Management

Activity	% of All Companies (503)			
	Extent of Personnel Department's Responsibility			No Such Activity at Company/Facility
	All	Some	None	
Relocation services administration	47	19	5	29
Supervisory training	43	44	9	3
Employee communications/ publications	40	34	19	7
Executive compensation administration	39	32	23	6
Human resource planning	38	48	4	10
Safety programs/OSHA compliance	38	39	20	3
Management development	34	49	9	8
Food services	32	8	34	26
Performance evaluation, nonmanagement	29	55	13	3
Community relations/fund drives	28	37	29	5
Suggestion systems	28	17	12	43
Thrift/savings plan administration	26	17	6	51
Security/plant protection	25	14	53	8
Organization development	22	50	13	15
Management appraisal/MBO	19	46	15	20
Stock plan administration	19	14	8	58
Skill training, nonmanagement	15	48	30	7
Public relations	13	30	52	5
Administrative services (mail, PBX, phone, messengers, etc.)	13	12	73	2
Payroll processing	10	26	63	1
Travel/transportation services administration	9	24	46	21
Library	9	6	48	37
Maintenance/janitorial services	6	8	81	5

*Less than 1 percent.

Source: Bureau of National Affairs, Inc., "Activities Handled by Personnel Departments," *ASPA–BNA Survey No. 41*, p. 2. With permission. Copyright © 1981.

been considerably higher in the personnel field, which is the ultimate indication of the worth of a function in private organization.

When a large corporation recently went looking for a manager to head its human resources division with an offer of over $100,000, it was obvious that it was not looking for a "picnic planner." The American Society for Personnel Administration surveys salaries of personnel executives on an annual basis. In 1982, managers in charge of personnel units with ten or fewer members received a median salary of $40,200, while those in larger units received $74,000.

To obtain a general picture of the typical responsibilities of the personnel unit, an annual survey of the Bureau of National Affairs covering approximately 500 establishments with a total employment of over 1 million persons reveals the activities commonly undertaken.[2] Figure 1-2 itemizes 46 typical activities with an indication of degrees of responsibility of the personnel unit. It should be noted that the greater bulk of these activities requires a sharing of responsibility with other units of the firm. Only in the narrow technical areas such as personnel records, insurance benefits administration, unemployment compensation administration, and personnel research are the units given almost exclusive responsibility. The heart of a personnel program itself requires considerable coordination, as well as coordination with units in the remainder of the organization.

CHALLENGES OF MODERN PERSONNEL MANAGEMENT

We need not look far to discover challenging problems in the field of personnel management. Managers may ignore or attempt to bury personnel problems, but these will not lie dormant because of the very nature of the problem component. Many problems are caused by constant changes that occur both within and without the firm. Among the many major changes that are occurring, the following five will illustrate the nature of the personnel challenge:

- Changing mix of the work force
- Changing personal values of the work force
- Changing expectations of citizen-employees
- Changing levels of productivity
- Changing demands of government

Changing Mix of the Work Force

Though each person is unique and consequently presents a challenge to our general understanding, one can also appreciate broader problems by categorizing personnel to delineate and highlight trends. Among the major changes in the mix of personnel entering the work force are: (1) increased numbers of minority members entering occupations requiring greater skills, (2) increasing levels of formal education for the entire work force, (3) more female employees, (4) more married female employees, (5) more working mothers, and (6) a steadily increasing majority of white-collar employees in place of the blue-collar.

The last challenge has had much to do with many of the above-listed changes. Prohibition of discrimination and requirements for positive action to redress imbalances in work force mix have led to greater numbers of minority personnel being hired for all

---

[2]Bureau of National Affairs—American Society for Personnel Administraiton, *Personnel Activities, Budgets, and Staffs: 1980–1981,* Survey No. 41, May 21, 1981, p. 2.

types of jobs. The proportion of blacks, for example, has increased significantly in professional, technical, managerial, clerical, sales, and artisan-type jobs. However, this group still holds a disproportionately large share of the less skilled and lower-paid jobs, such as those of service worker and laborer. Steady increases in the level of formal education would seem to bode well for continued change.

Improvement in the educational level for blacks has also been accompanied by increased levels all along the line. In 1981, the average formal educational level of the work force was in excess of 12 years.[3] In the 25-to-64 age group, approximately 40 percent were high school graduates and 22 percent had college degrees. Another 17 percent had 1 to 3 years of college. This portends a very serious problem to personnel managers who must effect a match between human needs and organizational requirements.

That this is not being done well is shown by the number of college graduates finding jobs in professional and technical areas. In 1981, only 54 percent were able to find such jobs, as compared with 67 percent in 1970.[4] A portion of this was caused by the lack of growth in demand for teachers as the baby-boom generation passed through the schools. That education, as personal capital, tends to pay off is indicated by hourly earnings. In 1981, those with 8 years' schooling or less received an average of $5.06 per hour; 1 to 3 years' high school—$5.50; high school diploma—$6.19; 1 to 3 years' college—$6.91; college graduate—$6.93; and 5 or more years of college—$7.92.[5]

The Bureau of Labor Statistics makes periodic predictions of the types of jobs that will be available in the years ahead. As portrayed in Figure 1-3, the two major growth areas in the coming decade are clerical workers and service workers. More specific projections by occupation are shown in Figure 1-4. Though declines are predicted in the teaching area, other technical fields are developing that can utilize our increasingly educated work force. One notes the 112 percent projected growth for computer systems analysts, the 75 percent increase for aeroastronautic engineers, and the 51 percent increase for professional nurses. Though the overall number of professional jobs is projected to rise about 30 percent, this is limited progress when considering steady increases in both the size of the work force and the constantly increasing levels of education. Rather than relaxing with the feeling that more of a good thing (education) is better, if we do not reorganize and redesign jobs to effect a match with better-qualified personnel, we are contributing only to frustration, absenteeism, grievances, and turnover.

Laws, as well as activist groups, have contributed to greater numbers of female employees entering the work force. Women have been entering the work force in recent years at a much faster pace than males. In 1982, 43 percent of the total work force was female, as compared with 33 percent in 1960 and 38 percent in 1970.[6] As portrayed in Figure 1-5, this trend is expected to continue. Also of significance to the manager is that an increasing proportion of female employees have children under the age of 6 years. This makes it difficult for them to become regular members of an organization, and personnel managers should seriously consider such practices as flexible hours of work,

[3]Anne McDougall Young, "Educational Attainment of Workers, March 1981," *Monthly Labor Review,* vol. 105, no. 4, April 1982, p. 52.
[4]*Ibid.,* p. 53.
[5]Earl F. Mellor and George D. Stamas, "Usual Weekly Earnings: Another Look at Intergroup Differences and Basic Trends," *Monthly Labor Review,* vol. 105, no. 4, April 1982, p. 23.
[6]Robert W. Bednarzik, Marilyn A. Hewson, and Michael A. Urquhart, "The Employment Situation in 1981: New Recession Takes Its Toll," *Monthly Labor Review,* vol. 105, no. 3, March 1982, p. 13.

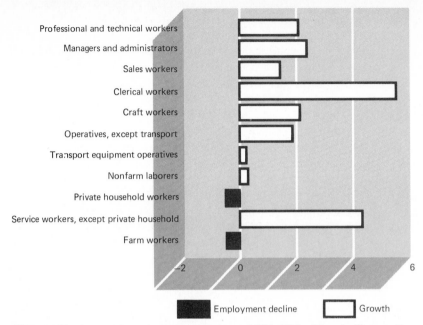

Figure 1-3 Projected changes in employment, 1978–90 (millions). (*Source: Bureau of Labor Statistics,* Occupational Outlook Handbook, 1980–81, *p. 21*)

FIGURE 1-4
Projected Changes in Employment by Occupation
1978–90 (thousands)

	Employment		Percent Change 1978–90
	1978	1990	
Aeroastronautic engineers	57	100	75
Computer programmers	204	361	77
Computer systems analysts	185	392	112
Data processing machine mechanics	63	162	157
Employment interviewers	51	88	72
Industrial engineers	109	148	37
Health technologists	1,246	1,820	46
Nurses, professional	1,026	1,551	51
Office machine servicers	49	91	87
Paralegal personnel	28	69	143
Personnel and labor relations	169	208	23
Personnel clerks	90	113	25
Physicians	447	631	41
Railroad conductors	33	32	−5
Teachers	3,877	4,074	5
Adult education	105	124	18
College	454	408	−10
Graduate assistants	131	109	−16
Secondary	1,229	1,068	−13

Source: Max L. Carey, "Occupational Employment Growth through 1990," *Monthly Labor Review*, vol. 104, no. 8, August 1981, pp. 42–55.

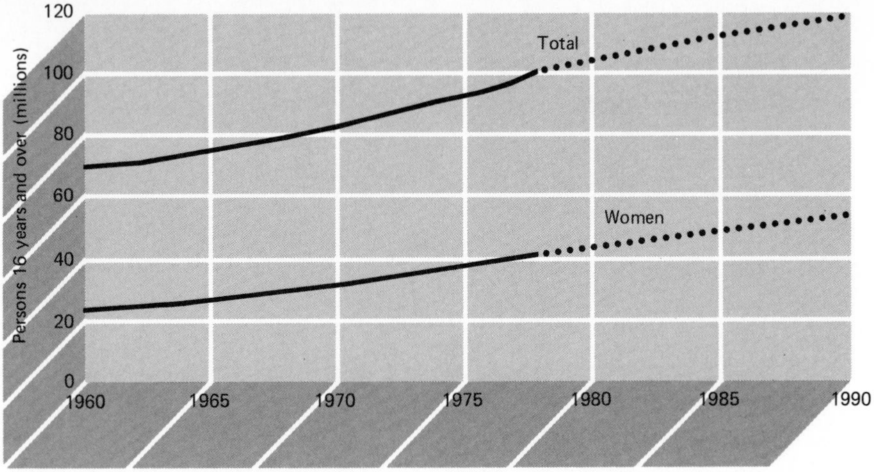

Figure 1-5 Changes in proportion of females in the work force. *(Source: Bureau of Labor Statistics, Occupational Outlook Handbook, 1980–81, p. 17)*

sharing of one job by two or more workers, and providing child care during working hours. Other more fundamental and lasting changes brought by female workers are briefly discussed in Box 1-1.

One of the more interesting changes in skill mix that has occurred in our society is depicted in Figure 1-6. In 1956, white-collar job-holders outnumbered blue-collar workers for the first time. By 1990, it is projected that over half of the total work force will be white-collar. These employees are typically less inclined to join labor unions, but, on the other hand, have greater expectations in terms of more individual treatment by management. Performance on these types of jobs tends to be more difficult to objectively evaluate, thereby leading managers toward more participative appraisal systems such as "management by objectives."

BOX 1-1
Changes Brought by Women Workers

"A record 12 million women entered the labor force in the 1970s. According to conventional wisdom, this massive influx of working women has now peaked. But new analyses show that because of a dramatic shift in the employment patterns of women, the pace will actually accelerate as 16.5 million more women find jobs in the 1980s. The impact of this speedup will have important economic and business implications that have not been adequately factored into the longrun prospects for the U.S. economy."

Among the changes foreseen are (1) an increase in consumer spending because of the increasing numbers of married women in the labor force, (2) increased adaptability to unemployment since many households will have two paychecks during ordinary times, (3) an overall rise in productivity as women become more acclimated to the working climate, (4) greater continuity in the female employee's work history with less time out for child rearing activities, and (5) an increased tendency to acquire professional education and training.

"In business, the number of graduating women rose from 3% to 23% (during the 1969 to 1980 period), while in medicine the increase was from 8% to 24%. Observes Geoffrey Greene of Wharton Econometric Forecasting Associates Inc: 'Female participation rates are a function of that generation's past educational achievements. A lot of the reason for this jump in graduate school enrollments is that these younger women perceived opportunities out there.' "

"The Lasting Changes Brought by Women Workers," *Business Week*, March 15, 1982, p. 59.

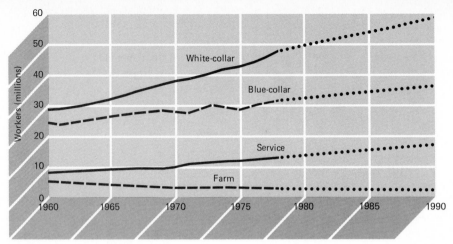

Figure 1-6 Changes in work force mix. *(Source: Bureau of Labor Statistics*, Occupational Outlook Handbook, 1980–81, *p. 21)*

Changing Personal Values of the Work Force

The changing mix of the work force inevitably leads to introduction of new values to organizations. In the past and continuing into the present, the work force of America has been heavily imbued with a set of values generally characterized by the term "work ethic." Work is regarded as having spiritual meaning, buttressed by such behavioral norms as punctuality, honesty, diligence, and frugality. One's job is a central life interest and provides the dominant clue in interpersonal assessment. A work force with this set of values is highly adapted to use by business organizations in their pursuit of the values of productivity, efficiency, and effectiveness.

There is growing evidence that the work ethic is declining in favor of a more existential view of life. Instead of organizations providing the basic guides to living, persons are responsible for exploring and determining for themselves what they want to do and become. With this philosophy, work becomes only one alternative among many as a means for becoming a whole person in order to "do one's own thing." Family activities, leisure, avocations, and assignments in government, churches, and schools are all equally viable means through which a person can find meaning and become self-actualized. The absolute worth of the individual is a value which is merged with the concept that all people are members of the great human family. Concerning specifics, full employment gives way to the full life. Climbing the organization ladder of success for its accompanying materialistic symbols becomes less important than self-expression through a creative accomplishment. Private lives outside the job and firm are relatively autonomous, accompanied by an increasing reluctance to sacrifice oneself or one's family for the good of the organization. Quality of life is preferred to quantity, equity to efficiency, diversity to conformity, and the individual to the organization.

With respect to an increasing emphasis upon the individual as compared with the organization, a number of changes in personnel programs have been tried. Attempts have been made to *redesign jobs* to provide challenging activities that meet needs of the human ego.[7] In one company, it being well realized that some individuals prefer more repetitive, less challenging assignments, a choice was provided between the assembly line and individual assembly for the *same* product. Concerning *pay,* a few firms have moved to pay the employee for skills possessed rather than for skills demanded by the job. With respect to *fringe benefits,* a cafeteria arrangement has been proposed where the employee can periodically choose what particular benefits he or she desires while remaining within an overall cost limit.

As a final illustration of the move toward the individual, the self-determination of work schedules is an interesting recent phenomenon in this country. ''Flexitime'' is a program that allows flexible starting and quitting times for the employee. The schedule used by one company is as follows: (1) 7 to 9 A.M. constitutes a flexible band during which the employee may choose the time he or she begins work, (2) 9 to 11:30 A.M. is core time—all employees must be present, (3) 11:30 A.M. to 1:00 P.M. is flexible time for taking a 30-minute lunch, (4) 1 to 4 P.M. is core time, and (5) 4 to 6 P.M. is flexitime for quitting. When allowed this freedom, slightly over half of the employees chose an earlier starting time and about a third kept on working the usual hours. All employees must still work the required total number of hours for the week or month. A variation of the plan is group-selected staggered hours. Rather than each individual choosing her or his specific starting and stopping times, the group votes as a unit for varying schedules that all will follow for designated periods of time. In a Conference Board survey of 2,400 firms, it was found that flexitime was being utilized by 15 percent for their white-collar workers and by only 3 percent for blue-collar employees.[8] The insurance industry showed the greatest interest in this type of schedule, with 34 percent providing for flexible programs.

Though flexitime fits quite well with the new values of the modern work force, such plans have also been found to have a number of advantages to the employer. Among those suggested are the following:

1. *Enhanced productivity.* Though there is little hard evidence, surveys indicate chances of improving productivity vary from one-third to one-half, with the probable size of the gain in the range of 5 percent to 14 percent.[9] Explanations for this include better morale, better fit of work time to the employee's ''body clock,'' improved handling of fluctuating workloads, increased customer service because the establishment is open longer, and less ''killing time'' until quitting time because of reluctance to begin a new task.

2. *Reduced employee tardiness and absenteeism.* When contemplating a late arrival under a fixed schedule, the employee is often tempted to skip work altogether. If the approved arrival time is within a two-hour flexible band, both tardiness and absenteeism from this source are eliminated. Personal errands can be taken care of without the necessity of being officially absent for all or a portion of the day.

3. *Improved morale and reduced turnover.* Flexitime provides the employee with some control over the workday, thereby constituting a type of job enrichment. Employees are treated substantially in the same fashion as managers and profes-

[7]See Chapter 5.

[8]Harriet Gorlin, ''An Overview of Corporate Personnel Practices,'' *Personnel Journal,* vol. 61, no. 2, February 1982, p. 128.

[9]Stanley D. Nollen, ''Does Flexitime Improve Productivity?'' *Harvard Business Review,* vol. 57, no. 5, September-October 1979, p. 18.

sional personnel. In Germany, where flexitime had its start, commuting time was reduced from 20 to 30 percent since the employee could adjust starting and finishing times to avoid peak traffic periods.

There are, of course, some disadvantages to the employer's utilizing a flexitime schedule. Utility costs are increased since the plant is open for longer periods of time. Not all necessary employees are present when a particular problem arises, thereby forcing its postponement until the core period. There are difficulties in recording hours actually worked, and the symbol of servitude, the time clock, may have to be reintroduced. There may also be conflicts with certain laws that require the payment of overtime for hours worked in excess of 8 per day. Supervision may become a problem since a single supervisor cannot be present for the full 11 or 12 hours of the authorized day. And finally, there may be some confusion for customers and suppliers who are not familiar with the varying attendance of personnel under flexitime arrangements.

And now from Europe, where flexitime was first developed, there comes the suggestion of "flexiyear" schedules.[10] Workers can sign contracts to work so many hours during a year. If, for example, one contracted to work 1,200 hours during a year, this could be fulfilled in 120 days of 10 hours, 240 days of 5 hours, or any particular combination that fits personal requirements. It is estimated that at least 12 firms with a total of 1,000 employees are using the working-year contract in West Germany.

Changing Expectations of Citizen-Employees

There are increasing signs that external rights of citizenship are penetrating the boundaries of business enterprises in the interest of improving the quality of work life. Two prominent illustrations are: (1) freedom of speech, and (2) the right to privacy. Should employees be allowed to speak up and criticize the organization's management and its products without jeopardizing their job security? In public organizations, this right of "whistle blowing" is fairly well protected. Though some private firms have voluntarily adopted policies favorable to employee freedom of speech, others have been forced to such practices through court cases. When a qualified medical doctor publicly protested the early release of a new medication, the court determined that the public interest required that she not be disciplined. However, when a salesman who had worked for U.S. Steel Corporation for 14 years was discharged for communicating his doubts about the safety of steel tubes under high pressure, the court upheld his discharge on the basis of the employer's right to terminate employment "at will."[11] In these court cases, a basic task is to determine the motivation of the employees—are they acting as Judas Iscariots or Martin Luthers? If the person is stimulated by a real desire to improve the organization or protect the public, freedom of speech may be protected. The court will also evaluate the qualification of the employee in making the judgment that was openly communicated to others. In addition, it is also expected that the employee first try the normal communication processes within the firm before going public and exposing the firm. Though true and justified, the firm may claim that interpersonal relationships have

---

[10]Bernhard Teriet, "Flexiyear Schedules—Only a Matter of Time?" *Monthly Labor Review,* vol. 100, no. 12, December 1977, pp. 62–65.

[11]Clyde W. Summers, "Protecting *All* Employees against Unjust Dismissal," *Harvard Business Review,* vol. 58, no. 1, January-February 1980, p. 132.

been seriously and permanently damaged by such "squealing," and thus the employee should be discharged. One research project concluded that organizations are more likely to retaliate against "whistle blowers" who have superior standing in terms of age, experience, and education.[12] Retaliation is thus directed toward persons who can do the most damage to the organization. Dow Votaw contends that freedom of speech within the organization is "a development which may well prove to be a necessary concomitant of effective corporate responsibility."[13]

Employees are also becoming more concerned with the information they must provide in order to obtain and hold jobs. They feel that many questions are an invasion of privacy, such as whether one is pregnant or not, drinking habits, kinds of friends, type of neighborhood in which one lives, records of arrests, ability to pay bills, and whether the job applicant has ever received psychiatric counseling. Again, the major restrictions upon employers have been largely in the public area. The Privacy Act of 1974 requires federal agencies to open personnel files for inspection by employees; the Family Education Rights and Privacy Act allows students to inspect educational records and prohibits universities from disclosing information without student consent. Employees perceive a greater invasion of privacy when (1) personal information is distributed to others without their permission, (2) personality information, as compared with productivity data, is disclosed, and (3) personal information is given to outsiders rather than those working within the firm.[14]

There has been more voluntary movement in the area of privacy than in conjunction with freedom of speech. Though the Conference Board survey of corporate practices in 1977 revealed very few companies that were considering action in this area, the 1982 survey indicated that 45 percent of the responding companies had written policies regarding the privacy of personnel records.[15] More than 85 percent provided employee access to records, and well over half required employee permission before revealing personal information other than work location, term of employment, and last position held. Currently, laws in California, Maine, Michigan, Oregon, and Pennsylvania grant employees the right to inspect their personnel files. As one example of a comprehensive privacy program, Figure 1-7 outlines the essential guidelines followed by the International Business Machines Corporation.

Changing Levels of Productivity

Perhaps the most serious current problem facing all managers, not just personnel managers, is the declining productivity of the American economy. Up until the 1960s, the typical annual increase in productivity was approximately 3 percent. This figure was even placed in the United Auto Workers contract as a guaranteed base for increasing employee income. In the last two decades, the level of productivity has fallen markedly. As indicated in Figure 1-8, the United States ranks behind many nations in its annual growth of real gross national product per worker.

[12]Marcia A. Parmerlee, Janet P. Near, and Tamila C. Jensen, "Correlates of Whistleblowers' Perceptions of Organizational Retaliation," *Administrative Science Quarterly,* vol. 27, no. 1, March 1982, pp. 17–34.

[13]Dow Votaw, *The Corporate Dilemma,* Prentice-Hall, Englewood Cliffs, N.J., 1973, p. 44.

[14]Paul D. Tolchinsky, Michael K. McCuddy, Jerome Adams, Daniel C. Ganster, Richard W. Woodman, and Howard L. Fromkin, "Employee Perceptions of Invasion of Privacy: A Field Simulation Experiment," *Journal of Applied Psychology,* vol. 66, no. 3, June 1981, pp. 308–313.

[15]Harriet Gorlin, "An Overview of Corporate Personnel Practices," op. cit., pp. 125–126.

FIGURE 1-7
IBM Guidelines on Employee Privacy

Entry to Firm
1 Restrict collection of data to essentials.
   a Do not ask for birthdate, employment of spouses, relatives at IBM, previous addresses, previous arrests, previous treatment of emotional illnesses, etc.
   b Do ask for name, address, previous employer, education, and convictions within past 3 years.
2 Undertake background checks only with consent and knowledge of applicant. No outside agencies are assigned this function.
3 Do not administer personality tests or polygraphs.
4 Do not give general intelligence tests if some other means of assessment are available.
5 Do administer valid aptitude tests.

Records maintenance
1 Performance appraisals, grades in IBM courses, and records of convictions that are 3 years old are purged from files.
2 Do not use social security numbers on identification badges or medical and dental claim cards. Do not give out number without employee's consent.
3 No taping of conversations without consent.
4 Keep employee's attendance, performance, vacation schedules, etc. for very limited time.

Access
1 Line managers allowed to see only job-related information. They do not see such information as medical benefits, payroll deductions, payments for educational programs, wage garnishments, and the like.
2 Outside organizations requesting references receive only job title, place of employment, and date of employment. Give out other information only with consent of employee.
3 Creditors, attorneys, and private agencies receive no information without consent of employee.
4 Employee is allowed to review personal file with the exception of business planning information concerning future salary schedules and promotions.

Source: "IBM's Guidelines to Employee Privacy—An Interview with Frank T. Cary," *Harvard Business Review*. vol. 54, no. 5, September-October 1976, pp. 82–90.

There have been many reasons proposed for the recent declines in productivity:

1. Numerous federal regulations and laws have added to the cost of doing business without enhancing productivity in the short run, such as environmental protection, health and safety, affirmative action, and so on.

2. Such laws have led to increased numbers of employees new to the business environment. The influx of females and minorities may have resulted in less productivity during the introductory period.

3. American managers typically have a short-term profit orientation in making business decisions. With pressures from stockholders, stock markets, and financial institutions, they tend to postpone vital research, development, and new plant investments in the interest of short-term showings. This leads to declining productivity over time. It is also contended that various tax laws have discouraged innovation and new plant investment.

4. With maturity, our economy has increasingly become more of a service, rather than manufacturing, type of system. Achieving gains in productivity when providing services is considerably more difficult than becoming more efficient in production processes.

FIGURE 1-8
Annual Growth, Real GNP Per Employed Worker

Country	1963–74	1973–79
Japan	8.7%	3.4%
Germany	4.6	3.2
France	4.6	2.7
Italy	5.4	1.6
Canada	2.4	0.4
United Kingdom	3.0	0.3
United States	1.9	0.1

Source: *Economic Report of the President, January 1980*, p. 85.

5. Adversarial relationships with labor unions reduce cooperative efforts that would enhance productivity. Numerous union-negotiated work rules designed to protect jobs and income in the short run have disastrous results when employers must compete on the world market.

6. Employee alienation leads to refusal to collaborate in the interest of improving productivity. It has been suggested that poor employee attitudes have been caused by such factors as high job insecurity, narrow and meaningless jobs, and autocratic managers who deny significant employee participation in decisions affecting the work and the quality of work life.

Though the personnel manager can do little to alter the fundamental competitive makeup of our economy, there are many areas where the challenges can be met. Major portions of this text will deal with personnel programs designed to enhance productivity. In particular, Chapter 17 will deal with motivational programs based on a collaborative mode, such as quality circles and semi-autonomous work groups. And under the pressures generated by worldwide competition, there is evidence that unions and managements are becoming less adversarial in their relations with each other.

Changing Demands of Government

Throughout this text, we will deal with pertinent national legislation when undertaking the discussion of particular functions of personnel management. It is well at some point, however, to recognize and appreciate the fact that personnel management is becoming increasingly *legalized* in our society. The following incomplete listing of major items of federal regulations pertaining to each personnel function should support this contention:

Procurement

- Civil Rights Act of 1964 (Prohibits discrimination in hiring on basis of race, color, religion, nationality, and sex.)

- Equal Employment Opportunity Act of 1972 (Empowers federal commission to undertake direct court action.)

- Executive Orders No. 11246 of 1965 and No. 11375 of 1967 (Requires contractors of the federal government to establish affirmative action programs in hiring groups protected by the Civil Rights Act.)

- Rehabilitation Act of 1973 (Requires government contractors to take affirmative action to hire handicapped personnel.)
- Pregnancy Discrimination Act of 1978 (Requires employers to treat pregnant employees in the same manner as other employees.)

Development

- National Apprenticeship Program Act of 1937 (Details basic program requirements for certification.)
- Manpower Development and Training Act of 1962 (Funds special programs for the unskilled.)
- Civil Rights Act of 1964 (Applies to training programs.)
- Economic Opportunity Act of 1964 (Funds special programs for the hard-core unemployed.)
- Comprehensive Employment and Training Act of 1973 (Emphasizes local control of job creation and training programs, primarily for hard-core unemployed and welfare families.)
- Job Training Partnership Act of 1982 (Greater private industry involvement in training the hard-core unemployed.)

Compensation

- Davis-Bacon Act of 1931 (Establishes minimum wages and overtime hours for government construction work.)
- Walsh-Healey Public Contract Act of 1936 (Sets minimum wages and overtime hours for government contracts in excess of $10,000.)
- Fair Labor Standards Act of 1938 (Establishes minimum wages and overtime hours for firms engaged in interstate commerce.)
- Equal Pay Act of 1963 (Requires that women and men on the same job get equal pay.)
- Civil Rights Act of 1964 (Applies to pay.)

Integration

- Norris-LaGuardia Act of 1932 (Limits employer use of injunctions against labor unions.)
- National Labor Relations Act (Wagner) of 1935 (Protects right to form unions, levies bargaining obligations on employer.)
- Labor Management Relations Act (Taft-Hartley) of 1947 (Levies obligations for proper bargaining upon the labor union.)
- Labor Management Disclosure Act (Landrum-Griffin) of 1959 (Protects union members from abuse by union officials and requires numerous reports to the government.)

- Civil Rights Act of 1964 (Applies to all phases of employment including discipline.)
- Age Discrimination Act of 1967 as amended in 1978 (Prohibits discrimination against workers aged 40 to 70.)

Maintenance

- Occupational Safety and Health Act of 1970 (Sets standards and enforces them through inspections and fines.)

Separation

- Social Security Act of 1935 (Sets up federal retirement benefits and stimulates establishment of state laws to provide unemployment compensation for those laid off by firms.)
- Employee Retirement Income Security Act of 1974 (Protects worker rights in private pension plans and requires some form of employee ownership of shares.)

In addition to these major pieces of federal regulation, all fifty states have legislation that impinges upon the personnel program. Prominent among these are workers' compensation laws that require employer insurance against injuries on the job, and unemployment compensation laws that require accumulation of funds for payment to workers in the event of layoff. Though one would not like to see a personnel manager design a program with a basic legalistic bent, it is undeniable that one requires the services of a lawyer to monitor compliance with the law. Our society is becoming increasingly legalistic in nature, and great emphasis has been devoted to the protection and enhancement of our human resources.

Predictions for new legislation for the future include (1) elimination of all age requirements for retirement purposes, (2) federal privacy legislation requiring personal files to be open and employee permission to disclose contents, (3) uniform workers' compensation benefits on a national basis, (4) revision of overtime laws to facilitate different work schedules, such as flexitime and the 4-day workweek, and (5) changes in the Social Security law to preclude bankruptcy of the system.

SUMMARY

A survey of the functions and challenges of personnel management supports the contention that the modern personnel manager must operate at the nexus of three major forces. First, one must plan, organize, direct, and control the procurement, development, compensation, integration, maintenance, and separation of a work force in order that the organization may accomplish its designated objectives. In this view, the work force is an instrument of the organization, and the personnel manager provides and shapes that instrument. Organization requirements change with time, as is illustrated by the growth of large, multinational corporations and the use of more complex and automated technology.

Second, the instrumental work force is composed of human beings of varying types with complex and changing needs and values. The personnel manager must assist the organization in adapting to changes in mix (better educated, more working parents, more minority employees) and values (demands for individual rights, treatment, and opportunities). The personnel manager searches for programs that have overlapping interests for both employee and organization, such as flexitime, which allows individual decision concerning working hours, yet returns values in the area of tardiness, absenteeism, turnover, and productivity.

Finally, the third major force is society, represented by multiple levels of government. A brief list of the statutes and regulations at only the national level serves to illustrate the nature of this burgeoning third force. The obligations of both the organization and the personnel manager toward society will be discussed in greater detail in Chapter 4.

BRIEF CASE

In July 1979, seven black employees at a Zellerbach plant in Los Angeles sent a letter to the Los Angeles school board protesting an award to the company for a project that brought minority students to the plant to show them possible jobs. Copies of the letter were also sent to company managers, the mayor, and several black organizations. Among other statements, the letter condemned the personnel director of the firm as "the standard bearer of the bigoted position of racism at Zellerbach," and demanded that the affirmative action program of the firm be examined.

The company management dismissed the seven employees for "disloyalty." They stated that any employee could complain to appropriate government agencies and the company would not retaliate. However, the school board was a major purchaser of company products, and no employee has the right "to injure the company and its employees by jeopardizing its reputation and relationships with its customers." The "Zellerbach Seven" filed a grievance under the labor contract contending that there was not just cause for their firing. They were supported by the United Paperworkers Union, the local American Civil Liberties Union, and a black community organization.

Questions

1. Assuming the case were appealed to you, an outside arbitrator, what would you rule concerning the discharge?

2. Do citizenship rights of freedom of speech give these employees any protection?

DISCUSSION QUESTIONS

1. Identify and distinguish among the four managerial functions and the six operative functions of personnel management.

2. In fulfilling the personnel management responsibility, what three forces are affecting the program? What is the chronological order of development of these forces?

3. With the educational level of the nation's work force steadily increasing, what problems and opportunities are created for the personnel manager?

4. With more females in the work force, what major changes are introduced into our society?

5. Assuming that we want to alter personnel programs in the direction of emphasizing the role of the individual, what suggestions are made in the areas of job design, pay, fringe benefits, privacy, and freedom of speech?

6. What are the values of flexitime to the organization? What problems are generated for the firm?

7. Is American business moving more rapidly than in the past in promoting employee privacy or in developing freedom of speech? Why?

8. What are the major sources behind the declining level of productivity in this nation? Which sources can be attacked by personnel managers?

9. For each of the six operative functions, itemize one piece of federal regulation that guides the personnel manager.

10. What forces are behind the steadily increasing status of the personnel manager in private business organizations?

SUPPLEMENTARY READING

CHUNG, KAE H., and MARGARET ANN GRAY: "Can We Adopt the Japanese Methods of Human Resources Management?" *Personnel Administrator,* vol. 27, no. 5, May 1982, pp. 41–46.

COOPER, M. R., B. S. MORGAN, P. M. FOLEY, and L. B. KAPLAN: "Changing Employee Values: Deepening Discontent?" *Harvard Business Review,* vol. 57, no. 1, January-February 1979, pp. 117–125.

ELLIG, BRUCE R.: "The Impact of Legislation on the Personnel Function," *Personnel,* vol. 57, no. 5, September-October 1980, pp. 49–53.

HATANO, DARYL G.: "Employee Rights and Corporate Restrictions," *California Management Review,* vol. 14, no. 2, Winter 1981, pp. 5–12.

PARMERLEE, MARCIA A., JANET P. NEAR, and TAMILA C. JENSEN: "Correlates of Whistleblowers' Perceptions of Organizational Retaliation," *Administrative Science Quarterly,* vol. 27, no. 1, March 1982, pp. 17–34.

SKINNER, WICKHAM: "Big Hat, No Cattle: Managing Human Resources," *Harvard Business Review,* vol. 59, no. 5, September-October 1981, pp. 106–114.

chapter 2

From Mechanics to Social Responsibility

There is usually something to be gained by taking a look at the past. We can often determine more correctly the direction in which we are headed if we view it from the perspective of past events, and we can often manage to avoid actions that have been proved, by past experience, to be mistaken. For the student of management, the past helps to give a clearer conception of the present status of the subject. For these reasons, in this chapter we shall present a brief summary of selected significant aspects of the history of personnel management.

MECHANICAL APPROACH TOWARD PERSONNEL

Industrial management in this country has done an excellent job in the mechanical and electronic implementation of production. For over a century managers have applied the principles of interchangeable parts, transfer of skill from human to machine, and operational specialization to machinery, equipment, layout, and the general plant. This has been accomplished with a high degree of success. It is not surprising, therefore, that the same basic mechanical approach should be applied to labor. If machines can be made more productive by extreme specialization, so can people. Jobs can be created requiring such little ability that bodies, properly numbered, can be interchanged readily. Just as we try to purchase machinery and plant with the lowest direct outlay, so we can hire labor as cheaply as possible. Just as we try to keep plant and equipment operating economically as long as possible and junk them for better when necessary, so we can use and discard human labor.

This basic approach, which we have labeled ''mechanical,'' has also been called the ''commodity approach'' or the ''factor-of-production concept.'' These titles are descriptive of the attitude that assumes that labor must be classified with capital and land as a factor of production to be procured as cheaply as possible and utilized to the fullest. The fact that a human being is involved in this factor is of little significance. In effect, we are adopting a *closed-system* stance or strategy in our approach to the management of personnel. We assume that personnel are controllable, predictable, and interchangeable. The firm is sheltered from outside forces such as government or labor unions that might attempt to "interfere" with the mechanistic approach to personnel. Related to this attitude was the "scientific management" movement, which also adopted a rationalistic, deterministic, and closed-system approach to the management of the enterprise. Its recognized founder, Frederick W. Taylor, introduced such techniques as motion study, time study, incentive wages, and specialized foremanship in the pursuit of technical efficiency. As he stated, "Each man must learn how to give up his own particular way of doing things, adjust his methods to the many new standards, and grow accustomed to receiving and obeying directions covering details, large and small, which in the past have been left to his individual judgment."[1] Man is viewed as an excessively simplistic human system who only strives to avoid pain and obtain money, the "economic-man" model.

Since labor is human, with multiple complex motives, the mechanical approach usually results in the creation of various management problems—personnel problems. Many of these problems are quite old and have their beginning with the original adoption of this approach toward labor. Without implying that these are the only such problems, we believe that this presentation should assist in providing some perspective for the personnel function as performed in the present. The selected problems are (1) technological unemployment, (2) security, (3) labor organization, and (4) pride in work. Some indication will be given of how the problems arose, what management did about them using the mechanical approach, and what the consequences were of such proposed solutions.

Technological Unemployment

Loss of jobs through the development of new machines or new techniques of work is termed "technological unemployment." Labor is replaced either by machines or by management innovations that result in more work being done by fewer people. The mechanical approach of management toward technical problems pays off in the immediate sense. In that same sense the losses to labor are obvious. Reactions of labor in the past were not greatly different from those of today to similar events—fear and resistance. Yesterday there were riots and attempts to sabotage the new machinery. Today there are more subtle types of resistance, such as slowdowns and union-negotiated introduction of laborsaving devices.

What are some of the proposed solutions to the personnel problem of minimizing the adverse effects of technological changes? First, it should be pointed out that for over a century industrial managers in general did not particularly worry about the problem and that they mechanically laid off the employee. This was the free-enterprise system, in which employees looked after themselves. But growing public dissatisfaction with the manner in which this problem was being ignored stimulated the proposal of some individual solutions. A few isolated companies, such as Procter and Gamble, advanced the philosophy of sharing part of the company's profits with employees in order (1) to allow workers to benefit from the company's improved position and (2) to provide some additional funds to help tide the worker over in case of unemployment. This solution was not widely accepted, to say the least, though the Procter and Gamble plan, started in

[1]Frederick W. Taylor, *Shop Management,* Harper & Brothers, New York, 1911, p. 133.

1886, exists to this day. A few companies, such as Nunn-Bush Shoe Company, Hormel Company, and again Procter and Gamble, proposed the idea of guaranteeing an annual wage for all eligible employees. Though they might work a short week or be laid off entirely, covered employees would continue to receive pay for a limited time, a year being, in most plans, the maximum. These employer-initiated guaranteed annual wage plans did not spread. In 1935 the federal government in the Social Security Act imposed a responsibility on private industry for partially financing the out-of-work employee through unemployment compensation. Funds collected from taxing employers are available to eligible persons seeking work. In the 1950s we had the union version of the guaranteed annual wage as an imposed solution to this problem. In most instances, this means an employer-financed supplementation of the unemployment compensation, which would raise the total amount paid to the employee to over 50 percent of the base wage. It should be noted that these plans cover all types of job losses other than discharge for cause and organized strikes. Perhaps the two most common reasons for job loss are technological change and layoff due to the reduction in the need for output.

All the above-cited plans—profit sharing, unemployment compensation, and guaranteed annual wages—will be discussed in this text. Our purpose at this point is to demonstrate (1) that we are dealing with a very old personnel problem, (2) that the problem was long ignored by private industry, (3) that the problem will not take care of itself through relying on the usual long-run economic adjustment, and (4) that solutions imposed from without, by government and labor unions, will fill the void left by private industry. Few thinking people oppose these technological improvements, but many are concerned with the manner and timing of their introduction in order to minimize the short-run effects on employment.

Security

It is evident that decreased economic security is also a current problem that results partially from other problems, such as technological unemployment, and in turn creates still other problems, which lead to the creation of labor organizations. The mechanization of production creates the factory system. With the forming of factories, labor must move from a predominantly agricultural environment to the locale of a city. The tool or machine assumes greater importance, and the worker is often relegated to the position of machine tender. The uncertainty of steady employment, coupled with the problem of coming old age, works to produce a greater feeling of economic insecurity.

Granting the increase in the insecurity of employees, we might ask why management should be concerned, in a free competitive society. Such unconcern was at one time the attitude of industry in general, a philosophy that was consistent with the mechanical approach. This reaction to the problem proved to be wrong, and outside forces stepped in to impose certain solutions. In the first place, the workers' insecurity led to the formation of labor unions in order that they might acquire a measure of control over some of the factors bearing on economic security. Second, the government again entered the picture with legislation requiring the recognition of labor unions to protect employee interests, requiring that retirement income be provided through Social Security, and protecting employee ownership rights in private pension plans.

This is not to say that many private employers are not today voluntarily installing various programs to promote employee security. But it is apparent that both unions and government feel that private enterprise by itself will not do enough. Increased employee security can be rationalized on the basis that it contributes to increased employee productivity.

Labor Organization

Management's indifference to the requirements of its personnel contributed heavily to the creation of labor unions. When unions were actually formed, various techniques were utilized to destroy them. Labor organizations grew at a very slow pace through the nineteenth century because of such factors as the following:

1. Periodic economic depressions, during which union members broke ranks to obtain any kind of employment

2. Immigration, which supplied workers willing to take less than union members

3. The frontier, which always beckoned when things got rough with an Eastern employer

4. The public attitude, which was generally opposed to labor organization, considering it antagonistic to private property rights and freedom of the individual

5. The attitude of all branches of government, which was a reflection of the public attitude cited above

6. The expenditure of union energy and funds for "uplift" unionism concerned with political reform, rather than with the "business" unionism of dealing with employers for better wages, hours, etc.

7. The aggressive efforts of most managements in actively combating the efforts toward unionization

These factors constituted a decided brake on the labor movement. As each was modified or eliminated, the membership of unions tended to grow.

The first attempt at national organization that met with any degree of success was the ill-fated Knights of Labor, a union that accumulated over 700,000 members in the 1880s. This organization had in it several defects that led to its early demise. Among them were (1) a highly centralized form of control under one man, (2) a heterogeneous membership, which included wage earners of all types and even some small employers, and (3) a great interest in "uplift" unionism. The American Federation of Labor, formed in 1886, profited by these mistakes and established a labor organization which lasts to this day. The federation based its form of unionism on the organization of homogeneous groups of employees along craft lines. The fact that it was formed as a federation is an indication of a decentralization of authority. In addition, the basic policy of the AFL was to refrain from direct participation in politics, a policy which was followed until the 1940s, when the passage of the Taft-Hartley Act jarred the organization away from this philosophy. A time line of labor union growth is presented in Figure 2-1. In addition, certain selected events important to the union movement are indicated.

Almost from its inception, the American Federation of Labor dominated the labor movement. During these years, industrial management was well aware of the efforts being made along the line of employee organization. Many attempts, mostly successful, were made to halt the spread of unionism. A large number of these attempts involved force and violence. One interesting example should demonstrate the attitudes of union and management and the types of activity utilized by both sides in these contests.

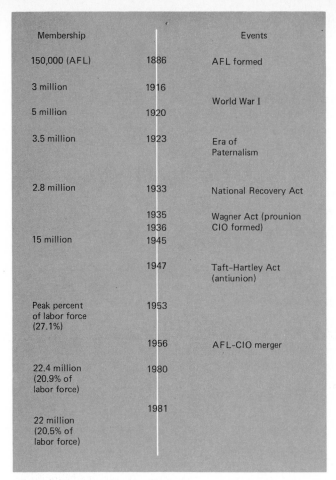

Membership		Events
150,000 (AFL)	1886	AFL formed
3 million	1916	
		World War I
5 million	1920	
3.5 million	1923	Era of Paternalism
2.8 million	1933	National Recovery Act
	1935	Wagner Act (prounion
	1936	CIO formed)
15 million	1945	
	1947	Taft-Hartley Act (antiunion)
Peak percent of labor force (27.1%)	1953	
	1956	AFL-CIO merger
22.4 million (20.9% of labor force)	1980	
	1981	
22 million (20.5% of labor force)		

Figure 2-1 Labor union growth.

The steel industry in 1892 had a union of skilled workers, the Amalgamated Association of Iron, Steel, and Tin Workers. It was a fairly strong union. The Homestead, Pennsylvania, plant of the Carnegie Steel Company had been struck by this union even though relations between company and union had been fairly friendly prior to this time. Andrew Carnegie, who had stated that he was wholly in favor of unions, was away in Europe and had left the factory in the hands of the plant manager, Henry Frick. A wage cut brought on the strike, whereupon Frick shut down the entire plant and prepared to protect it. The workers seized the mill property. Frick rose to the occasion by hiring some 300 Pinkerton detectives, whom he armed with Winchester rifles and placed on two barges, which were towed up the Monongahela River near the plant property. For 1 full day a battle that would have done credit to almost any small war raged on the banks of the Monongahela. The strikers tried to sink the barges with cannons, and when this failed, they poured oil on the water and set it afire. The detectives, with three dead and several wounded, surrendered and were marched out of town. Frick then appealed to the Governor of Pennsylvania for aid, and 1 week later the state militia took over the town. With this protection the company reopened the plant and started to bring in outside personnel. It was estimated that only 800 out of nearly 4,000 strikers got their jobs back. So thoroughly was the job done that it was not until the 1930s that another effective union was established in steel.

By 1916 there were approximately 3 million members of labor unions. During the next 4-year period, the number was almost doubled, because of wartime prosperity and favorable government attitudes. As usual, the movement suffered during the ensuing short depression and managed to stabilize again at about 3 million during the 1920s. With some further losses during the Depression of the 1930s, the membership stood at less than 3 million in 1933. *Twelve years later, there were approximately 15 million union members.* The most powerful factors contributing toward this increase were the favorable public attitudes, wartime prosperity, and passage in 1935 of the Wagner Act, the Magna Charta of labor. Collective bargaining was pronounced our national policy, and the right to organize was protected. Management's authority over another function was reduced and rigorously regulated.

In 1980, union membership stood at 22.4 million, a figure which is comprised of approximately 58 percent blue-collar and 42 percent white-collar employees. Most of the current membership are in unions affiliated with the American Federation of Labor–Congress of Industrial Organizations (AFL–CIO); the rest are in nonaffiliated unions such as the Teamsters, United Auto Workers, United Mine Workers, and various local independents.[2] Approximately 21 percent of the total labor force is organized into unions. This represents a decline from a high of 27.1 percent reached in 1953. It is evident, however, that despite this decline, turning back is impossible; the labor union is here to stay as a definite factor in our economy. We do not suggest that since unions have come this far, management should accept them completely. Such acceptance is neither desirable nor legal. But it should be evident that this problem of labor organization is one of the foremost of our time and requires more constructive thinking than has been evident in the past.

Decreased Pride in Work

Tightly designed organization structures and precisely planned work systems have played a role in lessening the freedom of the individual organization member. On the operative level, the increasing transfer of skills to machines has often left the worker with either a task of machine tending or no task at all. For managers, introduction of computers and data processing systems has served to regulate more closely their activities. Chris Argyris has suggested that industrial management in general has tended to underestimate the intelligence, resourcefulness, goodwill, and creativity of the American worker. He contends that jobs have been designed that call for docility, passivity, submissiveness, and short-term perspectives.[3] In his terms, the net result is psychological failure. We should, therefore, be concerned with a resulting absence of individual pride in accomplishment engendered by traditional structures of organization and operation.

As we consider this problem, we should first ask if pride in work is necessary. So long as the employee grinds the work out day after day, regulated by a system of production and managerial controls, why worry? Yet, when a problem is ignored, certain solutions are contributed by others which may not be the most desirable. This work

---

[2]See Chapters 19 and 20.
[3]Chris Argyris, ''Personality vs. Organization,'' *Organizational Dynamics,* vol. 3, no. 2, Autumn 1974, pp. 18–29.

situation, as we have briefly described it, is essentially the plight of the mass production worker. The CIO split from the AFL in 1936 for the specific purpose of representing this group of employees. The practice of ignoring the many requirements of the mass production worker has led to more unionization. The CIO, of course, later rejoined the AFL to form the AFL–CIO in 1956.

There are no laws or union demands that require management to create employee pride in work. The management with a mechanical approach toward labor has no interest; consequently, it can see no need and therefore no possible profit in considering the employee's psychology. Further analysis of this problem has led many to change their minds and, thus, their approach to labor. If stimulated, employees can often utilize their talents to make greater contributions than the minimum required. There is a large, relatively untapped reservoir of ability, loyalty, and interest.

Various other problems of personnel could be classified as a part of this series. But we feel that the essential point has been made—that management has played a large part in creating many of our modern personnel problems and that these problems have been too long ignored. Much of the progress made concerning these and similar problems has taken place within the last 20 years. Personnel management is a youthful, skilled profession dealing with some old and ingrained problems.

PATERNALISM

Although not all firms and managers held with the mechanical approach toward labor, it was fairly predominant in our economy up until the 1920s. Then suddenly there was a drastic reversal of form by a substantial segment of industrial managers. Some believe that a different approach was created by a fear of labor union growth, for during World War I the union membership almost doubled in number. Employees had demonstrated that they could escape from the managerially engineered closed system. As employers observed the breakdown of total control, they attempted to reclose the system by demonstrating to employees that there was little need for an outside force, the labor union. They began to undertake "voluntarily" a number of humanistic activities that they, the "fathers," felt that the employees needed.

Paternalism is the concept that management must assume a fatherly and protective attitude toward employees. The cold, impersonal attitude of the commodity concept is now replaced by a personal, and sometimes superpersonal, attitude of paternalism. The 1920s were the period during which personnel management became known as the glamor field of management. Here is where the need arose for the "backslapper," the "personality boy," and the person whose sole qualification was "liking people." During this time very elaborate personnel programs were developed, emphasizing such activities as company stores, company homes, recreational facilities, and the like. If the objective of this approach was to contain unions, it succeeded for a time, since the labor movement actually decreased in membership during this period. If the objective was that of buying employee loyalty and gratitude, it failed, since the employees considered themselves adults rather than children.

We do not believe that merely supplying many benefits, such as housing, recreation, and pensions, makes a management paternalistic. Of firms that offer identical benefits, one might be properly labeled paternalistic and the other might not. To be paternalistic, two characteristics are necessary. First, the profit motive should not be prominent in management's decision to provide such employee services. They should be offered because the management has decided that the employee needs them, just as a parent decides what is good for the children. This is not to say that the services may not prove to be profitable, but profit is not the prime reason for their installation. Second, the decision concerning what services to provide and how to provide them belongs solely to management. The *father* makes the decision that he feels is best for the child. If a firm offers a program of employee services because (1) it feels that such treatment of labor is a sensible and profitable undertaking that will advance the entire organization, or (2) the employees request and participate in the establishment of such programs, or (3) the labor union *demands* such programs, then that firm cannot properly be labeled paternalistic.

It is interesting to note that the paternalistic era coincided with the initiation of a second school of management thought. Just as the first, scientific management, developed in conjunction with the mechanical approach, the second school grew out of a series of lengthy experiments at the Hawthorne plant of the Western Electric Company beginning in 1924. This school, variously titled "human relations" and "behavioral," encouraged the adoption of a new model of the person. The pendulum swung from one extreme to another, from simplistic economic person to simplistic social person. Developing employee morale was viewed as a certain means to higher productivity. The interests of humans and organizations were deemed to be substantially identical. The impact of this school of thought, populated primarily by psychologists and sociologists, was felt primarily in the 1940s and 1950s. Just as the scientific management philosophy exacerbated certain human problems within the organization, the softer, human relations programs did not meet the requirements of organizational effectiveness in the experience of many managers. The problem is, instead, a highly complex one.

SOCIAL SYSTEM APPROACH

Paternalism died largely during the Depression of the 1930s, though certain managements still claim to utilize this basic approach even today. Having learned through experience of the values and dysfunctions of both prior approaches, managers and researchers began to realize that the management of personnel is no simple process. The pendulum has moved from its extreme simplistic positions to a more complex location involving analysis of multiple and often conflicting forces. We shall term this third view of personnel management a "social system" approach. In brief, the organization, or firm, is viewed as a complex central system operating within a complex environment which can be termed an "outer extended system." Managers recognize that the central system *cannot* be closed and directed in a mechanistic fashion. Options are available to central system members, both within the boundaries of the firm and on the outside with the aid of such external units as labor unions, government, and various public groups. Significant elements of the systems are depicted in Figure 2-2.

There are many and varied definitions of the term *system*. The definition by Beckett—"A system is a collection of interacting systems"—is perhaps most accurate, though confusing.[4] A system is a conglomerate of interrelated parts, each of which in turn can be viewed as a subsystem. Our central system, the firm, is a part of a larger system

---

[4]John A. Beckett, *Management Dynamics: The New Synthesis*, McGraw-Hill Book Company, New York, 1971, p. 29.

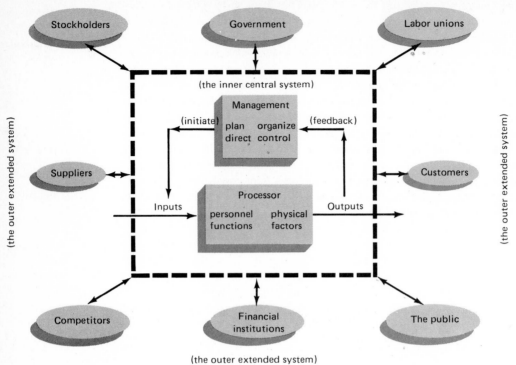

Figure 2-2 The social system.

generally known as the "economic system." The economic system is a part of the political system of our nation. Our country is a part of the political system of the world. The world is a subsystem of the solar system, which in turn is a subsystem of a largely uncharted space system. Thus, when we state that a system is a collection of interacting systems, we are emphasizing the inevitable interconnectedness and relationships that management must consider if it is to develop viable programs of personnel management.

The major components of any one system, as depicted in Figure 2-2, are (1) inputs from the outer environment; (2) a processor component, consisting of people, functions, and physical factors, which transforms these inputs into another set of utilities (e.g., steel into automobiles, ill patients into healthy people, uninformed students into knowledgeable citizens); (3) a set of outputs desired by members of the outer environment; and (4) a nerve system, usually designated "management," which regulates the inputs, processor, and outputs. One of the significant subsystems of the processor is termed "personnel." Though located *within* the boundaries, modern managers recognize that they do not have total control over the talents and attitudes of their employees, thereby requiring an open-systems strategy of adaptation, negotiation, persuasion, and compromise. Each individual employee is a complex human system. Employees tend to develop friendships, cliques, and associations that, in turn, become informal subsystems. We have learned that serious study of individual needs, as well as of informal group processes, can lead to personnel programs that help to align central system objectives (outputs) with the goals of the personnel component. It should also be noted that the subsystem of "management" has been divided, as suggested in the preceding chapter, into the functions of planning, organizing, directing, and controlling. After plans have been developed, the processor is designed and populated through the organizing function. Direction provides the initiating impulses for the processor to begin operation, while control works from the feedback of information concerning the nature and level of ensuing operations. Thus, the management component is also a subsystem.

Consideration of the members of the outer extended system provides the basis for a third school of management thought. An exclusively scientific or exclusively behavioral approach to managing gives way to one that has been termed "contingency" or "situational" management. If the outer system members are powerful, the central system will have to adapt and accommodate; if less powerful, the central system can try to close and operate on the basis of rational efficiency. And, as indicated above, if internal personnel have important powers of knowledge and cooperation, management must adapt and accommodate; if they possess less power because of substitutability, management may move closer to scientific processes. *There is no one way to manage that is applicable to all situations*. Thus contingency managers recognize that other system members, internal and external, possess powers that are important to the well-being of the enterprise.

TOWARD THE SOCIAL ROLE OF THE BUSINESS FIRM

In recent decades, there has been a growing concern about a redefinition of the proper role of the business firm within our society. That this is a problem is demonstrated by various surveys of public opinion concerning the design and operation of the business system. Over one-half of the public believe that the bad features of our business system either equal or outweigh the good.[5] The public estimate of the level of profits per dollar of sales is 28 cents; the actual amount is less than 5 cents. In addition, the general public has a low opinion of the caliber of business ethics. Though 70 percent contend that business has an obligation to help society even if it means less profit, less than half would accept that executives have a social conscience.

Inasmuch as the business system is a subsystem of organized society, the modern business executives must be concerned with societal expectations. Executive decisions concerning the direction and operation of business organizations have social consequences that can no longer be ignored. We have become increasingly concerned with the preservation and enhancement of (1) our physical resources on this planet, and (2) our human resources. Concerning the first, it has become only too apparent that our physical resources of air, land, and water are being seriously threatened by uncontrolled pursuit of economic goals. Second, with the labor union movement of the 1930s and 1940s and the civil rights movement of the 1950s and 1960s, society has demonstrated its marked interest in how business utilizes its citizens as employees. The personnel manager has an important and inescapable responsibility in helping the firm's management to recognize, define, and fulfill this enlarged concept of its social role.

---

[5]Thomas Benham, "The Factual Foundation," in Clarence H. Danhof and James C. Worthy, eds., *Crisis in Confidence II: Corporate America*, Sagamon State University, Springfield, Ill., 1975, pp. 21–53.

Bases of Social Responsibility

If one grants that the business firm is a subsystem of the economy, which in turn is a subsystem of the total society, it still remains to determine the nature and extent of that firm's societal obligation. Normative statements of what business *ought* to do with regard to social responsibility will not ensure that action will be undertaken. There are a number of rationales or theories upon which social action can be based. Among these are:

1. Long-run profit maximization and social responsibility are substantially similar concepts.

2. The changing ethics of business managers are in concordance with the changing norms of society.

3. Firms will prepare a list of goals in order of priority with noneconomic social values being included.

4. Firms will be socially responsible to the degree they perceive power threats in the environment.

With respect to the coincidence of a long-term view of profit and social responsibility, it has been stated, "The longer the range a realistic business projection is, the more likely it is to find a sound ethical footing."[6] When Henry Ford II explained Ford's extensive hard-core unemployed hiring and training program to stockholders, it was justified on the basis of preventing future riots in Detroit. When insurance companies undertook extensive investments in slum reconstruction, they explained to their stockholders that they were opening up future markets for life insurance. When money is contributed to private educational instutitions, stockholders are told that the firm's management is helping to develop professional employees for the future. All of these implications are logical, but exclusive benefit to the spending firm is difficult to prove.

There is some evidence that firms that are more socially active tend to be more profitable as well. Of the companies listed as *Fortune's* "Top 500" in 1973, 80 were selected as being significantly more active in multiple social areas than the remaining 420.[7] These 80 firms had significantly higher net income as measured as a percentage of sales, percentage of stockholder equity, and earnings per share. A second study suggests that excessive activity in the social area can be almost as detrimental to profits as too little activity. Those firms with a *medium* level of social activity provided a return on investment of 16.1 percent.[8] This compared with a return of 10.2 percent for those with little activity and 12.3 percent for those with a great many social programs. A highly plausible basis for the coincidence of profits and social activity is that the factor underlying both is superior, sophisticated, and intelligent management. Those who can solve technical and economic problems can also work out an effective relationship with members of the outer extended system. As indicated in Box 2-1, an initial investment in the area of social responsibility can turn into a profitable undertaking.

---

[6]Albert Z. Carr, "Can an Executive Afford a Conscience?" *Harvard Business Review,* vol. 12, no. 4, July-August 1970, p. 64.

[7]Robert Parket and Henry Eilbirt, "Social Responsibility: The Underlying Factors," *Business Horizons,* vol. 18, no. 4, August 1975, p. 8.

[8]Edward H. Bowman and Mason Haire, "A Strategic Posture toward Corporate Social Responsibility," *California Management Review,* vol. 18, no. 2, Winter 1975, pp. 52–54.

Ten miles from the Bronx, in Brooklyn's Bedford-Stuyvesant district, International Business Machines Corp. has been manufacturing computer components for 14 years with a work force drawn almost entirely from this black, working-class neighborhood. IBM admits it began the operation in 1968 as a social experiment. In the volatile climate following the 1960s race riots, some 120 persons were put to work in a converted warehouse at the lowest of high-tech tasks, reconditioning electronic cable.

The plant stayed, and by all accounts has prospered. Today a staff of 420, split 50–50 between production and management-engineering, works on a variety of tasks, from routine "board stuffing" to assembly of two components of the 3081 system, IBM's most powerful computer. In 1978 the workers moved five blocks to a new building put up by IBM.

Two other computer makers have built big inner-city manufacturing plants. Digital Equipment Corporation makes all its half-inch tape drives and flexible disk products on a 15-acre site in a predominantly black area of Springfield, Mass. Almost 60% of the 840 workers are minorities. Control Data Corporation's minority hiring push began in 1968 with a plant in Minneapolis' northside neighborhood.

The sociological view of a movement toward greater business social responsibility rests upon the impact of changing cultural values upon the firm's managers. It is contended that as concern for physical and human resources spreads throughout society, individual managers' consciences and codes of ethics will lead them to make more socially responsible decisions. One negative note is sounded by a survey and comparison of codes of ethics of practicing marketing managers and young college students in both business and liberal arts fields.[9] In asking over 1,500 students and business executives their views on questionable actions in 20 hypothetical situations, there were *no* significant differences in the answers from the three groups; business executives averaged 34 percent approval, business students 36 percent, and liberal arts students 33 percent. Lowest average approval was for an action involving hiding your spouse's expenses on a report of a recent business trip (4 to 8 percent), while highest approval was given to using "long-distance" telephone calls from nearby cities to reach busy executives (81 to 88 percent). Using hidden tape recorders in conducting personal interviews received approval by approximately a third of all respondents.

A more usable basis for injecting a greater measure of social responsibility into decision making is the contention that managers may preach "profit maximizing" but they practice "profit satisficing." Rather than exacting the last possible dollar profit out of each decision, one strives for a reasonable level that will satisfy significant members of the outer environment, such as stockholders, financial institutions, and so on. The manager then utilizes remaining resources in pursuing social values of lesser priority such as hiring the hard-core unemployed, utilizing the physically handicapped, or locating new plants in underdeveloped ghetto areas. Hired professional managers are more likely to use a profit satisficing approach than are owner-managers. The latter are more inclined to manage the firm using a more restricted number of goals.[10]

[9]Charles S. Goodman and C. Merle Crawford, "Young Executives: A Source of New Ethics?" *Personnel Journal*, vol. 53, no. 3, March 1974, pp. 180–187.

[10]Joseph Monsen, "Ownership and Management: The Effect of Separation on Performance," *Business Horizons*, vol. 12, no. 4, August 1969, p. 47.

The final basis is considered by many to be the only realistic approach to the concept of social responsibility. The firm will be socially responsible to the degree to which it perceives power threats from others in the system. As outlined in Figure 2-2, there are significant and powerful groups operating in the environment of the business firm. Labor unions and governmental units are perhaps the most powerful. Consumer groups, led by such people as Ralph Nader, are working to increase their power. Special-purpose groups, such as the Urban League and the National Organization of Women, try to bring pressure upon those in authority.

A problem of increasing concern in this country is the private company's responsibility to employees and communities when deciding to close down a plant. In many countries of the world, severe financial penalties are imposed upon firms in the form of substantial payments to employees for jobs lost. Plant closing legislation has been introduced into the United States Congress. Though none has been passed as yet, one bill would require a 1-year notice of a closing, give displaced workers the right to transfer to a new company location at company expense, provide employee severance pay equal to 85 percent of annual wages, and require companies to pay 100 percent of one year's tax loss to the community.

Managers will assess the power of each group and its potential threat to organization activities. They will attempt to reduce these threatening forces by such actions as (1) stockpiling products to reduce the effect of labor union strikes, (2) lobbying government officials and securing business personnel appointments to governing commissions, (3) advertising to influence customers, (4) appointing a few minority members to the firm's board of directors, (5) developing multiple sources of materials supplies to reduce influence of particular vendors, (6) retaining earnings to reduce power of financial institutions, and (7) seeking stockholder proxies in order to control board of director elections. To some, many of these actions designed to reduce central-system dependencies are antagonistic to a broader view of social utility. However, two points can be made. First, the basic requirements of all social systems involve this movement toward control and predictability; this is a source of much efficiency and effectiveness. Second, there is no way that the system can be entirely closed and made completely rational; we can never eliminate all of the contingencies. Thus, powerful others will always have impact on the decision processes of private managers. When managers go too long without responding, they risk the possibility of new legislation, new institutions, and perhaps even a new system.

Obligations of the Personnel Manager

Since society's expectations regarding appropriate treatment of its citizens are constantly changing, the personnel manager occupies a unique position in the firm. With respect to defining and fulfilling this enlarged social role, her or his obligations are primarily three in number: (1) ensuring that expectations concerning the quality of work life are met, (2) ensuring that the organization is in compliance with appropriate laws and regulations affecting employees, and (3) participating in the design and execution of periodic social audits.

Beyond adequate compensation and a safe work environment, there is evidence of a growing demand for challenging and interesting jobs, according respect for personal privacy, permitting greater individualism in dress and life-style, and assistance in planning lifelong careers. As indicated in the preceding chapter, a type of "corporate constitutionalism'' is beginning to enter private enterprises when the executive's power to make unilateral decisions is restricted. The employee does not give up his or her societal citizenship when entering the organization. There will be increasing expectations in terms of ''due process'' in deciding upon layoffs and discharges, freedom of speech in regard to revealing unsafe or illegal organizational activities, and the right to not reveal personal information of no concern to the organization. It has been suggested that firms should be measured in terms that will reveal the quality of work life, such as absenteeism, turnover, alcoholism, drug addiction, and mental illness.[11] If ''acceptable levels'' are exceeded, firms should be fined or taxed just as they are when they excessively pollute the air or water. Of course, measuring and determining what are acceptable levels would be very difficult tasks. In addition it is not at all certain that the quality of work life is the only possible cause for alcoholism, drug addiction, and mental illness.

Though some firms successfully ignore threats issuing from failures to improve the quality of work life, they are much less able to avoid the uniform measures imposed by governmental legislation. Each year, a greater obligation is placed upon the personnel manager to ensure organizational compliance with a host of laws and governmental rules concerning hiring, training, compensating, and utilization of various special groups in our society. Personnel management is increasingly becoming a legalistic process as society has become impatient with voluntary social action. And though a personnel manager would prefer to acquire higher status through the initiation of sound voluntary programs, the fact is that today's elevated status of the field owes much to the intervention of government.

Finally, the modern organization will display a concern for periodic auditing of social activities, both voluntary and required. Because of the coverage of human resources, the personnel manager has a significant role to play in its design and execution. A social audit is defined as ''a commitment to systematic assessment of and reporting on some meaningful, definable domain of a company's activities that have social impact.''[12] Its uses are to provide internal information to management which aids in decision making and to provide external information to the public in response to pressures upon the enterprise to be socially responsible.

Four possible types of audits are currently envisaged: (1) a simple inventory of activities, (2) compilation of socially relevant expenditures, (3) specific program management, and (4) determination of social impact. The inventory is generally the place where one would start. It would consist of a simple listing of activities undertaken by a firm over and above what is required for ordinary operation. For example, one firm itemized the following social activities: (1) minority employment and training, (2) support of minority enterprises, (3) pollution control, (4) corporate giving, (5) involvement in selected community projects by firm executives, and (6) a hard-core unemployed program.

A step forward in sophistication would be an attempt to itemize the costs incurred in these socially oriented activities. Such expenditures would be more impressive to external publics but more depressive to internal managers without some indications of offsetting benefits. One utility company determined that it had spent $30,000 in 1 year

---

[11]Edward E. Lawler III, ''Should the Quality of Work Life Be Legislated?'' *The Personnel Administrator*, vol. 21, no. 1, January 1976, pp. 17–21.

[12]Raymond A. Bauer and Dan H. Fenn, Jr., ''What *Is* a Corporate Social Audit?'' *Harvard Business Review*, vol. 51, no. 1, January-February 1973, p. 38.

in the human resources area, with an additional $90,000 being allocated to pollution control. Further documentation was provided in such areas as: (1) emission levels of particulate matter, sulfur oxides, and nitrogen oxides for coal, oil, and gas used, (2) temperatures of water received and discharged from the plant, (3) workdays lost due to employee injuries and illnesses, (4) number of minority and female employees hired and trained, and (5) charitable contributions.[13]

In the program management approach, each separate project is researched to ascertain not only its expenditures but also its outputs, in terms of specific management objectives. In the Bank of America, for example, the Small Business Administration-Minority Enterprise Program is evaluated in terms of additional costs incurred for this type of loan, compared with a projected goal of new successful minority enterprises established.[14] The Student Loan Program would involve a comparison of the costs of the lower rate of interest received with a goal concerning numbers of young people financed in college. This "Management by Objectives" approach permits managerial determination of the degree of success without invading the issue of the impact of goal accomplishment upon the welfare of society.

The ideal social audit would involve determination of the true benefits to society of any socially oriented business activity. Obtaining data for this ultimate impact not only is extremely difficult but involves decisions requiring value judgments. What is the value of a hard-core unemployed program to the community? Is it greater or less than the value of a program to promote minority business enterprises? Program management evades this issue by accepting a program as generally good on the basis of logic or pressure, and then evaluating it against specific program objectives. This does not deal, however, with the development of an overall, balanced, and integrated program that could issue from an analysis of social impact. Given the embryonic stage of development in which we find the social audit, management should be willing to settle for less than this ultimate form.

SUMMARY

Both the attitudes toward personnel and the philosophies of managing them have evolved through history. Figure 2-3 is a summary of some of these significant changes.

The social system approach to personnel is part and parcel of a larger system approach to management. Research has demonstrated that it is often possible to develop personnel programs that can simultaneously satisfy the needs of individuals, groups, managers, and the total organization. In other instances, such perfect alignment is not possible. Open system analysis and development of strategies characterized by discussion, confrontation, negotiation, and compromise will be required to manage conflicts that inevitably develop.

The task is further complicated by the forces that can be brought to bear by significant others in the outer environment. These forces have become more numerous and powerful and have led to increasing recognition that the private business firm has a social

---

[13]Steven C. Dilley and Jerry J. Weygandt, "Measuring Social Responsibility: An Empirical Test," *The Journal of Accountancy,* September 1973, pp. 62–70.

[14]Bernard L. Butcher, "The Program Management Approach to the Corporate Social Audit," *California Management Review,* vol. 16, no. 1, Fall 1973, p. 14.

FIGURE 2-3
Evolving Approaches toward Personnel

Personnel Approach	System Assumed	Union Strength	Management Philosophy
Mechanical	Closed	Weak	Scientific management (Taylor)
Paternalism	Attempted reclosing	Doubled before; declined during	Behavioral (Hawthorne experiments)
Social system	Open	Quintupled	Contingency

responsibility. Successful performance of the economic role is no longer sufficient in and of itself.

Whether one believes that long-run profit maximization and social responsibility are substantially similar concepts or that power analysis will ultimately force socially desirable behavior, it is certain that modern managers will pay more attention to the protection and enhancement of both physical and human resources. The personnel manager has an obligation to do more than ensure that the company is in compliance with the numerous laws detailing social minimums. Concern grows regarding improving the quality of work life within the firm for all employees, whether a special protected group or not. Corporate constitutionalism may soon require tolerance for dissent, participation in decision making, judicial review for complaints, and freedom to pursue individual life-styles. These additional obligations in no way decrease responsibility for providing the enterprise with a competent and capable work force making possible the effective accomplishment of traditional economic goals.

BRIEF CASE

One Monday morning, Dr. King happened to notice that the water in his swimming pool was not circulating. Having had an unending amount of difficulty with the pool pump, he had severed relations with Acme Pool Company almost a year ago. His new company had immediately replaced the pump, and he had had trouble-free service ever since. On investigating the situation, he discovered that the switch by the motor had not been turned on. He flipped it on and immediately blew out all the fuses. Looking more closely, he discovered that the motor was not his! Someone had taken the new motor and replaced it with another. Reasoning that only a pool company would do such a thing, a little detective work among the neighbors revealed that an Acme truck had been in his driveway about 4 days ago. On calling Acme, the secretary, after some delay, admitted that a mistake had been made. A worker had misread the address on the work order. Inasmuch as the severing of relationships with Acme a year ago had not been amicable, Dr. King told the secretary in no uncertain terms that the motor had better be returned that very day.

On returning home that evening, it was immediately apparent that the motor had not been replaced. Calling Acme the next morning, Dr. King demanded to speak to the manager. He told the manager that if the ''stolen property'' was not returned that day, a complaint would be filed with the police. The motor was reinstalled that afternoon.

Two days later, Dr. King received a letter from Acme apologizing for the error, but upbraiding him for his behavior during the episode. In part, the letter read: "We are a good, community-minded employer, and it has been our policy to employ the culturally disadvantaged. The worker who made the mistake on your motor is an older, minority worker who is gradually losing his eyesight. In view of this, we feel that your impatience and ill humor are inconsistent with modern management practice." Dr. King flung the letter down in disgust, saying, "Well, that's one brand of ethics!"

Questions

1. What does Dr. King mean by the term "brand of ethics"? What are the "brands" involved in this case?"

2. How does a firm reconcile the conflicting demands of social responsibility and the economics of competition?

DISCUSSION QUESTIONS

1. Define the three approaches to personnel and relate them to the development of various schools of management philosophy.

2. Define the three approaches to personnel and relate them to the history of the union movement.

3. What are the major components of a system? How can we characterize management as a nerve subsystem?

4. When private business organizations fail to solve such problems as technological unemployment, insecurity, and loss of pride in work, what usually happens next?

5. What major groups make up the extended outer environment? What actions can a manager take to reduce dependency on each group?

6. Discuss the four bases for a private business firm's assuming a social responsibility beyond that of producing a product or service for a profit.

7. Discuss the specific obligations of the personnel manager with respect to the social responsibility of the firm.

8. Define the social audit and indicate the varying types that have been identified.

9. Define and interrelate "profit maximizing," "profit satisficing," "hired-managers," "owner-managers," and "social responsibility."

10. What is meant by "quality of work life"? What role is there here for the personnel manager?

SUPPLEMENTARY READING

ARLOW, PETER and MARTIN J. GANNON: "Social Responsiveness, Corporate Structure, and Economic Performance," *Academy of Management Review,* vol. 7, no. 2, April 1982, pp. 235–241.

ERDLEN, JOHN D.: "Ethics and the Employee Relations Function," *The Personnel Administrator,* vol. 24, no. 1, January 1979, pp. 41–43.

FREDERICK, WILLIAM C.: "Free Market vs. Social Responsibility," *California Management Review,* vol. 23, no. 3, Spring 1981, pp. 20–28.

GOODPASTER, KENNETH E. and JOHN B. MATTHEWS, JR.: "Can a Corporation Have a Conscience?" *Harvard Business Review,* vol. 60, no. 1, January-February 1982, pp. 132–141.

JOHNSON, HAROLD L.: "Ethics and the Executive," *Business Horizons,* vol. 24, no. 3, May-June 1981, pp. 53–59.

NASH, LAURA L.: "Ethics without the Sermon," *Harvard Business Review,* vol. 59, no. 9, November-December, 1981, pp. 79–90.

chapter 3

Managing the Personnel Unit

Though personnel activities are common to all organizations, their assignment to a specialized unit occurs in only larger organizations. In one survey of approximately 500 companies, two-thirds of 74 firms with fewer than 250 employees had no separate personnel unit budgets.[1] In these firms, the procurement, development, compensation, integration, maintenance, and separation of personnel were being done by the various operating units.

The focus of this chapter will be on managing a specialized personnel unit as a part of a larger enterprise. As Figure 3-1 indicates, the typical personnel staff ratio (number of persons in the personnel unit compared to total employed) is 1 employee per 100 other employees in the firm. This ratio is larger in smaller organizations (1.5 to 100) and smaller in firms with more than 2,500 employees (0.8 to 100). This figure includes all personnel assigned. If confined solely to professional and technical staff members, the typical ratio is 0.5 to 100.

Other surveys support this finding. A survey of 404 organizations found the personnel unit to have 1 full-time person for every 100 employees on the payroll, and 1 professional/technical person per 177 employees on the payroll.[2] Ratios also tend to vary by industry with comparatively greater investments in personnel units in finance and manufacturing. Concerning government, a survey of two states, Iowa and Alabama, produced a ratio of 1.8 personnel workers per 1,000 employees.[3] This considerably lower public ratio is largely explained by the existence of civil service commissions that perform much of the work normally allocated to a private personnel department.

It was stated in Chapter 1 that the basic functions common to all managers are planning, organizing, directing, and controlling. In this chapter, we shall examine the

---

[1]Bureau of National Affairs, Inc., "Personnel Activities, Budgets, and Staffs: 1980–1981," *Bulletin to Management No. 1627*, May 21, 1981, p. 7.

[2]Steven Langer, "Budgets and Staffing: A Survey, Part II," *Personnel Journal*, vol. 60, no. 6, June 1981, p. 464.

[3]Myron D. Fottler and Craig Norrell, "State Government Personnel Directors: A Comparative Analysis of Their Background Characteristics and Qualifications," *Public Personnel Management*, vol. 8, no. 1, January-February 1979, p. 19.

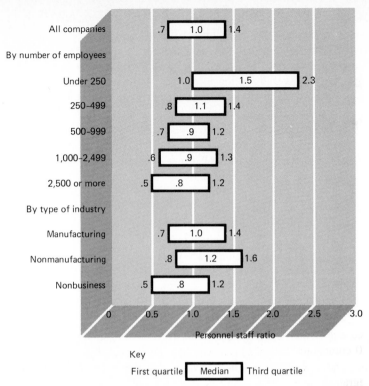

All companies .7 | 1.0 | 1.4

By number of employees

Under 250 1.0 | 1.5 | 2.3

250–499 .8 | 1.1 | 1.4

500–999 .7 | .9 | 1.2

1,000–2,499 .6 | .9 | 1.3

2,500 or more .5 | .8 | 1.2

By type of industry

Manufacturing .7 | 1.0 | 1.4

Nonmanufacturing .8 | 1.2 | 1.6

Nonbusiness .5 | .8 | 1.2

0   0.5   1.0   1.5   2.0   2.5   3.0

Personnel staff ratio

Key

First quartile | Median | Third quartile

Figure 3-1   Personnel staff ratios: number of persons on personnel staff per 100 employees in total work force. *(Source: "ASPA–BNA Survey No. 41, Personnel Activities, Budgets and Staffs: 1980–1981,"* Bulletin to Management *No. 1627, May 21, 1981, p. 6. With permission.)*

managing task of the leader of the specialized personnel unit. Attention will be given to only three of the functions—planning, organizing, and controlling—with discussion of the fourth, directing, delayed until coverage of the operative function of integration. The directing function is heavily concerned with motivation of others to contribute to organizational objectives, a task that is essential to integration. If the personnel manager is obligated to assist other managers in this area, it would seem logical that this same expertise could be brought to bear upon the immediate organizational unit.

That more attention should be devoted to management of personnel activities is substantiated by frequent and persistent criticism of personnel units as uneconomical and useless appendages to vital living structures of productive organizations. A former chairman of the Avis Rent-A-Car Corporation recommended "firing the whole personnel department."[4] Herzberg complains that the unit's major goal is too often that of "peace," thereby calling for numerous hygienic programs to "clean up" the workplace and prevent dissatisfaction.[5] Though criticism of specific company programs is often justified, it is undeniable that a considerable potential for value creation exists in specialized units whose primary concern is the organization's human resources. With increasing pressures brought to bear by both government and labor unions, there is little danger that the unit

[4]Robert Townsend, *Up the Organization,* Alfred A. Knopf, Inc., New York, 1970, p. 144.
[5]Frederick Herzberg, *Work and the Nature of Man,* The World Publishing Company, Cleveland, 1966, chap. 9.

will be "fired." However, a professional personnel manager will not settle for this protective, maintenance, and peacekeeping role and will search for approaches that will simultaneously enhance values derived by people, organizations, and society. That this is one of the most difficult tasks imaginable perhaps provides us with an excuse, but it does not serve to justify excessive absorption in relatively unimportant activities. Top management can lead the way by insisting that personnel managers establish definite goals for the personnel system, that continuous planning be practiced because of the dynamic nature of the subject, that more human resource information be made available in a form that facilitates sound decision making, and that the multiple, splintered, and technique-oriented operative activities be integrated into a coordinated system.

Opportunities do exist for personnel managers to act decisively and professionally. In a survey of large enterprises, 126 of the 249 top personnel executives carried the title "vice president."[6] In a second study of 1,708 senior-level executives in large, publicly held corporations, 117 identified themselves as personnel executives.[7] Approximately 48 percent had been in personnel work for their entire careers, the average tenure with the current organization being 15 years. With an average workweek of 50 hours, the median salary was $94,000 as compared with $116,000 for all other senior-level executives. Only about 1 percent of the total number of executives identified personnel management as the "fastest route to the top." Finance/accounting, marketing, and general management were deemed to be better routes to company presidencies. It should be noted, however, that a slowly increasing number of company presidents include a tour of duty in the personnel unit as a part of their career development. The chairman of the board of Delta Airlines as well as the chairman of International Paper Company spent time as personnel executives.[8]

In 1975, the American Society for Personnel Administration, an organization of 28,000 members, established an independent nonprofit organization, the Personnel Accreditation Institute, for the purpose of accrediting professionals in the personnel field. As a part of this process of examination for accreditation, the association developed the *ASPA Handbook of Personnel and Industrial Relations.* This is an attempt to establish a recognized body of knowledge in order to raise the quality of performance in the field. The personnel activities in this book cover the six functional areas associated with the accreditation examinations. Though further study and experience are necessary, familiarization with the field provided by this book should contribute to professional accreditation.

Organizing the Personnel Unit

In most organizations, the specialized personnel unit is typically designated as a staff unit. The denotation of "staff" indicates that it is producing values to be consumed by the organization itself. The organization may be established for various purposes such as producing and marketing automobiles, or providing a college education for qualified students. A specialized personnel unit creates secondary values to be consumed by the primary or line units within the enterprise, such values as screening new hires to work

---

[6]Allen R. Janger, "Personnel Administration: Changing Scope and Organization," *Studies in Personnel Policy, No. 203,* National Industrial Conference Board, New York, 1966, p. 14.

[7]John Sussman, "Profile of the Successful Personnel Executive," *The Personnel Administrator,* vol. 25, no. 2, February 1980, p. 78.

[8]"Personnel Widens Its Franchise," *Business Week,* February 26, 1979, p. 121.

in the primary areas, assisting in their training, and developing compensation programs that will enhance both a feeling of equity and motivation to work. The product of the unit is a willing and effective workforce. The product of the firm is a purchased automobile or a graduated student.

Bases of departmentation Within the personnel unit, a manager can organize on a number of different bases. Perhaps the functional base is most common within personnel departments. In the example shown in Figure 3-2, the basic grouping revolves around procurement (employment), development (training), compensation (wage and salary administration), integration (labor relations), maintenance (safety), and separation (employee services, retirement). The exact breakdown would obviously vary with the enterprise, inasmuch as it is affected by such variables as size, abilities of personnel, and top management philosophy regarding the role of the unit. If employment interviewers and personnel assistants are considered to be entry-level professional jobs in the personnel unit, a salary survey in one recent year produced the following median salaries expressed in terms of percentages of the entry positions.[9]

Training and organizational development manager	197%
Compensation and benefits manager	171
Employee benefits manager	165
Training manager	158
Recruitment, selection, and employment manager	157
Employment manager	137
Recruiter	127
Employee benefits administrator	125
Compensation analyst	123

One behavioral critic has suggested that most personnel time and budget have been improperly spent upon hygienic activities designed to prevent employee dissatisfaction. Though the importance and extent of such activities will not decline, Herzberg contends

[9]"Overview of Current Personnel Salaries, Part I: Personnel/Industrial Relations Report," by Steven Langer, copyright September 1979. Reprinted with the permission of *Personnel Journal*, Costa Mesa, Calif.; all rights reserved.

Figure 3-2 Personnel department—functional base.

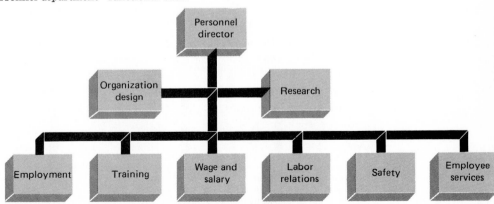

that an even more significant activity should be undertaken, that of promoting employee satisfaction.[10] As indicated in Figure 3-3, the first functional grouping should be on the basis of purpose or service: (1) prevent dissatisfaction through hygienic maintenance, and (2) promote satisfaction through motivators. The functional breakdown of the hygiene division would be similar to that in Figure 3-2. The suggested breakdown of the new motivator division would be as follows: (1) an educational function to convince all managers that satisfaction comes basically from the job content and not the surrounding environment, (2) a job design function to enhance interest and pride in work (see Chapter 5), and (3) a remedial function involving training and education to overcome technological obsolescence and poor performance of specific individuals and groups.

Sokolik suggests a third basis on which modern departments might be organized: clientele.[11] He feels that modern crises as well as the varying requirements of different types of employees might dictate specialization on this particular base. As indicated in Figure 3-4, he recommends that subunits be developed to concentrate separately upon scientific and technical personnel, workers new to industry (hard-core unemployed), managers, women, and labor organized into unions. Instead of a "total market" approach to all personnel, market or personnel segmentation would be more likely to lead to differentiation of programming and treatment. In most instances, the particular personnel department organization that is adopted is a combination of bases, rather than any single one.

Line and Personnel Staff Relationships

When a specialized staff unit is introduced into an organization, formerly clear interunit relationships often become highly complex. In organizing, what has been di-

[10]Frederick Herzberg, op. cit., pp. 171–181.
[11]Stanley L. Sokolik, "Reorganize the Personnel Department?" *California Management Review,* vol. 11, no. 3, Spring 1969, p. 48.

Figure 3-3 Personnel department—service base.

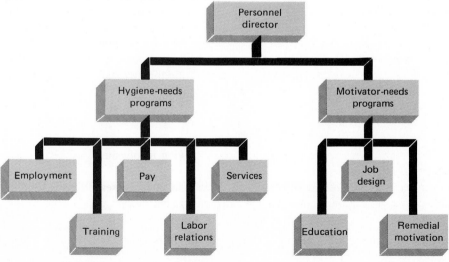

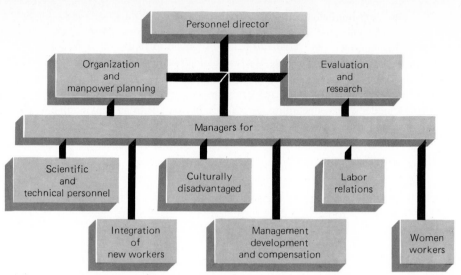

Figure 3-4   Personnel department—clientele base. *(Source: Stanley L. Sokolik, "Reorganize the Personnel Department?" California Management Review, vol. II, no. 3, Spring 1969, p. 48; © 1969 by The Regents of the University of California, reprinted by permission of the Regents of the University of California.)*

vided to secure specialized expertise must ultimately be combined to secure unity of organized action. Various guides or principles of line/staff relationships have been proposed as means of effecting greater coordination and cooperation. Four examples will be given, the first two of which emphasize the primary status of line; the latter two defend the necessary contribution of the personnel staff unit.

Principle of staff advice   This is the most frequently cited principle in this area and states that staff can only *advise* line what to do, never command or order. The wholeness or integrity of the line should not be broken. But what if the personnel manager has recommended that a superintendent follow a proposal and the latter refuses? According to the principle, personnel cannot force compliance. But the personnel manager is convinced that the proposal is sound. The formal organization allows appeal to a common superior, in this case the vice president of production. If this official agrees, the staff recommendation becomes a line order, which the superintendent must follow. The integrity of the line has been preserved, but the personnel manager may have difficulty in working with the superintendent in the future. Many staff specialists feel that they can be more effective in their work by avoiding such actions as this except in extremely important situations. They prefer to rely upon persuasion and sometimes upon "politicking" to achieve their aims. In a review of 556 transactions by personnel managers in 72 organizations, the reported role of "adviser" was attached to 505.[12] In only 51 cases were there reports of greater decision-making involvement, with over half of these being in the area of grievance processing.

In terms of specific grants of decision-making authority, research has discovered a high degree of variability, not only among different firms but also among different

---

[12]Charles J. Coleman, "The Personnel Director: A Cautious Hero Indeed," *Human Resource Management,* vol. 18, no. 4, Winter 1979, p. 18.

personnel operative functions within the single enterprise. In interviews with 75 executives in 25 firms varying in size from 100 to 15,000 employees, French and Henning discovered that the authority varied from little or none to unilateral rights of decision making in some personnel functions.[13] Over half reported that personnel directors are particularly strong in terms of unilateral action in decisions concerning the use of psychological tests, reference checks, and determination of bargaining strategy. They play a weaker role in decisions concerning the creation of new positions, maximum bargaining concessions, and granting of unusual and new fringe benefits. They are most authoritative in the procurement function and least authoritative in determining wage-level policies.

Principle of limitation of staff economy   This principle emphasizes the *service* relationship of staff. It states that in order for the line to operate at maximum economy and effectiveness, it is sometimes necessary for the serving staff to operate with reduced economy. The line is to be served by staff, not vice versa. Sometimes the staff official may have to run his or her department in a manner that is considered undesirable in order properly to serve the line. For example, a company may be desperately short of machinists. There is some chance that if the personnel department stays open at night some machinists may be encouraged to look around for another job after working hours. Also, these long hours may be extremely unpopular with personnel employees, and the budget may take a beating, but the hardship is necessary for the welfare of the line organization. Too often staff tends to prescribe what line must do to adjust to its requirements. The tail attempts to wag the dog.

Principle of compulsory staff advice   The first two principles stated above emphasize the importance of the line. If staff is necessary in an organization, its contribution must be defended. Staff functions are separated from the line and sometimes line resents this loss. There may be a tendency in the line to ignore or refuse to utilize staff, in the hope that they will go away and leave the line alone. If such is the case, a considerable investment has been made in staff personnel with little or no return. The line official is making all decisions with no assistance.

The principle of compulsory staff advice does not compel a line official to accept and follow the advice; it compels the line person only to listen. For example, the personnel unit should be consulted when jobs are being redesigned by line managers. Too often, only engineers and line managers are involved, thereby leading to job contents that may be technically feasible but humanly objectionable.

Principle of staff independence   Staff may not only be ignored by some line officials, but it may sometimes be dominated by others. The principle of staff independence indicates that staff personnel should have sufficient security to be able to give truthful advice to their superiors without fear of losing their jobs. If we are to profit by the presence of expertness, then that expertness requires a certain amount of freedom within which to operate. If the staff specialist is merely to echo line ideas, the investment is wasted and the function should be returned to the line, formally as well as informally.

An example of this concept has sometimes been observed with respect to pending unionization of a firm. Research and study may lead the personnel manager to conclude that cooperation with the unionizing attempt, within the confines of the law, may be to the long-run best interest of the organization. Recommendation of such a policy to an

---

[13]Wendell French and Dale Henning, "The Authority-Influence Role of the Functional Specialist in Management," *Journal of the Academy of Management*, vol. 9, no. 3, September 1966, pp. 187–203.

owner-manager in some instances has been tantamount to immediate discharge. Again, line officials are not compelled to accept or follow the advice of expert specialists; but they are exceedingly shortsighted if they refuse to listen at all, or if they punish and reward in a manner leading to suppression of rational thought.

PLANNING THE PERSONNEL PROGRAM

Defined in its simplest terms, *planning is the determination of anything in advance of action*. It is essentially a decision-making process that provides a basis for economical and effective action in the future. Effective planning sets the stage for integrated action to take place, reduces the number of unforeseeable crises, promotes the use of more efficient methods, and provides the basis for the managerial function of control, thereby assuring focus on organization objectives. Figure 3-5 portrays the personnel manager's working time as revealed in a study of 72 organizations. The unclassified category refers to such activities as professional reading and attending seminars.

Decision Making

The personnel manager, despite the nebulous and complex nature of the field, can increase program effectiveness through a more judicious decision-making process. The suggested sequence of steps in more scientific decision making would encompass the following: (1) recognize and define a problem that calls for action, (2) determine possible alternative solutions, (3) collect and analyze facts bearing upon the problem, and (4) decide on a solution. Recognition of personnel problems calls for experience and background that makes it possible for cues and clues to be observed and synthesized into patterns of probable cause and effect. In the personnel field, one must be always alert to possible dysfunctional human effects issuing from many technical programs promulgated in the name of rationality and profit; e.g., controls such as budgets often stimulate internal warfare. In generating solutions, creative imagination as well as interpersonal contacts will lead to generation of multiple possible answers. "Brainstorming" and other

FIGURE 3-5
The Personnel Director's Working Time

	Percentage of Time
Planning and directing the personnel department	21.8
Providing information and advice to others for decisions	21.2
Environmental relations (primarily with the union)	19.1
Gathering information	17.4
Control: where personnel approval is needed to complete an action	12.0
Unclassified	8.5

Source: Charles J. Coleman, "The Personnel Director: A Cautious Hero Indeed," *Human Resource Management*, vol. 18, no. 4, Winter 1979, p. 17. With permission.

artificial creative stimulants have been applied to personnel problems on occasion.[14] After imagination abates temporarily, judgment takes over in the collection and analysis of facts. Operations research and quantitative methods show some promise of being able to assist the personnel manager in collating and understanding gathered data. Ultimately, the essence of the manager's position is *choice*. One must extend one's neck and commit time and talent to a program that one figures will work.

Programs and Policies

Policies and programs are human-made guides to action. In theory, they are based on an analysis of enterprise objectives as well as on the available knowledge in the subject area concerned. Personnel managers are often called upon to establish guides in areas where the state of the art is incomplete, and able persons can differ concerning best approaches. For example, is it a true principle that the higher employees' morale, the higher their productivity? If this were a universal fact, the development of various programs would be a simpler task. The available research indicates, however, that the relationship is not a simple one. A review of a number of studies by Vroom, for example, shows a median correlation of plus .14 between employee satisfaction and output (1.00 would indicate a perfect relationship, while 0 would suggest that they are unrelated).[15] All is not lost, however, for certain of the studies in particular companies revealed a very high correlation (in the .60s and .70s), suggesting that personnel managers *here* would do well to develop morale-building activities. In a few firms, the correlation was inverse, placing the personnel manager in a considerable quandary, torn between moral and economic values.

The subject matter of personnel requires that the manager become somewhat familiar with decision-making techniques involving the use of probability estimates. Illustrative of this concept, the Xerox Corporation has developed an approach to permit more objective assessment of proposed programs. As Figure 3-6 indicates, a proposed personnel program in job enrichment can be assessed by the manager in four major areas: (1) the state of the art with respect to designing enriched jobs, (2) the ease with which it can be implemented in the organization, (3) the projected economic benefits to the firm, and (4) possible economic risks associated with the program. Under the category of economic benefits, it should be noted that the manager must estimate the probability of obtaining each specific benefit. There are no certain probabilities (1.0), but it is calculated that it is almost certain (.8) that job enrichment would reduce absenteeism because of greater interest in the job. With the assistance of accountants, estimates can be made concerning dollar savings. When these are multiplied by probability estimates, the *expected* values can be ascertained ($2,132,500 \times .8 = \$1,706,000$ for absenteeism).

Despite the high marks given the job enrichment program in areas of state of art, economic benefits, and economic risks, the very low score allocated to "ease of implementation" led the management to rate the proposal as "moderately desirable." As suggested above, technical quality is not enough. One must also consider line manager attitudes, organization structure, technology, the outer environment, and preferred lead-

---

[14]"Brainstorming" is a group ideation process where judgment is prohibited, "wild" ideas are encouraged, quantity rather than quality is the immediate goal, and chain reactions from idea to idea often develop. It has most often been used in the field of advertising.

[15]Victor H. Vroom, *Work and Motivation*, John Wiley & Sons, Inc., New York, 1964, p. 183.

1. Define and describe the program.	**PROGRAM NAME:** Service Force Job Enrichment Program Program No. 16

DESCRIPTION   (objectives, target population, implementation schedule):

To extend the job enrichment program for the service force—
as piloted in Spring Falls, Avon Hills, and Maplewood branches
— to all branches between 1972 and 1976.

2. Identify and segregate legally required efforts

Is program legally required?   ☐ Yes   ☒ No

3. Evaluate feasibility:

(a) State-of-the-art implications

STATE OF THE ART   ☒ High   ☐ Medium   ☐ Low

(b) Ease of implementation.

EASE OF IMPLEMENTATION   ☐ High   ☐ Medium   ☒ Low

(c) Net economic benefits . . .

ECONOMIC BENEFITS   ☒ High   ☐ Medium   ☐ Low

	Potential revenue impact	Probability of occurrence	Probable gross benefit (cost)
Identifiable benefits:			
Reduction in service force turnover of 1 point.	$ 450,000	.2	$ 90,000
Extension of 1.2 point reduction in absenteeism, as demonstrated in pilot project	$ 2,132,500	.8	$ 1,706,000
Extension of 5% increase in service force productivity, as demonstrated in initial efforts	$85,500,000	.1	$ 8,550,000
Total benefits	$88,082,500	.12	$10,346,000
Tangible costs to Xerox of acting:			
Group personnel staff time to develop program, and line management time to implement program in all branches.	($ 472,950)	.9	$ 425,655
Total costs	($ 472,950)	.9	$ 425,655
Probable net benefits (cost)			$ 9,920,345

. . . and intangibles

Intangible benefits

Increased morale in service force, with improved customer service and satisfaction.

"Contagious effect" of job enrichment to other groups, e.g., sales and clericals.

Improved service manager development with concurrent sharpening of their motivational skills. As an extreme example, one manager at Avon Hills increased his team's productivity 70%.

(d) Economic risks.

ECONOMIC RISKS   ☒ High   ☐ Medium   ☐ Low

Possible consequences of not acting:

Continued escalation of service costs as a percent of revenue.

ASSUMPTIONS AND OTHER CONSIDERATIONS:

Cost estimates assume 4.4 man years of group staff time, .26 man years of branch manager time, and 15.8 man years of service manager time to implement program in a population of 1,053 service managers.

Benefit estimates assume elimination of 3 days absenteeism per month for each of 1,053 service teams, favorable productivity, and that turnover experience in pilot branches can be cascaded to all branches.

Figure 3-6 Personnel program evaluation form. (*Source: Logan M. Cheek, "Cost Effectiveness Comes to the Personnel Function," Harvard Business Review, vol. 51, no. 3, May-June 1973, p. 99. Used with permission.*)

ership styles. A difficult implementation process is envisaged. Perhaps another program, an educational one, could be devised to reduce predicted managerial resistance, thereby upgrading the "ease of implementation" assessment to at least the "medium" level.

The "seat-of-the-pants" approach to decision making in the field of personnel is increasingly jeopardized by the size of the stakes involved. Systematic study and assessment of possibilities in all the functions of personnel will have to be undertaken to design value-producing programs as well as to reduce potential conflict with government agencies and labor unions.

The Computer and Personnel

It would appear that one hope for more scientific decision making in the personnel field issues from the steady invasion of computer processing. In many firms, the answers to personnel questions are highly dependent upon the memories of existing personnel specialists. Pertinent information exists within the file drawers, but the search process is of necessity highly limited. For example, who in the company is qualified for a new job opening in electrical engineering for a new plant to be opened overseas? A search of the files is a partial search. If a skills inventory were available in a computer memory bank, *all* qualified personnel would at least be brought to the attention of the personnel manager.

If a management wishes to develop an automatic data processing system for personnel data, certain minimum essentials must be met. In the first place, there must be established a personnel data base that includes each piece of personnel information necessary for making decisions. In the study of one organization, it was found that over 2,100 items of data were used, but further analysis reduced this to only 160 items or elements that proved to be distinctly different.[16] One of the significant by-products of the creation of this data base was a reduction in the costs of maintaining and transacting personnel information; in this instance, the reduction was in excess of $6 per employee per year.

Within this single personnel data bank, many items of information must be available and current. With respect to skills, each person's record should show past jobs held, preference for job type, geographic preferences, foreign languages known, level of formal education, and special courses completed both within and without the firm. When combined with the payroll and fringe-benefit data bases, many useful outputs can be generated for the personnel manager. As indicated in Figure 3-7, each of the six personnel functions can be adapted in part to computer processing.

The increasing numbers of periodic reports required under the Civil Rights Act, Occupational Safety and Health Act, and Employee Retirement Income Security Act makes computer processing highly attractive to the large firm. In addition, rapid manipulation of data makes many new and different kinds of information available. For example, a report of the rate with which salary increases are meted out to individuals in comparison with their performance ratings will doubtlessly prevent able, but unrewarded, personnel from quitting. The amount of time spent in each position in comparison with assessed potential will indicate the degree to which the firm is utilizing its prized human assets. Comparing the number of positions filled from within by promotion with those

[16]Philip L. Morgan, "Automatic Data Processing of Personnel Data," *Personnel Journal*, vol. 45, no. 9, October 1966, p. 554.

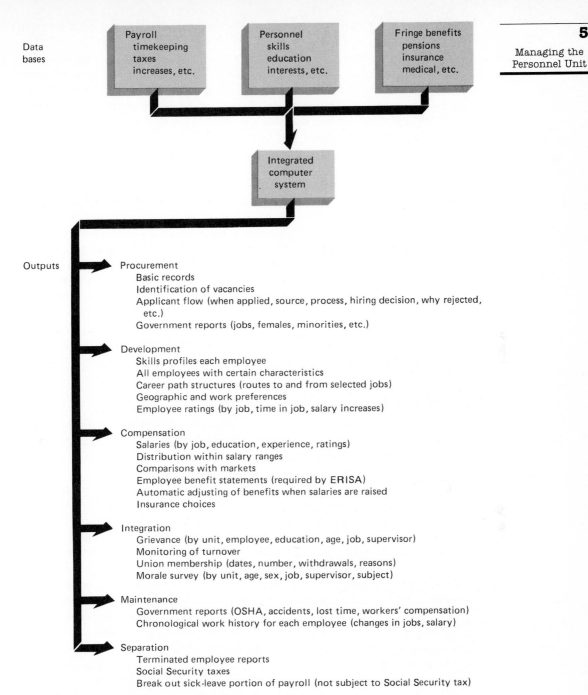

Data
bases

Outputs

Figure 3-7 Personnel management information system.

where the firm was forced to go outside gives some measurement of the effectiveness of personnel development programs.

The integrated personnel data processing system also facilitates the control function. Identification of significant exceptions to standards can be programmed for such on-going problems as determining those employees for whom salary increase are overdue, determining which specific recommended pay changes are in excess of or below authorized limits, flagging personnel or organizational units that have excessive lost time, and specifying employee requisitions that have remained unfilled for excessive periods of time.

Planning for the future is facilitated through projected simulations. Negotiators with labor unions might want to know the specific costs if vacation allowances were extended 1 additional week for employees with 10 years of service. What specific jobs will become open throughout the total organization by reason of retirement within the next 5 years? What has been the experience of this company with respect to the relationship between age and salary when educational level is held constant? There are many things that a manager would like to know in order to determine the direction and speed with which the organization is moving or drifting. An automatic personnel data processing system should make many of these answers available. Surveys of practice generally indicate increasing utilization of the computer in the personnel functions by the larger-size firms; e.g., of 210 firms with 500 to over 25,000 employees, 74 percent reported use of electronic data processing in personnel, particularly with respect to records, wages and salaries, and service benefits.[17]

Standards

A very important part of the personnel manager's responsibility for general administration of the personnel program is the establishment and maintenance of many standards by which performance can be judged. A *standard* can be defined as an *established criterion or model against which actual results can be compared.*

Many different types of standards can be used in controlling business activities. The foremost type would be standards governing the nature of the operating *results,* commonly called "performance standards." Operating results generally concern such variables as quantity, quality, time, and costs. At the present stage of development, the latter two variables, time and cost, are more adaptable to the personnel field than are quantity and quality. It is quite common to work against personnel budgets that specify cost standards. Similarly, work schedules that give time objectives are usually established for particular personnel functions. In the following section, we shall itemize and briefly discuss certain specific standards that are concerned with quantity and quality in the personnel field.

Sometimes it is difficult if not impossible to specify exactly the performance standards desired. In such cases, standards governing the process may be established and used as a basis for control in an attempt to promote the maximum in results. These other types of standards cover (1) *method or function,* (2) *personnel,* and (3) *physical factors.* If lack of knowledge prevents the establishment of exact and accurate standards of operating results, control over the *manner* of operative execution will contribute to a better result

---

[17]Frederick H. Black, Jr., "The Computer in the Personnel Department," *Personnel,* vol. 46, no. 5, September-October 1969, pp. 67–68.

than could otherwise be obtained. Thus, if the best-known methods of performance are utilized by high-quality personnel, who have available the latest in equipment, we can logically expect a high order of results in terms of quantity and quality.

With reference to standards of function, a basic method, often termed a standard operating procedure, can be devised and enforced. Presumably, if this procedure is followed, the desired result will be obtained. If it proves difficult to establish either or *both* a performance standard and a standard of function, selection of a high-quality person to do the job may effect the desired result. A specification of human characteristics required to execute a task thus constitutes a standard of personnel. Standards of physical conditions are also important since they can drastically affect the work of people. If the machinery, equipment, and general working conditions leave much to be desired, the best person using the best method may yield inadequate results in terms of quantity, quality, time, and costs. Examples of each of these seven types of standards are given in Figure 3-8 with reference to the hiring or procurement function.

CONTROLLING THE PERSONNEL UNIT

The personnel manager must oversee and collect information concerning the performance of personnel functions and compare these results with predetermined standards. Continuous comparison is expensive. The period tends to be shorter under conditions of highly centralized control and repetitive operations. In the personnel field the periods are relatively *long*. For example, it may take years to determine the true effectiveness of a new psychological testing program to be used in selection. *Monthly* reports on such factors as absenteeism, turnover, and accidents are quite typical of business operations; comparisons can be made with both past performance and the published data in the industry. *Yearly* comparisons are usually made on wages and fringe benefits. Training results as revealed through productivity rates can be made *daily* or even *hourly*.

When the comparison of performance with standards is made, there must be a decision as to the significance of the deviation discovered. If it is deemed a significant

FIGURE 3-8.
Examples of Standards Applicable to Procurement Function

Type of Standard	Example
Performance results	
1 Quantity	20 assembly technicians to be obtained for new project
2 Quality	Turnover rate for technicians to be less than 1 percent per month
3 Time	20 technicians to be obtained and placed by June 15
4 Cost	Budget for hiring not to exceed $4,000
Process	
1 Function	Hiring procedure to encompass reference checks, dexterity tests, and interviews
2 Personnel	Interviewers to possess college degrees and undergo retraining every 2 years
3 Physical factors	Testing and interviewing to be conducted in locations where total privacy is assured

exception to planned behavior, corrective action will follow. There are two general types of corrective action—immediate and basic. Those actions directed toward solution of the discovered exception are considered to be immediate, e.g., issue new instructions, work overtime, appeal for unusual cooperation, and revise the plan. Those actions directed toward correcting the underlying conditions that led to this and other similar emergencies are deemed to be basic, e.g., replace personnel, discipline personnel, revise the operating procedure, and change the organizational relationships. In general, immediate corrective action should be taken first in order to provide the time necessary for the analysis of underlying causes.

Strategic Control Points

In this text we are primarily concerned with the management of personnel. How does one ensure that the personnel program is returning value for the investment that was made in it? To understand the presentation that follows, the reader needs familiarity with the nature of personnel operations. Since operative performance precedes or is concurrent with control, the proper reading sequence might well demand that this be placed at the end of the text. But in the interest of demonstrating the interrelationships with the management cycle, we have included the discussion of control in this section.

Although we cannot separate precisely the operative functions of personnel one from another, we find it desirable to organize the presentation of control points by the operative functions. For example, if procurement is a basic operative function of personnel, how can one check to ensure that it is being done effectively? The specific measures that are applied to procurement may also shed light on integration or development, but we believe that some type of classification will help the reader to understand and remember.

Procurement The objective of the procurement process is to secure the proper number and kind of personnel for the organization. Successful procurement will result not only in the organization's acceptance of the person, but also in the person's acceptance and satisfaction with the job and the company. The following various points can be utilized to check upon the effectiveness with which the procurement process is administered:

1. *Formal placement follow-up* to determine (1) the supervisor's satisfaction with the employee, and (2) the employee's satisfaction with the job, department, supervisor, and company.

2. *Requests for transfer*. Such requests should be analyzed to determine whether they are caused by poor procurement activities or are created by causes outside the control of the organization.

3. *Voluntary quits*. The greatest number of voluntary quits ordinarily occur during the first few months on the job. This suggests poor selection and induction.

4. *Involuntary layoffs*. In these days of unemployment compensation and guaranteed annual wages, involuntary layoffs caused by poor planning of human resources requirements are to be avoided. Consequently involuntary layoffs can be taken as an index of the effectiveness of personnel planning, with, of course, proper consideration for the exigencies of particular situations, stage of the business cycle, etc.

5. *Unit efficiency*. If data processing facilities are available, such ratios as the following can be computed: number of hirees per recruiter, cost of hiring by

source of applicant, time spent interviewing per employee, relocation costs per employee, rejection rate per interviewer, retention rate per interviewer, etc.

We do not imply that the above-listed points constitute a complete coverage of the methods of controlling a procurement program. But the list does suggest that control is necessary and can be effected without watching every step that the line manager, recruiter, or employment interviewer may take. Among other points sometimes used to judge the quality of the personnel obtained are sales in dollars per employee, output in units per person-hour, and the level of aging of the work force.

Development   Measuring the effectiveness of training and development is one of the manager's more difficult tasks. In many instances, an evaluation of the program by the trainee is the prime source of information. This point is not to be ignored, but it is clear that a wide discrepancy often exists between trainee acceptance and trainee performance on the job. Some suggested control points are listed below.

1. *Productivity.* Where it is adaptable to the problem, specific information concerning productivity after training is the best control point for a training program. Often, however, the objectives of training are more intangible. For example, how does one measure the effectiveness of a human relations training program for first-line supervision? This is a highly subjective area, but even here managers should attempt to deal with concrete results by either observing the trainee in action or receiving reports from others with whom he or she comes in contact.

2. *Quality losses.* This index is closely related to the productivity record, emphasizing quality in addition to quantity. Trouble with quality control can issue from other sources besides training, but quality losses can provide a clue to the adequacy of training.

3. *Adequacy of talent reservoir.* How many incumbents of key jobs are backed up by trained replacements with the potential for promotion? What is the status of the available talent for new jobs to be created with the expansion of the firm? An index that may also be helpful in judging the adequacy of the talent reservoir is the number of higher-level positions that were filled from within the organization. Within particular development programs, points to watch would include the percentage of participants completing the course, costs per person-hour, and percentage of key personnel who are currently involved in organized development. Certainly, the developmental history of each key individual should also be reviewed from time to time.

4. *Unit efficiency.* Costs of training per employee-hour of instruction can be computed and compared among courses and between in-house training versus outside consultant training.

Compensation   The function of compensation, as defined in this text, is concerned solely with monetary remuneration. It would therefore seem that control points in this area should be more objective, since we are dealing with concrete figures. The determination of a correct wage, however, is not a completely objective process since "correctness" also denotes fairness and equitableness. The following measures of a compensation program are suggested for control purposes:

1. *Community wage rates.* The going wage in the community can be used as a basis for comparison with the company's wage structure. Though ordinarily some

argument is raised concerning the selection of firms to be surveyed and the geographic area to be covered, the community wage rate is a fairly objective measure of the entire compensation system.

2. *Wage and salary budgets.* In addition to ensuring that the firm is generally competitive in terms of salary, the manager must also make sure that expenditures are within allocated budgets. The average pay of employees in particular jobs can be compared with the midpoint in the salary range. Salary distribution by decile throughout each range will provide a more complete picture. Salary range limits for each job classification are monitored by the personnel specialist, and specific line approval must be sought when limits are to be exceeded.

3. *Grievances concerning compensation.* One of the objectives of any systematic wage and salary program is to reduce employee discontent with wages. The number of formal and informal complaints submitted by individuals is an indication of discontent.

4. *Incentive earnings: number of employees.* The number of employees earning a bonus in excess of the standard rate of pay constitutes an index of the effectiveness of the incentive compensation program. If only a very small percentage of the employees on incentive jobs actually earn extra income, obviously very little incentive exists and some part of the incentive program is not working.

5. *Incentive earnings: amount.* Analysis of the amount of incentive earnings per employee will provide valuable data for appraising the effectiveness of an incentive program. If we find that most or all employees are earning *uniform* bonus amounts, possibly the group has agreed concerning the amount that should be produced.

6. *Benefits.* Costs per employee can be calculated as a percent of salary. The percentage of participation can be determined for voluntary plans by job, organizational level, or department. Turnaround time per claim provides information concerning the efficiency of the benefits unit.

Integration   The function of integration is one of the most intangible and difficult parts of a personnel program to evaluate. In this area we are dealing with feelings and attitudes. Several measures have been developed that give clues to the effectiveness of an integration program:

1. *Morale surveys.* Surveys of opinions and attitudes on various and sundry subjects of interest to the organization can be made and will give an index of morale. Comparisons of results can be made in various ways—department by department, this company with other companies, or by comparing a present survey with one taken in the past. The direction of progress within the firm can thereby be determined, as well as progress in relation to other firms in the industry.

2. *Absenteeism, tardiness, and turnover.* The reasons for absenteeism, tardiness, and turnover are many. It is the belief of many in personnel management that these factors often reflect a basic attitude—a feeling of irresponsibility and indifference. Though this may not be true in any one particular instance, a record accumulated over a period of time can give a good measure of interest in and acceptance of the job and the company.

3. *Number of grievances.* The number of grievances submitted by employees is a frequently used index of morale in industry. It should be pointed out that a simple statistical count can be misleading. Other important variables to be considered along with the number are the types of grievances submitted, the orga-

nization source, and the timing of other related actions such as the introduction of a new program. In many instances the number of grievances filed is compared with the number settled as well as the number entering arbitration proceedings. This comparison can give some indication of the degree of successful grievance processing within the company.

4. *The future.* Monitoring the number and type of counseling sessions can provide an early warning system for probable trouble areas in the future.

Maintenance   The maintenance of personnel is concerned primarily with preserving the physical, mental, and emotional condition of employees. Measures of the effectiveness of programs designed to achieve this are as follows:

1. *Accident rates.* Using the accepted measures of accidents and comparing company rates with those of one's competitors provide a basis for considering the desirability of corrective action. The most commonly used measures of accidents are frequency rates and severity rates.
2. *Insurance premiums.* One of the most telling measures of a safety program is the out-of-pocket costs in the form of insurance premiums. When we realize that other indirect costs of an accident amount to four times the out-of-pocket insurance premium costs, we appreciate more the material importance of this particular measure.

Separation   Effective separation of employees requires carefully designed programs of retirement, layoff, and discharge. Among the control measures are the following:

1. *Number of retirees participating in retirement programs.* Research shows that the more information one has about retirement, the more successful is the transition.
2. *Number of requests for information and help after retirement.* The greater the number, the more inadequate the retirement program.
3. *Challenges of requests for unemployment compensation.* If none are challenged, it is likely that the firm is paying compensation when not deserved, e.g., voluntary resignation, discharge for cause, on strike, etc.

The Personnel Audit

Few top managements fail to see the necessity for periodic internal and/or external audits of the financial resources of the enterprise. The obtainment, preservation, and expenditure of the human resources would appear to be an equally important responsibility of a management interested in long-term viability of the enterprise. The personnel audit is a systematic survey and analysis of all operative functions of personnel, with a summarized statement of findings and recommendations for correction of deficiencies. In many cases, the auditing tool is a simple worksheet of basic questions to be answered during interviews with personnel specialists and, at times, selected personnel throughout the enterprise. This systematic interviewing process should be preceded by collection and comparison of pertinent statistical data available in the control points previously discussed.

The orientation of the auditing process is toward the ways and means of program execution. A series of questions, which can be answered either "yes" or "no," is prepared, covering the five operative functions. Many of the questions deal with the myriad of details pertaining to the establishment of systematic procedures in any field. For example:

1. Are the required federal and state labor bulletins properly posted?
2. Is the firm in compliance with labor laws concerning overtime hours and rates, female employees, rest periods, and employment of minors?
3. Is the firm in compliance with state and federal minimum wage laws?
4. Are multiple sources for personnel utilized in recruitment?
5. Have employee handbooks on rules, policies, and benefits been prepared and distributed?
6. Are enrollment cards for available life insurance programs on file for each insured employee?
7. Does each job have a written description that has been approved by the personnel manager during the past 12 months?
8. Has each specified key employee had a formal appraisal during the past 12 months?
9. Has each employment interviewer undergone retraining during the past 2 years?
10. Do new employees receive an orientation tour?
11. Are line supervisors satisfied with the services of the personnel unit?
    a. Whenever they have a questions, do they know whom to contact in the unit?
    b. Does the department pay attention to supervisors' suggestions?
    c. Do they get different answers from different persons in the unit?
    d. Does the unit give enough information about the job applicants referred?
    e. Does the unit do a good job in interpreting new government laws and regulations?
    f. Does personnel keep them informed ahead of time of personnel policy changes that will affect supervisors?
    g. Does the personnel unit find a needed new employee within a reasonable period of time?
    h. Does the personnel unit give the supervisors a free hand in deciding whether or not to hire an applicant they have referred?

The above list of questions by no means covers the entire personnel program, but it does indicate the basic nature and approach of an audit. The fact that a personnel manager knows that she or he is subject to periodic systematic inspections by outside consultants, or representatives of top management, tends to stimulate a serious concern for internal planning and control.

Human Resources Accounting

Though extremely difficult to implement, interest is growing in the possibility of establishing a system of accounting for human resources. The significance of this is highlighted by the following question: Supposing that tomorrow a major catastrophe wiped out all of the human resources in your organization, how long would it take and how much would it cost to replace them with equivalent talent and interpersonal competence? Typical estimates of costs range from three to five times present payroll.[18]

Among the firms that have experimented with human resources accounting (HRA) are R. G. Barry Corporation, Touche, Ross, and Company, and the American Telephone and Telegraph Co. AT&T has developed an approach involving the capitalization of procurement and development costs for operators. The intent is to make management cost-conscious about the loss of human assets through resignation and discharge. It is suggested that the most sophisticated system is one developed by Lester Witte and Company, certified public accountants.[19] Whereas the AT&T plan is cost-outlay based, the Witte system values human assets by discounting back to the present the anticipated cash income to be generated by the employee. This CPA firm is able to predict billable hours and fees at various stages of employee tenure.

Likert contends that even more important aspects of human resources lie in the area of general employee satisfaction and motivation. Consequently, he suggests periodic measures of attitudes toward the job, company, supervision, security, and opportunity. Though these can be obtained and evaluated on a comparative basis, conversion into dollar costs is quite difficult. At the present stage of development, the greatest potential use for HRA is to focus attention upon internal personnel problems in the hopes of developing more sophisticated managers. Attempts to incorporate human assets figures into the standard financial statements for external consumption are premature.

SUMMARY

The management of a specialized unit charged with accomplishment of nebulous but important goals is no easy task. The personnel manager should not rely on the "softness" of the field to provide exemption from improving managerial practices. In organizing the unit, choice lies among multiple bases of departmentation—functions, clientele, and service. A considerable obligation must be assumed in tying the unit into the entire organization, following such guides as compulsory staff advice, limitation of staff economy, and staff independence.

In planning the personnel program, the manager should approach the decision-making process in a systematic and objective manner, calculating and comparing probabilities, costs, risks, and benefits. Specific policies, procedures, and standards will have to be established, even in subject areas where the state of the art is not well developed. The introduction of the computer and electronic data processing present new opportunities to manipulate data and obtain answers to questions of considerable significance to managing human resources more effectively.

In controlling the personnel unit, the manager must identify selected strategic control points that can be monitored on an exception basis. Periodically, a systematic and comprehensive audit of personnel activities and practices can be undertaken to assure that the program is being accomplished as planned. If in the future a reasonably accurate and

[18]Rensis Likert and David G. Bowers, "Organizational Theory and Human Resource Accounting," *American Psychologist*, vol. 24, no. 6, June 1969, p. 588.

[19]James A. Craft and Jacob G. Birnberg, "Human Resource Accounting: Perspecitves and Prospects," *Industrial Relations*, vol. 15, no. 1, February 1976, p. 8.

acceptable system of accounting for human resources is developed, personnel management will improve in practice, visibility, and status.

BRIEF CASE

After ten years of experience in various phases of personnel management in a large corporation, Harry Jonas accepted a position as personnel manager in a small manufacturing firm located in a small city close to St. Louis, Missouri. Harry was tired of taking orders on every small detail, and was anxious to head an operation where he could introduce some innovative ideas. The owner of the firm had largely retired, leaving the everyday direction of the plant to George Wolfe. Harry and George got along very well, and the first year saw considerable progress in establishing better relations between the work force and management.

Despite these advances, Harry was well aware of a labor union effort to organize the production force of some 200 employees. He took soundings periodically and was convinced that the greater bulk of the employees would vote for a union if given the chance. Treatment accorded them by the owner and previous plant managers had built up substantial resentment which could not be quickly overcome by new policies. Harry also investigated the union that was making the organizing effort, and discovered that it was basically a well-managed and responsible organization. As a consequence, he prepared a policy recommendation for the plant manager and owner. The essence of his position was that the firm should not make any moves to forcefully oppose the union effort. Upon reading this memorandum, the owner said, "Either he is for us or against us." He instructed George to ask for Harry's resignation.

Questions

1. What principle of line and staff relationships is involved in this incident?
2. What values are being emphasized by the owner? by Harry?

DISCUSSION QUESTIONS

1. Suppose that you have been appointed the new manager of a newly created personnel department in a firm of some 600 employees. What size personnel department would you recommend be established? How would you organize it? How would you set up the working relationships with other departments in the firm?

2. If the president of the firm issues a policy statement that you, the personnel manager, must be contacted prior to altering any job's content, what principle is he or she following? What is the logic of the principle?

3. If the president asks for your resignation because your research report has proposed that the firm not oppose employee unionization, what principle is he or she violating? What is the logic of the principle?

4. If you, the personnel manager, have recommended that line supervisor training classes be held at 8 A.M. daily because you will be the instructor, what principle are you likely to be violating? How?

5. For each of the seven types of standards, cite one example that a personnel manager might use in controlling her or his hiring section.

6. For each of the six operative functions of personnel, cite two examples of strategic control points.

7. In what ways can an integrated computer processing system help a personnel manager perform more effectively?

8. If a subordinate, who is a fan of Herzberg, recommends inauguration of a program of job enrichment for production employees, how would you go about reviewing the recommendation?

9. What is human resources accounting? What are its possible values?

10. Compare and contrast the various bases of departmentation on which a personnel unit can be organized.

SUPPLEMENTARY READINGS

COLEMAN, CHARLES J.: "The Personnel Director: A Cautious Hero Indeed," *Human Resource Management*, vol. 18, no. 4, Winter 1979, pp. 14–20.

FITZ-ENZ, JAC: "Quantifying the Human Resources Function," *Personnel*, vol. 57, no. 2, March-April 1980, pp. 41–52.

LANGER, STEVEN: "Budgets and Staffing: A Survey, Part II," *Personnel Journal*, vol. 60, no. 6, June 1981, pp. 464–468.

MATHIS, ROBERT L. and GARY CAMERON: "Auditing Personnel Practices in Smaller-sized Organizations: A Realistic Approach," *The Personnel Administrator*, vol. 26, no. 4, April 1981, pp. 45–49.

McAFEE, R. BRUCE: "Evaluating the Personnel Department's Internal Functioning," *Personnel*, vol. 57, no. 3, May-June 1980, pp. 56–62.

SUSSMAN, JOHN: "Profile of the Successful Personnel Executive," *The Personnel Administrator*, vol. 25, no. 2, February 1980, pp. 77–81.

PART TWO

PROCUREMENT

The management functions are to plan, organize, direct, and control. The operative functions of personnel are procurement (Chapters 4 to 8), development (Chapters 9 to 11), compensation (Chapters 12 to 14), integration (Chapters 15 to 19), maintenance (Chapters 20 and 21), and separation (Chapters 22 and 23).

In this part, we discuss the procurement process. The first step in a personnel program is to obtain personnel to carry out organizational tasks. Before the hiring process can be started, we must be familiar with the many laws and regulations governing its execution (Chapter 4). Next the job unit must be designed (Chapter 5) and its content analyzed to determine the number and quality of personnel required (Chapter 6). With this foundation created, the firm may proceed to recruit and screen applicants for job openings (Chapters 7 and 8). Procurement ends with the induction and orientation of the newly hired employee to the job, to other employees, and to management.

chapter **4**

Fair Employment Practices

Before undertaking coverage of the procurement practices followed by organizations, we must first examine a major environmental constraint upon the process—fair employment practices imposed by government. Not content with voluntary social responsibility programs, various components of government have decreed that certain employment practices must be followed. These have taken the forms of laws, Executive orders, agency guidelines, and judicial decisions pertaining to them.

In this chapter, we shall briefly survey five major pieces of federal legislation and two Executive orders that bear upon fair employment practices. We shall indicate their impact upon multiple protected employee groups in our society—minority races, religious groups, nationalities, female employees, handicapped personnel, and older workers. This impact will be portrayed through not only the laws, orders, and court decisions, but also by surveying some of the guidelines put forth by the two major administering agencies—the Equal Employment Opportunity Commission (EEOC) and the Office of Federal Contract Compliance Programs (OFCCP). Our federal courts have accorded considerable weight to these guidelines even though they are specific regulations formulated by the executive branch.

That some changes have been effected in the proportion of minorities and females in various occupations are shown in Figures 4-1 and 4-2. Overall, the female portion of

Figure 4-1 Changes in minority employment, 1970–1979. *(Source: Equal Employment Opportunity Commission.)*

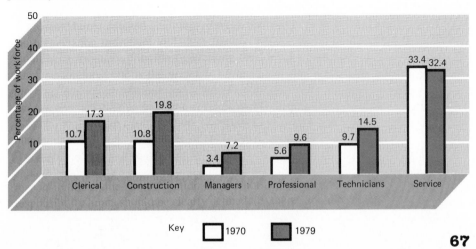

Key ☐ 1970 ■ 1979

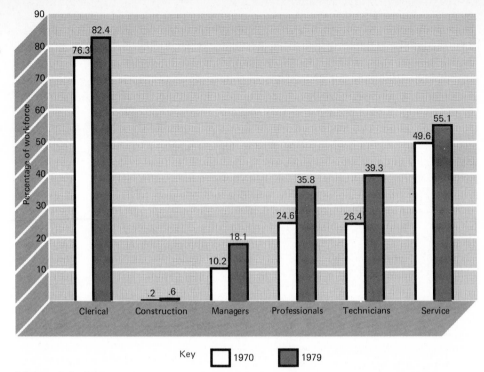

Figure 4-2 Changes in female employment, 1970–1979. *(Source: Equal Employment Opportunity Commission.)*

the labor force stands at 42 percent, and thus they are overly represented in both clerical and service occupations. Considerable improvement has been made in moving more females into managerial, professional, and technical occupations. Progress in the construction jobs such as carpenters, electricians, and painters, has been extremely slow, this despite an OFCCP-announced goal of 6.9 percent females in all construction occupations. Minorities are overly represented in the service occupations, but have steadily improved their position in all other areas.

FEDERAL LEGISLATION AND EXECUTIVE ORDERS

Though the first law governing fair employment practices was passed by the state of New York in 1945, it was not until the middle 1960s that major federal legislation was passed. As outlined in Figure 4-3, the first landmark legislation was the Civil Rights Act of 1964. Its amendment, the Equal Employment Opportunity Act of 1972, empowered the administering agency, the Equal Employment Opportunity Commission (EEOC), to undertake direct court action against alleged offenders. The Civil Service Commission is charged with the responsibility in this area for all federal employees. In brief, the act prohibits discrimination in hiring, firing, pay, or other conditions of employment because of race, color, religion, sex, or national origin. The law does not require affirmative action programs, but a federal court may impose one upon employers found guilty of discrimination.

FIGURE 4-3

69

Fair Employment
Practices

**Major Federal Legislation and Orders Relating to Fair
Employment Practices**

Law/Order	Objectives	Applies to	Enforcement Agency	Possible Penalties
Civil Rights Act	Equal opportunity for races, religions, sexes, nationalities	Employers and unions with 15 employees/members, employment agencies, hiring halls, federal, state, and local governments	Equal Employment Opportunity Commission	Court-ordered affirmative action Back pay
Exec. Orders No. 11246, 11375	Equal opportunity and affirmative action	Government contractors in excess of $10,000, federal government agencies, U.S. Postal Service	Office of Federal Contract Compliance Programs Civil Service Commission	Contract cancellation
Age Discrimination in Employment Act	Equal opportunity for ages 40–70	Employers with 20 employees, unions with 25 members, employment agencies, federal, state, and local governments	EEOC	Court-ordered affirmative action Back pay, fines up to $10,000, possible imprisonment
Vocational Rehabilitation Act	Equal opportunity and affirmative action for handicapped personnel	Government contractors in excess of $2,500, federal government agencies	Office of Federal Contract Compliance Programs Civil Service Commission	Contract cancellation
Equal Pay Act	Equal pay for equal work regardless of sex	Employers subject to Fair Labor Standards Act	EEOC	Back pay, fines up to $10,000, possible imprisonment
Pregnancy Discrimination Act	Equal treatment of pregnant employees	Same as Civil Rights Act	EEOC	Back pay

In general, there are three main types of discrimination: (1) disparate treatment, (2) disparate effect, and (3) present effects of past discrimination. Disparate treatment is the most easily understood type of discrimination. If persons of one race, sex, or ethnic group receive *different* treatment from persons of another race, sex, or ethnic group who are otherwise *similarly situated,* this constitutes discrimination. For example, a black employee with five unexcused absences is discharged, while a white with five unexcused absences is retained on the job. Disparate effect occurs when any particular practice has an *adverse impact* upon a protected group. For example, requiring a high school degree for employment will rule out more blacks than whites, or refusing to hire employees who have been arrested will rule out more minorities than whites. If any practice results in disparate effects, the employer must prove that it is *job related*. An organization can continue to require a high school degree if it can prove that those with the degree are more effective employees than those without. In the absence of such proof, the practice is discriminatory.

In the case of *National Educational Association v. South Carolina*, the Supreme Court in 1978 upheld South Carolina's use of a teacher-testing system that disqualified 83 percent of black applicants but only 17.5 percent of the whites. The court maintained that tests administered had been validated to establish a rational relationship between high scores and professional skills. In the case of *Griggs v. Duke Power Company*, the Supreme Court in 1971 declared a high school diploma minimum hiring requirement to be illegal because of its disparate effect on blacks accompanied by an unproved relationship between the diploma and job performance.

In reference to present effects of past practices, a basic principle issuing from the *Griggs* case was that procedures and practices, neutral on their face, cannot be maintained if they operate to freeze prior discrimination into the present situation. This concept was most frequently applied to seniority systems that served to keep minorities and females in less desirable positions. In some cases, lower federal courts ordered overturn of existing seniority systems that perpetuated past discrimination. In 1977, however, in *Teamsters v. U.S.* and *United Airlines Inc. v. Evans,* the Supreme Court exempted seniority systems from this principle if they were established before the Civil Rights Act took effect, and if the organization did not *intend* to discriminate through the system. And in a 5-to-4 vote in 1982 in a case involving two Richmond, Virginia, plants of the American Tobacco Company, the Supreme Court ruled that seniority systems established since 1965 are legal even if they unintentionally hurt minority and female workers. Thus the *Teamsters v. U.S.* decision has been extended to cover all seniority systems. Employees must prove the employer intended to discriminate against them. The EEOC has issued a set of guidelines that will make it easier to prove such intent, but these rules of evidence have not, as yet, been subjected to court tests.

Executive Orders No. 11246 and No. 11375 go further than the Civil Rights Act. Not only is equal opportunity protected, but contractors with the federal government must develop an affirmative action program whereby percentages of employed females and minorities are to be increased. A written program of employment goals for hiring, training, and promotion must be filed with the Office of Federal Contract Compliance Programs (OFCCP) by contractors with 50 or more employees, possessing contracts with values in excess of $50,000. The Reagan administration has proposed that the minimums required for filing written programs be raised to 250 employees and $1 million contract size. Abbreviated programs would be required of those with 250 to 500 employees. Those with contracts ranging from $10,000 to $1 million must still have a program but it need not to be filed. The content of such programs will be discussed in a later section of this chapter.

The Age Discrimination Act was passed in 1967 and proposes to reduce discrimination against older employees. An amendment in 1978 extended the range of protection from ages 40–65 to 40–70. Objection to mandatory retirement at age 65 was the major force that led to passage of the amendment. The law applies to firms that are involved in interstate commerce as defined under the Fair Labor Standards Act.

In 1974, action was undertaken to give protection against discrimination to another group, the handicapped. Like the setup for Executive orders, this law pertains only to federal agencies and government contractors with contract values in excess of $2,500. And in 1978, still another protected group was established—the pregnant employee. Stimulus for this amendment to the Civil Rights Act came from a Supreme Court decision that pregnancy need not be covered in employer's fringe benefit program to be in compliance with the Civil Rights Act. The Pregnancy Discrimination Act requires inclusion of benefits for pregnancy if the employer offers any type of medical benefit program.

Finally, the EEOC administers an act designed to effect equal pay for equal work. The passage of the Equal Pay Act was in response to data that steadily show that female employees on the average receive about 60 percent of the pay given to males. In the following sections, we shall consider discriminatory practices with regard to each of the protected groups.

MINORITY RACES

Because of the energy with which their leaders have attacked the problem of employment discrimination, blacks would constitute a good single illustration of a special racial group. This high degree of activity is stimulated by employment statistics that show that black unemployment is typically twice that of whites, and black employees are overly represented in the lower-paying positions in most organizations. The EEOC requires that employment records be maintained for blacks, American Indians, Asians, and Hispanics.

Since the 1960s, there have been many suits won on behalf of blacks. For example, the Albemarle Paper Company and the United Paperworkers and Papermakers Union recently agreed to pay $205,000 in back wages to 144 black workers who filed a discrimination suit 11 years ago. The black employees contended that they were not promoted in the same manner as whites and that the firm's job qualification test discriminated against blacks.

Much of the major legal activity with regard to blacks has been in reference to the adverse effects of perpetuating seniority systems. Though the recent court decisions exempted systems created without intention to discriminate against protected groups, these decisions in no way affected the operations of the OFCCP that administer Executive orders. Employers can still be ordered to alter seniority systems to open up greater opportunity for minorities and females.

Some companies have been required to use plant-wide seniority rather than more narrow job or department seniority in making promotion decisions. Others have been ordered to administer layoffs in such a manner as to preserve the gains in employment percentages of protected groups. The basic thrust has been based on the principle of restoring such employees to their "rightful place" had such discriminatory practice never been in effect. In many instances this has involved back wages and increased seniority levels. As indicated previously, the EEOC is still sympathetic to this position and is attempting to overcome the court's decision through issuance of guidelines. Consequently, a state of confusion exists among many employers and unions concerning what is and is not likely to be legal in the eyes of the EEOC, OFCCP, and the various federal courts. Such confusion is leading industry to seek other ways of softening the impact of layoffs through work sharing, shorter workweeks, earlier retirements, suspending operations for limited periods, and encouraging voluntary leaves of absence.

When a management wishes to introduce a special racial group into the enterprise, it is wise to be aware of possible human relations difficulties. However, studies have indicated that most managements are overly fearful of the reactions of the white majority, and that careful advance planning and preparation can do much to smooth the transition.

The first essential of such an introductory program is the adoption of a definite policy by top management. This serves the same purpose for the firm as law does for the community. If trouble does arise, supervisors are given more confidence by the existence of an explicit directive from top management. If persuasion fails, they can use the policy to force at least a minimum degree of acceptance.

The communication of the policy is of central importance. All managers must *understand* that the policy exists. As has been suggested previously, attitude changes are effected more readily through processes of discussion and conference than through orders and commands. The philosophy and techniques of group dynamics can serve to develop supervisory understanding and acceptance of minority-group members. Willing acceptance is always preferable to forced obedience. However, subordinate managers must be assured that top management mean what they have said and promulgated. Employment agencies and the union must also be informed and convinced. As usual, actions in hiring and upgrading will mean far more than a planned publicity campaign alone.

If the firm is serious about improving significantly the percentages of blacks employed, special efforts such as the following will have to be forthcoming in the area of recruitment: (1) Pacific Telephone and Telegraph Company uses walking employment offices—Hispanic and black recruiters go to people's homes, barbershops, poolrooms, and bars; (2) Michigan Bell sends recruiting trailers to the ghetto areas; (3) Westinghouse Electric provides 1-day plant orientation sessions for students from predominantly black high schools; and (4) General Electric took legal steps to open up housing for a newly hired black engineer.

In the placement process, application blanks will have to be altered to eliminate questions bearing upon race, religion, and nationality, and interviewers will have to be retrained to assure equal treatment of all applicants. If the black applicant must be rejected on the basis of inadequate qualifications, frankness is important. Acceptance of such rejections is facilitated if it is realized that other blacks have already been hired successfully by the firm. The black is sensitive because of past discrimination, and any rejection must be handled skillfully. At the least, careful rejection records must be kept.

Concerning introduction and orientation of the new black employee, the supervisor is of utmost importance. Certainly, the new employees must be carefully oriented. Though technically qualified, the new black employees may need help in adjusting not only to the industrial environment, but also to the probable "cold" initial acceptance by the majority. They should be placed in departments where supervisors are both sympathetic to the company policy and respected by present subordinates. Supervisors should speak frankly of possible prejudice and the necessity for patience and good performance. They should indicate that they and the company will not tolerate fellow employee actions when they definitely interfere with work processes or when they make it too uncomfortable for the new employees to carry on. If overt resistance is encountered, firm action in consonance with the policy is an absolute necessity. In regard to the employee himself or herself, the manager should expect acceptable levels of job performance, criticize constructively when necessary, and handle disciplinary problems in the same manner that would be employed for those of majority members.

FEMALE EMPLOYEES

In the last two decades, the proportion of the work force that is female has been increasing at a rapid pace. In 1960, approximately 33 percent of the labor force was female; currently, the percentage is somewhat in excess of 40 percent and still growing. Some of this increase can be attributed to changes in cultural beliefs and norms; yet the assurance of greater opportunities through the civil rights legislation has also contributed to these increased numbers.

Since 1964 there have been numerous major federal court decisions regarding the employment of females. Among the illegalities discovered are: (1) refusal to hire women, but not men, with young children; (2) refusal to hire married women; (3) refusal to hire a female because she might become pregnant; (4) discharging an unmarried pregnant female; (5) requiring pregnant employees to take leave without regard to ability to perform the job; (6) refusal to hire females because heavy weights must be lifted; and (7) taking away seniority rights after pregnancy leave.

The Civil Rights Act specifically provides for the possibility of a bona fide occupational qualification (BFOQ) in regard to sex. For example, one may specify hiring a male or female for the job of actor or actress. In the case of *Dothard v. Rawlinson,* a female applicant for a job of correctional counselor in an Alabama state prison was turned down because she could not meet the state's 5'2", 120-pound minimum requirement. It was shown that these minimums excluded 41 percent of the female population of the United States while excluding less than 1 percent of the males. The court determined that there was little evidence that these minimums were required to perform the job adequately. However, the court went on to specify that sex, rather than height and weight, *was* a BFOQ because of the "jungle" nature of state prisons. It was determined that a female's ability to maintain order in a male, maximum security penitentiary would be directly reduced by her womanhood.

Despite the law and many specific legal decisions, it is true that equal opportunity is denied to female employees in many subtle ways on a daily basis. When identical scenarios are provided research subjects, the mere change of a name for "John" to "Joan" revealed significantly different attitudes toward hiring females for traveling sales jobs, sending females to management training programs, transferring females to positions in other states, and expecting the female spouse to support the male's occupational career and not vice versa.[1] Employment interviewers may describe the same job differently to females than males, in the one case emphasizing congenial colleagues and in the other pointing out the developmental opportunities. A supervisor may give a female a rather superficial performance appraisal on the immediate job with no discussion of career advancement. When a man that a firm really wants is found on the market, the job may be redesigned to suit; but in self-consciously seeking a female, the job may be designed with such detailed care that the "perfect" female candidate surprisingly cannot be found.

When an employer is desirous of providing truly equal opportunity for females, such practices as the following are recommended: (1) remove sex labels from all jobs; (2) formulate a policy statement of firm declaration of intent regarding treatment of

---

[1]Benson Rosen and Thomas H. Jerdee, "Sex Stereotyping in the Executive Suite," *Harvard Business Review,* vol. 52, no. 2, March-April 1974, pp. 45–58.

females; (3) establish company-wide posting of job openings; (4) make available educational and training programs to females, with emphasis upon developmental experiences on the job, such as "assistant-to" positions, internships, and temporary assignments; (5) establish a procedure where career-ambitious females can have contact with higher-level executives to pose questions, suggest actions, and define problems; (6) provide for reinforcement contacts among similarly career-ambitious female employees; and (7) provide more flexibility in work times through flexitime, sharing jobs, and leaves of absence. The government will provide surveillance over the statistics of hiring and promotion; only management can provide surveillance over the activities that really count in providing truly equal opportunity.

PREGNANT EMPLOYEES

In the Supreme Court decision in the *General Electric Co. v. Gilbert* case, it was held that exclusion of pregnancy from the risks covered by an employer's disability benefits plan does *not* violate the Civil Rights Act. It was reasoned that pregnant women were seeking additional compensation that was not available to nonpregnant women and men. This ruling was nullified by Congress in the passage of the Pregnancy Discrimination Amendment to the Civil Rights Act in 1978.

This amendment makes it an unfair employment practice to discriminate on the basis of pregnancy, childbirth, or related medical conditions in hiring, promotion, suspension, discharge, or any other term of employment. The bill requires no new programs to be established; rather it requires that pregnant employees be treated the same as other employees on the basis of their ability or inability to work.

Guidelines issued by the EEOC would appear to require the following:

1. An employer cannot refuse to hire a pregnant applicant so long as she is able to perform the major functions of the job. Hiring cannot be refused merely because of preference by coworkers or customers.

2. If employers accommodate other temporarily disabled workers, they must make similar accommodations for pregnant workers, such as temporary relief from having to lift heavy materials.

3. The employer cannot require female employees to take leave arbitrarily at a set time in their pregnancy. Leave times are to be determined by the ability of the employee to do the job.

4. Full reinstatement rights must be given to female employees on leave for pregnancy-related reasons, including credit for previous service, seniority, and accrued retirement benefits.

5. Fringe benefits or insurance programs, if such exist, must include coverage for pregnancy of employees in the same manner as for other employee disability or sick benefits.

6. Employers providing extended medical insurance benefits to husbands of female employees must cover *equally* the medical expenses of wives of male employees, including pregnancy.

Though a district court had previously ruled that the Pregnancy Discrimination Amendment was designed only to protect female employees and not female dependents, the Fourth Circuit Court ruled otherwise in the case of *Newport News Shipbuilding and Dry Dock Company v. EEOC*. A second Court of Appeals in the state of Washington ruled in the opposite manner, contending that Congress intended to limit the act to women employees. Obviously, the Supreme Court will have to resolve this issue.

SEXUAL HARASSMENT

Though the Civil Rights Act is designed to prohibit discrimination on the basis of sex, and thereby protects men as well as women, the obvious intent was to protect and enhance opportunities for female employees. Most cases brought to the attention of the EEOC and federal courts involve accusations of discriminatory treatment against females. Recent court cases and EEOC guidelines have declared that sexual harassment is sex discrimination under Title VII of the Civil Rights Act.

Section 1604.11(a) of the EEOC guidelines issued in 1980 define the term "sexual harassment" as "unwelcome sexual advances, requests for sexual favors and other verbal or physical conduct of a sexual nature." The guidelines are written in such a manner as to make clear beyond reasonable doubt that protection against sexual harassment extends to both male and female employees.

The guidelines set up three circumstances under which the above definition will apply:

1. *Employment condition*—when submission to such sexual conduct is made explicitly or implicitly a term or condition of an individual's employment.

2. *Employment consequences*—when submission to or rejection of such conduct is used as a basis for employee decisions, such as promotion, retention, and so on.

3. *Job interference*—when such conduct has the effect of interfering with job performance or creating an intimidating, hostile, or offensive working environment.

The EEOC guidelines impose an absolute liability on employers for the acts of supervisors regardless of whether the conduct was known to, or authorized, or forbidden by the employer. Liability for acts of coworkers and third-party customers appears to be somewhat less, particularly if the employer takes immediate action to eliminate such practices.

In *Miller v. Bank of America,* the Ninth Circuit Court of Appeals ruled that even though the employer had an announced sexual harassment policy plus a grievance mechanism, it was still liable for the supervisor's actions. In *Kyriaki v. Western Electric,* the female employee linked her discharge to sexual misconduct by male coworkers in the form of tasteless behavior, joking, and innuendos. A District Court ruled she was entitled to reinstatement and coworkers who engaged in the harassment and supervisors who were aware of the behavior were each fined $1,500. In *Bundy v. Jackson,* Sandra Bundy charged that she had been subjected to numerous propositions, but had not been denied tangible employee benefits as a result of her resistance. The Court of Appeals accepted EEOC guidelines holding the employer liable for creating a hostile and offensive working environment, even though she had not been denied any tangible benefit.

In general, the employer can limit its liability by showing that it took immediate corrective action when the sexual misconduct was discovered. The foundation of an acceptable program is a strong policy statement from top management that sexual harassment will not be tolerated. Training programs for both current employees and managers, and orientation programs for new employees would also be necessary to ensure that the policy is fully understood. Problems exist in determining exactly what is considered to be sexual harassment. In surveying over 1,800 subscribers to the *Harvard Business Review,* significant percentages indicated that the following may possibly constitute sexual harassment: (1) whenever I go into the office, my supervisor eyes me up and down, making me feel uncomfortable; (2) my supervisor puts his hand on my arm when making a point; and (3) my supervisor starts each day with a sexual remark, insisting that it's an innocent social comment.[2] On the other hand, there was substantial agreement that the following constituted sexual harassment: (1) I can't seem to go in and out of my boss's office without being patted or pinched; and (2) my boss told me that it would be good for my career if we went out together. And finally, the program will only be effective if employees and supervisors can see evidence that top management will take action when sexual misconduct is discovered. In one incident, a male supervisor had a habit of making jokes with sexual overtones to a female subordinate who appeared to take no offense and made no complaints.[3] Two years later, she filed a complaint with EEOC contending that she was denied a promotion given to a male employee. She cited the supervisor's sexually oriented comments in her complaint. The EEOC investigated and disapproved her claim for the promotion, but substantiated the sexual joking by the supervisor. To limit the company's liability, the EEOC office recommended a 1-week suspension for the supervisor; the company accepted.

THE OLDER EMPLOYEE

The original Age Discrimination in Employment Act passed in 1967 prohibited discrimination in employment based upon age with respect to individuals who were at least 40 years of age but less than 65 years. The practices included were failure to hire, denial of opportunities, discharge, and discrimination in regard to conditions of employment. In 1978, the act was amended to prohibit mandatory retirement for those under the age of 70. The act applies to private employers who employ at least 20 workers, and to state and local governments. Specific exemptions include certain high-risk jobs such as police officers and fire fighters, and high-paid private employees who could retire with very liberal pensions. The amendment also defers the age-70 ceiling if lower ages are contained in retirement benefit plans or seniority systems provided by collective bargaining agreements; the delay in this case was until January 1, 1980 or until the termination of such an agreement. In regard to federal government employees, mandatory retirement is prohibited at *any* age.

Much of the court activity under this act has been in reference to discharge and forced retirement. Recently, Exxon Research and Engineering Company was found guilty

---

[2]Eliza G. C. Collins and Timothy B. Blodgett, "Sexual Harassment . . . Some See It . . . Some Won't," *Harvard Business Review,* vol. 59, no. 2, March-April 1981, pp. 84–85.

[3]George K. Kronenberger and David L. Bourke, "Effective Training and the Elimination of Sexual Harassment," *Personnel Journal,* vol. 60, no. 11, November 1981, p. 882.

Age discrimination has long been a fact of corporate life in the U.S. Wall Street's emphasis on 'youthful, dynamic management' and the actuarial costs of an older staff have shortened many an executive's career. For some companies, firing or forcing early retirement on highly paid older executives has two perceived advantages: It cuts salary costs and pension liabilities and, at the same time, makes room at the top for young achievers. It is a particularly tempting option in a recessionary period when corporations seek to trim expenses."

Utilizing the protection of the Age Discrimination in Employment Act, a number of suits have been brought against companies. Among these are (1) Standard Oil Company of California paying $2 million to 264 employees in a 1974 age bias case, (2) Hartford Fire Insurance Company paying $240,000 in 1979 to 72 employees allegedly fired, demoted or denied promotion on the basis of age, and (3) a 1981 court order of Heublein Inc. to pay $425,000 to a former executive for failing to promote him to a vice-presidency. Higher-level executives have filed age bias cases against such firms as Consolidated Edison, National Broadcasting, Japan Air Lines, and Equitable Life Assurance.

"In all such cases, say lawyers and management consultants, the odds are heavily in favor of the employee, particularly since amendments to the ADEA in 1978 assured the availability of jury trials. 'When you put a large corporation against an employee in front of a jury on an issue like this, there is rarely any question as to the outcome,' says George P. Sape, vice-president of Organization Resource Counselors Inc., a New York-based employee relations consultant.

"Wounded Executives Fight Back on Age Bias," *Business Week,* July 21, 1980, p. 109.

in U.S. District Court of pressuring a research chemist to retire at the age of 60. The chemist had been assigned to menial tasks when he refused to retire voluntarily. In another instance, three supervisors, ages 57 to 59, were discharged for failure to get the work out. When the company immediately ran recruitment advertisements seeking supervisors aged 30 to 35 years, the discharged supervisors sued for damages and won. The act does not prevent discharge of older workers who are unable to perform satisfactorily. In another instance, a court upheld the discharge of a 52-year-old sales manager when evidence was provided of lower sales for him in combination with continuation of a number of older managers with higher sales. Other instances of discrimination on the basis of age are listed in Box 4-1. Population trends suggest that more cases will be filed in the years ahead. By 1985, over one-third of the work force will be more than 40 years of age, while members of the postwar baby boom will be pushing for higher-level jobs. As talent becomes more plentiful, companies will be tempted to retire older managers, and they will be required to demonstrate measurable differences in performance. As stated by one observer, "a sophisticated employer who wants to get rid of an older, too-highly paid executive nowadays is going to do it in a subtle way over a period of time by building up a dossier on little ways he screwed up."[4] An equally sophisticated older executive will start building his or her own dossier, keeping notes and copies of commendations.

The law also provides for the possibility of age being a BFOQ in hiring. Greyhound Lines, Inc. specifies that new hires cannot be older than 35 years of age. When evidence was produced proving that the safest intercity bus driver is between ages 50 and 55 with 16 to 20 years of experience, age was approved as a bona fide occupational qualification for hiring. Similarly, the Federal Aviation Agency regulation which establishes the age of 60 as the maximum for airline pilots is a BFOQ. The EEOC guidelines indicate that

[4]"Wounded Executives Fight Back on Age Bias," *Business Week,* July 21, 1980, p. 114.

age discrimination is permissible when it is necessary to protect the public safety. Authorization is also given when hiring actors for either youthful or elderly characterizations, and when selecting persons used in advertisements or product promotions aimed exclusively at particular age groups.[5]

As in the case of females, a stereotype of the typical older employee exists in the minds of many managers. Older employees are often considered to be inflexible, resistant to change, less creative, and unable to deal with crisis situations. When treated in this fashion, it may well become a self-fulfilling prophesy. When given equal opportunity, studies show that they are the equal of the younger in terms of quantity and quality of output. In addition, they offer maturity derived from experience. Older workers are less prone to accidents than the younger; caution and experience may compensate for loss in agility and dexterity. They are also usually superior in terms of turnover inasmuch as they are, ironically, fully aware of the discrimination that exists and thus more appreciative of the job they now hold.

RELIGIONS

There have been relatively few cases involving charges of discrimination on the basis of religion. Though the original Civil Rights Act prohibited discrimination on a religious basis, there was little elaboration of its meaning. The 1972 amendment to the act indicated that not only religious beliefs, but religious observances and practices were to be protected. In addition, contrary to all other protected groups under the act, employers are required to ''accommodate to the religious needs of employees'' when such accommodation can be made without serious inconvenience to the firm. The argument is that a requirement that bears on only one religious group has a disparate effect, and cannot be legal unless justified by business necessity.

As an example of employer problems in this area, Trans World Airlines operates its stores department 24 hours a day, 365 days per year. Saturday and Sunday assignments are generally undesirable and a skeleton crew is operated. One employee, a member of the Worldwide Church, observed his Sabbath on Saturday. Assignment to weekend work was made on a seniority basis. The company has tried to find the employee another job and attempted to persuade the union to arrange swaps with other employees. The Circuit Court ruled that TWA had not made sufficient effort to accommodate the employee's religious practices. It suggested that the employee could work a 4-day week with another employee taking his place, or other personnel could have filled in on Saturday with overtime pay. This ruling was overturned by the Supreme Court which maintained that TWA had made a good attempt to accommodate, that an agreed-upon seniority system must not give way to accommodate religious observances, and that anything more than a minimum cost to accommodate is an undue hardship on the company. The rights of the many should not be sacrificed for the rights of a few.

In response to this setback, the EEOC proposed new guidelines to indicate what actions are necessary to provide reasonable accommodation. These suggest that accommodation without undue hardship is possible when voluntary substitutes are available, and the employer must assist in their identification. Employers are also asked to explore

---

[5]Patricia Linenberger and Timothy J. Keaveny, ''Age Discrimination in Employment: A Guide for Employers,'' *The Personnel Administrator*, vol. 24, no. 7, July 1979, p. 89.

creation of flexible work schedules such as flexitime, floating holidays, and flexible work breaks. When these fail, employers are asked to investigate possible transfers and change of job assignments. Some religious organizations do not permit payment of dues to labor unions, and the guidelines require that the union accommodate the employee by permitting him or her to donate a sum equivalent to dues to a charitable organization other than one associated with the employee's religion. The last item was placed into a 1980 amendment to the Taft-Hartley Act exempting from compulsory union membership employees whose religious convictions prohibit them from joining labor organizations.

Members of religious groups have been using the religious accommodation provisions of the Civil Rights Act in bringing lawsuits against their employers. In one instance, a Roman Catholic employee of the Internal Revenue Service charged that he was denied a promotion because of his unwillingness to audit organizations involved in abortion procedures. In another, an Orthodox Jew brought suit against a city in an effort to have it schedule his civil service examination on a day other than Saturday.[6]

NATIONALITIES

There are also relatively few charges of discrimination on the basis of national origin. EEOC guidelines suggest that possible discrimination on this basis could be involved in language requirements, height and weight requirements, membership in organizations promoting rights of particular groups, and having a surname indicative of a particular national origin. In one case involving the County of Los Angeles, it was charged that requiring a minimum height of 5'7" for fire fighters excluded 45 percent of otherwise eligible Mexican-American applicants. The County failed to show that the requirement was job related, though the Chief, who stands 5'8" himself, said that he believed that a smaller person might have difficulty in working with taller persons in removing long ladders.

In the 1980 guidelines issued by the EEOC, national origin discrimination is defined as including, but not limited to, the denial of equal employment opportunity because of an individual's or her or his ancestors' country of origin; or because an individual has the cultural or linguistic characteristics of a particular national origin. The latter phrase suggests that any expression of ethnic identity such as clothing, hair style, jewelry, slang words, and phrases that are peculiar to a national origin are protected.

The EEOC has included fluency in English as a selection criterion for which the employer must bear the burden of proof. In *Garcia v. Gloor Lumber and Supply Inc.*, the court upheld the employer's right to prohibit employees from speaking Spanish on the job, unless they were talking to Spanish-speaking customers. The rule did not apply anywhere except in the sales room. Employees have the right to speak their primary language when there is no clear business need. However, if the company required its sales people to speak English without an accent, it would have to prove that this degree of fluency was a business necessity.

A difficult problem encountered in this area is the requirement of citizenship for employment. In response to the *Espinoza v. Farah* case where the company was permitted to require U.S. citizenship when it was proved that the requirement did not rule out large

---

[6]"Religious Accommodation and the Courts: An Overview," *Personnel,* vol. 58, no. 3, May-June 1981, p. 48.

numbers of Hispanics, the EEOC guideline permits citizenship requirements as long as there are no discriminating effects. Despite this, lack of citizenship can rarely be an acceptable reason for not hiring legal aliens in the private sector. In 1979, the Supreme Court upheld the constitutionality of Executive Order No. 11935 barring aliens from Federal civil service positions. In a previous case, *Amback v. Norwick,* states were permitted to limit alien participation "when exercising the function of government."

Finally, the EEOC guidelines state that ethnic slurs and other verbal or physical conduct relating to an individual's national origin constitute harassment when this conduct creates an intimidating or hostile working environment, interferes with the individual's work performance, or adversely affects employment opportunities. Just as in the instance of sexual harassment, the employer is responsible for not only acts of supervisors, but also those of fellow workers and "nonemployees." Employers should be aware that bathroom graffiti, ethnic slurs, certain ethnic jokes, and arbitrary task assignments may be viewed as harassment.

THE HANDICAPPED

The Vocational Rehabilitation Act of 1973 requires firms receiving $2,500 or more annually in federal contracts to (1) take affirmative action to employ and advance in employment qualified handicapped persons, and (2) make a reasonable accommodation to the physical and mental limitations of handicapped employees. It is estimated that there are over 20 million handicapped people in this country, of which some 7 million are employed.[7] A handicapped person is one who has a physical or mental impairment that substantially limits one or more of life's major activities, or one who has a record of such impairment or is regarded as having an impairment. Thus, one who had been in a mental hospital, but is now mentally sound, might still be regarded by some employers as handicapped because of the record of mental illness.

The affirmative action requirement would entail the following actions: (1) positive steps to recruit qualified handicapped workers, (2) modification of personnel practices to meet handicapped needs, such as special training for personnel interviewers concerning barriers facing the handicapped, (3) reasonable accommodation to the physical and/or mental limitations of an applicant, and (4) training of supervisory personnel to provide strong internal support. There are no affirmative action requirements in terms of employment goals and timetables. The definition of "qualified handicapped," according to proposed OFCCP guidelines, means such individuals must be able to perform the "essential functions," though perhaps not the marginal or secondary functions, of the job. However, in *Southeastern Community College v. Davis,* the Supreme Court ruled that "an otherwise qualified person is one who is able to meet *all* of a program's requirements in spite of his handicap." The college had refused to admit a deaf woman to its nursing program solely because of her handicap. The court ruled that the ability to understand speech without reliance on lip reading was necessary for patient safety. However, the door was left open for "reasonable accommodation" when modifications can be made "without imposing undue financial hardship and administrative burdens."[8]

[7]Gopal C. Pati, "Countdown on Hiring the Handicapped," *Personnel Journal,* vol. 57, no. 3, March 1978, p. 145.

[8]"Significant Decisions in Labor Cases," *Monthly Labor Review,* vol. 102, no. 10, October 1979, p. 70.

Various companies have developed extensive programs to find suitable jobs for handicapped workers. In some instances, one with a handicap is often more suited to a particular job than the so-called normal person. DuPont studied 1,452 employees with a variety of handicaps and discovered that 96 percent rated average or better in safety records both on and off the job, 79 percent had average or better attendance, and 91 percent had average or better job performance.[9] This is certainly one area where a little affirmative effort on the part of firms will pay good dividends to both the organization and the handicapped person. Rather than requiring unlimited expenditures for special equipment, the DuPont study showed that relatively few disabled workers required unusual work arrangements. Accommodations such as raised hallway signs to assist the blind, telephone amplifiers to help the hearing-impaired, and curb cuts to help the wheelchair-bound employees cost relatively little. As one manager stated, "It's peanuts when you compare the job performance and loyalty of these people."[10]

The Minnesota Mining and Manufacturing Company has been particularly innovative in developing a program for the handicapped.[11] This company has a rehabilitation committee along with a full-time, professional counselor. The first step is usually the referral of an individual who meets with the counselor to evaluate the handicap. The full committee reviews the information and develops a rehabilitation process for the employee. The next step is exploring job possibilities, and the counselor must be familiar with all departments and may suggest modification of job content. After placement is made, the counselor checks with the employee and her or his supervisor to see how the new situation is working out. The 3M Company also has a handivan program for transporting employees in wheelchairs, an opticon (a special reading device for the blind), and amplified telephones for hearing-impaired employees.

ORGANIZATION AND PROCEDURES

As indicated in Figure 4-3, there are a number of different agencies in the federal government that are involved with administering fair employment practices legislation and orders. Often they issue conflicting instructions, such as detailing different requirements for validating selection devices. A reorganization plan has been submitted whereby the EEOC would become the "super agency," taking over first the Civil Service Commission's civil rights authority over government workers, then equal pay and age discriminations programs from the Department of Labor, and ultimately the functions of the OFCCP in monitoring government contractors. The EEOC and OFCCP still remain separate. The EEOC is not empowered to conduct compliance reviews. It can work only when receiving a valid charge. The OFCCP does conduct compliance reviews of firms holding contracts with the federal government. The EEOC consists of five commissioners and a general counsel appointed by the President and confirmed by the Senate. It has responsibility for processing individual charges of discrimination and stipulating various rules and guidelines in the interpretation of the Civil Rights Act.

---

[9]Robert B. Nathanson, "The Disabled Employee: Separating Myth from Fact," *Harvard Business Review,* vol. 55, no. 3, May-June 1977, p. 7.

[10]Gopal C. Pati, op. cit., p. 150.

[11]"Finding a Place for the Handicapped Worker," *Personnel,* vol. 56, no. 5, September-October 1979, p. 41.

Organizations covered by the Civil Rights Act must maintain records that reflect the composition of their work forces as well as those pertaining to the normal course of business, such as hirings, transfers, promotions, and layoffs. All organizations with 100 or more employees must file an annual information report showing the relationship of minority and female workers to both the total labor force and for the following job categories: officials and managers, professionals, technicians, sales workers, office and clerical, craft workers, operatives, laborers, and service workers. No one person can be counted in more than one race-ethnic category. These data are compiled and integrated on a geographic and industrial basis to reflect trends in employment.

Concerning the individual or group charge procedure, one must be filed at an EEOC district office within 180 days after occurrence, or 300 days if the alleged offense took place in a state with its own fair employment practices agency. If in such a state, the charge must be referred to the state agency first. If not settled by the state within 60 days, the EEOC can assume jurisdiction. Once the charge is accepted, notice must be served upon the employing organization concerned within 10 days.

There then follows an investigation of the charge to determine whether it has reasonable cause. The Commission is empowered to issue subpoenas, require attendance, and take testimony. Field investigators obtain affidavits from the charging party, respondent, and witnesses on both sides. On the basis of the evidence, the Commission will reach a decision. If it concludes that discrimination has taken place, it will then enter into a process of conference, conciliation and persuasion with the organization in the hope of working out some settlement that will remedy the situation. If one is developed, it becomes a tripartite agreement signed by the EEOC, charging party, and respondent. If one is not developed, the EEOC has the option of litigation in the federal courts. Should they elect not to sue, and relatively few cases are brought to court, the charging party will be given the statutory right to sue. This must be done within 90 days of receiving such authorization.

Because of the formidable backlog of unprocessed charges, the EEOC is experimenting with a faster and more informal procedure. In a few model offices, EEOC specialists are turning from making charges automatically to putting the accuser and accused together on a face-to-face basis as quickly as possible. In these experimental districts, the number of formal charges has dropped about 40 percent. In one instance, a black truck driver complained that his employer had discriminated against him by requiring a road test when it made no such requirement for white drivers. The quick, informal investigation revealed that other black drivers took no such test, but they required one of him since he had experienced two accidents and received a speeding ticket in the first few weeks on the job. No charge letter was written. In another case, a real estate company explained its rejection of a woman by claiming that she lacked training and a real estate license. When she whipped out her license, the company agreed to give her a job on the spot.[12]

It should be noted that Title VII of the Civil Rights Act states that it is an unlawful practice for an employer to discriminate against any employee who (1) has opposed an unlawful employment practice, and (2) participates in a discrimination proceeding through filing charges, testifying, collecting data, and so on. Courts have held that the employee need only to "reasonably believe" that a practice violates Title VII, whether or not it does so in fact. Employers must be extremely careful in changing their treatment of

---

[12]"The Troubled Drive for Efficiency at the EEOC," *Business Week*, Dec. 19, 1977, p. 91.

employees involved with a charge, such as if shortly after filing the employee begins to get critical performance appraisals. However, the employer need not tolerate any unreasonable behavior on the part of the employee. In one instance, a female biologist complained frequently about her salary, insulted her boss, circulated rumors that the organization would lose funding, and invited a reporter to examine confidential files.[13] The court concluded that her actions justified discharge even though the subject of salary differentials was covered by the act.

AFFIRMATIVE ACTION PROGRAMS

In contrast to the equal opportunity policy of the Civil Rights Act, laws and Executive orders enforced by the OFCCP require affirmative action programs for covered government contractors. An affirmative action program would encompass the following elements: (1) analysis of the firm's current utilization of females and minorities; (2) comparing ethnic and sexual composition of the firm with the availability of qualified females and minorities in the relevant recruiting area; (3) establishing goals and hiring rates to correct discrepancies; (4) development of action-oriented programs in recruitment, training, and promotion to enable goal accomplishment; and (5) constant auditing of applicant flow and personnel records to insure steady progress toward goals.

Affirmative Action Court Cases

In the first Supreme Court case that pertained directly to the constitutionality of affirmative action programs, the court ruled in *Regents of the University of California v. Bakke* that quotas for university admission based entirely on race, in situations where no previous discrimination had been found, are flatly illegal. In the 5-to-4 decision, the court, however, authorized consideration of race as *one factor* among many in making the admission decision. As Justice Lewis Powell stated, "in such an admission program, race or ethnic background may be deemed a 'plus' in a particular applicant's file, yet it does not insulate the individual from comparison with all other candidates for the available seats." Whether the 16 of 100 seats reserved at the university for blacks, Hispanics and Asian-Americans were called "quotas" or "goals," the court prohibited drawing a line solely on the basis of race and ethnic status. Thus the Court authorized the establishment of "soft goals." "In short, in evaluating a black and white candidate, whether for hire or promotion, both of whom are qualified, it is proper to give consideration to the distance which each has traveled and the handicaps which each has overcome in achieving the personal characteristics and abilities which each has at the particular point in time."[14]

---

[13]Bette Bardeen Durling, "Retaliation: A Misunderstood Form of Employment Discrimination," *Personnel Journal,* vol. 60, no. 7, July 1981, p. 558.

[14]Barbara Lindemann Schlei and Paul Grossman, *Employment Discrimination Law,* The Bureau of National Affairs, Inc., Washington, 1976, p. 730.

One year later, in 1979, the Supreme Court in *United Steelworkers of America v. Brian Weber* moved one step further. Kaiser Aluminum signed a bargaining agreement with the United Steelworkers that included a quota for admitting black workers to on-the-job training for craft positions. For each two training vacancies, one black and one white would be selected according to seniority within two separate lists. Though Kaiser admitted no past discrimination, blacks made up only 1.83 percent of the company's craft workers, while they made up 39 percent of the local labor force. Brian Weber, a white worker, filed suit charging "reverse discrimination" when he was not selected after black workers with less seniority were included. The Supreme Court upheld the affirmative action program for the following reasons: (1) the Civil Rights Act cannot require such a program, but it does not prohibit an employer from voluntarily undertaking such efforts to remedy an obvious racial imbalance, (2) the program did not harm white employees unnecessarily or excessively since none were fired or replaced with blacks, and (3) the program was temporary and would be discontinued when the imbalance was eliminated. Thus, there is no blanket endorsement of all "hard goal" systems; rather each program will be examined on the basis of need and minimal harm to the majority.

Finally, in 1980 in *Fullilove v. Klutznick,* the Supreme Court upheld the right of Congress to pass specific laws encompassing the use of quotas. It upheld a 1977 law that specified that out of $4 billion that the government would spend in financing public works, at least 10 percent had to go to contracting firms owned by citizens of minority status. With steady emphasis on proper qualifications, government officials can waive the 10 percent requirement if they could not find enough qualified minority contractors to meet it.

Program Content

Written affirmative action programs have been required by the OFCCP of all government vendors with 50 or more employees and $50,000 or more in contract value. With the objective of reducing paperwork costs, the federal administration has proposed raising the limits to 250 employees and $1 million in contract value. Firms with 250 to 499 employees may submit abbreviated programs. Though such programs cannot be ordered under the Civil Rights Act, the EEOC has announced that such activity is probably necessary to be fully in compliance with the act. The Weber decision provides employers with protection from suits should they voluntarily establish such programs. And of course, should a firm be found guilty of discrimination in litigation under the Civil Rights Act, the court may specify its own affirmative action program to redress the situation.

The first step in developing an affirmative action program is to compute how many minorities and females are currently employed in each major job classification. A hypothetical situation is detailed in Figure 4-4 and shows percentage utilization in seven job categories. For example, of all managerial jobs, 4 percent are held by females and 6 percent by minorities. On the other hand, 98 percent of all secretarial and clerical jobs are held by females, 12 percent by minorities.

The second step is perhaps the most difficult. One must determine the number of available *qualified* personnel in the market area for each job category. The market area for a management job is likely to be broader than one for an operative or security job. In the past, the OFCCP has required consideration of eight major factors in making this determination. It has proposed reducing these to the following four: (1) percentage of minorities and women in the civilian labor force in the immediate labor area; (2) percentage of minorities and women with requisite skills in the immediate labor area; (3) percentage of minorities and women with requisite skills in the relevant recruitment area; and (4) percentage of minorities and women among those promotable or transferable within the contractor's organization. The federal government has proposed that if an employer has achieved 80 percent of the percentage of qualified personnel available, no action against the firm will be undertaken.

In Figure 4-4, it has been determined that there is underutilization of females in managerial positions. Some 20 percent of the available qualified work force is female. In the case of secretarial and clerical positions, we have overutilization; 98 percent of XYZ's clerks and secretaries are females. Though the qualified market is predominantly female, 95 percent, the XYZ corporation plans no additional hiring goals in excess of 50 percent. No one will be dismissed, but the firm plans to encourage more males to enter these types of positions. For AT&T, such a program resulted in a net decrease in the number of females in the entire organization. With respect to minorities, the worker market in managerial jobs is estimated at 10 percent, with the firm's utilization percentage at 6 percent; in the clerical jobs, the figures are 20 percent and 12 percent, respectively.

In establishing employment goals, the upper limit would be the percentage of such personnel in the total population of the appropriate area. The more practical ultimate goal would be the percentage of qualified personnel in the work force population. Goals for lower-skilled jobs may be met fairly quickly if the firm is growing. Goals for the professions will often consume longer periods of time. When the firm is stable or contracting in size, the task of more equitable utilization is a formidable one. Courts have ruled that existing bona fide seniority systems for layoff cannot be circumvented in order to retain newly hired females and minorities. Returning to the XYZ firm, the company plans to increase the percentage utilization of females in managerial positions to 6 percent after 1 year and 12 percent after 5 years. This would still not meet the estimated worker market percentage. For minorities in these same managerial jobs, the XYZ Corporation has established the market percentage as its target at the end of 5 years. Concerning the secretarial and clerical positions, the firm will make no special effort to hire females, but will strive to meet the market percentage of 20 percent in the case of minority personnel.

FIGURE 4-4
Affirmative Action Plan, XYZ Corporation

	Utilization plan for females and minorities by job category							
	Females				Minorities			
Job Category	% Util- ization	% Worker Market	% Goal 1 Year	% Goal 5 Years	% Util- ization	% Worker Market	% Goal 1 Year	% Goal 5 Years
Management	4	20	6	12	6	10	8	10
Professionals	11	35	13	18	0	5	1	3
Secretary/clerical	98	95	*		12	20	16	20
Telephone	100	95	*		5	15	10	15
Security	2	20	6	15	10	25	15	25
Skilled crafts	15	25	17	20	5	15	7	12
Operatives	25	35	30	35	20	25	22	25

*This plan does not increase female representation beyond 50%.

There has been much discussion concerning the effects of equal opportunity, soft goals, and hard goals. Equal opportunity would support the hiring of the currently most able person, providing that one can provide objective evidence of this superiority. A soft goal could still end up with the most able, providing that the additional credit given to certain groups was not sufficient to overcome the differences in current ability. A hard goal would require selection of qualified persons in underutilized groups, but their current qualifications could well be less than other qualified persons not so protected. The reasoning is that the currently less-qualified underutilized groups will, in time, develop through training and experience to the point where we can go back to equal opportunity. Affirmative action programs can be viewed as temporary protective measures that provide training opportunities for the underutilized.

Despite the great concern about goals, the meat of an affirmative action program lies in all the activities necessary to make the plan work. An equal employment opportunity policy must be formulated and announced in the policy manual, company newspaper, bulletin board, and communications with recruiting sources and company vendors. A specific executive should be appointed as director of the program and given top management support and staffing. Recommended specific activities would include: (1) broadened recruitment efforts in areas where females and minorities are likely to be found; (2) formal career counseling programs to include attitude development, education aid, and job rotation; (3) possible child-care, housing and transportation programs designed to improve employment opportunities; and (4) including equal employment opportunity efforts in the performance appraisal of all supervisors.

THE CULTURALLY DISADVANTAGED

Though no national laws require that currently unqualified personnel be hired and utilized by private business firms, the federal government has attempted to encourage help for the culturally disadvantaged through various forms of subsidies. There are in our society a number of persons whose consideration for employment on the basis of current qualifications would lead to their exclusion with little hope for change in the future. Perhaps the more commonly used label for this group would be the "hard-core unemployed." In one group of 98 so identified by the Lockheed Aircraft Corporation, all were male, most were single, three-fourths were black, two-thirds were 20 years old or younger, and two-thirds were school dropouts.[15] For these persons to enter the typical business firm, regular hiring standards must be relaxed.

The Civil Rights Act of 1964 would not prohibit the exclusion of a hard-core unemployed applicant on the basis of lack of job skills. In many instances, the formal education level possessed is no higher than fourth or fifth grade. Consequently, the federal government has become involved on a promotional basis and has appropriated money to subsidize unusual costs of training, personal counseling, and transportation to and from

---

[15]James D. Hodgson and Marshall H. Brenner, "Successful Experience: Training Hard-Core Unemployed," *Harvard Business Review,* vol. 46, no. 5, September-October 1968, p. 150.

work. This program is labeled "Job Opportunities in Business Sector" (JOBS) and is administered through a voluntary organization of business executives, the National Alliance of Businessmen.

The NAB encourages employer participation in assisting the culturally disadvantaged through either contracts that compensate for unusual expenses or a signed pledge in voluntary recognition of a social responsibility. Examples of such expenses sometimes include serving breakfast to create regular eating habits, education in personal hygiene, transportation door-to-door for the first week, provision of specialized counselors, and even purchasing alarm clocks to re-regulate sleeping and working hours. In a survey of 350 corporations, it was discovered that the retention rate (a crucial success factor) of firms collaborating with JOBS programs averaged 57 percent.[16] This compared with an average of 39 percent for those without formal affiliation with the program. The retention rate is of great importance because of the necessity to convert the culture of the hard-core unemployed to that deemed necessary by the hiring organization in regard to dress, work habits, punctuality, attendance, and so on.

In a study of practices of five large organizations (Boeing, Eastman Kodak, Westinghouse, UAL, Inc., and Bankers Trust Company), it was concluded that an extensive and special effort is necessary to implement a successful hard-core unemployment program. Key elements of the program include top management commitment that gets through to "majority" members, pretraining preparation of the trainee, considerable support while in training, clear linkages of training with the future job, and follow-up activities after the employee assumes the regular job. This and other studies emphasize the very crucial nature of the support activities. The assignment of a specialized counselor is one of the most effective means of increasing successful trainee adaptation. Successful programs also require committed and understanding supervisors who are willing to work in an empathic and counseling manner.

Review of over a decade of experience with employing the culturally disadvantaged has resulted in a number of general conclusions.[17] The most basic one was emphasized in the preceding paragraph—the more supportive the environment and the closer the training linkage to an actual job, the more successful the program. The greater top management's support of the program and the more skilled the supervisors in interpersonal relations, the higher the retention of culturally disadvantaged employees. In terms of what not to do, the more the firm relies on conventional recruiting sources and traditional screening practices, the more likely that potentially qualified personnel will be missed. When the disadvantaged employee is present at work, the quantity and quality of output are comparable with other employees. The major difficulty lies in the higher rates of tardiness and absenteeism of such trainees. Of 81 employers studied in one survey, 31 percent relaxed their rules on absenteeism and 12 percent on tardiness.[18] In correlating these practices with retention rates, an inverse relationship was found. Supportiveness should not be translated into permissiveness.

---

[16]Robert C. Sedwick and Donald J. Bodwell, "The Hard-Core Employee: Key to High Retention," *Personnel Journal,* vol. 50, no. 12, December 1971, p. 951.

[17]James L. Koch, "Employing the Disadvantaged: Lessons From the Past Decade," *California Management Review,* vol. 17, no. 1, Fall 1974, pp. 68–77.

[18]Elchanan Cohn and Morgan V. Lewis, "Employers' Experience in Retaining Hard-Core Hires," *Industrial Relations,* vol. 14, no. 1, February 1975, p. 58.

SUMMARY

The federal government's administration of fair employment practices ranks right along with labor union growth as a force causing revolutionary changes in personnel management. Major pieces of legislation and executive orders include: (1) the Civil Rights Act of 1964 which calls for equal opportunity; (2) Executive Orders No. 11246 and No. 11375 which call for equal opportunity and affirmative action for employees for government contractors; (3) the Age Discrimination Act of 1967 which prohibits discrimination against the older employee; (4) the Vocational Rehabilitation Act of 1973 which calls for equal opportunity and affirmative action for the handicapped; (5) the Equal Pay Act of 1963 which requires equal pay for equal work; and (6) the Pregnancy Discrimination Amendment of 1978 which requires equal treatment of pregnant employees.

Groupings of citizens that receive special protection in their civil rights in employment include (1) minority races; (2) minority nationalities, (3) religious groups, (4) females, (5) those aged 40–69, (6) handicapped personnel, and (7) pregnant employees. This protection develops through either assuring equal opportunity in covered firms or special affirmative action programs to enlarge the pool of qualified minorities and females. The actions of the Equal Employment Opportunity Commission and the Office of Federal Contract Compliance Programs are undergoing surveillance through various federal court decisions on a constant stream of cases. In many areas, there is confusion as one agency conflicts with another, one law conflicts with an Executive order, and the Supreme Court conflicts with multiple lower courts thereby overturning guidelines of years' standing. Nevertheless, the basic thrust of the movement is clear. Employers, labor unions, and employment agencies must continue to work toward truly equal opportunity for all of this nation's citizens. As far as the day-to-day process is concerned, one personnel manager stated, "We do our best and pray a lot."

BRIEF CASE

George Smith, personnel manager for a small family-owned manufacturing plant, returned to his office on Monday after a 1-week vacation. On his desk, among a pile of other work, was a telephone memo dated last Thursday, which stated "Please call me at once. Urgent!" Smith recognized the name of Georgia Wilson, the secretary to the vice president of finance, John Dickerson. After completing a few essential items, he dialed Wilson's extension. When he identified himself to her, she said that she would call him back in about 10 minutes.

Ten minutes later, Wilson called and said, "I'm calling from a phone booth. I'm calling you Mr. Smith to see if you can help me. If you can't help me, or won't help me, I'm going to have to go to the EEOC. I love my job, Mr. Smith, and I need the money, but I can't take any of this anymore. I'm being sexually harassed by Mr. Dickerson. Now I know that he is the brother-in-law of the firm's owner, but I don't see why I have to put up with stuff like this." Mr. Smith said, "What kind of stuff?" Wilson said, "Well the first time he talked to me about a raise in his office, he put his hand on my knee. At least twice a week, he drops by my desk just before quitting time and drops little hints about having a little fun, going out for a drink, and sometimes, suggesting dinner. I have given him absolutely no encouragement, but I haven't directly told him to cut it out either. A friend of mine told me that this kind of behavior is prohibited by the Civil Rights Act. Now I don't know anything about how to file a charge, but my friend said that she would help me.''

Questions

1. Does the Civil Rights Act prohibit sexual harassment? Is this sexual harassment?

2. If you were George Smith, what would you say to Wilson? What action would you undertake?

DISCUSSION QUESTIONS

1. Define and distinguish among the three discrimination types of (1) disparate treatment, (2) disparate effect, and (3) present effect of past discrimination. Give an example of each type.

2. Define and distinguish among (1) equal opportunity in hiring, (2) soft goals, and (3) hard goals. What are the qualifications of the personnel hired under these three systems?

3. What are the major differences between the Civil Rights Act and Executive Orders No. 11246 and No. 11375?

4. Compare and contrast the Bakke and Weber Supreme Court decisions.

5. What two protected groups require the employer to "accommodate" them? What is the nature of this accommodation?

6. What is sexual harassment? What are the employer's obligations in this regard?

7. What is national origin harassment? What are the employer's obligations in this regard?

8. What is a bona fide occupational qualification? Cite one example in regard to age. Cite one in regard to sex.

9. Identify the major elements of an affirmative action program. Which decision is most difficult to make accurately?

10. Which group in this chapter is not protected by the cited laws, regulations, and guidelines? Should the employer voluntarily undertake to employ this group, what key elements contribute to success?

SUPPLEMENTARY READING

CHACKO, THOMAS I.: "Women and Equal Employment Opportunity: Some Unintended Effects," *Journal of Applied Psychology,* vol. 67, no. 1, February 1982, pp. 119–123.

COLLINS, ELIZA G. C. and TIMOTHY B. BLODGETT: "Sexual Harassment . . . Some See It . . . Some Won't," *Harvard Business Review,* vol. 59, no. 2, March-April 1981, pp. 77–94.

GREENLAW, PAUL S. and JOHN P. KOHL: "Age Discrimination in Employment Guidelines," *Personnel Journal,* vol. 61, no. 3, March 1982, pp. 224–228.

NORWOOD, JOHN M.: "But I Can't Work on Saturdays," *The Personnel Administrator,* vol. 25, no. 1, January 1980, pp. 25–30.

PETERSEN, DONALD J.: "Paving the Way for Hiring the Handicapped," *Personnel,* vol. 58, no. 2, March-April 1981, pp. 43–52.

ORNATI, OSCAR A. and MARGARET J. EISEN: "Are You Complying with EEOC's New Rules on National Origin Discrimination?" *Personnel,* vol. 58, no. 2, March-April 1981, pp. 12–20.

TROTTER, RICHARD, SUSAN RAWSON ZACUR, and WALLACE GATEWOOD: "The Pregnancy Disability Amendment: What the Law Provides," *The Personnel Administrator,* vol. 27, no. 2, February 1982, pp. 47–54.

chapter 5

Organizational and Job Design

Organizations are systems of relating resources that will make possible the accomplishment of specified ends or goals. They are social and technological devices made up of people and physical factors. With the aid of technological implementation, these people execute functions or tasks that lead to the accomplishment of rationally determined objectives. Organizations are processing units that transform certain inputs from the environment into specified outputs desired by society; for example, a hospital transforms ill patients into healthy people, and a manufacturing firm transforms raw material into usable products.

Organizational design is the beginning point for procurement. As a part of this design process, specific units of responsibility, commonly designated as "jobs," will be set up. The performance of these jobs will lead to the accomplishment of overall organization objectives. Procurement is concerned with the process of obtaining personnel who are best suited to performing the tasks assigned to specific jobs. A continuing admonition of our courts and administrative agencies in promoting fair employment practices is that the job should dictate the type of person to be hired. Discrimination on the basis of job requirements is the societally approved type of discrimination in making personnel decisions.

Every manager has the responsibility of organizing subordinates into patterns of interactions that will facilitate accomplishment of unit goals. However, the basic, overall design of the total organization has always been the responsibility of the chief executive. As the organization grows in size, its complexity increases at an even more rapid rate. Consequently, in the larger organizations, there have been evolved specialized people and units to advise and assist the chief executive in this organizing function. One survey indicated that 100 of the nation's top 500 companies had established specialized staff units for the purpose of assisting in organizational design and development.[1]

There is growing evidence that the personnel department is the one that will be responsible for the organization design unit, at least until the unit merits separate status under the chief executive. The study cited above revealed that *most* of the 100 existing departments were subdivisions of personnel departments. In another study of 244 per-

---

[1]William F. Glueck, "Where Organization Planning Stands Today," *Personnel,* vol. 44, no. 4, July-August 1968, pp. 19–26.

sonnel departments in large companies, 82 percent had been given general responsibility for organization planning.[2] In those companies placing the unit outside of that department, it was usually grouped with such personnel activities as management development and human resource planning.

The above studies strongly suggest that the personnel manager should develop a special interest and expertise in organization planning and design in order to provide the service desired by the chief executive. This view also makes sense, considering the nature of the operative functions of personnel. If the three key components of any organization are people, jobs, and physical factors, the personnel manager has special knowledge of the first two. Organizations are dependent upon the caliber of personnel available, and it is no accident that organizational design is frequently grouped with personnel activities like executive training and development and the forecasting of human resource needs. The personnel unit also collects information about job content which can be of material assistance in organizational design.

The function of organizing is basically a process of tying these key components together and harnessing them so that they may be directed toward enterprise objectives. Thus, a technical definition of the formal process of organizing would be as follows: it is the process of establishing *relationships* (responsibility, authority, and accountability) among key *components* (personnel, functions, and physical factors) for the purpose of *harnessing* (line, line/staff, functionalized, and project structures) and directing toward organizational *objectives*. Thus, experts in organizational design require knowledge of such subjects as objectives, components, relationships, and structures. If the personnel manager is to provide sound and effective advice in this area, this executive must study the theory and practice of organizing as avidly as the more traditional content of the personnel functions. Brief coverage of the major elements of this definition will be presented in the following sections.

ORGANIZATIONAL OBJECTIVES

Inasmuch as organizations are intendedly rational devices established to achieve objectives, it is logical to begin a consideration of organization design with a consideration of those objectives. One of the first things recognized by most managers is that any organization has *multiple* objectives. One classification of goals of business organizations is as follows:

I   Primary objectives
   A   Create and distribute a product or service
   B   Satisfy personal objectives of the members of the organization, such as:
      1   Profits for owners
      2   Salaries and other compensation for executives
      3   Wages and other compensation for employees

---

[2]Allen R. Janger, *Personnel Administration: Changing Scope and Organization*, National Industrial Conference Board. Studies in Personnel Policy, no. 203, New York, 1966, p. 23.

4 Psychic income for all, including:
  a Pride in work
  b Security
  c Recognition
  d Acceptance
  C Meet community and social obligations, such as:
    1 Protection and enhancement of the human resources of society
    2 Protection and enhancement of the physical resources of society
II Secondary objectives
    A Economy of operation in meeting the primary objectives
    B Effectiveness of operation in meeting the primary objectives

A careful study of the above outline should reveal much concerning the nature of organizational objectives. Reasonable accomplishment of all is prerequisite to managerial success, a fact that should create some appreciation of the difficulty of the managerial task.

Product or service objectives   Every business organization must have as one of its basic purposes the creation and distribution of some good or service. The tangible representation of this objective is the automobile, refrigerator, can of beans, or haircut. The personnel engaged in the actual creation, distribution, or financing of this product are performing the basic work of the organization. They are carrying the ball. A personnel department is *not* so engaged. It is charged with the responsibility of *assisting* those in production who are creating the product, those in sales who are distributing it, and those in finance who provide the funds for its creation and distribution. Thus, the goals of a personnel department must be derived from the objectives of the entire organization.

Personal objectives   An organization is composed of two or more people. These people have various and often conflicting personal objectives, which must be reasonably satisfied or individuals will withdraw from the organization. Such withdrawal can lead to collapse of the enterprise and failure to accomplish the product or service objective.

These personal objectives are of two general types, monetary and nonmonetary. In recent years, management has become increasingly aware of the nonmonetary goals of people. When the wage or salary is somewhat reasonable, other desires come to the fore, and they form the basis of today's human relations program.

On personnel management rests a large measure of the responsibility for ensuring satisfactory accomplishment of the personal objectives of employees. If the personal objectives of all groups are not reasonably achieved, the basic objectives of the entire organization will suffer. Consideration of the nature and techniques of fulfilling many of these objectives constitutes a major portion of this text.

Community and social obligations   Society has imposed upon business a number of broad social obligations, which thereby become business objectives. It is apparent that appreciation of superordinate societal goals, discussed in preceding chapters, will have considerable impact upon the design of complex organizations in the future.

Secondary objectives In labeling economy and effectiveness of operation as secondary objectives, one should not imply that they are unimportant. If these goals also are not satisfactorily achieved, all other goals will suffer. But again, we are not in the business of providing more economy and effectiveness in a vacuum. Some other objective must be the basic goal, which we hope to accomplish with a reasonable expenditure of money and effort.

Primacy of product or service objective Aside from their multiplicity, one aspect of the outline of business objectives that seems unusual is the emphasis on the product or service objective. The thesis of the primacy of the service objective can be defended in three areas. The first might be labeled the political area. Society, through the Constitution, has granted us the right to own property and establish a business. The right was not granted solely to enable an owner to make a profit; rather, *the right to make a profit was granted in order to provide an incentive to produce the goods and services that society needs*. Profit is the personal motivation; the good or service is the end or objective. Ours is known as the profit system, a system which is a means to the end of creating the necessary and desirable goods. The service objective exists in other types of economic systems where the profit objective does not.

The second defense lies in the area of organization. It is a principle of organization that all members must have one *common* goal in order to secure cooperation and coordination of action. The product or service objective is the only one in which all are immediately interested. Thus, while the objective of the business manager or owner is profit, the objective of the business organization is the product or service.

The last defense of this thesis is economic in nature. Under our competitive system, there is substantial freedom of choice in the markets for goods and services. The theory of the system is that resources will flow to the organizations that produce the best product at the lowest price. In the political area, a business may be voted out of existence or hampered by means of legislation. In the marketplace, it may be voted out or restricted by the customer's dollar. Thus, the rationale of our system is that resources, income for profits and wages, will flow to the organization that creates the best goods and services.

In the final analysis, the manager who is aware of the tremendous importance of the product or service objective, already being aware of the profit objective, will have a philosophy of management that will not be too far wrong. An *intelligent* pursuit of profits, with equitable consideration for labor and the customer, will usually lead to the same position as the principle of the primacy of the service objective.

FUNCTIONS

Objectives do not accomplish themselves. Work must be executed by people or machines in order that objectives may be achieved. The word "function" can be defined simply as *work that can be distinguished from other work*. The function of production, for instance, can be defined and distinguished from sales, just as planning can be separated from control. In manufacturing concerns, three functions are considered to be primary or organic: they are sales, production, and finance. These functions contribute directly toward the accomplishment of the basic objective of the firm, that is, the product or service objective. Since these are primary, they are generally referred to as "line" functions.

In the one-person firm, all functions are bound up in one person. This person produces, sells, and finances the product. As the volume of business increases, a process of functional differentiation occurs. This is essentially a separation of certain functions from the original performer and an assignment of them to other people who are added to the enterprise. Functional differentiation takes place in two directions—downward and outward. The results of both directions of growth are the same, i.e., more functional specialization.

Functional Differentiation Downward

Staying with the one-person firm for the moment, we see that as the business grows, a helper will be hired. Thus, a function has been differentiated, possibly in the area of production, and assigned to the second person, as shown in Figure 5-1. The process of downward differentiation is under way, and we now have two levels of organization. As volume continues to grow, additional personnel are added to the organization, as depicted in Figure 5-2. Perhaps one or two of the subordinates are engaged in the function of selling. At some point in this process of functional splitting, the owner will encounter a basic principle of organization known as the *span of control*.[3] This principle is basically a statement of human limitations; that is, there is a limit to the number of people and functions that one person can supervise effectively. Assuming that our owner-manager has reached that limit, we must push down to another level of organization. One of our present employees is perhaps appointed a supervisor, and now this span of control can be utilized when we add other personnel to the company. With further growth, three full levels will come into existence, as shown in Figure 5-3.

As the limits of anyone's span of control are reached, we are forced to push down and create another level of organization. In organizations of several thousand members, there may be as many as fourteen different levels. Were there no such principle as the span of control, there would be one manager, to whom all others would report.

FIGURE 5-1 Functional differentiation downward.

[3]As in the case of the exception principle, the span-of-control concept is quite old. Exodus 18:25 states, "And Moses chose able men out of all Israel, and made them heads over the people, rulers of thousands, rulers of hundreds, and rulers of fifties, and rulers of tens."

FIGURE 5-2 Further downward differentiation.

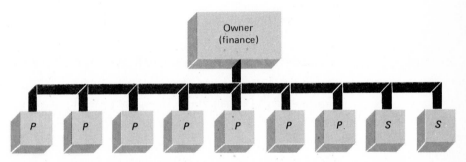

P, production employee; *S*, salesperson

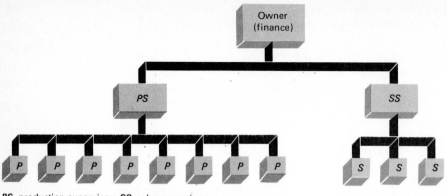

PS, production supervisor; SS, sales supervisor;
P, production employee; S, salesperson

Figure 5-3 Three full levels of organization.

Let us examine this span-of-control principle more closely. What are the limits? The number of functions and personnel that one person can supervise effectively will depend upon such factors as that *person's ability,* one's *subordinates' abilities,* the *complexity* of the functions performed, the *similarity* of the functions to one another, the degree of *situational stability,* and the degree to which separate work assignments *interlock.* A series of subprinciples can thus be devised as follows: (1) the greater the degree of functional complexity, the fewer the functions that can be supervised effectively, and (2) the greater the degree of dissimilarity of functions, the fewer the functions that can be controlled effectively.

Research indicates that people are more satisfied in "flat" organizations with wide spans of control.[4] The "tall" organization, with its larger number of supervisors, provides less opportunity to engage in behavior characterized by freedom, independence, and personal accomplishment. In comparing reactions of outside sales personnel in tall versus flat organizations, those in the latter experienced: (1) greater felt autonomy, (2) higher self-actualization, and (3) less anxiety stress.[5] There were no differences in absenteeism rates, but those in the flat organizations had higher efficiency ratings.

Traditional managers tend to prefer smaller spans, which permit a higher degree of control of communication and operations. Psychologists and sociologists, on the other hand, advocate broader spans, which necessitate a greater degree of freedom for the subordinate. It is apparent that there are no valid formulas that will indicate the theoretically perfect span for any situation. The particular philosophy of management, analysis of the limiting fractors cited above, and a reasonable amount of trial and error will all doubtlessly be involved in answering this question for each manager.

Functional Differentiation Outward

The lack of managerial specialization becomes increasingly serious with increased growth in size of organization. This situation results from the effect of another principle known sometimes as *the law of functional growth.* This law states that as the volume of

[4]Edwin E. Ghiselli and Douglas A. Johnson, "Need Satisfaction, Managerial Success, and Organizational Structure," *Personnel Psychology,* vol. 23, no. 4, Winter 1970, p. 572.

[5]John M. Ivancevich and James H. Donnelly, Jr., "Relation of Organizational Structure to Job Satisfaction, Anxiety-Stress, and Performance," *Administrative Science Quarterly,* vol. 20, no. 2, June 1975, p. 277.

business grows, the complexity of the functions necessary for performance increases at an even more rapid pace. For example, the establishment of a wage and salary structure for a shop of four or five people is considerably less difficult than the performance of the same function for a concern of several hundred or thousand employees. The effect of this principle is to emphasize the need for managerial assistance through specialization. Certain activities are differentiated outward from the chain of command previously established by means of downward differentiation. Secondary or staff functions are established in areas *other* than production, sales, or finance. The objective of these secondary functions is the assistance and facilitation of the performance of line functions. Thus a staff function is *one that has been separated from the line for purposes of specialization.* Its separation is justified only so long as it is believed that the function can be performed more effectively and economically by a specialist than by the line from which it was evolved.

The above description can be clarified by an example. Functional differentiation downward of the three primary functions creates a pure line organization. All members are producing, selling, or financing, or are in the direct chain of command above these three functions. The production supervisor in Figure 5-4 has been having trouble training new personnel because of the rapid growth of the firm. He or she has asked that a line machine operator be assigned as a training assistant to assume much of the responsibility in that area. Training done by the training assistant is a staff function. As the business continues to grow, there may be more work than the training assistant can handle alone. He or she is provided with a subordinate, which means, of course, that functional differentiation is pushing downward within the staff function of training. This movement results in the formation of a staff section, the training section.

While the above functional differentiation outward and downward is going on, the law of functional growth has forced other functions out of the line into staff assignments. The production supervisor may have the usual subordinate line personnel but will also

Figure 5-4 Addition of staff to a line organization.

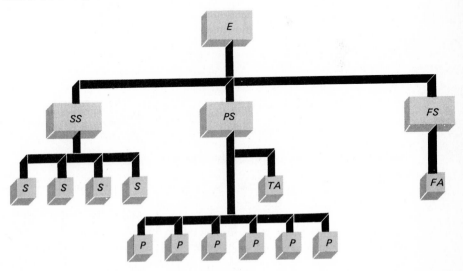

E, executive; *PS*, production supervisor; *SS*, sales supervisor; *FS*, financial supervisor; *TA*, training assistant (staff); *S*, salesperson; *P*, production worker; *FA*, financial assistant

have a multitude of staff engaged in such activities as training, production control, inspection, hiring, safety, and the like. To reduce the span of control, one may prefer to regroup some of the staff sections to form a staff department. Thus, a personnel department may be formed through combining the sections of hiring, training, and safety.

Functional differentiation outward can take place at *any* level in the primary chain of command. It may take place gradually and go through the above-described steps: (1) assignment of the function to one person, a staff assistant; (2) creation of a staff unit by adding personnel; and (3) creation of a larger staff unit by grouping with related specialized units. In addition, with further growth the staff unit may develop an internal support structure. For example, if the training effort becomes sufficiently large, the organization may be able to afford a training *research* subunit. Thus, if production is primary to the goal, and training secondary in that production is facilitated, then training research is tertiary in that it facilitates the secondary function of training. In effect, we have experienced functional differentiation downward in training to create a secondary chain of command, followed by functional differentiation outward to create a "staff-to-staff."

The pattern of functional growth is universal—first *down* in the primary or line functions and secondly *out* into staff functions. This can be summarized as follows:

Principle	Process	Result
Span of control	Functional differentiation downward	Operative specialization and added organizational levels
Law of functional growth	Functional differentiation outward	Managerial specialization and creation of staff

Finally, if the firm grows quite large, the staff function can be separated on multiple levels from top to bottom in the organization. As shown in Figure 5-5, there can be a

Figure 5-5 Parallel personnel staff.

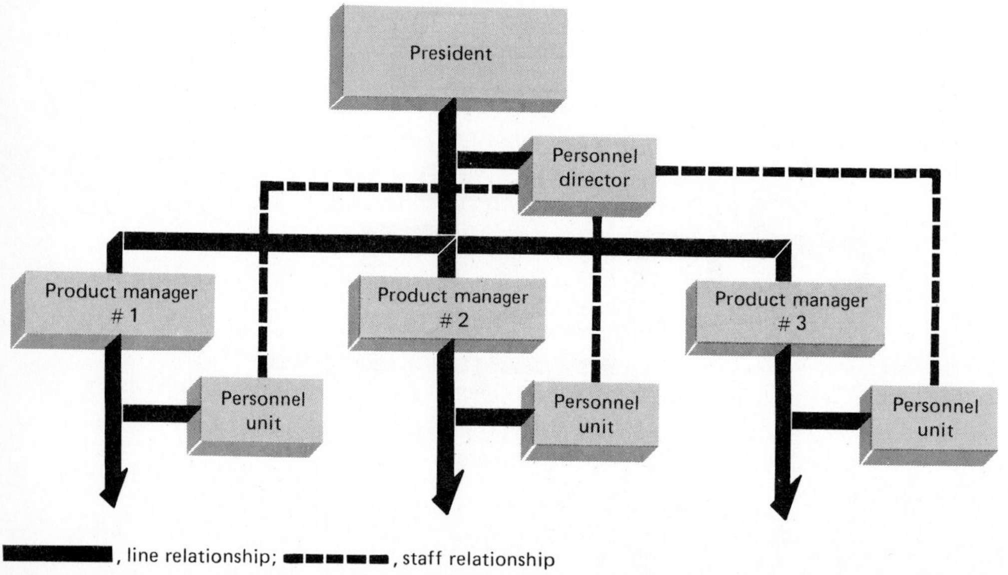

━━━━━ , line relationship; ━ ━ ━ ━ , staff relationship

personnel director for the entire organization, as well as personnel units for each of the product managers. The top central unit serves as a clearinghouse for personnel information and activities throughout the enterprise. It may also provide certain central services, such as negotiating the master contract with the labor union. This parallel functional development also acts as a specialized channel of communication and constitutes a career promotion ladder. It should be noted that even though the staff director is reporting directly to the president, and may even be accorded vice-presidential standing, this in no way transforms the unit into line status. The incidence of service toward primary organizational goals is still controlling.

RELATIONSHIPS

The process of organizing is one of *relating* the component parts of the organization to one another and to the organization objective. Knowledge of these parts—functions, personnel, and physical factors—is prerequisite to understanding the relationship that should exist among them. Characteristics of personnel and physical factors assigned to differentiated functions will also, of course, have impact upon the design. Though treatment of these these two components will not be undertaken at this point, various illustrations will appear in this and later chapters. Organizing is the process of binding the parts together into a unified whole that can operate effectively. The immediate result of this process is the establishment of organization structure, a subject that will be discussed later in this chapter.

The relationships that will be established among the components of organization are of two general types, formal and informal. Formal relationships are those that are *officially* established and prescribed in the organization manual, charts, and job descriptions. The three basic relationships of this category are *responsibility, authority,* and *accountability*. Informal relationships are those that emerge from the formal and are established unofficially by particular persons employed. They would include such relationships as power, status, and politics.

Responsibility

Responsibility is *one's obligation to perform the functions assigned to the best of one's ability in accordance with directions received.* It is logically the first relationship that should be established and is based on an analysis of *functions* required to accomplish the organization *objective*.

There are many principles governing the formal assignment of responsibility. Perhaps the foremost one is the *principle of functional similarity*. This principle states that *the functions assigned to an individual should be grouped on the basis of similarity to one another in order to facilitate specialization.* Insofar as possible, the functions to be assigned to make up a job, section, department, or division should be sufficiently related one to another to take advantage of specialized backgrounds. The greater the volume of work, the greater is the opportunity to apply the principle of functional similarity.

Other principles applicable to responsibility are: (1) there should be no overlapping responsibilities—the same function should not be assigned to two or more persons; (2) responsibility limits should be clearly defined; (3) there should be no gaps in responsibility assignments—work that should be done must be assigned to some person; and (4) responsibility should not be assigned for work that is unnecessary and does not contribute toward organization objectives. It should be noted that responsibility is assigned through delegation from superiors. The significance of the word ''delegation'' is that the process in no way reduces the superior's original amount of responsibility. This concept is what puts the risk in a manager's job. Responsibility is still full and complete although execution of the task has been largely relegated to others.

Authority

Authority is the *right to decide what should be done and the right to do it or to require someone else to do it*. The basic principle governing this relationship is the principle of coequal authority and responsibility. This principle states that a commensurate amount of authority should accompany a delegation of responsibility. Just as responsibility is derived from functional analysis, authority is derived from responsibility. A person should have no authority without having a prior responsibility.

The source of formal authority is from above through delegation. One receives official organizational rights to hire, fire, spend money, and so on, from one's superior, and ultimately from organization owners and society at large.

Accountability

Accountability is the *requirement of answerability for one's performance*. It is the opposite phase of responsibility, in that responsibility is delegated downward while one is accountable upward to some superior for proper performance. If one has been delegated an amount of authority commensurate with responsibility, one can, logically, be held accountable for results. Just as responsibility is a derivative of functions and authority is a derivative of responsibility, accountability is a derivative of authority. If insufficient authority has been delegated, it is not logical to hold a person fully answerable.

Perhaps the foremost principle governing the formal relationship of accountability is that of single accountability. This principle states that *the most desirable relationship is that each person be accountable to only one superior*. Divided accountability to multiple superiors imposes considerable difficulties upon the subordinate. As the size of the organization increases with concurrent expansion in the number of staff specialists, the principle of single accountability is placed in considerable jeopardy.

It has been suggested that a related concept, the principle of unity of command, is more important than single accountability. Though a person has two bosses, *if* those bosses are coordinated, unity of command can be preserved despite the loss of single accountability. It may well be that future large-size organizations will see the increased introduction of ''plural executive,'' that is, a number of executives operating as one office.

Figure 5-6 is a summary of the organizing process up to this point. We start the design of organization with a selection of organization objectives. Analysis of these objectives will tell us what functions will have to be performed. In dividing up these functions among our personnel, units of responsibility will be established. Given this amount of responsibility, sufficient authority must be delegated to enable meeting these obligations. Assuming sufficient authority, then accountability can be imposed. Thus, the logical derivation is in the sequence indicated in Figure 5-6.

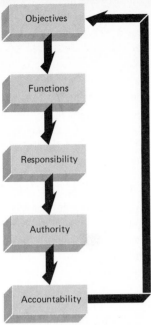

Figure 5-6 Derivation of relationships.

ORGANIZATION STRUCTURE

The immediate result of the organizing process is the creation of organization structure. This structure is a framework of the formal relationships that have been established. The purpose of the structure is to assist in regulating and directing the efforts put forth in an organization so that they are coordinated and consistent with organization objectives.

There are several basic types of organization structure, any one of which may be adopted. If responsibility, authority, and accountability are established in one way, the result is *line structure*. If these relationships are set up in another way, the *line and staff structure* is created. The third arrangement of relationships is known as the *functional type of structure*. Each of these structures will be briefly described and the location of the personnel functions noted. In addition, the project structure will be briefly discussed to indicate how activities can be fitted into this most recent structural adaptation.

Line Organization Structure

The nature of line organization has been largely described in the earlier discussion of functional differentiation. Line structure is created by the functional differentiation downward of primary or basic functions. In manufacturing, these basic functions are production, sales, and finance. Thus in the line organization, all personnel are either producing, selling, or financing, or are in the direct chain of command above these three functions. There is no functional differentiation outward.

In the line organization, the personnel functions exist but are performed by line personnel. A supervisor is responsible for procurement of personnel and their development and integration in the workplace. He or she has no assistance in these matters beyond what a superior can supply.

One of the decisions common to all types of structure is the selection of bases for grouping divided activities. What has been divided must be combined, if possible, to effect coordinated and unified progress toward organization goals. Perhaps the two most signficant bases of grouping are (1) functions and (2) product or service. Line organizations typically group on the basis of the first—that is, all activities related to production, for example, are placed in one unit, while all those related to the selling function are placed in another. This ensures specialization and requires the top manager of the enterprise to coordinate the total task.

With increasing size, firms typically move to the product or service base. Each unit has its own production and sales subgroupings, thus leading to a seeming duplication of activities throughout the firm. Each may be established as a separate profit center designed to produce such values as a "whole" approach to each product, more rapid decision making, and a greater development and motivation of personnel responsible.

In addition to these two bases of grouping, other choices available are (1) geography, (2) customers, (3) time, and (4) numbers. Recognition of the first will result in territory managers. The second reflects recognition of peculiar customer requirements, such as teenage shops and budget basements in department stores. Time and numbers may call for multiple supervisors on different work shifts.

Line and Staff Organization Structure

Functional differentiation downward *and* outward produces a line and staff organization. Most business organizations, except the very small, have this type of structure. The problems of management have become sufficiently complex so that presumably expert attention will produce more effective results in selected areas. This expertise is introduced into the organization in an advisory or facilitative manner. In theory, line managers are free to reject the specialized advice or service on the basis of overriding general objectives. Examples of specific guides for combining line and staff activities were discussed in Chapter 3 with specific reference to the staff personnel unit.

Functional Organization Structure

The adoption of the functional form of organization structure involves the violation of some principles of organization previously cited. A functional relationship is established when *a staff function is brought directly to bear on the line functions with authority to command rather than to advise.* Thus, the integrity of the line is broken and some personnel are accountable to multiple superiors. If the personnel unit, for example, is set up on a functional basis, it does not recommend that a supervisor accept an applicant; it *orders* that it be done. The unit can overrule lower line managers on matters of wages, grievances, training, and the like. Thus in matters pertaining to personnel, the supervisor must look to the personnel unit; in other areas, the supervisor looks to the appropriate line superior.

No firms today are completely functionalized in all specialized functions. The significance lies in the provision of a third alternative. Organizers can choose among the following: (1) a function such as hiring can be allocated to the supervisor (line organization); (2) it can be given to a specialized personnel unit with rights of advice only (line and staff); or (3) it can be assigned to the personnel unit with rights of command (functionalized). The third alternative should be used sparingly to prevent distortion of basic general objectives.

Project Structure

A variation of the functionalized form now coming into wider use, particularly in the aerospace industry, is the project structure. If a management desires to emphasize strongly a specific undertaking or project, a special structure can be created. Such projects are usually unique and unfamiliar to the existing organization and complex in nature. They require interaction among specialists and have limited time objectives. A project manager is given authority to assemble temporarily the necessary talents and facilities to accomplish an undertaking. In some instances, the usual line and staff departments do the work, but the project manager specifies what effort is needed and when it will be performed. The operating unit manager may decide who in his or her unit is to help and how the work is to be accomplished. It is apparent that, though the unit manager has line or command authority over personnel, the project manager has functionalized authority in connection with the work on the particular project.

Business managers have found the project structure supplement to be highly effective in assuring the accomplishment of important goals. The project cannot get lost between departments. It has been found that one person can work for two or more ''masters,'' and that a ''master'' can effectively influence those over whom he or she has no clear authority. The possibility of conflict and frustration is great, but the opportunity for prompt, expeditious, and effective accomplishment is even greater. The coordinative power of the knowledge and expertise of the participating specialists makes up in part for the vagueness and complexity of formal organizational relationships. Both project managers and supporting unit managers must maintain an open mind and be willing to negotiate.

The typical role of personnel managers in project structures is to provide supporting personnel specialists and to be willing to share in their supervision. For example, a task force may be set up to open a new branch of a discount chain in a distant city. The personnel unit may be asked to supply an employment interviewer to help in selecting personnel for the new outlet. This interviewer works not only for the project director, but also for his more permanent superior, the personnel director. Conflicts can develop when the project director wants more speed in selecting personnel, while the personnel manager wants all laws and policies followed to the letter. On occasions, the personnel specialist can be a project leader who is authorized to draw temporary help from various parts of the organization. For example, if the firm wants to put the force of authority behind a program for hiring the culturally disadvantaged, a task force can be formed of line supervisors who temporarily report to the project leader from the personnel unit. One can again visualize possible conflicts between the special project objectives and the continuing objectives of the line units. The project structure is utilized when one wishes to emphasize two different sets of values. Rather than the ensuing conflicts being settled by the chain of command, the project structure relies upon negotiating skills of project leaders and functional bosses, both of whom possess overlapping formal authority.

CONTRAST OF FORMAL
AND INFORMAL ORGANIZATION

The formal organization structure provides a minimal basic blueprint for the guidance of behavior. Most of the relationships within organizations are informal and unofficial in nature as particular people work out day-to-day problems. As Figure 5-7 indicates, the informal emerges from the formal. A formal job may be assigned but its execution involves additional *role* expectations. A role would consist of the total pattern of expected behavior, interactions, and feelings that one should display, such as dress like a manager, demonstrate loyalty to the firm, stick up for one's subordinates, etc. Whereas the *formal* structure will set up an official unit, such as a production division, particular employees will *informally* establish *primary work groups* involving helping and supporting relationships, providing members adhere to group norms.

Power can be defined as the capacity to apply "any force that results in behavior that would not have occurred if that force had not been present."[6] As such, it includes, but goes beyond the authority provided by the formal organization. Other sources of power would include knowledge, rewards, punishments, personality, friends, and the ability to control significant contingencies that affect organizational performance.

The formal organization allocates levels of responsibility and authority, and these can have a considerable effect upon one's *status* or social rank. Other sources of status would include seniority, associates, and education. One can tell much about a person's status in an organization by observing such symbols as uniforms, desks, rugs, paintings, office location, number of secretaries, automobile, and privileges accorded.

As power and status are used in an organization, we become involved in a political process. Organization members may choose to cooperate, reward their friends and punish enemies, bend or break formal regulations, cover for each other, and a host of other activities. It would be naive to insist that political action does not take place in organizations. They can be overdone and work contrary to the formal goals, but in many

[6]David Mechanic, "Sources of Power of Lower Participants in Complex Organizations," in David R. Hampton, Charles E. Summer, and Ross A. Webber (eds.), *Organizational Behavior and the Practice of Mangement,* Scott, Foresman, Glenview, Ill., 1968, p. 426.

Figure 5-7 Formal and informal concepts.

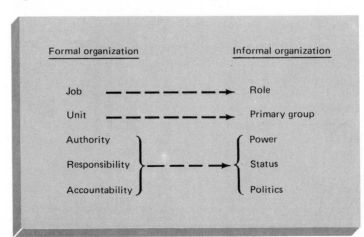

Figure 5-8 Formal and informal organization structure. (*Source: Ross Martin Company, Systemation Letter, © 1959, Tulsa, Okla. By permission.*)

instances they enable complex situations to be dealt with in a reasonably effective manner. If only the formal organization and its accompanying rules and procedures were followed religiously and without deviation, most organizations would be seriously harmed. We do not mean to suggest in Figure 5-8 that the informal organization consists solely of drinking and sleeping on the job, gossip, sabotage, and backstabbing. What we do intend to suggest is that there is far more to organizations than that prescribed by the formal.

JOB DESIGN

Moving from general groupings to the specific, the personnel manager should have an even greater interest in the design and specification of individual jobs within the organization. Excessive specialization and concentration upon technical efficiency have had an adverse impact upon the motivation of personnel responsible for executing these narrow jobs.

The design of an effective work unit for an individual employee is a highly complex task. It should not be left solely to the line supervisor, the union business agent, or the industrial engineer. The personnel manager has a responsibility to represent the interests of the individual, which hopefully will be reflected to some degree in the interests of the total organization. Among the many factors that will affect job design are (1) the proven values of specialization and repetitive operations, (2) changing technology, (3) labor union policies, (4) abilities of present personnel, (5) available supply of potential employees, (6) the interaction requirements among jobs within the system, and (7) psychological and social needs of human beings that can be met by the job.

Specialization tends to lead to greater productivity as well as ease of hiring. The resulting unit of work undergoes constant modification because of the impact of mechanization and automation. Some jobs are eliminated, others created, and still others altered in content, resulting in different specifications of education, experience, personality, and breadth of viewpoint. Labor unions are necessarily involved and seek to retain both present employee security and union control of these units of work. Thus, the firm may be required to respect jurisdictional lines of traditional crafts or to delay alteration of job content despite advances in technology. Economic and organizational values lost in job design may be recouped in part through enhanced union cooperation.

Management must also be concerned with the practical considerations of quantity and quality of personnel presently available, both within the firm and in the labor market generally. It does little good to design a job in terms of the ideal if the resulting unit cannot be supplied with workers. Consequently, changes in job content may be made to reflect particular characteristics of specific people available for transfer or hire.

It is apparent that the interrelationships among various jobs will levy an interaction requirement upon job incumbents. Work systems should be designed to minimize points of friction. For example, Whyte's restaurant study found that when lower-status personnel, such as runners, initiated action for higher-status personnel, such as chefs, the potential for explosions and dish breakage was increased.[7] He hypothesized that work will flow more smoothly when those of higher status are in a position to originate work for those of lower status. What appears to be personality conflicts between two individuals may actually be defects in job design, which tend to go counter to the needs and cultures of personnel handling the jobs.

Behavioral scientists have continually stressed the importance of designing jobs and systems of work in a manner that will satisfy psychological and sociological needs of people. One of the most commonly cited human relations problems in this area of job design is employee dissatisfaction with jobs that are repetitive, narrow, meaningless, and routine. Engineering efficiency has led to the creation of the production and assembly lines. Such lines have proved themselves on the basis of the quantity and quality of production that can be exacted from such a productive arrangement. The major deficiency, however, lies in the human relations area, with such specific problems resulting as the boredom of the worker, loss of pride in work, insecurity, and obsessive thinking. These problems are compounded when a moving conveyor links all positions together. The conveyor is a "monster" whose pressure never ceases.

Traditionally, the solution of excessive specialization of job assignments has in-

---

[7]William Foote Whyte, *Organizational Behavior,* The Dorsey Press and Richard D. Irwin, Inc., Homewood, Ill, 1969, chap. 4.

volved some means of periodic rotation to provide variety, such as change tasks every few hours, or work up the moving assembly line. In recent years, considerable research has been undertaken with respect to more unusual and seemingly risky changes in job content. Among these are job enlargement, job enrichment, and semiautonomous groups.

Job Enlargement

In response to criticisms concerning the dehumanization of work through excessive specialization, an obvious suggestion would be to enlarge job content to utilize more of the abilities of employees. If the additional responsibilities are of a horizontal nature, variety has been introduced and the process is termed "job enlargement." If the additional responsibilities are of a vertical nature encompassing self-control, the process is termed "job enrichment." Job enrichment is the approach to job design most recommended by behaviorists and will be discussed in the following section.

Variety can be produced by adding functions, thus possibly reducing monotony. An added psychological value can be derived if the added functions make possible the completion of an identifiable unit, thereby producing a sense of closure. In one instance, a hospital appliance that had been assembled by nine workers spaced along a moving conveyor was changed to a new system where each operator completed an entire unit.[8] Thus the job was enlarged from one operation to nine operations. Though there was a drop in quantity, the quality was immediately and significantly improved. A behaviorist would attribute this result to the greater variety and sense of closure produced by the job enlargement. A classicist would attribute it to increased accountability since it is now clear who produced what.

In a study of various assembly line jobs in a home laundry manufacturing firm, attempts were made over a 5-year period to increase the number and variety of tasks in single jobs.[9] For example, a pump assembly line of six operators required an average of 1.77 minutes per unit. In moving to single-operator work stations where the operator would perform the full assembly, the time was reduced to 1.49 minutes. In thirteen other similar job changes, there was an average decrease in quality rejects from 2.9 to 1.4 percent. However, there was an average decrease in output efficiency from 138 percent to 126 percent.

Job Enrichment

Though variety and closure are helpful, they are often not enough to effect the improvements visualized by behaviorists. The theory of job enrichment is outlined in Figure 5-9. Behaviorists contend that the employee will become "turned on" to his or her job if (1) the work is meaningful, (2) the worker has knowledge of operating results, and (3) the worker is personally responsible for these results. Meaning can be placed into a job by providing for skill variety, task identity, and task significance. Knowledge of operating results can be effected by opening feedback channels to the worker, and if

[8]Louis E. Davis, "Job Design: Historical Overview," in Louis E. Davis and James C. Taylor, eds., *Design of Jobs,* Goodyear Publishing Company, Inc., Santa Monica, Calif., 1979, p. 31.

[9]E. H. Conant and M. D. Kilbridge, "An Interdisciplinary Analysis of Job Enlargement: Technology, Costs, and Behavioral Implications," *Industrial and Labor Relations Review,* vol. 18, no. 3, April 1965, p. 377.

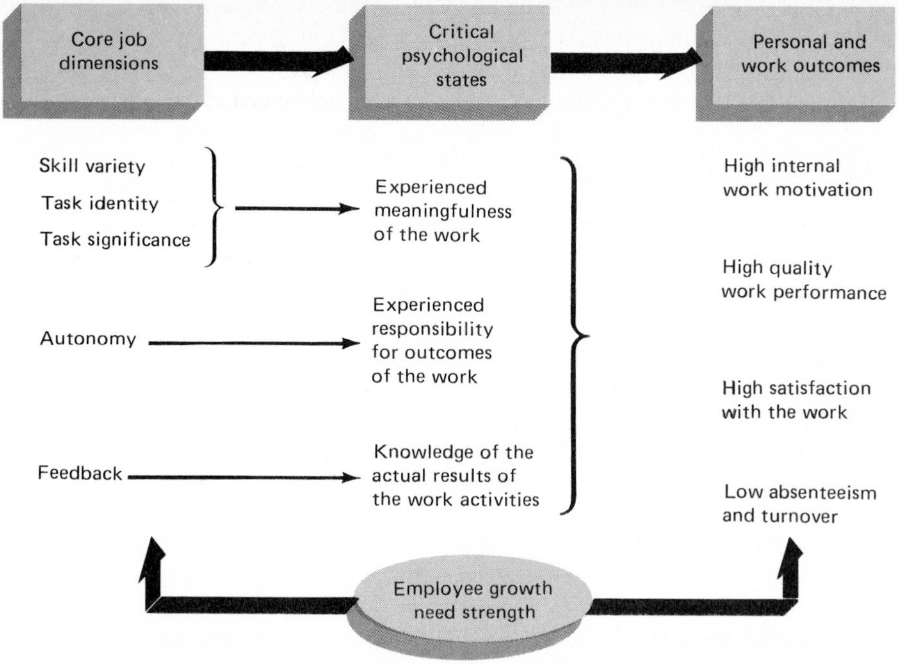

Figure 5-9 Model of job enrichment. *(Source: J. Richard Hackman and Greg R. Oldham, "Development of the Job Diagnostic Survey," in* Journal of Applied Psychology, *vol. 60, no. 1, April 1975, p. 161.)*

the employee is granted some degree of discretion and autonomy over the job, that worker's sense of responsibility is increased.

Moving from theory to practice, one inquires as to how the five core job dimensions can be designed into a unit of work. To effect the first, *variety*, the job can be enlarged as discussed earlier. One can move backward in the work flow, and add preparation functions; or move forward and combine the task with finishing or quality control functions. If sufficiently broadened, the task will take on a separate *identity*. The combination of tasks should be a natural one, such as the worker makes a whole item, provides services for one department, and so on. A natural unit of work tends to promote a sense of job ownership, a feeling of responsibility for an identifiable unit of work.

The establishment of identifiable and natural work units will serve to demonstrate the service provided by the worker. If one can perceive that one's performance has impact upon others, task *significance* is enhanced. Naturally, the greater the impact, the greater the degree of task signficance, e.g., a design engineer on a space probe versus a design engineer in a toy factory. Research indicates that this significance can be manipulated to some degree. When coworkers say to the employee, "This is interesting, it's nice to use the skills I developed in school," the levels of both satisfaction and productivity tend to increase.[10] With identical jobs, the social cues of "this isn't very interesting, the more you do this job the less meaningful it is" can create the opposite effect. Thus, a well-redesigned job can be sabotaged by social cues received from coworkers.

[10]Sam E. White and Terrence R. Mitchell, "Job Enrichment versus Social Cues: A Comparison and Competitive Test," *Journal of Applied Psychology,* vol. 64, no. 1, February 1979, p. 1.

Many feel that the most critical dimension is that of job *autonomy*. It certainly is the critical difference between job enlargement and job enrichment. Autonomy is created through a process of "vertical loading," that is, the worker is given self-management rights in multiple areas. In various programs, such additional responsibilities as the following have been given: (1) setting one's own work schedule and work breaks, (2) establishing work methods, (3) making one's own quality checks, (4) varying the workplace, (5) changing duties with others, (6) setting priorities as to work performed, (7) making crisis decisions in problem situations rather than relying on the boss, (8) training less-experienced workers, (9) establishing direct relationships with the users of one's output (the client), and (10) setting one's own work pace.

The fifth core dimension, opening *feedback* channels, is necessary to the other four. One of the joys of bowling or playing golf is the immediate feedback on performance results. One can imagine the problems involved if we were forced to bowl through a curtain. Though there would still be some feedback in terms of sound, the specific results are missing. Too often this is the case in various organizations. The supervisor "sees" the results and may or may not have the time and inclination to feed them back to the worker. Job-provided feedback is preferred to supervisor-provided feedback.

Numerous job enrichment experimental programs have been reported in the literature. For example, the job of a keypunch operator in the Travelers Insurance Company was enriched to include: (1) working for only one particular department, (2) communicating directly with the user-client, (3) checking one's own quality, (4) establishing personal work schedules, and (5) correcting one's own errors.[11] Results of the project include an increase in quantity of output (39 percent versus 8 percent for a control group), a decrease in the error rate (.9 percent versus a previous 1.5 percent), and a decrease in the absenteeism rate (*minus* 234 percent versus a 27 percent increase for the control group). A recent survey of 58 companies with job enrichment programs revealed that two-thirds felt that product quality had improved, half said employee turnover was down an average of 18 percent, over one-third reported decreases in absenteeism of 15 percent, and one-third indicated that employee satisfaction had improved with grievances dropping by 16 percent.[12] The average cost of introducing the program was slightly in excess of $1,000 per employee whose job was enriched.

Despite the well-developed behavioral theory and the many reports of program success, one must conclude that job enrichment is no panacea. When one large insurance company attempted to introduce job enrichment, most affected employees (82 percent) reported liking the jobs but almost as many (68 percent) stated that employee morale was lower because they were not being paid in proportion to increased duties.[13] As Figure 5-9 indicates, the enrichment process is mediated by the strength of employee growth needs. Those high in the need for achievement, (*n* Ach) are more likely to respond to job enrichment opportunities.[14] Employees low in the need for achievement (low *n* Ach) are often unaffected by such changes. A person with a high *n* Ach is one who feels

---

[11]J. Richard Hackman, Greg Oldham, Robert Janson, and Kenneth Purdy, "A New Strategy for Job Enrichment," *California Management Review,* vol. 17, no. 4, Summer 1975, p. 69.

[12]"PAIR Potpourri," *The Personnel Administrator,* vol. 22, no. 9, November 1977, p. 12.

[13]Paul J. Champagne and Curt Tausky, "When Job Enrichment Doesn't Pay," *Personnel,* vol. 55, no. 1, January-February 1978, pp. 30–39.

[14]See Richard M. Steers and Daniel G. Spencer, "The Role of Achievement Motivation in Job Design," *Journal of Applied Psychology,* vol. 62, no. 4, August 1977, pp. 472–479, and William F. Giles, "Volunteering for Job Enrichment: A Test of Expectancy Theory Predictions," *Personnel Psychology,* vol. 30, no. 3, Autumn 1977, pp. 427–435.

a need to accomplish something important, to compete against a challenging standard of excellence, and prefers to receive clear and prompt feedback of results. Employees who are younger and more educated are more responsive to job enrichment. A survey of some 1,500 employees revealed that white-collar employees ranked "interesting work" as most important, whereas blue-collar employees ranked it in seventh position *after* such items as security, pay, helpful coworkers, and clearly defined responsibilities.[15] Thus management should not assume that all employees are alike in their growth needs.

It should be apparent that the same concepts for developing enriched jobs could also be applied to team activities. The latter system would require additional interpersonal skills as well as requiring some mechanism for team self-management. One study contrasting 25 job enrichment programs with 28 team-oriented enrichment programs produced the same type and level of values, but with substantially greater costs for the latter.[16] The median investment costs per employee for the job enrichment effort was $417, while that for the team-oriented projects was $1,519. Discussion of the process and problems of team management will be presented in Chapter 17.

SUMMARY

This chapter has ranged from the general to the specific, from the basic overall objectives of an organization to the specific job content of an individual task. On the thesis that the personnel manager will be increasingly called upon for advice and expertise in the field of organizational design, knowledge must be obtained on such diverse subjects as objectives, functions, relationships, structure, job enlargement, and job enrichment.

Organizing is the process of establishing formal relationships (responsibility, authority, and accountability) among key components (functions, personnel, and physical factors) for the purpose of harnessing (line, line/staff, functionalized, or project structure) and directing toward common enterprise objectives (service, member, and social). Objectives govern the specification of functions, which tend to be differentiated, both downward and outward, with increasing size of organization. Primary, secondary, and tertiary contributions to the primary objective can be identified. These analyses of objectives and functions are necessary for the understanding and design of basic instrumental structures.

Whether an organizational expert or not, the personnel manager must study the design of specific job assignments. Psychological and sociological research suggests that redesign of work content to provide variety, closure, significance, autonomy, and feedback can often provide considerable returns to the organization. Returns in the areas of product quality, and such human values as morale, absenteeism, and turnover are highly probable. The major concerns usually encountered revolve around the considerable investment in time and talent required for such redesign, accompanied by doubts about the net impact upon work output.

[15]Bernard J. White, "The Criteria for Job Satisfaction," *Monthly Labor Review*, vol. 100, no. 5, May 1977, pp. 30–35.
[16]Antone Alber and Melvin Blumberg, "Team vs. Individual Approaches to Job Enrichment Programs," *Personnel*, vol. 58, no. 1, January-February 1981, p. 73.

As a part of the hiring process, Jane Darr, an applicant for the job of Personnel Specialist, was given the following assignment. Having been provided with the current job description for a janitor in a large public university, she was asked to redesign the job incorporating whatever concepts from job enlargement and job enrichment that she felt was feasible.

Janitor

I   Function
   A   Performs routine manual work in the general cleaning of interior spaces.

II   Typical Duties/Responsibilities
   A   Sweeps, mops, vacuums, and polishes floors in rooms and halls according to prescribed schedule.
   B   Dusts and polishes furniture, windows, blinds, mirrors, and equipment according to prescribed schedule.
   C   May make beds, collect and replace soiled linens or towels.
   D   May replace light bulbs and perform minor repairs or maintenance.
   E   May wash dishes or utensils.
   F   Moves furniture, equipment, or fixtures as required.
   G   Runs errands and performs similar duties as required.

III   Distinguishing Characteristics
   A   Employees of this class differ from the corresponding level of laborer and groundskeeper in that the work of janitor is primarily that of interior cleaning. Work is performed under very close supervision with no latitude given for independent action.

IV   Qualifications
   A   Required
      1   Elementary education or equivalent.
      2   Ability to follow verbal instructions.
   B   Desired
      1   Some knowledge of work methods and machines commonly used in janitorial duties.

Questions

1.   How would you redesign the job?

2.   For each change you made in the job, what concept of job enrichment were you applying?

DISCUSSION QUESTIONS

1. Give the complete definition of the formal process of organizing.

2. Compare and contrast concepts of formal and informal organization.

3. Define and distinguish between job enlargement and job enrichment.

4. Indicate the core job dimensions entailed in job enrichment, and explain how they may be inserted into a new job design.

5. What is the span of control and what is its impact upon the design of organizations?

6. Beginning with training being performed by immediate line supervisors, trace the process of functional differentiation, outward to its organizational position in a large, multiplant firm.

7. For each of the three basic types of organization structure—line, line/staff, and functionalized—indicate the location and authority of those performing personnel functions.

8. Describe the relationship of a personnel department manager to a project manager under the project form of organization structure.

9. What are the derivative relationships among the concepts of function, authority, responsibility, accountability, and objectives? What, therefore, is the justification for authority?

10. Defend the thesis of the primacy of the service or product objective for a private business organization.

SUPPLEMENTARY READING

ALBER, ANTONE and MELVIN BLUMBERG: "Team vs. Individual Approaches to Job Enrichment Programs," *Personnel,* vol. 58, no. 1, January-February 1981, pp. 63–75.

KOLODNY, HARVEY F.: "Managing in a Matrix," *Business Horizons,* vol. 24, no. 2, March-April 1981, pp. 17–24.

MINTZBERG, HENRY: "Organization Design: Fashion or Fit?" *Harvard Business Review,* vol. 59, no. 1, January-February 1981, pp. 103–116.

MONTANA, PATRICK J. and DEBORAH F. NASH: "Delegation: The Art of Managing," *Personnel Journal,* vol. 60, no. 10, October 1981, pp. 784–786.

ROBERTS, KARLENE H. and WILLIAM GLICK: "The Job Characteristics Approach to Task Design: A Critical Review," *Journal of Applied Psychology,* vol. 66, no. 2, April 1981, pp. 193–217.

WEAVER, CHARLES N.: "Job Satisfaction in the United States in the 1970s," *Journal of Applied Psychology,* vol. 65, no. 3, June 1980, pp. 364–367.

chapter 6

Human Resources Planning

We are now at the point in the procurement process where the type and number of persons to be hired must be determined. The fair employment practices discussed in Chapter 4 will definitely have impact upon the hiring decision. The specific jobs that have been designed as a part of the organizing process discussed in Chapter 5 must now be analyzed to determine the type of person who can best perform the assigned duties. The government places much weight on the desirability of having adequate job analyses as the foundation for making personnel decisions.

Decisions concerning human resources requirements are not confined to a personnel department. It will be found that the line supervisor has much to contribute, as well as certain other staff elements such as time study and production control. This chapter is devoted to the general question of human resources requirements and is divided into two parts. The first part deals with the process of determining the kind or quality of personnel needed. This is followed by a presentation and analysis of the problem of determining the quantity of personnel required to operate the organization properly. The immediate tangible result of these two analyses is the creation of an *employee requisition* authorizing the hiring of a certain number of people of a specified type.

QUALITY OF PERSONNEL

In order to hire personnel on a scientific basis, one should establish in advance a standard of personnel with which applicants can be compared. This standard should establish the minimum acceptable qualities necessary for adequate performance of the job duties and responsibilities to determine human abilitites required for execution. The establishment of the job is a part of the organizing process, and was discussed in Chapter 5. The study of job content to determine human requirements is termed "job analysis." Personnel specialists in large organizations should be intimately involved in both activities. In the small firm, these two tasks must also be performed and, of necessity, will be executed by line managers.

Job Terminology

In most areas of study, a certain amount of technical terminology is necessary in order to facilitate communication. It is therefore desirable to list and define terms in the job analysis field, as well as some terms that are related to and often confused with job analysis.

Position[1]   A position is a *group of tasks assigned to one individual*. There are as many positions in a firm as there are personnel. The term is used in this narrow technical sense to facilitate more precise analysis of the job analysis technique.

Job   A job can now be defined as a *group of positions that are similar as to kind and level of work*. In some instances only one position may be involved, simply because no other similar position exists. For example, in the typical firm the position of personnel manager also constitutes a job since there is only one personnel manager in the organization.

Occupation   An occupation is a group of jobs that are similar as to kind of work and are found throughout an industry or the entire country. An occupation is a category of work found in many firms. The United States Employment Service has attempted to survey and define the occupations of the United States in the Dictionary of Occupational Titles.[2] It has also prepared occupational descriptions for various industries. These descriptions are necessarily general in nature and can be used only for background purposes for a particular firm's job analysis program. To show the relationship among these first three definitions, we can say that one person can hold a position, a job, and an occupation simultaneously. One must always have a position and a job, but may not be in a type of work that is found generally throughout an industry and thus may have no occupation.

Job analysis   Job analysis is the *process of studying and collecting information relating to the operations and responsibilities of a specific job*. The immediate products of this analysis are job descriptions and job specifications, which are defined below.

Motion study   Job analysis is often confused with motion study, which also involves study of the job. There are two different ways of studying the same job. Motion study is a *process of analyzing a job to find the easiest, most effective, and most economical method of doing it*. As such, motion study is a part of the job design function. If a job is subjected to both processes of study, motion study should *precede* job analysis.

Job description   A job description is an *organized, factual statement of the duties and responsibilities of a specific job*. In brief, it should tell *what* is to be done, *how* it is done, and *why*. It is a standard of function, in that it defines the appropriate and authorized content of a job. A more complete explanation of this document follows in a later section.

Job specification   A job specification is a *statement of the minimum acceptable human qualities necessary to perform a job properly*. In contrast to the job description, it is a standard of personnel and designates the qualities required for acceptable performance. This product of job analysis is also covered at greater length in a later section.

Job classification   A job classification is a *grouping of jobs on some specified basis such as kind of work or pay*. It can refer to a grouping by any selected characteristic but probably is used most often in connection with pay and job evaluation. The *Dictionary of Occupational Titles* utilizes a number of different classification bases as indicated by

---

[1]This definition is not widely used in business, but we do need some term to designate the assignment of each individual, e.g., ''position,'' ''work station,'' etc. There can be minor variations in task assignments of individuals working on the same job.

[2]*Dictionary of Occupational Titles,* vol. 1, U.S. Department of Labor, 1978.

FIGURE 6-1

FIGURE 6-1
Job Codes in the Dictionary of Occupational Titles

Data (Fourth Digit)	People (Fifth Digit)	Things (Sixth Digit)
0 Synthesizing	0 Mentoring	0 Setting up
1 Coordinating	1 Negotiating	1 Precision working
2 Analyzing	2 Instructing	2 Operating-controlling
3 Compiling	3 Supervising	3 Driving-operating
4 Computing	4 Diverting	4 Manipulating
5 Copying	5 Persuading	5 Tending
6 Comparing	6 Speaking-signaling	6 Feeding-offbearing
7 No significant relationship	7 Serving	7 Handling
8 No significant relationship	8 No significant relationship	8 No significant relationship

Source: *Dictionary of Occupational Titles (Vol. 1)*, U.S. Department of Labor, 1978, p. xvi.

the following codes: "0" and "1" cover professional, technical, and managerial occupations; "2" refers to clerical and sales; "3" is for service occupations; "4" is used for farming, fishery, and forestry work; "5" is for processing work; "6" for machine trades; "7" for bench work; "8" is reserved for structural work; and "9" is for miscellaneous occupations. The second and third digits of a code number provide a finer breakdown with respect to function or industry. For example, "50" is for metal processing, "52" for food processing, and "56" for wood processing.

The DOT system also encompasses a classification dealing with the relation of the occupation to three components: (1) data, (2) people, and (3) things. As shown in Figure 6-1, each of these components is further divided into eight areas. As an example, the occupational code number for a Chief Housekeeper is 187.168. The "1" indicates that it is a managerial occupation, and the "87" identifies the service industry. The final three digits show the occupation's relation to data, people, and things. The "1" indicates a coordinating function with respect to data, the "6" shows a speaking-signaling relationship with people, and the "8" reveals no significant relationship with things. It is apparent that an occupational analysis must be completed before this type of classification can be established.

Job evaluation   Job evaluation is a *systematic and orderly process of determining the worth of a job in relation to other jobs*. The objective of this process is to determine the correct rate of pay. It is therefore *not* the same as job analysis. Rather it should *follow* the job analysis process, which provides the basic data to be evaluated. Job evaluation is discussed at length in a later chapter and is included at this point in order to reduce confusion with the term "job analysis."

Job Analysis Process

The process of analyzing a job after its design is essentially one of data collection. Various approaches can be utilized, and the four currently most popular are (1) questionnaires, (2) written narratives, (3) observation, (4) interviews. A survey of 899 firms ranging in size from under 500 employees to over 100,000 revealed that the most widely used method was the interview: 85 percent reported using this research method for both salaried and hourly workers.[3] The second most popular was observation, which was used more widely for hourly employees. Questionnaires and written narratives were about equally divided in popularity, ranking behind the other two. In addition, there were many miscellaneous sources of information such as old job descriptions, time and motion studies, and daily diaries or logs.

The questionnaire technique places great faith in the jobholder's ability to organize the reporting of the job. The information received is often found to be incomplete, unorganized, and sometimes incoherent. Such a questionnaire can be used, however, in providing background information for the interview, which must necessarily follow, in order to analyze the job properly.

Narrative descriptions can be requested of both the job incumbent and the supervisor. This approach is used more often on salaried jobs. A more detailed reporting of this type would be the daily diary or log. Under this system, the employee keeps a daily record of major duties performed, marking the time when each task is started and finished. Narratives, logs, and questionnaires can be of material assistance to the job analyst, but as single techniques unsupported by follow-up interviewing and observation, they leave much to be desired.

The third and fourth methods of collecting job information hold the greatest promise of completeness, accuracy, and better utilization of time. If a particular job is simple and repetitive, observation may be the only technique required. In most cases, however, interviews coupled with observation constitute the preferred approach. The interview will provide information not readily observable plus the verification of information obtained by means of other techniques.

Since the job analyst will use the interview as a prime method of data collection, there are several basic attitudes and techniques that will serve to elicit the maximum of accurate and complete information. These attitudes and techniques will also help to reduce the natural suspicion of both employee and supervisor toward a staff specialist operating out of the personnel unit. Among these are the following:

1. *Introduce yourself so that the worker knows who you are and why you are there.* The supervisor can be of material assistance in helping to explain in advance what the job analysis program is and how it affects various personnel activities such as procurement and compensation. The employee should be assured that the objectives of the process are not detrimental to his or her well-being. On the contrary, the program may easily result in more realistic training, better organization, and more equitable compensation for the job.

2. *Show a sincere interest in the worker and the job being analyzed.* It is difficult to fake sincerity, and a periodic, mechanical "uh huh" in response to worker contributions is insufficient and often irritating. The job constitutes a large proportion of this employee's life. If the analyst can demonstrate a sincere interest in both the job and the employee, increased receptivity and openness generally follow.

3. *Do not try to tell the employee how to do the job.* In this process, the incumbent is the job expert and the analyst's task is to extract the information and organize it in a significant manner. The job analysis process is basically descriptive in nature. Correction of mistakes and possible changes in job content should be

---

[3]*Summary of National Job Analysis Methods Survey,* California State College, Bureau of Business Research, Long Beach, 1968, p. 9.

initiated by those with authority in the area concerned. The job analyst should view herself or himself as an expert in studying and reporting jobs, not as an expert in the job itself.

An interesting question might be raised at this point. What type of background should a job analyst possess? To ask intelligent questions about a job, one must know something about it. Yet, if a large number of different types of jobs are covered, how can one be expert in all? The preceding paragraph gives the correct answer. The job analyst's skills are in extracting correct information, organizing that material in logical order, and presenting it in understandable and usable form. One need not be expert in the job, though preliminary familiarization with certain aspects is necessary in order not to appear too ignorant during the interview.

4. *Try to talk to the employees and supervisors in their own language.* This will involve some preparation, particularly when the analyst covers many different fields; but the establishment of rapport is facilitated if the worker feels that the analyst is not a complete novice. This process can, however, be overdone. It is wise to confine oneself to the jargon that a member of the firm would reasonably be expected to acquire; an attempt to use all the shop terminology smacks of "getting down to their level" and thereby incurs resentment.

5. *Do not confuse the work with the worker.* The particular worker being interviewed is the medium through which information is derived about the job. The objective is not to describe this particular employee but rather the job that the incumbent performs and, later, the abilities necessary for proper execution of job duties. The fact that this particular jobholder has a college degree does not necessarily mean that such a degree is a minimum requirement. In this process of data collection, the basic approach should be scientific insofar as it attempts to distinguish between fact and inference and between fact and opinion.

6. *Do a complete job study with the objectives of the program.* The information desired in job analysis is of the type that will assist in various personnel activities. Job analysis is not motion study, and we do not need a "blow-by-blow" physical description of what the worker does. Suppose that the worker tells the analyst that a production part is placed in a solution to be electroplated and is taken out when done. A motion study analyst may be interested in how the item is dipped and how it can be removed most efficiently. The job analyst must have information that will reveal the *skill* and *knowledge* required. One may ask the worker, "How do you know when the item should be removed from the solution?" The usual response is, "I just know by experience." This is not sufficient to show skill level, and the job analyst must get *behind* the "just know how." Knowing *what* information one wants and knowing *how* to question an employee to get that information are different things.

7. *Verify the job information obtained.* Data collected from one employee should be checked by consultation with others holding the same job. The analyst may thus obtain additional information and may find some contradictions and inconsistencies. Resolution of such discrepancies, if they are factual, is the responsibility of supervision. The analysis should *not* be confined to work done by the best worker on the job; a reasonable sample is necessary when the job is composed of a considerable number of positions.

In the previously cited survey, most large organizations assigned the responsibility for job analysis to the wage and salary section of the personnel department. The average time for completing the analysis of one job was less than 4 hours for hourly jobs, and 4 to 8 hours for the salaried. Automatic data processing systems for storage of job information were reported by only 10 percent of the surveyed companies.[4]

The Job Description

The first and immediate product of the job analysis process is the job description. As its title indicates, this document is basically descriptive in nature and constitutes a record of existing and pertinent job facts. These facts must be organized in some fashion in order to be usable. A suggested order is as follows:

1. Job identification
2. Job summary
3. Duties performed
4. Supervision given and received
5. Relation to other jobs
6. Machines, tools, and materials
7. Working conditions
8. Definitions of unusual terms
9. Comments that add to and clarify the above

The identification section includes such information as job title, alternative titles, department, division, plant, and code number for the job. The job summary has two purposes: (1) to provide a short definition that will be useful as additional identification information when the job title is not sufficient, and (2) to serve as a summary to orient the reader toward an understanding of the detailed information that follows. In practice, it is easier to write this section *after* writing section 3.

The duties-performed section is the heart of the job description and is the most difficult to write properly. It is supposed to tell what is being done, how it is done (without involving the detail of a motion study), and the purpose behind each duty. It is often found advisable to list major duties with a statement of "what" and "why," followed by subduties detailing the "how." These should, if possible, be arranged in chronological order. In addition, an estimate concerning the approximate percentage of time devoted to each major duty is helpful. Research has indicated that employees are reasonably accurate in estimating these time percentages. When checking the actual times against the estimates, Hinrichs discovered that 232 technical employees were within 5 percent of the time proportions obtained through work sampling.[5] A study of 16 clerical workers, done in the same manner, revealed that differences were no larger than 6 percent, one of the larger errors being in an excessively small estimate of idle time.[6] Despite these differences, the estimates are sufficiently accurate to be used as a general guide in recruitment, training, compensation, and reorganizing.

[4]Ibid., pp. 5, 8, and 9.
[5]J. R. Hinrichs, "Communications Activity of Industrial Research Personnel," *Personnel Psychology,* vol. 17, no. 2, 1964, pp. 193–204.
[6]Stephen J. Carroll, Jr., and William H. Taylor, Jr., "Validity of Estimates by Clerical Personnel of Job Time Proportions." *Journal of Applied Psychology,* vol. 53, no. 2, 1969, pp. 164–166.

It should be noted that there is a definite writing style for the duties-performed section. It is terse and direct, giving the impression of action. There are many detailed rules, such as: (1) start each sentence with an action verb; (2) use present tense; and (3) use the word "may" when only some workers perform the duty and the word "occasionally" when all workers perform at irregular intervals. The purpose of this style is to facilitate communication through completeness, conciseness, and clarity. It should be noted, however, that a job analyst with a facility with words can make a job appear much more impressive than it actually is. What is the worth of the job whose duties are described in Figure 6-2? A more terse description is found at the end of this chapter.

The remaining sections of the job description are based on the duties-performed section. The section on supervision tells (1) the titles of jobs that are immediately over and under this job and (2) the degree of supervision involved, such as general direction, intermediate, or close supervision. The section on relation to other jobs identifies vertical relationships of promotion and the horizontal relationships of work flow and procedures. The machines, tools, and materials portion lists and defines each major type, giving trade names when necessary. This information is helpful in devising training programs. Checklists are often used to indicate working conditions, using such alternatives as hot, cold, dry, dusty, oily, noisy, and so on. Hazardous conditions should be particularly noted. Any technical or unusual words used in the duties-performed section should be listed separately and defined; they thus become a kind of job glossary.

The job descriptions of managers tend to be more concerned with goals and situa-

Figure 6-2
An Example of How Job Descriptions Can Mislead

Proposed job description
1 Job identification
   a Title: Director of Industrial and Agrarian Priorities
   b Dept.: Maintenance

2 Job duties
   a Directs, controls, and regulates the movement of interstate commerce, representing a cross section of the wealth of the American economy. Exercises a broad latitude for independent judgment and discretion without direct or intermediate supervision.
   b Integrates the variable factors in an evolving situation utilizing personal judgment, founded on past experience, conditioned by erudition, and disciplined by mental intransigence. Formulates a binding decision relative to the priority of flow of interstate and intrastate commerce, both animate and inanimate, such decisions being irreversible and not subject to appellate review by higher authority or being reversed by the legal determination of any echelon of our judicial complex. Influences the movement, with great finality, of agricultural products, forest products, minerals, manufactured goods, machine tools, construction equipment, military personnel, defense materials, raw materials, end products, finished goods, semifinished products, small business, large business, public utilities, and government agencies.
   c Deals with all types of personalities and all levels of education, from college president and industrial tycoon to truckdriver, requiring the exercise of initiative, ingenuity, imagination, intelligence, industry, and discerning versatility. Implements coordinated motivation on the part of the public, which is consistent with the decision of the incumbent, failure of which could create a complex objurgation of personnel and equipment generating a catastrophic loss of mental equilibrium by innumerable personnel of American industry, who are responsible for the formulation of day-to-day policy, and guidance implementation of the conveyances of transportation, both interstate and intrastate.
   d Appraises the nuances of an unfolding situational development and directs correction thereof commensurate with its seriousness and momentousness.

Figure 6-3
Job Description Which Identifies Situational Factors, Goals,
and Activities

Name: John Doe   Title: General Plant Manager
Supervisor: President   Company: General Paper Company
Number of employees in the plant: 40 exempt, 36 nonexempt salaried, and 150 hourly paid.
Reporting directly to him are 7 department heads. General manager has full authority to take
action necessary to meet the goals for which he is responsible. He is supported fully in this
by the company president.

Objects (Physical Resources)	
Goals	Performance Activities
1 To assure acquisition, operation, and maintenance of physical facilities.	1 Plans for authorized expenditures for plant physical resources.
2 To improve and develop products and equipment.	2 Plans for and coordinates product and equipment development and improvement.

Sequences and Events (Process, Schedules, and Accounting Systems)	
Goals	Performance Activities
1 To assure the development and use of systematic and effective work flow, operation processes, and accounting systems.	1 Coordinates the processes, schedules, and accounting controls between departments.
2 To schedule work operation and transportation.	

Other Persons (Human Relations)	
Goals	Performance Activities
1 To maintain a favorable organization climate.	1 Maintains an atmosphere of acceptance and support.
2 To maintain a warm and friendly relationship with employees and associates.	2 Communicates well the expectations and results of subordinates.
	3 Reduces threat to security.
	4 Recognizes the needs of others in working with them.
	5 Cooperates with others in work.

tional factors. As shown in Figure 6-3, situational information is provided that indicates size of work group, type of employees, and degree of delegation. This particular illustration suggests that goals should be subdivided according to physical resources, sequences of functions, other persons, achievement, and groups. Opposite each set of goals are the prescribed activities that will lead to their accomplishment.

As an alternative to the above-described task-oriented approach, E. J. McCormick has developed a worker-oriented inventory that can be used to establish a profile of any job.[7] The Position Analysis Questionnaire is a statistically derived instrument and is divided into six categories: (1) information input, (2) mental processes, (3) work output, (4) relationships with other persons, (5) job context, and (6) other job characteristics not

---

[7]E. J. McCormick, ''Job and Task Analysis,'' in M. D. Dunnette, (ed.), *Handbook of Characterizational and Organizational Psychology,* Rand McNally, Chicago, 1974.

Figure 6-3 (*continued*)
**Job Description Which Identifies Situational Factors, Goals,
and Activities**

121

Human Resources
Planning

Achievement (Profitability, Productivity, Marketing, etc.)	
Goals	Performance Activities
1 To establish policies, objectives, and plans for overall plant profitability, productivity, marketing, physical and financial resources, and personnel. 2 To assure efficient operation and coordination of department functions for maximum profitability, productivity, and sales.	1 Prepares written policies, broad objectives, and plans for the plant. 2 Participates in group meetings with department heads for the establishment of objectives. 3 Stimulates accomplishment of objectives and conduct of plans. Discusses results of performance with subordinates. 4 Approves product grade change and allocates new grades to machines. 5 Maintains cost control and proper balance of financial expenditures.

Purposeful Groups (Organization and Leadership)	
Goals	Performance Activities
1 To provide the overall leadership functions for the plant. 2 To assure the effective design, development, and staffing of the organization. 3 To motivate and develop subordinates. 4 To assure participation of all subordinates in group management. 5 To initiate and assure completion of actions.	1 Performs leadership functions for the plant. 2 Works with subordinates to provide organization structure, proper delegation, and coordination. 3 Establishes effective managerial control through delegation and coordination. 4 Establishes policies and procedures for personnel programs to maintain group satisfaction, stimulate their achievement, and evaluate performance. 5 Works effectively with superiors, peers, and subordinates. 6 Conducts regular participative meetings. 7 Initiates the actions toward meeting broad goals.

Source: J. C. Wofford, "Behavior Styles and Performance Effectiveness," Personnel Psychology, vol. 20, no. 4, Winter 1967, pp. 470–471.

classifiable in the previous categories. Each of these divisions is composed of several dimensions. Job context, for example, has such dimensions as potentially stressful environment, hazardous situations, and demanding situations.

Role Analysis

Dissatisfied with the somewhat simple and sterile nature of existing job descriptions that highlight formal duties, various critics have suggested that job analysis should be extended to include *role analysis*. The concept of role is broader than that of job. A role would consist of the total pattern of expected behavior, interactions, and sentiments for an individual holding an assigned job. As such, the job incumbent is exposed to a number of personnel who often expect different attitudes and behavioral patterns, thus establishing the potential for substantial role conflict. For example, the supervisor is expected by assigned subordinates to protect and promote their interests in the organization. Simultaneously, superiors levy expectations of operating the unit at its most productive and efficient level, which often entails actions deemed detrimental by subordinates. The ability to cope with such built-in job conflicts is a definite and important job requirement. Mere listing of official duties will not necessarily reveal the behavioral expectations of multiple and various groups that impinge upon the job incumbent.

Role analysis of personnel holding boundary-spanning jobs provides a good example of its potential value in the making of personnel decisions.[8] A boundary-spanning job is one whose incumbent is commissioned to deal with some significant element of the *outer* environment, e.g., credit officer, purchasing agent, finance officer, sales personnel, and personnel manager. The credit officer, for example, is expected by the finance department to minimize losses due to bad debts, thereby lessening organizational dependency upon outside banks. Simultaneously, the sales department views the task as one of facilitating growth of sales and creation of new customers. Thus, the credit officer, finance officer, and sales manager are all boundary-spanners, providing the basis for conflict spillover into the organization itself. The personnel manager is also a spanning agent as new employees are obtained from the outside. When strong labor unions are present in the environment, particularly stressful conflicts are generally encountered. Coping with these inevitable internal and external conflicts is a role requirement.

With reference to contacts with significant external personnel, the boundary-spanning agent must deal with persons and organizations over whom absolute control is denied. Thus, flexible personalities and pragmatic personal value systems are often requisites. Such roles often require superior verbal skills, sensitivity to the values of external personnel, and an aptitude for remembering details. Thus, when the personnel manager is required to deal with a powerful labor union, effective role behavior requires the selective use of words that do not incite emotional resistance, an understanding of union leadership values and motives, and the ability to remember names, dates, places, and events of significance to union negotiators.

Organizations, viewed as entities, also establish different climates based on different philosophies, thereby leading to different behavioral expectations. The job descriptions for two supervisors in two different companies may look the same, but the role requirements could be substantially different. If one company's philosophy regarding leadership is basically democratic, role requirements would necessitate behavior characterized by helping, supporting, persuading, talking freely and cheerfully, and empathic understanding. If the second company's philosophy is more authoritarian, the expected behavioral pattern is likely to include aggressiveness in relation to others, insistence upon adherence to prescribed patterns, impatience with faulty performance, and supportive relationships with superiors rather than with subordinates.

A survey of the chief officers of 306 of our largest corporations revealed expectations that are often never written down on paper.[9] Among other items, the executives worked from 60 to 70 hours per week, traveled 6 to 10 days a month, and in three out of four cases, placed the business ahead of their families' needs. Little items often make the difference in the hiring decision. One executive lost a $55,000-a-year job because he

---

[8]Dennis W. Organ, "Linking Pins between Organizations and Environment," *Business Horizons,* vol. 14, no. 6, December 1971, pp. 73–80.

[9]Frank Allen, "Chief Executives Typically Work 60-Hour Weeks, Put Careers First," *The Wall Street Journal,* August 19, 1980, p. 31.

referred to his wife as "mommy." Another lost a $300,000-a-year job because he attacked an artichoke with a knife and fork. The chairman of the board said that he just didn't want a guy who didn't know how to eat properly. One recruiter maintains that "more than half of the time, the technically best-qualified person isn't hired."[10]

Though the importance of the expected behavioral style cannot be denied, it is seldom diagnosed, recorded, and used systematically in the hiring process. For this reason, the face-to-face interview will doubtlessly remain an important part of the hiring process despite its frequently reported low validity as a predictor of job success. The accuracy of the job analysis process would be improved considerably if attention were given to role expectations surrounding each prescribed activity or duty.

Job Specification

Preparing a complete and correct *job description* is relatively simple as compared with preparing a complete and correct *job specification*. After reading a job description, we may find ourselves in considerable disagreement concerning the human requirements for the work. Does this job properly call for a high school diploma or is some college education necessary? What is the minimum degree of intelligence required? What experience level and how much? One manager suggests that each requirement be classified as "mandatory" or "desirable." If mandatory, one should specify (1) if the attribute is basic or advanced in nature, and (2) if it should be possessed from the very beginning or can be developed soon after, on the job. If the characteristic is described as desirable, one indicates its level of importance to job performance. For example, the requirement that a computer system supervisor "understand computer software systems in use" is described as (1) basic knowledge, (2) mandatory knowledge, and (3) possessed at entry to job. "Advanced understanding of software systems" is described as (1) desirable, and (2) important.[11]

The establishment of basic minimum human requirements for work is a decision of concern to our entire society. It has been commented by some observers that organizations in general establish excessively high requirements for formal education and training backgrounds, a process that results in overly qualified personnel being placed on routine jobs, such as requiring a college engineering degree for a routine draftsman's job. Not only do such practices lead to frustrated and discontented personnel, the Supreme Court decision in the *Duke Power* case indicates that it may be illegal if such requirements work to the proven disadvantage of certain classes of citizens.[12] Section 703 of Title VII of the Civil Rights Act of 1964 specifies that "it shall be an unlawful employment practice for an employer—to limit, segregate, or classify employees in any way which would deprive or tend to deprive any individual of employment opportunities or otherwise adversely affect his status as an employee, because of such individual's race, color, religion, sex, or national origin." In the Duke Power Company, a minimum hiring requirement of a high school diploma had been established for initial assignment to any department except labor. Such a requirement worked to prevent the employment of larger

[10]Roger Ricklefs, "The Hidden Hurdle: Executive Recruiters Say Firms Tend to Hire 'Our Kind of Person,' " *The Wall Street Journal,* September 19, 1979, p. 1.

[11]Edward O. Joslin, "Career Management: How to Make It Work," *Personnel,* vol. 54, no. 4, July-August 1977, p. 69.

[12]Floyd L. Ruch, "The Impact on Employment Procedures of the Supreme Court Decision in the Duke Power Case," *Personnel Journal,* vol. 50, no. 10, October 1971, pp. 777–783.

numbers of blacks than whites. This does not mean, however, that the high school requirement is illegal per se. As Chief Justice Burger's opinion stated, "Congress has placed on the employer the burden of showing that any given requirement must have a manifest relationship to the employment in question." In other words, the employer can stipulate possession of a high school diploma *if* it can be proven that such possession results in better job performance than by those without the degree. This would, of course, be merely sound personnel practice. Nevertheless, the court decision requiring such research has led many firms to abandon stipulations of human minimums, particularly in the area of formal education.

Uses of Job Analysis Information

Job analysis is one of the most pervasive tasks of personnel management. Its products—descriptions and specifications—have many and varied uses beyond those mentioned previously. A brief listing of these uses is as follows:

1. *Validation of hiring procedures.* Under the Civil Rights Act, courts have required employers to prove that selection devices that tend to exclude protected groups are in actuality predictive of job success. Content validity is authorized and defined as "systematically examining selection criteria or predictors to determine whether they are closely related to the behavior domain of the job."[13] In other words, is there a representative sample of those behavior domains which are required on the job encompassed in the hiring device (test, interview, reference, etc.)? Content validation begins with a thorough and accurate job analysis.

2. *Training.* Description of duties and equipment used is of material assistance in developing the content of training programs.

3. *Job evaluation.* Job descriptions and specifications of human requirements are evaluated in terms of worth, with the ultimate objective of determining dollar value.

4. *Performance appraisal.* Instead of rating an employee on characteristics such as dependability and initiative, there is now a tendency toward establishing job goals and appraising the work done toward those goals. In this type of appraisal, a job description is useful in defining the areas in which job goals should be established.

5. *Career development.* Job information helps the firm to chart channels of promotion, and provides the employee with data concerning opportunities and requirements for careers within the organization.

6. *Organization.* Job information obtained by job analysis often reveals instances of poor organization in terms of the factors affecting job design. The analysis process, therefore, constitutes a kind of organization audit.

7. *Induction.* For the new trainee, a job description is most helpful for orientation purposes.

8. *Counseling.* Job information is, of course, very valuable in occupational counseling. More of such counseling is advisable at the high school level, since many graduates are unaware of the types of jobs that exist.

[13]Craig Eric Schneier, "Content Validity: The Necessity of a Behavioral Job Description," *The Personnel Administrator,* vol. 21, no. 2, February 1976, p. 41.

9. *Labor relations*. A job description is a standard of function. If an employee attempts to add to or subtract from the duties listed therein, the standard has been violated. The labor union as well as the management is interested in this matter. Controversies often result, and a written record of the standard job jurisdiction is valuable in resolving such disputes.

10. *Job reengineering*. If employers wish to adapt to any special group, such as the physically handicapped, they must usually alter the content of certain jobs. Job analysis provides information that will facilitate the changing of jobs in order to permit their being filled by personnel with special characteristics.

The survey of 899 firms showed that 75 percent used the results of the job analysis process in making job specifications, approximately 60 percent for training, over 90 percent in setting wage and salary levels, approximately 60 percent in appraising personnel on salaried jobs as compared with 44 percent on hourly jobs, 70 percent in transfers and promotion, 50 percent in organizing, 36 percent in orienting new employees, 25 percent in counseling, 25 percent in restructuring hourly jobs for the handicapped, and 33 percent and 43 percent, respectively, for conducting labor negotiations and handling grievances in hourly jobs.[14] The job is one of the major "stocks in trade" of a personnel manager. Whether job knowledge is gained formally or informally, it is necessary for scientific management of personnel. Only in this way can we adequately determine the type of personnel we need in the organization.

HUMAN RESOURCES REQUIREMENTS

The second decision concerning the organization's need for human resources is a determination of the *number* of personnel of each type that should be provided. As outlined in Figure 6-4, this problem can be logically divided into three parts: (1) resource demand forecasting, (2) resource supply forecasting, and (3) human resource actions. The purpose of human resources planning is to assure that a certain desired number of persons with the correct skills will be available at some specified time in the future.

Resources Demand Forecasting

The forecasting of human resources requirements is often subdivided into long-range and short-range forecasts. The latter type is almost unavoidable in most firms, but a survey of 589 members of the American Society of Personnel Administration revealed that only 32 percent reported any long-range planning of human resources needs in their organizations.[15] From the report of activities in Box 6-1, however, it would appear that various firms are moving in this direction. When this activity is included in the personnel executive's unit of responsibility, the average salary in 1979 was $79,000. This compared to $52,000 when the executive was not involved in this very important activity.

---

[14]*Summary of National Job Analysis Methods Survey*, pp. 4–5.
[15]Barry C. Campbell and Cynthia L. Barron, "How Extensively Are HRM Practices Being Utilized by the Practitioners?" *The Personnel Administrator*, vol. 27, no. 5, May 1982, p. 70.

BOX 6-1
Personnel Widens Its Franchise

Until three years ago, the personnel department at Standard Brands, Inc. was virtually indistinguishable from those that have existed since the dawn of the corporate era. Composed of a director of labor relations and a director of benefits—each with a salary in the $30,000 range—and a staff of about 20, the department routinely administered hiring and firing procedures, handled labor negotiations, maintained employee records, administered benefits, and saw to it that paychecks went out on time. Its decisions could vitally affect individual employees, but they had little impact on the direction of the corporation, and the department was buried well below finance, marketing, and planning in the corporate bureaucracy.

The old personnel staff is still performing many of the same functions at Standard Brands today, but now it is part of a new human resources department, four times the size of the original personnel department and headed up by a corporate vice-president, Madelyn P. Jennings, whose salary and responsibilities are easily double those of the two directors combined. Part of that growth is the result of a flood of new government regulations that have increased the importance and the complexity of traditional personnel administration tasks. Since joining the company in 1976, Jennings has instituted a national compensation program, overhauled benefits, and developed an employee appraisal system.

But much of the stunning growth of Jennings' department is the result of a brand-new role that has been assigned to personnel administration at Standards Brands: the development and implementation of the company's first manpower planning system, one that is directly tied to carrying out corporate strategies. This new personnel function at Standard Brands is typical of similar changes taking place in most other large corporations that promise to lift top personnel administrators, who increasingly are adopting the human resources designation, into prominence as powerful officers in the corporate hierarchy.

Already, experts estimate, such human resources executives—whether they carry the title or not—now hold key manpower planning responsibilities in almost all of the nation's 500 largest industrial companies, compared with only a handful of companies five years ago.

While their staffs handle such mundane chores as allocating spaces in the company parking lot, they are also expected to work closely with senior operating managers to create staffing plans that are designed to meet corporate goals and to satisfy the growing demands by employees for clear career paths they can follow. "Management realizes that its important assets are not simply financial resources but having the people on hand at the right time and in the right place to make a thing go," observes Thomas C. Stevens, who in 1974 filled a new post as corporate director of human resources at J. L. Case Co., the construction and farm equipment subsidiary of Tenneco, Inc.

Not surprisingly, personnel executives able to tackle such herculean tasks are commanding top dollar. A recent study by Heidrick & Struggles, Inc., a Chicago-based executive-search firm, shows that the average salary of senior human resources executives is $79,000 compared with $52,000 for personnel executives who normally do not perform manpower planning. Even senior personnel executives who may handle human resources responsibilities but do not have the title average $61,000. And one human resources officer recently told *Business Week* that, counting performance incentives, his annual compensation can top $250,000. "Today corporations recognize that the right executive in human resources can add to profits," comments Lester B. Korn, president of Korn/Ferry International, an executive-search firm that conducted 28 searches for human resources vice-presidents in the last two years, a 30% increase from the prior two years.

Chief executive officers are increasingly taking an active role in such searches, a clear indication that the

human resources position is gaining importance. Standard Brands' Jennings recalls one prehiring interview with F. Ross Johnson, the company's chairman, that lasted seven hours. William M. Buck, Jr., who holds the new post of senior vice-president of human resources at Peabody Coal Co., was hired by President and Chief Executive Officer Robert H. Quenon. And at American Express Co., Chairman James D. Robinson III and President Roger H. Morley insisted on interviewing all potential candidates for the job themselves before hiring Philip H. Prince last August as AmEx's senior vice-president for personnel and management development.

The pipeline to the top rarely stops after hiring. Many human resources executives such as Buck report directly to the CEO. Others—Jennings is one—sit on corporate policy committees. "More and more, key human resources people are sitting at the CEO's right elbow," notes Gerard R. Roche, president of Heidrick & Struggles.

Tenneco is typical of the trend to relate manpower planning to corporate goals and strategies. The company recently started requiring vice-presidents to submit a five-year "executive resources" projection along with their five-year business plans. Both are closely reviewed by Kenneth L. Otto, senior vice-president of employee relations, who determines if they are compatible. If a division, for example, is planning to shift from a marketing to a production orientation, Otto must make certain that it is planning not only to develop a large enough production staff to meet the new demands in that area but also to make a suitable reduction of marketing specialists. "We're looking at how people figure into the equation as a long-range problem," says Otto.

Such planning is essential for companies with ambitious growth goals. AmEx, for example, has plans to expand into new business areas that will double its employee population to 70,000 over the next ten years. Even without this growth, the company's annual turnover rate produces a need

Continued following page

for more than 500 new people a year. As a result, a manager's performance will be judged on how well he has been able to grow people in his own organization, and up to 10% of an executive's bonus could be negatively affected for failure to meet management development goals. That, in turn, is already placing a heavy demand on Personnel Senior Vice-President Prince to develop new programs to teach AmEx executives necessary skills in employment recruitment, training, and career counseling.

The new stress on human resources planning has resulted in a major expansion in the entire area of personnel, and experts estimate the number of specialists in the field has doubled in the last five years. At Hibernia Bank, in San Francisco, Max H. Forster, the new vice-president and director of personnel, more than doubled the size of his unit from 6 to 14 people in only six months. At Levi Strauss & Co., Harold M. Goldstein, director of employee selection and development, recently was authorized to hire human resources staffers "at a time when we were trying as a company to hold the line."

Unlike its precedessors in personnel, who thought mostly in terms of answering or silencing employee complaints, the new breed of human resources executives focuses much more sharply on profits. That often means reorienting personnel staffs toward a bottom-line view that once seemed alien to them. Laurence E. Mullen recalls that when he became vice-president of personnel and organization at Allegheny Ludlum Industries Inc., in 1974, his staff "not only lacked awareness of how they could impact the profitability of a business, but they weren't aware that people wanted them to." Mullen's solution: A series of intensive training seminars in corporate finance were given to the company's entire personnel staff.

Luckily, corporations are starting to get an influx of people with both an interest in human resources and a thorough grounding in business. In many companies, personnel was once considered a dumping ground for executives who could not succeed in running operating divisions. More common now are executives such as James W. Kennedy, manager of hu-

man resources planning and employment for General Foods Corp., who switched careers after 12 years as a successful marketing executive. Also typical are a growing number of line managers who believe that two-to three-year stints as human resources executives can be a major way station in their route to the top. And they can point to a lengthening list of examples to support that belief, including W. Thomas Beebe, chairman of Delta Airlines Inc., and J. Stanford Smith, chairman of International Paper Co., both of whom spent time as personnel executives.

Business schools are accommodating this trend by turning out more MBAs who believe that human resources is where the action is. "Since 1975, we've had a 50% increase in the number of graduates who are interested in this position," comments J. Frederic Way, associate dean of placement and career services at Columbia University's Graduate School of Business. Similarly, Frank H. Cassell, professor of industrial relations at Northwestern University's Graduate School of Management, watched attendance at his seminar for human resources soar from only six students eight years ago to 275 students this year—roughly 80% of the entire graduating class. And at the University of Pennsylvania's Wharton School of Business, three to five students each semester are taking independent majors in human resources, majors that were not even provided five years ago.

While a variety of factors explain the growing role of corporate human resources departments, the one most commonly cited is government. Dozens of new federal laws—from the Employee Retirement Income Security Act to the Equal Employment Opportunity Act—spell out how companies must treat existing and prospective employees, and compliance often involves expensive new programs. Peabody Coal's human resources department, for example, began supervising a program costing more than $500,000 in 1973 that simulates various mining conditions in order to train some 15,000 miners a year—all to ensure compliance with the Mining Safety & Health Act. And Standard Brands' Jennings notes that the number of statutes enforced by the Labor Dept. has increased from

40 in 1960 to 130 now.

A less obvious but equally important reason for the closer attention large companies are giving to human resources is the skyrocketing cost of employee benefits, which has risen from just above 20% of an average employee's salary five years ago to 35% today. With so much invested in an employee, reducing turnover rates is crucial. At Tenneco's J. L. Case subsidiary, the human resources department is credited with helping the company reduce its monthly turnover rate to 1.1%, compared with an industry average of 1.5% a month, by developing clearer job performance criteria and better training programs and by emphasizing promotion from within. Thanks to a new system for spotting and tracking internal managerial talent, Case fills 80% of its salaried slots with insiders, up from 50% five years ago.

Yet human resources executives are by no means over all of the hurdles in establishing their new role in the corporation. The problem of putting manpower training programs in place and "getting management to buy them" still remains, observes Ruben Krigsman, manager of personnel research at Union Carbide Corp. But he notes that a "new breed" of operating managers is coming along who show far more respect for personnel executives. Five years ago, Krigsman figures, he initiated 90% of all of his contacts with top management. Now they come to him about 60% of the time.

One major reason for that, says Krigsman, is that top management increasingly appreciates the profit potential of human resources executives. To illustrate, he recalls how in 1976 he was dispatched to Carbide's Pleasantville (N.Y.) plant to try to boost employee productivity and morale. After running various surveys, Krigsman instituted new training programs and reorganized the workplace to give blue-collar workers more responsible jobs. In just three months, productivity soared by 25%; the amount of finished goods passing inspection jumped from 60% to 80%; and absenteeism dropped from 5% to 3%. As a result of such triumphs in human resources management, says Krigsman, "managers recognize that there's a payoff for both the business and the employees."

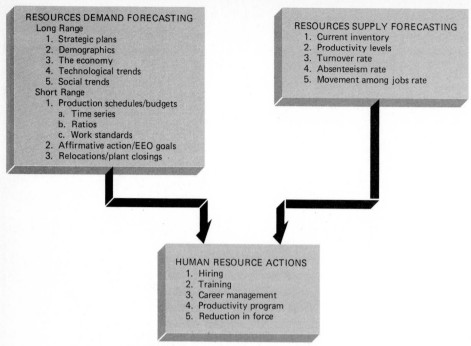

RESOURCES DEMAND FORECASTING
Long Range
    1. Strategic plans
    2. Demographics
    3. The economy
    4. Technological trends
    5. Social trends
Short Range
    1. Production schedules/budgets
       a. Time series
       b. Ratios
       c. Work standards
    2. Affirmative action/EEO goals
    3. Relocations/plant closings

RESOURCES SUPPLY FORECASTING
    1. Current inventory
    2. Productivity levels
    3. Turnover rate
    4. Absenteeism rate
    5. Movement among jobs rate

HUMAN RESOURCE ACTIONS
    1. Hiring
    2. Training
    3. Career management
    4. Productivity program
    5. Reduction in force

FIGURE 6-4 Human resources planning.

Long-range factors. Though specific numbers are difficult to develop in forecasts encompassing two to five years, those responsible for planning human resource requirements must be aware of a number of basic factors.

1. *The firm's long-range business plans.* When Heublein's United Vintners management decided to split its wine operations into two divisions, it was determined that a wine professional was required for its premium wine business, and a personal products manager, from some firm like Gillette, should manage the standard wines unit.[16] In General Electric, strategic objectives for various products are classified as "grow," "defend," and "harvest," depending upon the stage of the product life cycle. General Electric managers are also classified by personal styles as "growers," "caretakers," and "undertakers." In this same company, when it was projected that the firm should move from electromechanical to electronic products, this required actions in the present to ensure a supply of electronic engineers some five or so years down the road. If plans call for more efforts on the international market in the future, then decisions must be made now regarding the utilization of host-country nationals and third-country nationals.

2. *Demographics.* We have gone from the "baby dearth" of the 1930s depression (2.1 fertility rate) to the "baby boom" of the 1950s (3.8) to the "baby bust" of the 1970s (1.8).[17] As demonstrated in Figure 6-5, these fluctuations affect the labor supply available in various age categories. The baby boom group has been likened to a watermelon moving through a snake's body. There will be a relative

[16] "Wanted: A Manager to Fit Each Strategy," *Business Week,* February 25, 1980, p. 166.
[17] "Americans Change," *Business Week,* February 20, 1978, pp. 64–77.

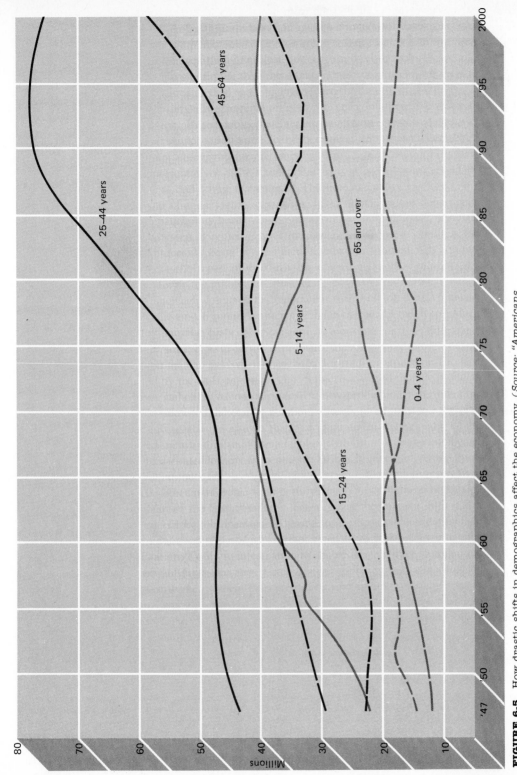

FIGURE 6-5 How drastic shifts in demographics affect the economy. (*Source: "Americans Change," "Business Week, February 20, 1978, pp. 64–65. Reprinted by special permission. Copyright © 1978 by McGraw-Hill, Inc., New York. All rights reserved.*)

oversupply of persons from ages 25 to 44 in the coming decade, resulting in some slowing down in career progress. On the other hand, the latter portion of the decade shows a smaller number of 15- to 24-year-olds entering the work force. The personnel manager will be simultaneously faced with a labor shortage for entry jobs and much competition among the middle aged for promotion to higher-level jobs.

The overall rate of growth of the labor force has fluctuated from decade to decade. During the 1950s, the annual percentage growth was 1.25; this increased during the 1960s to 1.65, and moved still higher during the 1970s to 2.3. The decade of the 1980s will see a contraction in the growth rate with the annual percentage increase falling to 1.9 percent from 1980 to 1985, and declining even further to 1.1 percent from 1985–1990.[18] With continued growth of the economy, these declining percentages provide a sound argument for undertaking the task of human resources planning.

3. *The economy.* Movements from prosperity to recession and back to prosperity pose considerable problems for the personnel executive. Though economic predictions are considerably difficult to make with accuracy, some consideration must be given to the level of economic activity in planning for human resources requirements. According to one set of predictions, portrayed in Figure 6-6, the growth in projected job openings will vary according to the occupation, while outright declines are anticipated among private household workers and farm workers.

[18]Donald E. Pursell, "Planning for Tomorrow's Personnel Problems," *Personnel Journal,* vol. 60, no. 7, July 1981, pp. 559–561.

FIGURE 6-6 Predicted job openings, 1978–1990. (*Source: Bureau of Labor Statistics, Occupational Outlook Handbook, 1980–1981, p. 22*)

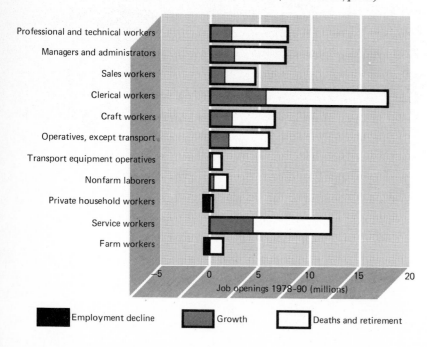

4. *Technological trends.* Advances in technology have definite effects on the nature and mixture of jobs available. For example, advances in computer technology resulted in a decrease in the number of bookkeepers, and an increase in the number of computer programmers. The use of robots in place of some kinds of human labor is beginning to take off. Some observers say that the current level of technology for building robots would enable the replacement of two-thirds of today's factory work force. General Motors is planning to use "sighted robots" that can recognize thirty different automobile body styles and adjust their spray-painting accordingly. General Electric has plans for replacing nearly one-half of its 37,000 assembly workers with "steel collared workers."[19] Resistance by organized labor so far has been minimal inasmuch as most current applications relieve people of work that is hazardous, dirty, or monotonous, such as loading presses or spraying paint in confined areas.

5. *Social trends.* Looking back, the impact of the Civil Rights Act and Executive orders have had major effects on human resource planning. Looking ahead, managers must anticipate and adapt to other potential changes in both customs and laws. For example, personnel appear to be increasingly immobile as the number of refusals to move to other locations increases. This reduction in flexibility will have impact upon resource planning in the future. In the area of possible new laws, two bills were introduced in a recent session of Congress requiring not only advance notice of pending plant closings, but heavy financial penalties in the form of payments to displaced employees and lost revenue to the cities and states involved. One manager believes that nearly every social trend that will affect business twenty years from now is being "previewed" somewhere.[20] Firms are increasingly employing "scanners" to do extensive reading of publications to identify various social and political factors that will help shape the future business environment.

In considering the above factors and making a specific long-range projection, one method that can be utilized is termed the "Delphi technique." Essentially, it is an iterative questionnaire technique in which recognized experts are asked to make separately specific estimates of human resources needs in the future. This is followed by feedback of summarized results, followed by a request for a new estimate. After three or four iterations, there tends to be some convergence in specific future estimates. In effect, it is a "judgment refining" process, but the numbers resulting should still be regarded with considerable suspicion.

Short-range factors. Though long-range planning may appear to be a luxury to most firms, the personnel unit does require some lead time to provide the personnel required by the firm in the short run.

1. *Production schedules and budgets.* Specific sales forecasts for the coming year must be translated into a work program for the various parts of the enterprise. For production, this is variously titled "production program," "master schedule," and "department schedule." In the sales division, the problem revolves around sales quotas and sales territories. Some plans must be made concerning the amount of work that each segment of the firm is expected to accomplish during some coming period.

[19]"Robots Join the Labor Force," *Business Week,* June 9, 1980, p. 68.
[20]"Capitalizing on Social Change," *Business Week,* October 29, 1979, p. 106.

Various techniques can be used in making a short-term projection of both the amount of work to be done and the number of personnel necessary to do it. Time series analysis can be used to identify trends in the past. This should enable some understanding of how the organization has changed over time. The bias in such analysis is in favor of the past, and must be altered by review of many of the long-range factors discussed above.

Various ratios can be computed, such as the number of sales personnel in relation to the level of sales, or the number of telephones in relation to the number of customer service representatives. Thus, the number of new sales personnel to be added can be derived from the projected increase in sales, assuming that everything else remains unchanged. It was pointed out in Chapter 3 that the typical ratio of number of persons working in the personnel unit as compared to total personnel in the firm is 1 to 100. Again, this approach is based upon the past.

The establishment of work standards can be approached in a more systematic manner. Given that a unit of output must be produced by an employee, systematic time study can be used to determine a more accurate time for processing. Such work standards are established for the average employee, exerting average effort working under average conditions, such as 0.09 hour to process a single voucher. If the employee averages 0.07 to 0.08 hour, per voucher, he or she is working faster than standard. If more time is taken than 0.09 hour, then the schedule will not be met. Human resources planning in this case is based on a work rate of slightly in excess of 11 vouchers produced for each hour worked.

2. *Affirmative Action/EEO goals*. If the firm has a government contract in excess of $10,000, or has been convicted in court of purposeful or inadvertent discrimination, or voluntarily undertakes to improve its employment percentages of minorities and females, then specific numbers in the form of goals will be reflected in the human resource plan. In some court-ordered instances, the employer is required to hire one minority or female for every other type of employee added to the firm.

3. *Relocations/plant closings*. The recession of the early 1980s saw major retrenchments on the part of many firms. The reductions in force that follows such major changes are particularly stressful for not only the employees involved, but the personnel unit as well. The personnel unit should be informed as soon as possible that such closings are scheduled. Provisions must be made for determining which personnel are to be offered transfers and the degree of help to be given to those terminating employment with the firm.

In making the short-term projection of human resources needs, ''the most common approach is to rely most heavily on the judgemental (sic) forecasts of unit managers, supplemented with some basic statistical analysis.''[21] Though arguments abound as to whether the process should be from the top down (top management projections with subordinate reactions), or from the bottom up (subordinate recommendations with top management review), the unit manager is a key person in making this determination.

---

[21]Richard B. Frantred, ''Human Resource Planning: Forecasting Manpower Needs,'' *Personnel Journal,* vol. 60, no. 11, November 1981, p. 854.

Resources Supply Forecasting

Though the available supply of human talent would appear to be easier to determine than projected needs, there are a number of complexities in this decision as well. In projecting future availability, the following factors are usually considered.

1. *Current inventory*. Personnel records should be summarized in some systematic manner to indicate the talent available in various jobs and units within the firm. As an example of an "inventory card" for one employee, Figure 6-7 shows various bits of information that indicate the specific talent that is now available. Filing these records on the basis of organizational units has the advantage of grouping together the records as they would most probably be used in human resources planning.

2. *Productivity level*. As indicated earlier, future projections of resource needs are often made on the basis of past experience. For example, let us suppose that ratio analysis shows that average sales per person last year was $250,000 per year. Reviews of changes in productivity levels reveal that sales per person have been increasing at the rate of 10 percent per year. If next year's projected sales is $25 million, we would not anticipate a need for 100 salespersons ($25 million divided by $250,000), but rather for only 91 salespersons since we expect an increase in productivity per person to $275,000. As technology improves the productivity levels of a work force, the number of persons required per unit of output will decline.

3. *Turnover rate*. Our current inventory records show, for example, that we have 100 assemblers on the payroll to process the production schedule for the coming month. Can we project that we will still have those 100 persons at the end of the month? To answer this question concerning predicted supply, we must look

FIGURE 6-7 Sample inventory record.

(Front)

```
┌─────────────┐
│             │
│             │
│             │
│ Photograph  │
│             │
│             │
│             │
└─────────────┘
```

Birth date: <u>3/1/30</u>   Service date: <u>5/22/68</u>   Retirement: <u>3/1/95</u>
Family status: Married, 3 children
Outside activities: Member of Big Brothers and Boy Scouts; interested in boating and hobby-shop work connected with boating; has been member of city council and chief of volunteer fire department
Education: 2 years high school; quartermaster service school, auto mechanic and body-work course, 2 weeks, 1966; State College, basic management course, 2 weeks, 1968
Military history: U.S. Army 1969–1971, S./Sgt. in charge of basic training platoon; not in reserves
Previous employment: 1950–1968 auto mechanic (self-employed)
In-plant experience: 1968, patrolman (85); 1972, sergeant (85)

(Reverse)
JOHN DOE

Appraisals

Date	By	Reviewer	Result
6/15/75	A. K. Allison	H. J. Bright	Potential for future promotion
8/20/77	A. K. Allison	H. J. Bright	Potential for future promotion
5/25/79	A. K. Allison	D. G. Doll	Immediately qualified for promotion

Interests: Strong in mechanical, computation, persuasive, musical, social service, and clerical
Personality: Normally stable, extroverted, dominant, and confident
Mental alertness: 40th percentile
Mechanical comprehension: 85th percentile
Remarks
Centerville credit bureau: Credit rating satisfactory, no record of convictions
Management screening investigation: Reported to be industrious, civic-minded, quiet, and a good neighbor
Health: Has recurring bronchitis and acute asthma

at turnover data. If we find that our monthly separation rate is a not unusual 2 percent, the answer is that if we need 100, we will be 2 persons short by the end of the month. Retirements are predictable but other turnover must be computed on a percentage basis.

The turnover rate can be expressed by a number of different formulas. These involve such terms as *accessions,* addition to payroll; *separations,* quits, discharges, retirement, deaths; *replacements,* one accession plus one separation; and *average work force,* number at the beginning of the period (usually a month) plus number at the end, divided by 2. If our work force averages 800 employees this month, during which time there were 16 accessions and 24 separations, the accession rate is 2 percent, the separation rate is 3 percent, and the replacement rate is 2 percent.

4. *Absenteeism rate.* "Absenteeism" is the title given to a condition that exists when a person fails to come to work when properly scheduled to work. The most common measure is the percentage of scheduled time lost and is computed as follows:

$$\frac{\text{Number of person-days lost}}{(\text{average number of persons}) \times (\text{number of workdays})} \times 100$$

There is probably some irreducible overall minimum of absenteeism, and 3 percent is projected as this figure. In one year, for example, the overall average rate was 3.5 percent, in mining 5.2 percent, in manufacturing 4.0 percent, in trade 2.8 percent, for white-collar employees 2.6 percent, for blue-collar 4.4 percent, and for managers 1.8 percent (the lowest of any occupation).[22]

Absenteeism obviously reduces the number of personnel actually available. If the monthly absenteeism rate among our 100 assemblers is 4 percent, this means that on the average only 96 are present each day and ready to work.

5. *Movement among jobs.* Some jobs are sources of personnel for other jobs; for example, secretaries may be obtained by the promotion of typists, and branch managers are obtained from a pool of section managers. If, for example, we anticipate a need for five new branch managers seven years from now, *more* than five potential branch managers should have entered the firm *this* year, assuming that seven years is the average development time. Obviously, some will quit before the seven years are up and others may not qualify for promotion.

To determine the rate of movement, we need to go over past records to obtain the following: (1) normal rate of branch managers who quit; (2) normal rate of section managers who quit; (3) normal rate of promotion from section to branch manager; and (4) normal rate of demotion of branch manager to section manager. In Figure 6-8, we assume that other transfers are not possible. Thus 85 percent of the section managers will remain section managers, 5 percent will

---

[22]Janice Neipert Hedges, "Absence from Work—Measuring the Hours Lost," *Monthly Labor Review,* vol. 100, no. 10, October 1977, pp. 16–23.

FIGURE 6-8
Annual Flows of Employees

Time I (T)	Time II (T + 1 yr.)			
	Section Managers	Branch Managers	Out	Σ
Section managers	85%	5%	10%	100%
Branch managers	10	80	10	100

be promoted, and 10 percent will quit the system. On the other hand, 80 percent of the branch managers will remain at their present post, 10 percent will go back to section head, and 10 percent will quit the system. Application of these percentages to our present talent inventory will tell us what things will look like in one year if we do not add anyone to the system. Assuming that we now have 100 section managers, and 20 branch managers, at the end of the coming year we will have 87 section managers (85 retained plus 2 demotions) and 22 branch managers (16 retained and 5 promotions). If we want more or less in either category, we must take such actions as recruitment, accelerating or slowing or promotion rates, and accelerating or slowing of exit rates.

Human Resource Actions

The matching of projected human resource needs with projected human resources available provides the basis for undertaking various actions to ensure that supply will equal demand at the time specified. Such actions as the following can be undertaken:

1. *Hiring.* If projected supply is short of projected demand, the addition of new personnel is a likely possibility. Let us suppose, for example, that the projected work load for a clerical department during the coming month is to process 22,000 vouchers. Time study has set 0.09 hour as the work standard for processing one voucher. Multiplying 0.09 times 22,000 vouchers produce a total projected workload of 1,980 hours for the coming month. Theoretically, one person can contribute approximately 180 hours of work next month through working 4 ½ weeks. Dividing 1,980 by 180 gives an answer of 11 persons required to undertake the predicted workload.

   What if the numbers do not come out even? Overtime can extend one individual's capacity beyond 180 hours, though it should be recognized that the 0.09 standard will probably increase to 0.10 or 0.12 during the overtime hours. If similar skills exist, perhaps an employee can be transferred and used part time. In some situations part-time help can be leased. It must also be remembered that neither of the figures, the 0.09 person-hour standard or the 22,000 projected volume, is highly exact and accurate.

   In calculating the projected supply, let us assume that our current inventory shows 11 names on the payroll. Is there any assurance that these 11 will be available for work every day? Investigation of absenteeism rates shows an excessively high figure of 9 percent. This rate demands investigation, but if the situation continues, we shall require 12 names on the payroll to ensure that an average of 11 show up each day. We now must factor in possible turnover, and our records may indicate one retirement coming up next month. Thus, our workload analysis may indicate a need for 11 clerks. Absenteeism rates require the addition of 1 more, and an analysis of turnover factors and rates adds another. Though we now have 11 voucher clerks on the payroll, a requisition to hire 2 additional clerks would be the necessary human resource action.

2. *Training.* Analysis of trends in General Electric showed that the utility electrical equipment portion of the business had dropped from 80 percent to 47 percent of income during the 1970s.[23] Movement from electromechanical to electronic products required not only a stepping up of campus recruitment, but also a massive retraining of electrical/mechanical engineers into electronic engineers. Hiring was not the only solution attempted.

[23]"Conversation with Reginald H. Jones and Frank Doyle," *Organizational Dynamics,* vol. 10, no. 3, Winter 1982, p. 49.

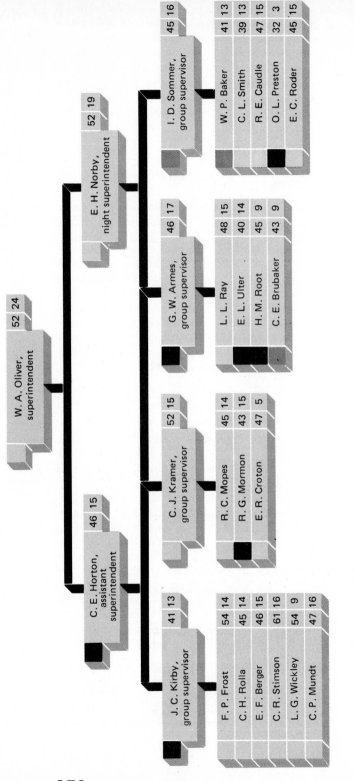

FIGURE 6-9 Promotability chart.

3. *Career management.* It is to the advantage of both the employee and the firm that changes in job assignments be planned to form a career. The personnel unit should have some system of recording and tracking career moves through the organization. A simple system used by one organization is shown in Figure 6-9. It is basically a modified organization chart that highlights age, seniority, and promotion status. It also identifies key jobs for which there are no qualified replacements in the unit, for example, J. C. Kirby, group supervisor. Analyses of this type can also lead to a discovery of an excess of talent in another area, such as G. W. Armes, group supervisor. Perhaps either Ulter or Root can be moved to replace Kirby when that position becomes vacant. There still may be difficulties since Frost, Rolla, Berger, Stimson, Wickley, and Mundt may well resent such a promotion as infringing on their rights of succession.

4. *Productivity programs.* Because of the steady decline in productivity rates in the United States during the last decade, various firms have undertaken specific programs to increase the effectiveness of the work force. Many of these will be discussed in this book, but most revolve around some type of participative employee involvement in work planning and execution. Improving productivity levels will increase the supply of human resources available without increasing the number of personnel. Organized labor has also been involved in the process through participating in improved quality of worklife programs, and agreeing to alter various work rules that hold down productivity. "If an electrician can use a screwdriver to take the cover off an electrical contact instead of waiting for a millwright to perform the nonelectrical task, you save a lot of money in terms of downtime."[24] Even some union leaders estimate that eliminating inefficient rules could produce a one-time productivity increase of 10 percent.

5. *Reductions in force.* If the projected supply of human resources is in excess of projected demand, the firm may well have to close plants and layoff personnel. Recent agreements between the United Auto Workers and General Motors and Ford have involved a promise by the former to improve productivity in exchange for guarantees not to close plants. The hope is that such reductions in costs will lead to greater sales in competition with the Japanese. A reduction in force is always a difficult process for everyone—the employee, the management, the union, the government, and the community. But in a competitive economy of the type that we have in the United States, such human resource actions are not uncommon.

SUMMARY

Before recruitment and selection of personnel can be undertaken, one must know the nature of the problem to be solved. The requirements for human resources must be analyzed in terms of quality of personnel needed as well as the number of each type. Job design and analysis are the basic processes that provide information leading to the establishment of personnel standards regarding quality. The immediate result of the processes is the creation of a job description (standard of function) and a job specification (standard of personnel). These two documents have multiple uses in a well-planned personnel program, but their immediate use at this stage of the text is as a standard by which we can measure applicants for jobs. A somewhat more terse statement of the duties

[24]"Can GM Change Its Work Rules?" *Business Week,* April 26, 1982, p. 116.

described in Figure 6-2 is: "At highway construction projects where only one-way traffic is possible, the person waves a red flag and tells which car to go first." Job analysis jargon can be misleading. It can also be misleading in that it leaves out the many values provided by proper role analysis. Common job descriptions in two different organizations often have different behavioral expectations.

The second major question concerning human resources requirements is that of specifying the number of each type of personnel needed at some specified time. This involves a forecasting of the number required, an inventory of current talent, and specific actions to bring demand and supply into balance. The longer the lead time in making such determinations, the more room the personnel unit has to adjust the supply of human resources. Long-range demand forecasting is highly subjective and involves consideration of such factors as the firm's strategic plans, demographics, the general economy, and technological and social trends. Short-range determinations basically evolve from next month's or next year's work-load schedule. In determining the level of human resources actually available, we not only count "heads" but we must modify this count with productivity, turnover, and absenteeism rates. Bringing supply into balance with demand necessarily involves such human resource actions as hiring, training, career management, and reductions in force.

BRIEF CASE

John Edgar was recently hired by a manufacturing firm as a personnel assistant. One of his first assignments was to prepare a job description for an engine lathe operator. He first familiarized himself with the operations of the lathe department and tried to learn what he could about lathe work. He observed George Halton, a highly skilled lathe operator, for an hour or so and followed this up with an interview. During all of this time, John took the following notes as each item of information came up:

"Sets up machine. Looks at blueprints and then adjusts various dials on the machine. Attaches tool holder to machine. Also a chuck to hold material. Puts material in chuck and makes sure it doesn't wobble during rotation. Sets speed control. Starts lathe. Makes trial cut. Measures workpiece with calipers. Adjusts tool. Makes first cut. May make several cuts after checking blueprints. When satisfied, puts a cutoff tool in place of the cutting tool. Cuts the correct length of the part off. Removes scrap stock from chuck. Lubricates lathe when necessary. Grinds own tools. Supervises and instructs two engine lathe operator learners. Assigns them work that they can do. Reads blueprints and route sheet received from foreman. Orders own stock from stock room, and cuts it to desired lengths with a power hack saw. May use steel, aluminum, brass. There are three other highly skilled operators in addition to George. Next job up is supervisor. The shop is well lighted but somewhat dirty. George said he had been an apprentice for four years and had graduated from high school. He has been on this job for three years. Place is pretty noisy. Has to stand up all the time."

In gathering the above information, George had been reasonably cooperative, though he didn't really see any point to the whole idea of the study. He was somewhat suspicious at first, but John explained that he wanted to learn and that George was the expert. After the information was collected, George was laughing and joking with one of the other workers about John being a job analyst. "How can he analyze something he knows nothing about? Oh well, guess it's harmless."

Questions

1. Does John need to know how to run an engine lathe in order to write an accurate job description?

2. How would you write up the collected information?

DISCUSSION QUESTIONS

1. What is the difference between job design and job analysis? Which requires greater skill to do effectively?

2. How is it possible for one employee to have both a position and job, and yet have no occupation?

3. If you were doing a role analysis for the job analyst position, what types of behavior would you specify?

4. What are the two major products of a job analyst? To what uses can these be put?

5. In what way is private-firm establishment of job specifications subject to review and approval by government?

6. Why should a personnel executive be interested in the birthrate? What problems do you foresee in this area?

7. In making long-range demand forecasts of human resources requirements, what major subject areas require attention? How does the Delphi technique fit into such forecasts?

8. What impact do productivity levels have on determining the supply of human resources?

9. If the work schedule requires processing 44,000 vouchers during the next month (22 ½ working days of 8 hours each), and time study has set 0.09 person-hour as the voucher processing time, how many persons will be required to meet the schedule? If the average absenteeism rate is 5 percent, how would this change your answer?

10. Why isn't a current inventory of human resources sufficient to determine the supply of human resources?

SUPPLEMENTARY READING

FRANTZREB, RICHARD B.: "Human Resource Planning: Forecasting Manpower Needs," *Personnel Journal*, vol. 60, no. 11, November 1981, pp. 850–857.

GORDON, PAUL J. and PAUL H. MEREDITH: "Creating and Using a Model to Monitor Managerial Talent," *Business Horizons*, vol. 25, no. 1, January-February 1982, pp. 52–61.

LEVINE, EDWARD L., RONALD A. ASH, and NELL BENNETT: "Exploratory Comparative Study of Four Job Analysis Methods," *Journal of Applied Psychology*, vol. 63, no. 5, October 1980, pp. 524–535.

LINDROTH, JOAN: "How to Beat the Coming Labor Shortage," *Personnel Journal*, vol. 61, no. 4, April 1982, pp. 268–272.

LOPEZ, FELIX M., GERALD A. KESSELMAN, and FELIX E. LOPEZ: "An Empirical Test of a Trait-Oriented Job Analysis Technique," *Personnel Psychology,* vol. 34, no. 3, Autumn 1981, pp. 479–502.

SCARBOROUGH, NORMAN and THOMAS W. ZIMMERER: "Human Resources Forecasting: Why and Where to Begin," *The Personnel Administrator,* vol. 27, no. 5, May 1982, pp. 55–61.

WALKER, JAMES W.: *Human Resource Planning,* McGraw-Hill Book Company, 1980, Part 2.

chapter 7

Recruitment and Hiring

Once a determination of human resources requirements has been made, the recruitment and hiring processes can begin. *Recruitment* is the process of searching for prospective employees and stimulating them to apply for jobs in the organization. It is often termed ''positive'' in that its objective is to increase the selection ratio, that is, the number of applicants per job opening. Hiring through selection is negative in that it attempts to eliminate applicants, leaving only the best to be placed in the firm. In this chapter, we shall be concerned with both these processes; in the following chapter more attention will be devoted to testing and the identification of managerial talent.

HIRING AND THE LAW

The major effort thus far of the Civil Rights Act and the various Executive orders has centered upon entry into the organization. Though these directives also apply to internal programs of training, promotion, and appraisal, the first task has been to promote the initial hiring of minorities and females.

The various agencies responsible for insuring fair treatment of special groups have attempted to develop ''Uniform Guidelines on Employee Selection Procedures.'' The major thrust has been centered upon three issues: (1) the right of organizations to select employees on the basis of qualifications, (2) the responsibility of the organization to prove validity and job relatedness of selection devices that have adverse impact on protected groups, and (3) the responsibility to use alternative methods of selection with less adverse impact when feasible. The agencies involved are the Equal Employment Opportunity Commission, the Office of Federal Contracts Compliance Programs, the Civil Service Commission, and the Department of Justice.

After the fundamental decisions in the *Griggs v. Duke Power Company* and *Albemarle Paper Company v. Moody* Supreme Court cases, the accent has been on the right to hire persons with superior qualifications to do the job. However, unfair discrimination exists when persons with *equal* probabilities of success on the job have *unequal* probabilities of being hired for the job. The courts are heavily concerned about the use of particular selection devices that have an adverse impact upon females and minorities. This disparate effect exists when (1) larger proportions of one special group would be excluded by a selection device than would be the case for other groups, (2) larger percentages of minorities and females actually applying for jobs are rejected during the hiring process, and (3) the existing levels of employment in the firm of minorities and females are out of line with the existing levels of population in the area. An example of the first effect would be the specification of a height and weight requirement that would include most white males, but exclude most females and Mexican-Americans. The second effect can be determined only by examining company hiring records classified by employee groupings. The third effect is general, in that it looks at resulting hiring patterns. If, for example, 15 percent of the surrounding population are black, but are only 3 percent black employees in the firm, a disparate effect is inferred.

The most recent revision of the Uniform Guidelines took effect in 1978. Three major changes were highlighted: (1) a numerical definition of disparate effect, (2) suggested alternatives to selection procedures that have disparate effects, and (3) approval of "bottom-line" analysis to reduce the overall number of validations required.

The numerical definition of disparate effect (adverse impact) deals with selection rates for various groups. The selection rate is the number of applicants hired or promoted, divided by the total number of applicants. The EEOC has established an 80 percent rule. A selection rate for any race, sex, or ethnic group which is less than 80 percent of the selection rate for the group with the highest rate will be considered a substantially different rate. For example, in Figure 7-1, the highest selection rate is 40 percent for the white group. If one divides the selection rate of all other groups by this 40 percent, an impact ratio is developed. If this ratio is less than 80 percent, then adverse impact is inferred. In the example, there is no adverse impact for Hispanics since their rate was 82 percent of the top rate. There is inferred adverse impact for American Indians with a 50 percent impact ratio and blacks with a 62 percent ratio.

A critical consideration in determining the selection rate is the definition of "applicant." As defined by the EEOC, an applicant is anyone who might have been considered for the job, regardless of interest or qualifications. Private firms prefer the term to be "qualified applicant," meaning that the person (1) has personally completed and filed a formal written application, (2) possesses at least minimal qualifications, and (3) completes all steps necessary for consideration until either turned down or accepted. Qualified applicants making inquiries about jobs for which the employer is not currently accepting qualification should not be placed in the applicant pool. The rule also may penalize an employer who makes an affirmative action effort to encourage applications from specific minority groups. If the number of qualified applicants among the groups are few, the tendency of the EEOC to count the total applicant flow will result in presumed numerical adverse impact.

FIGURE 7-1
Adverse Impact Analysis
(80% Rule)

	White	American Indian	Hispanic	Black
Applications	50	10	30	40
Hired	20	2	10	10
Selection rate	40%	20%	33%	25%
Impact ratio		*50%	82%	*62%

*Does not meet 80% rule.

Perhaps the most controversial new guideline is that which allows an affirmative action program to be used to offset adverse impact on minority groups. No mention is made of validating the selection devices that make up this affirmative action program. The major impact of Supreme Court decisions has been on forcing proper validation of selection procedures. As one court stated, if a selection device has been properly validated, it makes no difference how many minorities and females it tends to reject. Adverse impact is legal if the device chooses the better employee. Thus, the employer who chooses a hiring numbers approach to offset adverse impact runs the risk of violating the Civil Rights Act as interpreted in the *Griggs v. Duke Power* and *Albemarle Paper v. Moody* cases. The latter decision shifted the burden for proving the existence of valid alternatives to the plaintiff rather than the firm.

The EEOC and employers also differ on the degree to which the firm must search for alternatives with less impact on protected groups. Whereas the employer, in agreement with the *Griggs* decision, seeks only to prove job relatedness of the selection device, the Commission emphasizes the requirement of business necessity. Thus, if the employer could move to another method thereby incurring greater costs that do *not* threaten the continuation of the business, the EEOC could contend that the "business necessity" criterion has not been met. However, in a 1982 Supreme Court decision, *Connecticut v. Teal,* it was held that adverse impact at one stage of the selection process could *not* be cured by a final selection result that did not reflect adverse impact. Title VII focuses on the individual rather than the minority group as a whole. Thus, an acceptable bottom line does not eliminate the discrimination suffered by an applicant who had been eliminated by a nonvalidated test.

Finally, the new guidelines have widened the definition of selection devices to include unstandardized, informal, and unscored selection procedures. The employer is now faced with many separate validations on each of several steps that go into the hiring process. A "bottom-line" strategy is authorized which relieves the employer of the responsibility for validating each selection device, so long as the total combined effect of the entire process does not produce adverse impact on any protected group. To do this, one must keep detailed records of applicants and hires by sex, race, ethnic background, religion, and so on.

RECRUITMENT

In general, the sources of employees can be classified into two types, internal and external. Filling a job opening from within the firm has the advantages of stimulating preparation for possible transfer or promotion, increasing the general level of morale, and providing more information about job candidates through analysis of work histories within the organization. An internal search of the computer personnel data bank can flag personnel with minimum qualifications for the job opening. Dissatisfaction with such skills inventories have led some to a more personalized job posting and bidding system. Such a system is more compatible with adapting the organization to the needs of individuals.

A job posting system has a number of advantages. From the viewpoint of the employee, it provides flexibility and greater control over career progress. For the employer, it should result in better matches of employee and job, in addition to meeting EEOC requirements for equal opportunity for advancement of all employees. A survey of over 2,000 organizations revealed that job posting is used for production jobs in three out of four firms, while the rate for office jobs is three of five.[1] In most instances, the jobs are posted on bulletin boards, though some carry listings in the company newspapers. The posting period is commonly 1 week, with the final decision for hiring being completed within 4 weeks. Internal applications are often restricted to certain employees, the guidelines for one company including (1) "good" or "better" on most recent performance review, (2) dependable attendance record, (3) not under probationary sanction, and (4) having been in present position for 1 year.[2] The present supervisor must at some time be informed of his or her subordinate's interest in another job. Some require immediate notification, while others inform only if the employee becomes a prime candidate for the listed opening. The personnel unit acts as a clearinghouse in screening applications that are unrealistic, preventing an excessive number of bids by a single employee, and counseling employees who are constantly unsuccessful in their attempts to change jobs.

Inevitably, the firm must go to external sources for lower-entry jobs, for expansion, and for positions whose specifications cannot be met by present personnel. Figure 7-2 shows search methods used by over 3 million persons that resulted in finding a job. Thus, the firm has a number of outside sources available, among which are the following:

1. *Advertising*. There is a trend toward more selective recruitment in advertising. This can be effected in at least two ways. First, advertisements can be placed in media read only by particular groups; for example, *The Tool Engineer* is ordinarily read by production engineers. Secondly, more information about the company, the job, and the job specification can be included in the ad to permit some self-screening. When time is limited, the daily newspaper, particularly the Sunday edition, will reach the maximum number in the shortest period.

2. *Employment agencies*. Additional screening can be effected through the utilization of employment agencies, both public and private. Today, in contrast to their former unsavory reputation, the public employment agencies in the several states are well-regarded, particularly in the fields of unskilled, semiskilled, and

[1]Harriet Gorlin, "An Overview of Corporate Personnel Practices," *Personnel Journal*, vol. 61, no. 2, February 1982, p. 126.
[2]Thomasine Rendero, "Job-Posting Practices," *Personnel*, vol. 57, no. 5, September-October 1980, p. 6.

FIGURE 7-2
Method used to obtain job (3.5 million persons)

Job Search Method	Percentage
Applied directly to firm	34.9
Asked friends and relatives	26.2
Answered advertisements	13.9
Private employment agency	5.6
Public employment agency	5.1
School placement office	3.0
Labor union	2.3
Took Civil Service test	2.1
Teacher/professor job leads	1.4
Other	5.5

Source: Carl Rosenfeld, "Jobseeking Methods Used by American Workers," Monthly Labor Review, vol. 98, no. 8, August 1975, p. 40.

skilled operative jobs. In the technical and professional areas, however, the private agencies appear to be doing most of the work. Many private agencies tend to specialize in a particular type of worker and job, such as sales, office, executive, or engineer. A recent innovation, the videotaped interview, promotes more effective decision making with easier scheduling and more time saving for the hiring organization. When job specifications are somewhat nebulous, as they generally are in the higher types of jobs, the addition of a 30-minute videotaped interview to the usual, more sterile résumé enables representatives of the hiring organization to quickly narrow the pool of candidates to a few finalists.

3. *Recommendations of present employees.* When present employees are asked to recommend new hirees, a type of preliminary screening takes place. The present employee knows both the company and the acquaintance and presumably would attempt to please both. In one company employing 1,600 clerical workers, it was found that long tenure was related to obtaining employees from this source.[3] The separation rate of referred employees was lower than that of those obtained through either want ads or employment agencies. A second study of clerical employees in three insurance firms tended to confirm this finding with the additional modifying elements of (1) degree of friendship, (2) accuracy of company information conveyed, and (3) subsequent employee performance rating.[4]

4. *Schools and colleges.* Jobs in business have become increasingly technical and complex to the point where high school and college degrees are widely demanded. Consequently, many firms make special efforts to establish and maintain constructive relationships with school faculties and administrations. In recruiting at the college level, inquiries from 255 new technical college graduates, both before and 1 year after hiring, revealed that the most important influences affecting choice of firm and job were work-related factors, such as the nature of the assignment, degree of responsibility, and possibilities for advancement.[5] Bachelor's-degree candidates were more interested in training opportunities and precise definition of the initial assignment in order to reduce first-job anxiety. Master's candidates were also interested in the nature of the work but, in addition, exhibited considerable concern about the human organization and the personalities with whom they would be working. Doctoral-degree candidates indicated a significantly greater interest in the first job assignment than in future allocations. They were also interested in the human organization as well as the status of the industry in which the employing organization was located.

5. *Labor unions.* Firms with closed or union shops must look to the union in their recruitment efforts. Disadvantages of a monopolistically controlled labor source are offset, at least partially, by savings in recruitment costs. With one-fifth of the labor force organized into unions, organized labor constitutes an important source of personnel.

6. *Casual applicants.* Unsolicited applications, both at the gate and through the mail, constitute a much-used source of personnel. These can be developed through provision of attractive employment office facilities and prompt and courteous replies to unsolicited letters.

---

[3]Joseph C. Ullman, "Employee Referrals: Prime Tool for Recruiting Workers," *Personnel*, vol. 43, no. 3, May-June 1966, p. 33.

[4]Raymond E. Hill, "New Look at Employee Referrals as a Recruitment Channel," *Personnel Journal*, vol. 49, no. 2, February 1970, p. 147.

[5]J. R. Beak, "Where College Recruiting Goes Wrong," *Personnel*, vol. 43, no. 5, September-October 1966, pp. 22–28.

7. *Nepotism.* The hiring of relatives will be an inevitable component of recruitment programs in family-owned firms. Such a policy does not necessarily coincide with hiring on the basis of merit, but interest and loyalty to the enterprise are offsetting advantages.

8. *Leasing.* To adjust to short-term fluctuations in personnel needs, the possibility of leasing personnel by the hour or day should be considered. This practice has been particularly well developed in the office administration field. The firm not only obtains well-trained and selected personnel but avoids any obligation in pensions, insurance, and other fringe benefits.

RECRUITMENT EVALUATION

Not every firm can afford to develop every source of labor to the fullest extent. Sources utilized should be evaluated and judged in terms of the degree of success in obtaining competent personnel. For each major category of jobs, present personnel can be evaluated in terms of job success. If a correlation is discovered between successful personnel and particular labor sources, those sources should be further developed with money and effort. Within certain general sources, such as schools and colleges, the firm may find that particular schools provide better personnel for its purposes than other schools. A continuing study by the Division of Research, Harvard Business School, suggests that a firm's image or style has something to do with the type of student talent it can attract.[6] Firms are characterized by such variables as size, discouragement of risk taking, stability, emphasis upon profits, plainly stated policies, and well-structured chain of command. In correlating student preferences concerning these variables and student preferences regarding religion, the study suggested that Jewish students may wish to work for a smaller and less well-structured company. Catholics tend to prefer the well-structured company with clear policies, while Protestants and agnostics tend to fall in between Catholics and Jews. Thus, if firms wish to attract personnel from diverse ethnic backgrounds, certain alterations in practices and image may facilitate this process.

If the most successful sources of employees can be ascertained, the recruitment program can be more carefully aimed. A large insurance company has discovered that three sources of personnel provide them with most of their better employees. These are (1) high schools, (2) present-employee recommendations, and (3) newspaper advertising. Michigan Bell discovered that present-employee recommendations constituted the best single source.

In terms of job survival rates, another study of new hires for banks and insurance companies found that employee referral was a consistently good source, while newspaper ads and employment agencies were among the worst.[7] For hiring high-performing research scientists, journal advertisements and convention contacts were the best sources, while newspaper ads and college placement offices produced poorer results.[8] Differences were attributed to the amount of information transmitted, with the more productive and

[6]"How Does Religion Influence Job Choice?" *Business Week,* April 17, 1965, p. 178.

[7]Phillip J. Decker and Edwin T. Cornelius III, "A Note on Recruiting Sources and Job Survival Rates," *Journal of Applied Psychology,* vol. 64, no. 4, August 1979, p. 463.

[8]James A. Breaugh, "Relationships between Recruiting Sources and Employee Performance, Absenteeism, and Work Attitudes," *Academy of Management Journal,* vol. 24, no. 1, March 1981, p. 146.

satisfied employees being hired through sources that provided the greater amount. And finally, a New York bank, regularly utilizing seven sources, discovered that quit rates varied from a 21 percent low for one source to a 40 percent high for another, a pattern that was sustained over a 4-year period.[9] If the bank had confined its recruiting to the best four sources (reemployment of former workers, referees from high school, present-employee recommendations, and walk-ins), it would have reduced its quit rate by 9 percent, resulting in estimated savings of $180,000 over the 4 years.

The computer is readily adaptable to recruitment problems where job requirements must be matched with human characteristics and capabilities. One private employment agency for middle executives requires a 6-page questionnaire to be completed by all job applicants. Information extracted from this is placed into a computer. When a client company sends in a job specification to be filled, the agency can obtain from the computer a list of candidates who most nearly match the position. A similar approach has been used in some universities for graduating seniors, thus providing company recruiters with the names and addresses of students who appear to qualify for their job specifications.

Success in the funciton of recruitment can be judged by utilizing a number of criteria, among which are, in order of increasing importance: (1) the number of applicants, (2) the number of offers made, (3) the number of hirings, and (4) the number of successful placements. The number of job applicants would appear to have least value in determining the effectiveness of the program, for applicants can be attracted by methods that do not result in successful hirings. The number of offers made is a better indication of the quality of the recruits. The number of acceptance of hirings is getting closer to the real objective of securing an adequate number of qualified personnel. But the true test of a recruitment program can be determined only by means of a hiring follow-up. Was the placement successful? Did the employee quit because of misunderstanding the nature of the job and company? Is the person a good employee in terms of productivity and attitude? Admittedly, such an evaluation will include an appraisal of the selection procedure as well, but we believe that one cannot properly evaluate recruitment without considering the end result, a successful placement. Placing the control point earlier in the cycle could well lead to an overemphasis on the wrong types of recruitment.

NATURE OF THE HIRING PROCESS

In order to initiate the procedure for hiring, we must satisfy the three preliminary requirements depicted in Figure 7-3. First, there must be the authority to hire, which comes from the employment requisition, as developed through analysis of the work load and work force. Secondly, we must have a standard of personnel with which we can compare prospective employees. This is represented by the job specification, as developed through job analysis. And finally, we must have job applicants from whom we can select the persons to be hired. A planned recruitment program provides us with these applicants.

The hiring procedure is essentially a series of methods of securing pertinent information about the applicant. At each step we learn more about the prospect. The information obtained can then be compared with the job specification, the standard of per-

[9]Martin J. Gannon, "Sources of Referral and Employee Turnover," *Journal of Applied Psychology*, vol. 55, no. 3, June 1971, pp. 226–228.

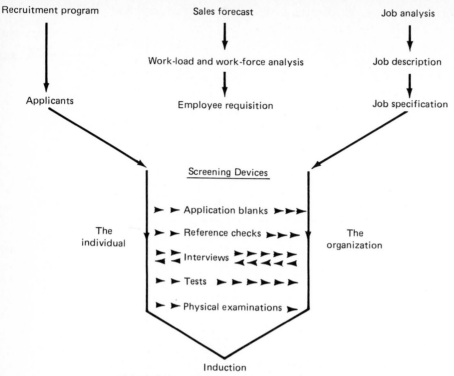

FIGURE 7-3 Framework for procurement.

sonnel. If the applicant qualifies, he or she advances to the next step. Thus, the job specification and the job applicant are present at each step in the hiring procedure. The step constitutes the means by which the applicant's qualifications can be compared with the minimum requirements established in the job specification.

Evaluating the abilities of a human being is an extremely difficult task. There are no easy shortcuts, and the hiring procedures used by the more advanced firms are long and complicated. This fact has not entirely prevented the use of various techniques of quick appraisal, some of which are well organized and can be called "pseudosciences." Among such practices are phrenology (skull protrusions), physiognomy (facial features), astrology (birth date), pigmentation (blonde-brunette), and graphology (handwriting).

Most people do not consciously practice any of these pseudosciences, but many have favorite techniques of their own, judging by such things as how a person shakes hands, whether one looks you in the eye, and how one holds a cigarette. Again we must emphasize that there is no easy shortcut to the accurate evaluation of a human being under any circumstances. The length and complexity of the modern selection procedure are tangible evidence of this fact.

THE HIRING PROCEDURE

As we have learned more about studying and measuring the individual, we have seen a continuous development of hiring procedures over the years. There are, of course, numerous aspects of a person that can be accurately measured, such as the attributes of height, weight, age, and eyesight. Other qualities, such as hearing and hand dexterity, are subject to less accurate evaluation. Psychological capabilities are even more difficult to measure, but even here there is a hierarchy of accuracy ranging from the testing of abstract intelligence, which can be done quite well, to the judging of that most nebulous of all qualities, personality. Though personality is probably the most difficult characteristic of all to measure, it is one of the most important determinants of job success.

In the hiring procedure varying methods are used to discover significant information about an applicant, which can then be compared with the job specification. Though there is no standard procedure adopted by all firms, the following is an example of a popular method:

1. Initial or preliminary interview
2. Application blank or blanks
3. Check of references
4. Psychological tests
5. Employment interview
6. Approval by the supervisor
7. Physical examination
8. Induction or orientation

It is not suggested that these specific steps or this particular sequence constitutes a model to be followed. The procedure will vary with the size of the company, the type of job to be filled, and the philosophy of the personnel management. In a survey of 202 Canadian manufacturing firms, 40 percent of those with over $50 million in sales utilized four or more selection instruments, as compared with only 7 percent of those with sales under $500,000.[10] It will be noted in Figure 7-4 that the procedure followed by the Champion Paper and Fibre Company very nearly approaches the one outlined above.

Preliminary Interview

The more nonselective the recruitment program, the more likely it is that a preliminary interview will be required. This initial interview is usually quite short and has as its object the elimination of the obviously unqualified. In many instances it is a stand-up interview conducted at a desk or railing.

The more obvious facts and impressions are of the type generally obtained in an initial interview. Appearance and facility in speech are quickly evaluated. Applicants are often asked *why* they are applying for a job with this particular organization. Salary requirements are ascertained. An idea of education and experience can be obtained by asking for the last grade finished in school and the names of jobs previously held. Many firms do not bother to initiate any paperwork at this early stage. If the applicant appears to have some chance of qualifying for existing job openings, he or she is given the application blank to complete.

---

[10]Harish C. Jain, ''Managerial Recruitment and Selection in the Canadian Manufacturing Industry,'' *Public Personnel Management*, vol. 3, no. 3, May-June 1974, p. 212.

FIGURE 7-4
Example of Hiring Procedure

Champion Paper and Fibre Company Employment Procedure

1 The first step in hiring an applicant into the Champion organization is the initial interview, during which time an attempt is made to screen out undesirable candidates.

2 If the results of the initial interview are favorable, the applicant is given an application blank to fill out. This can be filled out while in the employment office or at his home and mailed back to the employment office.

3 After reviewing the application, the applicant may be called to the employment office to take a battery of screening tests such as: Wonderlic A (general intelligence), PTI Numerical (arithmetic achievement), Bennett Mechanical AA (mechanical comprehension), Brainard Occupational Interest (occupational interest), and Thurstone Temperament (personality).

4 A check of references is next made and a phone call made to the present employer, if any.

5 The next step in the procedure is a call to the Hamilton Credit Bureau for credit references on the applicant. The credit report is a written report and includes the credit ratings and a check for police record, if any.

6 A final interview is arranged, at which time all facts at hand are considered and a decision is made as to whether or not the applicant will be hired. During this interview the employment-section representative discusses with the applicant conditions of work, type of job, rate of pay, bonuses, etc.

7 The final step in the employment procedure is to arrange for a physical examination in the medical department. Employment, of course, is based on any applicant's passing a physical examination.

8 After the examination, the applicant is returned to the employment office for a brief discussion concerning rules and regulations, payday, and hours of work. He is then taken to the clock house and shown how to ring his timecard. After this he is introduced to his supervisor.

Source: Champion Paper and Fibre Company, Hamilton, Ohio. By permission.

Application Blank

As a result of the Civil Rights Act and interpreting court decisions, the application blank is slowly undergoing transformation. Obviously, one can no longer ask for a photograph, religious affiliation, coloring, sex, or ancestry. The only exception is when the prohibited inquiry concerns a bona fide occupational qualification; for example, one needs to be a Presbyterian minister to work in a Presbyterian church. More specifically, questions have been altered as follows:

1. You can ask if the applicant has a legal right to work in the United States, but you cannot ask if one is a naturalized or native-born citizen.

2. You can ask if the applicant is between 18 and 70 years of age, but you cannot ask how old one is.

3. You can ask for the applicant's place of residence, but you cannot ask for one's birthplace.

4. You can ask what languages the applicant speaks and writes, but you cannot ask how this ability was obtained.

5. You can ask for educational background, but you cannot ask for the religious affiliation of the schools in which it might be obtained.

6. You can ask if the applicant has ever been convicted of a crime that is related to the job, such as embezzlement for a bank teller job, but you cannot ask if he or she has ever been arrested.

7. You can ask if the applicant has any physical or mental impairment that would interfere with job performance, but you cannot ask for a listing of all disabilities or treatments for various diseases.

8. You can ask about willingness to work the firm's required work schedule, but you cannot ask about willingness to work any particular religious holiday.

Of course, *after* hiring, the photograph and birth date can be obtained for identification and record-keeping purposes.

One of the general principles of hiring procedures is to assign to each step information objectives that can be best obtained by the methods of that particular step. Factual information should be obtained by means of an application blank. We should not ask embarrassing questions or questions that can be easily misinterpreted. We should not automatically assume, however, that all information written on the blank by the applicant is accurate. In a study of 111 blanks completed by applicants for the job of nurse's aide, systematic checking with previous employers produced some marked discrepancies: one-fourth disagreed on "reasons for leaving prior position," while over half of the applicants overstated both salaries received and duration of previous employment.[11] It was also discovered that 15 percent had never worked for employers they had indicated on the blank. On hopefully rare occasions, newspapers carry stories of the highly successful medical doctor who has never graduated from medical school, the reasonably effective professional who does not have the degrees claimed, and the properly credentialed and classroom-effective professor who held three *full-time* college jobs simultaneously within a 100-mile radius.

Some firms are now attempting to increase the value of the application blank by studying the relationship between certain biographical data ordinarily requested on the form and success on the job. If the specific value of any of the factual items can be determined, these items can then be weighed. In general, the approach is that of studying carefully the qualities of both your present successful employees and the unsuccessful ones. If one group possesses certain qualities and the other does not, these may well be distinguishing characteristics. For example, it may be discovered that successful employees are married and have families and that unmarried ones have poorer records. If so, a scale of points can be established for such variables as single, married, and married with children. There are several factors that have been discovered to be of value in specific business situations. Weights have been determined for such items as educational level, amount of life insurance, experience, age, and number of jobs held in the last 5 years. In a study of 1,525 life insurance salespersons in Metropolitan Life Insurance Company, a combination of high prior income and more than two dependents at the time of application was found to be descriptive of subsequent high producers.[12] When one company was pressured by a union into granting a new fringe benefit of company-paid automobile insurance, analysis of driver risk designations revealed that the "low-risk" employee-driver averaged 7 days' absence per year, the "average-risk" driver had 11

---

[11]Irwin L. Goldstein, "The Application Blank: How Honest Are the Responses?" *Journal of Applied Psychology,* vol. 55, no. 5, October 1971, p. 492.

[12]Robert Ranofsky, R. Ronald Shepps, and Paul J. O'Neill, "Pattern Analysis of Biographical Predictors of Success as an Insurance Salesman," *Journal of Applied Psychology,* vol. 53, no. 2, pp. 136–139.

days per year, while the "high-risk" driver averaged 13 days per year.[13] Good drivers also were less likely to receive reprimands, have their wages garnished, be late to work, or receive injuries on the job. A review of twenty-one studies of biographical blanks by Schuh revealed one or more items with a predictive relationship with turnover in almost every case.[14] Contrast of the predictive accuracies of biographical data versus psycho-

[13]Dale Zechar, "Auto Insurance Rating: Measure of the Man?" *Personnel Journal,* vol. 49, no. 4, April 1970, p. 315.

[14]A. J. Schuh, "The Predictability of Employee Tenure: A Review of the Literature," *Personnel Psychology,* vol. 20, no. 2, Summer 1967, pp. 133–152.

FIGURE 7-5
Weighted Application Blank for Secretary

	Percentage		
Item	Short Term	Long Term	Weight
Age:			
20 or under	10	0	0
21–25	50	12	−4
26–30	20	12	0
31–35	10	23	0
Over 35	10	53	+5
Marital status:			
Married	20	47	+2
Single	63	41	−1
Widowed	0	0	0
Divorced	10	6	0
Separated	7	6	0
Education:			
Attended grade school	0	0	0
Grade school graduate	0	0	0
Attended high school	0	12	0
High school graduate	33	41	0
Attended college	40	41	0
College graduate	27	6	−1
Business school	10	29	0
Years on last job:			
Less than 1	50	0	−5
1 to 1½	7	35	+2
1½ to 2½	37	12	−1
2½ to 3	0	6	0
More than 3	10	35	+2
Years of experience:			
0	3	18	0
Less than 1	20	0	−1
1 to 2	20	0	−1
2½ to 3	30	0	−3
More than 3	27	71	+5

Use of the cutting source of +2 would have eliminated 83 percent of the short-term employees and 13 percent of the long-term employees. *Source: Stanley R. Novack, "Developing an Effective Application Blank," Personnel Journal, vol. 49, no. 5, May 1970, pp. 421–422. Used with permission.*

logical tests (intelligence, aptitude, interest, personality) with regard to job proficiency showed substantially higher validities for the former.[15]

Review of 58 studies revealed an average validity coefficient of .35, a level which compares quite favorably with validities obtained through psychological tests.[16] In general, personal history data has less predictive value for higher-level management jobs than it does for operative jobs.

The weighted application form must be established and used with caution. First, objectives must be determined. Many firms have established as the prime objective the selection of more stable employees to decrease labor turnover. They have discovered and utilized the particular data that denote stability—facts relating to time at present residence, marital status, age, and sex. An example of the weighting process is shown in Figure 7-5 with respect to one's company's experience in retaining secretaries. Other firms have established job proficiency as the major objective and have correlated biographical items with production records, merit-rating scores, or sales volume. The criterion of success must be selected before significant factors can be determined.

A second problem is concerned with the breadth of coverage of any particular factor in success. It may be found that age, for example, is a distinguishing factor in one company or one department but not so in another. Job conditions differ substantially, and the differences alter the relationship between any one factor and job success. Consequently, each firm must develop its own weighted form, taking cognizance of the varying conditions within the organization. In addition, the blank must be continuously updated. A survey previously cited demonstrates consistent decreases in predictive accuracy of the blank with the passage of time.[17] It is recommended that the entire blank be restudied and reweighted every 3 years at the minimum.

At present the weighted application blank is not under active judicial review. If it were, the empirical process of validation would suggest that it might be acceptable. However, the personnel manager would do well not to depend solely upon this raw empiricism; it is likely that if challenged one will have to provide logic to back up discovered relationships. For example, one study discovered that those employees more likely to steal in a Detroit chain store (1) weighed 150 pounds or more, (2) did not wear eyeglasses, (3) had a Detroit address, (4) had two or more previous jobs, and (5) carelessly prepared the application blank.[18] A judge would probably challenge the Detroit address as creating disparate impact upon blacks. But the personnel manager should also be prepared to explain the relationship between stealing and eyeglasses or weight.

References

The purposes of the reference check are to obtain information about past behavior of applicants and to verify the accuracy of information given on the application blank. A survey of 122 private and public organizations revealed that 90 percent checked the applicant's work references, 84 percent verified his or her educational background, 28

[15]James J. Asher, "The Biographical Item: Can It Be Improved?" *Personnel Psychology*, vol. 25, no. 2, Summer 1972, p. 255.

[16]Richard R. Reilly and Georgia T. Chao, "Validity and Fairness of Some Alternative Employee Selection Procedures," *Personnel Psychology*, vol. 35, no. 1, Spring 1982, p. 6.

[17]A.J. Schuh, op. cit., p. 146

[18]Larry A. Pace and Lyle F. Schoenfeldt, "Legal Concerns in the Use of Weighted Applications," *Personnel Psychology*, vol. 30, no. 2, Summer 1977, p. 160.

percent checked personal references on a regular basis, and only 4 percent ran regular credit checks.[19] The most common method of checking was a combination of letters and telephone calls. Letters of reference carried by the applicant are of little value; one knows what is in them.

The reference check is subject to the same restrictions as all selection devices under the Civil Rights Act. It is unlawful to utilize reference information that has an adverse impact on protected groups unless it can be shown to be valid and job related. The civil right of privacy has led to many other laws that affect the reference checking process. Among these are: (1) the Privacy Act of 1974, which requires federal agencies to open personnel files for inspection of employees, (2) the Fair Credit and Reporting Act, which allows a person to know the nature and substance of personal credit files, and (3) the Family Education Rights and Privacy Act, which allows students to inspect educational records and prohibits universities from disclosing information without student consent. Predictions are that the stringent requirements of the Privacy Act will soon be extended to the private sector. It is probable that employees will acquire rights of access to their personnel files, will be able to respond to derogatory information found in the file (including references), must be notified of pending release of reference information to third parties with rights of preventing release, and will be entitled to find out how file information is being used. Information that does not pertain to job performance will be prohibited from being collected.

Some firms are increasingly reluctant to respond to requests when the information is unfavorable to the employee. Only factual and job-related information is provided, even to the point of reporting an actual numerical score on a merit-rating record rather than providing a subjective statement, such as, "average" or "good." The safest reference would include only (1) dates of employment, (2) job title, (3) absentee record, (4) promotions and demotions, (5) compensation, and (6) stated reasons for termination. It is likely that reference processing will be increasingly centralized to make sure that privacy is protected and that the firm will not risk being sued concerning the nature of the information provided. Subjective statements concerning employee character and performance have been the "meat" of the reference check in the years past. In the future, "basically, the reference check will become a process of verifying that the prospective employee was at a certain place doing a certain job for a specified period of time at a verified compensation level."[20]

Psychological Tests

The next step in the procedure outlined above is that of testing. If all organizations, large and small, are considered, it is apparent that most are *not* using psychological tests. However, there is a direct relationship between the size and firm and the use of tests in hiring. Most of the larger companies that can afford to have a more detailed and accurate selection procedure do utilize some form of employment testing. It is the smaller company that frequently does not bother with tests, but places greater reliance upon the interview. Since psychological testing is a complex subject, it will be discussed at greater length in the next chapter.

[19]George M. Beason and John A. Belt, "Verifying Applicants' Backgrounds," *Personnel Journal,* vol. 55, no. 7, July 1976, p. 346

[20]John D. Rice, "Privacy Legislation: Its Effect on Pre-employment Reference Checking," *The Personnel Administrator,* vol. 23, no. 2, Fall 1978, p. 51.

Interviewing

Interviewing is probably the most widely used single method of selection. A substantial amount of subjectivity, and therefore, unreliability, is to be expected from interviewing when used as a tool of evaluation. One human being is evaluating another under somewhat strained and artificial circumstances. The specific sources of unreliability are several in number. First, the interview is allocated information objectives that cannot be obtained otherwise; thus it deals with intangible goals such as assessing leadership potential, role fit, and inner motivation. Secondly, much research of specific sources of subjectivity has demonstrated the following: (1) those interviewed immediately after a weak candidate are appraised more favorably, (2) excessive weight is given to unfavorable information, with only one negative item leading to rejection in about 90 percent of the cases in one study,[21] (3) interviewer stereotyping exists with more females recommended for such jobs as editorial assistant and more males for personnel technician, (4) interviewers sometimes make a decision very early and conduct the rest of the interview searching for substantiating information, (5) when favorable information is received prior to unfavorable, the applicant fares better, (6) the greater the number of job vacancies, the more favorable the applicant evaluation, and (7) interviewers are often affected by appearance and nonverbal clues having little to do with job performance. With respect to the last item, two groups of subjects followed identical scripts in interviewing for a job.[22] The first group concentrated on greater eye contact, smiling, gestures, smaller interpersonal distance, a direct body orientation, and an attentive posture. The second group avoided eye contact, slouched, turned away, and sat at a greater distance. Despite the identical verbal content, 86 percent of the first group were recommended for hiring as compared to only 19 percent of the second.

Though most of the attention of the EEOC has been directed to psychological testing, Sec. 1607.13 of the Guidelines states: "Selection techniques other than tests . . . may be improperly used so as to have the effect of discriminating against minority groups. Such techniques include, but are not restricted to, unscored or casual interviews and unscored application forms . . . the person may be called upon to present evidence concerning the validity of his unscored procedures." In one instance, a federal court declared the subjective judgment of interviewers to be unlawful where white interviewers were judging employees utilizing no structured or written format for conducting the interview.[23] Since the resulting employment showed a disparate effect upon blacks, the court concluded that heavy reliance upon this type of interview was unlawful.

Despite its subjectivity the interview is useful and can be improved in accuracy. The use of structured formats with the same or similar questions used for all applicants for a particular job will increase reliability.[24] Research indicates that the provision of more detailed job information to the interviewers will increase the accuracy of appraisal.[25]

---

[21]E. C. Webster, *Decision Making in the Employment Interview*, Industrial Relations Center, McGill University, Montreal, 1964, pp. 16–34.

[22]Andrew S. Imada and Milton D. Hakel, "Influence of Nonverbal Communications and Rater Proximity on Impressions and Decisions in Simulated Employment Interviews," *Journal of Applied Psychology*, vol. 62, no. 3, June 1977, p. 299.

[23]Robert D. Gatewood and James Ledvinka, "Selection Interviewing and EEO: Mandate for Objectivity," *The Personnel Administrator*, vol. 21, no. 4, May 1976, p. 16.

[24]E. C. Mayfield, "The Selection Interview: A Revaluation of Published Research," *Personnel Psychology*, vol. 17, no. 3, Autumn 1964, pp. 239–260.

[25]J. A. Langdale and J. Weitz, "Estimating the Influence of Job Information on Interviewer Agreement," *Journal of Applied Psychology*, vol. 57, no. 1, February 1973, pp. 23–27.

Though taking notes may contribute to some deterioration of rapport, studies indicate that those who do retain far more information to evaluate at the end of the interview.[26] A separation of data collection and data evaluation processes can lead to increases in reliability. In the American Telephone and Telegraph management assessment center, each 2-hour interview was recorded on tape and later evaluated by multiple raters. The degree of agreement among these raters was considerably higher than normal, .72 for noncollege interviewees and .82 for college-educated as compared with more typical .40 to .60 levels (1.0 would indicate perfect agreement).[27] Another study discovered that voices are even distracting to the interviewer. In selecting dishonest interviewees, listening to a tape was a more accurate process than interviewing in person, but reading a transcript was the most accurate method of all.[28] Evidently, the presence of the interviewee serves to lessen the concentration of the interviewer on what is actually being said.

Types of Interviews

In general, there are two types of interviews, guided and unguided. Alternative titles sometimes used are "directed and nondirected" and "patterned and unpatterned." In the guided interview, a list of questions is prepared based on an analysis of the job specification. Such a list is quite helpful to the untrained interviewer, but with the passage of time and development of skill, one tends to depart from this detailed pattern. A survey of 273 firms revealed that only 26 percent used a patterned interview form.[29] The typical employment interview is guided, nonetheless, as its average length is 30 minutes for plant employees and 45 minutes for office employees.

The unguided interview is more often used in situations other than hiring, such as counseling, processing of grievances, and exit interviews. This type of interview is largely unplanned, and the interviewee does most of the talking. The theory of the unguided interview is that the interviewee will reveal more of her or his desires and problems. The greater use of this type is by skilled counselors in seeking to help disturbed people. Advice and reassurance are avoided, and listening is emphasized. Although the typical employment interview is guided, the use of the unguided approach for higher types of job openings is not unknown. More time is devoted to interviewing the candidate, frequently by many different interviewers. In the study cited above, the average length of the unguided employment interview was 90 minutes for college graduates, 2 hours for engineers, and 3 hours for supervisors and executives.

Another basis for classifying interviews is the situation in which the interview is conducted. We are discussing here primarily the employment interview. In addition to this type, there is the counseling interview, the merit-rating or appraisal interview, the grievance interview, and the exit interview. A list of this kind emphasizes the fact that the interview is a basic management tool that is used in many situations.

[26]R. E. Carlson, P. W. Thayer, E. C. Mayfield, and D. A. Peterson, "Improvements in the Selection Interview," *Personnel Journal,* vol. 50, no. 4, April 1971, p. 271.

[27]Donald L. Grant and Douglas W. Bray, "Contributions of the Interview to Assessment of Management Potential," *Journal of Applied Psychology,* vol. 55, no. 1, 1969, p. 28.

[28]Norman R. F. Maier and James A. Thurber, "Accuracy of Judgments of Deception When an Interview Is Watched, Heard, and Read," *Personnel Psychology,* vol. 21, no. 1, Spring 1968, pp. 23–30.

[29]Milton M. Mandell, *The Employment Interview,* American Management Associations Research Study 47, New York, 1961, p. 23.

Principles of Interviewing

There are many principles of good interviewing, and it is helpful to classify them in some manner to facilitate their retention. Perhaps the most useful means of classification is by the typical sequence of functions that occur within the interview: (1) preparation, (2) setting, (3) conduct of the interview, (4) close, and (5) evaluation.

Preparation   There should be preparation of some type for all interviews, scheduled or unscheduled. Obviously, a considerable amount of planning is needed for interviews that are scheduled in advance, such as employment and appraisal interviews. However, many interviews conducted on the spot, such as the initial processing of a grievance, allow for no preparation. The following principles are still applicable:

1. *Determine the specific objectives of the interview.* In employment interviews, some decision must be made as to which information objectives are to be accomplished in the interview. There should be little overlap with other employment steps; the interviewer should not, for example, repeat all of the basic information questions given on the application blank. In general, the employment-interviewing objectives are largely intangible, dealing with such traits as character, social adjustment, attitude, oral expression, and capacity for growth and advancement.

   The objectives of other types of interviews should be similarly spelled out. The general purpose of a grievance interview is resolution of the controversy to the satisfaction of both the employee and the company. The purpose of an exit interview is to obtain the real reason for quitting the employ of the company, and, at times, it is an attempt to persuade an employee to remain. The purpose of an appraisal interview is to inform the employee of his or her standing concerning performance and to motivate the individual toward improvement.

2. *Determine the method of accomplishing the interviewing objective.* In general, this principle involves a decision to utilize either the guided or the unguided approach. It involves such questions as whether to use a standard rating form or a less systematic evaluation; whether to take notes or to rely upon the memory. Managers who retain less information tend to systematically rate the interviewee higher and with less variability on component traits and abilities, a type of halo effect. Those with more information allocate lower ratings and recognize intraindividual differences.

3. *Inform yourself as much as possible concerning the known information about the interviewee.* For the employment interviewer, this means a study of the application blank. For the supervisor handling an unexpected grievance, this emphasizes the traditional need of "knowing your people."

Setting   Establishment of the setting is not exactly a separate step in the interviewing process, but it deserves special emphasis. The setting for an interview is of two types, physical and mental.

1. *The physical setting for the interview should be both private and comfortable.* The value in the use of this principle lies in the encouragement of talk on the part of the interviewee. A few firms are taking advantage of the principle of comfort. An individual who is sitting in a comfortable padded chair has a tendency to relax and talk more freely, thus providing more and truer information for the interviewer to evaluate.

2. *The mental setting should be one of rapport.* An initial effort should be made by the interviewer to establish an atmosphere of ease. Instead of plunging directly into the business at hand, some seemingly idle conversation should take place first. Some interviewers still use the weather as the favorite ice breaker; others utilize more specialized subjects gained from a reading of the interviewee's application blank. The interviewer must be aware of nonverbal behavior. Impatience, irritation, hostility, and resentment can be conveyed by body language. If one seldom smiles and always keeps a physical barrier between oneself and the interviewee, very little rapport will be established.

Conduct of the interview   This is the step in the process where most of the action takes place. It is here that we obtain the information desired and supply the facts that the interviewee wants to know.

1. *The interviewer should possess and demonstrate a basic liking and respect for people.* This principle is considered by some to be the most fundamental in interviewing. It is not a specific rule to follow but, rather, a fundamental philosophy. The interviewer who likes to talk with people and is truly interested in them will find out the most about them. He or she creates a general atmosphere which leads the interviewee to open up.

2. *Questions should be asked in a manner that encourages the interviewee to talk.* Instead of asking if the person being interviewed has trouble getting along with supervisors, the interviewer should ask what type of supervisor the interviewee would like to work for and why. Questions that can be answered by "yes" or "no" are not the type that will reveal the true nature of the applicant. Examples of employment interview question are given in Figure 7-6. In addition, some interviewers use "simulation questions," such as, "Your spouse and two teenage children are sick in bed with a cold; there are no relatives or friends available to look in on them; your shift starts in 3 hours; what would you do?"[30] It is possible to establish scoring keys for answers that are weighted in terms of the behavior desired by the organization.

3. *Listen attentively and, if possible, projectively.* At the very least the interviewee must have the full attention of the interviewer. Marginal listening not only prevents the obtaining of full information but is insulting to the interviewee. One cannot successfully fake attentive listening.

   To understand fully the meaning of what is being said by the interviewee, projective listening is required. The interviewer who can listen much faster than the interviewee can talk must utilize that time by attempting to project into the position of the interviewee. This will require an imaginative study of the personal background of the individual as revealed by his application blank. Projection does not necessarily mean that the interviewer must agree with everything that is said. One still must retain a measure of objectivity by means of which the applicant and her or his capabilities can be assessed.

Close   Some have compared this interview to a situation of controlled polite conversation. Civility makes certain requirements—for instance, that the interview should open and run smoothly, without awkwardness and embarrassment. There is a similar requirement for its close.

---

[30]Gary P. Latham, Lise M. Saari, Elliott D. Pursell, and Michael A. Campion, "The Situational Interview," *Journal of Applied Psychology,* vol 65, no. 4, August, 1980, p. 424.

FIGURE 7-6
159

Recruitment and
Hiring

FIGURE 7-6
Sample Questions in Employment Interviews

Basic Attitudes

1 What caused you to consider leaving your present job?
2 What part of your last job did you like best?
3 If you could have changed your last job, what particular things would you have wanted changed?
4 What do you consider to be your greatest achievement?
5 What is the most difficult situation that you have ever faced?
6 How do you spend your spare time?

Specific Skills

1 You say that you have conducted training sessions ...
   a What types of employees were involved?
   b How did you handle hostile participants?
   c What learning concepts did you use in designing the session?
2 You say that you have supervised other people ...
   a What types of jobs did your subordinates have?
   b In terms of education and experience, what type of subordinates did you have?
   c What was your greatest concern? How did you handle it?

Ambitions

1 If you could write your own job description, what would it look like?
2 What do you eventually want to do in your career?
3 Where do you hope to be in five years? ten years?

Adaptibility

1 This job requires extensive traveling and you may be away from home one week out of four. What experience have you had with this type of situation?
2 This job requires you to be here promptly at 8 a.m. every day and to stay late frequently. What type of hours have you worked in the past?
3 This job requires you to handle confidential information. Have you had this type of experience before? How did you handle it?

---

1. *The interviewer should make some overt sign to indicate the end of the interview.* One of the problems often mentioned by applicants is that they are never sure when the interview is ended. In employment situations, the interviewer has a definite responsibility for bringing the conversation smoothly to a close and so indicating in some obvious manner, thus enabling the interviewee to make a reasonably poised exit. The interviewer may lay a pencil down, push back a chair, stand up, or do any of a number of things to indicate that the conversation is coming to a close. The interviewee is often highly appreciative of such signs, particularly after having been caught in embarrassing situations in the past.

   With reference to the requirements for civility, the above principles are applicable to most employment-interviewing situations. Some firms, however, employ the "stress" interview and purposefully place the interviewee in demanding and embarassing situations in order to observe the person's resulting behavior. In this type of interview, many of the above-cited principles are not applicable. The stress interview should be used, however, only where the job specification justifies its use as a technique of selection.

2. *The interviewee should be given some type of answer or indication of future action.* One should not be left hanging in the air, wondering what, if anything, happens next. This is true even for the processing of gripes and grievances, when

the supervisor is not in a position to give a definite answer. In such a case the complainants should be told of the steps that will be undertaken to provide an answer, and, if possible, another interview should be scheduled to communicate the results.

In employment interviewing, any one of several things can happen. The applicant can be accepted, in which case she or he is informed of further employment processing. Or the applicant can be rejected for not measuring up to the job specification. Many prefer to avoid a face-to-face rejection and rely upon more impersonal means, such as a letter. Others prefer to speak frankly to interviewees and inform them of the rejection and of the reasons for it.

Evaluation   When the door closes, the interviewer must immediately undertake the task of evaluating the candidate while the details are fresh in mind. If notes have not been previously taken, details should be recorded now. If a rating sheet has been provided for the structured interview, entries and supporting information should be entered. Some decision must be reached concerning the applicant.

In addition to evaluating the candidate, the interviewer should always evaluate herself or himself at this point. Interviewing is largely an art, the application of which can be improved through practice.

Approval by the Supervisor

Following the outlined procedure, we should now be of the opinion that a candidate who has successfully completed all steps thus far should be hired. At this point in the process, a third interview is conducted. The information objectives of this interview may well overlap those of the preceding one. This overlap is not undesirable for at least two reasons. First, the organizational relationships often require that the supervisor be given the right to pass upon personnel; otherwise he or she cannot be held accountable for their performance. Thus we preserve the equality of authority and responsibility. Second, the qualities that are generally appraised in an interview are highly intangible, such as personality, ability to get along with others, and leadership potential. In such matters it is helpful to have an appraisal by both the staff employment interviewer and the supervisor, who is better acquainted with the actual job conditions and the type of personnel at present in the department.

In executing the personnel unit screening functions, the emphasis tends to be more on formal qualifications and general suitability. When the supervisor takes over, the emphasis tends to switch toward more specifically job oriented worker characteristics such as training and relevant past experience.

Physical Examination

The physical examination is an employment step found in most businesses. It can vary from a very comprehensive examination and matching of an applicant's physical capabilities to job requirements, to a simple check of general physical appearance and well-being. In the hiring procedure the physical examination has at least three basic objectives. First, it serves to ascertain the applicant's physical capabilities. Can the applicant work standing up? Can a 10-pound weight be lifted? Is his or her eyesight sufficiently keen to meet the job requirements? This is a particularly important step when hiring the physically handicapped.

The second objective of the examination is to protect the company against unwarranted claims under workers' compensation laws, or against lawsuits for damages.[31] As lawsuits are won, physical examinations change. In recent years, employees have won settlements for loss of hearing even though no lost time occurred on the job. If a record of a new employee's physical condition at the time of entry does not exist, a claim could possibly be filed for injuries greater than were incurred after starting to work.

A final objective of the physical examination is to prevent communicable diseases from entering the organization. It is obvious that this is a continuing objective and will constitute part of the regular work load of a medical department after personnel are hired and placed.

Induction

If the physical examination has been passed successfully, the employee is hired. The examination is the last step at which a rejection can be made, and thus it is the actual end of the selection process. The induction function, however, immediately follows and is generally considered to be a part of the hiring procedure.

Induction is concerned with the problem of introducing or orienting a new employee to the organization. Inasmuch as various firms report that over half of their voluntary resignations occur within the first 6 months, proper orientation can do much to reduce this problem and its accompanying costs.

All organizations have some type of formal or informal induction program. A survey of 196 companies revealed that 56 percent had organized formal programs.[32] The first phase is usually conducted by the staff personnel unit. Subjects covered include products of the company, employee benefits, salary schedules, safety, probationary period, time recording and absences, holidays, equal employment opportunity programs, parking, and the grievance procedure. Research has shown that providing a realistic preview of the organization, as compared with a sales indoctrinational pitch, will reduce the number of voluntary resignations. In a controlled experiment with 80 newly hired telephone operators, half were shown a 15-minute film of the traditional type—mostly good information about the company.[33] The other half were given a 15-minute film containing both good and bad information about the job and company. Those given the realistic film had a slightly higher survival rate in the job. Reasons proposed for this favorable effect include (1) greater self-selection among applicants who withdraw, (2) lower initial expectations about the job and organization, (3) more information to enable the new hire to cope, and (4) more positive new hire attitudes because of an atmosphere of honesty presented by the firm. Reviews of eleven studies show little support for each explanation, but generally demonstrate small improvements in survival rates.[34] The greater effect was in connection with more complex jobs.

---

[31]See Chapter 22.

[32]American Society for Personnel Administration—The Bureau of National Affairs, Inc., "Employee Orientation Programs," *Bulletin to Management, No. 1436*, Aug. 25, 1977.

[33]John P. Wanous, "Tell It Like It Is at Realistic Job Previews," *Personnel*, vol. 52, no. 4, July-August 1975, p. 55.

[34]Richard R. Reilly, Barbara Brown, Milton R. Blood, and Carol Z. Malatesta, "The Effects of Realistic Previews: A Study and Discussion of the Literature," *Personnel Psychology*, vol. 34, no. 4, Winter 1981, p. 830.

It has also been demonstrated that "work previews" contribute to the survival rate. A work preview is a realistic sample of the type of work actually done on the job in question. The survival rates for life insurance sales personnel were significantly increased when inductees were required to learn a sales talk and go into the field to experience the sales process. The survival rate in one agency moved from 14 to 52 percent after 1 year, and from 29 to 40 percent in another.[35]

The second phase of most organized induction programs is performed by the immediate supervisor. The inductee is introduced to fellow employees, given a tour of the department, and informed about such details as locker and rest rooms, supply procedures, hours of work, overtime, call-in procedures, rest and lunch periods, and lunching facilities. Research has again substantiated the benefits of doing a thorough job in this category, as well.

In a study of 405 operators at Texas Instruments, it was discovered that the first days on the job were anxious and disturbing ones.[36] A special experimental induction program was devised with the specific goals of assuring new hires that their chances of success were good, asking them to disregard the hazing games of older employees, and encouraging them to approach their supervisors with questions and problems. As indicated in Figure 7-7, the experimental group achieved a competence level during the second month of training, as compared with the fourth month for a control group that had been inducted in the more traditional manner. It was concluded that the reduction in anxiety accounted for the entire gap between the two curves.

The complete induction program will provide for phase three—a follow-up some weeks later. This interview, conducted by either the supervisor or a personnel specialist, is concerned with (1) employee satisfaction with the job and organization, and (2) supervisor satisfaction with the employee. Dissatisfactions may be cleared up by explanations or actual transfers to a different job. In any event, the interest in the employee evidenced by the mere act of having a follow-up interview will help to increase the level of employee satisfaction.

[35]Michael A. Raphael, "Work Previews Can Reduce Turnover and Improve Performance," *Personnel Journal*, vol. 54, no. 2, February 1975, p. 97.

[36]Earl R. Gomersall and M. Scott Myers, "Breakthrough in On-the-Job Training," *Harvard Business Review*, vol. 44, no. 4, July-August 1966, pp. 62–72.

FIGURE 7-7 Mastery attainment by experimental and control groups. (*Source: Earl R. Gomersall and M. Scott Myers, "Breakthrough in On-the-job Training,"* Harvard Business Review, *vol. 44, no. 4, July-August 1966, p. 69.*)

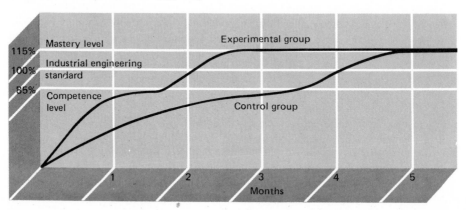

A hiring procedure works best on a foundation provided by job analysis, labor budgeting, and recruitment. Job analysis, through a job specification, tells us the kind of person that is necessary to fulfill properly the responsibilities of the job. An analysis of work load and of the characteristics of the present work force enables us to budget or plan our work-force requirements from the standpoint of number. Skillful recruitment provides a number of reasonably satisfactory job applicants. Thus, knowing what kind of people we want and how many are to be hired, we can choose from the available job applicants.

The selection or hiring procedure is basically a series of personnel studies. We are attempting to discover the qualifications and characteristics of the job applicant. Each step in the sequence should contribute new information. Information objectives should be assigned to the step that can best extract that type of data. A preliminary interview can do little but effect a "meat-ax" type of selection—elimination of the obviously unfit. The application blank can elicit more factual information. A reference check can provide the experience of others. Psychological tests can measure such qualities as intelligence and aptitude. To the interview is assigned a number of difficult objectives. If we can obtain information in no other way, we will usually attempt to obtain it through an interview.

The supervisory interview can also make a contribution toward successful selection and placement by adding the specialized, on-the-job knowledge of the department head. The physical examination enables us to match the applicant's physical capabilities with the job requirements. Though induction is not actually a step in selection, it is *always* the final step in the hiring process. Proper orientation and introduction, both in general for the company and specifically for the workplace, can be justified on a dollars-and-cents basis.

BRIEF CASE

Joan Johns applied for a job of clerk-typist in a small manufacturing firm. She did not complete several parts of the application blank, and demanded to speak to the personnel manager. In talking with him, she particularly protested answering the following:

1. Do you rent or own your own home?
2. Have you ever changed your name? If so, from what?
3. Are you married?
4. What are the ages of your children if any?
5. Height? Weight?

Joan protested that the above items were none of the company's business. The personnel manager said that it was company policy that all blanks on the application must be filled if the person is to be considered for employment.

Questions

1. For each of the items, provide a rationale for the company to justify asking the question.
2. Are any of these questions illegal? Why or why not?

DISCUSSION QUESTIONS

1. In determining numerically whether or not an organization's hiring practices result in adverse impact upon protected groups, what particular approaches can be used?

2. In applying the 80 percent rule, what is the definition of an "applicant?" How do employers and the EEOC differ? Why?

3. What is the "bottom line" rule and what is its relation to professional personnel practices? to government policy?

4. What is a weighted application blank? How does one go about the process of setting one up? Is it legal?

5. Discuss the accuracy of the employment interview. What causes inaccuracy? What can we do about it?

6. How many interviews were specified in the procedure presented in this chapter? What are the goals of each?

7. Outline the total framework of the procurement function, indicating major components and their interrelationship.

8. What is a "realistic job preview?" What impact does it have on survival rates? Why?

9. What does the reference step of the hiring procedure have to do with the right to privacy? What rights to privacy do employees have?

10. Indicate ways in which the recruiting process can be evaluated.

SUPPLEMENTARY READING

ARVEY, RICHARD D. and JAMES E. CAMPION: "The Employment Interview: A Summary and Review of Recent Literature," *Personnel Psychology,* vol. 35, no. 2, Summer 1982, pp. 281–322.

FELTON, BARBARA and SUE RIES LAMB: "A Model for Systematic Selection Interviewing," *Personnel,* vol. 59, no. 1, January-February 1982, pp. 40–48.

GORLIN, HARRIET: "An Overview of Corporate Personnel Practices," *Personnel Journal,* vol. 61, no. 2, February 1982, pp. 125–130.

LAWRENCE, DANIEL G., BARBARA L. SALSBURG, JOHN G. DAWSON, and ZACHARY D. FASMAN: "Design and Use of Weighted Application Blanks," *The Personnel Administrator,* vol. 27, no. 3, March 1982, pp. 47–53.

NOVIT, MITCHELL S.: "Employer Liability for Employee Misconduct: Two Common Law Doctrines," *Personnel,* vol. 59, no. 1, January-February 1982, pp. 11–19.

REILLY, RICHARD R. and GEORGIA T. CHAO: "Validity and Fairness of Some Alternative Employee Selection Procedures," *Personnel Psychology,* vol. 35, no. 1, Spring 1982, pp. 1–62.

chapter 8

Psychological Tests and Identification of Management Talent

Ever since Hugo Munsterberg fathered the field of industrial psychology at the beginning of this century, psychological testing has occupied a prominent place in personnel management. Munsterberg identified his role as helping to find employees best suited to a job and determining under what psychological conditions the greatest output per person could be achieved.[1] The seeming precision of the measurement process being applied to humans fitted very well into the philosophies of scientific managers.

In this chapter, we shall briefly survey the complex field of psychological testing in order to indicate its place and importance in personnel procurement. Emphasis will be given to the influence of government inasmuch as this particular selection device has probably received the greatest amount of attention from the various regulatory agencies. We conclude with a discussion of techniques of identifying one particular type of person, a potential manager for the organization.

PSYCHOLOGICAL TESTS

An employment test is an instrument designed to measure selected psychological factors. The purpose of this measurement process, at least in business, is to enable one to predict what a person will do in the future. Actually we are measuring what we feel to be a representative sample of human behavior and utilizing that measurement to predict future behavior. The factors measured are usually of the psychological type, such as ability to reason, capacity for learning, temperament, and specific aptitudes. Usually the term also includes those tests designed to measure certain physical or motor abilities, such as manual dexterity or hand-eye coordination.

---

[1]Claude S. George, Jr., *The History of Management Thought*, Prentice-Hall, Inc., Englewood Cliffs, N.J., 1968, p. 103.

Though the impact of federal regulatory agencies has had a chilling effect upon the use of tests in industry, one survey shows that 63.5 percent of 2,500 organizations make use of tests in hiring and/or promotion.[2] Only 39 percent of firms with fewer than 100 employees reported using tests, as compared with over 60 percent for those with 5,000 or more. Test usage was greatest in transportation, communication, public utilities, and insurance firms, and least in hospitals, manufacturing, and retail stores. Clerical jobs were subjected to the greatest amount of testing; applicants for unskilled hourly jobs were tested least. The most commonly used and important selection device reported in this survey was not the test, but rather the interview.

In the discussion that follows, emphasis will be given to two aspects of a testing program. First, we shall present certain basic testing concepts that are necessary to a successful and governmentally approved program. Second, we shall survey briefly the various types of tests given in industry. The purpose of this survey is to give some conception of the nature of tests and the factors that are being measured. Obviously, no comprehensive listing of the literally thousands of tests being published and sold today could be attempted in a book of this type.[3]

BASIC CONCEPTS OF TESTING

In terms of philosophy, perhaps the first concept should be acceptance of the fact that testing cannot do the job by itself; it is only one part of a comprehensive hiring procedure. There has not been developed as yet any test, or any battery of tests, that can fully capture the complex nature of the human being. Other important concepts follow.

Job analysis basis Since the purpose in testing is to predict future success in a job situation, the beginning point of analysis is obviously the job. What are the basic human qualifications that are required for successful job performance? We must return to the job specification. At this point a decision must be made concerning which of the required characteristics are adaptable to measurement by tests. If we have specified a requirement for a certain level of ability to reason, we can select some type of intelligence test that will measure this characteristic satisfactorily. If we have specified a requirement for some type of capacity for leadership and motivation of others, we must find out whether or not a relevant test is available or can be designed. If an important selection factor cannot be measured by a test, we shall have to measure it by means of some other technique. As government challenges of testing programs are increasing, it is extremely important that such programs rest on a solid foundation of job descriptions and job specifications.

Reliability A second basic concept in testing is to ensure that the test is a reliable instrument. "Reliability" refers to the degree of *consistency* of results obtained. If a test possesses high reliability, a person who is tested a second or third time with the same test under the same conditions will obtain approximately the same score. If the results

---

[2]Prentice-Hall, Inc., American Society for Personnel Administration, *Personnel Management: Policies and Practices,* Prentice-Hall, Inc., Englewood Cliffs, N.J., 1975, p. 658.

[3]For a comprehensive listing of tests, see O. K. Buros, *The Eleventh Mental Measurements Yearbook,* The Gryphon Press, Highland Park, N.J., 1981.

obtained vary drastically, it is doubtful if we are testing anything. Certainly, no decisions can be based on any one of these highly variable scores. If consistent scores are obtained, we are assured that we are measuring something. Whether that measurement is of value in predicting job success is another subject, that of validity.

The degree of reliability can be determined by such techniques as test-retest or split-half correlations. The method of presentation is typically in terms of correlation coefficients. These coefficients range from 0, indicating a complete absence of a relationship between two variables, to 1, which indicates a perfect relationship. If scores on the first test are identical with the retest, the measurement has a reliability of 1. If the scores vary slightly, the coefficient may drop to the .90s. When one considers the nature of reliability, it is obvious that coefficients must be quite high to make the test usable for hiring. Coefficients in the .90s are quite common for these types of tests, and some place the cutoff point, below which the test will not be used, at .85. It will be recalled that the reliabilities of interview evaluation processes are generally much lower.

Validity   Tests used in employment must possess the characteristic of validity. Does the test do what we want it to do? Validity is highly specific in nature. A particular test may be valid for one objective and invalid for another. Thus, by means of job analysis we may have determined that a certain level of intelligence is required for adequate job performance. We select a well-known and valid intelligence test. It has been determined, through previous research, that the selected test is valid for the objective of measuring intelligence. However, we have now *altered* the objective to that of predicting success on a particular job. For this specific purpose, the test's degree of validity is generally much lower, for many other variables influence job success besides intelligence.

Not only is validity specific with respect to objective, but it is also specific with respect to the particular business situation. It has happened that one firm has achieved a measure of validity in using a particular test for predicting future job performance. You have determined that your company has a similar problem, that is, the selection of satisfactory personnel for the same type of job. It is dangerous to assume that the same test will be of equal validity in both situations. The factors which influence job success under certain conditions may not have equal influence under other conditions.

The specific nature of validity leads to an obvious conclusion: one must determine degree of validity for oneself. An employer can generally accept with some assurance the research of others concerning reliability, for this is a determination of the degree of precision that a particular instrument possesses; but with validity, each employer has a somewhat differing set of objectives and situations. Relying upon the claims of other companies or pointing to the reputation of the test designer does not constitute a defense when the testing program is challenged.

The doctrine of situational specificity is currently undergoing attacks by some theorists.[4] It is maintained that though we often find varying validities in similar situations, these variances are caused by such factors as (1) differences in test reliabilities, (2) differences in criterion reliabilities, (3) differences in range of subjects covered, and (4) sampling errors. Regarding the last item, small sample sizes lead to underestimation of the power of the test to predict accurately. With a sample size of 30 to 50, the typical validities reported vary from .25 to .50. Thus, if the test is truly valid, studies with such

---

[4]Frank L. Schmidt and John E. Hunter, "The Future of Criterion-related Validity," *Personnel Psychology*, vol. 33, no. 1, Spring 1980, p. 44.

small samples will detect this only 25 to 50 percent of the time. To obtain the power of .90, one would need 200 to 300 in the sample. It should be noted that the selection guidelines of the EEOC require a minimum sample size of only 30.

As in the case of reliability, validity is often presented in the form of a coefficient of correlation. Perhaps the most popular correlation technique is the Pearson product-moment correlation. The basic assumption underlying this technique is that both the X variable and the Y variable are normally distributed in the population, though not necessarily in the sample. In the example presented in Figure 8-1, the X variable is a test score and the Y variable is a merit rating score. As indicated in the computations, the correlation coefficient for these two variables is a very high .785. It should be noted that we are not only concerned with the reliability of the test, but the accuracy of the criterion, the merit score, as well. One should seek indicators of job performance that are high in reliability. Production output, quality of output, promotions received, number of complaints, accidents, tardiness, attendance, turnover, and training success are all somewhat reliable measures of performance on the job. A recent Supreme Court decision in *Washington v. Davis* accepted success in a well-designed training program as an acceptable criterion, even without evidence that training grades were related to actual job performance. One of the more popular criteria is the general supervisory rating obtained through periodic appraisals. These appraisals are characterized by many of the same sources of unreliability as the interview. As such, they are regarded with suspicion by compliance agencies when they are used as the sole or primary means for validating tests that have disparate impact.

FIGURE 8-1
Example of Pearson Product-Moment Correlation

	Test Score (X)	Merit Score (Y)	X²	Y²	XY
	78	40	6,084	1,600	3,120
	73	50	5,329	2,500	3,650
	70	45	4,900	2,025	3,150
	65	40	4,225	1,600	2,600
	64	44	4,096	1,936	2,816
	59	35	3,481	1,225	2,065
	56	34	3,136	1,156	1,904
	54	40	2,916	1,600	2,160
	51	32	2,601	1,024	1,632
	45	30	2,025	900	1,350
Sums	615	390	38,793	15,566	24,447

$$\text{Correlation } (r) = \frac{n\Sigma XY - (\Sigma X)(\Sigma Y)}{\sqrt{[n\Sigma X^2 - (\Sigma X)^2][n\Sigma Y^2 - (\Sigma Y)^2]}}$$

$$r = \frac{10(24,447) - (615 \cdot 390)}{\sqrt{[10 \cdot 38,793 - 615^2][10 \cdot 15,566 - 390^2]}}$$

$$= \frac{244,470 - 239,850}{\sqrt{[387,930 - 378,225][155,660 - 152,100]}}$$

$$= \frac{4620}{5877.9}$$

$$= .785$$

In conducting validation studies, we can choose between two groups of persons: present employees or new applicants. If present employees are used, the result is termed "concurrent validity" since we are comparing two measures that exist simultaneously in the present. If new applicants constitute the data source, we are developing "predictive validity" since much time elapses between the two measures. Using present employees has the prime advantage of speed; we already have the criterion on job performance and need now only the test score. This measure is considered less desirable than the predictive type since (1) present employees may lack incentive to do well on the test, (2) poorer performers have probably been terminated and better ones promoted resulting in restriction of job performance range, and (3) the disparate effect of past hiring practices may have resulted in the presence of no minority or female employees in the work force. Using new applicants will solve the problem of incentive, as well as provide a wider range of personnel to study. However, the problem of obtaining the criterion has been created. We shall have to hire various types of people, store the test data, and collect job performance measures over an extended period of time.

If a test predicts job performance perfectly, it has a validity coefficient of 1. If, by using the test, we are still operating at no higher level than sheer chance, the correlation is 0. Many years of experience have shown that validity coefficients in hiring seldom exceed .50, and are higher in predicting training success than job success. "Taking all jobs as a whole . . . it can be said that by and large the maximal power of tests to predict success in training is of the order of .50, and to predict success on the job itself is of the order of .35."[5] The range of validity coefficients discovered by Ghiselli in a survey of published research was from .27 to .59 for training criteria and from .16 to .46 for job success criteria. Over the years, there has been little movement toward greater validities.

The reasons for this prediction ceiling lie on both sides; the human being is an open system and works within a larger, varied system. "The same digit span score can be obtained by a strategy of grouping or by a wax-like memory . . . the same score on a verbal analogy test by a good vocabulary or by superior ability to see the relationships. . . ."[6] Thus the same score on a particular test may come from two people using very different basic processes. These processes, rather than the test score, are the basic determinants of training or job success.

On the other side, job success means different things in different environments. In a firm with an authoritarian climate, the "good" employee will be different from the "good" employee in a democratically administered organization. In addition, various research studies have *not* shown specific types of behavior to be always successful. In the same organization, it is entirely possible that both autocratic supervisors and permissive superiors will achieve the same results as measured by quantity and quality of output. Thus, the other half of the equation, the criterion of job success, also contributes to the creation of a prediction ceiling.

The relationship between test scores and criteria of job success can be presented in other ways than coefficients. Figure 8-2 portrays this information by means of a scatter diagram. Such a diagram is of assistance in determing the critical score required to pass the test. If we place the minimum acceptable score on the test at 30 and the minimum

---

[5]E. E. Ghiselli, *The Validity of Occupational Aptitude Tests,* John Wiley and Sons, Inc., New York, 1966, p. 125.

[6]Edward A. Rundquist, "The Prediction Ceiling," *Personnel Psychology,* vol. 22, no. 2, Summer 1969, p. 11.

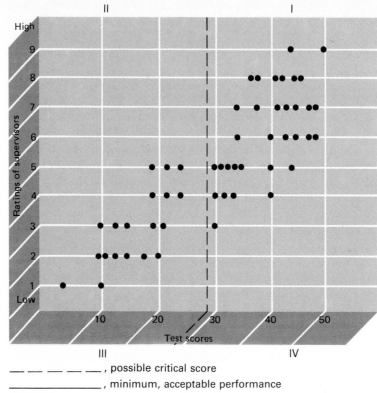

_ _ _ _ _ , possible critical score

_____ , minimum, acceptable performance

FIGURE 8-2 Scatter diagram of test scores and supervisory ratings.

acceptable performance rating at 5, Figure 8-2 can be formed into four quadrants as follows:

- Quadrant I   — 28 true positives
- Quadrant II — 3 false negatives
- Quadrant III — 16 true negatives
- Quadrant IV — 5 false positives

The efficiency of the test under these circumstances can be determined by summing Quadrants I and III (44) and dividing by the total (52), resulting in an index of 85 percent. Though this sounds very good, it can only be compared with the *base rate,* which can be developed by determining the percentages of good employees that would have been hired were there no screening tests. The base rate is developed by summing Quadrants I and II (31), dividing by the total (52), and deriving a base rate of 60 percent. Thus, our use of the test has resulted in a hiring improvement from 60 percent to 85 percent.

TESTING AND THE LAW

As indicated in preceding chapters, Title VII of the Civil Rights Act of 1964 prohibits discrimination in employment because of race, color, religion, sex, or national origin. Psychological testing, perhaps because of its presumed objectivity, has received a substantial amount of challenge and criticism by aggrieved applicants and federal agencies. In one year, 20 percent of the complaints filed under Title VII concerned the use of tests, two-thirds of which were decided in favor of the aggrieved. Agencies have received substantial backing from various federal courts, such as *Griggs v. Duke Power Company,* wherein the Supreme Court not only declared a high school diploma stipulation illegal because of unproved relationship to job performance, but also directed its verdict toward similar use of the Wonderlic Personnel Test and the Bennett Test of Mechanical Comprehension. In 1973, a federal district court ordered Detroit Edison to pay $4 million and Local 223, Utility Workers of America, to pay $250,000 in punitive damages to blacks victimized by union-supported company practices in hiring. In addition, the company was ordered to increase the number of black employees from 8 percent to 30 percent, and to halt the use of intelligence and aptitude tests that worked to exclude blacks with no substantiating validation data.

The thrust of both agencies and the courts is to require personnel managers to provide validating proof of the effectiveness of procurement practices. Among various guidelines established, perhaps the foremost one concerns the manner of establishing validity. *Empirical statistical validity,* showing a significant relationship between the predictor and specific measures of job performance, has been the preferred approach. Within this category, "predictive validity" studies on incoming applicants are deemed to be better evidence. If "concurrent validity" based on present employees is utilized, there may be no representative groups of minorities among the work force.

Though formerly deemed less desirable than empirical studies, the Uniform Guidelines on Employee Selection issued in 1978 have elevated *content* and *construct* validities to equal status. In content validity, the test itself must be a representative sample of the domain of job duties, such as a typing test for a clerk, or a welding test for a welder. To utilize this defense, the firm must present (1) comprehensive job descriptions, (2) explanation of the rationale of test and job content, (3) evidence of soundness of test construction, and (4) the manner in which minimum passing scores are determined. Thus, the determination of content validity is fundamentally a judgmental process concerned with the adequacy of a test as a sample of job activities.

The development of construct validity requires both judgmental and statistical processes. In the judgment of a manager, based on job analysis, a particular trait or construct, such as spatial relations, stress tolerance, or empathy, is deemed necessary for job performance. Evidence of a statistical nature is now needed to prove that a particular test is valid for measuring that construct. This evidence comes from an accumulation of many studies by various organizations in the testing field to prove its validity.

In all statistical studies of validities, the compliance agencies expect the correlation coefficients to be significant at the .05 level, that is, where there is only one chance in twenty that the correlation was obtained by chance. In a previously cited survey, only about two out of ten smaller companies had conducted validation studies, as compared with two out of three firms with over 10,000 employees.[7] Twenty-eight percent reported that such validation studies cost more than $5,000 per job studied.

There is some evidence that the U.S. Supreme Court is beginning to reject the rigid preference for predictive criterion-related validities that has received such strong support in the past. In *Tyler v. Vickery,* the Court refused to review a decision made by a lower court that allowed continued use of the Georgia bar examination even though no evidence existed concerning correlations of scores and performance as a lawyer. In *U.S. v. State*

[7]Prentice-Hall, Inc., American Society for Personnel Administration, op. cit., pp. 669–677.

of North Carolina, teacher certification was authorized on the basis of the National Teacher Examinations even though there was no empirical evidence that knowledge tested was necessary for effective teaching. And in *Washington v. Davis*, the Supreme Court accepted training success as a proper criterion. All three tests had disparate effects upon minority groups. The general thrust seems to be one of looking at all evidence, judgmental as well as statistical, in declaring a selection device to be valid.

TYPES OF TESTS

Various ways of classifying psychological tests bring out and emphasize certain characteristics. Tests may be taken by pen or pencil or by trying out through performance, such as a typing test. Most tests have time limits and are designated "speed" tests; while others, classified as "power" tests, have no time limit but questions asked become progressively more difficult. Tests may also be classified by the type of questions, such as objective, descriptive, or projective. For the present purpose of briefly sketching the nature of psychological testing in business, we may classify the various methods as (1) intelligence tests, (2) aptitude tests, (3) achievement tests, (4) interest tests, and (5) personality tests.

Intelligence tests   The intelligence test is probably the most widely administered standardized test in industry. It is also one of the first types developed by psychologists. Intelligence has been given various definitions. One of the first intelligence tests, the Binet-Simon, assumed that intelligence was a general trait, a capacity for comprehension and reasoning. Thurstone later differentiated primarily mental abilities from the general trait of intelligence and created more specialized types of intelligence tests; they were reasoning, word fluency, verbal comprehension, numbers, memory, and space.[8] The Wechsler-Bellevue Intelligence Scale utilizes a multiple measurement of such factors as digit spans both forward and backward, information known, comprehension, vocabulary, picture arrangement, and object assembly.

Various reviews of studies have shown varying validities depending upon the type of job. Validity coefficients tend to be higher when selecting skilled workers, supervisors, and clerical workers. They are substantially lower in predicting job success for unskilled workers and sales clerks. The fact that average validity coefficients for intelligence tests in selecting skilled workers are higher than those for selecting supervisors does not mean that the former are more intelligent than the latter. Rather, it indicates that the supervisory job involves a much larger domain of activities, and though intelligence is required it is not sufficient to insure success. One author suggests for managers a baseline level of 120 IQ as measured by the Weschler Adult Intelligence Scale.[9]

Intelligence tests, though among the more widely used, have come under serious attack as discriminating against minority-group members with little or no validation being effected. The general measure, in particular, suffers from imprecision. For example, occupants of both drafting and secretarial types of jobs tend to have about equal scores

---

[8]L. L. Thurstone and T. G. Thurstone, "Factorial Studies of Intelligence," *Psychometric Monograph*, no. 2, University of Chicago Press, 1941, p. 37.

[9]Charles Bahn, "Can Intelligence Tests Predict Executive Competence?" *Personnel*, vol. 56, no. 4, July-August 1979, p. 58.

on general intelligence tests. However, those in drafting tend to have higher component scores in spatial relations and numbers, while those holding secretarial positions have higher component scores in perceptual speed and verbal fluency. Thus, the general intelligence test may prove to be too dull a tool to utilize for procurement in a society that proposes to eliminate inadvertent and unintended discrimination.

Aptitude tests   Whereas intelligence is frequently defined as a general trait, an aptitude is a more specific capacity. "Aptitude tests measure whether an individual has the capacity or latent ability to learn a given job if given adequate training."[10] The use of aptitude tests is advisable when an applicant has had little or no experience along the lines of the job opening. We are interested in selecting persons who will show a higher degree of success after the training period.

Examples of specific capacities or aptitudes are as follows: mechanical, clerical, linguistic, musical, and academic. In addition to these examples, some psychologists include in this category certain motor capacities such as finger dexterity, hand dexterity, and hand-eye coordination.

Two of the more widely known mechanical-aptitude tests are the Bennett Test of Mechanical Comprehension and the Stenquist Mechanical Aptitude Test. Questions are asked which fall into the general area of understanding mechanical relationships. Some questions relate to knowledge of actual shop machines, tools, and similar equipment. Others deal with certain practices such as the type of fastener to be used to fasten a board to a box or a hinge on a door. In one study conducted by Tiffin, a correlation of .36 was found between the Bennett Test and a supervisor's ratings of job performance of forty-seven paper-machine operators.[11] Such a correlation was usable in differentiating the better employees by means of the test.

Tests of clerical aptitude deal with questions concerning office vocabulary, arithmetic, spelling, and detail checking. There are many tests in the manipulative and dexterity field. The O'Connor Finger Dexterity Test requires the applicant to place three pins, 1 inch in length and 0.072 inch in diameter, into a hole 0.196 inch in diameter. The holes are spaced ½ inch apart, ten in each row. The reliability of this test has been found to be .98. A correlation obtained with the Otis Test of Mental Ability was .07, thus indicating that these two tests are measuring widely different characteristics.

Achievement tests   Whereas aptitude is a capacity to learn in the future, achievement is concerned with what one has accomplished. When applicants claim to know something, an achievement test is given to measure how well they know it. Trade tests are the most common type of achievement test given. Questions have been prepared and tested for such trades as asbestos workers, punch-press operators, electricians, and machinists. There are, of course, many unstandardized achievement tests given in industry, such as typing or dictation tests for an applicant for a stenographic position. Obviously all tests, aptitude and intelligence included, reflect some degree of achievement on the part of the applicant. If the test—achievement, intelligence, or aptitude—will enable us to predict job success, its specific classification as to type is of secondary importance. With the courts demanding a more demonstrable relationship between test content and job performance, it is predicted that the usage of achievement tests will grow at the expense of the more intangible general intelligence, aptitude, and personality tests.

[10]Joseph Tiffin and Ernest J. McCormick, *Industrial Psychology*, 6th ed., Prentice-Hall, Inc., Englewood Cliffs, N.J., 1974, p. 137.
[11]Ibid., p. 119.

Interest tests   Most people realize that a person who is interested in a job or task will do much better than one who is uninterested. At times superior interest offsets lack of basic ability.

Two of the more widely used tests of interest are the Strong Vocational Interests Blank and the Kuder Preference Record. These tests utilize two basically different approaches. The Strong has been validated in specific occupations; that is, it determines the degree of agreement between the applicant's interests and the interests of successful personnel in specific professions and occupations. The applicant is asked whether he likes, dislikes, or is indifferent to many examples of school subjects, occupations, amusements, peculiarities of people, and particular activities. Patterns of interests have been developed for some sixty occupations, among which are accountant, architect, dentist, engineer, personnel manager, production manager, and teacher. When instructed to fake specific interests, individuals can increase their scores by one to five standard deviations, suggesting extreme caution in the use of the Strong in a selection situation. However, research with respect to the degree of faking that does occur under actual selection conditions indicates that "there is neither a significant nor consistent tendency for applicants to increase their selection scores."[12] Thus, test-taking behavior under artificial faking instructions may not parallel that usually practiced under actual conditions.

The Kuder Preference Record is scored in terms of more basic interest groupings. These areas are mechanical, computational, scientific, persuasive, artistic, literary, musical, social service, and clerical.[13] Techniques of scoring the Preference Record have been developed to differentiate between the honestly answered blanks and those designed to make a good impression. Methods also exist for identifying the carelessly or randomly completed test. Both interests and personality measures are of considerably greater value in counseling situations where the subject is sincerely interested in finding out more about herself or himself in an attempt to solve pressing personal problems.

Personality tests   The importance of personality to job success is undeniable. Often an individual who possesses the intelligence, aptitude, and experience for a certain job has failed because of inability to get along with and motivate other people.

Personality tests are similar to interest tests in that they, also, involve a serious problem of obtaining honest answers. Such tests have been of great use in counseling situations. In the employment situation, however, the applicant is highly motivated to make a good impression. Consequently an applicant is often led to alter answers when that is possible. In one study of the Humm-Wadsworth Temperament Scale, 65 college students were asked to answer the 318 questions on the test as frankly and honestly as possible. After this they were asked to answer as if they were applying for a job. The desirable personality traits showed a marked increase and the undesirable a substantial decrease.[14]

In an attempt to obtain a more realistic assessment of personality, projective tests have been designed. One of the more popular projective tests is the Thematic Apperception Test. The subject is shown a series of pictures, one at a time, and is asked to make up as dramatic a story as he can for each. Examples of such scenes are (1) a short, elderly woman stands with her back turned to a tall young man, and (2) a boy lies on

---

[12]N. M. Abrahams, Idell Neumann, and W. H. Githens, "Faking Vocational Interests: Simulated versus Real Life Motivation," *Personnel Psychology,* vol. 24, no. 1, Spring 1971, pp. 5–12.

[13]*Kuder Preference Record: Vocational,* Science Research Associates, Inc., Chicago, Ill.

[14]Tiffin and McCormick, op. cit., p. 175.

the floor next to a couch with a revolver by his side. The subject is asked to tell what led up to the event, what is happening at the moment, what the characters are feeling and thinking, and what the outcome of the situation will be. The psychologist analyzes the story in terms of such factors as length, vocabulary, cohesiveness, bizarre ideas, plot, mood, and symbols used. The well-known Rorschach test is also projective in technique; the subject is asked to organize unstructured inkblots into meaningful concepts. The resulting projections are analyzed in terms of such factors as use of color and shadings, use of part or the whole of a blot, seeing of movement, and definiteness and appropriateness of forms seen. An integrated picture of the subject's personality is then formulated. The use of all personality tests, whether of the projective or questionnaire types, requires the service of a trained psychologist.

Surveys of the testing literature reveal lower levels of validity for personality tests as compared with intelligence tests. The range of reported validities varies from .15 to .40. Many feel more confident with projections based on biographical data obtained through more sophisticated application blanks.

TO TEST OR NOT TO TEST

In determining whether or not to test, there are other factors besides the surveillance of compliance agencies and the threat of court actions. If, for example, there is a selection ratio of one applicant to one opening, testing will not be necessary. Also of concern is the range of performance existing in the presently untested group of employees. If the best performer is ten times as good as the worst, testing can make a material contribution in screening future applicants. If the work environment is closely structured, as in the case of an assembly line operation, the performance range may well be one of 10 to 9. Testing in this situation is not likely to improve hiring effectiveness. Haire points out that if the selection ratio is 10 to 4 (10 applicants for 4 openings), if the test's validity coefficient is .45, and if the range of performance among present personnel is a not unusual 3 to 2, the improvement in hiring effectiveness will be about 4 percent.[15] He suggests that performance improvements through good training and supervision of unscreened personnel could easily be 30 to 40 percent, thus downgrading the role of selecting in comparison with subsequent training and supervision. Where the range of possible performance qualities is great, such as in executive and management positions, screening through testing can easily improve placement effectiveness as much as 10 to 15 percent.

William H. Whyte, Jr. suggests that testing, particularly personality testing, constitutes an invasion of privacy. In his popular book, *The Organization Man,* he provides a psychological set to enable the applicant to pass any personality questionnaire, thereby evading the firm's invasion of his privacy.[16]

Research concerning the seriousness of the invasion of privacy contention does not indicate that it is a widespread, general phenomenon. It is more a matter of significant subgroupings. In one study, younger females expressed annoyance at 35 out of a total

[15]Mason Haire, *Psychology in Management,* 2nd ed., McGraw-Hill Book Company, New York, 1964, p. 135.

[16]William H. Whyte, Jr., *The Organization Man,* Doubleday & Company, Inc., Garden City, N.Y., 1957, pp. 449–456.

of 361 questions; older males found all but 4 questions to be acceptable.[17] In a second study of approximately 1,400 subjects, more precise patterns were encountered: (1) older employees were less concerned about questions concerning values and interests than were younger, (2) the more educated were less concerned about personal history items but more concerned with questions about personal finances, and (3) female employees were less concerned with personal financial inquiries but more concerned with topics involving personal history data.[18] Greatest general sensitivity was experienced with questions concerning religious beliefs, racial or ethnic background, description of brothers and sisters, loans being paid, savings, other sources of income, and how income is budgeted. It should be recalled that inquiries about the first two items are prohibited by law.

Others are concerned about the use of polygraphs or lie detectors in attempts to verify information provided on the application blank without the necessity of undertaking a background check. Sometimes the applicant, faced with a week's delay before beginning work, and the organization, faced with an expensive background check, will both agree to quicker and cheaper polygraph checks on the accuracy of the information given. Such tests are also used for making periodic security spot checks in organizations where theft is likely, as well as in situations where a specific investigation of a theft is being undertaken. The Zale Corporation, a retail jewelry chain, reports that 10 to 15 percent of applicants for positions in that organization fail to pass the polygraph test.[19]

The typical polygraph examination lasts 45 minutes to an hour, but the candidate is connected to the instrument for only 5 to 10 minutes. Changes in breathing, blood pressure, and perspiration are measured by various sensors attached to the body. Reputable examiners will go over each question to be asked prior to that time the polygraph is turned on. Such questions as the following are asked: (1) are the statements on your application blank true?, (2) have you ever stolen from a previous employer?, (3) do you use drugs?, (4) have you ever committed a serious crime?, and (5) do you currently have a serious illness? The candidate is cautioned to be honest about having taken pencils and supplies from the office, as well as mildly padding expense accounts. After the test, the subject is shown the results and given the opportunity to explain unusual reactions, such as "oh yes, I once used the office postage meter for my Christmas cards." The test is then repeated with these additional stipulations phrased into the questions. Subjects should refuse to answer questions not pertaining to the job application, such as religion, politics, marriage, sexual activities, and so on.

The use of polygraphs in employment has been objected to on the basis of invasion of privacy, self-incrimination, violation of human dignity, and questionable accuracy of measurement in the hands of unskilled practitioners. Such testing is opposed in principle by both the American Civil Liberties Union and the American Federation of Labor–Congress of Industrial Organizations. Only nineteen states have polygraph licensing laws stipulating minimum educational and training backgrounds as necessary for operating the device. Fifteen states have laws restricting its use in employment processes.[20] A survey of 143 corporations indicated that 20 percent used the polygraph; the most

[17]Ronald C. Winkler and Theodore W. Mathews, "How Employees Feel about Personality Tests," *Personnel Journal,* vol. 46, no. 8, September 1967, pp. 490–492.

[18]Bernard L. Rosenbaum, "Attitude toward Invasion of Privacy in the Personnel Selection Process and Job Applicant Demographic and Personality Correlates," *Journal of Applied Psychology,* vol. 58, no. 3, December 1973, pp. 333–338.

[19]"Corporate Lie Detectors Come under Fire," *Business Week,* January 13, 1973, p. 88.

[20]Alaska, California, Connecticut, Delaware, Hawaii, Idaho, Maryland, Massachusetts, Minnesota, Montana, New Jersey, Oregon, Pennsylvania, Rhode Island, Washington.

common use was for theft investigation, and the most common industries involved were banking and retail outlets.[21]

Though the justification of any test must first rest on proved contributions to organizational effectiveness, any business practice is subject to veto by society. Labor arbitrators of grievance disputes generally show a considerable distaste for use of polygraphs in disciplinary and discharge cases. Though the employer justifiably is concerned about more effective hiring and prevention of theft and embezzlement, it would appear that the trend in social values may well restrict the choice of screening instruments.

Finally, there is a concern about the possibility of "differential validity," that is, that scores on the same test will mean different things for different cultural groups. It is contended that the makeup and validation of most standard psychological tests have been geared to the majority, white, middle-class segment of our population. As a result, other groups with equal probabilities of job success may produce lower test scores and not be hired. The Uniform Guidelines require graphical presentation of cutoff scores in order to ascertain their impact upon separate groups of employees.

In a study reported by Lopez, three selection instruments were used to screen applicants for the job of toll collector; there were a clerical speed and accuracy test, a mental ability test, and a standardized 10-minute biographical data interview.[22] Criteria of job success used in the validation process were absence rates, toll-accuracy rate, continued employment, and supervisor's ratings. In the study of 182 toll collectors, it was found that black applicants achieved significantly lower scores on the mental ability test and the interviewer's rating sheet. However, there was *no* significant difference in job performance between white and black employees. On other criteria, high scores on the predictors meant poor attendance, high toll accuracy, and high turnover for blacks, and only poor toll accuracy and high turnover for the white group. If the supervisory rating is used as a single criterion, the two tests were predictive of job success for the whites but showed no significant relationship, pro or con, for the black group. The interview was predictive for black job success but showed no relationship for the white group. It is apparent that different hiring practices could be justified depending upon the groupings utilized.

Despite the Uniform Guidelines and much publicity, some researchers have indicated that the jury is still out on the issue. Of 297 instances in which some validity was obtained in studies involving black and white persons, only 8.1 percent were cases of differential validity.[23] When comparing the rigor of the research methodologies followed, the cases of differential validity were accorded lower methodological ratings in the selection of the criterion and similarity between predictor and criterion. Two reviewers of research stated "as a general rule, most studies showing *lack* of differential validity have used better than average criterion measures, while most of the studies supporting differential validity rely on subjective, poorly determined rating criteria."[24] Nevertheless, even if true differential validities are not as widespread as reported, even the occasional instance can have undesirable social repercussions. Probably few personnel programs have ever been harmed from over research.

---

[21]John A. Belt and Peter B. Holden, "Polygraph Usage among Major U.S. Corporations," *Personnel Journal,* vol. 57, no. 2, February 1978, p.82.

[22]Felix M. Lopez, Jr., "Current Problems in Test Performance of Job Applicants," *Personnel Psychology,* vol. 19, no. 1, Spring 1966, pp. 10–18.

[23]Virginia R. Boehm, "Differential Prediction: A Methodological Artifact?" *Journal of Applied Psychology,* vol. 62, no. 2, April 1977, pp. 146–154.

[24]D. W. Bray and J. L. Moses, "Personnel Selection," *Annual Review of Psychology,* vol. 23, 1972, pp. 545–576.

IDENTIFICATION OF MANAGEMENT TALENT

Though much of psychological testing is devoted to predicting success in the immediate job, the organization is also concerned with predicting future potential, particularly with respect to managerial jobs. In general the research has taken two directions: (1) a determination of significant personal characteristics or behavior that seem to presage future success, and (2) the establishment of clinically oriented assessment centers modeled somewhat after the Office of Strategic Services Assessment Program of World War II.

Early Identification through Characteristics

Since the managerial development process consumes extended periods of time, it would be helpful to identify particular human talents that give rise to potential managerial success. One early measure that can be assessed is performance in college as measured by grades. Two research programs of the American Telephone and Telegraph Company found a definite relationship between grades in college and salary level achieved.[25] In the 1960 study of 10,000 managers, 51 percent of those in the top tenth of their college class were located in the top third of the salary levels in the company. The correlation between grades and salaried level was .33; in the earlier study of 1,300 managers, it was .37. In a study of top managers at General Electric, it was found that individuals who received salary increases of 30 percent or more at least once in a single year had a much higher probability of reaching the top within this company.[26] Such increases reflected one or more rewards for outstanding behavior.

One of the earliest research programs, undertaken by Sears, Roebuck in 1942, resulted in the development of a number of significant characteristics and attitudes that were associated with successful managerial performance.[27] Among these were a marked preference for orderly thought, overt and even aggressive self-confidence, a leaning toward "number-related tasks," personal values of a practical and economic nature, and high general activity. The Sears researchers used a battery of standard tests, and it has been discovered that though the test scores of the same person can differ significantly until the age of 30 is reached, thereafter personality tends to stabilize and test results show little change. A study of 443 managers of Standard Oil of New Jersey attempted to relate job success to measurements produced by such devices as a general intelligence test, a nonverbal reasoning test, personality tests, an individual background survey, a management judgment test, a self-performance report, and an attitude inventory.[28] The most significant relationships were found between the background survey (.64) and the management judgment test (.51). The latter test described managerial problems and

---

[25]F. R. Kappel, "From the World of College to the World of Work," *Bell Telephone Magazine,* Spring 1962, pp. 3–21.

[26]Lawrence L. Ferguson, "Better Management of Managers' Careers," *Harvard Business Review,* vol. 44, no. 2, March-April 1966, p. 146.

[27]*Research toward the Development of a Multiple Assessment Program for Executive Personnel,* Sears, Roebuck, and Co., Psychological Research and Services Section, June 1965.

[28]*A Summary of the Early Identification of Management Potential Research Project,* Standard Oil Co. of New Jersey, Social Science Research Division, Employee Relations Department, August 1961.

presented several choices for action or decision. The least valuable predictive device was the personality test. The criteria for job success included the organization level of job held, salary, and general ratings.

Moving from abilities that could possibly signal success in management, Miner proposes that motivation is equally important. Ability is impotent if not accompanied by desire. Research has discovered a steadily decreasing trend in college student motivation to aspire to managerial positions. The measurement scale consists of ascertaining degree of possession of the following attitudes: (1) favorable attitude toward authority, (2) desire to compete, (3) assertive motivation to take charge and make decisions, (4) desire to exercise power, (5) desire for attention of others, and (6) a sense of responsibility.[29] Research has indicated that high scores on these six measures correlate with managerial success. In a study of 61 managers in one oil company, those whom the company "would rehire" had average scores of 8.9, while those whom they would "not rehire" averaged 3.3, a significant difference. In another study, executives who had not been promoted scored 3.7, those promoted one or two levels had 6.2, and those promoted three or more organizational levels scored 8.6. Business managers in general have an average score of 6 points, nonbusiness managers (largely school administrators) score 1 point, while the average scores of 1,400 students in five universities have declined from approximately 4 points to minus 2 points over the period of 1960 to 1972. In research comparing personnel managers with general managers, the former tend to score lower.[30] These motivational measures are designed to predict managerial success in hierarchical organizations. The environments of both colleges and personnel departments tend to be less hierarchical in nature than those in line managerial positions.

Research has also indicated that one's peers are fairly successful in the prediction of future managerial success. Validities tend to run in the .30s and .40s in correlating peer appraisal with future success in training, promotion, and performance. In one particular study, peer appraisals correlated in the .30s with future promotional success for lower managers and future performance success for higher managers.[31] The major factors centered around "impact" (aggressiveness, originality, capacity, and general impression) and "tactfulness" (cooperation, emotional maturity, and perceptiveness). These ratings were gathered during training sessions where conditions were standardized for all and candidates were not in direct competition with each other.

Assessment Centers

The assessment center concept for examining and identifying personnel with potential for managerial success began with the German military in World War II. It spread to Great Britain in the form of a War Office Selection Board, moved to the United States in selecting agents for the Office of Strategic Services, and was finally introduced to American business by the American Telephone and Telegraph Corporation in the mid-1950s. It was estimated that in 1972 there were approximately a dozen large business

[29]John B. Miner, "The Real Crunch in Managerial Manpower," *Harvard Business Review,* vol. 51, no. 6, November-December 1973, p. 148.
[30]John B. Miner, "Levels of Motivation to Manage among Personnel and Industrial Relations Managers," *Journal of Applied Psychology,* vol. 61, no. 4, August 1976, p. 425.
[31]Allen I. Kraut, "Prediction of Managerial Success by Peer and Training-Staff Ratings," *Journal of Applied Psychology,* vol. 60, no. 1, February 1975, p. 17.

firms operating executive assessment centers.[32] Predictions now vary from 2,000 to 4,000 companies being involved with this type of activity.[33]

The two basic purposes of an assessment center are: (1) to make selection and promotion decisions, and (2) to identify strengths and weaknesses of candidates for developmental purposes. Analysis of returns from 64 companies revealed that 48 percent used the center for screening purposes, while 46 percent stated that training and career planning was its dominant purpose.[34] The average yearly costs were placed at $88,000 with the average estimated return being $364,000.

The Third International Congress on the Assessment Center Method set forth certain minimum requirements before a selection procedure could be termed an assessment center.[35] Among these requirements are: (1) multiple assessment techniques must be used; (2) multiple assessors must be used; (3) judgments made must be based on a pooling of information among assessors; (4) an overall evaluation of behavior must be made at

[32]Allen I. Kraut, "Management Assessment in International Organizations," *Industrial Relations,* vol. 12, no. 2, May 1973, p. 175.

[33]Treadway C. Parker, "Assessment Centers: A Statistical Study," *The Personnel Administrator,* vol. 25, no. 2, February 1980, p. 65.

[34]Stephen L. Cohen, "The Bottom Line on Assessment Center Technology," *The Personnel Administrator,* vol. 25, no. 2, February 1980, p. 53.

[35]J. L. Moses et al., "Standards and Ethical Considerations for Assessment Center Operations," Task Force on Development of Assessment Center Standards, Quebec, Canada: Third International Congress on the Assessment Center Method, May 1975.

FIGURE 8-3
Typical Assessment Center Schedule

Day 1:
Orientation of dozen candidates
Break-up into groups of four to play a *management game* (observe and assess organizing ability, financial acumen, quickness of thinking, efficiency under stress, adaptability, leadership).
Psychological testing (measure and assess verbal and numerical abilities, reasoning, interests, and attitudes) and/or *depth interviews* (assess motivation).
Leaderless group discussion (observe and assess aggressiveness, persuasiveness, expository skill, energy, flexibility, self-confidence).

Day 2:
In-basket exercise (observe and assess decision making under stress, organizing ability, memory and ability to interrelate events, preparation for decision making, ability to delegate, concern for others).
Role-playing of employment of performance appraisal interview (observe and assess sensitivity to others, ability to probe for information, insight, empathy).
Group roles in preparation of a budget (observe and assess collaboration abilities, financial acumen, expository skill, leadership, drive).

Day 3:
Individual case analyses (observe expository skill, awareness of problems, background information possessed for problems, typically involving marketing, personnel, accounting, operations, and financial elements).
Obtain *peer ratings* from all candidates.
Staff assessors meet to discuss and rate all candidates.

Weeks later:
Manager, with assessor experience, meets with each candidate to discuss assessment with counseling concerning career guides and areas to develop.

a time separate from the observation of behavior, and (5) simulation exercises must be used.

Figure 8-3 presents a skeleton outline of a typical 2½-day assessment center schedule. A survey of 33 companies reveals that the three most widely used simulations are in-basket exercises (31 firms), business games (30 firms), and leaderless group discussion (31 firms).[36] An in-basket is a set of notes, messages, telephone calls, letters, and reports that the candidate is expected to handle within a period of 1 or 2 hours. The candidate's decisions can be rated by assessors with respect to such abilities as willingness to take action and organizing of interrelated events. A business game is a competitive simulation where teams are required to make decisions concerning production, marketing, purchasing, and finance in competition with each other. The leaderless group discussion simulation involves asking groups of candidates to engage in discussions without having anyone designated as head; for example, each sponsors a subordinate for promotion, utilizing materials supplied concerning the subordinate. Candidates can be observed and measured in such activities as taking the discussion lead, influencing others, summarizing and clarifying, mediating arguments, and speaking effectively. In addition, various other exercises are often designed to fit the firm's particular situation; for instance, J. C. Penney utilizes the Irate Customer Phone Call, made by an assessor, in order to rate the candidate's ability to control emotions, demonstrate tact, and satisfy the complaint.[37] Another example of a specially designed simulation exercise used by Merrill Lynch, Pierce, Fenner and Smith Inc., is shown in Box 8-1. Psychological tests and depth interviewing are frequently used techniques but generally show lower levels of accuracy in predicting future success. Personality tests, in particular, appear to be the weakest predictor.

In determining the predictive accuracy of the assessment center approach, the initial study of AT&T was most impressive. Assessor ratings were not communicated to company management for a period of 8 years in order not to contaminate the results. In a sample of 55 candidates who achieved the middle-management ranks during that period, the center correctly predicted 78 percent of them.[38] Of 73 persons who did *not* progress beyond the first level of management, 95 percent were correctly predicted by the assessment staff. As a result, this company has maintained its centers, processing an average of 10,000 candidates a year. Reviewing ratings and actual progress of 5,943 personnel over a 10-year period demonstrated a validity coefficient of .44 for assessment center predictions.[39]

Continued research supports use of the assessment center in making selection and promotion decisions. Interrater reliabilities range from the .70s to the .80s, while reported validities in predicting future performance range from .30 to .60.[40] It has been found to be effective with female candidates, one study producing *a validity coefficient of .37 for* almost 5,000 females and .44 for almost 9,000 men.[41] The overall assessment rating

[36]Joseph M. Bender, ''What Is 'Typical' of Assessment Centers?'' *Personnel*, vol. 50, no. 4, July-August, 1973, p. 51.

[37]William C. Byham, ''Assessment Centers for Spotting Future Managers,'' *Harvard Business Review*, vol. 48, no. 4, July-August 1970, p. 158.

[38]Douglas W. Bray and Donald L. Grant, ''The Assessment Center in the Measurement of Potential for Business Management,'' *Psychological Monographs*, whole no. 625, vol. 80, no. 17, 1966, p. 24.

[39]James R. Huck, ''Assessment Centers: A Review of the External and Internal Validities,'' *Personnel Psychology*, vol. 26, no. 2, Summer 1973, p. 198.

[40]Wayne F. Cascio and Val Silbey, ''Utility of the Assessment Center as a Selection Device,'' *Journal of Applied Psychology*, vol. 64, no. 2, April 1979, p. 107.

[41]Joseph L. Moses and Virginia R. Boehm, ''Relationship of Assessment-Center Performance to Management Progress of Women,'' *Journal of Applied Psychology*, vol. 60, no. 4, August 1975, p. 529.

BOX 8-1
Going for Broker: Our Man Takes Part in Stock-Selling Test
Lawrence Rout

My "in" basket is brimming with memos and unanswered letters. My desk calendar shows that conflicting appointments haven't been taken care of, and a client may pop in at any moment. Ignoring it all, I call a local industrialist who, I have been told, may be willing to buy some stock.

"You've got to be kidding," he screams when I make my pitch. "Based on your recommendation, my brother lost $97,000 on a $100,000 investment, and now he is going to sue you."

Who me?

Well, sort of. Welcome to the Merrill Lynch account-executive simulation exercise, or, as dubbed by some, the Merrill Lynch stress test. It's a nail-biting three hours filled with alternating despair and satisfaction that leaves many longing for the good old days of calculus finals. Still, whether you leave in frustration or imbued with self-confidence, the exercise can't help but get you keyed up.

"I just can't calm down," says 25-year-old Michael Schrimmer about an hour after the exercise has ended. "It was a real high."

Stakes also High

The stakes are high, too. Those taking part in the simulation, except me, are applicants for the job of account executive, or stockbroker, at Merrill Lynch, Pierce, Fenner & Smith Inc., the nation's largest securities firm. The simulation exercise is designed to gauge how they will perform under conditions similar to those that a real stockbroker faces.

It's a method that is becoming increasingly popular in hiring and promoting. Three years ago, only about 1,000 companies of any sort used simulations; that figure has doubled to about 2,000 today, according to William C. Byham, president of Development Dimensions International Inc., a Pittsburgh-based consulting firm.

Mr. Byham stresses that simulation is only part of a more extensive hiring process. At Merrill Lynch, for in-

stance, the applicants taking the simulation have already undergone a written test and a personal interview.

Neither of those, however, prepares you for the simulation, which works like this:

You have taken over for Frank Jones, a stockbroker who has been transferred to another office. Frank has left you his client book, with individual descriptions of each client's portfolio and investment objectives, a hot-prospect book, and various unanswered letters and memos. There is a constantly changing stock market, news releases every five minutes, research reports and a book describing the stocks and defining the terms used in the game.

The First Half-hour

Sound complicated? It is, especially when it's all thrown at you at once. "The first half-hour was the part that really unnerved me," says Meg Roggensack of Lancaster, Wis., who took the test here on another occasion. "I felt totally out of it."

This time, nine people take the test at a Merrill Lynch office here one night. A tape recording is played throughout the test, giving forth the sounds of a bustling daytime brokerage office. The ticker-tape clicks, salesmen shout.

After a while, the phones start ringing, as three trained Merrill Lynch stockbrokers, holed up in a back room except when they keep appointments with us, play the roles of Frank Jones's clients. Applicants are told to field their requests after explaining that Frank has been transferred.

Even that can confuse the harried stockbroker candidates who are trying to decipher the reams of material on their desks. Just ask Sylvia DeWitt, a 28-year-old jobseeker from Ames, Iowa. When she took the test and her first caller asked for Frank Jones, Mrs. DeWitt put the receiver down, looked around the room and asked: "Anybody here named Frank Jones?"

Few of her colleagues noticed. They were all absorbed in their own efforts

to sell stock to Mr. Jones's former clients.

Approaches differ widely. One applicant was asked by a client whether a particular stock was too risky. "No guts, no glory," he replied. To the same question another candidate said: "I don't really know if this is the stock for you. I would hate to recommend it."

Neither response is necessarily correct or incorrect. "There is no one answer," says Russell Scalpone, a manager in the Los Angeles office of A. T. Kearney Inc., management consultants. "A simulation exercise allows a person a number of different ways of dealing with a situation—he can put his best foot forward."

But it's pretty easy to stumble. One situation we are faced with is a rise in the market price of a stock before an order is completed. When I call the client back to explain, he is upset. "We made a deal," he says. "How come you're backing out?" Helped, no doubt, by the fact that I really don't want the job anyway, I manage to keep cool, mollifying the client with something like "these things happen."

Another candidate explodes under the same circumstances. "What the hell do you want me to do?" he tells the client. "I've only got two hands." That candidate ultimately received a poor rating, and he speculated that the blow-up "may have sealed my fate."

The test is designed so that someone without prior knowledge of the stock market isn't operating at a disadvantage. Still, for applicants who actually have no prior knowledge, the test can be unnerving. When the candidate behind me tells someone on the phone that a particular stock is a good buy if the investor wants to "preserve capital; it's got a real good yield," some of the applicants are awed by such professional language. "What's the matter with this guy?" the candidate next to me asks. "He got tired of working for Paine Webber?"

Continued following page

Tapping the Fundamental

Our clients avoid technical jargon. Lowell Hellervik, president of Personnel Decisions, a Minneapolis-based psychological-consulting firm that helped develop the test, says: "There are relatively simple concepts involved. We did that on purpose so that we would be tapping something very fundamental in the individual."

This idea of looking for something fundamental is instilled in the "evaluators," the three stockbrokers who will eventually rate our performance—the same three people who play the role of our contacts.

The evaluators play three different characters each, and most of them find that the roles hit close to home. "I deal with guys like this all the time," says Anthony Faath, talking about his role as the irate local industrialist. "It's fun to be on the other side for a change."

It's hard work too. The evaluators take detailed notes on each conversation, and since they each play three parts and there are usually nine candidates, they can end up as frazzled as their prospective colleagues.

After the simulation has ended, the evaluators discuss each individual separately, spending as much as a half-hour on each candidate. Their final decisions are based on everything from successful sales to letter writing. Nervous laughter, overblown promises—everything is considered. And since all evaluations are clocked, the assessors are able to determine if a candidate improves as the exercise proceeds.

60% Recommended

In the end, about 60% of the applicants taking part in the simulations are recommended for hiring. That is 60% of a group already considered the best of account-executive applicants; after the written test and the interview, only 10% of the 30,000 applicants who will come to Merrill Lynch this year will make it to the simulation.

The evidence is that the test works. In 1977, Merrill Lynch gave it to a group of new account executives who already had been hired but hadn't yet started working. Sixteen months later, the personnel department compared the production of the stockbrokers who did well in the simulation to those who didn't. The result: The former group's production was 25% to 30% greater than the latter's.

The test has been just as valuable in helping candidates decide whether they really like the job. "It never really occurred to me," one candidate said, "that I would be personally responsible for making recommendations about other people's money." Another candidate, in Dallas, got up after an hour and said, "I don't know whether I'm coming or going, so I'm leaving."

As for me, I did well. (The evaluators didn't know my identity, but Merrill Lynch did.) My overall rating was the highest possible—"outstanding potential, definitely recommended for hire." But then, I had to do well. After all, the other applicants' scores would never go beyond the evaluators and the Merrill Lynch files. I was going to have to tell you.

tends to be the best single predictor and has been found to work for minority groups as well.[42] Predictions tend to be more accurate for future advancement than they are for present jobs.[43]

In a survey by Korman of over thirty such studies, he concludes that "judgmental" prediction methods as exemplified particularly by assessment procedures are better predictors than psychometric procedures alone.[44] Intelligence tests are ruled out since the restriction of the range of applicants does not allow significant differentiation between the successful and unsuccessful. Personal history data as predictors are usable primarily for first-level managerial jobs but tend to be less valuable for higher positions. Personality inventories tend to have the least predictive value in assessing executive potential on all levels.

Assessment centers are not without disadvantages. Obviously, there are considerable costs involved, particularly when a large number of assessors is used. Most assessors are higher line managers, who are thus provided a valuable by-product in their training to evaluate personnel more effectively. Psychologists are also used, particularly when the techniques of psychological tests and depths interviews are being utilized. Possible

[42]James R. Huck and Douglas W. Bray, "Management Assessment Center Evaluations and Subsequent Job Performance of White and Black Females," *Personnel Psychology*, vol. 29, no. 1, Spring 1976, pp. 27–28.

[43]James O. Mitchel, "Assessment Center Validity: A Longitudinal Study," *Journal of Applied Psychology*, vol. 60, no. 5, October 1975, p. 578.

[44]Abraham K. Korman, "The Prediction of Managerial Performance: A Review," *Personnel Psychology*, vol. 21, no. 3, Autumn 1968, p. 319.

dysfunctional consequences of the use of the center include the "crown prince or princess effect," the "kiss of death effect," and possible demotivation of low-rated personnel who are competent in present positions. Studies of the operations of the International Business Machines center over a 5-year period indicate that fears concerning these adverse by-products are not well founded.[45] High ratings received in the center were not sufficient in and of themselves to secure a promotion for a particular individual. High ratings increased the likelihood of advancement but did not assure it. Low ratings were

[45]Allen I. Kraut and Grant J. Scott, "Validity of an Operational Management Assessment Program," *Journal of Applied Psychology*, vol. 56, no. 2, April 1972, pp. 124–129.

FIGURE 8-4 Assessment center profile. (*Source: Louis Olivas, "Using Assessment Centers for Individual and Organization Development,"* Personnel, *vol. 57, no. 3, May-June 1980, p. 65. With permission of the publisher. © 1980 by AMACOM, a division of American Management Associations. All rights reserved.*)

Name of participant: _____ Date: _____

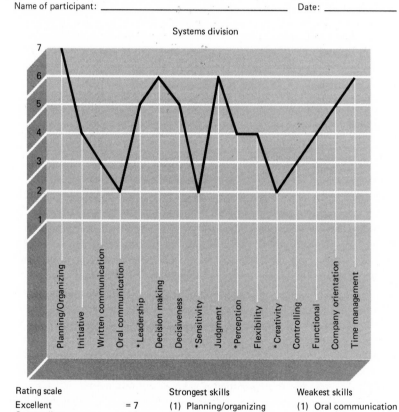

Rating scale

Excellent	= 7
Outstanding	= 6
Better than satisfactory	= 5
Satisfactory	= 4
Less than satisfactory	= 3
Much less than satisfactory	= 2
Weak	= 1

Strongest skills

(1) Planning/organizing
(2) Judgment
(3) Decision making
(4) Time management

Weakest skills

(1) Oral communication
(2) Creativity
(3) Sensitivity

(Each assessment center will give a full definition of the skills measured.)

*Skills essential to the successful operation of the division.

not necessarily the "kiss of death," but they did slow a candidate down. Concerning possible disillusionment leading to resignation, this study showed that the proportion of low-rated candidates who quit was not significantly different from the proportion of the high-rated group. Touchy human relations problems do exist with respect to those not receiving invitations to attend a center, as well as in the stress situations created by the obvious competitive elements of assessments through simulation. However, most organizations evidently conclude that the values far outweigh the costs and problems.

In recent years, there has been some movement toward converting the assessment center to a nonthreatening skills analysis center for the purpose of helping candidates in their careers. Participants are more likely to behave more naturally since they know the experience is designed to help, not select, them. More people are likely to benefit since they are not divided into "winners" and "losers." All develop more insight and some will make the hard decisions themselves rather than relying upon management to deliver the news, such as "your real strengths are more technical than managerial." Subjects are more willing to attend a development center when they know it will help, and not be a critical making or breaking of an entire career. An example of an individual report is given in Figure 8-4. In this example, the subject's major weaknesses, sensitivity and creativity, happen to be in areas that are essential to this portion of the organization. This analysis is then followed by remedial suggestions, most of which lie in the next section of this text, the development function.

SUMMARY

In hiring, one is concerned with assessing a human being in order to predict performance. Systematic and objective measurements are highly attractive processes in making these predictions more accurate. Management has tested in such areas as (1) intelligence, (2) aptitude, (3) achievement, (4) interest, and (5) personality. The intelligence test was the first developed but is now under fire by various minorities. The personality test is largely in a developmental stage as far as its use in selection is concerned. The cardinal concept in the use of a test of any type is that it must be validated under the actual conditions of use. Validity is highly specific in nature and must be proved to exist for each proposed use. That this is no longer just a requirement of the profession is made evident by the Civil Rights Act and accompanying guidelines published by the compliance agencies. Empirical statistical validity utilizing new applicants and objective criteria is the preferred method; concurrent statistical validity and content and construct validities are also acceptable. Special attention must be given to the problem of testing minority groups using instruments generally validated on characteristics of a white majority class.

The task of predicting employee success is even more difficult when one is concerned with future potential to become a manager. Numerous studies have attempted correlating success with such variables as college grades, personal values, intelligence, attitudes, motivation to manage, personality, and peer appraisals. Thus far, the most accurate method of predicting managerial success is the clinically oriented assessment center. The hallmark of the assessment center is the use of such simulations as in-baskets, business games, and leaderless group discussions.

BRIEF CASE

An assessment center for a company was set up in 1967, in which 47 individuals were assessed. In addition, two members of the organization with no knowledge of the assessment center results were asked to review the personnel files of the 47 people and make predictions as to management potential. Eight years later, both sets of predictions were revealed, and the correlation coefficient between the assessment center rating and management level attained was a significant .46. The correlation between the managers' estimates and level attained was .55.*

Questions

1. If we are merely trying to predict advancement, is the assessment center an overly expensive and involved technique for doing so? Why do you think the two managers were just as accurate as the assessment center?

2. Accepting the above as factual, is there any reason to have an assessment center?

DISCUSSION QUESTIONS

1. What is a correlation coefficient? How is it used in testing?

2. How can one compute the efficiency and base rates for a test?

3. Define and distinguish between reliability and validity. Is one prerequisite to the other?

4. If you used calipers to measure the size of your head in order to determine your level of intelligence, is this process valid, reliable, or neither valid or reliable? Change the statement so that it is both reliable and valid.

5. Define and differentiate among the following types of validities: empirical statistical predictive validity, concurrent validity, content validity, and construct validity.

6. Discuss the use of polygraphs and personality tests with respect to their social implications versus their contributions to organizational effectiveness.

7. What are the basic characteristics of an assessment center?

8. How good is an assessment center in predicting future performance?

9. What is a simulation? What are the most common simulation exercises used in assessment centers?

10. What is differential validity? Is this an important problem? Why or why not?

*John R. Hinrichs, "An Eight-Year Follow-up of a Management Assessment Center," *Journal of Applied Psychology*, vol. 63, no. 5, October 1978, pp. 596–601.

SUPPLEMENTARY
READING

187

Psychological Tests
and Identification
of Management
Talent

BARRETT, GERALD V., JAMES S. PHILLIPS and **RALPH A. ALEXANDER:** "Concurrent and Predictive Validity Designs: A Critical Reanalysis," *Journal of Applied Psychology,* vol. 66, no. 1, February 1981, p. 106.

DREHER, GEORGE F. and **PAUL R. SACKETT:** "Some Problems with Applying Content Validity Evidence to Assessment Center Procedures," *Academy of Management Journal,* vol. 6, no. 4, October 1981, pp. 551–560.

FRANK, FREDRIC D. and **JAMES R. PRESTON:** "The Validity of the Assessment Center Approach and Related Issues," *The Personnel Administrator,* vol. 27, no. 6, June 1982, pp. 87–95.

NICHOLS, LELAND C. and **JOSEPH HUDSON:** "Dual-Role Assessment Center: Selection and Development," *Personnel Journal,* vol. 60, no. 5, May 1981, pp. 380–386.

SCHMIDT, FRANK L. and **JOHN E. HUNTER:** "The Future of Criterion-Related Validity," *Personnel Psychology,* vol. 33, no. 1, Spring 1980, pp. 41–60.

WYSOCKI, BERNARD: "More Companies Try to Spot Leaders Early, Guide Them to the Top," *The Wall Street Journal,* February 25, 1981, pp. 1, 20.

EXERCISE AND CASES
FOR PART TWO

Exercise: Weighted Application Blank

The Rolla Store is a large establishment with a current roster of 20 sales personnel. The turnover has been high and management is interested in reducing it through the hiring process. Ten of the current 20 people have been with the store a relatively long time. Their characteristics are given in the table on page 188. Analyze the above information for "stayers" and "leavers," and develop a scoring system that would keep more of the stayers and reject more of the leavers. Calculate the percentage efficiency of your cutoff score.

Case: The Dekker Company

The Dekker Company was a large manufacturer of electrical equipment for control devices and for the radio and television industry. In its Louisville, Kentucky, branch plant the company manufactured a complicated switching mechanism used in specialized electrical apparatus. The switching mechanism was produced in Department C, one of the three major operating departments shown in Figure 1.

The works manager was responsible to the company-wide vice president of production for plant operations. Reporting to the works manager were six division managers. Each division was separated into departments, such as the switch department (Department C). Each department was further divided into sections and groups.

The production employees of the company, including those in Switch Department C, were represented by a local of an international labor union. The labor contract specified a typical grievance procedure of five steps beginning with "informal, oral discussion

Weighted Application Blank

Name	Age When Hired	Education	Experience Previous Job	Total Previous Experience	Experience Rolla Store	Marital Status	Number Children	Ht.	Wt.	Time at Present Address	Merit-rating (high—1; low—7)
Phyllis	23	h.s.	3 yrs.	4 yrs.	7 yrs.	Single	0	5'5"	115	5 yrs.	4
Ann	26	h.s.	4	8	6	Married	1	5'6"	120	6	3
June	21	h.s.	2	2	6	Married	0	5'2"	105	5	3
Beverly	23	h.s.	4	4	6	Married	1	5'7"	130	6	4
Ed	22	h.s.	3	3	7	Married	1	5'11"	175	6	6
Ruth	24	2 yrs. coll.	3	4	5	Married	0	5'4"	110	7	6
Julie	23	g.s.	1	4	7	Married	2	5'5"	111	7	3
Wayne	24	2 yrs. coll.	3	3	8	Married	2	5'11"	170	2	6
George	25	2 yrs. h.s.	4	8	5	Married	1	6'	180	8	6
Jane	22	h.s.	3	3	6	Married	0	5'8"	135	5	4

Going through the records, the following 10 employees had either resigned or had been fired:

Name	Age When Hired	Education	Experience Previous Job	Total Previous Experience	Experience Rolla Store	Marital Status	Number Children	Ht.	Wt.	Time at Present Address	Merit-rating (high—1; low—7)
Charles	25	coll.	2	8	1	Single	0	5'10"	175	1	7
Mary	19	h.s.	1	1	½	Single	0	5'9"	135	½	5
Joe	21	g.s.	1	6	2	Single	0	5'9"	165	2	4
Peter	24	2 yrs. coll.	2	2	1	Married	1	6'	190	7	6
Bill	23	g.s.	½	4	½	Single	0	5'11"	185	2	6
John	23	h.s.	1	7	2	Single	0	5'11"	175	1	5
Bob	24	h.s.	4	6	1	Single	0	5'8"	180	1	3
Lucy	26	coll.	1	3	1	Single	0	5'4"	105	2	5
Sam	24	2 yrs. coll.	1	2	2	Married	1	5'10"	170	1	3
Dick	25	coll.	1	4	½	Single	0	5'8"	145	1	2

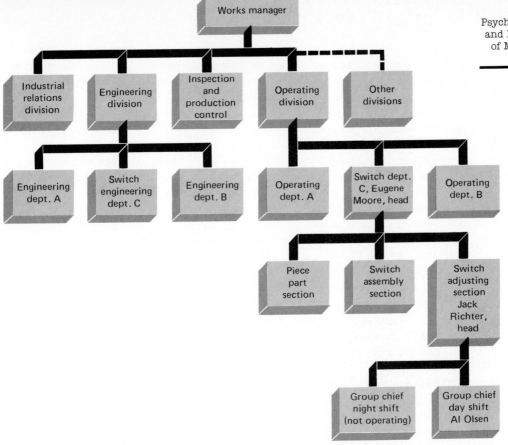

FIGURE 1   The Dekker Company (Louisville branch) partial organization chart.

between the Section Chief and the Authorized Representative, except that grievances regarding a job wage rate could not be initiated until ''60 days subsequent to the setting of such rate,'' in order to give the new rate a fair trial.

About 75 piece parts were required for each switch made in the switch department. The switches were assembled on an ''assembly conveyor'' by about 15 employees. They were then placed on an overhead conveyor that carried the assembled switches to an ''adjusting conveyor'' in an adjoining area. Here, 13 men performed about 50 electrical and mechanical adjustments on each switch. The adjusted switches were sample-inspected by members of the inspection division, and then loaded on a transport rack for a delivery to another building. The standard output from this adjusting conveyor was 60 switches per hour. The adjusting line was set up on this basis.

The 50 switch adjustments were broken down by the engineering department so that each of the 13 workers performed only a few adjustments on *each* switch as it went past on the conveyor belt. Through the use of time-study data, the engineer on the job balanced the line so that each position required an equal amount of time.

Certain adjustments were more difficult to make than others. In recognition of this, the workers who made the difficult adjustments were assigned a higher labor grade. The four labor grades on the adjusting line ranged from Grade 10 (the second lowest grade in the factory) to Grade 14. The rate difference between each grade was 5 cents, and each grade had a within-grade range of 8 cents. All adjusters were paid a day rate.

Engineering Department C serviced the switch shop. The engineers determined the method of manufacture, established time standards for each job, and authorized the purchase of all new machines and equipment. They prepared manufacturing layouts which the operating department was responsible for following. For example, a written layout by the engineering department covered the switch-adjusting operations for the 13-person assembly line. The sequence of adjustments and the duties of each position on the conveyor were described in this layout.

The department head in the switch shop, Eugene Moore, had been with the company for 24 years. He had been a department head for 12 years. His subordinates considered him to be a "company man," that is, he had a firm management viewpoint and lacked close touch with employees in his department.

The section head in the switch-adjusting section, Jack Richter, was a young man about 30 years of age. He had been recently transferred to his present line supervision job, after working several years at a desk job in the production-control department. He was energetic and aggressive. He wanted to "get ahead." The adjusters did not like him, although he got along well with most other persons in the switch department.

The group chief on the adjusting conveyor, Al Olsen, had been with the company less than 2 years. He was young, had a pleasant personality, and was well liked by the adjusters. He was conscientious but not aggressive. He found it difficult to discipline his charges, many of whom were young men in their first job.

Ten weeks ago the daily production schedule was increased from 480 switches to 720 switches by management in the company home office. Thus the standard hourly production, or "SHP" as the workers called it, had to be increased from 60 to 90 switches, if the plant was to remain on a one-shift basis. It was not feasible to install another conveyor, and it was company policy to manufacture on a one-shift basis insofar as possible. The existing conveyor, with minor modification, was capable of taking care of as many as 24 people.

Upon notification of the new schedule, the engineer revised the adjusting operations, adding some preliminary operations and changing the sequence of others, in such a manner that 18 workers could adjust 90 switches per hour. Time standards, previously established for each element of work, were used as the basis for rebalancing the "line" to turn out the increased schedule. Because each adjuster had less time to spend on each switch, it was necessary in some cases to divide a complicated or lengthy adjustment into two parts, a preliminary adjustment and a final adjustment. One person would make the preliminary adjustment, and a second worker on the line would make the final adjustment. The new method used the same number of higher labor grades that the old one used.

From the engineering standpoint, the new method of adjusting switches was just as good as the old method. The new method was covered by an engineering layout and given to switch-shop supervision through regular channels (that is, lines of authority). The project engineer realized that some "bugs" might develop in a change of this magnitude, so he notified Al Olsen informally that when the new method was introduced on the conveyor, the engineers would watch operations carefully for possible trouble.

When Richter and Olsen received the new engineering layout and instructions, they protested that they did not want to use the new method because:

1. They believed they could not meet the higher SHP, even though the time standards indicated that they could.

2. They did not have the 5 additional trained switch adjusters required by the new layout.

They wanted to continue adjusting according to the old method on the day shift, but to hire 5 new employees to work on this day shift, thus relieving experienced people to work on a second shift. The second-shift line would run on a kind of partial conveyor basis. Operating in this manner, and by working an overtime day on Saturdays, they believed that the increased schedule could be met.

At Moore's insistence, backed by the project engineer, the 18-person line was placed in operation without giving much consideration to the alternate proposal. Some minor "bugs" in the adjusting procedure were discovered but readily eliminated, and it was proved to the satisfaction of the engineering department that the new method would work. The SHP of 90 was not met at first, but this was expected by the engineers, since the employees needed time to gain experience.

From the very first day, however, the adjusters did not like the new arrangement. They felt that the new sequence of operations would not work. They did not like the idea of subdividing some of the lengthy adjustments into two parts. They thought that the new SHP was too high. In general, they griped to Olsen, to the engineer, and to anybody who would listen. One habit they developed at this time was to place metal tote boxes on the floor under the adjusting table and drum and pound on them with their feet while they worked. Often they did this in unison several times a day, making a terrific noise which disturbed nearby departments. The employees were not disciplined because Richter felt he needed their goodwill and cooperation in order to meet the increased schedule. The schedule had to be met within a few weeks; otherwise the backlog of adjusted switches would be exhausted, which would idle several hundred employees in later production stages.

This unsettled situation continued for 4 weeks. Output gradually increased, but it leveled at 5 to 10 switches above the old SHP of 60 switches. In addition, the quality declined precipitously. The inspector rejected many of the completed lots. The stock of adjusted switches became so short that Richter took the following emergency actions:

1. He established a partial second shift using 4 new employees and 5 regular adjusters. The regular adjusters were replaced on the first shift by 5 new employees.

2. He placed both shifts on a 10-hour day. This required that the two shifts overlap from 1:30 to 5:30 P.M. Since there was adequate space, the second shift during this overlap sat at side benches and reworked switches that had been rejected by the inspectors.

3. He scheduled one Saturday shift using as many persons from both shifts as wished to work.

While checking the night shift, about 6 weeks after the change, Richter privately approached one of the adjusters who was quite friendly with him, and asked him to "check up" on the activities of the other adjusters. Richter wanted him to report any adjuster who was not working diligently. The adjuster told several of the other adjusters, and the men began to "simmer." At about 10 P.M. the adjusters refused to work any longer. One of the men called Al Olsen, who was at home, and told him about the trouble. Olsen called Moore and they both came to the plant. The adjusters were told by Moore to go back to work, and they did. So much hard feeling developed from this incident that management decided to transfer Richter to another plant in another city during the following week to give him a fresh start. An experienced supervisor named Gene Smith was brought from another department to fill Richter's job.

Aside from this incident, whenever the supervisors did advise and lecture the employees about maintaining high quality, the employees answered by pointing a finger of blame at defective switch parts. They claimed that adjustments were too difficult to make because of poor piece parts which made up the switch.

Some adjustments concerned a clearance between moving parts. For example, one part had to clear another part by at least 0.005 and not more than 0.01 inch. The first part also had to be parallel to the second part. Therefore, if during piece-part manufacture the parts were not deburred properly, were not milled properly, or were not polished smoothly, the adjustments were very difficult to make.

Another adjusting trouble resulted because one adjustment might affect adversely a prior adjustment. For example, the thirteenth worker might make an adjustment which would "throw out" the adjustment that the ninth one made. In a case of this kind, the thirteenth worker was supposed to recheck the adjustment made by the ninth one to make sure that it was not disturbed. All of the adjustments were involved to this extent. It was, therefore, difficult for inspectors to pinpoint causes of poor quality without a special investigation. There was a special investigating staff for that purpose.

Ten weeks after the changeover, production was still below 90 switches hourly, quality was bad, and the stock of finished switches was almost exhausted. The operating division manager called a conference to try to determine a solution to the adjustment problem. He invited the project engineer and his manager, the project inspector and his manager, the switch-department head (Moore), the three switch-section heads, and Olsen.

Questions:

1. What is the number of units per employee-hour being produced when the case opens? What is this at the end? How do you account for the difference?

2. What approach to job design is being used by Dekker? What are the alternatives? What impact would these alternatives have on quantity and quality?

Case: Two Masters

The Adamson Aircraft Company has in the last decade expanded its product line to include the design, development, and production of missiles for the United States government. For this purpose a missile division was established, and over 5,000 personnel were gathered to man this portion of the firm.

The traditional type of organization in aircraft manufacturing calls for functional specialization like that found in the automobile industry. Aircraft are made up of such items as engines, radios, wheels, and armament. The manufacture of component parts was standardized and the aircraft put together on an assembly line. It was quickly recognized that such a simplified approach would not meet future requirements, as the demand for greater capability and effectiveness increased and forced the designers to insist upon optimum performance in every part or component. Several components, each with an operational reliability of 99 percent, may have a combined reliability of only 51 percent. Even with the most judicious selection and usage of standard parts, a system could end up with a reliability approaching zero. To overcome this reliability drop, it became necessary to design the entire system as a *single* entity. Many of the parts that were formerly available off the shelf must now be tailored to meet the exacting demands of the total system. Thus, the "weapons system" concept was developed, which necessitated a change in organization and management.

For each weapons system project, a chief project engineer is appointed. He assembles the necessary design personnel for every phase of the project. In effect, he organizes and creates a small, temporary company for the purpose of executing a single weapons system. On his staff are representatives of such functional areas as propulsion, secondary power, structures, flight test, and "human factors." The human factors specialist, for example, normally reports to a human factors supervisor. In the human factors department are people with training in psychology, anthropology, physiology, and the like. They do research on human behavior and hope to provide the design engineers with the basic human parameters applicable to a specific problem.

James Johnson, an industrial psychologist, has been working with the missile division of Adamson for 6 months as a human factors specialist. His supervisor, George Slauson, also has a Ph.D. in psychology and has been with the firm for 2 years. Johnson is in a line relationship with Slauson, who conducts his annual review for pay purposes, and prepares an efficiency report on his work. Slauson is responsible for assembling and supervising a group of human factors experts to provide Adamson with the latest and most advanced information in the field of human behavior and its effect on product design.

Johnson has been assigned to a weapons system project, which is under the direction of Bernard Coolsen, a chief project engineer. In a committee meeting of project members, Coolsen stated, "I am thinking about a space vehicle of minimum weight capable of 14 days' sustained activity, maneuverability, and rendezvous with other vehicles for maintenance and external exploration. How many people, how big a vehicle, and what instruments, supplies, and equipment will we need?" Johnson immediately set to work on his phase of the project. The data for the answer to this request were compiled and organized, and a rough draft of the human factors design criteria was prepared in triplicate. Johnson took the original to his supervisor, Slauson, for review, retaining the other two copies. Using one of the copies, he began to re-edit and rewrite, working toward a smooth copy for presentation to Coolsen. A week later Johnson was called in by Slauson who said, "We can't put out stuff like this. First, it's too specific, and secondly, it's poorly organized." Slauson had rewritten the material extensively and had submitted a draft of it to *his* immediate superior, the design evaluation chief. In the meantime Coolsen had been calling Johnson for the material, insisting that he was holding up the entire project. Finally, taking a chance, Johnson took his original copy to Coolsen, and they sat down together and discussed the whole problem. An illustrator was called in, and in 2 days the whole vehicle was sketched up ready for design and specification write-up. The illustrator went to his board and began converting the sketches to drawings. Coolsen started to arrange for the writing of component and structural specifications, and Johnson went back to his desk to revise his human engineering specifications in the light of points brought out during the 2-day team conference.

Three days later the design evaluation chief called Johnson into his office and said, "Has your supervisor seen this specification of yours?" Johnson replied that he had and that this was Slauson's revision of the original. The chief then asked for the original, and Johnson brought in the third original copy. Two days later the chief's secretary delivered to Johnson's desk a draft of his original specification as modified by Slauson as modified by the design evaluation chief. Johnson edited this for technical accuracy and prepared a ditto master. Slauson and the design evaluation chief read the master, initialed it, and asked for 30 copies to be run off. One copy was kept by Johnson, one by Slauson, one by the chief, five put into company routing, and the balance placed in file. Those in company routing went to the head of technical staff, head of advanced systems, and finally to the project engineer, Coolsen. Coolsen filed one copy in the project file and gave the other to Johnson. The latter dropped it in the nearest wastebasket, inasmuch as several days previously, Coolsen had combined his, the illustrator's, and Johnson's material and submitted it to publications. Publications had run off six copies, one each for Coolsen, the illustrator, Johnson, the head of advanced systems, the U.S. Patent Office, and one for file. Also, by this time, the vehicle had been accepted by the company management as a disclosure for patent purposes. Johnson breathed a sigh of relief, since he thought that he gotten away with serving two masters.

Questions:

1. Why does the organization wish to have two bosses for Johnson?

2. Coolsen and Slauson are both interested in "good quality" work from Johnson. What is each manager's definition of "good quality?"

Case: The Worried Attorney

George Helms paced the floor of his den. It was 2 A.M., and his wife had urged him to stop worrying and go to bed. George felt, however, that he had to make a decision before he could sleep. Which of the two young law graduates should their law firm of Harrison, Holmes, and Helms hire? Since the one chosen would presumably be a partner some day, the decision was doubly important.

As he worried about the choice, his thoughts returned to his own graduation day 15 years ago. While growing up near San Francisco, he had always felt that his family, especially his father, had kept him on a particularly tight leash. Sometimes Helms resented the fact that his father was such a prominent judge in the Bay area. Despite doing well in school and sports, he was never sure he had done as well as his father had expected. Upon graduation from law school he had been accepted by the State Department for a foreign assignment in France. Instead of his father's being pleased, he had strongly advised him to turn down the appointment and come back to San Francisco to enter the firm of Harrison and Holmes. The discussion concerning this had been long and sometimes bitter. In the end, George had returned to San Francisco, and as he reflected now, it had been for the best. He had been quite happy with this old San Francisco law firm.

Helms's mind next moved to the first of the two applicants who were being considered. Eleven in total had applied or been asked for the opening in the firm. All were recent law school graduates. The field had been narrowed to two, Bruce Hargraves, who had received his law degree from Michigan 4 years ago, and Roger Parnes, who was graduating from Stanford this year. As George pondered his decision, he asked himself why Harrison and Holmes had left so much of this decision on his shoulders. Bruce

Hargraves . . . surely a top-flight student . . . second in his class . . . had been one of the editors of the school's law review . . . had also done some teaching . . . was active in local Democratic politics . . . wonder where he got the time for all of this? Helms recalled that Hargraves had taken a job with an oil company in Iran after graduation. He recalled in the interview that he had asked why, and that Hargraves had snapped back that it was for the money. Hargraves then had told him about his childhood and teenage years in Columbus—how he had always had some kind of job since he was 12, and how he had been arrested for street fighting when he was 15. Helms recalled that Hargraves had won an engineering scholarship at MIT but had turned it down. He had gone to Michigan instead. Hargraves told how he had it figured out that he had enough money to get through the football season without taking a job. In the winter, he got a 6-hour-a-day factory job in Willow Run and also received a small athletic scholarship. Helms recalled asking if he had ever played varsity ball at Michigan. Hargraves had replied that he and the coach had had an argument, and that he quit the squad as a result. Hargraves added that he was able to make more money playing semipro industrial football on Saturdays and Sundays. George recollected that Hargraves's grades in college were surely outstanding; in fact, he had graduated a member of Phi Beta Kappa. Other data concerning Hargraves came to mind. He had turned down a bid from a fraternity because he could not afford it. He had been quite active in campus political clubs. That, he said, had helped him get a summer job in the Governor's office one year. When Hargraves graduated from college, he was almost immediately drafted. He had told Helms that he had become a sergeant and had seen quite a bit of action. When asked about his marital status, Hargraves had artfully dodged the question. He said he had no plans to settle down until he was a tired old man of 40. Helms remembered smiling at the remark but thought it a little brash. George decided that there was something in Hargraves's manner that disturbed him. He remembered the day the two of them had driven to Oakland in Hargraves's Austin-Healey. He had felt the same way that day. He just could not put his finger on what it was, though.

Helms's attention now shifted to Roger Parnes. He could not quite get used to the idea of young Roger Parnes becoming a member of his or any other law firm. Though he had not really known Roger before he had made application to the firm, he had seen him around the San Francisco area for years. Roger's father had been a friend of the family, though he could not remember his ever coming to the house. He and Roger had played golf in the same foursome a time or two. George laughed to himself as he recalled that until recently he had thought that golf was Parnes's greatest accomplishment in life. Reading Roger's transcripts had shown George that Roger's brain was more agile than he had realized. Though not brilliant, he had been in the top third of the Stanford Law School class during his first 2 years. This did not stack up to Hargraves's record, but it was certainly acceptable. Actually, Roger had a bit more legal experience than the other man. He had spent the past six summers working as a law clerk. Hargraves's job with the oil company had not been in the legal field, though he was hired for his law training. Thinking back to Hargraves, George reflected he had sort of a take-charge quality that many people probably admired. He was unable to find such a quality in Roger, though he knew that Roger got along well with people. He reasoned, therefore, that people must certainly have looked to Roger for leadership. When Roger was very young, he had considered him to be a ''mamma's boy'' with his carefully combed hair and almost too well-groomed clothes. Later recollections included him on the golf course, racing his sailboat, and at a dance or two with Charlotte Gilmour. Charlotte's family had been very close friends of George's, so he had gotten to know Roger a little in this way. Roger's only years away from California were two spent in the service. George did not recall where.

George lighted another cigarette and paced some more. Why had Fletcher Harrison and Charles Holmes left the decision up to him when they were the senior partners? He very well knew how each stood. Fletcher had said that George should make the decision, and then added that, from the interviews, young Parnes appeared to be very capable. George then thought back to his own father's comments that when Helms, Sr., and Harrison were in law partnership, Fletcher sometimes took days to express an opinion or make a decision. Charles Holmes had made his feelings more obvious. Charles had been given his first job by George's father. He said he thought Hargraves was the sharpest young fellow he had seen in a long time.

Helms smoked and paced some more. He sat down and decided that Roger Parnes would make a fine member of the firm. Feeling relieved, he went to bed. On getting up the following morning, he thought a bit more about his decision. Although not completely satisfied, he decided that all had worked out for the best.

Questions:

1. What are the specific major differences in characteristics between the two candidates?

2. What type of firm image is implemented by the hiring decision?

3. How do job analysis and role analysis differ in this case?

PART THREE

DEVELOPMENT

The final phase of the procurement function is induction. Immediately following, and usually combined with it, is the function of developing the employee's ability to do the job. In this section, we shall examine the training of operative employees and the development of executives and organizations (Chapter 9). Also essential to the development process is performance appraisal and the establishment of performance goals (Chapter 10). And finally, both employee and employer should be concerned with the former's long-term career objectives (Chapter 11).

chapter 9

Individual and Organization Development

After the employee has been recruited, selected, and inducted, he or she must next be developed to better fit the job and the organization. No one is a perfect fit at the time of hiring, and some training and education must take place. No organization has a choice of whether to develop employees or not; the only choice is that of method. If no organized program exists, then development will largely be self-development while learning on the job. Development would include both training to increase skill in performing a specific job and education to increase general knowledge and understanding of our total environment.

Planned development programs will return values to the organization in terms of increased productivity, heightened morale, reduced costs, and greater organizational stability and flexibility to adapt to changing external requirements. Such programs will also help meet the needs of individuals in their search for work assignments that can add up to life-long careers. Our society as a whole is also vitally interested in training and educational programs in order to promote employment and utilize the talents of its citizens. One of the earlier legislative attempts in this regard was the Manpower Development and Retraining Act of 1962, which was designed to assist in the conversion to new skills of those persons thrown out of work by changing job requirements. In 1964, the Economic Opportunity Act was directed toward providing training assistance for young entrants in the job market. Neighborhood youth corps, job corps, and college work-study programs were formed to help younger persons whose unemployment rates are typically double the average.

In 1973, because of the confusion generated by literally thousands of publicly financed training programs, the Comprehensive Employment and Training Act was passed. Its objective was to decentralize the control of programs to local and state level, and to focus most funds on assisting the unskilled and long-term unemployed. In 1978, this single act constituted the fastest growing portion of the federal budget with over $12 billion appropriated for training and job formation. As practiced, it has become a type of ''revenue sharing'' with local governments with emphasis on job creation to reduce unemployment.

After an experimental program in the late 1970s, the Job Training Partnership Act of 1982 allocated $3 billion to Private Industry Councils to implement training for the hard-core unemployed. These councils, under the control of private business persons rather than local government officials, were designed to train for long-lasting jobs. The typical CETA job lasted for only 18 months. The philosophy of most Private Industry Councils is that no training will be offered unless there is a job at the end of the line, and attention will be given to developing skills that lead to long-term employment, such as how to take an interview, adapt to supervision, and behave on the job.

In this chapter, we shall concentrate on three subjects: (1) training programs for nonmanagers to develop skills to perform a job, (2) training and educational programs for executives to develop the ability to manage, and (3) programs designated to develop organizational units as entities. With respect to the last item it has often been found that individual training may be wasted if the organizational unit does not permit such acquired skills to be practiced. As a result, a major training effort has evolved under the title of "organization development" whose major objective is the enhancement of interpersonal and intergroup collaboration.

OPERATIVE TRAINING

The development of operatives calls for specific increases in skill and knowledge to perform a particular job. There are primarily four basic methods in use: (1) on-the-job training, (2) vestibule school, (3) apprenticeship, and (4) special courses.

On-the-job training Since most jobs in industry can be learned in a relatively short period of time, this method is the most widely used. It has the advantage of strongly motivating the trainee to learn since it is not located in the artificial situation of a classroom. The fact that the success of the system depends almost entirely upon the immediate supervisor, the trainer, means that the personnel unit has a major responsibility for making a good, effective teacher out of every supervisor. As outlined in Figure 9-1,

FIGURE 9-1
Training Procedure

Step	Suggestions
Instructor preparation	1 Divide task into logical parts to create lesson plan. 2 Select teaching techniques, e.g., demonstration.
Trainee preparation	1 Place trainee at ease. 2 Relate training to trainee needs, e.g., promotion
Present the task	1 Present overview of task. 2 Proceed from known to unknown, easy to difficult. 3 Adjust pace to individual differences. 4 Go through task and explain each step. 5 Have trainee tell instructor what to do.
Tryout performance	1 Have trainee explain each step prior to execution. 2 Be aware of learning plateaus to sustain motivation. 3 Provide feedback on progress.
Follow-up	1 Positively reinforce continuously at start. 2 Move to variable positive reinforcement schedule as trainee matures.

the supervisor typically follows a set procedure in training an employee to perform a particular task. The suggestions accompanying each step are general guides evolved from both experience and research.

Vestibule schools   These are adapted to the same general type of training problem that is faced by on-the-job training. A vestibule school is operated as a specialized endeavor by the personnel department. It usually trains for the same type of job as on-the-job training, that is, work of the semiskilled machine operator or tender. Why, then, have a vestibule school? The reason lies in the law of functional growth, as described in Chapter 5. When the amount of training that has to be done exceeds the capacity of the line supervisor, a portion of this training is evolved from the line and assigned to staff through a vestibule school.

It should be noted also that this situation sometimes creates typical line-staff difficulties of the kind that were discussed in Chapter 3. The staff school trains the employee and turns him or her over to the supervisor. If the employee is deficient in performance, who is to blame? The supervisor may ''pass the buck'' to the school and attribute the poor performance to improper training. The school may return the ball to the supervisor and attribute it to poor induction that led to the confusion of the employee. Any time a staff function is evolved from line, myriad opportunities for conflicts arise.

The advantages of using the vestibule-school system are the advantages of specialization. The instructor, a specialist, should be more skilled at teaching. The student avoids the confusion and pressure of the work situation and thus is able to concentrate on learning. One can also often attain a given level of skill more quickly in the specialized learning situation. We have more assurance that adequate time and attention will be given to training and that it will not be slighted in favor of other problems. More individualized instruction can be given, and training activities do not interfere with the regular processes of production. Among the disadvantages are the aforementioned organizational problems, artificiality of the training situation, and the necessity for additional investment in training equipment.

Apprenticeship programs   The third system of training, apprenticeship programs, is designed for a higher level of skill. As shown in Figure 9-2, apprenticeship programs tend toward more education than on-the-job training or vestibule schools, in that knowledge in doing a craft or a series of related jobs is involved. The usual apprenticeship program combines on-the-job training and experience with classroom instruction in particular subjects.

The basic federal law establishing apprenticeship policy is the National Apprenticeship Act of 1937, which is administered by the Bureau of Apprenticeship and Training of the Department of Labor. In addition, some 30 states have their own apprenticeship laws.

A survey of approximately 400 members of the American Society of Personnel Administration resulted in one-third reporting use of apprenticeship programs.[1] The incidence was greater among manufacturing firms, hospitals, and utilities. They were relatively rare in banks and insurance companies.

Specific apprenticeship programs are administered by joint labor and management

[1]*Employee Training*, Prentice-Hall Editorial Staff for the American Society for Personnel Administration, Prentice-Hall, Inc., Englewood Cliffs, N.J., 1979, p. 3.

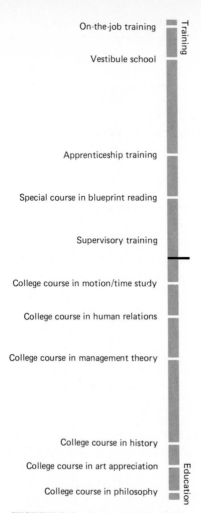

On-the-job training — Training

Vestibule school

Apprenticeship training

Special course in blueprint reading

Supervisory training

College course in motion/time study

College course in human relations

College course in management theory

College course in history

College course in art appreciation

College course in philosophy — Education

FIGURE 9-2   A training-education continuum.

committees for each craft. These committees, called JACs, establish the selection qualifications for entry into a program. Though they vary from craft to craft, general requirements include a high school education, letters of recommendation, specified intelligence
and aptitude scores on standard tests, and willingness of a particular employer to hire
the applicant for the apprenticeship period, usually 3 to 5 years. The JACs are responsible
for the content of apprenticeship training programs under the general guidelines established by the government. This includes decisions concerning course content, means of
instruction and examination, and allocation of time between organized group instruction
and work on the job. Federal guidelines call for a minimum of 144 hours of classroom
time each year. Programs registered with the government are required to use "objective
standards" and to provide "full and fair opportunity for application." The Civil Rights
Act of 1964 specifically prohibits discrimination in all phases of employment, including
training.

Apprenticeship programs are available in a number of crafts such as machinists, electricians, pipefitters, welders, tinners, carpenters, and millwrights. The mechanical apprenticeship program in Champion Paper and Fibre Company, for example, encompasses a period of 4 years. Four hours per week must be spent in classroom training for which instructors are provided by the company. Progress reports are given every 3 months for the first year and every 6 months thereafter. The apprentice has the same status as other employees with respect to insurance, vacations, and bonuses. In a survey of 193 manufacturing firms, approximately 14 percent reported having formal apprenticeship programs.

Special courses The last system of operative training may be classified by some as education rather than training. Yet special courses, such as shop math or blueprint reading, cannot be labeled as general education and can be directly related to a person's particular job.

The teaching machine, a device originated by Sidney L. Pressey of Ohio State University in 1924, has become a popular technique in the past two decades. Programmed learning has been used in a number of ways, as in a textbook, for example, but its adaptation to a machine has stimulated more widespread use. Advantages to the trainee are that one can select a personal pace of learning, go back over material when desired, and use the machine when it is convenient. A slow learner will be forced to go through every portion in the program, while correct responses by fast learners will permit more rapid completion. This method of instruction utilizes the basic learning concepts of (1) establishing explicit goals, (2) breaking the subject into bits of logically sequenced knowledge, (3) requiring an active role on the part of the learner, (4) making learner self-pacing possible, and (5) providing immediate reinforcement of learning through feedback of results.[2]

Concerning the relative effectiveness of programmed learning as compared with other more conventional methods, attention can be allocated to three factors: savings in learning time, amount of immediate learning, and long-term retention. A survey of over 150 studies reveals that programmed instruction is clearly superior in only the first factor, learning time.[3] On the average, the time saved was approximately one-third of that normally taken by competitive methods. Time saved issues largely from individual flexibility in establishing one's own pace. In a survey of 193 firms, 20 percent used some form of programmed instruction.[4]

There is no one best system of operative training. In any one firm, it would not be unusual to find all four systems in use simultaneously. As stated earlier, the on-the-job system is by far the most commonly used. With the advent of automation and the consequent upgrading of skill level, it may be that special courses and classroom instruction will receive a much greater degree of emphasis in the future.

[2]John W. Buckley, "Programmed Instruction in Industrial Training," *California Management Review,* vol. 10, no. 2, Winter 1967, p. 73.

[3]Allan N. Nash, Jan P. Muczyk, and Frank L. Vettori, "The Relative Practical Effectiveness of Programmed Instruction," *Personnel Psychology,* vol. 24, no. 3, Autumn 1971, pp. 410–411.

[4]National Industrial Conference Board, *Personnel Practices in Factory and Office: Manufacturing,* Studies in Personnel Policy, no. 194, New York, 1964, p. 56.

MANAGEMENT DEVELOPMENT

Perhaps the foremost justification for a planned and systematic management development program is the very complex nature of the job itself. The executive job is typically open-ended, fragmented, interpersonal, verbal, and active. Job descriptions, if they should exist, cannot possibly capture the nature of the job in its entirety. Though we may theoretically specify that the executive plans, organizes, directs, and controls, the typical day is not that neat. A few minutes might be devoted to checking up on a project (control), followed by a few seconds to issue an order on another project (direct); then follows a meeting to coordinate with a fellow manager on a continuing conflictual situation (organizing), interrupted by an emergency telephone call from the assistant manager (control), and so on. An immediate supervisor may have over 500 separate incidents during the day, many of which are of limited importance. In many instances, the manager may devote no more than one-half of her or his time to contacts with subordinates, the remainder being allocated to persons outside of the chain of command, so that skills of persuading, negotiating, coordinating, and facilitating are called for.

Though arguments abound as to whether or not management constitutes a profession, the complex and essential nature of the task requires that conscious and systematic attention be allocated to development of managerial skills. There are no specified formal educational requirements, as in the cases of law and medicine. There is, however, a strong tendency on the part of the larger firms to require possession of a college degree for admission to executive development programs. Some have suggested that the Master of Business Administration (MBA) will become for the manager what the M.D. is to the physician and the LL.D is to the lawyer. Given the open-ended, complex, and variable nature of the task, this situation is less likely to come about on the basis of proven need. Executive development typically calls for a combination of experience, training, and education, thus requiring collaboration among employing organizations and a variety of private and public educational enterprises.

MANAGER NEEDS AND DEVELOPMENTAL PROGRAMS

Among firms which profess to believe in some type of planned systematic executive development, a great variety of developmental techniques are used. The selection of techniques must rest on one's philosophy of development. In Figure 9-3 is a portrayal of the various types of development needs typically required by an executive position. In each of the categories, a number of alternative methods are available to achieve the designated goal. *Decision-making skills* can be enhanced through use of such techniques as the in-basket, business games, and case analysis. Much-needed *interpersonal skills* can be promoted through a variety of means, including role playing, behavior modeling, sensitivity training, transactional analysis, and structured insight. Obviously, the executive requires *job knowledge* in the assigned position, and thus the methods of on-the-job experience, coaching, and understudies are available. The job is performed within an organizational environment, and such required *organizational knowledge* can be obtained through position rotation and multiple management.

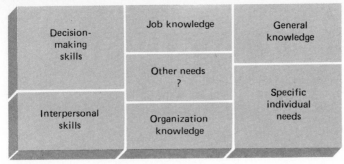

FIGURE 9-3 Executive development needs.

In the interest of long-run general development of executive talent, efforts are often allocated to the acquisition of *general knowledge*. It is here that a variety of educational organizations are usually involved in offering special courses, meetings, and selective reading lists. In adapting to the principle of individual differences, analysis of managerial candidates may reveal *specific individual needs* unique to them. Special projects and selected committee assignments are often utilized to attack these developmental problems. Again, demonstrating the open-ended nature of the managerial task, Figure 9-3 portrays a category of "Other Needs." Though the above itemization covers most of the standard developmental methods utilized in business organizations, one cannot contend that they cover all the foreseeable developmental needs on all types of management jobs.

There is no ideal best combination of management development methods. Each organization must design its own particular program to suit the climate of the firm, the organizational level for which training is required, the particular characteristics of the personnel to be developed, the recognized specific developmental needs, and the availability of economic resources that can be allocated to training and education. Without itemizing the listed methods used by any one firm, a survey of 225 personnel directors in firms having at least 1,000 employees reported the following rank order of importance for development methods: (1) on-the-job experiences and transfers, (2) seminars, (3) conferences, (4) role playing, (5) in-basket technique, (6) quantitative techniques, and (7) sensitivity training.[5] Over two-thirds designated on-the-job methods as most effective.

Both on-the-job and off-the-job developmental approaches have a place in a well-rounded management development program. In the sections that follow, we shall briefly outline the content of the various training and educational methods, classified by the developmental needs to which they are directed.

Decision-making Skills

To many, the essence of the executive job is making decisions, the great majority of which are correct. Though this skill can be approached in a variety of ways, including special courses in decision making, there has been a marked tendency to utilize methods entailing simulation of the executive environment. Among these methods are the in-basket, business games, and case studies.

---

[5] William J. Kearney and Desmond D. Martin, "Quantitative Methods in Management Development," *Business Horizons,* vol. 17, no. 4, August 1974, p. 55.

In-basket   As indicated in an earlier chapter, the in-basket is a popularly used device in identifying executive potential in executive assessment centers. It can also be utilized in teaching decision-making skills. After trainees are given background information on a simulated company and its products, organization, and key personnel, they are provided with an in-basket of assorted memoranda, requests, and data pertaining to the firm. The trainee must make sense out of this mass of paperwork and prepare memos, make notes, and delegate tasks within a limited time period. Not all the items are of equal importance, and one must often relate one item to another. Abilities that can be developed encompass (1) situational judgment in being able to recall details, establish priorities, interrelate items, and determine need for more information, (2) social sensitivity in exhibiting courtesy in written notes, scheduling meetings with involved personnel, and explaining reasons for actions taken, and (3) willingness to make a decision and take action. In one variation, the trainee is allowed to place simulated phone calls for more information. If he or she calls the correct person in the organization, more written data on the issue will be provided. Group conference discussions on separate individual handlings of the in-basket can elicit further developmental values.

Business games   Over the years, a variety of simulations have been developed to portray the operations of a firm, or some component part. These exercises introduce some uncertainty inasmuch as they are often played on a competitive basis. Teams of trainees are formed to meet, discuss, and arrive at decisions concerning such subjects as production amounts, research and development, inventories, sales, and a myriad of other activities for a simulated firm. Games can be relatively simple, permitting rapid decision making to be effected, or extremely complicated, entailing long and detailed analysis of trends in cost, inventories, and sales. The requirement that decisions be made as a team provides trainee experience in cooperative group processes. The multiple facets of a realistic simulation lead to appreciation of the complex and interlocking nature of business systems, necessitating decisions that require breadth of viewpoint as well as attention to detail.

As in the case of the in-basket, playing a business game provides practice in sticking one's neck out and making a decision. Immediate feedback of results demonstrates the relative accuracy of the decision, taking into account the uncertain nature of competitors' decisions. Interjection of major changes in the environment can give practice in achieving flexibility. Organizational ability, financial acumen, quickness of thinking, and the ability to adapt under stress can also be developed through the use of game simulations.

Case studies   The case method of development utilizes actual case examples collected from various organizations for diagnostic purposes. The trainee must (1) identify the major and minor problems in the case; (2) filter out the significant facts from the insignificant; (3) analyze the issues and use logic to fill in the gaps in the facts; and (4) arrive at some means for solving the identifiable problem. Cases in personnel management are presented after each major section in this text.

In ensuing group discussions concerning the case, the trainee will usually see that other candidates differ from himself or herself about what is important and what action should be undertaken. One is thus taught tolerance of others' viewpoints as well as the difficulty of arriving at absolutely correct answers in complex problems. It has been found that some candidates are excellent in analysis and can pursue ramifications endlessly, sometimes to the point of self-immobilization. They clearly see that any decision chosen will have some undesirable dysfunctional consequences. Nevertheless, the instructor must press for some stand to be taken. Decision choice is an inescapable responsibility of a manager.

Interpersonal Skills

Traditional managers are likely to emphasize the rational portion of a manager's task, thereby emphasizing its decision-making elements. Behaviorally oriented managers contend that acceptance of the decision is just as important as its quality, thereby emphasizing the necessity for developing interpersonal competence.

Role playing   Role playing is a simulation in which the trainee is asked to play a part in a problem situation requiring interaction with others. Basic mental sets are stated for all participants, but no dialogue is provided. For example, a supervisor, on the advice of a motion and time study engineer, has decided to change the work methods of subordinates. The supervisor's role may contain, among other items, such statements as, "You get along well with your people; this idea of the methods man makes pretty good sense for both the employees and the company; the data provided by the expert are fairly clear." Roles are also provided for each of the subordinates. One may exhibit great suspicion against the motion and time study expert. Another may be structured as a potential ally of the supervisor in the projected change. Still another may show a fear of working himself or herself out of a job if methods are improved. All will probably reflect the usual human resistance to any change, good or bad. No dialogue is provided, and the trainees attempt to play themselves in the roles as structured.

Role playing is close to a laboratory situation in dealing with people in job situations. Playback of the tape, if recorded, provides opportunities for the trainee to examine his or her performance with the additional insight of participants and experienced observers.

Multiple role playing can be utilized in large groups. The same situation can be given to four or five groups simultaneously. Observers in each group can report the approach taken by the supervisor as well as the reactions of the persons playing the subordinate roles. In the above-described situation, it has been found that if a problem-solving approach is taken by the supervisor, there is a greater chance of coming up with multiple answers that will meet varying sets of values. If a "hard-sell" or "soft-sell" approach is taken, the more likely result is a "yes" or "no" to the single proposed solution.

Behavior modeling   Though sometimes confused with role playing, behavior modeling is a more structured approach to teaching specific supervisory skills. It is based on social learning theory insofar as the trainee is (1) provided with a specific model of behavior and (2) informed in advance of the consequences of engaging in that type of behavior.[6] The approach taken generally involves the following steps:[7]

[6]A. Bandura, *Social Learning Theory,* Englewood Cliffs, N.J., Prentice-Hall, 1977.
[7]Jerry I. Porras and Brad Anderson, "Improving Managerial Effectiveness Through Modeling-Based Training," *Organizational Dynamics,* vol. 9, no. 4, Spring 1981, p. 64.

1. A conceptual presentation is made in the proper handling of a particular problem. Each key action step is identified and emphasized.

2. A videotape of the effective handling of the problem is presented. Each key action step is performed.

3. A behavioral rehearsal period is then undertaken. Though this may look like role playing, the trainee is not free to select a response. Rather, he or she *rehearses* the behavior presented in the first two steps.

4. During and after the rehearsal period, the trainee is given feedback on performance, and is positively reinforced when demonstrating the behavioral model.

5. Finally, the trainee is encouraged to try the behavior out on the job and to report back for discussion the results of that tryout.

Sorcher and Goldstein report effective use of behavior models for such interpersonal problem areas as giving recognition to an employee, handling a complaining employee, stimulating acceptance of proposed changes, conducting a performance appraisal, and inducting a newly hired employee into the organization.[8]

In the handling of interpersonal problems, the fundamental approach to all such situations involves (1) description of the desired behavior, (2) justification for the necessity of such behavior, (3) active listening to employee responses, and (4) active involvement of the employee in the solution. As an example, the behavior model in handling a complaining employee emphasizes the following key action steps:[9]

1. Avoid responding to the complaint with hostility and defensiveness.

2. Ask for and listen openly to the complaint.

3. Restate the complaint to insure thorough understanding.

4. Recognize and acknowledge the complainant's viewpoint.

5. State your position nondefensively.

6. Set specific date for follow-up meeting.

Each of these key points is demonstrated in handling a specific complaint that has been videotaped. The trainee then practices the above-prescribed behavior in dealing with another complaint during the rehearsal session. In comparing 20 trained supervisors with 20 nontrained supervisors in one company, the former achieved significantly higher scores on the company's traditional performance appraisal instrument.[10] Behavior modeling for supervisors is used by a variety of organizations including General Electric, Xerox, Atlantic Richfield, and Lukens Steel Company.

Sensitivity training As the title indicates, the general goal of sensitivity training is the development of awareness and sensitivity to behavioral patterns of oneself and others. More specifically, goals frequently announced include (1) increased openness with others, (2) greater concern for others, (3) increased tolerance for individual differ-

---

[8]Melvin Sorcher and Arnold P. Goldstein, "A Behavior Modeling Approach in Training," *Personnel Administration*, vol. 35, no. 2, March-April 1972, pp. 35–40.

[9]Gary P. Latham and Lise M. Saari, "Application of Social-Learning Theory to Training Supervisors through Behavioral Modeling," *Journal of Applied Psychology*, vol. 64, no. 3, June 1979, p. 241.

[10]Ibid., p. 244.

ences, (4) less ethnic prejudice, (5) understanding of group processes, (6) enhanced listening skills, and (7) increased trust and support. Unlike content-oriented methods, sensitivity training swings to the other extreme in establishing a laboratory situation in which one learns about oneself. It involves face-to-face learning about ongoing behavior within a small group that meets continually for periods as long as 1 or 2 weeks. It is less artificial than role playing inasmuch as the trainee plays *himself* or *herself* rather than a structured role. The technology of sensitivity training usually includes (1) absence of structure, (2) catalytic role by trainer, (3) isolation, (4) groupings of strangers, (5) discussions of the "here and now," and (6) emphasis upon honest, but supportive feedback.

The general goal of this type of training is to open up the organization through increasing managerial sensitivity and trust, as well as increasing respect for the contributions of others, whether peers, subordinates, or superiors. The technique has not received majority approval by business managers. Among the reasons for this resistance is limited acceptance of the open, supportive, and trusting organizational model that various behavioral theorists have visualized. It is contended that most managers must make unpleasant decisions that work to the short-term detriment of particular people. Excessive empathy and sympathy will not necessarily lead to a reversal of the decision, and may exact an excessively high emotional cost from the manager. As one critic stated, "The normative prescriptions implied in laboratory training may be totally inappropriate for the business environment.[11] The single executive who undergoes effective sensitivity training and returns to the company may well be a "sitting duck" if others continue to behave as before. For this reason, the emphasis in various companies has switched from individual sensitivity training to group organization development.

Transactional analysis Though characterized by some as instant, do-it-yourself psychology, various organizations have taken advantage of the understandable concepts of transactional analysis to improve interpersonal relations. The emphasis is upon (1) understanding the three ego states possessed by all, and (2) analyzing interpersonal transactions in terms of these states. The system was developed and popularized by Eric Berne and Thomas Harris.

As outlined in Figure 9-4, the ego states are parent, child, and adult. The parent tends to be judgmental, condescending, and punishing with frequent use of such words as "should," "ought," and "mustn't." The child is of two types, a free-spirited one of creativity and spontaneity, and an adaptive and inhibited one that can be either overly rebellious or overly submissive. The adult within us deals with here and now reality, listens with an open mind, states opinions tentatively, and is actively engaged in probability estimating and rational decision making. Trainees are taught to analyze their interactions with others in terms of the ego state being expressed. As suggested in Figure 9-4, complementary transactions tend toward improved communications, whereas the crossed lines shown in part *b* will probably end up in arguments and misunderstandings. It has been suggested that one who generally is low in parent, high in adult, and high in free child is likely to be most effective in dealing with others.[12]

---

[11]John Drotning, "Sensitivity Training Doesn't Work Magic," *Management of Personnel Quarterly*, vol. 7, no. 2, Summer 1968, p. 19.
[12]Dudley Bennett, "Transactional Analysis in Management," *Personnel*, vol. 52, no. 1, January-February 1975, p. 39.

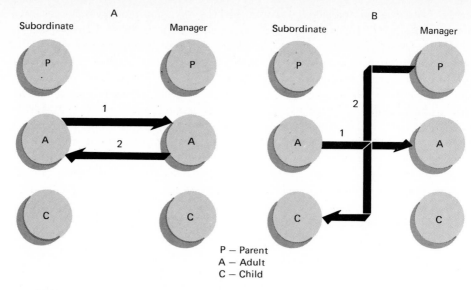

P — Parent
A — Adult
C — Child

Transaction A
   1. Subordinate: Have you reviewed my set of goals for the coming period?
   2. Manager: Yes and we should get together soon and talk about possible changes and ways in
      which I can help you achieve your goals.

Transaction B
   1. Subordinate: Have you reviewed my set of goals for the coming period?
   2. Manager: Yes and it's apparent that you don't know what a management-by-objectives pro-
      gram is all about.

FIGURE 9-4 Complementary and crossed transactions.

Structured insight   In attempting to obtain some of the values of sensitivity training
and role playing without their accompanying costs, trainers have used various instruments
to systematically collect data concerning trainee attitudes and values. These are then
compared to a model of behavior in the hope that trainees will develop some insight into
makeup and implications of their chosen modes of behavior. In one particular scheme,
these assessments are located upon a 9-by-9 "managerial grid," with concern for people
shown on the vertical scale and concern for output on the horizontal.[13] A score of 1
indicates trainee low concern and a score of 9 indicates high concern. Such assessments
are then followed by thorough group discussion of the meaning of the measured location
of each trainee, usually with the admonition that the group should move to a more
balanced position of equal concern for both people and productivity.

   Chris Argyris suggests the use of another method that will provide self-insight into
leadership practices of top-level executives.[14] Executives are first asked to write out
descriptions of their espoused theories of leadership, particularly in reference to how
they deal with people. Second, a tape recording is made of an actual meeting conducted
by the executive. In a later gathering of all executives involved in the development
program, each is asked to diagnose and describe the actual theory in use revealed by his

---

[13]Robert R. Blake and Jane S. Mouton; Louis B. Barnes and Larry Greiner, "Breakthrough in Organization Development," *Harvard Business Review,* vol. 42, no. 6, November-December 1964, p. 133.

[14]"Conversation with Chris Argyris," *Organizational Dynamics,* vol. 3, no. 1, Summer 1974, pp.
51–55.

or her own tape. In addition, they must do the same for the tape of one other executive in the group. The ensuing discussion involves a comparison of the espoused theory with the theory actually in use as revealed by the two separate tape diagnoses. The goal of this process is to reveal the inevitable difference between stated beliefs and actual behavior; to reduce dissonance, one must change either the espoused theory or the theory in use. Assuming a desire to change behavior, a specific program of action is then prepared by each executive. Rather than presenting general resolutions such as "I'll be less autocratic," the executive is asked to specifically indicate what will be said and done in probable situations. Three months later, another tape is made of an actual meeting conducted by the subject executive, and this is analyzed in a fashion similar to that described above. Any systematic device that furthers understanding of one's actual behavior in comparison with preferred behavior can be labeled "structured insight."

Job Knowledge

Regardless of the degree of prior possession of decision-making and interpersonal skills, the executive must acquire knowledge concerning the actual job to which he or she is assigned. As shown in the survey of personnel directors previously cited, on-the-job approaches are simultaneously most widely used and most highly valued.

On-the-job experience   Learning by experience cannot and should not be eliminated as a method of development, though as a sole approach it is wasteful, time-consuming, and inefficient. On-the-job learning is not confined to personnel assigned to relatively simple tasks. In a survey of 290 scientists and engineers engaged in research and development activities, it was found that they keep up to date through a variety of activities which are largely unrelated to formal continuing-education courses.[15] On-the-job problem solving and colleague interaction were reported as being most important for professional growth by 62 percent of the respondents. Interactions with fellow professionals on the job were seen as a major source of both motivation and information. Publishing, independent reading, formal courses, and outside profesional meetings were deemed important, but not as important as on-the-job activities.

Coaching   On-the-job experience in conjunction with a skilled coach with authority, one's boss, is deemed by many to be the single most effective training technique. Teaching is individualized and one learns by doing. There is increased motivation for the trainee, with minimization of the problem of learning transfer from theory to practice. The foremost disadvantages lie in frequent neglect by the superior, both in time and quality of teaching efforts, and the tendency to perpetuate customary practices and solutions.

Effective coaching is a difficult skill to master. It requires a delicate balance of direction and freedom. The coach should help by explaining the relevance of information and through helping to generate alternatives for problems. Trainees must also be given the "right to fail" on occasions, if they are ever to stand on their own. Coaching also involves teaching by example. If an open problem-solving organization is deemed desirable, the superior must demonstrate this in her or his own style by asking for suggestions, encouraging subordinate participation in the superior's own decisions, and generally encouraging a free flow of information.

---

[15]Newton Margulies and Anthony P. Raia, "Scientists, Engineers, and Technological Obsolescence," *California Management Review*, vol. 10, no. 2, Winter 1967, p. 44.

Understudy   The understudy system can be considered a somewhat different approach from those described above, in that a certain person is specifically designated as the heir apparent. The understudy's future depends upon what happens to his or her superior. The advantages of this technique pertain to the practical and realistic situation in which the training is conducted. In addition, on-the-job learning is acquired in a situation where the trainee is not responsible for operating results. Serious mistakes are thus reduced, and the strain on the trainee is relieved. The disadvantages are numerous. Since the understudy has been specifically designated, there is often the feeling that the competition for promotion is over, with a consequent reduction in motivation for both the one designated and the other personnel as well. Besides, progress is uncertain, since the position must be vacated before the understudy can move up. Full-time understudies are somewhat expensive to maintain over a long period. And finally, this approach to training suffers the same disadvantages as all on-the-job training. The trainee learns the ways of the superior, who in turn learned them from *his* or *her* superior. Outside contacts through other development techniques constitute a desirable supplement.

Organizational Knowledge

Programs designed to increase the trainee's knowledge of the total organization necessarily involve exposure to information and events outside the confines of the immediate job. Perhaps the most popular of these methods is that of position rotation. If a firm espouses the participative philosophy as a way of managing, the multiple management method can also be utilized.

Position Rotation   The major objective of position-rotation development is that of broadening the background of the trainee in the business. On-the-job experience, coaching, and understudying are narrow, in the sense that the trainee acquires skill and knowledge in the one job. If the trainee is rotated periodically from one job to another, he or she acquires a general background. In a planned rotation program, the job switches are made in periods of from 6 months to a year. In the Procter and Gamble Company, for example, a trainee may enter a department as an assistant supervisor. Gradually, the assistant learns the supervisor's job, function by function. Over a period of time, the supervisor is trained *out* of a job by transferring the duties, one by one, to the assistant supervisor. The original supervisor is then rotated to another department as an assistant and will there undergo a similar process.

The advantages of planned position rotation are: (1) it provides a general background and thus an organizational point of view; (2) it encourages interdepartmental cooperation, since managers have seen multiple sides of issues; (3) fresh viewpoints are periodically introduced to the various units; (4) it promotes organizational flexibility through generating flexible human resources; (5) comparative performance appraisal can be accomplished more objectively; and (6) it acquires all the advantages of on-the-job coaching in each situation. Position rotation can also be used as a "new experience" reward to competent managers without the qualities to move higher. The primary disadvantages of this method are that productive work may suffer because of the obvious periodic disruption caused by such changes, and the limitation on the amount of job skill that can be developed during these shorter periods of time. Managers on planned rotation programs may be discouraged in developing and pursuing long-term projects. They may also be tempted to "liquidate the human assets" in the interest of enhancing personal records for maximum output and minimum cost. These drawbacks can be ameliorated somewhat by lengthening the interval of rotation, limiting the rotation to positions of assistants, and measuring the "human assets" through morale surveys.

Multiple Management In 1932, Charles P. McCormick, president of McCormick and Company of Baltimore, introduced the idea of establishing a junior board of directors. The greatest value of this additional board was the training of junior executives. The board was given the authority to discuss any problem that the senior board could discuss, and its members were encouraged to put their minds to work on the business *as a whole*, rather than to concentrate on their specialized areas. From such a method, a value may be derived similar to that achieve by rotation—the encouragement of a general viewpoint.

The junior board at McCormick consists of 16 department managers or their assistants. At the end of each 6-month period, on a ballot taken among themselves, 6 of these members are dropped from the committee. Nominations are then made, and an election by the remaining 10 is conducted to fill the 6 vacancies. Membership on this board is considered to be a high honor as well as an excellent training experience. In addition, membership on the junior board has become a prerequisite to membership on the senior board of directors.

The junior board of directors discusses a wide variety of subjects. All recommendations that are forwarded to the senior board must be unanimous, and they remain as recommendations until the senior board approves them. In practice, the senior board turns down a negligible number of these submitted recommendations. Thus, though the major objective is training, the firm is also being benefited by productive ideas.

General Knowledge

It has been suggested that executive development, as compared with operative training, tends to move toward the education end of the training-education continuum. Thus, it is not surprising to find a considerable role for formal educational institutions of various types. In these developmental attempts, there are unusual problems of learning transfer from class or conference room to the job situation.

Special courses The method of special courses requires the trainee to leave the workplace and devote her or his entire time to development objectives. Special training and/or educational courses can be established in numerous ways by a business organization as a part of its executive development program. First, there are the courses which the firm itself establishes, to be taught by members of the firm. Some companies have regular instructors assigned to their training departments. In the case of General Motors, this approach grew into the General Motors Institute of Technology, which is actually an industrial university.

A second approach is for the business organization to work with a school or college in establishing a course or a series of courses to be taught by school instructors. In the training-education continuum, these courses usually tend toward the education end. There is an increasing amount of cooperation between schools and business organizations in the area of business and management education.

A third approach is for the firm to send personnel to programs established by schools, colleges, consultants, or associations formed for the purpose of management development. As indicated in Box 9-1, the "yearn to learn" is most often attributed to the need to keep up with rapid changes in the environment. The first such program was the Sloan

BOX 9-1
The Executive Yearn to Learn
Jeremy Main

The scene was familiar. The speaker droned on in hypnotic cadences, reading his paper on "controlling structural disequilibration." The 1,000 or so in the audience, mostly middle-aged male executives, were lulled by the warm air and soft lights in the grand ballroom of New York's Waldorf-Astoria Hotel. No one snored, but nor did anyone seem to be taking notes. People appeared to be napping with their eyes open. Some drifted out to the phone booths to check with their secretaries for messages that would tell them the real world still needed them. For two days the 1,000 were in the grip of a meeting on the financial outlook sponsored by the Conference Board.

In the name of management education, a good crowd of American executives will turn out for almost any seminar, listen to any speaker, or travel to any conference that is offered, and hang the expense, which is usually steep. Prices normally start at about $500 for a two-day seminar, not including the participant's salary and living and travel expenses, and go as high as $15,200 for 13 weeks at Harvard's Advanced Management Program and more for a year at MIT's Sloan school.

The number and variety of offerings are vast. Presidents can mingle with other presidents at posh resorts in seminars held exclusively for them. Underlings can attend one of the 5,000 one- to three-day courses offered this year by the American Management Associations (AMA). The crown princes of great corporations get to go to Harvard or some other prestigious business school. Senior executives who have reached such heights that they can turn their minds to lofty thoughts may attend the Aspen Institute for Humanistic Studies in Colorado. There, in the description of one participant, they may read a few pages of Plato and then adjourn to an outdoor barbecue, contemplating at once the magnificence of the Rockies and their own place in the universe.

Executives who have attended almost any sort of management training usually recall the experience warmly. Of course, no one is likely to come back from Aspen and admit that he has just wasted two weeks. But if asked to specify exactly how his company has benefited from a course or seminar he just took, the executive may have trouble coming up with the answer. Off the record, he will often admit that the course he took was boring, irrelevant, or misleadingly marketed. Short seminars get the most criticism. The academically rigorous and well-organized courses lasting two weeks or more at the better-known business schools are generally highly rated. Clients seem particularly pleased with courses specially designed by consulting firms for the entire top management of a particular corporation in transition or crisis, even though these tailor-made programs run up bills of hundred of thousands of dollars.

The management-education market is so diverse and changing that it has not yet been measured as a whole, but isolated numbers that emerge here and there show exceptional growth. The nonprofit AMA, the biggest purveyor of management training, has tripled the annual number of its sessions since the mid-1970s, when management education seems to have taken off. The AMA's annual income from education has climbed from $11 million to $60 million in ten years. The profitmaking companies selling education are smaller than the AMA, but growing fast: Xerox Learning Systems, acquired by Xerox in 1960, became a "gold-plated" investment in 1976, according to its president, Stanley E. Sanderson Jr., and has been growing 32% annually for the past five years. Two firms that specialize in management training, Wilson Learning and Forum Corp., are growing by 30% and 45% a year, respectively. All the Big Eight accounting companies have gone into management training. Control Data established its Management Institute two years ago.

Consulting firms such as Arthur D. Little both use and sell executive training extensively.

The hunger for management education is most often attributed to the - need-to-keep-up-with - increasingly -rapid-change-in-this-ever-more-complex-world. The middle-aged manager especially may need help. Arnold K. Weinstein, dean of Arthur D. Little's Management Education Institute, explains, "You're 45 years old with a bachelor of arts degree and you have bright young MBAs with the latest techniques working for you. You can't understand the language. You feel obsolete and threatened."

So you go to school. Subjects that weren't taught a while back at business school, like productivity and information systems, have become important, while traditional subjects, such as strategic planning, need a new look. Younger executives may realize that all the quantitative and analytical thinking they acquired at business school left out the human side of management. So the curriculum abounds in "soft subjects," such as the art of criticizing subordinates constructively.

The business schools were first in management education and remain foremost in prestige. The Sloan school at MIT started its year-long advanced-management program in 1931 and the Harvard Business School launched its 13-week version of the course during World War II (current cost is $15,200). Dozens of other colleges added similar courses and, in recent years, shorter courses lasting one or two weeks or even just a few days. For reasons not altogether clear, some professors regard two weeks as instructionally respectable but anything less too short a time to teach anything. The Harvard Business School has dropped most of its very short courses, but increased the number of two- and three-week courses. On the other hand, the Wharton school will stage 160 two- and three-day seminars around the U.S. this year.

Fellowship Program, established in 1931 at the Massachusetts Institute of Technology. Most have been established since 1950. Among them are the programs at Michigan State University, Harvard University, Indiana University, Marquette University, University of Arizona, and a host of others. The American Management Associations is a private organization engaged in the business of management education and offers seminars in the various specialized fields of finance, management, insurance, international management, manufacturing, marketing, office management, packaging, personnel, and research development. It also operates an academy at Saranac Lake, New York, where a basic 4-week course in management principles is offered.

Special Meetings   In the category of special meetings are placed such activities as the 1- or 2-day meetings on special subjects held by various organizations. For example, one of the activities of the American Management Associations is the holding of periodic 2- to 3-day conferences in various fields, such as personnel or production management. Attendance varies from a few hundred to over 2,000 participants. The meeting consists of a series of speeches with subsequent question periods. The practice of the Society for the Advancement of Management is to hold local chapter meetings once a month. At each of these meetings a talk or demonstration is presented on some management subject.

Schools and colleges are also engaged in the business of holding 1- or 2-day conferences. Many of these are annual conferences, such as the Personnel Institute of Ohio State University. Various associations, such as the American Institute of Industrial Engineers, the Industrial Relations Research Association, and the American Society for Personnel Administration, also conduct a series of meetings in their respective fields. Many firms are interested in sending selected personnel to special meetings held in their geographic area. The values are largely educational in nature, adding to the general knowledge of these personnel. An additional value is the interchange of information among personnel of various companies in informal sessions outside of the formal presentations.

Selective reading   Many executives claim that it is very difficult to find time to do much reading other than that absolutely required in the performance of their jobs. In most instances proper organization of the daily routine will provide some time for reading that will advance the general knowledge and background of the individual.

Business magazines, such as the *California Management Review* and *Harvard Business Review,* are purchased by some firms for management personnel. The management of the Johnson and Johnson Corporation feels that higher-level executives, who have progressed well beyond the stage where their needs can be met by organized classes, can be stimulated by an attractive book-reading program. Their "Ideas and Authors" program involves face-to-face small-group discussions with authors of stimulating books. Executives are given 4 to 6 weeks to read assigned books, after which a dinner meeting is arranged with the author to discuss his major ideas. These meetings take place about 6 evenings a year and are designed to develop greater conceptual ability, to stimulate new ways of looking at issues that are both internal and external to the business firm, and, in general, to broaden the executives' thinking.

Specific Individual Needs

Most of the previously described programs require placement of the executive trainee into a group situation of a somewhat uniform character. If we are to tailor the development program to individual differences, each candidate will have to be studied to determine which of these programs will meet an observed need. In addition, this study is likely to reveal specific needs peculiar to the individual for which no standard developmental program is available. The two most popular methods of attacking this problem are special project assignments and judiciously chosen committee memberships.

Special projects   A special assignment is a highly useful and flexible training device. Such assignments ordinarily grow out of an individual analysis of weaknesses and, thus, are likely to be highly valuable training. An example of this would be to ask a trainee to develop a system of cost collection in the production of an order. This project not only would provide valuable experience in systems analysis, but would also have the other values of indoctrinating the trainee with the importance of costs and increasing

FIGURE 9-5
Individual Development Program

Name: Oak, T.   Position: Shift Foreman, Rolling

Department: Continuous-weld Pipe

Description of Development Need	Recommended Method of Development	Proposed Dates		Date Completed	Comments
		From	To		
Planning and organizing	Increased attendance at departmental planning meetings.	As scheduled			
	More guidance in formulating plans in own group.	As need for planning occurs			
Development of subordinates	Discuss importance of systematic methods of training subordinates, delegating authority and responsibility, and reviewing their performance.	At once		3/20/79	Realizes problem, but requires more help.
	Coach him in development of subordinates and delegation of authority. Review his performance and offer help.	Monthly			
Working with and utilizing staff departments	Have him assist in budget preparation and review performance figures.	Regularly			
	Have him work with engineers and maintenance department on relocation of equipment	Now	3/31/75	3/31/79	Excellent response. Repeat whenever possible, including other departments.

the trainee's knowledge of organizational relationships with the accounting department. At times, a task force is created consisting of a number of candidates representing different functions in the organization. Trainees not only acquire knowledge of the assigned subject but also learn how to work with and relate to others possessing different viewpoints. Other examples of this type of training are given in Figure 9-5.

Many able young college graduates have been "turned off" by routine, extended, and unexciting developmental programs to the point where a substantial majority change jobs within 3 years of graduation. In response, a few firms have begun special projects programs of a fast-track, "high-risk/high-reward" type. In one instance a recently graduated trainee was given a list of canceled accounts adding up to a half-million dollars in sales.[16] His project was to design a strategy for recouping these accounts; he was then shoved out the door to carry out the plan. Other unusual challenging assignments included developing a plan to recruit minority employees, preparing material for proxy battles in attempted organization take-overs, composing position papers for executive testimony in court, and designing and introducing a personnel program into a small branch plant.

Committee assignments   Committee assignments differ from special projects in that they are regularly constituted or ad hoc committees. They are not training committees per se. Each has assigned objectives and responsibilities related to the work of the organization, and as such they must be peopled by competent personnel. This does not prevent them from being used as training devices under special conditions. If a certain executive seems to be unappreciative of the contributions of another department, appointment to a committee involving members of that department may lead to a change in attitude; or another executive may require a broader knowledge of a problem that involves diverse elements of the firm. Committee assignments could very well provide the necessary general background.

EVALUATION OF MANAGEMENT DEVELOPMENT PROGRAMS

There is no one generally best method of developing effective managers. In surveying over 50 training directors from among the nation's 200 largest firms, it was found that only the case study method ranked number one on two of six suggested training objectives.[17] As portrayed in Figure 9-6, the top-rated methods were as follows: (1) case studies for problem-solving skills and participant acceptance, (2) conference discussion for knowledge acquisition, (3) sensitivity training for changing attitudes, (4) role playing for developing interpersonal skills, and (5) programmed instruction for knowledge retention.

For the individual firms, there are various methods of evaluating program effectiveness. The one most frequently found and least effective is measurement of the group *after* the training has been completed. In most programs, the opinions obtained from trainees about the worth of the experience are almost always favorable.

---

[16]Lawrence Stessin, "Developing Young Managers: 'Immediacy' Sets the Tone," *Personnel*, vol. 48, no. 6, November-December 1971, p. 34.

[17]John W. Newstrom, "Evaluating the Effectiveness of Training Methods," *The Personnel Administrator*, vol. 25, no. 1, January 1980, p. 58.

FIGURE 9-6
Perceived Effectiveness of Nine Training Methods for Six Objectives

Training Objectives

Method	Knowledge Acquisition		Changing Attitudes		Problem-Solving Skills		Interpersonal Skills		Participant Acceptance		Knowledge Retention	
	Mean	Rank	Mean	Rank	Mean	Rank	Mean	Rank	Mean	Rank	Mean	Rank
Case study	3.35	4	2.63	5	3.89	1	2.69	5	4.40	1	3.04	4
Conference (discussion) method	3.72	1	2.93	3	2.91	5	2.89	4	3.45	5	3.26	2
Lecture (with questions)	2.57	8	2.35	7	2.47	7	1.72	8	2.79	8	3.15	3
Business games	3.27	5	2.75	4	3.68	2	2.93	3	3.57	2	2.98	7
Movie films	2.98	6	2.41	6	2.06	9	2.00	6	3.50	4	3.00	5
Programmed instruction	3.49	3	2.21	8	2.85	6	1.81	7	2.69	9	3.87	1
Role playing	3.59	2	3.63	2	3.33	3	4.06	1	3.55	3	3.00	5
Sensitivity training (T-group)	2.74	7	3.65	1	3.00	4	3.80	2	2.86	6	2.57	9
Television lecture	2.43	9	2.20	9	2.15	8	1.67	9	2.81	7	2.76	8

Rating Scale 5 = Highly effective 4 = Quite effective 3 = Moderately effective 2 = Limited effectiveness 1 = Not effective

Source: John Newstrom, "Evaluating the Effectiveness of Training Methods." Reprinted from the January 1980 issue of Personnel Administrator, © 1980, The American Society for Personnel Administration, 30 Park Drive, Berea, Oh. 44017.

A sounder approach is that of measuring the group both before and after the training. Comparisons can then be made to determine if organizational behavior has improved within the group. A still better method is measuring the group both before and after training and applying an identical measurement process to a *control* group that has been carefully selected as equivalent to the trained group in all things except the training experience. Finally, an even more effective method is to use a "post-post" research design by adding an additional measure some time after training, such as 6 months or a year. In one study of the effects of training sessions on leadership styles, the immediate postmeasure after completion of training showed no significant difference between the experimental and control groups.[18] Another measure 18 months later showed that the experimental group had significantly higher scores on self- and other sensitivity measures and in showing consideration for others, both of which were goals of the training course. With reinforcement by organizational superiors, the values taught by the training program began to take form in the work situation.

A final example illustrates the interesting, but often frustrating, nature of training evaluation. In a course specifically designed to improve problem-solving and decision-making abilities, a measurement of group opinion at the end of the course revealed that 87 percent thought the course was worthwhile.[19] The Watson-Glaser Critical Thinking Appraisal was administered to the group both before and after the training. A control group of managers on the same organizational levels in another plant of the firm was also administered this test both before and after the training of the first group. The results showed a *decline* in posttraining scores for the trained group and an *increase* for the untrained control group. The differences were not statistically significant, but they still serve to illustrate the often discouraging nature of management development.

ORGANIZATION DEVELOPMENT

When personnel are subjected to individually oriented training and development programs, the applications of accepted evaluation research designs often "proves" that learning was accomplished. Despite such proof, in all too many instances the impact upon organizational functioning was nil. The trainee must reenter the culture of the ongoing organization, and if it has been unchanged during training, it, rather than the training, is more likely to ultimately control actual behavior. As a consequence, beginning in the 1960s, there sprang up a considerable interest in altering the organization's culture through an *organization development* program.

Bennis defines organization development (OD) as "a *complex educational strategy* intended to *change* the beliefs, attitudes, values, and structure of organizations so that they can better adapt to new technologies, markets, and challenges, and the dizzying rate of change itself."[20] It is a planned and calculated attempt to move the organization

---

[18]Herbert H. Hand and John W. Slocum, Jr., "A Longitudinal Study of the Effects of a Human Relations Training Program on Managerial Effectiveness," *Journal of Applied Psychology,* vol. 56, no. 5, October 1972, pp. 412–417.

[19]Dannie J. Moffie, Richard Calhoon, and James K. O'Brien, "Evaluation of a Management Development Program," *Personnel Psychology,* Winter 1964, pp. 431–440.

[20]Warren G. Bennis, *Organization Development: Its Nature, Origins, and Prospects,* Addison-Wesley, Reading, Mass., 1969, p. 2. Emphasis added.

as a unit to the climate of the behavioral, open, organic model. More specific goals are (1) decision making on the basis of competence rather than authority, (2) creatively resolving conflict through confrontation designed to replace win-lose situations with win-win types, (3) reducing dysfunctional competition and maximizing collaboration, (4) increasing commitment and a sense of "ownership" of organization objectives throughout the work force, (5) increasing the degree of interpersonal trust and support, (6) creating a climate in which human growth, development, and renewal are a natural part of the enterprise's daily operation, and (7) developing a communication system characterized by mutual openness and candor in solving organizational problems.

In a sample of 63 companies in Indiana, 38 reported using one or more educational interventions of an OD type.[21] Team development devices were used by 33 firms while 8 reported use of attitude or opinion survey feedback. Other reported techniques were sensitivity training, management by objectives programs, and use of the managerial grid.

Team Development

The dominant technique in the arsenal of the OD consultant is team development. Instead of sending isolated individuals off to a sensitivity training session attended by strangers, a type of sensitivity session is conducted for the members of an operating unit, off-site, away from the job. A systematic comparison of individually oriented sensitivity training with group-oriented team development is given in Figure 9-7. To overcome the natural reluctance for subordinates to exhibit candor with colleagues and superiors, the services of an outside third-party consultant are deemed essential. In effect, the outsider serves three functions: (1) contacting all members separately to determine what they feel are the major obstructions to effective functioning of the unit, (2) feeding this gathered information to the convened group in a manner that preserves the confidence of information contributors, and (3) serving as a catalyst in the ensuing discussion, which is designed to encourage honest feedback, leveling, and candor. In large organizations, the third party is often a member of the staff personnel unit. The data collection can be either through interview or questionnaires.

With the support of the consultant, the supervisor may be expected to demonstrate openness to constructive comment and suggestions concerning how the unit's collaborative processes are functioning. When one group generated the courage to tell the boss that he was a cold, unfeeling, and impersonal supervisor, he admitted it but simultaneously reported his intention *not* to change. He did provide the reason for his style, issuing from unhappy wartime experiences when many close friends were lost in combat; he had

[21]W.J. Heisler, "Patterns of OD in Practice," *Business Horizons*, vol. 18, no. 1, February 1975, p. 82.

FIGURE 9-7
Contrast of Sensitivity Training and Team Development

Characteristic	Sensitivity Training	Team Development
Participants	Strangers	Fellow workers
Location	Isolated	Isolated
Subject	"Here and now"	Company problems
Structure	Little or none	Some
Trainer	Yes	Yes
Feedback	Honest	Somewhat honest

resolved never to become close to anyone again. Though there was not desired behavior change, the climate was significantly improved because of general understanding of the supervisor's behavior. Also, members of the group discovered that he was equally unfriendly to all—he did not discriminate. In another instance, the superior was disturbed with failures of subordinates to follow instructions communicated by memo, feeling that there might be instances of outright insubordination. At the suggestion of the consultant, several of his memos were gathered, with instructions to all who had received any to write out their interpretations. The net conclusion was that there was no insubordination—just confusion. The executive resolved to rely less on memos and more on face-to-face oral instructions.

Survey Feedback

Though morale surveys have long been conducted by many organizations, such surveys can be turned into an OD strategy by feeding the results back to those who answered the questionnaires. Employee task forces can be formed to analyze results in such areas as the reward system of the firm, leadership style, communication processes, careers, and conflict. Recommendations are made to management and final decisions are discussed and fed back to the employees concerned. Not only are changes made in specific areas, but an atmosphere of mutual respect and trust may well be created.

The Bank of America utilizes an Open Meeting Program to generate change.[22] Small groups of a dozen employees of the same grade level are invited to meet with a member of the personnel unit to talk about their jobs and the work environment. Candor is the rule and anonymity is assured. A detailed and confidential report is prepared for the department head, who shares this upwards or with other units as he or she sees fit. The department head then undertakes some type of action program to address the difficulties uncovered in the open meetings. Although participation is voluntary, over 60 percent have chosen to become involved.

Intergroup Sessions

In most organizations, there is dysfunctional competition and conflict among some units; for instance, engineering makes life tough for production, production causes problems for sales, and personnel brings everything to a halt while enforcing the law. All specialized units have a tendency to turn inward and project their problems on some other group. When a particular interface has approached something close to open warfare, a type of intergroup OD session is sometimes held.

The two groups, or their major representatives, are asked to prepare separate lists of things that the other group does that make life difficult. They are asked to stick to the "here and now" and not complain about last year's slights and hurts. They are prohibited from telling the other group what to do about a problem; they only report what it does to them. Each group is then asked to predict what the other group will write about them. When the two groups meet face-to-face and compare lists, they often realize that all lists are fairly similar, that each group's behavior is frozen in relation to the other. With the facilitation of the third party, who favors only unity, the groups are encouraged to work out action plans to alleviate difficulties.

[22]Adri G. Boudewyn, "The Open Meeting—A Confidential Forum for Employees," *Personnel Journal*, vol. 56, no. 4, April 1977, pp. 192–194.

SUMMARY

Development consists of (1) training to increase skills and knowledge to do a particular job, and (2) education that is concerned with increasing general knowledge, understanding, and background. There are two broad groups of individuals to be trained, operatives and managers. The four basic systems of operative training are (1) on-the-job training, (2) vestibule schools, (3) apprenticeship programs, and (4) special courses. Effective operative training should increase productivity, reduce costs, heighten morale, and promote organizational stability and flexibility.

With the more complex nature of the executive job, manager development involves both training and education. Decision-making skills are enhanced through business games, case studies, and in-basket exercises. Interpersonal skills can be promoted through role playing, behavior modeling, sensitivity training, transactional analysis, and structured insight. Job knowledge can be acquired through experience, coaching, and understudy systems, while organizational knowledge can be developed through position rotation and multiple management. In addition, one's general educational background can be developed through special courses, meetings, and a reading program, while specific individual deficiencies can be addressed through special projects and committee assignments.

Both operative and managerial training can go for naught if the organizational environment precludes learned skills from actually being utilized. Organization development is an intervention strategy whereby the general environment is altered to emphasize collaboration, competence, confrontation, trust, candor, and support. Particular intervention techniques would include team development processes, survey feedback, and intergroup confrontation sessions.

BRIEF CASE

A New York firm recently decided to install word processing equipment in order to increase clerical productivity. The new centralized center was staffed with six secretaries who learned to operate the processors from books and audio-visual aids. The word processor manufacturer stated that the new generation of equipment is so much easier to use that companies can take someone with typing skills off the street and put them into word processing with a minimum of training.

One year after the installation of the new center, the output averaged only 370 lines a day from each operator. This is less than most people achieve hunting and pecking on a manual typewriter. In addition, five of the original operators had resigned. One division manager, who had lost his secretary to the new center, stated, "Just as in the case of introducing the computer, unless there is proper planning and training, people will use word processors like very expensive typewriters." The tension between the operators in the center and the divisions served was great. The operators were miserable because they were being deluged with more work than they could handle, and division managers were unhappy because their work was not being done as quickly and as well as before.

Questions

1. What do you think went wrong here?

2. Is this a training problem? An organizational problem? Why?

3. What suggestions would you make to increase the productivity of the word processing center? In meeting the requirements of the division executives?

1. Contrast the four systems of operative training from the viewpoints of purpose, organization, and educational characteristics.

2. Discuss programmed learning in terms of learning concepts and effectiveness.

3. Compare and contrast sensitivity training with team development.

4. Identify the major elements of training technology utilized in sensitivity training.

5. Contrast and compare sensitivity training and structured insight.

6. Describe the role of the OD consultant.

7. Classify the executive development techniques into on-the-job versus off-the-job methods.

8. Identify and briefly describe one executive training technique in each of the following areas: (1) decision making, (2) interpersonal skills, (3) organizational knowledge, and (4) job knowledge.

9. What is organization development? What type of organization is envisaged?

10. Compare and contrast role playing and behavior modeling.

SUPPLEMENTARY READING

BOURGEOIS, L. J. III and MANUEL BOLTVINIK: "OD in Cross-Cultural Settings: Latin America," *California Management Review,* vol. 23, no. 3, Spring 1981, pp. 75–81.

DECKER, PHILLIP J.: "The Enhancement of Behavior Modeling Training of Supervisory Skills by the Inclusion of Retention Processes," *Personnel Psychology,* vol. 35, no. 2, Summer 1982, pp. 323–332.

MAHONEY, FRANCIS X.: "Team Development, Part 5: Procedure Meetings," *Personnel,* vol. 59, no. 3, May-June 1982, pp. 30–41.

PORAS, JERRY I. and BRAD ANDERSON: "Improving Managerial Effectiveness Through Modeling-Based Training," *Organizational Dynamics,* vol. 9, no. 4, Spring 1981, pp. 60–77.

SIMS, HENRY P. JR. and CHARLES C. MANZ: "Modeling Influences on Employee Behavior," *Personnel Journal,* vol. 61, no. 1, January 1982, pp. 58–65.

STARCEVICH, MATT M. and J. ARNOLD SYKES: "Internal Advanced Management Programs for Executive Development," *The Personnel Administrator,* vol. 27, no. 6, June 1982, pp. 27–38.

chapter 10

Performance Appraisal and Management by Objectives

Despite the multiplicity and complex nature of many training and educational programs, most development occurs on the job. But such development is slowed and less effective if the employee is not systematically appraised and fed back information concerning her or his quality of performance. All employees are appraised on their job performance in some manner or another. In general, it can be said that the choice lies among three possible approaches:

1. A *casual,* unsystematic, and often haphazard appraisal
2. The *traditional* and highly *systematic* measurement of (a) employee characteristics, (b) employee contributions, or (c) both
3. Mutual goal setting through a Management by Objectives program (MBO)

Though the casual approach is perhaps the most commonly used, various studies have revealed an increase in the number of firms choosing some formal type of appraisal. A survey of 426 firms resulted in 67 percent reporting a formal rather than casual attempt to evaluate employees.[1] There was a direct relationship between size of firm and incidence of formal plans, with 87 percent of those having more than 5,000 employees using a systematic approach. A survey of approximately 1,000 firms indicated that 80 percent have some type of formal appraisal system.[2] One-third of the firms having programs reported utilization of the most recent innovation, Management by Objectives.

---

[1] National Industrial Conference Board, ''Personnel Practices in Factory and Office: Manufacturing,'' *Studies in Personnel Policy,* no. 194, New York, 1964, p. 17.
[2] Glenn H. Varney, *''Performance Appraisal: Inside and Out,''* The Personnel Administrator, vol. 17, no. 6, November-December 1972, p. 16.

PERFORMANCE APPRAISAL AND THE LAW

Title VII of the Civil Rights Act covers performance measurement systems in the same fashion as it applies to selection devices used during the hiring process. EEOC guidelines concerning adverse impact are also applicable. In *Friend v. Leidinge,* it was determined that the company, utilizing an appraisal system, had promoted 4.5 percent of all black employees and 5.3 percent of all whites during a specified time. Inasmuch as 4.5 was not less than 80 percent of 5.3, no adverse impact was inferred. In this case, *all* employees were considered to be applicants for promotions; again, the employer would prefer a smaller pool through restricting the term "applicant" to those either applying for advancement or those deemed eligible for consideration.

Other statistical analyses have been used to determine the existence of adverse impact on protected groups.[3] One court made internal comparisons of the percentages of minorities in high- and low-level positions, versus the percentages for the white majority. Still another compared the percentage of minorities in higher positions as compared to the percentage of the external labor market in the standard metropolitan area. Finally, interest has been shown in the mean scores of minorities on performance appraisal instruments as compared with the means of majorities.

In analysis of 66 legal cases involving charges of discrimination in the use of performance appraisal systems, companies successfully defending against the charges utilized one or more of the following practices:[4]

1. Job analysis was used to develop the system. The dimensions being measured on the instrument were developed from analysis of job duties, thereby constituting a type of content validation.

2. The appraisal instrument was behavior-oriented rather than trait-oriented. When subjective traits are utilized, it is believed that these can be used to hide conscious or unconscious bias on the part of the rater. On one occasion, 47 executives were asked to define the trait of "dependability"; 75 different definitions were generated.[5] Thus, if specific behaviors are defined and measured, the company is better able to defend its assessments.

3. Appraisers are given definite instructions and training in how to make the appraisals. Since validating the instrument is extremely difficult, validating the skills of the rater will help.

4. Results of the appraisal process are communicated to the employee and provision is made for appeal in the event of disagreement.

In various decisions, the courts have made such statements as "ratings should be examined for evidence of racial, ethnic, or sex bias," and "criteria should represent important or critical work behaviors or outcomes." In one of the first major cases, *Rowe v. General Motors Corporation,* the performance appraisal system was overturned be-

---

[3]Lawrence S. Kleiman and Richard L. Durham, "Performance Appraisal, Promotion and the Courts: A Critical Review," *Personnel Psychology,* vol. 34, no. 1, Spring 1981, pp. 105–106.

[4]William H. Holley and Hubert S. Feild, "Will Your Performance Appraisal System Hold Up in Court?" *Personnel,* vol. 50, no. 1, January–February 1982, p. 61.

[5]Wayne F. Cascio and H. John Bernardin, "Implications of Performance Appraisal Litigation for Personnel Decisions," *Personnel Psychology,* vol. 34, no. 2, Summer 1981, p. 215.

cause (1) the supervisor's recommendation was indispensable to promotion, (2) supervisors were given no written instructions, and (3) the standards used were vague and subjective. These factors coupled with significantly fewer promotions for blacks and exclusive reliance upon the recommendations of an all-white supervisory force, led the court to decide that the company was in violation of the Civil Rights Act.

With the passage of the amendment to the Age Discrimination Act that prohibits compulsory retirement prior to the age of 70, companies will also have to protect against charges of discrimination on the basis of age in removing inadequate personnel. Rather than just allowing marginal personnel to wait it out until retirement at 65, this extension will force earlier systematic appraisal that can be defended against charges of bias on the basis of age.

SYSTEMATIC APPRAISAL BY SUPERIORS

Appraisals of subordinates by superiors is deemed by many to be an essential part of the executive job. A systematic and periodic appraisal process is deemed superior to a casual, intuitive, and, at times, haphazard evaluation, which will always take place in the absence of such preplanning. In the sections that follow, we shall examine the particular values issuing from systematic appraisal, survey several alternative measurement systems, and indicate the prominent features of a program of installation.

Values of the Systematic Approach

Perhaps the first and basic value of systematic performance appraisal is that it provides information of great assistance in making and enforcing decisions about such subjects as promotions, pay increases, layoffs, and transfers. It provides this information *in advance* of the time when it may be needed, thereby avoiding spot judgment when a decision must be made. The reported uses of formal appraisal in one survey of 132 companies was 43 percent for reward allocation, 28 percent for employee development, 16 percent for feedback of operating performance, 7 percent for making promotions, and 4 percent for human resources planning.[6] When the decision is made in a systematic fashion, it is not colored unduly by the events that have happened most recently or by those the appraiser can remember. In addition, the systematic approach provides the information in *a form that permits the making of comparisons*. All persons have been appraised in the same manner. It has been found that the records established by the systematic rating of personnel are of great value in *backing up decisions* that have been challenged.

A second value of systematic appraisal of employee performance is that it serves to *stimulate and guide employee development*. Most people like to know how they are doing. A good appraisal program provides this information in a form that can usually be communicated to the employee. The factors utilized in the rating process form a pattern of desired behavior, and a comparison of the individual's performance with the approved pattern will indicate areas of weakness.

[6]Ralph F. Catalanello and John A. Hooper, "Managerial Appraisal," *The Personnel Administrator*, vol. 26, no. 9, September 1981, p. 77.

The requirement for periodic and accurate appraisal levies a burden upon supervision that tends to produce *better and more competent supervisors*. An immediate superior should be well acquainted with employees and their performance. The existence of a formal requirement tends to condition and train her or him in the essential functions of judging and helping personnel. Additional values of systematic appraisal would include provision of one criterion for validation of selection and training devices, and attraction of higher-caliber personnel to an organization that recognizes and rewards better-than-average performance.

TRADITIONAL PERFORMANCE APPRAISAL SYSTEMS

There are a number of different types of systems for measuring the excellence of employee performance. As suggested in Box 10-1, looking for the ideal appraisal system is comparable to looking for the Holy Grail. Many of the same systems that are utilized in measuring the worth of jobs (job evaluation) are also used in measuring the worth of a person on the job. These two techniques, job evaluation and performance appraisal, often provide the rational foundation for a wage and salary system.

In the discussion that follows, several performance appraisal systems will be described briefly. Among them are:

1 Ranking

2 Person-to-person comparison

3 Grading

4 Graphic scales

5 Checklists

6 Forced-choice description

7 Behaviorally anchored rating scales
   a Expectation scales (BES)
   b Observation scales (BOS)

8 Essay

We shall present briefly the rationale of each system and make some comparison of its merit with those of other approaches.

Ranking

The oldest and simplest system of formal systematic rating is to compare one person with all others for the purpose of placing them in a simple rank order of worth. In doing this, the appraiser considers person and performance as an entity; no attempt is made to systematically fractionize what is being appraised into component elements.

One of the objections to the ranking process is that we are asking the rater to perform an impossible feat. The analysis of one person's performance is not simple. Yet we are asking the rater to compare several people simultaneously and turn out an accurate rank order. Can the human mind handle all these variables at one time? To simplify this problem, the paired-comparison technique of ranking can be used. Each person can be compared with every other person, one at a time. For example, suppose there are five employees. Employee A's performance is compared with B's, and a decision is made concerning whose is the better performance. Then A is compared with C, D, and E in order. The same approach is used for the other personnel. Thus, the use of the paired-comparison technique with these five employees would mean a total of ten decisions, only two people being involved in each decision. The number of decisions can be determined by the following formula:

$$\text{Number of comparisons} = \frac{N(N-1)}{2}$$

In this formula, N equals the number of personnel to be compared. The results of these comparisons can be tabulated, and a rank created from the number of times each person is considered to be superior.

Person-to-Person Comparison

One of the first attempts to break the person's performance apart and analyze its components was the person-to-person rating system, used by the Army during World War I. Certain factors, such as leadership, initiative, and dependability, were selected for purposes of analysis. A scale was designed for each carefully defined factor. Instead of defining varying degrees of leadership, *particular people* were used to represent these degrees. The rater had to develop his or her own scale by evaluating the leadership qualities of persons known in the past. The person who demonstrated the highest degree of leadership was placed at the upper end of the scale, and particular other key people were assigned to the lowest and intervening degrees. Thus a scale of persons was created for each selected factor.

It is apparent how the title "person-to-person" was derived. Instead of comparing whole people to whole people, personnel are compared to *key persons*, one factor at a time. This system of measurement is utilized today in job evaluation, being known as the "factor-comparison" system.[7] Though it is highly useful in measuring jobs, it is of very limited use in measuring people. The devising of scales would evidently be extremely complicated. If each rater must use, for different degree definitions, particular people one has known, the ratings would not be comparable from one department to another.

Grading

In the grading system, certain categories of worth are established in advance and carefully defined. In the federal civil service, for example, there are three categories of personnel: outstanding, satisfactory, and unsatisfactory. Employee performance is then compared with these grade definitions, and the person is allocated to the grade that best describes his or her performance. The employee can receive an O, S, or U. There can, of course, be more than three grades. This is the same basic system of measurement that is used in the job evaluation system, called "grade description." The federal civil service is consistent in that it uses the grading approach for both people and jobs.

The grading system is sometimes modified into a forced-distribution system, in which certain percentages are established for each grade. For example, 10 percent of the total personnel *must* go into the top grade, 20 percent *must* be assigned to the second grade, 40 percent to the middle, 20 percent to the fourth, and 10 percent to the bottom grade. It has the advantage of forcing a separation of the personnel in the group, so that the rater cannot relax and judge them all as average, superior, or below average. As in all systems that force the rater to do something, there is considerable resistance on the part of the evaluator. This system also introduces a zero-sum game for all ratees. Even though a person rated in the bottom 10 percent should significantly improve performance, he or she would not rise in ratings if all others had improved similarly. Imagine the frustration of such an employee, as well as the dismay of the superior while communicating recognition of the improved performance with the same low rating.

Graphic Scales

Perhaps the most commonly used traditional, systematic method of performance appraisal is that of establishing scales for a number of fairly specific factors. In one survey of 216 organizations, 57 percent used graphic rating scales.[8] It is an approach similar to that of the person-to-person system except that the degrees on the factor scales are represented by *definitions* rather than by key people. Figure 10-1 is one type of rating form that is considered to be graphic. The rater can choose one of five degrees for each factor. If one desires more freedom for the rater to make fine distinctions, each degree can be considered to be a continuum and the location of the check mark can be high,

---

[7]See Chapter 12.

[8]Alan H. Locher and Kenneth S. Teel, "Performance Appraisal—A Survey of Current Practices," *Personnel Journal*, vol. 56, no. 5, May 1977, p. 247.

CP F 8472
APPRENTICE PERFORMANCE RATING—Training Section, Industrial Relations Department

NAME	CLOCK NUMBER	DEPARTMENT	JOB CLASSIFICATION
DATE STARTED ON JOB	DATE OF LAST RATING		DATE OF THIS RATING

TO THE RATER: This rating will represent your appraisal of the trainee's actual performance on his present job or in related classroom work. The value of it depends upon the impartiality and sound judgment you use. You should keep in mind both the interest of the company and the personal interests of the individual, when making the rating.

TO HELP YOU MAKE A CAREFUL ANALYSIS, THE FOLLOWING SUGGESTIONS ARE OFFERED:
1. Consider only one factor at a time. Do not let your rating in one trait influence your rating of another.
2. Base your judgment on the requirements of the job and his performance in it as compared to others doing similar work.
3. Carefully read the description of each trait and specifications for each grade before making your entry, then check the space which most nearly describes your opinion.
4. Upon completion, review and check your rating.
5. Make any comments in provided space which you believe will furnish additional information concerning trainee.

PERFORMANCE RATING

PERFORMANCE FACTORS	Does not meet job requirements	Partially meets job requirements	Meets job requirements	Exceeds job requirements	Far exceeds job requirements
QUALITY OF WORK: Accuracy, skill, thoroughness, neatness	Consistently unsatisfactory	Occasionally unsatisfactory	Consistently satisfactory	Sometimes superior	Consistently superior
	☐	☐	☐	☐	☐
QUANTITY OF WORK: Output; consider not only regular duties, but also how promptly he completes "extra" or rush assignments	Consistently below requirements	Frequently below requirements	Usually meets requirements	Frequently exceeds requirements	Consistently exceeds requirements
	☐	☐	☐	☐	☐
DEPENDABILITY: Follows instructions, good safety habits, initiative, punctuality and attendance	Requires constant supervision	Needs occasional follow-up	Ordinarily can be counted on	Needs very little supervision	Completely trustworthy in job requirements
	☐	☐	☐	☐	☐
ATTITUDES: Toward company, job and fellow workers; cooperation	Seldom works with or assists others; indifferent	Frequently uncooperative; too critical of others	Generally works well with others; normal interest	Eagerness often displayed; a good team worker	Extraordinary interest; inspires others to work
	☐	☐	☐	☐	☐

COMMENTS:

DEPARTMENT SUPERVISOR	CLASSROOM SUPERVISOR

FIGURE 10-1 Graphic rating scale for hourly personnel. (*Source: Champion Paper and Fibre Company, Hamilton, Ohio. By permission.*)

middle, or low within each degree. The degree of interrater reliability should be higher when only five decisions are permitted on each factor, as compared with a much larger number when multiple decisions are allowed within each degree. It is interesting to note that this same basic approach is the most commonly used system for measuring the worth of jobs—the "point system" of job evaluation.

The selection of factors to be measured is a crucial part of the graphic scales system. As indicated previously, they are of two types: (1) characteristics, such as initiative and dependability, and (2) contributions, such as quantity and quality of work. Since certain areas of job performance cannot be objectively measured, it is likely that graphic scales will continue to use a mixture of characteristics and contributions, with the emphasis upon the latter.

The number of factors ordinarily used varies from nine to twelve and is adjusted to the particular occupational category being considered, such as hourly personnel, sales and financial, and so on. Commonly used factors are quantity and quality of work, cooperation, personality, versatility, leadership, safety, job knowledge, attendance, loyalty, dependability, and initiative. Research shows that it makes no appreciable difference in rating results ". . . whether (a) the 'good' end of a graphic scale is located at the left, right, top, or bottom, (b) graphic scales or numerical ratings are used, or (c) the order of presentation is one name at a time, one trait at a time, or a matrix with free choice or order. . . ."[9] Such research usually demonstrates that there should be less concern with form and technique and more emphasis placed upon rater selection and training.

Though popular in use, graphic scales impose a heavy burden upon the rater. One must report and evaluate the performance of subordinates on scales involving as many as five degrees on twelve different factors for perhaps twenty to thirty people. The fact that the manager actually reports a decision for each factor in all cases does not necessarily mean that an accurate decision can be made.

Checklists

To reduce the burden upon the appraiser, a checklist system can be utilized. The rater does not evaluate employee performance; it is merely reported. The evaluation of the worth of *reported* behavior is accomplished by the staff personnel department.

An example of the checklist system is shown in Figure 10-2. In this form a series of questions is presented concerning the subject employee and his or her behavior. The rater checks to indicate if the answer to a question about the employee is yes or no. The value of each question may be weighted. The rater is not aware of the specific values, but can distinguish the positive questions from the negative and thus introduce bias if desired. It will be noted that an attempt is made to determine the degree of consistency of the rater by asking the same question twice, but in a different manner (numbers 33 and 40).

One of the disadvantages of the checklist system is that it is difficult to assemble, analyze, and weigh a number of statements about employee characteristics and contributions. In addition, a separate listing of questions must be prepared for different types of jobs, since those used for clerical positions cannot be used for management. The checklist approach does have the advantage of requiring only a reporting of facts from the rater. One does not have to distinguish among various degrees for each of nine to twelve factors for each of twenty to thirty employees.

[9]Herbert H. Blumberg, Clinton B. DeSoto, and James L. Kuethe, "Evaluation of Rating Scale Formats," *Personnel Psychology*, vol. 19, no. 3, Autumn 1966, p. 253.

FIGURE 10-2
Checklist for Appraising Supervisors

		Yes	No
31	Does he or she usually volunteer good ideas?	___	___
32	Is a marked interest shown in the job?	___	___
33	Is consistent treatment meted out to all subordinates?	___	___
34	Does he or she usually back up subordinates?	___	___
35	Is equipment maintained in good condition?	___	___
36	Does the supervisor display a good working knowledge of the job?	___	___
37	Does he or she know and try to follow the provisions of the labor contract?	___	___
38	Do subordinates show respect?	___	___
39	Is the departmental area usually maintained in a neat and clean condition?	___	___
40	Does the supervisor show favoritism to particular subordinates?	___	___
41	Does he or she usually find time to listen to employee troubles?	___	___
42	Has he or she ever reprimanded an employee in public?	___	___
43	Does he or she complain about treatment accorded by superiors?	___	___
44	Does the supervisor maintain control over emotions?	___	___
45	Is the buck usually passed to higher management?	___	___
46	Are orders usually followed?	___	___
47	Are the supervisor's orders usually followed?	___	___
48	Is recognition and praise accorded a well-done job?	___	___
49	Are schedules usually met?	___	___
50	Does he or she ever make mistakes?	___	___

Forced-Choice Description

None of the above-described systems can eliminate one of the major criticisms of performance appraisal, the charge that the rater may be biased or prejudiced. One of the fundamental objectives of the forced-choice approach is to reduce or eliminate the possibility of rater bias by *forcing* a choice between descriptive statements of seemingly equal worth. For example, a pair such as the following will be presented to the rater:

1. Gives good, clear instructions to subordinates

2. Can be depended upon to complete any job assigned

The rater is asked to select the one statement most characteristic of the ratee. Even though one may claim that both are equally applicable or inapplicable, he or she is *forced* to select the one that is closer to describing the person in question.

The rater is also forced to choose between statements that are seemingly equally unfavorable, such as the following pair:

1. Makes promises that he or she knows cannot be kept

2. Shows favoritism toward some employees

Again, though feeling that neither or both are applicable, one must select the statement that is more descriptive. Only one of the statements in each pair is correct in identifying the better performance, and this scoring key must be kept secret from the raters. In one research project involving the rating of fourteen instructors by 1,046 students, the use of a forced-choice scale effectively eliminated the leniency error, while the use of a graphic scale format allowed bias to be introduced.[10]

[10]Amiel T. Sharon and C.J. Bartlett, "Effect of Instructional Conditions in Producing Leniency on Two Types of Rating Scales," *Personnel Psychology*, vol. 22, no. 3, Autumn 1969, pp. 251–263.

The manner in which the secret scoring key is devised is substantially as follows: The correct answers are determined on the basis of a *study of present personnel*. By some other method of rating, present employees are placed into two or more categories. A committee can often pretty well agree upon which employees are the best and which are the poorest. A great deal of time, discussion, and effort are put into the process of dividing up present employees as to overall worth, for the committee must be assured that these resulting divisions are as accurate as they can be made. For accurate assessment of human performance and potential, there is no substitute for group evaluation utilizing a number of measuring devices.

The next step in the process is to devise a series of paired statements similar to the examples given previously. At first there may be as many as 100 such pairs. Present employees are then rated in a forced-choice manner. A pair of statements must definitely distinguish between the better and the poorer employees to be accepted and incorporated into the system. If, for example, the statement, ''Can be depended upon to complete any job assigned,'' is checked as being most descriptive for most of the good personnel and the other statement is checked for the poor employees, this pair is discriminating and can be used in the system, with the second statement indicated as the correct answer. It is often found that many paired statements do not distinguish among the categories of personnel; such pairs must be eliminated.

In effect, the forced-choice system represents an attempt to devise an objective method of arriving at the *same answers* that the committee reached after their long discussions and hard work. At the same time, it is an attempt to eliminate rater bias, since the correct answers are not apparent. Reports of reliability coefficients as high as .70 to .90 have indicated in various studies. This compares with the usual reliability of from .60 to .80 for most merit ratings.

There are certain primary disadvantages of the forced-choice system. First, it is difficult, if not impossible, to keep the key secret. Secondly, the system is a very poor one to use if employee development is to be emphasized. Neither the rater nor the ratee can figure out from the form the desired mode of behavior, and in fact, if the form is shown to the ratee, he or she is usually unable to accept it or the philosophy behind it. In addition, raters often object to being *forced* to make decisions which they feel cannot or should not be made. Because of these disadvantages, the use of forced-choice systems is not widespread.

Behaviorally Anchored Rating Scales

A different approach to performance appraisal grew from research conducted during World War II when *critical incidents* that make the difference between success and failure were spotlighted. The supervisor's prime task is to observe and record these critical incidents when performed by an employee. For example, such incidents in a purchasing agent's job might include: (1) treated a salesperson in a markedly discourteous manner, (2) rejected a bid that was excessively overpriced, (3) persuaded a local vendor to stock an important item, and (4) failed to return an important phone call.[11] Such a systematic record would also be of great assistance in backing up personnel decisions when challenged by the employee, labor union, compliance agencies, or federal courts; it constitutes ''hard evidence.''

[11]Richard D. Scott, ''Taking Subjectivity Out of Performance Appraisal,'' *Personnel*, vol. 50, no. 4, July-August 1973, pp. 45–49.

More recently, the critical-incident approach has been merged with the graphic-rating concept to produce behaviorally anchored rating scales (BARS). These include two types: (1) Behavior Expectation Scales (BES), where anchors are illustrations that help the rater to define as superior, average, or below average the behavior of the employee, and (2) Behavior Observation Scales (BOS), where the rater reports the *frequency* with which the employee engages in the behavior specified in the anchor. A survey of six studies of the reliability of BARS resulted in a range from .52 to .76.[12]

Behavior expectation scales   The process of developing a BES system is quite complex. The following is an outline of the major steps:

1. A group of knowledgeable personnel (jobholders, supervisors) study the job description for the purpose of developing five to ten performance dimensions, such as verbal communication, dispatching equipment, and maintenance of equipment.

2. The group is then asked to generate multiple bits of behavior (anchors) that illustrate varying levels of performance for each dimension; for instance, the operator could be expected to ignore the operational status of the equipment, or the operator could be expected to inform supervisors immediately if problems arise. A well-stated behavior anchor avoids use of adjective qualifiers, such as "the supervisor does a good job in understanding complaints." One should also avoid anchors that make assumptions about employee knowledge, such as "the operator knows how to run the machine in an efficient manner." Specific examples of behavior should be used, which can later be scaled in terms of good, average, or below average performance.

3. All generated anchors are listed in random order and members of the group are asked to allocate them to specific dimensions. Anchors for which there is not 75 percent agreement are discarded as being too subjective.

4. At times, the random list of anchors along with the list of dimensions will be given for classification to a second group of knowledgeable personnel. Again, if there is not 75 percent agreement with the first group, the anchor is discarded.

5. Finally, the retained anchors under each dimension are ranked in the order of desirability, and a scale is formed. The net result is a rating scale that has examples of behavior anchoring for each degree.

Figure 10-3 is an example of a BES scale on the dimension of "supervision" for a sales manager.

Doubts still exist as to whether the increased accuracy of rating is worth the effort described previously. One study indicated that BARS was superior to traditional graphic scales in reducing halo errors and leniency, but the differences were small.[13] Researchers surveying several studies concluded that "despite the intuitive appeal of BARS, findings from research have not been encouraging."[14] Another study found that more cognitively complex raters do better with BARS, but those with less discriminating ability are more

[12]Rick Jacobs, Ditsa Kafry, and Sheldon Zedeck, "Expectations of Behaviorally Anchored Rating Scales," *Personnel Psychology,* vol. 33, no. 3, Autumn 1980, p. 629.

[13]Walter C. Borman and Marvin D. Dunnette, "Behavior-Based versus Trait-Oriented Performance Ratings: An Empirical Study," *Journal of Applied Psychology,* vol. 60, no. 5, October 1975, p. 561.

[14]Donald P. Schwab, Herbert G. Heneman III, and Thomas A. DeCotiis, "Behaviorally Anchored Rating Scales: A Review of the Literature," *Personnel Psychology,* vol. 28, no. 4, Winter 1975, p. 561.

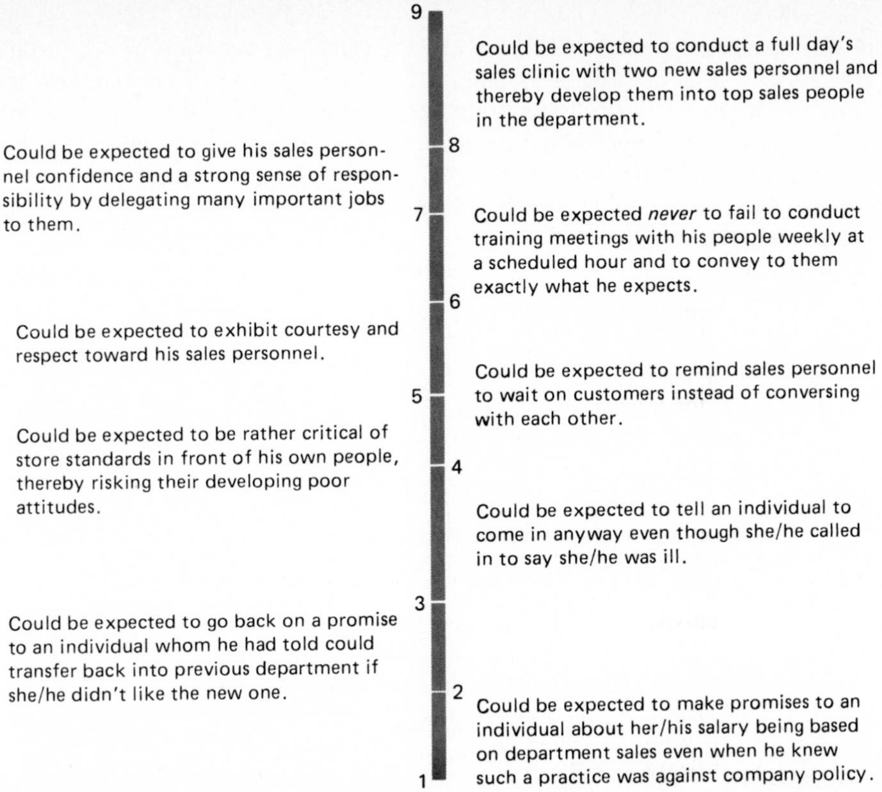

FIGURE 10-3 Behaviorally anchored rating scale for sales supervisor. (*Source: John P. Campbell, Marvin D. Dunnette, Richard D. Arvey, and Lowell V. Hellervik, "The Development and Evaluation of Behaviorally Based Rating Scales," Journal of Applied Psychology, vol. 57, no. 1, January 1973, p. 17. Used with permission.*)

accurate with simpler systems.[15] The approach is complex and costly inasmuch as different systems must be designed for separate groups of jobs. It would appear, however, that BARS would hold up well if challenged by compliance agencies and courts. It requires job analysis, involvement of jobholders, checking separate groups of evaluators against each other, and identification of critical incidents of behavior. In addition, though it is not demonstrably superior to other systems in evaluating levels of performance, the construction process is beneficial in training personnel and in generating acceptance of the appraisal results. In one firm, use of a BES system over a 20-month period resulted in more favorable employee attitudes toward both the appraisal process and the resulting ratings.[16]

Behavior observation scales When employing a BES, endorsement of a behavioral anchor above the neutral point would also seem to include all behaviors from the neutral point up. For example, if in Figure 10-3 an employee is allocated an "8," it

[15]Craig Eric Schneier, "Operational Utility and Psychometric Characteristics of Behavioral Expectation Scales: A Cognitive Reinterpretation," *Journal of Applied Psychology*, vol. 62, no. 5, October 1977, p. 541.

[16]John M. Ivancevich, "A Longitudinal Study of Behavioral Expectation Scales: Attitudes and Performance," *Journal of Applied Psychology*, vol. 65, no. 2, pp. 139–146.

would also say that he or she would be expected to exhibit the behaviors of ''5,'' ''6,'' and ''7'' as well since they are all neutral or favorable. This may or may not be true. In response to this problem, BOS systems have been developed. For *each* of the behaviors listed, the employee is rated on a 5-point scale as to the frequency with which the supervisor has observed that behavior. When numerous anchors are rated, the internal reliability of the scale can be calculated by correlating the odd-numbered items with the even-numbered. These internal consistency correlations have been found satisfactory for a wide variety of jobs.[17] An example of a portion of a BOS form for the job of waiter/waitress is given in Figure 10-4.

[17]Gary P. Latham and Kenneth N. Wexley, *Increasing Productivity through Performance Appraisal,* Addison-Wesley Publishing Company, Reading, Mass., 1981, p. 67.

FIGURE 10-4
Behavior Observation Scales Waiter/Waitress

In completing this form, circle a 1 if the employee has exhibited this behavior less than 50 percent of the time; a 2 if 50 to 64 percent of the time; a 3 if 65 to 79 percent of the time; a 4 if 80 to 89 percent of the time; and a 5 if 90 to 100 percent of the time.

12. Uses the words "thank you" and "please" when talking to customers.

    Almost never   1   2   3   4   5   Almost always

13. Chats with customers who have already been served while other customers are waiting to order.

    Almost never   1   2   3   4   5   Almost always

14. Smokes behind the counter.

    Almost never   1   2   3   4   5   Almost always

15. Stops talking to fellow employees as soon as a customer approaches.

    Almost never   1   2   3   4   5   Almost always

16. Serves customers their drinks immediately after the food order is taken.

    Almost never   1   2   3   4   5   Almost always

17. Puts hands in hair.

    Almost never   1   2   3   4   5   Almost always

18. Smiles when the customer asks for change.

    Almost never   1   2   3   4   5   Almost always

19. Makes suggestions like "would you like some dessert?"

    Almost never   1   2   3   4   5   Almost always

20. Complains about fellow employees within hearing distance of customers.

    Almost never   1   2   3   4   5   Almost always

Essay Description

Perhaps in response to the complexities of rating scales and formats, some organizations have reverted to simple essay descriptions of employee performance. In one survey of 139 firms, the essay or discussion format was used by 47 percent of the sample, ranking ahead of traditional graphic scales.[18] One company asks the supervisor to appraise overall performance as "marginal," "competent," or "excellent," and then to compose a narrative explaining this rating. If the appearance of subjectivity presented by this approach is not backed up by systematic accumulation of performance information (critical incidents), it may present some difficulties if challenged by governmental compliance agencies.

THE APPRAISAL PROGRAM

More important than the rating form or method is the quality of the rater. Certainly adequate time and attention must be given to the selection and design of a rating system, but even more time and effort must be expended in deciding such questions as who is to rate, how he or she should be trained, and how the accuracy of the ratings can be maintained.

Who Is to Rate

In most situations, the rater is the immediate superior of the person to be rated. Because of frequent contact, he or she is most familiar with the employee's work. Supervisor ratings are often reviewed and approved by higher management, thereby maintaining hierarchical control over the appraisal process.

If more involvement is deemed desirable, the appraisal process can be undertaken by a group of raters. Various surveys show that 15 to 18 percent of business firms utilize group ratings of administrative and professional personnel.[19] Members of the group can be superiors, peers, and subordinates. If they are all superiors, group appraisal ventures only a small distance from classical management theories. If they are all subordinates, it involves a considerable move toward behavioral theories. A few firms have given serious consideration to evaluation by peers. For example, over 3,000 agents in three life insurance companies have been asked to nominate three other agents with whom they work in connection with such questions as, "Who would you prefer to have accompany you on a tough case?"[20] Such "buddy nominations" were not turned over to the firms, but were kept to assess their effectiveness in identifying future successful assistant managers. In general, the higher the "buddy score," the higher the success rate as managers. A similar study of middle managers at International Business Machines Corporation revealed that those receiving the higher peer ratings were definitely more likely to be promoted.[21]

[18]Bureau of National Affairs Inc., "Employee Performance Evaluation and Control," *Personnel Policies Forum,* no. 108, February 1975.

[19]Mitchell Novit, "Performance Appraisal and Dual Authority: A Look at Group Appraisal," *Management of Personnel Quarterly,* vol. 8, no. 1, Spring 1969, p. 3.

[20]Eugene C. Mayfield, "Peer Nominations: A Neglected Selection Tool," *Personnel,* vol. 48, no. 4, July-August 1971, p. 40.

[21]H. E. Roadman, "An Industrial Use of Peer Ratings," *Journal of Applied Psychology,* vol. 48, no. 4, August 1964, pp. 211–214.

The final possibility, which is most behavioral in orientation, is to allow subordinates to rate themselves. The major values lie in the development and motivation areas, it being claimed that this approach (1) results in a superior upward flow of information, (2) forces the subordinate to become more personally involved and to do some systematic thinking about self and work, (3) improves communication between superior and subordinate, in that each is given more information by the other when disagreements are discovered, and (4) improves motivation as a result of greater participation.

The usual fear of this approach is that of excessively high ratings. This fear has some basis in research. In a study of 92 technical employees, subordinates rated themselves more favorably than did their supervisors.[22] There was good agreement on ratings concerning creative ability and human relations skills, but little concerning technical competence.

On the other hand, a study of 81 subordinates in the General Electric Company resulted in multiple values to the organization when self-ratings were requested.[23] Forty subordinates were asked for self-ratings, while 41 were rated in the usual manner by their managers. More defensiveness was noted among those rated by superiors, 8 of the 41 feeling that criticisms brought up in the interview were unwarranted. Only 2 of the 40 who were interviewed after self-ratings felt that ensuing criticism was unwarranted. In a 3-month follow-up after the appraisal interviews, superiors reported that 16 of the 41 manager-appraised subordinates were not measuring up to the job, as compared with only 8 of the 40 self-rated subordinates. Twenty-three of the 35 managers involved believed that the self-rating approach was clearly superior.

If the basic participatory management approach continues to grow, it is certain that the self-rating aspect of the process will also become more widespread. In most instances where its use is noted, the ratees are managerial and professional personnel. It is also suggested that if the subordinate knows that the superior is also preparing ratings, the former is more likely to do a realistic job. The use of self-ratings as an additional input of information to provide the basis for a mutually beneficial interview has considerable merit.

When to Rate

The most frequent rating schedules are semiannual and annual. New employees are rated more frequently than older ones. The practice of one insurance company calls for ratings (1) annually on the employee's anniversary date, (2) after first 6 months of employment, (3) upon promotion or within 3 months after promotion, (4) when the job occupied has been reevaluated upward, (5) upon special request, as when the employee's salary is below the average pay, and (6) upon the employee's termination. When ratings are given on anniversary of employment, ratings of all employees will not fall due on the same day. When the supervisor must rate 20 to 30 employees at the same time, the pressure of other duties will probably prevent her or him from giving adequate time and attention to this task.

---

[22]W. K. Kirchner, "Relationship between Supervisory and Subordinate Ratings for Technical Personnel," *Journal of Industrial Psychology*, vol. 3, 1965, pp. 57–60.

[23]Glenn A. Bassett and Herbert H. Meyer, "Performance Appraisal Based on Self-Review," *Personnel Psychology*, vol. 21, no. 4, Winter 1968, pp. 421–430.

Training of the Rater

The initial training of raters must, of course, incorporate complete explanations of the philosophy and nature of the rating system. Factors and factor scales, if any, must be thoroughly defined, analyzed, and discussed in conference sessions. Though training should be positive in nature, it has been found advisable to stress certain negative aspects of the rating process and to warn the raters about the more common errors of traditional rating in order that they may be on guard against them. Among these errors are:

1 The halo error

2 The central tendency

3 Constant errors
 a too harsh
 b too easy

4 Miscellaneous errors
 a similar-to-me
 b contrast
 c position
 d biases of sex, race, religion, and nationality

The halo error can be recognized quite easily on factor scales. It takes place when the rater allows one aspect of a person's character or performance to influence the entire evaluation. No person is likely to be either perfectly good or perfectly bad; one is generally better in some areas than in others. The best correction for the halo error is education. Often a rater is not aware of this tendency and needs only to have it pointed out to correct it.

The central tendency is perhaps the most commonly found error in performance rating. This error is evidenced when the rater marks all or almost all personnel as average. In this manner the rater avoids "sticking one's neck out" when in doubt, or possessing inadequate information, or giving the rating process little time, attention, and effort.

There are "easy" raters and "tough" raters in all phases of life. There are teachers who rarely award A's and those who give them to most of the class. These errors are known as constant or systematic errors. Figure 10-5(*a*) illustrates the situation created by a lenient rater. Ratings are distributed in a normal curve, but the supervisor is utilizing only the upper half of the scale; the average rating is 7. The harsh rater utilizes the lower half of the scale, as shown in Figure 10-5(*b*). He or she also has a normal distribution, with an average rating of 3. If these ratings are valid for these two groups, we have no rating problem. If they are constant errors, the rating of 7 by the first rater is equal to the rating of 3 by the second. Education, again, is the basic solution. Should this educational process fail, there is a system, used by some organizations, that translates the raw rating score into percentiles. The rating of 7 becomes a rating of the 50th percentile, as does the rating of 3. In general, the better solution is to reeducate the rater rather than manipulate the ratings.

Because of the complexity of evaluating another human's performance, there are a number of miscellaneous errors to guard against. The "similar-to-me" mistake is a tendency for the rater to judge more favorably those who appear to be similar to herself

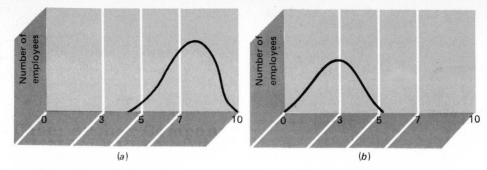

(a) By the lenient rater
(b) By the harsh rater

FIGURE 10-5 Distribution of ratings.

or himself. Unless corrected, individuality and creativity may ultimately be eliminated. Contrast errors occur in the sequencing of ratings. If superior performers are rated first, average performers are likely to be rated down; if poorer performers come first, the average performer will be rated more highly. Awareness of this human evaluation error does much to overcome it. There is also a tendency to rate the occupant of a higher position more favorably than one in a lower position. And despite the steady bombardment in the area of civil rights, one must constantly reemphasize the absolute necessity of guarding against prejudice and bias. In contrasting the accuracy of managers trained through group discussion and those developed through workshops, utilizing videotapes, the latter group made significantly fewer similarity, contrast, and halo errors.[24]

Finally, the supervisor must be trained to conduct the periodic appraisal interview. This, to many, is the most painful part of the process. Supervisors do not mind "playing God" if they can be a benevolent god. But when criticism is deemed necessary, they resort to the widely used "human relations sandwich"—criticism sandwiched between initial statements concerning one's good points and ending exhortations that improvement will be forthcoming in the future. In the traditional interview, the appraiser is clearly superior and acts in judgmental fashion. The distaste for this process, as well as research findings indicating its negative effects, have led a great many organizations to consider Management by Objectives programs.

Monitoring the Effectiveness of the Appraisal Program

Maintaining surveillance over the systematic appraisal program is usually a job for a staff personnel department. Systematic performance appraisal is a measurement process and as such must be reliable, which means that it must be accurate and consistent. The reliability of a rating system can be obtained by comparing the ratings of two individuals for the same person. It can also be obtained by comparing the supervisor's rating given now with another rating in the future, allowing for possible changes that can be justified by facts. Whereas the reliability coefficients for psychological tests are generally in the

[24]Gary P. Latham, Kenneth N. Wexley, and Elliott D. Pursell, "Training Managers to Minimize Rating Errors in the Observation of Behavior," *Journal of Applied Psychology*, vol. 60, no. 5, October 1975, p. 555.

.90s, and .85 is often taken as a minimum, the coefficients for merit-rating systems are generally lower. In fact, an .85 would be considered quite good for merit rating. Ordinarily, the performance appraisal reliabilities, when determined, range from .60 to .80.

Validity is concerned with the truthfulness of the measurement results. How can we be sure that the ratings obtained are true and representative of the ratee? Since reliability is a prerequisite to validity, some courts have checked interrater reliabilities in making determinations about instrument validity. Ratings can also be checked against certain objective evidence such as production quantities, quality, and absenteeism. Other comparisons can be made with a curve of normal distributions, if the number of ratees is sufficiently large. There are some systems that attempt to incorporate checks for bias or inconsistencies by comparing the answers with several related questions about the ratee. Sometimes validity is determined by comparing the results of one system with those of another. For example, the ratings of the forced-choice system are compared with the prior categorization of selected personnel by means of committee discussions, hard work, and serious individual study.

The ratings must be made by the immediate superiors of the ratees, but a staff department can assume the responsibility of monitoring the system. The personnel department should not change any ratings. They do have the obligation to point out certain inconsistencies to the rater, such as harshness, leniency, central tendency, and inconsistencies. If the firm has a strong equal opportunity program as well as emphasizing the use of trained raters, courts are more likely to judge the system as valid despite the difficulties of proving it quantitatively.

MANAGEMENT BY OBJECTIVES

In all of the methods of traditional and systematic appraisal, the manager is sitting in judgment on the performance of subordinates, hoping to obtain an impartial, objective, factual, and acceptable measurement score. In recent years, the critics of this philosophy of rating have increased in number and loudness. Though an attack has been mounted upon the low reliabilities and validities of traditional systems, the fundamental criticism has been based on the judgmental role of the manager and the antagonistic response of the subordinate. The initial leading critic was Douglas McGregor, who seized upon an approach previously suggested by Peter Drucker in 1954. Instead of sitting in judgment, the superior should devote attention to establishment of goals, so that subordinates can exercise self-control in pursuit of those goals—Management by Objectives. Though early efforts inspired by McGregor led to subordinate self-determination of goals followed by self-appraisal of subsequent accomplishment, such programs have evolved into ones where management takes a more prominent role. Early efforts tended to enter the firm through the personnel department as a program for motivating subordinates. Admitting the increment in motivation, management was nevertheless concerned that a multitude of individuals ''doing their own things'' might not add up to the common good of the organization. Consequently, modern Management by Objectives (MBO) approaches tend to emphasize a participative but *joint* determination of objectives, followed by a participative but *joint* evaluation of success in periodic appraisal interviews. Each of these major program elements will be discussed in the following sections.

Establishment of Objectives

Management by Objectives is far more than just an appraisal process. To many, it is a fundamental way of managing, in which periodic appraisal is but a part. Organizations are composed of a multitude of people, performing various and specialized activities, supposedly thereby contributing to basic organizational objectives. Sociologists pointed out long ago the dysfunctional consequences of activity specialization and rules: that such organized segmentation and directives often lead to human behavior characterized by rigidity, impersonality, and inward orientation; to wit, a pathological bureaucrat. Odiorne, in his development of an MBO philosophy, has characterized this phenomenon as an "activity trap"; the individual becomes so enmeshed in performing assigned functions that he or she loses sight of the goal, the reason for performance.[25] Even greater dysfunctions occur when the goals change but the individual activities do not.

The statement that objectives should be established for key positions is a simple one that belies its complexity. It often requires days, rather than hours, to compose a set of meaningful and measurable goals that will objectify the everyday fuzzy world of work. The first step usually entails a conference between superior and subordinate with

[25]George S. Odiorne, "Management by Objectives: Antidote to Future Shock," *Personnel Journal,* vol. 53, no. 4, April 1974, p. 263.

FIGURE 10-6
Examples of Objectives for MBO Program

Position	Objectives
Director of finance	Reduce bad debt losses from 5 percent to 3 percent of sales by January 1.
	Reduce number of accounting employees 10 percent, through transfer of operations to computer, by June 1.
Director of management information systems	Add "return on assets employed" to reports for each cost center by January 1.
	Reduce by 20 percent the number of copies of EDP reports prepared by June 1.
Marketing manager	Complete field testing of Product X by June 1, and add to regular line by January 1.
	Increase share of market of Product J from 15 percent to 20 percent in Northeast territory by January 1.
Personnel manager	Decrease turnover of clerical employees from 20 percent to 10 percent by January 1.
	Complete planning and installation of supervisory training program on grievance processing by June 1.
Production manager	Reduce welding rejects from 6 percent to 3 percent by January 1.
	Improve percentage of due dates met on production schedule from 90 to 95 percent by June 1.
Research and development manager	Complete design and development of Product X by June 1, within a cost budget of $150,000.
	Provide two new products for marketing field testing within the next 12 months.

the purpose of securing agreement upon the *key tasks* included in the job description. More accomplishment will be achieved if one focuses on a limited number of goals. It is here that the superior ensures that the objectives developed are actually related to the needs of the enterprise.

Various classifications of objectives have been suggested, but most could be designated as routine, problem-solving, innovative, and personal development. Referring to the examples in Figure 10-6, the objective of the production manager to improve the percentage of due dates met could be classified as a *routine* type of objective. The personnel manager's objective of installing a new supervisory training program is a *problem-solving* objective to cope with inadequate grievance processing. Adding a "return on assets employed" section to reports for cost centers on the part of the director of management information systems could well be a nonroutine objective of the *innovative* type. A *personal development* objective would specify planned accomplishment in training, education, or experience, for instance, to attain reading competence in a foreign language within 1 year.

Research and practice indicate that the well-established goal has the characteristics of specificity, challenge, and acceptance. In a study of appraisal systems in General Electric, it was found that when specific, quantitative goals were mutually established, the average accomplishment noted later was 65 percent. In cases where such specific goals were not set, the average accomplishment was estimated to be 27 percent.[26] Thus, in writing goals, special attempts should be made to phrase them in such terms as volume, costs, frequency, ratios, percentages, degrees, phases, and calendar dates. Developing the characteristics of "challenging" and "acceptable" calls for an artful balance of opposing forces. Research indicates that challenging objectives lead to greater accomplishment only if the subordinate truly accepts the goal as reasonable.[27] Acceptance can be enhanced through participative practices in goal establishment. Acceptance is also moderated by personality. Those with high needs for achievement (seek out challenges, want personal responsibility, seek feedback) prefer success probabilities at about the .5 level.

For each objective suggested by the subordinate and accepted by the superior, a basic strategy for assessment should be planned. The superior should do what he or she can to help in providing information that will enable the subordinate to evaluate and measure on-going accomplishment. For example, in proposing an objective within the Department of Health, Education, and Welfare, an agency head specified that 10,000 additional alcoholics would be treated during the coming year.[28] Feeling that the real goal was actual *rehabilitation,* information had to be developed as a basis for assessment of this more advanced and intangible objective. "Rehabilitation" was then defined as being gainfully employed 1 year after treatment. In such an instance, the previously suggested numerical objective of 10,000 may have to be scaled downward if applied to the more fundamental end result.

[26]Herbert H. Meyer, Emanuel Kay, and John R. P. French, Jr., "Split Roles in Performance Appraisal," *Harvard Business Review,* vol. 43, no. 1, January-February 1965, pp. 123–129.

[27]Gary P. Latham and Gary A. Yukl, "A Review of Research on the Application of Goal Setting in Organizations," *Academy of Management Journal,* vol. 18, no. 4, December 1975, p. 835.

[28]Rodney H. Brady, "MBO Goes to Work in the Public Sector," *Harvard Business Review,* vol. 51, no. 2, March-April 1973, p. 73.

Appraisal Interview

Though abhorred and often feared in the traditional approach to appraisal, the interview is one of the more fruitful elements of an MBO program. In the previously cited General Electric study, it was found that the traditional approach resulted in such responses as the following: (1) criticism issues from the very nature of the system, (2) criticism within the appraisal interview had a negative effect upon improvement and tended to increase antagonism and defensiveness, and (3) praise during the interview has *little* effect, either good or bad.[29] The very nature of the traditional interview where the superior acts as judge tends to stimulate one to adopt a role stereotype of supervisor—critical, evaluative, and often defensive.[30] One tends to display superiority, lack of concern, an inclination toward control or manipulation, and an attitude of certainty and finality at the end of the interview.[31]

In the MBO appraisal interviews, the atmosphere for discussion tends to be characterized by empathy, mutual respect, equality, supportive informational contributions, shared definitions, and provisional, rather than definitive, conclusions on the part of the superior at the end. The sequence of interview phases carried out in one large corporation is as follows.[32] First, the subordinate usually takes the lead in a discussion of accomplishment and failures since the last meeting. The superior participates through asking questions and interjecting comments. Reasons for nonaccomplishment are examined and suggestions for changes in objectives or strategies are discussed. The atmosphere is that of two persons working on common problems with common goals, rather than of one sitting in judgment upon the other. In the second stage, the manager takes the lead in establishing goals for the next period that will fit into organizational purposes. The subordinate will submit proposals for the new set of goals. During the third stage, both manager and subordinate are equally involved in establishing criteria for assessing progress toward goals arrived at in stage two. The fourth and final stage is devoted to discussions about the subordinate's future and a determination of personal development goals. In this stage, the superior acts in the capacity of counselor.

When interviews are conducted in this performance-goal-oriented fashion, the level of satisfaction on the part of both parties tends to be high. Burke and Wilcox correlated the interview characteristics of (1) high level of subordinate participation in appraisal, (2) helpful and constructive (not critical) attitude by superior, (3) solution of job problems hampering performance, and (4) mutual setting of specific goals, with ensuing attitudes and behavior of the subordinate.[33] In a study of 323 employees in six offices of a large public utility, a composite of the above four variables correlated .75 with subordinate satisfaction with the interview, .56 with subordinate's stated motivation to improve performance, and .44 with actually improved performance.

[29]Meyer, Kay, and French, op. cit., pp. 123–129.

[30]Philip G. Hanson, Robert B. Morton, and Paul Rothaus, "The Fate of Role Stereotypes in Two Performance Appraisal Situations," *Personnel Psychology,* vol. 16, no. 3, Autumn 1963, pp. 269–280.

[31]William N. Butler, "Supportive Communication and Performance Appraisal," *Personnel Administration,* vol. 32, no. 1, January-February 1969, p. 50.

[32]Edgar F. Huse, "Putting in a Management Development Program That Works," *California Management Review,* vol. 9, no. 2, Winter 1966, p. 78.

[33]Ronald J. Burke and Douglas S. Wilcox, "Characteristics of Effective Employee Perforamance Review and Development Interviews," *Personnel Psychology,* vol. 22, no. 3, Autumn 1969, pp. 290–305.

Limitations of MBO

Like all basically good and simple ideas, widespread overly enthusiastic exhortations and poorly prepared installations can move them to the status of "fads." MBO is no cure-all, no panacea for all managerial ills. It, too, has its dysfunctional consequences. Meeting the 95 percent goal in due dates on the part of the production manager may lead him or her to interfere with the objectives of the quality control manager; production tries to slip marginal products by the inspectors. When multiple activities are closely interrelated, one will have to move to establishment of *group objectives* prior to identifying individual responsibilities. "A medium-size service company experimented with this approach [teams] and finally decided to ignore individual objective altogether, reasoning that too much interlinking, support, and cooperation are required to blame or reward any individual for the production of any single end result."[34]

A second limitation of the approach is the difficulty of applying it to many nonmanagerial positions. Certainly, such an approach to blue-collar employees on the assembly line would be impracticable, though Herzberg would suggest that such jobs be redesigned so that meaningful goals and feedback of information could be developed. Considering the time and effort that must be allocated to a well-designed MBO plan, most firms restrict its application to managerial, technical, and professional personnel.

A final limitation is that MBO makes *comparative* assessment of multiple personnel rather difficult. In traditional assessment methods, all personnel are rated on common factors. In MBO, each person will have different sets of goals of noncomparable complexity and difficulty of accomplishment. Management must still make various decisions on a comparative basis—who gets the pay increase or who is to be promoted. Superiors will, however, develop a strong impression of a subordinate's effectiveness in a MBO program, not only in performances related to goal accomplishment, but also in his or her conception of the job and its major goals. Certainly, the joys of intrinsic satisfaction from goal accomplishment will wear thin if not accompanied by a fair share of extrinsic rewards available in the system, such as money, promotion, status symbols and so on.

SUMMARY

In all probability, the attention being given by governmental compliance agencies to fair employment practices will be enlarged to encompass the performance appraisal task. Casual and subjective appraisals will not be able to stand the tests of fairness and legality if challenged. Firms are thus being forced into some type of formal, systematic evaluation system to provide evidence to withstand charges of bias.

Traditional systems can vary from the simple ranking and essay description plans to the enormously complicated forced-choice and behaviorally anchored rating scales. The popular graphic scale with its hazy definitions will have to be bolstered in some manner to increase objectivity, such as providing an example of behavior to justify ratings on each factor. The key to the process is the rater, and considerable attention should be given to the avoidance of halo, leniency, harshness, and central tendency errors.

---

[34]Richard E. Byrd and John Cowan, "MBO: A Behavioral Science Approach," *Personnel*, vol. 51, no. 2, March-April 1974, p. 48.

Management by objectives is a philosophy of management that incorporates a differently oriented appraisal process. Central to MBO is joint and mutual establishment of end results for individual key personnel. Equally essential is periodic joint appraisal when assessments are made concerning degrees of accomplishment. When organizational activities are closely interlocking, it is recommended that team or group goal establishment precede the identification of individual responsibilities and goals.

BRIEF CASE

The president of the Academy Employment Service has inaugurated a Management by Objectives program in order that more accurate appraisals may be made of professional personnel. Frank Bank, an employment interviewer, has for the past year established relations with Small Business College, a privately run school in the southern part of the state. It graduates about 25 people per month and Bank had agreed to place as many of those who wanted placement in training-related jobs. Between 15 and 20 people per month signed up for this service. When the president asked Bank to prepare objectives for his job, this seemed to be one of the easy places to do it. Inasmuch as Bank was now placing about 35 percent of the applicants, the president asked if he thought he could raise this to 50 percent. Bank assured him that he could. In reviewing Bank's accomplishments at the end of the 6-month period, it was concluded by the personnel unit that Bank was placing only 5 to 7 percent of the graduates in training-related jobs. Several lengthy and heated discussions took place regarding just what was meant by *training-related*. Bank considered any job to be training-related, while the personnel unit contended that the job content had to bear some relationship to the training acquired in school. Moreover, if the placed student quit before 90 days of work, the personnel unit would not classify this as a successful placement. Continuous documentation of Bank's 5 to 7 percent performance against the 50 percent objective led to Bank's serious consideration of early retirement.

Questions

1. Is this objective a well-stated one? Why or why not?

2. If you were the president, how would you resolve the dispute between Bank and the personnel unit?

DISCUSSION QUESTIONS

1. What problems are there in applying the EEOC 80 percent rule to performance appraisal systems?

2. Why are firms moving more and more toward formal appraisal systems?

3. Compare and contrast Behavior Expectation Scales with Behavior Observation Scales.

4. Compare the types of definitions found on a (a) person-to-person scale, (b) graphic scale, (c) BES, and (d) BOS.

5. Compare and contrast the measurement processes of the following pairs: (a) graphic scales—checklists, (b) person-to-person—graphic scales, (c) forced choice—forced distribution, (d) grading—graphic scales, (e) graphic scales—Behavior Expectation Scales.

6. Compare and contrast the appraisal interviews conducted in a systematic performance appraisal program with that given in a Management by Objectives program.

7. Describe the characteristics of a well-stated objective in a Management by Objectives program.

8. Identify common errors of rating in systematic programs of performance appraisal.

9. What characteristics of a performance appraisal program will contribute to successful court defenses when a firm is charged with violations of the Civil Rights Act?

10. Describe the process of developing a Behavior Expectation Scale.

SUPPLEMENTARY READING

CEDERBLOM, DOUGLAS: "The Performance Appraisal Interview: A Review, Implications, and Suggestions," *Academy of Management Review*, vol. 7, no. 2, April 1982, pp. 219–227.

FAY, CHARLES H. and GARY P. LATHAM: "Effects of Training and Rating Scales on Rating Errors," *Personnel Psychology*, vol. 35, no. 1, Spring 1982, pp. 105–116.

GARLAND, HOWARD: "Goal Levels and Task Performance: A Compelling Replication of Some Compelling Results," *Journal of Applied Psychology*, vol. 67, no. 2, April 1982, p. 245–248.

HOLLEY, WILLIAM H. and HUBERT S. FEILD: "Will Your Performance Appraisal System Hold up in Court?" *Personnel*, vol. 50, no. 1, January-February 1982, pp. 59–64.

IVANCEVICH, JOHN M. and J. TIMOTHY McMAHON: "The Effects of Goal Setting, External Feedback, and Self-Generated Feedback on Outcome Variables: A Field Experiment," *Academy of Management Journal*, vol. 25, no. 2, June 1982, pp. 359–372.

PRINGLE, CHARLES D. and JUSTIN G. LONGNECKER: "The Ethics of MBO," *Academy of Management Review*, vol. 7, no. 2, April 1982, pp. 305–312.

chapter 11

Career Development

The employee having been trained, educated, and appraised, it would seem that the development function is at an end; the employee is properly qualified and effectively performing the assigned job. Modern personnel managers must look beyond the present assignment, since neither organizational requirements nor individual attitudes and abilities are ever constant. Concern for long-term *career* development must always accompany any comprehensive employee development program.

The need to plan for employee careers issues from both economic and social forces. First, if the organization is to survive and prosper in an ever-changing environment, its human resources must be in a constant state of development. A planned program of internal resource development typically pays greater dividends than relying upon chance or frantic outside recruitment when needs suddenly appear. In addition, too many employees "retire on the job" when there is no managerial concern for proper career progressions. Further, work is losing its premier position as the sole value to be sought in life by all personnel. Modern employees are beginning to insist that work demands be effectively integrated with the human need for personal growth, expectations of one's family, and the ethical requirements of society. The work ethic is not dead; rather, it lives in consonance with a more complex set of values. "It is ironic that what is most precious to the individual insofar as work is concerned, that is, the career, is given the least attention by the organization."[1]

NATURE OF CAREERS

A career can be defined as a *sequence of separate but related work activities that provides continuity, order, and meaning in a person's life*. Careers are both individually perceived, and societally constrained; not only do people make careers out of their particular experiences, but career opportunities provided in society also influence and "make" people. As discussed in Box 11-1, the concept of a career in Japan is significantly different than the approach taken in the United States.

---

[1]John Leach, "The Notion and Nature of Careers," *The Personnel Administrator*, vol. 22, no. 7, September 1977, p. 50.

The Broad Career Path of Japanese Executives
William Ouchi

A frequently overlooked but very important feature of Japanese organizations is the principle of lifelong job rotation. Americans often switch jobs from organization to organization but they tend to stay within the same specialty. In Japan, by contrast, people often switch specialties while conducting their careers within a single organization.

The French scholar Jean-Louis Bouchet has studied the career paths of top officers in 50 of the largest U.S. firms. He found that on average they had worked in fewer than two functions on their way up the corporate ladder. Marketing executives tend to have come up through the sales division, technical executives through engineering, controllers through accounting. In many cases, they have been hired away from other companies, but seldom from other specialties.

In Japan, career paths are much less specialized. An electrical engineer may go from circuit design to fabrication to assembly. A technician may work on a different machine or in a different division every few years. And almost all managers will rotate through different areas of the business.

Consider the varied assignments of a typical management trainee who joins a Japanese bank after graduating from his university. Under the guidance of a mentor, he will be exposed in his first 10 years to almost all the bank's operations. He will be given jobs in commercial banking, retail lending to customers, personnel, back-of-the-office clerical work. He will work at both branches and headquarters, and he will have to learn how to manage tellers, and to deal with both individual customers and larger company clients. After 10 years, it's typical to gain the first promotion, perhaps to another branch in charge of new business. A few years later, it may be back to headquarters, this time in the international division.

By the time the Japanese banker reaches the peak of his career, he is familiar with all his bank's services, specialties and offices and can think of them as an integrated whole. Compare this pattern with an advertisement that appeared not long ago for one of the major U.S. banks. In bold type it said: "Bank with us. Why? Expertise." Below the large type were photos of three of the bank's senior officers. "Meet Fred," it read. "For 30 years Fred has done nothing but make commercial loans to forest product companies in the Pacific Northwest. He's an expert."

The typical Japanese bank will not have an expert with Fred's detailed knowledge of the needs, the people and the problems of one industry. That is a weakness of the Japanese system of lifelong job rotation. However, when it comes time to coordinate functions, the Japanese form has great advantages.

Suppose a bank wants to computerize commercial lending information, and therefore needs cooperation between lending and back-of-the-office operations. In the Japanese case, virtually every department will include someone who knows the people, problems and procedures of any other part of the organization. And since there is a good chance that the computer people might later be transferred to the lending department, there's a strong incentive to cooperate.

In many U.S. companies, by contrast, specialists often develop the goals and outlook of their profession—goals which don't always match their companies'. Computer systems groups, for example, often try to show off their technical wizardry in designing information systems—even if company goals might better be achieved with a less sophisticated system.

Plant managers tend to be concerned almost exclusively with production efficiency—even at the expense of a company's marketing objectives. Different functions have trouble expressing their needs to each other. And since promotion—or transfer to another company—is mostly within the same specialty, there's little incentive to learn about the needs of other parts of the organization.

Japanese job rotation, of course, is intimately linked with the mutual promise of lifetime employment. In the U.S. specialists often run off with their expertise to a competitor; indeed in the aerospace and semiconductor industries, raiding skilled engineers and supervisors from competitors is one of the principal means of technology transfer. But in Japan you cannot take any worker from one company and expect him to be productive in another. Training in Japan is much more firm specific. It has less to do with learning a technical field and more with how to make a specific, unique business operate as well as it possibly can.

Let's not overstate the differences between the U.S. and Japan. A number of American companies—for example General Motors and Hewlett-Packard—make fairly systematic efforts to shift managers around and give them different experiences. At General Electric, a corporate vice president for executive development is in charge of broadening managers' exposure to different parts of the organization. It's perhaps no coincidence that all these companies tend to promote mostly from within.

There have been times, too, when departments within U.S. organizations have given up their local objectives and narrow professional point of view for the sake of the larger enterprise. The Apollo project to put an astronaut on the moon was perhaps the outstanding example, but building early aircraft and computers also yielded such sacrifices. Indeed, NASA, Boeing and IBM are known for the ways that talented workers have put aside the normal politics of specialization and professionalization and cooperated in very complex projects.

We probably don't want to adopt the Japanese career path entirely. But some significant movement in the direction of company-centered rather than skill-centered careers could yield many benefits.

A series of work-related experiences does not have to constitute a profession, in the sense of law or medicine, to be regarded as a career. There are, for example, career plumbers, soldiers, electricians, homemakers, factory workers, prostitutes, and criminals. Even in careers with low-opportunity ceilings, one can progress through such forms as receiving higher pay on the same job, more security, cleaner working conditions, greater freedom from supervision, or more respect for length of service. In the more commonly cited case, a career consists of a series of properly sequenced role experiences leading to increasing levels of responsibility, status, power, and rewards. Some careers are characterized by early exit (professional football players) while others have late entry (judges). Some people pursue a "career" of multiple careers, changing from one to another as attitudes and opportunities change. "Thus, whether mobile or stable, the career represents an organized path taken by an individual across time and space."[2]

There are multiple forces that lead to the development and shaping of a career. As indicated in Figure 11-1, fundamental inputs consist of physical and mental characteristics, parents, schooling, ethnic groupings, sex, peers, organizational experiences, and age. From these, the individual will develop a notion of a career that is closely related to his or her need for self-esteem. A direction will be selected and goals or levels of aspiration will emerge. For example, one young man decided upon a collegiate academic career and established the following timetable: (1) Ph.D. degree by age 26, (2) assistant professor by 27, (3) first book published by 30, (4) professor and department head by 35, (5) dean of a college by 40, and (6) president of a university by 45.

As the model in Figure 11-1 indicates, this internal career notion must be tested by external realities. Specific decisions will have to be made as to organizations in which the career will unfold. Particular strategies and tactics will be selected in the light of situational factors. Outcomes, both failures and successes, will lead to modification of the internal career notion. The aspiration level may have to be lowered if the success timetable is not met. This, in turn, will have impact on one's self-esteem. Unforeseen opportunities will arise, often out of presumed failures. Though the basic direction may not be altered, specific forms may change; for instance, the young man became president of a specialized graduate-level institute. Though it would appear that this is all the business of the individual and the organization is only marginally concerned, the more that success can be programmed, the more valuable is the individual to the organization.

CAREER ANCHORS

In longitudinal research conducted by Schein, it was discovered that certain attitudinal syndromes that served to guide many people throughout their careers were formed early in life.[3] These syndromes were composed of a combination of needs, values, and talents, and serve to "anchor" the person to one or a few related types of careers. Five such anchors were identified: (1) managerial competence, (2) technical-functional competence, (3) security, (4) creativity, and (5) automomy-independence.

---

[2]John Van Maanen and Edgar H. Schein, "Career Development," in J. Richard Hackman and J. Lloyd Suttle, eds., *Improving Life at Work,* Goodyear Publishing Company, Inc., Santa Monica, Calif., 1977, p. 31.

[3]Edgar H. Schein, "How 'Career Anchors' Hold Executives to Their Career Paths," *Personnel,* vol. 52, no. 3, May-June 1975, pp. 11–24.

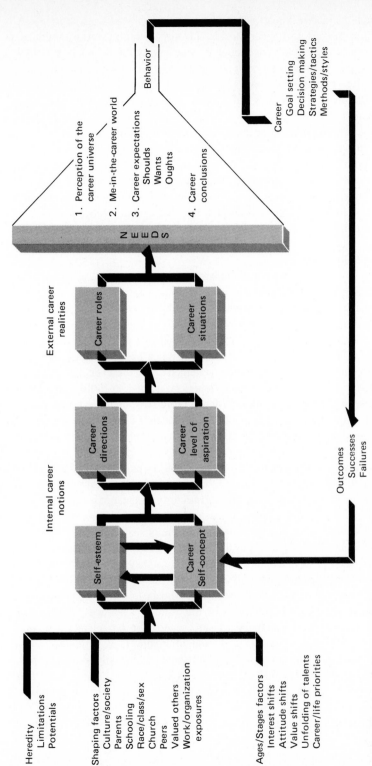

FIGURE 11-1 Sources of our career behavior. (*Source: John Leach, "The Notion and Nature of Careers," The Personnel Administrator, vol. 22, no. 7, September 1977, p. 53. Used with permission.*)

Heredity
Limitations
Potentials

Shaping factors
Culture/society
Parents
Schooling
Race/class/sex
Church
Peers
Valued others
Work/organization
exposures

Ages/Stages factors
Interest shifts
Attitude shifts
Value shifts
Unfolding of talents
Career/life priorities

Internal career
notions

Self-esteem

Career
Self-concept

Career
directions

Career
level of
aspiration

External career
realities

Career roles

Career
situations

Outcomes
Successes
Failures

N
E
E
D
S

1. Perception of the
career universe

2. Me-in-the-career world

3. Career expectations
Shoulds
Wants
Oughts

4. Career
conclusions

Behavior

Career
Goal setting
Decision making
Strategies/tactics
Methods/styles

The fundamental characteristics of those persons anchored by an overriding interest in management included a capacity to bear considerable responsibility, ability to influence and control others, and skills in solving problems with incomplete information. Those identifying with this anchor agree with such statements as "the process of influencing, leading, and controlling people at all levels is important to me." It is suggested that those who wish to be effective managers should possess analytical, interpersonal, intergroup, and emotional competences.

On the other hand, those with the technical competence anchor leave no doubt that they are primarily interested in the functional work performed. They agree with such statements as "I would leave my company rather than be promoted out of my area of expertise."[4] They look upon administrative duties as an irritant. The third group of persons seem primarily driven by a search for security. They are more attached to a particular organization and geographical area than they are to their work. This type of person will accept with little question the organizational prescriptions for his or her career, and agree with such statements as "I am willing to sacrifice some of my autonomy to stabilize my total life situation."

Those adhering to the fourth anchor demonstrate an overriding interest in creating or developing something new. They agree with such statements as "I have been motivated throughout my career by the number of products that I have been directly involved in creating." Many of these persons are entrepreneurs who have established separate businesses, less for the sake of making money than for creating a product or service that could be identified as theirs. The final group demonstrates an overriding interest in freedom and independence, agreeing with such statements as "a career that permits a maximum of freedom to choose my own work hours, tasks, and so forth, is important to me." Among these are private consultants, college professors, and free-lance writers. In terms of median incomes of each group, those with anchor (1), managerial competence, received the most, and those with anchor (5), autonomy-independence, were paid the least.

In planning for career development, personnel managers require knowledge of the basic drives and needs of employees. There has been considerable research concerning the varying amounts of managerial, technical, and security orientations among professional personnel in business organizations. Some professionals disclaim any interest in managerial responsibilities. Their dominant posture is one of dedication and service to the pursuit of professional knowledge, using the present organization as a means to that end. This attitude is labeled "cosmopolitan" inasmuch as they are quite mobile and willing to move to any organization that will enhance the practice of their profession.

If, on the other hand, the organization is accorded primary loyalty, with professional skills being exclusively adapted toward its ends, the attitude is termed "local." Obviously, any professional who is employed by an organization has elements of both "localism" and "cosmopolitanism." As suggested in Figure 11-2, attitudes can be positioned in one of four quadrants: (1) relatively indifferent, (2) heavily oriented toward the profession (technical competence), (3) heavily oriented toward the organization (managerial and security competences), and (4) oriented significantly toward both the profession and the organization.

In a study conducted by Miller and Wager, these four different orientations were

---

[4]Thomas J. DeLong, "Reexamining the Career Anchor Model," *Personnel,* vol. 59, no. 3, May-June 1982, pp. 56–57.

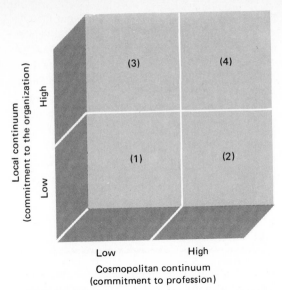

Local continuum
(commitment to the organization)

High

Low

Low   High

Cosmopolitan continuum
(commitment to profession)

FIGURE 11-2 Cosmopolitan and local orientations.

discovered among 390 engineers and scientists in two units of a major American aero-space company.[5] The researchers utilized a questionnaire technique and labeled 31 per-cent "cosmopolitans," since they exhibited high professional orientation accompanied by a low bureaucratic attitude. Members of this group were largely physical scientists with Ph.D degrees working in the basic science research laboratory. They exhibited such attitudes as "I would most like to publish a paper in the leading journal of my profession, even though the topic might be of *minor* interest to the company," and "In the long run, I would rather be respected among specialists in my field outside the company." Thus, the cosmopolitans view the universe as the field of their profession, wherever they find themselves. They often ask questions and make critical comments that traditional managers feel to be bordering on disloyalty to the organization. Yet, the skills and scientific viewpoint of the cosmopolitan are the fountainhead of the ideas that contribute to organizational progress and growth.

Twenty-seven percent of the 390 engineers and scientists were characterized as "locals," since they possessed a relatively low orientation to professional values with a high concern for and loyalty to the organization. The greater bulk of these were engineers without the Ph.D. If the professionals remain with a single organization for a considerable time, the attitude tends to become more local in character. They tend to agree with such statements as "being able to pursue a career in management is very important to me," and "having a job which permits me to take on progressively more administrative re-sponsibility is important to me." Engineers, more often than scientists, are likely to move toward this set of values. The significant reference group is management rather than outside professionals in the field. "Locals" are usually more cooperative and willing to take direction from management. Follow-up research discovered that cosmopolitans had stronger feelings of alienation and more role conflict than did locals.[6]

[5]George A. Miller and L. Wesley Wager, "Adult Socialization, Organizational Structure, and Role Orientations," *Administrative Science Quarterly*, vol. 12, no. 2, June 1971, pp. 151–162.

[6]Charles N. Greene, "Identification Modes of Professionals: Relationship with Formalization, Role Strain, and Alienation," *Academy of Management Journal*, vol. 21, no. 3, September 1978, p. 489.

The remaining personnel in the Miller and Wager study were divided into the two hybrid types: 15 percent were "indifferents," with low orientation to both sets of values, and 27 percent were "local-cosmopolitans," who exhibited high orientations to both the profession and the organization. The "indifferents" were mostly engineers with long service with the organization. This suggests that an entering engineer might have begun with high orientation to either the profession or the organization or both, but was slowly transformed into an "indifferent" as he or she experienced lack of progress in both areas. The previously cited research project indicated that the indifferents were the most alienated of all groups. The "local-cosmopolitan" was more likely to be an engineer who had worked for the company for a shorter period of time. It is apparent that the management of highly educated and skilled personnel poses a considerable challenge to personnel management.

AN INTEGRATED LIFE

The work life of a person does not stand in isolation. Too often, managers make seemingly routine career decisions for subordinates, with little or no concern about the impact upon personal lives. Figure 11-3 outlines three significant life cycles that are interrelated. The first depicts the usual stages of life in moving from infancy to old age. In each stage, certain characteristics are highlighted—trust in infancy, conscience in childhood, a search for identity in adolescence, intimacy with others in young adulthood, concern for guiding the next generation in adulthood and ego integrity in old age.[7] The adolescent stage marks the beginning of the search for identity with the prospective work career playing a major role. Such a stage encompasses a good deal of extremes in both commitment and repudiation in the search for new values. Identity develops when the person knows where he or she fits in the environment and there is a coinciding among one's capacities, values, and opportunities.

There is also a related family development cycle that the employing organization cannot ignore. Unmarried employees are more inclined to accept career decisions calling for frequent transfer and movement among organizational units. If a person is married and the spouse is unemployed, this willingness to relocate may well continue, though some nonworking spouses are no longer docile. With the steady increase in greater female employment, we are seeing a new variety of career conflict developing.[8] Major accounting firms require auditors to sign oaths annually that no marriage partners work for clients. A major national retailer expressed some concern when it discovered that an important compensation specialist in its personnel department was married to a personnel specialist in a competing firm. Should a competitor try to persuade executives to switch organizations, it would be helpful to know their exact salaries.

When the employee has a family, career moves involving relocation are particularly disruptive. The problems are greater when there are children in school, and even more severe when there are teenagers involved. In any move to a different community, there are social losses for the family in the disruption of selling a home, leaving friends,

---

[7]Erik H. Erikson, "Youth and the Life Cycle," in Jay W. Lorsch and Louis B. Barnes, eds., *Managers and Their Careers,* Richard D. Irwin, Inc., and The Dorsey Press, Homewood, Ill., 1972, pp. 86–87.

[8]Joann S. Lublin, "Working Couples Find an Increasing Chance of Conflicts in Jobs," *The Wall Street Journal,* Nov. 18, 1977, p. 1.

FIGURE 11-3
Cycles of Life

255

Career
Development

Self-development	Family Development	Career Development
Infancy Childhood	Child	Growth (age 0–14)
Adolesence		Exploratory (ages 15–24)
Young adult	Unmarried	
	Married—spouse is	
	1 Unemployed	
	2 Supplemental employment	
Adult	3 Career qualified: partially employed	Establishment (ages 25–44)
	4 Career qualified: fully engaged	
	Married—family has	
	1 One infant	
	2 Two or more preschool children	Maintenance (ages 45–64)
	3 One or more in school	
	4 First child leaves home	
	5 All children have left	
Old age	Loss of spouse	Decline (age 65 plus)

purchasing a new house, and reestablishing the family unit in a new community. This involves a myriad of problems in locating doctors, dentists, appliance repair personnel, and the like. The disruption of schooling of children was so severe in one case that tutors were provided at the expense of the company. These worries undoubtedly have some effect upon the short-term performance of the transferred employee. The pains of uprooting a settled family have led some employees to jeopardize their careers by refusing the developmental transfer. In several organizations, refusal of such a transfer is the "kiss of death," and almost tantamount to dismissal. Again, proper career development on the part of the organization should allow a greater decision role to be played by the employee concerned. Changing values make the old "take it or leave it" policy increasingly out-of-step with modern society.

The career development cycle depicted in Figure 11-3 is modeled after the one proposed by Super.[9] The organization's responsibility begins with the "exploratory" stage as the employee enters the organization. Realizing that a young adult is still uncertain as to permanent direction, one should make provision for some organizational experimentation. The entering employee will encounter "reality shock" inasmuch as neither prior education nor elaborate induction programs can fully prepare one for the actual job in practice. Research indicates that the more challenging the job in the first year of service, the more effective and successful the employee will be 5 or 10 years later.[10] Alternatives for initial training include a "sink or swim" approach, full-time training with no job responsibility, and work while training. The sooner the trainee is given a definite job assignment, the more rapidly development will occur.

[9]Donald E. Super and Martin J. Bohn, Jr., *Occupational Psychology,* Wadsworth Publishing Company, Inc., Belmont, Calif., 1970, p. 136.
[10]David E. Berlew and Douglas T. Hall, "The Socialization of Managers: Effects of Expectations on Performance," *Administrative Science Quarterly,* vol. 11, no. 2, June 1966, p. 222.

After some reality testing of one's career notion, some specific direction is usually chosen. Super indicates that this *establishment* stage usually begins about age 25 and continues for many years. Successful career development requires organizational feedback of progress information to the employee. The first performance appraisal, the first completed project, and the first promotion are all extremely important occasions for the young adult on the job. One moves from apprentice to "independent" contributor, with a definite field of expertise. One relies less upon the superior and more upon peer interaction in developing ideas and solving problems. These are the highly productive years in many careers.

The *maintenance* stage is a holding action where the employee attempts to retain what he or she has established. In competitive situations, this will require continued learning and updating in order to maintain the continued role in the organization. To many, this period also brings shock, contributing to a mid-career crisis. Some will make the attempt to switch to entirely different careers to once again experience the challenge of growth; for example, various successful business executives often attempt to move into collegiate teaching as a new career. One study of the creative careers of great painters, composers, poets, writers, and sculptors revealed a sudden surge in the death rate between the ages of 35 and 39.[11] The greater the genius, the higher was the death rate. Reasons given included an increasing awareness of physical aging, a realization that life was half over, and understanding that this was about as far as one can go (Is that all there is?).

The final stage of "decline" is also a shock to many employees. Discussion of the retirement event will be covered in a later chapter in this text inasmuch as it is an important part of the sixth personnel function, separation.

THE CAREER DEVELOPMENT PROGRAM

A properly designed career development program involves three main ingredients: (1) assisting employees in assessing their own internal career needs, (2) developing and publicizing available career opportunities in the organization, and (3) aligning employee needs and abilities with career opportunities.

Career need assessment A person's career is a highly personal and extremely important element of life. The basic stance of the organization should be to permit each person to make her or his own decision in this regard. The role of the personnel manager is to assist in this decision-making process by providing as much information as possible about the employee to the employee.

Just as there is considerable confusion among many college students as to proper choice of major, organizational employees are often uncertain as to the type of work that would suit them best. There are a number of evaluation instruments available that will assist the person in determining his or her primary interests and basic aptitudes to perform different types of work. As indicated in an earlier chapter, the Strong Vocational Interest

---

[11]Elliott Jacques, "Death and the Mid-Life Crisis," *International Journal of Psychoanalysis*, vol. 46, 1965, pp. 502–514.

Blank is validated on known interests of successful persons in specific occupations. There are life-planning workbooks that facilitate career decision making.[12] Candidates are urged to consider the relative importance of such things as prestige, independence, money, and security. They are also asked to think about whether they are basically loners or socially oriented, whether they prefer to lead or follow. Some large firms provide formal assessment center workshops where small groups of employees are subjected to psychological testing, simulation exercises, and depth interviewing. With the aid of expert observers, employees are helped to make decisions concerning proper career goals and specific development needs appropriate to those goals. The objective in these assessment programs is not that of selecting future promotees, but rather to help individuals to do their own planning.

Career opportunities   Realizing that employees have definite career needs, there naturally follows the obligation of charting specific career paths through the organization. Low-ceiling jobs, where there are limited opportunities for significant progression, should be identified and made known to possible applicants. Employees heavily affected by the ''security career anchor'' may find these jobs to be highly acceptable.

Though sometimes neglected in career workshops, the employee needs to know what types of jobs are now and will be available in the immediate future, as well as in the medium and long range. Information should be provided concerning actual duties of these jobs, as well as what is required in the way of training and development. Employees need to know how they become eligible for training, and the selection criteria for those who have completed training. And finally, it is important to know what jobs lead to other jobs.

As pointed out in Chapter 6, job analysis provides the fundamental information required to chart the lines of promotion within an organization. A careful analysis of the duties of the lower job must be made to determine the adequacy of preparation for higher jobs. Too often lines of advancement are restricted to a single department and are more or less obvious to anyone who studies an organization chart. Analysis of job duties generally leads to the discovery of multiple lines of advancement to several jobs in different areas.

Figure 11-4 is a chart depicting two avenues of advancement to the top personnel job in a large manufacturing firm. With a common entry point of personnel assistant, one avenue emphasizes advancement through a series of management positions in various-sized plants, while the other route is through multiple specialized functions within the personnel area. Figure 11-5 portrays a more complicated career ladder in a manufacturing unit. Not only are internal sequences identified, but ways of direct entry from the outside are noted as well. Choices are then made known; for example, one can become a mechanic by rising through the ranks from helper or laborer, or by completing a community college technology program.

One of the more interesting questions concerning lines of promotion is the identification of the route to the top job, the presidency of an organization. In a survey of the presidents of 239 of the 500 largest industrial firms during the period from 1945 to 1964, it was found that the main routes lay in general management, production, marketing,

---

[12]See H. A. Shepard and J. A. Hawley, *Life Planning: Personal and Organizational,* National Training and Development Service, Washington D.C., 1974; and G. A. Ford and G. L. Lippitt, *A Life Planning Workbook,* NTL Learning Resources Workbook, Fairfax, Va., 1972.

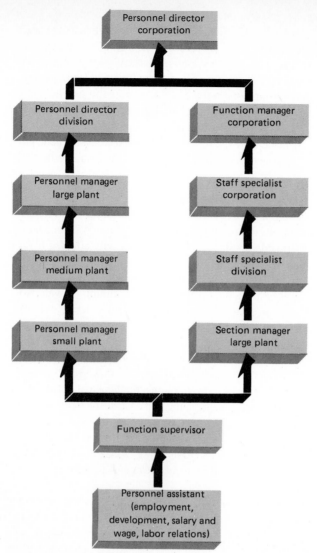

FIGURE 11-4 Line of promotion in personnel management—large manufacturing firm.

and finance.[13] The proportion of presidencies contributed by these fields remained fairly stable over the 20-year period, the average being 21.6 percent for general management, 21.5 percent for production, 17.6 percent for marketing, and 15.9 percent for finance.

The environmental situation facing the firm will exert a considerable influence upon the choice of chief executive officer. During the early 1950s, production received most attention. Later in that decade, marketing took over. With capital in plentiful supply during the 1960s, financial experts who could make acquisitions necessary for rapid growth and diversification were in the saddle. And now the serious inflationary problems

---

[13]William P. Dommermuth, "On the Odds of Becoming Company President," *Harvard Business Review,* vol. 44, no. 3, May–June 1966, p. 66.

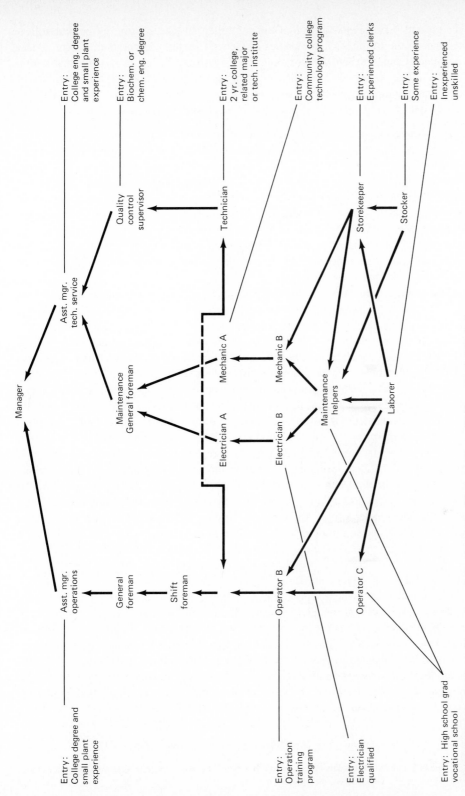

FIGURE 11-5 Career ladders: manufacturing unit. (*Source: Elmer H. Burack and Nicholas Mathys, "Career Ladders, Pathing and Planning: Some Neglected Basics," Human Resource Management, vol. 18, no. 2, Summer 1979, p. 6. With permission.*)

of the present period mark the rise of the controller. In recent years, former controllers have risen to the top in such companies as General Motors Corporation, Singer, Pfizer Incorporated, and Fruehauf Corporation. The significant increases in personnel within controller offices also provide evidence of this most recent trend. As the controller of J.C. Penney Company stated, "Sheer economic pressure has dictated that we have to get more out of things already in place—that is, people, bricks, and mortar."[14]

Need-opportunity alignment   When employees have accurately assessed their career needs and have become aware of organizational career opportunities, the remaining problem is one of alignment. All of the developmental techniques discussed in Chapter 9 can be incorporated into a planned career development program. Greater emphasis should be given to the more individualized development techniques such as special assignments, planned position rotation, and supervisory coaching. In performance appraisal and Management by Objectives programs, discussed in Chapter 10, special attention should be allocated to career progress and counseling. It will be recalled that modern MBO programs incorporate personal development objectives in addition to the more basic work objectives.

The specific transfer and promotion decisions made by management for each employee are the final payoff of a career development program. Appraisal, counseling, training, and education go for naught if the employee does not progress along his or her individually perceived career path. Both productivity and morale are facilitated if these personnel decisions are based on objective assessments of present and potential capability. That such is not always the case is substantiated in a study by Powell of 240 managers in forty firms.[15] As developed from carefully introduced questionnaires, it was concluded that there were many factors leading to an advancement in rank. Managerial capability was first to be stipulated but lost its importance as a screening device for higher positions as it was deemed to be a common denominator held by the entire pool of candidates. Beyond this, such factors as the following were reported: spouse and family, religion, ethnic group, educational level, seniority, luck, influence of important customers, informal relations in the firm, and refusal of a prior promotion offer. On the basis of the 240 case studies of actual promotions, Powell characterized the successful promotee as being a capable leader, male, white, Anglo-Saxon, healthy and energetic, Protestant or Catholic, an effective decision maker, a college graduate, ambitious, loyal, a member of a reputable social club, aided socially by his wife, a Republican, member of the Chamber of Commerce, tall, clean-cut, conservatively dressed, a social drinker, participant in charitable and professional community organizations, and lucky.

The Equal Employment Opportunity Commission and other compliance agencies are taking closer looks at the advancement opportunities for females and minorities. In one celebrated case, AT&T was committed to increasing the number of females in second-level management jobs by 33 percent and in upper-level jobs by 50 percent. General Motors planned to promote one female for every three males on most organizational levels. In these instances, the personnel manager must be prepared to deal with dissatisfactions and complaints of "reverse discrimination" from qualified candidates from the majority group.

---

[14]"The Controller—Inflation Gives Him More Clout with Management," *Business Week,* Aug. 15, 1977, p. 84.

[15]Reed M. Powell, "Elements of Executive Promotion," *California Management Review,* Winter 1963, pp. 83–90.

Two major problems in career management have arisen as a result of major changes in our work force. The first is the problem of ''plateaued'' personnel who have temporarily or permanently stopped in their career progression. The second is an increasing incidence of the dual-career family.

Plateaued personnel   It appears that the decade of the 1980s will be a time of scarce promotions for persons born during the baby boom of 1945–1964. From 1980 to 1990, the number of persons in the 35-to-44-year range will increase from 25.4 million to 36.1 million, an increase of 42 percent.[16] During this same period, the Bureau of Labor Statistics predicts an increase in available managerial jobs of only 21 percent. This slowness of promotion could result in more stress, ''burnout,'' and psychological withdrawal by members of this prime ''middle manager'' candidate group.

Various activities can be undertaken to deal with the plateaued person. For one, mentors can help in altering expectations, pointing out that the rapid progression opportunities of the past are simply no longer available during the coming decade. A *mentor* is an older and respected manager or professional who counsels protégés, exhibits genuine concern, listens for feelings as well as facts, and stimulates people through ideas and information. The mentor can act as a *sponsor* when he or she mentions and says good things to others about protégés, gets them assigned to committees and task forces, and applies pressure to place persons on promotion lists.

A second possiblity is the establishment of additional career ladders. One can advance from junior scientist to senior scientist, as well as from professional to manager. Attention must be given to status symbols and ''perks'' for this second ladder in comparison to the more usual managerial ladder. Advancement in career learning can be enhanced through judiciously planned transfers to parallel but different jobs. Special task forces can be formed for which the plateaued person can be given leadership responsibility. And in time, the plateaued person can undertake a new task, that of acting as mentor to younger personnel entering the organization. Not everyone rises to become president and the plateau can be encountered on various organizational levels.

Finally, it should be noted that the plateaued person must also share the responsibility for dealing with this situation. As suggested by Manfred Kets de Vries, this coping process can take four main forms: defensive, depressed, underachievement, and constructive. Figure 11-6 lays out these processes on the dimensions of (1) orientation to what is going on and (2) degree of activity. The defensive person has a distorted view of reality and actively fights the situation through resistance to change, unwillingness to help develop younger personnel, and blaming or scapegoating others. Depressed persons feel that they have not met their original career aspirations and they begin to dwell in the past since the present is painful. Their psychological withdrawal from work often leads to inactivity and constant pessimism. Both the underachievement and constructive modes have a better view of reality. The underachievers are passive and are easily satisfied. They are reasonably happy with the plateaued situation, keep a low profile, and reduce their level of organizational participation. The style recommended for dealing

[16]Earl C. Gottschalk, Jr., ''Promotions Grow Few As 'Baby Boom' Group Eyes Managers' Jobs,'' *The Wall Street Journal,* October 22, 1981, p. 1.

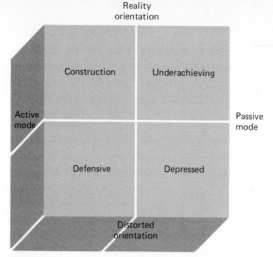

FIGURE 11-6 Four main styles of manager-environment interaction. (*Source: Manfred F. R. Kets de Vries, "The Midcareer Conundrum,"* Organizational Dynamics, *vol. 7, no. 2, Autumn 1978, p. 51. Reprinted by permission of the publisher, from* Organizational Dynamics, © AMA-COM, *a division of American Management Associations. All rights reserved.*)

with the mid-career transition is that of realistically recognizing the situation and constructively dealing with it. One may accept moving from the state of "mentee" to that of mentor. One could decide to change to a different career. Or one can accept the disappointment of not achieving original aspirations, and move to different or lesser aspirations with a minimum of bitterness.

Dual-career families As discussed in Chapter 4, the percentage of females in professional occupations has moved from 25 percent in 1970 to 36 percent in 1979; for managerial occupations the increase during this same period was from 10 percent to 18 percent. Though our society in the past has been geared to one career per family, it is clear that the number of dual career families will increase. And these two-career families are already posing difficult problems for various organizations. In one survey of 617 firms, the number reporting one or more employees refusing to transfer and relocate for personal or family reasons stood at 42 percent, an increase of over 10 percent in one year.[17] And hiring two members of the same family can cause certain difficulties for firms with strict nepotism policies.

Dual-career couples can be one of three types: (1) couples following the same career and working for the same firm, such as two chemists working for DuPont, (2) couples following different careers working for the same firm, such as a professor of economics and a research technician in the physical sciences, or (3) couples working for different firms regardless of similarity of career choice, such as a compensation specialist in Firm A's personnel department and a personnel recruiter in Firm B's personnel department.[18] Each of these types pose certain problems for the firm. For same career—same firm

---

[17]Cathleen E. Maynard and Robert A. Zawacki, "Mobility and the Dual-Career Couple," *Personnel Journal,* vol. 58, no. 7, July 1979, p. 469.

[18]Carol B. Gilmore and William R. Fannin, "The Dual Career Couple: A Challenge to Personnel in the Eighties," *Business Horizons,* vol. 25, no. 2, May-June 1982, p. 37.

couples, alterations in the recruitment process must be made so that each can be interviewed together as well as separately. Transfers are affected, and some firms will not transfer one without the other. Others will provide special allowances for separate living. And more importantly, if dual transfers cannot be effected, the refusal of one to transfer should not automatically be taken as disloyalty and lack of ambition. Certainly, the nepotism policy will have to be reviewed; various firms will not allow couples to work in the same section, let alone have one member of the couple as the supervisor of the other.

When pursuing different careers in the same firm, the nepotism problems are decreased. Transfer problems still remain, as well as certain other problems in the scheduling of time, such as vacations, child care, and so on. It is strongly recommended that the dual-career couple be involved in working out time-scheduling problems. Prescriptions following rigid company policies often tend to drive the career couple to other, more flexible organizations.

On some occasions, the firm is interested in only one member of the dual-career couple. In this case, firms increasingly are helping spouses of the preferred employees to locate new jobs. A survey of activities undertaken by 603 companies indicated that 84 percent made special attempts to find jobs in other companies; from half to two-thirds will help in counseling and preparing résumés.[19] Relatively few will pay employment agency fees or reimburse for extra job-finding trips.

As in the case of the plateaued person, the dual-career family itself has major obligations in career management. Couples must view job offers on a package basis, rather than pursuing one career objective to the exclusion of the other. If one person has generalized skills, such as high school or collegiate teaching, the couple may choose to locate where the more specialized person would have the greatest opportunity. On occasions, jobs are available in two cities close enough for the couple to locate the home halfway in between. On still other occasions, the opportunities are so far apart that the couple will have to either give up one or both, or settle for a commuter marriage. Child care poses definite problems, and in the majority of instances, the female is expected to assume a greater burden than the male. As will be noted in the following chapter, this may well have a deleterious effect upon the wife's salary and career progression.

LOW-CEILING CAREERS

There are many jobs where there is little room for advancement in career terms. Nevertheless, personnel will still seek some form of career progression. One of the most common measures of such progression is *seniority* which can be defined as the length of recognized service in an organization. Low-ceiling careers often lead to the formation of labor unions to provide some sense of control over one's organizational life. The seniority provisions are always a very important part of any labor contract that specifies rights of employees, unions, and managements.

There are at least four major tasks in the design and establishment of a seniority system. The first is specifying *when* seniority is to begin, how it may be affected by a number of different types of service interruptions, and under what conditions it terminates. In effect, this is the problem of establishing the ground rules that govern the

---

[19]Earl C. Gottschalk, Jr., "Firms Increasingly Help Spouses of Transferred Employees Find Jobs," *The Wall Street Journal*, January 21, 1982, p. 25.

accumulation of seniority. The second duty is determining what groups are to be given special treatment in the seniority system. Often both labor union and company want to favor their respective key personnel in the union and the firm. The third task is determining the range or area over which seniority can be accumulated, that is, whether over the entire plant or over some organizational element thereof. The final problem is determining what aspects of the employment situation will be affected by seniority. Should it be applied to promotion, layoff, and other related problems? In all such tasks, it is important that rules be carefully and specifically spelled out. If clear rules exist for every eventuality, the reliability of the measurement of seniority can approach a coefficient of 1. The validity of its use for making various personnel decisions is quite another matter.

Accumulation of Seniority

In many companies, seniority does not begin immediately upon hiring. There is usually a probationary period of 1 to 6 months. After this period it is usual for the recognized service to start as of the time of original employment. Even here, problems arise. Frequently, when several people are hired on the same day, it becomes important to keep exact times of hiring during the day. When there are several hires at the same time, some predetermined rule for distinguishing among personnel must be established, such as alphabetical by last name, lowest employee identification number, and so on. Seniority's greatest asset is its ability to distinguish among all personnel on an objective basis. Details, therefore, are highly important in defining the exact length of service.

One of the more difficult problems in the accumulation of seniority is that of specifying the effect of interruptions in service. If, for example, the employee leaves a job to enter military service, many firms will allow the continued accumulation of seniority and will thus create a type of "synthetic seniority." Another, more serious type of interruption is that of leaving the collective bargaining unit through promotion to a supervisory job. It is important that the company protect the seniority of persons so promoted, for otherwise there is a great loss of incentive to accept the higher job. When such protection is provided, the newly appointed supervisor usually continues to accumulate seniority. A smaller number of companies provide that when one reenters the bargaining unit after serving as supervisor, one's seniority stands where one left it at the time of promotion.

There are a number of conditions under which seniority is usually terminated. Among them are:

1. Being discharged for proper cause
2. Voluntary resignation
3. Overstaying leave of absence
4. Absences in excess of a stipulated period, such as 3 working days, without notifying the company
5. Failure to report to work after layoff when properly notified
6. A layoff in excess of a stipulated period, such as a year or 18 months

The last two reasons are the source of much controversy. To reduce the controversy surrounding reason 5, the manner of notification of the recalled employee should be spelled out in the policy or in the labor contract.

The controversy concerning the sixth reason is that many people feel that no employee should lose seniority for reasons beyond his or her control. Seniority is a highly valuable commodity, and the trend is in the direction of an increase in its value. Involuntary layoffs are outside the employee's control. From the company's viewpoint, there must be a time limitation, in order that it may maintain some control over the situation. In two-thirds of 1,845 union-management contracts covering almost 8 million employees, a stipulated period of layoff is designated for loss of seniority, one-half specify periods of less than 2 years, while the rest stipulate periods ranging from 2 to 5 years.[20]

Special Groups

The second task in establishing a seniority system is that of deciding what groups are to be given special treatment in the form of exemptions from the rules. The labor union generally requires that its officials and shop stewards be awarded a superseniority over all others. The reason for this stipulation is to keep the representative personnel intact, particularly in times of layoff and cutbacks when they are most needed. Unless accompanied by requirement of ability to do assigned work, this superseniority can result in the layoff of highly qualified employees and the retention of stewards and union officials who may not be qualified. The essential question is whether or not the superseniority is paramount or whether it is operative only when the union official can actually perform the job in question.

If the union requires that its organization be protected through the granting of superseniority, it is not unreasonable that the company should be able to trade those exceptions for some special treatment for certain key employees. For example, such special groups as the following may be exempted from the seniority provisions: (1) tool and die makers, (2) graduates of technical and professional schools, (3) personnel classified by management as indispensable for maintaining the flow of production, and (4) apprentices or those receiving special training and schooling. Sometimes it is specified that the number of management-protected personnel cannot exceed the number of union personnel who are granted superseniority.

Seniority Unit

Our third problem in setting up a seniority system is that of specifying the area or unit over which it operates. Seniority can be computed on the basis of company, plant division, department, or occupation. Any one or all of these areas can be used for different objectives. For example, the influence of seniority in promotion may be confined to occupational seniority, whereas in the matter of vacation choice it may be company-wide. When decisions have to do with matters involving employee competence to do work, management generally prefers the narrower area.

When the seniority unit is restricted, the problem of "bumping" during layoff is reduced. A longer-service worker can displace personnel of shorter service in only a restricted unit. When the area is company-wide, the layoff of one person might well generate a dozen or more "bumps." The disruptive effects of "bumping" can be reduced by stipulating that the displaced employee can "bump" only the least senior employee

---

[20]Winston L. Tillery, "Layoff and Recall Provisions in Major Agreements," *Monthly Labor Review,* vol. 94, no. 7, July 1971, p. 44.

in a unit, or that the number of "bumps" per displacement cannot exceed a certain number.

It is important specifically to indicate the particular units in which seniority can be accumulated. It is also important for the company to maintain exact and accurate seniority lists of all personnel. To management, company-wide seniority for most objectives seems rather ludicrous. However, though occupational seniority does ensure a certain minimum of job competence, such units may be too narrow. When a job is eliminated by changes in work processes, the seniority of all assigned personnel is wiped out. If occupational seniority is utilized, it is quite important to utilize also other seniority units, such as the department or division. Departmental seniority provides some flexibility, because it is unlikely that an entire department will be eliminated. It also ensures that the employee will have some general knowledge of the jobs to which he or she might fall heir in case of layoff.

Employment Decisions Affected by Seniority

The last and perhaps most important problem in designing a seniority system is to specify the employment privileges that seniority can affect and the weight of that effect. Certain employment factors are often affected by seniority. Among them are (1) promotion, (2) layoff, (3) transfer, (4) choice of shifts, (5) choice of vacation periods, (6) separation or severance pay, and (7) choice of machine, jobs, runs, and so on. For some factors, management is often entirely willing that seniority shall be *completely* controlling. The choice of vacation periods, machinery, and shift assignments is an example of this type. Decisions concerning transfer, layoff, and promotion are more complex, and management often wishes to use the merit base in place of or in addition to seniority.

A transfer is a change in job where the new job is substantially equal to the old in terms of pay, status, and responsibilities. There are various types of transfers such as (1) those designed to enhance training and development, (2) those making possible adjustment to varying volumes of work within the firm, and (3) those designed to remedy a problem of poor placement.

It is important that company policy be formulated to govern the administration of all types of employee transfers. Rather than decide each case solely on the characteristics of that case, effective management needs to establish some uniformity of treatment. The policy should cover such subjects as (1) the acceptable reasons for a transfer, (2) the organization area over which a transfer can be made, (3) the effect of seniority on such changes as shift transfers, (4) the posting of available job openings, (5) the classification of transfers as permanent or temporary, and (6) the effect, if any, of the transfer upon the pay of the employee. In general, the policy governing transfers should consider first the interests of the organization as a whole. This policy does not, however, prevent the granting of requests for remedial personnel transfers. Ordinarily company policies are flexible enough to permit some individual treatment of particular employee problems.

Layoff is a very difficult problem not only for the employee but for the company and the labor union as well. Since layoff involves the loss of income, the employee and the union are prone to restrict the company's freedom of decision. The company again is desirous of emphasizing the factor of ability and merit in layoff. It wishes to be sure that employees who "bump" other employees can adequately fulfill the job requirements.

On the other hand, because of the seriousness of the event to the employee, the employee tries to regulate layoff decisions through seniority systems. It is generally found that seniority is a *stronger* factor in layoff than it is in promotion. In a previously cited analysis of union-management contracts, seniority was the sole factor controlling layoff decisions in 25 percent of the contracts, a primary factor in one-half (seniority controlled if employee could meet minimum performance requirements), and a secondary factor in the remainder (seniority controlled only if the displaced employee was relatively equal to the person to be "bumped")[21].

With respect to promotion, management feels that it has the strongest case in advocating merit as the sole or most important basis for the decision. Unions and employees still contend that seniority should be given significant influence. Many compromises have been worked out between the extremes of pure seniority and pure merit, one of which can be phrased, "When ability is substantially equal, seniority will govern." This is weighted in favor of ability, since ability is rarely if ever equal. Obviously, there will be many disputes over the word "substantially," and labor arbitrators in deciding upon union appeals to overturn management decisions will define this term in practice.

A second type of compromise is written more in favor of seniority. This would be an agreement that the senior person meeting *minimum* requirements would be given preference. Suppose, for example, persons A, B, and C were being considered for a job opening. A has 10 years of service, B has 5, and C, 3. If A can meet the *minimum* requirements for the job, it is assigned to him or her even though B and C may be of substantially higher ability. Our problem here is how to tell whether A can do the job. The labor union generally insists that A be given a trial on the job. If after a few weeks he or she proves inadequate, the company may then turn to B. It is evident that the administration of this compromise agreement can consume a substantial amount of time. In a few instances, the union has accepted the results of various written and performance tests as a shortcut in a procedure of this type. Minimum scores are established, and the person with the greatest seniority among those who have passing scores is the one who gets the job.

Seniority and the Law

In the *Griggs v. Duke Power Company* case, the U.S. Supreme Court established the principle that procedures and practices, neutral on their face, cannot be maintained if they operate to freeze the status quo of prior discriminatory practices. This meant that the organization must be responsible for the present effects of past discrimination.

In following this principle, many district and circuit courts have overturned seniority systems as perpetuating past discriminatory practices. The Crown Zellerbach Corporation and the United Paperworkers and Papermakers Union, for example, were ordered to replace a job seniority system with a plant-wide system for making promotion decisions. The existing system was effectively utilized as an instrument in maintaining a pattern of discrimination against blacks with respect to promotion and training opportunities. Though there is nothing in a seniority system that is inherently prejudicial to blacks, its continued use in conjunction with past discriminatory practices in hiring led to the order to abolish the system.

[21]Ibid., p. 42.

In 1977, however, the U.S. Supreme Court issued two decisions that rejected the approach taken by the lower courts.[22] This was based on a section in Title VII of the Civil Rights Act that provided special protection for the legality of seniority systems *existing at the time the law took effect*. Such a provision was included to obtain the backing of significant labor union leaders in getting the law passed in 1964. However, only bona fide existing systems were protected by this provision. Such systems were ones that were neither established nor maintained with an *intent* to discriminate. Intent is very difficult to prove in court, and it would appear that substantial protection exists for systems established prior to 1964.

In response to this decision, the Equal Employment Opportunity Commission issued an interpretative memorandum.[23] The Commission will infer intent to discriminate if (1) unions and organizational units were segregated prior to 1964, or (2) the employer and union are made aware that they are presently locking minorities or females into discriminatory positions when an alternative system is available. It remains to be seen whether the courts will accept this position of the Commission. These Supreme Court decisions also shifted the burden to individual employees to prove that they had personally suffered from past discrimination. Class actions are no longer possible. The employee must prove that either he or she personally applied for a position and was turned down, or that the "chilling effect" of old segregrated policies discouraged application. And in a Supreme Court decision in 1982 involving two plants of the American Tobacco Company, the court ruled 5 to 4 that seniority systems established *since 1965* are legal even if they unintentionally hurt black and female workers. As in the Teamster ruling, employees must now prove that the employer *intended* to discriminate against them through the seniority system. The date of establishment of the system no longer matters.

SUMMARY

Individual employee careers must be of concern to organizations and managers in order that human resources may be developed to meet constantly changing environmental conditions. A career is a sequence of separate but related work activities that provides continuity, order, and meaning to a person's life. It is shaped by a myriad of factors including heredity, culture, parents, schooling, age level, family cycle, and actual experiences in one or more organizations.

An effective career development program provides substantial employee assistance in self-diagnosis of interests, aptitudes, and capabilities. It also provides complete information concerning career opportunities within the organization. The third major ingredient is that of aligning individual careers with career opportunities through a continuing program of training, education, transfer, and advancement. Major current problems in career management would include dealing with the plateaued employee and recruiting and utilizing dual-career couples.

The low-ceiling career provides an unusual challenge in alignment of human needs and organizational requirements. Perhaps the major factor in the management of low-ceiling careers is that of seniority. Precision of measurement of seniority calls for a

---

[22]*Teamsters v. U.S.*, No. 75-636 (U.S. Supreme Court, May 31, 1977) and *United Airlines, Inc., v. Evans*, No. 76-333 (U.S. Supreme Court, May 31, 1977).

[23]*Interpretive Memorandum Concerning International Brotherhood of Teamsters v. United States*, Equal Employment Opportunity Commission, July 12, 1977.

multitude of detailed rules governing techniques of accumulation, special treatment of protected groups, and units (occupation, department, company) in which it can be accredited to the person. Under the Civil Rights Act, the government is highly involved when such objective systems work to discriminate against protected groups of employees.

In making the many necessary personnel decisions in an organization, seniority can be mixed with ability in various ways; for example, when ability is equal, seniority governs. In any event, career development requires proper recognition of employee increases in experience, seniority, skills, and abilities.

BRIEF CASE

At the insistence of the labor union, talks have opened concerning the proper role of seniority in making promotion decisions. Management prefers the clause, "when ability is substantially equal, seniority will govern the decision." The union prefers, "the senior employee able to meet the minimum requirements for the job will be preferred in promotion decisions." In researching the impact of these two clauses, the personnel unit secured the following information for one department opening:

	Ability Index	Seniority (years)
George	95	2
John	85	8
Lucas	78	15
Harry	71	20
Julius	68	30
Jim	62	5
Ed	60	26

The union objects to the ability index as a way of determining capability. Rather than testing, it prefers job tryout.

Questions

1. Under the management-preferred clause, who would be selected for promotion? Is there a "substantial" difference? How can we tell?

2. If we set a score of 70 as the minimum acceptable level, who would get the job under the union-preferred clause?

3. If we accept the union's demand for job tryout along with its clause, what would be the process of making the promotion decision?

DISCUSSION QUESTIONS

1. Why should a private business organization be concerned with long-term career development of individual employees?

2. What is a career, and what factors go into the shaping of one?

3. What is a career anchor? Identify the five types of anchors discovered in the cited study. Using these anchors, describe the behavioral patterns exhibited by varying types of police personnel.

4. With respect to professionally trained employees, what are the nature and significance of designations such as ''local'' and ''cosmopolitan''? What two other categories can be developed using these concepts?

5. Integrate the cycles of self-development, family development, and career development.

6. What is a ''plateaued employee?'' How can the firm deal with him or her? What are the action alternatives from the view of the plateaued employee?

7. What are the peculiar problems of recruiting, developing, and keeping dual-career couples?

8. Discuss seniority systems in terms of their reliability and validity.

9. What is the current legal status of seniority systems that were developed prior to 1964? after 1964?

10. What are the various types of compromises that can be effected between ability and seniority in making personnel decisions?

SUPPLEMENTARY READING

GILMORE, CAROL B. and WILLIAM R. FANNIN: ''The Dual Career Couple: A Challenge to Personnel in the Eighties,'' *Business Horizons,* vol. 25, no. 2, May-June 1982, pp. 36–41.

GORDON, MICHAEL E. and WILLIAM J. FITZGIBBONS: ''Empirical Test of the Validity of Seniority as a Factor in Staffing Decisions,'' *Journal of Applied Psychology,* vol. 67, no. 3, June 1982, pp. 311–319.

HASTINGS, ROBERT E.: ''No-fault Career Counseling Can Boost Middle- and Upper-Management Productivity,'' *The Personnel Administrator,* vol. 27, no. 1, January 1982, pp. 22–27.

DeLONG, THOMAS J.: ''Reexamining the Career Anchor Model,'' *Personnel,* vol. 59, no. 3, May-June 1982, pp. 50–61.

LEACH, JOHN, J: ''The Career Planning Process,'' *Personnel Journal,* vol. 60, no. 4, April 1981, pp. 283–287.

LOUIS, MERYL REIS: ''Managing Career Transition: A Missing Link in Career Development,'' *Organizational Dynamics,* vol. 10, no. 4, Spring 1982, pp. 68–77.

EXERCISE AND CASES FOR PART THREE

Exercise: Promotion Decision

You are head of a highly regarded computer center in one plant of a multiplant organization. The work of your center involves design and operation of a plant management information system, as well as tying into the multiplant system. These activities involve the processing of a large amount of data and the preparation of detailed reports, which are then sent to different divisions within the plant, and then to the headquarters office. While some of the work is routine, much of it requires technical expertise. Some of it requires high interpersonal skills to handle conflicts with other organizational units.

On a recent visit by the headquarters vice president in charge of data processing, you were asked to nominate one of your subordinate managers to be the computer center head in a large plant that the firm has recently purchased. The vice president has asked for the person to be from your center because of some of the excellent results that your center has produced, both in developing new data processing techniques and in getting them successfully implemented within your plant. As you consider the personnel in your center, only two stand out in your mind, both of whom head up sections.

Georgia Summers is a 32-year-old college graduate with a master's degree in management informations systems. Though fairly young for the level of responsibility in her present position, her performance has been outstanding. One of her strengths is her ability to get people to work with her and for her. She has taken the lead in getting department heads to go along with new and different data processing ideas. The fact that she is attractive has opened doors for her. Summers is single and has mentioned several times that she is very career-minded.

The other candidate, John Winter, has also done an outstanding job as section head. He is 48 years old, has an undergraduate degree in general business, and has been in the center for 12 years. His progress has been slow but steady. In reviewing his work history, you realize that many of the creative innovations in data processing have come as a result of his suggestions. He has been able to devise a number of very effective, yet simple, procedures. He typically comes to work an hour before everybody else, and leaves an hour or so after the regular quitting time. On the job, he is all business and expects the people working for him to be the same. As a result, he seems somewhat abrupt in his interpersonal contacts. He is married, has two children, and has mentioned his great interest in advancing further up the career ladder.

As you consider these two candidates, you think about such aspects as the following: (1) effects of the promotion on Summers and Winter and their careers, (2) effects on the two present work groups, (3) effects on the total organization, (4) effects on you if you lost either of these two valuable people, and (5) effects on the newly purchased plant, which would require introduction of the firm's management information system. Whichever person is selected, you know that you will have to inform the other, and you worry about what to say. You realize that you, personally, will feel a loss since you do not have the technical skills of Winter, nor the superior interpersonal leadership qualities of Summers.

Procedure

1 Working individually, develop the criteria that you would use in making the decision to promote Summers or Winters. Organize them into (1) organization effects, (2) personal effects on you, and (3) effects on the two candidates.

2 Form into groups of four or five people. Discuss the criteria that each of you has developed, and agree on one set for your group. Without classifying as above, place these criteria in the order of importance that your group feels is proper.

3 Based on the information and the criteria, decide whom to promote.

4 Additional variations:

    a Have one group read its list of criteria in the order of importance, and have the class determine if it can predict the group's final decision.

    b Role play the task of informing the losing candidate of your decision.

Case: Archer Company*

Upon the death of their father, the two sons of Frederick Archer each took part of their father's original business and set up separate establishments. James Archer set up the Archer Company, an advertising specialty manufacturing firm, making metal, wood, and paper advertising items.

The Archer Company organization was set up by James Archer when he was 40 years old. He operated the business as its sole owner and principal executive for 15 years. The company employed about 150 people in the plant, on the average, and had a staff of nine salesmen. Most of the business of the firm was special order work. The Archer Company was highly regarded for the quality of its work.

James Archer, at the age of 55, began formulating plans for the future of his organization in the light of his planned retirement from active management a few years hence. His primary objective was to leave a strong, going concern. The plan, as matured by Archer, provided for the establishment of three key positions in the organization. These three positions were general manager, sales manager, and factory manager. It was Archer's purpose to have the men holding these three positions act as the executive committee of the company in determining policy and making important decisions. Initially, Archer would maintain active connection with the company, but he would gradually give over operating authority to the general manager, who would make use of the executive committee in formulating policy.

Up to the time this plan was developed, the Archer Company was a one-man organization operated by Archer himself. After a careful survey of his existing staff, Archer felt it necessary to go outside the firm to fill the newly created positions.

As general manager of the concern, Archer selected his son-in-law, Samuel Barton. At the time of his employment, Barton was not well acquainted with the business. He was rated by associates as a man of superior mental ability. He demonstrated an excellent capacity at long-range planning and organizing and was considered an average administrator. Some of his associates said he was moody at times and attributed what was called "personality difficulties" to the fact that he was hard of hearing and used a hearing aid. Barton had an obvious personal interest in the position by virtue of family connections and undertook his new job with enthusiasm.

For the position of sales manager, Archer selected James McCarthy. McCarthy was an outstanding salesman with a record of great success in this industry. He had a tremendous amount of drive and had achieved his reputation through his personal sales efforts. He had limited experience as a sales executive. At the time he was hired, his administrative skill in directing a sales force was an unknown quality. Archer was motivated in selecting McCarthy by the belief that his knowledge of salesmanship in this

*Robert Dubin, *Human Relations in Administration,* 2d ed., Prentice-Hall, Inc., Englewood Cliffs, N.J., 1961, pp. 485–490. Used with permission.

industry and his obvious success would serve as an example and inspiration to the sales force.

William Stevens was hired by Archer for the position of factory manager. Stevens had no direct production experience in this industry. However, for some years he had sold equipment throughout this industry and had a thorough knowledge of the machinery, its use, and its capabilities.

Shortly after these three principal executives were installed in office, they made plans for achieving an annual volume of business of 1 million dollars. The business was to be expanded over a 5-year period to reach this goal. This represented a substantial increase from the present volume of about $600,000 a year. Archer participated in this planning as the source of final authority in approving the work of the new executive committee.

Anticipating the expanding business, a decision was made to hire two additional specialists. Will Harrison was selected to fill the job of plant superintendent under Stevens. Harrison had worked in the industry for many years and had a fine reputation for his technical knowledge. Arnold Jefferson was hired as chief designer. He came to the Archer Company with an excellent background in product design, having done such work with several companies and with a design consulting firm in New York.

Also in line with the expansion program, an order was placed for a considerable amount of new production equipment. At this time a major contract was secured covering a 10-year period and calling for an estimated annual sales of $250,000 to this single account, the largest in the company's history.

In the face of sales expansion and plant modernization, Archer personally hired Sidney Fremont, an industrial engineer, to work on plant layout and production processes. Fremont was hired only on a project basis, but did such a creditable job that he was retained permanently to work out industrial engineering problems.

The final stage of staff expansion was reached when a decision was made to secure a new man to take over the job of Jefferson, the chief designer. Jefferson was considered a competent designer capable of developing other people's ideas. He was considered weak, however, on originality in design. The decision was made to move him into the sales department, where his talents would be particularly useful in servicing established accounts. To replace him, Wayne Klinger was employed as chief designer. In previous positions, Klinger had demonstrated exceptional promotional talents; he gave every promise of being the idea man desired for the position.

About a year after the organization began to expand, its structure was as shown in the chart (Phase I) on page 274.

In the course of the development of Phase I in the growth of the Archer Company, a number of problems arose. First of all, it became reasonably clear that the executive committee idea was not serving in the manner intended by Archer. He had retained very direct participation in the organization and his staff continued to look to him as the active chief executive. This was particularly true of McCarthy, the sales manager. Although nominally reporting to Barton, McCarthy often bypassed Barton and took problems directly to Archer. Archer's reaction to this was to continue to permit Barton to be bypassed. Archer viewed such action by McCarthy as a natural continuation of the sort of consultation he was used to as active head of the business.

At the same time that McCarthy seemed to be making an effort to work around Barton, he was frequently a minority of one in the executive committee in opposing the creation of new jobs and persons hired to fill them. This was particularly true of Klinger,

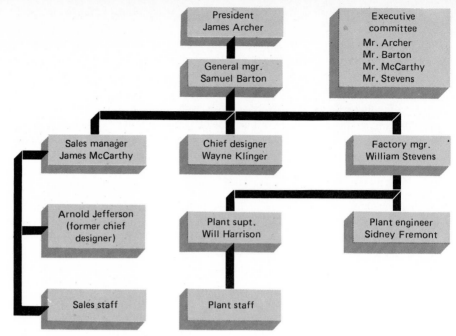

Archer Company organization: Phase I.

to whom McCarthy took an instant dislike. Part of McCarthy's dislike for Klinger may have been related to the fact that Klinger soon developed direct contacts with customers and was responsible for securing some important accounts on his own. In the nature of his work as new-idea man in the organization, Klinger had a lot of opportunity to contact customers and, if possible, secure their accounts through such contacts.

McCarthy was the object of considerable discontent among the salesmen. They felt that he was seldom at the office to help them, and in fact, was never really available for consultation or help with sales problems. McCarthy was on the road a great deal. Some of his sales staff undoubtedly viewed him as a potential threat in their own territories, since, by virtue of being sales manager, he could work in any territory he chose.

Barton soon found himself on the most friendly and cordial terms with Klinger. This friendship extended even to after-hours recreation, in which the two men spent considerable time together. This friendship was ultimately viewed by many of their associates as the cause of Barton's wife divorcing him. These observers said that Barton and Klinger had developed quite a reputation for "painting the town red" to the point where Mrs. Barton could no longer ignore her husband's activities.

McCarthy had by this time become so enraged with Klinger that he successfully delved into Klinger's past and sent a report to Archer outlining some of the more un-desirable features of Klinger's career. Archer was not disposed to fire Klinger, since, on business grounds, his work was entirely satisfactory. However, the report from Mc-Carthy, together with Klinger's connection with the events leading to the Barton divorce, put him in a frame of mind to accept Klinger's resignation when it was offered at the time of the divorce. (Klinger also had gained knowledge of the fact that Archer had the McCarthy report on Klinger's unsavory past. The combination of Klinger's close con-nection with Barton's divorce and Archer's knowledge of his past probably led him to submit his resignation.) The removal of Klinger from the organization tended to relieve McCarthy's feelings only temporarily.

Barton also offered his resignation to Archer at the time of the divorce. In spite of Archer's obvious hurt at seeing his daughter seek a divorce, he told Barton that he was doing a good job and did not have to resign. Archer pointed out that ''a man's personal life has nothing to do with his business life. He would be judged on the job only as he was successful in the latter.''

At about this juncture in the affairs of the company, Archer became increasingly aware that the strong organization he had envisioned had not yet materialized. He had this view confirmed when a personnel consultant hired by Barton discussed the organization with him. Archer came to the conclusion that he would have to shake up the organization drastically.

McCarthy was let go. In his place, Sidney Fremont, the industrial engineer, was appointed. Arnold Jefferson, the former chief designer, was given his old position back to take the job left vacant by Klinger's resignation. William Stevens was moved up from factory manager to general manager in place of Barton, who was retained in the company but given no specific assignment other than to be available for work on special projects. Finally, Will Harrison, plant superintendent, was moved up to factory manager and his old position was abolished. The executive committee was discontinued.

In the second phase of the growth of the Archer Company, the organization was as shown in Phase II.

The replacement of McCarthy by Fremont has been viewed by the sales staff as a distinct improvement. Fremont spends considerable time working individually with the salesmen and confines most of his work to the office, leaving direct sales to the salesmen. Jefferson is said to have improved and seems to display more creative ability than he first showed upon joining the organization. Stevens occasionally encounters difficulties in making decisions, according to some of his associates, but he has easy access to Archer's advice and counsel on such occasions. Harrison is doing a capable job of running the factory. Barton is called in on special projects to lend his assistance whenever and wherever needed.

Archer Company organization: Phase II.

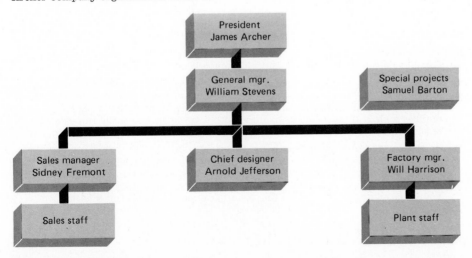

Questions

1. Is Archer unable or unwilling to retire? Document supporting evidence for your choice.

2. How does a chief executive go about the process of exiting from a firm?

Case: The Training Staff Meeting*

The Central Corporation had four plants, each employing at least 1,000 people, and a central office with a staff of approximately 250. At the central office James R. Simpson headed the training division with general staff responsibility in the area of company-wide training, and specific responsibility for running the training programs of the central office. Each of the four plants had a plant training staff operating under a director of training responsible for carrying out the plant training programs. The plant training directors reported directly to their respective plant managers. Mr. Simpson had no direct line authority over the plant training directors. His position, however, in the central office, and particularly his direct contact with the principal officers of the corporation, permitted him to exercise a great deal of influence over the plant training directors.

The board of directors had determined to undertake an executive training program and gave a general directive to Mr. Simpson to develop such a program to be worked out in detail with the plant training directors. The four plant managers were informed of the directors' decision to carry on the executive training program, and were urged to get their plant training staffs working on the program in the near future. As a result, Mr. Simpson had called a conference of the plant training directors and they were meeting with him at the central office. The discussions at the meeting were recorded as the simplest means for providing each participant with a record of discussions and decisions. Following is a segment of the recorded staff meeting on the first day. As Mr. Simpson indicates in his opening comment, the group has been talking about the program prior to the incident recorded here.

Mr. Simpson. We seem to be in general agreement as to what the executive training program ought to accomplish—what we're shooting at. Perhaps it would be a good idea to take a look at methods—how are we going to do it. There are lots of different methods—conferences, group discussions, lectures, workshops, and the like—and we ought to have some agreement among us on which we propose to use at our plants. I, of course, can't tell any of you what methods should be used here, but I do want to throw out the idea that we consider using role playing in our training. I have had. . . .

Carl Halvorsen (Plant 1 training director). I've read a little bit about that role-playing stuff, Jim, but I can't say it has impressed me particularly.

Mr. Simpson. I've used it some here and I think I can say without any qualification that it is successful. We have had amazing results with it after we once broke the ice. I know it is kind of a new thing and some of you may hesitate to undertake it because you are not familiar with it. If we decide to go ahead with it we could very easily run some practice sessions here before we break up and that would give us all a chance to see it in operation.

Harold Hicks (Eastern plant training director). Jim, before we talk about this role playing maybe we ought to find out what plans the fellows already have, if any. Some of us have been thinking about this program ever since we knew it was coming and I'll bet some of us have even been doing some executive training already. What I mean is, let's not decide on a method until we find out what some of the ideas on that are.

*Robert Dubin, *Human Relations in Administration*, 2d ed., Prentice-Hall, Inc., Englewood Cliffs, N.J., 1961, pp. 575–578. Used with permission.

Mr. Simpson. That's a good point, Hal. I guess I just assumed that would come out in the discussion, but let's do it that way to start. What are some of the plans you fellows have? How about your plant, Randy?

F. R. Randall (Plant 2 training director). Well, as you know, our plant manager hires personally all the executives at our plant and he is pretty proud of his executive staff. I think I will be able to sell him on this training program. I frankly haven't given much thought to methods—of course, we all know the usual methods—but I'll go along with anything we decide here.

Charles Pinkerton (Western plant training director). I know this role-playing business is supposed to be hot stuff; but we have used it for some time. I think all of us used it some way during the war with JMT and JRT.* I've found it works all right with workers and supervisors. But executives are likely to think it is kid stuff and just laugh it off. I have some reservations about using it in this executive training program.

Mr. Simpson. I'm glad you brought that point up, Charley. We were kind of worried about the same thing. Once we tried it here, however, we found that the executives ate it up. I know it takes some real technique in introducing it but if you do a careful job it will work. I remember one of our top executives here who just acted bored when the others were role playing. I could see he didn't like it. Then he played the role of a department head catching hell from his division chief. He really did a superb job and had the boys in the aisles with his acting. After that he was really enthusiastic about the method. After all, executives are human, too, and they get a kick out of really participating in the training. That's what role playing does—it gives everyone a chance to participate without having to make speeches and shoot the bull.

Mr. Pinkerton. Well, maybe the executives here at the home office have time to play games like that. But seriously, Jim, I wonder if we are going to have the time at our plants to make use of this role playing. If we are going to do a well-rounded training program we'll have to cover an awful lot of ground. I think you'll admit that role playing is slow going, particularly, as you say, when you have to spend so much time to put it over in the first place.

Mr. Simpson. You are right, Charley, and I wouldn't argue with you for a minute about the time it takes to do role playing. My own feeling about the matter—and this is, of course, just my personal opinion—is that the lessons learned in role playing are really learned and stick with people. Sure, you can cover more ground quicker by the conference method or by lectures, but how much of that stuff sticks with a person?

Mr. Halvorsen. That's just one of the things I've worried about in role playing. Now, I'm not an expert on it like you, Jim—I can only speak about what I've read about it—but I wonder how you evaluate its effectiveness. That's one of our biggest headaches in training—evaluation—and I don't think we know enough about evaluating role playing to be sure we have a good thing in it.

Mr. Simpson. Carl, we all know that evaluating is a headache, and I'd be the first to admit that we are a long way from having that one licked. My own observations are that role playing sticks with the participant and does a teaching job. What do you think, Charley?

Mr. Pinkerton. Oh, sure, I go along with you in saying it sticks with the participants, but so does at least some of most training. I still feel that we would have a real problem of getting executives to take it in the first place, and I don't think we will have the time back home at the plant to use it anyway.

Mr. Simpson. You haven't said much, Randy. What's your reaction to this?

Mr. Randall. As I said, I'll go along with anything you decide here. If you want us to try role playing, I'll try it. It doesn't make much difference to me because training is training, after all.

---

*Job Management Training and Job Relations Training, standardized training programs used during World War II.

Mr. Simpson. I'm sorry you put it that way, Randy, I'm not trying to force anything on you. You all know you are perfectly free to run your training programs as you please. I don't want any of you to have the impression that we at the home office are trying to insist on anything. Our purpose in getting together is to exchange ideas and develop a unified program so we will all be accomplishing the same things when we get our executive training under way. I just threw out this suggestion on role playing because I thought it was valuable, but of course that is just one of many things out on the table. We have a lot to get over in the next couple of days so maybe we ought to move on to something else and come back to methods later.

Questions

1. If functional authority is given to Simpson, what are the implications in terms of objectives and line/staff relationships?

2. What forms of resistance are shown by the plant training directors?

3. How can Simpson develop a company training program with no command authority?

PART FOUR

COMPENSATION

If the abilities of employees have been developed to the point where they meet or exceed job requirements, it is now appropriate that they be equitably compensated for their contributions. The factors affecting the determination of equitable compensation are many, varied, and complex, and management must come to some decision concerning the basic wage or salary (Chapter 12). To motivate improved performance on the job, many systems of variable compensation have been devised (Chapter 13). And finally, organizations have developed numerous ways of providing supplementary compensation in the form of fringe benefits (Chapter 14).

Base Compensation— Job

O ne of the most difficult functions of personnel management is that of determining rates of monetary compensation. Not only is it one of the most complex duties, but it is also one of the most significant to both the organization and the employee. It is important to the organization, because wages and salaries often constitute the greatest single cost of doing business; in 1929 employee compensation amounted to 58 percent of the nation's income, as compared with 75 percent in recent years. It is important to the employee because the paycheck often is the sole means of economic survival; it is also one of the most influential factors determining status in society.

As far as the organization is concerned, employee compensation programs are designed to do three things: (1) to attract capable employees to the organization, (2) to motivate them toward superior performance, and (3) to retain their services over an extended period of time. As a consequence, our discussion is divided into three chapters, with the first subject being that of determination of base pay. Though no science of pay exists, systems of job evaluation are widely used to make this first important decision. When coupled with surveys of rates paid by competing firms, the organization can establish a pay policy that will meet its desired goal of attracting sufficient personnel to accomplish work tasks.

In many cases, organizations prefer that their employees perform at a rate higher than average. In the following chapter, we shall examine methods of varying individual pay through merit evaluation and incentive pay plans, as well as systems of promoting group productivity through profit sharing and production bonuses. Finally, the third chapter in this part will deal with the fastest-growing segment of total compensation, the provision of all types of supplementary pay or fringe benefits. Such programs are more effective in maintaining a work force that they are in motivating higher levels of performance.

SIGNIFICANT FACTORS AFFECTING COMPENSATION POLICY

Though a considerable amount of guesswork and negotiation are involved in salary determination, certain factors have been extracted as having an important bearing upon the final dollar decision. Among these factors are the following: (1) supply and demand for employee skills, (2) labor organizations, (3) the firm's ability to pay, (4) productivity of the firm and the economy, (5) cost of living, and (6) government. Each of these will be discussed briefly in order to demonstrate the exceedingly complex nature of compensation. Perhaps a realization of these complexities will lead to a greater appreciation and acceptance of job evaluation despite its arbitrariness and scientific failings.

Supply and demand   Though the commodity approach to labor, as discussed in Chapter 2, is not completely correct, it is nevertheless true that a wage is a price for the services of a human being. The firm desires these services, and it must pay a price that will bring forth the supply, which is controlled by the individual worker or by a group of workers acting in concert. The primary practical result of the operation of this law of supply and demand is the creation of the ''going-wage rate.'' It will be demonstrated later how the wage and salary survey of this going rate is incorporated into a job evaluation approach to wage determination. We shall discuss the charges of certain groups that the market going rate reflects fundamental biases toward female employees.

This simple statement of the effect that the demand and supply of labor have on wages belies its complexity. It is not practicable to draw demand-and-supply curves for each job in an organization, even though, theoretically, a separate curve exists for *each* job. But in general, if anything works to decrease the supply of labor, such as restriction by a particular labor union, there will be a tendency to increase the compensation. If

FIGURE 12-1
Labor Unions and Earnings

	Median Weekly Earnings	Percent Represented by a Union	Percent Who Are Women
All full-time workers	$289	29	39
Highest-paying industries:			
Petroleum and coal products	433	36	20
Mining	423	36	15
Railroad transportation	422	82	7
Aircraft and parts manufacture	414	50	23
Ordnance	410	37	22
Motor vehicle and equipment manufacture	407	63	15
Lowest-paying industries:			
Private households	114	1	90
Apparel manufacture	170	27	79
Eating and drinking places	174	8	55
Leather and leather products	185	24	61
Personal services	188	18	59
Agriculture	189	4	16

Source: Earl F. Mellor and George D. Stamas, "Usual Weekly Earnings: Another Look at Intergroup Differences and Basic Trends," *Monthly Labor Review*, vol. 105, No. 4, April 1982, p. 19.

anything works to increase the employer's demand for labor, such as wartime prosperity, there will be a tendency to increase the compensation. The reverse of each situation is likely to result in a decrease in employee compensation, provided other factors, such as those discussed below, do not intervene.

Labor unions　In the structure of economic relationships, the labor union attempts to work primarily on the supply side. In a strike for higher wages, the employer's demand for labor to meet a market need is pitted against a supply withheld by the union. Union leaders are often very adroit in selecting the appropriate time to strike as judged by the markets for the employer's products.

To strengthen their control over the supply of labor, unions seek such goals as union or closed shops, regulated or restricted substitution of capital for labor through technology, and controlled entry into apprenticeship programs. All of these activities serve to restrict the number of alternatives open to the employer, who must see that other groups besides labor are properly compensated. All compensation must come from products sold in a market that is usually competitive in nature. Inequitable compensation to any or all will create trouble in maintaining the health of the organization. The increase in the strength of labor unions is due, in part, to the fact the employees' interests had not been receiving attention equal to that given to other components of the enterprise. The impact of this strength is shown in Figure 12-1. In the six highest-paying industries, approximately half of the full-time workers are organized. In the six lowest-paying industries, only 14 percent are organized. It should also be noted that the percentage of female employees is lowest among the highest-paying industries.

Ability to pay　Labor unions have often demanded an increase in compensation on the basis that the firm is prosperous and able to pay. However, the fundamental determinants of the wage rate for the individual firm issue from supply and demand. If the firm is marginal and cannot afford to pay competitive rates, its employees will generally leave it for better-paying jobs. Admittedly, this adjustment is neither immediate nor perfect because of problems of labor immobility and lack of perfect knowledge of alternatives. If the firm is highly successful, there is little need to pay far more than the competitive rate to obtain personnel. Such a firm, however, may choose to adopt a policy of paying above the competitive rate in order to attract a superior caliber of personnel. If firms in general are prosperous and able to pay, the tendency is to bid up the price of labor as a whole.

Productivity　Beginning with the famed General Motors contract with the United Automobile Workers (UAW) in 1948, much attention has been paid to the effect of general productivity increases in the economy upon the specific compensation of huge aggregations of employees. In the battle against inflation, representatives of the federal government have attempted to use computed productivity gains as guidelines in the settlement of wage disputes between managements and unions. Between 1947 and 1966, the computed average annual productivity increase in manufacturing was set at 2.9 percent, leading to the establishment of a "noninflationary" guideline for wage increases of 3.2 percent.[1] With growing inflation, resulting briefly in short-term wage and price controls, the validity of this guideline suddenly vanished. With inflation reaching double-

[1] Martin Ziegler, "Productivity in Manufacturing," *Monthly Labor Review*, vol. 90, no. 10, October 1967, p. 3.

digit levels, the government approach of "jawboning" to influence negotiated settlements has been placed under serious handicaps. An even more serious problem is that the average annual productivity increase in the United States during a recent 11-year period has sunk to 1.9 percent as compared with 9 percent in Japan, 5.5 percent in West Germany, 5.1 percent in France, and 2.8 percent in Great Britain.[2] During this same period, however, hourly pay has increased over 100 percent. A part of this problem of pay speedup and productivity slowdown is characteristic of a maturing economy; service businesses now account for 70 percent of all jobs. Productivity advances in services are more difficult to effect than in manufacturing.

Though some have hailed the widespread use of productivity index as a major breakthrough in compensation, there are several serious drawbacks to its use. Among these are the following: (1) there is no precise and accurate measure of productivity acceptable to all; (2) the reported percent increases are generally a long-term average and are not achieved each year; (3) not all industries participate equally in productivity gains; and (4) use of any index does not materially reduce controversy in bargaining, since the index is used as the base from which to bargain.

Cost of living   Another formula hailed by many as the answer is the cost-of-living adjustment of wages. Among the problems engendered by this approach are the following: (1) no cost-of-living formula will indicate what the base compensation should be—it merely indicates how that rate should vary; (2) this approach tends to vary monetary income but freeze real income, a result with which labor is not content; and (3) as in the case of productivity indexes, there are certain measurement problems in ascertaining cost-of-living increases. The Consumer Price Index of the Bureau of Labor Statistics, however, is widely accepted and followed by many employers and labor organizations.

Cost-of-living adjustment of compensation constitutes no fundamental solution to equitable compensation to employees. It is useful as a stopgap device in times of inflation when labor is pressed to keep up with the rise in prices. It is an essential ingredient of long-term labor contracts unless provision is made to reopen the wage clause periodically. The United Auto Workers agreement, for example, provides for quarterly cost-of-living adjustments amounting to a 1-cent increase for every 0.3 percent advance in the Consumer Price Index.

Government   Our varying levels of government often have very specific things to say about wages and salaries despite the theoretical and nebulous nature of equitable compensation. There are at least three major federal laws that deal directly with the subject of compensation. The Fair Labor Standards Act, often called the Wage and Hour Law, specifies a *minimum hourly wage* and *a standard workweek* for all firms engaged in interstate commerce. Since the law's inception in 1938, the minimum wage has moved from 25 cents to $3.35 per hour in 1982. The law applies to enterprises engaged in interstate commerce with gross annual volumes of sales of at least $362,500. Over 50 million employees are covered.[3]

The Equal Pay Act of 1963 is an amendment to the Fair Labor Standards Act and specifies that equal work requiring equal skill, effort, and responsibility under equal working conditions shall be accorded equal pay, regardless of sex of employee. Any

[2]Alfred L. Malabre, Jr., "Labor Costs Have Soared for a Decade Now, and Pay Outlook Points to More of the Same," *The Wall Street Journal,* March 14, 1978, p. 40.

[3]Peyton Elder, "The 1977 Amendments to the Federal Minimum Wage Law," *Monthly Labor Review,* vol. 101, no. 1, January 1978, p. 10.

differences must be rationally justified through systematic study, usually in the form of a job evaluation plan. Adjustment of differences cannot take the form of reducing pay of the higher-paid person.[4] One airline has been ordered to pay about $25 million in back wages to stewardesses who since 1968 were paid less than male employees doing the same work.

Hours worked in excess of 40 per week must be compensated at the regular rate *plus a penalty* of half time. Thus, if an employee's rate is $4 an hour, a 50-hour workweek would result in straight-time pay of $200 (50 × $4) and overtime pay of $20 (10 × $2) for a total of $220. Employees assigned to executive, administrative, or professional positions are usually excluded from coverage by the act. Labor organizations constantly press for increases in the minimum wage, decreases in the standard workweek, and increases in the penalty for overtime hours, all in the interest of increasing total compensation for labor.

The Walsh-Healey and Davis-Bacon Acts apply to employers dealing with the federal government as contractors, the former applying to those with contracts whose value is in excess of $10,000 and the latter to those having public works contracts with values in excess of $2,000. Under these two acts, the minimum wage is a rate established by the Department of Labor; it has been higher than that set by the Fair Labor Standards Act. The prevailing minimum wage is paid to a majority of workers in a particular craft in a specific geographic area. If there is no prevailing wage for a majority, the amount is determined on a weighted-average basis.[5] The standard straight-time period is the 8-hour workday rather than the week. Hours worked in excess of this standard must be compensated with the half-time penalty.

In addition to these three acts, there are numerous state laws specifying minimum wages. Usually these rates are lower than those placed in federal legislation, but some 20 states have minimums of $3.35 or higher. It can also be contended that the federal government is instrumental in salary determination through its insistence upon collective bargaining with organized labor as required by the Wagner and Taft-Hartley Acts.

EQUITY AND COMPENSATION

If our first goal of attracting capable employees to the organization is to be achieved, personnel must perceive that the compensation offered is fair and equitable. Equity is concerned with felt justice according to natural law or right. Homans's exchange theory predicts greater feelings of equity between people whose exchanges are in equilibrium.[6] When an employee receives compensation from the employer, perceptions of equity are affected by two factors: (1) the ratio of compensation to one's inputs of effort, education, training, endurance of adverse working conditions, and so on, and (2) the comparison of this ratio with the perceived ratios of significant other people with whom direct contact

[4]Robert D. Moran, "Reducing Discrimination: Role of the Equal Pay Act," *Monthly Labor Review*, vol. 93, no. 6, June 1970, pp. 30–34.

[5]The old rule for determining the prevailing minimum rate was an amount paid to only 30 percent of workers in a particular craft. In most instances, this meant that the union set wages. The change in definition is expected to result in savings of over a billion dollars per year.

[6]George C. Homans, *Social Behavior: Its Elementary Forms*, Harcourt Brace Jovanovich, Inc., New York, 1961.

is made. Equity usually exists when a person perceives that the ratio of outcomes to inputs is in equilibrium, both internally with respect to self and in relation to others.

In Figure 12-2, nine different situations are proposed. Equity theory would hypothesize that the correlation of pay and contribution that exists in cells 3, 5, and 7 would result in feelings of equity. In all other cells, feelings of dissonance are likely to exist. Research conducted with respect to under-reward situations (6, 8, and 9) clearly indicates that employee satisfaction is lower than in either the equity or over-reward situations.[7] Employee contributions exceed their outcomes of money. Resulting dissatisfaction often leads to efforts to reestablish equilibrium, such as ''borrowing'' from the supply room to increase rewards, trying to adversely affect the efforts and pay of others, convincing self that pay is not out of line, quitting or frequently absenting oneself from the organization, promoting labor organization, and so on.

Concerning the over-reward situations (cells 1, 2, and 4), original research conducted by Adams suggested that feelings of discomfort and guilt resulting from inequitably higher pay would lead to actions to reduce dissonance. He led an experimental

---

[7]David J. Cherrington, H. Joseph Reitz, and William E. Scott, Jr., ''Effects of Contingent and Noncontingent Reward on the Relationship between Satisfaction and Task Performance,'' *Journal of Applied Psychology*, vol. 55, no. 6, December 1971, pp. 531–536.

FIGURE 12-2   Equity in compensation.

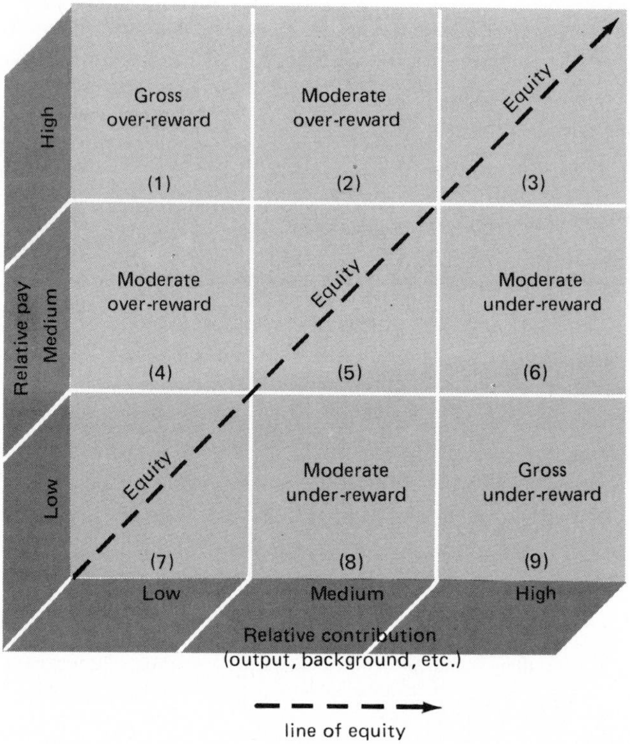

line of equity

group of employees to believe that the pay allocated was significantly in excess of their qualifications.[8] In one experiment, the overpaid group, compensated on an hourly basis, produced a quantity significantly *in excess* of an appropriately paid control group. In a second experiment under a system of incentive piecework, the overpaid group tended to reduce dissonance by *restricting output* so that total pay was more in line with equity expectations. And in a final experiment, the overpaid group restricted its quantity but increased its quality in order that total pay received might be in line with contributions. Other research has not demonstrated the same strength of impact upon an overpaid group as for an underpaid one. For example, a second study supported hypotheses with respect to underpaid personnel; they tended to *decrease* inputs over a period of time in comparison with those equitably paid as well as with those overpaid.[9] The overpaid group, however, tended to parallel the equity group in output. Concerning satisfaction, however, overpaids did express more *overall* dissatisfaction than did those from equitably paid groups. Thus, there is some indication of guilt from receiving more compensation than deserved, but such feelings were not translated into action.

It has been observed that many organizations pursue a pay increase policy characterized by cells 4, 5, and 6. The employee of average contribution is accorded an average increase in pay, but those above and below average are allocated compensation amounts *not* significantly different. Thus superior personnel are moderately under-rewarded, leading to lower contributions or withdrawal from the firm. Inferior personnel are moderately over-rewarded, leading to little or no change in behavior but effecting acceptable levels of employee satisfaction. It is this condition that led Herzberg to conclude that pay *cannot* be an effective motivator of employee behavior.[10] Figure 12-2 and equity theory would suggest that the problem may be one of improper design of compensation systems, rather than the fundamental inability of pay to motivate.

To cope with possible feelings of inequity, various organizations follow a practice of imposing secrecy with respect to compensation received. This is particularly true for salaries of executives and other personnel not covered by union contracts. Research has shown that personnel often underestimate pay of higher-level managers and overestimate the pay of both peers and those one level below.[11] Thus even if conditions exist that would favor equity, it will not be perceived if compensation is kept secret. On the other hand, if a firm desires to "go public" with its salaries, it had better be able to evaluate performance levels in an objective manner. There are many situations where job outputs are both intangible and intertwined in a dependent fashion with other jobs. Unless some form of acceptable objective assessment can be developed, public pay systems may well lead to lower performance and morale, accompanied by strained relationships between superiors and subordinates.[12]

[8]J. Stacy Adams, "Wage Inequities, Productivity, and Work Quality," *Industrial Relations,* vol. 2, no. 4, October 1963, pp. 9–16.

[9]Robert D. Pritchard, Marvin D. Dunnette, and Dale O. Jorgenson, "Effects of Perceptions of Equity and Inequity on Worker Performance and Satisfaction," *Journal of Applied Psychology,* vol. 56, no. 1, February 1972, pp. 75–94.

[10]See Chapter 15.

[11]Edward E. Lawler III, "The Mythology of Management Compensation," *California Management Review,* vol. 9, no. 1, Fall 1966, pp. 11, 17–19.

[12]Paul Thompson and John Ronsky, "Secrecy or Disclosure in Management Compensation," *Business Horizons,* vol. 18, no. 3, June 1975, p. 72.

COMPARABLE VALUE

As indicated earlier, the Equal Pay Act prohibits employers from discriminating between employees on the basis of sex by paying at a rate less than that paid to employees of the opposite sex. This applies when the jobs are equal, requiring the same skill, effort, and responsibility, and performed under similar working conditions. However, unequal pay is authorized if pay is based on a seniority system, a merit system, an incentive wage system, or any other system based on factors other than sex.

Despite this 20-year-old law, the average compensation of females has been running at approximately 60 percent of that for males.[13] As shown in Figure 12-3, this varies by major occupational areas, with the least discrepancy found in professional, technical, operative, and service occupations. Research shows that even when men and women begin their careers as equals, in the same type of job, the former soon move ahead. In comparing 40 male graduates and 40 female graduates from the Columbia Graduate School of Business, the average starting salaries in 1969 were approximately the same. Ten years later, females were receiving an average of $34,036 per year while males were making $48,000 per year. Various explanations for this difference have been suggested as follows:

1. Supervisors subconsciously or consciously undermine female subordinates by not giving them difficult assignments, thereby not violating the Equal Pay Act on the surface.

2. Supervisors assume that female employees are not as interested in promotions and fail to introduce them to senior officials in the firm.

3. Females may perform at a lower level caused by the stress and tension of working in a male-dominated environment.

4. Females are more likely to choose staff positions because of the nature of the work. Staff typically pays less than more vital line positions.

[13]That this 60 percent figure is extremely ancient is demonstrated by a verse in the Judeo-Christian Bible, Book of Leviticus, specifying two different levels of monetary contributions for males and females.

FIGURE 12-3
Median Weekly Earnings in Occupations with Total Employment of 50,000 or More, by Sex (1981)

Occupation	Male	Female	Ratio Female/Male	Percent Female
Professional/technical	$439	$316	71.8	42.8
Managers	466	283	60.8	28.4
Sales workers	366	190	52.0	33.0
Clerical	328	220	67.0	78.4
Crafts	360	239	66.5	5.6
Operatives (except transport)	298	187	62.9	38.8
Transport operatives	307	237	77.2	4.9
Nonfarm laborers	244	173	79.3	10.4
Service workers	238	170	71.3	50.3
TOTAL	347	224	64.7	39.5

Source: Nancy F. Rytina, "Earnings of Men and Women: A Look at Specific Occupations," *Monthly Labor Review*, vol. 105, no. 4, April 1982, pp. 26–29.

5. Women are more likely to bear the brunt of family duties if married. Though the married male may receive the career benefits of a nonworking wife, the married female manager is not as likely to have such support from her husband. One study indicated that a male married manager with a nonworking wife would make on the average $3,801 more than a male manager who was single.[14] If the male manager had a working wife, he made approximately $2,000 more than a single man. Other studies have suggested that women managers may be more successful in career attainment if they are not married.

6. Related to the above, female employees are more likely to turn down critical transfers and job relocations for the sake of the family.

7. Females tend to have more discontinuous work experiences, dropping out of the labor market more frequently than do males. This discontinuity is reflected in reduced pay.

Though a portion of the 40 percent discrepancy in pay can be attributed to the arguments above, it is contended that the greater bulk is created by a labor market that separates females and males into different occupational areas. As was noted in Figure 12-1, the lowest-paying industries are heavily populated by females. The going rates for jobs held predominantly by females tend to be considerably lower than those rates for predominantly male jobs. Rather than accept the market rate as the proper rate, it is suggested that comparisons be made concerning the true value of jobs. Rather than equal pay for equal work, we should give *equal pay for comparable value*. It has been noted that the major civil rights issue of the 1980s will be this of comparable value.

As in the case of most civil rights issue, we must turn to the courts to determine what constitutes discrimination. In a landmark case, *County of Washington v. Gunther,* the Supreme Court decided that this issue was covered by the Civil Rights Act, and not the Equal Pay Act alone. The case was remanded to lower courts to determine if Gunther's charge of sexual discrimination had merit. In deciding the merit issue, it will be difficult to predict the basic approach to be sustained by the courts. In an earlier case, *Christiensen v. State of Iowa,* the court refused to overturn the employer's pay policy based on meeting market rates. The court noted: ''The value of the job to the employer represents but one factor affecting wages. Other factors may include the supply of workers willing to do the job and the ability of the workers to band together to bargain collectively for higher wages. We found nothing in the text and history of Title IV suggesting that Congress intended to abrogate the laws of supply and demand or other economic principles that determine wage rates for various kinds of work. We do not interpret Title VII as requiring an employer to ignore the market in setting wage rates for genuinely different work classifications.''[15] Box 12-1 summarizes the difficulties to be encountered in measuring the comparable values of a secretary versus a plumber, a librarian versus a computer programmer, and so on. One observer suggests that the ultimate solution will be to reduce the barriers to entry to all male-dominated jobs.[16] This will increase the labor supply for the higher-paying jobs and reduce the supply for the lower-paying jobs, resulting in a reduction of the pay gap between females and males.

[14]Jeffrey Pfeffer and Jerry Ross, ''The Effects of Marriage and a Working Wife on Occupational and Wage Attainment,'' *Administrative Science Quarterly,* vol. 27, no. 1, March 1982, p. 78.

[15]*Christiensen v. State of Iowa,* 8th Circuit Court of Appeals, 1981.

[16]Michael F. Carter, ''Comparable Worth: An Idea Whose Time Has Come?'' *Personnel Journal,* vol. 60, no. 10, October 1981, p. 794.

BOX 12-1
Comparable Worth?
Graef S. Crystal

Quick! Who was worth more to society: Beethoven or Aristotle? Shakespeare or Albert Schweitzer? Einstein or Florence Nightingale?

Maybe those choices are too tough to judge. How about something more down to earth, like a secatary versus a tool and die maker?

Recently a commissioner of the Equal Employment Opportunities Commission [sic] raised this very question, for the agency has been thinking of pushing beyond "equal pay for equal work" to "equal pay for work of comparable worth."

Until now, the EEOC has been striving to assure that companies give equal pay to female and male secretaries who perform essentially the same duties, and equal pay to female and male tool and die makers who perform similar tasks. But on the basis of prevailing wages in the marketplace, companies have been paying secretaries less than tool and die makers.

That might be discrimination, too, according to the doctrine of comparable worth. Everyone knows that secretaries most of whom are females, have been discriminated against in the past. Small wonder that wage surveys pick up the low pay of secretaries. The real question, according to the doctrine, should be whether secretaries' work is as valuable to the organization as tool and die makers'. If it is, they should be paid the same, prevailing wages be damned.

The legal status of "comparable worth" is uncertain. Nurses recently lost a suit against the city and county of Denver, charging it was sex discrimination for the governments' plumbers and maintenance workers to be paid better. But more such suits can be expected. Eleanor Holmes Norton, chairman of the EEOC, suggests that comparable worth will be "the issue of the 1980s" for working women.

But how do you determine the comparative usefulness of different kinds of work? Under contract with the EEOC, a panel of the National Academy of Sciences is now studying whether existing job evaluation plans are sophisticated enough to compare widely different jobs. They aren't. There isn't one such plan that can't be torn to pieces by an impartial observer. And I doubt that NAS can come up with a good one.

Even if a plan could be built to universal acclaim, what about the forces of supply and demand? Just because two jobs are deemed to have the same worth doesn't mean, at any one time, that the number of openings and the number of candidates will be in balance for both occupations. If it's easier to find good secretaries than skilled tool and die makers, market forces require companies to pay the latter more, just to attract and keep them. Raising their wages will encourage more people to become tool and die makers. If, by contrast, secretaries' wages are kept artificially high, more people will try to become secretaries, and the imbalances will worsen.

That's just what "comparable worth" might do. Carried to its extreme, the idea represents a subtle form of wage controls. At some point, the government will benignly inform companies that disparate occupations really have the same worth, even if their "going rates" differ. The companies will have to pay both occupations the same, and managers will face some awful headaches. If they lower one occupation's wages, managers will have trouble attracting people with skills in short supply. If they equalize pay by raising the other occupation's wages, their payroll costs will soar.

Look at how nicely the market has worked with engineers. In the 1930s, too many engineers sought not enough jobs, so engineering graduates had to start out as draftsmen—if they were lucky. Then came the real war and the cold war and the space program, and the demand for engineers skyrocketed. So did pay rates, with the result that enrollments in engineering schools increased dramatically.

In due course, supply and demand came into balance until the end of the space program, when engineers were laid off, and some had to take a pay cut. Meanwhile, high school seniors became disenchanted with the profession, so engineering school enrollments started to decline. Once more, supply and demand came back into balance.

Once again, now, the economy can't seem to find enough engineers. The pricing mechanism will call forth the additional supply, just as it has reduced supply when there was a surplus. It would be a terrible shame to kill off a good act.

With a little more patience, the EEOC will likely achieve its underlying objectives without interfering in the labor market. Consider what is happening now with secretaries. As discriminatory barriers against women are hacked down, in large part because of the EEOC's earlier efforts, the most talented and overqualified secretaries are leaving the secretarial labor force and taking on more responsible positions. At the same time, the demand for secretaries is increasing, with the result that pay rates have started to soar. The market may yet validate the proposition that secretaries are worth more than tool and die makers.

Decreeing that one job must be paid the same as another represents interference at its worst. But barriers that keep women or minorities from realizing their full potential also represent interference at its worst. Mounting a full-scale attack on those barriers can only help the market to be more efficient. That—and not metaphysical excursions into the murky world of comparable worth—is, and should continue to be, the primary mission of the EEOC.

P.S. Beethoven was worth more than anyone else.

JOB EVALUATION

As a first step in the pursuit of equity, there should be established a consistent and systematic relationship among base compensation rates for all jobs within the organization. The process of such establishment is termed "job evaluation" and is not to be confused with job analysis, which is concerned with collection of data about jobs. In job evaluation, one attempts to consider and measure the inputs required of employees (skill, effort, responsibility, etc.) for minimum job performance, and to translate such measures into specific monetary returns.

The immediate objective of the job evaluation process is to obtain internal and external consistency in wages and salaries. Internal consistency is concerned with the concept of relative wages within the firm. If, for example, the supervisor is paid less than a subordinate, these rates are inconsistent. The scatter diagram of wage rates shown in Figure 12-4 depicts an internally inconsistent wage structure. The horizontal portion of the scale shows a hierarchy of jobs from low value to high value. The vertical portion shows the wage rates. Each dot shows the wage rate of a particular job. If these were internally consistent, the higher-worth jobs would be paid more than those deemed to be of lower value. The dots would form an upward-sloping line to the right. Of importance to internal consistency also are the specific amounts of wage differentials between any two jobs.

External consistency refers to a desired relativity of an organization's wage structure to that of the community, the industry, or the nation. The organization may choose to pay the going rate, more than the rate, or less. Wage and salary surveys are necessary for the determination of external consistency. It is here, also, that collective bargaining must enter the picture. Job evaluation and collective bargaining are not incompatible; they can and do exist within the same organization. Job evaluation would reduce the area of collective bargaining by systematizing the determination of internal consistency, which is concerned with proper wage differentials. Collective bargaining must still work to attain the objective of external consistency, the raising or lowering of the entire wage structure. Job evaluation should determine the *shape* of the wage structure and collective

FIGURE 12-4 Scatter diagram of wage rates showing inconsistent structure.

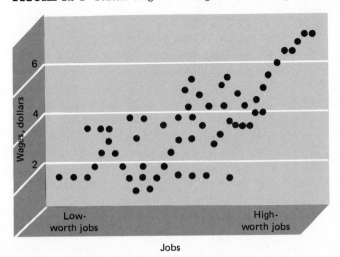

bargaining the *location* of the entire structure as a unit. Labor unions can also participate in the design and administration of the job evaluation system. In a sample of 38 unions questioned in 1972, 26 had job evaluation provisions in their contract, with union leader preference for the point system.[17]

Though internal and external consistency are the immediate objectives of job evaluation, its ultimate objective is employee and employer satisfaction with wages and salaries paid. Management wishes the employee to perceive that his or her compensation is fair and equitable. Management hypothesizes that development of rational consistency, both internally and externally, will increase the likelihood that compensation will be seen as just and equitable.

As a method of personnel management, job evaluation is not old. Early attempts along this line took place in the 1920s, and the period of most rapid growth occurred during the 1940s. The increasingly widespread adoption of job evaluation has been due to the growing size and complexity of modern organizations, as well as to societal requirements for justification of pay differentials accorded female employees and various minority groups. This demands a systematic and defensible approach to measurement and recording of job worth.

In establishing this systematic approach to measuring job worth, there are a number of necessary prerequisites. First, reasonably clear and accurate job descriptions and specifications must be available to provide data concerning the factors to be measured. Secondly, a decision must be made concerning what groups of employees and jobs are to be covered by a single evaluation system. Often, there are separate systems for production and maintenance, clerical and administrative, scientific and professional, and managerial employees. If all personnel are deemed to be in one market as they are all in one firm, there will have to be some means of relating these multiple systems to assure equitable treatment. A final prerequisite is the ''selling'' of the idea of systematic evaluation to all participants in the system. Selling the approach is the first step and the last step, and the insistence upon it is consistent with the concept that a correct salary must be satisfactory to both employee and employer.

JOB EVALUATION SYSTEMS

There are in use today four basic systems of job management. They fall into two categories. The first category covers the simpler methods, which make no use of detailed job factors. The job is treated as a whole, and job descriptions, rather than job specifications, are often utilized. In this category we place two systems sometimes known as the nonquantitative systems, (1) simple ranking and (2) grading. These systems are most popular among governmental organizations, one survey showing that over 85 percent of state and county governments make use of the grading method (sometimes called ''classification'').

The second category covers systems which use a more detailed approach. Job factors are selected and measured, and the firm's job analysis program must result in job spec-

---

[17]Harold D. Janes, ''Issues in Job Evaluation,'' *Personnel Journal*, vol. 51, no. 9, September 1972, pp. 675–679.

ifications that describe requirements for each of these factors. This category is known as the quantitative approach and includes (1) the point system and (2) the factor-comparisons system. These systems are most widely used in private industry, with the point system being used by approximately 75 percent of the firms that undertake job evaluation. Many firms use more than one system. Though the ranking system would seem most adaptable to the smaller enterprise, various large organizations use a simple ranking process in aligning middle- and upper-manager positions, while applying a more detailed point system to the many operative jobs. In addition, an excellent way of ascertaining the accuracy of one system is to check its answer by applying *another* system to the same jobs; there should be a substantial amount of agreement between the answers obtained by the two systems. In a survey of 39 unions representing over 20,000 locals, the order of use for factory jobs was (1) point system, (2) factor comparison, (3) ranking, (4) a combination of methods, and (5) grading.[18] When applied to office jobs, the usage was the same except for a switching of positions by the point and factor comparison systems.

SIMPLE RANKING

Since most of the business organizations of the United States are relatively small in size, as measured by the number of personnel, a simple and inexpensive system of job measurement has great potential usefulness. Ranking should involve the preparation of brief job descriptions, although some firms merely attempt to rank job titles. These descriptions are handed to a committee of judges, with instructions to place them in the order of worth, without respect to persons at present performing these jobs or to the present wage rates paid. No specific factors are selected for consideration.

Several techniques of ranking can be of value in this process of evaluation. First, the top and bottom jobs should be selected as bench marks for the remainder of the ranking process. They, at least, provide a point of departure on which there is generally full agreement among the judges. Secondly, the paired-comparison technique, previously discussed, can be applied. Each job can be compared with every other job, one at a time. A third technique is that of using a committee for the judging. Admittedly, there is a great deal of conjecture and some arbitrariness in any system of job evaluation, and the averaging of ranks by a group of informed evaluators often results in a more accurate judgment. A fourth device that can be used in ranking is the organization chart, if one exists. Job evaluation ranks should not violate the organizational ranking of jobs depicted on the chart, or, if they do violate the chart, perhaps the chart should be modified.

The defects of the simple ranking system are many. Its greatest virtue, simplicity, is also a disadvantage, in that the measurement is somewhat crude. It is hard to measure whole jobs. In addition, there is no predetermined scale of values, or yardstick, for the judges to use. Each judge has her or his own set of criteria, and it is difficult to explain the results to a job incumbent. The end result of this system is a list of jobs in the order of worth, as shown in the following table.

[18]Harold D. Janes, "Union Views on Job Evaluation 1971 vs. 1978," *Personnel Journal*, vol. 58, no. 2, February 1979, p. 81.

Rank	Job
1	X
2	Y
3	M
4	N
5	A
6	B
7	C
8	D
9	U
10	R

Are we to assume that the difference between X and Y is equal to that between Y and M or between M and N? Obviously these differences are not necessarily equal. A fifth technique of ranking can be introduced here to correct this difficulty to some degree. The rank order can be spaced along a numbered line, as in Figure 12-5. X, the highest-ranked job, is placed at the far end of the abscissa. A judgment is now necessary concerning the closeness of X to Y, and Y is therefore located at some selected distance from X. Considering this space and the estimated closeness in job requirements of X and Y, how close is M to Z? If a large committee has been used in the ranking process, the fractional values derived from the averaging of ranks can be used to determine the varying differentials. For example, if the average of all raters for Y is 2.4, for M is 2.8, and for

FIGURE 12-5 Ranking along a numbered line.

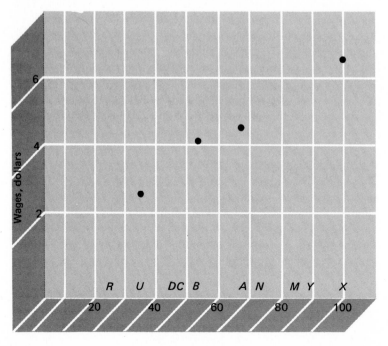

N is 4.1, then Y and M should be located more closely than M and N. The rank order given above is not violated in Figure 12-5. One can turn these ranks and spacings into wage rates by making wage surveys of selected key jobs and computing a wage curve. For example, going rates have been determined for jobs U, B, A, and X. A wage line can be drawn that is closest to the four rates charted for these jobs. All other rates can be interpolated from this line. The process of making a wage survey is explained under the subject of the point system discussed later in this chapter.

JOB GRADING

In the ranking system there is no predetermined yardstick of values. In the job grading approach there is *one* such yardstick consisting of job classes or grades. Jobs are measured as whole jobs. A scale of values is created with which jobs and their job descriptions can be compared. This scale consists of grades and *grade descriptions*. For example, it may be determined that twelve job grades are to be utilized for a category of jobs. Twelve grade descriptions must then be prepared. Such descriptions must be sufficiently broad to include several jobs. In a sense, a grade description is a job-*class* description, as compared with a job description.

There are two approaches to writing grade descriptions that will create a single scale of values for measuring the worth of jobs. Jobs may first be ranked and natural classes determined. If, for example, X and Y jobs are in one class, and A, N, and M are in another, these job descriptions can be used to create the two grade descriptions. It is also possible to convert a factor-comparison system and a point system into a grade-description system through this same process. The second approach is to ask a committee to determine in advance a series of grade definitions. Such definitions can be checked by grading some known key jobs against them.

When the scale of values is established, the process of job evaluation through the grading system consists in reading the job description, reading the grade descriptions, and then allocating the job to one particular grade. All jobs within one grade are treated alike in the matter of base salary.

Job grading is considered to be an improvement over ranking in that a predetermined scale of values is provided. In addition, this method arrives at a series of classes or grades, which is precisely the point at which both the point and factor-comparison systems also arrive. The grading system merely goes there *directly* by evaluating the job as a whole job; the other two systems create job classes out of a detailed measurement of job factors. Evaluation under the grading system can be supported by the evidence of job descriptions and job grade descriptions. It is also a relatively simple and inexpensive system to operate.

The primary disadvantage of the job grading approach is that broad generalities must be used in defining grades. These somewhat vague statements often lead to heated arguments between the jobholder and management, but the definitions must be general in order to include several jobs, since whole jobs are being measured. Another difficulty is that the grading approach usually requires multiple systems for different types of jobs; for example, grade descriptions for office jobs differ widely from those for production jobs.

POINT SYSTEM

The most widely used job evaluation method is the point system. It, along with the factor-comparison system, involves a more detailed, quantitative, and analytical approach to the measurement of job worth. This system can best be described through the presentation and discussion of a series of steps for its design and installation. A suggested procedure is as follows:

1. Select job factors or characteristics.
2. Construct a scale or yardstick of values for each job factor.
3. Evaluate all jobs in terms of the yardsticks.
4. Conduct a wage survey for selected key jobs.
5. Design the wage structure.
6. Adjust and operate the wage structure.

Selection of the Job Factors

In contrast to the ranking and grading methods, which measure jobs as whole jobs, the point system is a more analytical approach and deals with job components or factors. A job factor is a specific requirement levied upon the jobholder, which she or he must contribute, assume, or endure. In general, there are four major job factors in use: (1) skill, (2) responsibility, (3) effort, and (4) working conditions. In another sense, these are the values for which an employer pays money. One buys a certain amount and level of skill and effort. One also buys the abilities to assume certain amounts of responsibility and to endure certain specific working conditions.

The number of factors used in any one system varies with the organization. Some use only the four listed above. More frequently, these four major factors are divided into a number of smaller factors; the most common number used is approximately ten or eleven. Figure 12-6 lists the subfactors used by the trade associations in the electrical and metal trades, Xerox, the joint management-union system used in the steel industry, and a widely known system designed by a consulting firm, the Hay Associates.

The measurement of skill is accomplished indirectly through the evaluation of the job requirements for education, experience, and initiative. Responsibility is more specifically evaluated through a measurement of the *amount* and *value of things* and the *number* and *kind of personnel* for which the job incumbent is accountable. In most instances, effort is divided into mental and physical energy required to be expended, though occasionally the requirement for emotional effort is considered important. Working conditions constitute one factor which labor and management are agreed is directly and specifically compensable. Its measurement is concerned with the necessity for enduring disagreeable and hazardous conditions.

The selection of specific job factors to be used in any one system must be made by the organization concerned, as each system should be tailored to specific requirements. In various instances, statisticians have proved that the use of a limited number of key factors will provide the same final evaluation as the use of three times as many factors. Nevertheless, if employees perceive that twelve factors are more believable than four, then the former is the correct number for the system.

FIGURE 12-6
Typical Factors in Job Evaluation Systems

General Factors	NEMA/NMTA*	Xerox	Steel Industry	Hay Associates
Skill	Education Experience Initiative and Ingenuity	Education Training and Experience Job complexity	Preemployment training Employment training and experience Mental skill Manual skill	Know-how Problem solving
Responsibility	Equipment or process Material or product Safety of others Work of others	Accountability for efforts Internal contacts External contacts Guidance of others' work Confidential information	Materials Tools and equipment Operations Safety of others	Accountability
Effort	Physical Mental and visual	Physical	Mental Physical	
Working conditions	Work conditions Hazards	Work surroundings	Surroundings Hazards	Working conditions

*National Electrical Manufacturers Association–National Metal Trades Association.

As the contents of jobs are altered by technology and automation, it is logical that job evaluation systems should change in response. Traditional approaches are difficult to apply because of the greater degree of interdependence among automated jobs. There must be greater concentration upon interrelationships. In addition, it is common practice to introduce a greater degree of flexibility in job assignments; jobs are enlarged and people are rotated from station to station. In general, it is suggested that increased automation will cause greater job evaluation weights to be given to the value of the equipment, amount of discretion and initiative required, increased responsibility, increased tension, and required higher educational levels.[19]

Elliott Jacques has recommended that all job factors be discarded and replaced by a single index—the time span of discretion.[20] This is the length of time that elapses between the point at which a subordinate begins a task and the point at which the supervisor would normally examine performance against quantity and quality standards. He proposes the existence of an intuitive awareness of equity derived from an unconscious estimate of one's capacity, level of work to which assigned, and compensation received. As a single index, many researchers are doubtful that it will give satisfactory results. One study found that the time span measure and the results of the government grading system correlated .82.[21] In effect, the evaluation of the job is moved from the specialist

---

[19]Julius Rezler, "Effects of Automation on Some Areas of Compensation," *Personnel Journal*, vol. 48, no. 4, April 1969, pp. 282–285.

[20]Elliott Jacques, "Taking Time Seriously in Evaluating Jobs," *Harvard Business Review*, vol. 57, no. 5, September-October 1979, pp. 124–132.

[21]Thomas Atchinson and Wendell French, "Pay Systems for Scientists and Engineers," *Industrial Relations*, vol. 7, no. 1, October 1967, p. 53.

in the personnel department to the supervisor as he reports the time spans of discretion. Doubts concerning its reliability are introduced inasmuch as there are multiple raters instead of a centralized core applying a common set of scales to all jobs.

With respect to pay systems for scientists and engineers, there is evidence of basing compensation upon *no* job factors directly. In a sample of 120 major companies 'in aerospace, chemical, electrical, petroleum, and research industries, 56 percent used maturity curves.[22] Pay is thereby governed by the number of academic degrees, the *years* of professional experience, and the *quality* of performance, all of which are personal factors and not job factors. It is assumed that management will assign the maturing scientist and engineer to progressively more difficult tasks, thereby introducing the job factors. This approach avoids the problems of having to define jobs in a precise fashion. A study previously cited discovered a correlation of .64 between a job grading system and results obtained by a maturity curve.[23] This same study indicated that there was *less* perceived equity on the part of engineers and scientists when the maturity curve was used.

Construction of the Factor Scales

For each factor selected as important, a yardstick or scale of values must be constructed to permit measuring the factor in each job. The first decision is that of deciding the *total number of points* that will be utilized in the entire system. A more important decision is a determination of the percentage of these points that will be allocated to skill, effort, responsibility, and working conditions.

In most systems, the factor of skill is allocated the greatest percentage of value. Responsibility is ordinarily second in importance, with effort and working conditions given approximately the same value. The NEMA–NMTA breakdown is as follows:

Factor	Number of Points	Percentage
Skill	250	50
Responsibility	100	20
Effort	75	15
Working conditions	75	15

In the Xerox plan, a grouping of the ten functions would produce 55 percent for skill (education, training, experience, complexity), 40 percent for responsibility (accountability, contacts, guidance of others, confidential information), 2.5 percent for working conditions, and 2.5 percent for physical effort.

In recent years, there has been a definite tendency, in many plans, to *decrease* the importance of skill and *increase* that of responsibility. As suggested above, the reasons for this are the mechanization and automation that transfer more skill from humans to machines, thus decreasing the requirement for worker skill and increasing worker responsibility for equipment, processes, and results.

[22]Sang M. Lee, "Salary Administration Practices for Engineers," *Personnel Journal*, vol. 48, no. 1, January 1969, p. 36.

[23]Atchison and French, op. cit., p. 53.

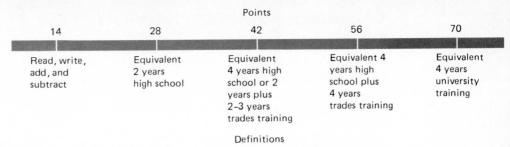

FIGURE 12-7 Scale of value for the education factor in NEMA–NMTA job-evaluation system.

Just as a committee should select the factors to be used, so should the weights be determined. Assignment of relative values is largely subjective in nature. With the total value of each factor thus determined, yardsticks can now be derived. These yardsticks are composed of *points* and *definitions* of degrees of the particular factor. For example, let us consider the education factor of the NEMA–NMTA plan. The total value is 70 points of the 250 allocated to skill. Five degrees of education have been established with an arithmetic progression of 14 points. As Figure 12-7 indicates, a job requiring only the ability to read and write will be allocated 14 points, while one requiring a college degree will be awarded the maximum of 70 points.

Thus, a scale of values for education has been derived which can be used to measure that factor in *any* job in the system. Similar yardsticks must be derived for all other factors. Some systems are enormously complex with many definitions and possible point allocations. In the Hay plan, for example, the know-how factor has 360 possible point totals while the accountability factor has 540. The more objective the definition of degrees, the higher the reliability of each scale. The reliabilities of the education and experience factors in the NEMA–NMTA system have ranged in the .90s. The reliability of the total system in one instance was .94, meaning that raters using this *same system* on the *same set* of job derived substantially the *same answers*.

Evaluation of the Jobs

If reliable scales for each factor have been constructed, and if detailed job specifications are available, the evaluation process has been greatly simplified. It consists of reading the job specifications carefully, comparing that information with degree definitions on factor scales, and deciding at which degree the job falls on each factor. A totaling of the points for all factors will give the evaluation of the job in terms of points.

In practice, the evaluation of jobs is generally done by a committee, the members of which may have varying degrees of familiarity with the job to be rated. In one study of twelve raters evaluating five jobs on each of fourteen factors, it was determined that the degree of rater familiarity had a significant effect on five of these factors—adaptability, decision making, mental work, working conditions, and managerial requirements.[24] It has also been determined that the more detailed the job specification, the higher the ratings are likely to be. Reliable scales and detailed, but consistently written, job specifications will do much to prevent trouble and controversy in these rating meetings.

[24]Joseph M. Madden, ''The Effect of Varying the Degree of Rater Familiarity in Job Evaluation,'' *Personnel Administration*, November-December 1962, pp. 42–46.

Conducting the Wage Survey

As a result of the preceding step, jobs have been evaluated and differentials established in terms of points. In effect, we have established the spacing of jobs on the horizontal axis of the chart shown in Figure 12-5, except that this time the *spacing is measured* rather than estimated. We now must translate these point values into monetary values. The basic means of accomplishing this translation is through the wage survey. At this point, the going rate enters the picture. Through the survey we hope to discover the going rate for various jobs and to key our entire structure to these rates. In a 1981 survey of 183 organizations, the vast majority (93 percent) used wage and salary survey data as an aid in administering their compensation programs.[25]

The first step in a wage survey is to select key jobs, ones whose duties are clearly defined, reasonably stable, and representative of all levels of job worth. Thus, a sample of jobs is created. Secondly, a sample of firms in the labor market area must be chosen. The labor market for different jobs can vary from local to regional to national in scope. With both samples selected, the final task is to obtain appropriate wage information, being careful to ensure that the job comparisons being made are valid. Job content, the varying qualities of personnel on these jobs, and the total compensation program must be carefully analyzed, compared, and equated.

The data obtained from the survey are analyzed and averaged. Dollar values of key jobs can now be plotted on the wage chart, shown in Figure 12-8. By drawing a wage-trend line that is closest to all points plotted, we have a line that approximates the going rates for all jobs in the structure. This line can be drawn freehand or by using the "method of least squares." Wage rates for all other jobs can now be interpolated by reading up from the point values to the wage line.

[25]"The Impact of Inflation on Wage and Salary Administration," *Personnel,* vol. 53, no. 6, November-December 1981, p. 53.

FIGURE 12-8 A wage trend line.

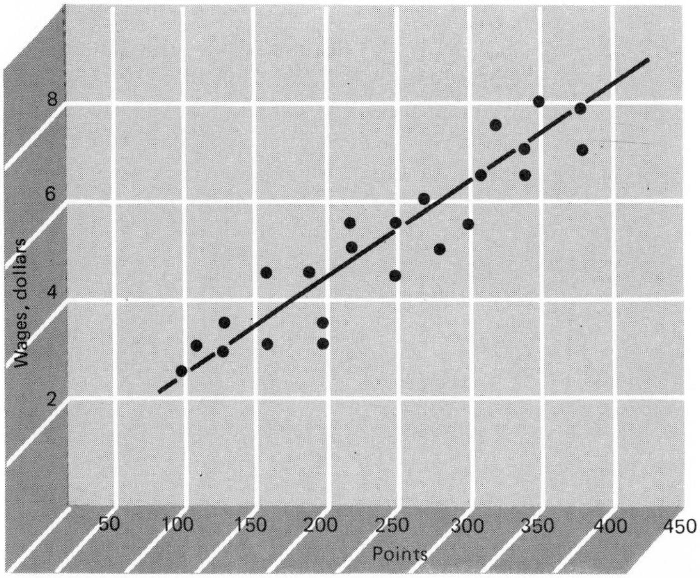

The obtainment of current and accurate compensation data can be greatly facilitated by a computer-assisted data exchange. System Development Corporation has been active in forming a group of thirty firms which have agreed to contribute to a large, centralized compensation data base on a semiannual basis.[26] Standard job family and subfamily codes have been developed, and the system staff takes the lead in ascertaining comparability of company job descriptions with these codes. Data are collected on rate ranges, actual high and low salaries, and number of job incumbents. Three reports can be requested by each company: (1) a complete breakdown of all rates within the requesting company, (2) compensation data for bench mark *key jobs* from all participating companies, and (3) detailed comparisons with selected companies with whom the requesting company has a mutual agreement.

Policies of Wage Structure Design

In many instances, the design of the wage structure revolves around the establishment of job classes and rate ranges. Ordinarily, jobs are not treated separately but are grouped to form a job class. All jobs within a class are treated in the same way. In a point system, classes are established by dividing the point range into the desired number of classes; that is, from 120 points to 150 points could constitute one class, 150 to 180 would be the spread for another, and so on. Almost all firms group jobs into classes for purposes of economical wage administration.

The firm has a choice of paying *flat rates* for each job class or *varying rates* within a rate range for each class. Flat rates would result in the wage structure shown in Figure 12-9a. Rate ranges would result in the creation of the structure shown in Figure 12-9b. If the structure consists of flat rates, there are usually a greater number of job classes, since promotion from one class to another constitutes the primary method of obtaining a higher base rate. A survey of 382 of *Fortune's* directory of the 500 largest industrial firms revealed that 42 percent use the flat-rate structure for blue-collar employees, as compared with only 2 percent for clerical and 1 percent for professional employees.[27]

---

[26]Kenneth E. Foster, "Job Worth and the Computer," *Personnel Journal*, vol. 47, no. 9, September 1968, pp. 619–626.

[27]William A. Evans, "Pay for Performance: Fact or Fable," *Personnel Journal*, vol. 48, no. 9, September 1970, p. 731.

FIGURE 12-9 Wage structures.

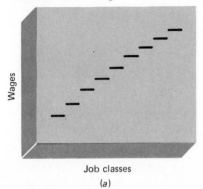
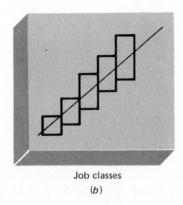

Wages

Job classes   Job classes

(a)   (b)

Rate ranges permit varying compensation within the same job class. The location of the rate ranges in relation to the going rate trend line is a matter of compensation policy. Most choose to be competitive and will pay the going rate for about the midpoint in each rate range. Some firms choose to pay above-average rates in the hope of attracting above-average personnel; in this case, the firm's trend line could be located along the tops of the rate ranges in Figure 12-9b. Other firms follow a policy of lower than average base rates, with emphasis being placed on additional income possible through various incentive arrangements. The ways in which one can progress through the rate range are discussed in the following chapter.

Adjusting and Operating the Wage Structure

The wage structure that has been developed constitutes a *standard* according to which wages can be administered. Ideally, all wages paid should be within the limits established by the structure. In the beginning, there will be some out-of-line rates, "red-circle" rates, of those who are receiving *more* than the proper amount, as well as substandard rates of those receiving *less*.

It is a cardinal principle of wage and salary administration that no individual shall receive a cut in pay as a result of the installation of job evaluation. Consequently, the firm will live with the red-circle rate until it can be placed into the proper structure through such means as a general increase in the rate structure, promotion of the individual to a job of higher worth, or waiting until the job is vacated through transfer, retirement, or resignation. The substandard rate can be raised immediately to the minimum authorized level. All future pay-rate changes should be in line with the designed limits of the systematic wage structure.

FACTOR-COMPARISON SYSTEM

The fourth system of job evaluation is the factor-comparison system. In essence, it is an application of the person-to-person system of merit rating to job evaluation. The steps in this system are as follows:

1. Select job factors.
2. Select key jobs.
3. Determine correct rates of key jobs.
4. Rank key jobs under each job factor.
5. Allocate the correct rate of each key job among the job factors.
6. Evaluate all other jobs in terms of these factor yardsticks.
7. Design, adjust, and operate the wage structure.

The first step is the same as for the point system, the selection of job factors. The factor-comparison system uses fewer factors, usually not more than seven. The selection of key jobs and the determination of correct rates are similar to the steps described for the point system above. The fourth step constitutes a refinement of the ranking system. Instead of being ranked as whole jobs, the jobs are ranked by one factor at a time. For example, a committee of judges may rank five key jobs as follows:

Skill	Responsibility	Effort	Working Conditions
A	B	E	D
B	A	D	E
C	C	B	C
D	D	C	B
E	E	A	A

The correct pay is then divided among the factors for each key job. Thus, if the pay for job A is $6, it is divided among skill, responsibility, effort, and working conditions, as the committee feels these factors are important in the job. The results of this allocation are portrayed in Figure 12-10.

We have now created a series of four scales or yardsticks. Each scale consists of *key job titles* and *money,* as contrasted with similar scales in the point system, which consisted of degree definitions and points. Other jobs are now evaluated by comparing them with the list of key jobs in each scale. If new job X is most similar to B in skill ($2.20), C in responsibility ($1.20), A in effort ($0.40), and B in working conditions ($.60), its correct rate is $4.40. If it is considered to be slightly different from any of these key jobs, varying amounts can be allocated and the new job X placed into the factor scale as a new level of that factor.

FIGURE 12-10
Factor Scales of a Factor-Comparison System

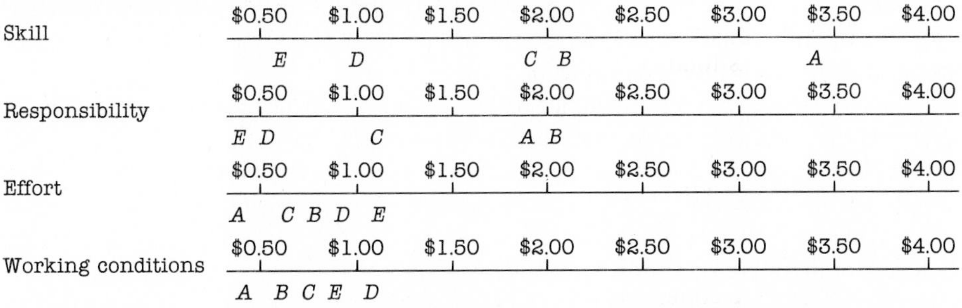

Skill	$0.50	$1.00	$1.50	$2.00	$2.50	$3.00	$3.50	$4.00
		E	D		C B			A	

Responsibility	$0.50	$1.00	$1.50	$2.00	$2.50	$3.00	$3.50	$4.00
	E D		C		A B				

Effort	$0.50	$1.00	$1.50	$2.00	$2.50	$3.00	$3.50	$4.00
	A	C B D E						

Working conditions	$0.50	$1.00	$1.50	$2.00	$2.50	$3.00	$3.50	$4.00
	A B C E D							

Correct job rates	Skill	Responsibility	Effort	Working conditions
A–$6.00	A–$3.40	B–$2.00	E–$1.20	D–$1.20
B–$5.60	B–$2.20	A–$1.80	D–$1.00	E–$0.90
C–$4.40	C–$1.80	C–$1.20	B–$0.80	C–$0.80
D–$4.00	D–$1.10	D–$0.70	C–$0.60	B–$0.60
E–$3.50	E–$0.90	E–$0.50	A–$0.40	A–$0.40

Factor comparison thus incorporates a job-to-job type of rating. It is a refinement of simple ranking in that comparisons are accomplished *job to job, by factors,* rather than as whole jobs. Instead of using money values today, most firms convert the dollar amounts into points to avoid adjusting their scales to changing price and wage levels. The final step of designing and operating the structure involves substantially the same problems as described under the point system.

HUMAN RELATIONS EFFECTS OF JOB EVALUATION

Job evaluation is a systematic, rather than a scientific, process of establishing wages and salaries. It possesses a high degree of reliability, but its validity must be determined by ascertaining the impact upon employee satisfaction. One way to do this would be by collecting and analyzing data with respect to employee complaints and grievances concerning pay. Morale surveys could also be adapted to this purpose. In addition, realizing the impact of relative pay upon perceived equity, a comparison of organization pay rates with going rates in the local community should provide some evidence bearing upon probable validity. There is no basis for contending that job evaluation and wage/salary surveys are scientific and provide incontestable answers. Consequently, we must be heavily concerned with employee and labor union reactions to specific challenges to the system and its results.

A second difficulty arising from the installation of job evaluation is that it will usually promote an *immediate* increase in the number of grievances concerning wages. Job evaluation gives the wage structure a sharp definition that it did not have before and, in effect, turns a spotlight on wages. When this new clarity of structure is combined with the system's admitted lack of infallibility, it is obvious that grievances will be filed. It is not so certain that these same grievances were not already present prior to job evaluation; the sharp definition provided by job evaluation merely provides a basis on which the grievance can be filed. The solution to this problem is to *wait* and process all grievances judiciously and fairly. If the system has a reasonable degree of reliability and validity, the first burst of grievances will die down, leaving the level of satisfaction higher than it was before job evaluation.

Finally, there is often a conflict between worker and management values in job evaluation. As indicated earlier, management generally considers, in rating a job, the general factors of skill, responsibility, effort, and working conditions. To these, workers would add the values of (1) the type of supervision received, (2) the congeniality of other workers, (3) the steadiness of the work, (4) the amount of overtime, and (5) the tightness of incentive standards. Obviously, no job evaluation system could ever encompass all the variables of a job that make it attractive to a worker. At times the job evaluation system may reverse the order of worth which the employees themselves have established. The solution to this type of problem usually lies in the managerial ability to be flexible rather than rigid. Where two jobs were reversed, it may be possible to consider both jobs to be in the same class and at least minimize the difference between workers and management.

Inasmuch as the Gunther decision specifies that pay systems can be challenged under the Civil Rights Act, the EEOC has moved to establish some guidelines in the use of job evaluation procedures. Some groups have challenged existing systems as mechanisms for perpetuating higher pay for male-dominated jobs. For example, the more weight given to the working conditions factor, the better traditional male jobs will fare under the system.

Though at the time of this writing, no official guidelines have been presented, the following are likely candidates for adoption:

1. A firm should use a single system encompassing all jobs to reduce potential for discriminating against certain classes of jobs.

2. The choice of factors should be equally appropriate to all jobs and not biased in favor of jobs held mainly by one particular sex or race.

3. If scores for predominantly female jobs are generally lower, the employer may be required to defend the use of such factor scales on the basis of business necessity.

4. Uses of existing wages to derive factor weights may be unacceptable unless it can be shown that such weights are unbiased by sex.

5. The system as a whole should (a) be documented, (b) be explained to all, (c) use well-trained raters, (d) be regularly audited to update job descriptions, (e) provide for an appeal mechanism, and (f) involve representatives of employees in its design and administration.

SUMMARY

The first and most difficult problem in wage and salary administration is the establishment of base compensation for the job. This problem is enormously complicated by such factors as supply and demand, labor organizations, the firm's ability to pay, variations in productivity and cost of living, and governmental legislation, including the Civil Rights Act. In order to attract and retain needed personnel for the organization, employees must perceive that compensation offered is equitable in relation to their background inputs and relative contributions. Outside of haphazardly establishing or bargaining over each individual rate, the only usable method of solving this problem at present is job evaluation, a systematic and orderly process for establishing the worth of jobs.

There are four alternative methods of job evaluation; (1) simple ranking, (2) job grading, (3) the point system, and (4) factor comparison. The significant elements of these systems are summarized in Figure 12-11.

The introduction of a pay system is an event of major importance to employees, and its effects upon them cannot be ignored. It is a valid system if it results in a structure acceptable to both employee and employer. In general, structures that are internally and externally consistent have the greatest chance of effecting overall satisfaction. Under-reward, over-reward, and inconsistency of reward not only tend to lead to lower satis-

FIGURE 12-11
Comparison of the Attributes of the Job Evaluation Systems

Attributes	Job Evaluation Systems			
	Simple Ranking	Job Grading	Point System	Factor Comparison
Type of comparison	Job-to-job	Job-to-category definition	Job-to-category definition	Job-to-job
Number of factors	None	None	Average of 11	Not more than 7
Type of yardstick	None	Single scale of job class descriptions	Multiple scales of points and factor degree definitions	Multiple scales of money (or points) and key job titles
Similarity to other job evaluation systems	Crude form of factor comparison	Crude form of point system	Refinement of job grading	Refinement of simple ranking
Similarity to performance appraisal systems	Corresponds to ranking system of appraisal	Corresponds to grading system	Corresponds to graphic scales	Corresponds to person-to-person system

faction but encourage behavior that often proves dysfunctional to organizational objectives. A sound, systematic, consistent system of compensation determination will do much to promote equity and satisfaction, provided that such a system is understood and reasonably accepted by most employees.

BRIEF CASE

A small group of nurses employed by Central City filed charges against the city for violating Title VII of the Civil Rights Act for systematically discriminating in pay on the basis of sex. They maintained that though the city did not intend to discriminate, it systematically underpaid nurses in comparison with other jobs in the city. They pointed out that of the accounting jobs, only 18 percent were held by females; in engineering, only 2 percent. However, females held 98 percent of the city nurses jobs as well as 74 percent of the social work positions. Though the average pay in accounting and engineering jobs was in excess of $20,000 per year, the starting salary of a graduate nurse with a college degree was $12,000. The city defended its policy on the basis that it made periodic wage and salary surveys and paid the competitive pay rate in the community.

Questions

1. What are the comparable values of nurses, social workers, accountants, and engineers? How could you measure this?

2. What is your view of the city's defense of using competitive market rates? Should commissions and courts overrule markets? Why or why not?

1. What does an organization expect an effective compensation system to do for it? What corresponding types of compensation will meet these objectives?

2. Relate the process and objectives of job evaluation to the development of equity in the eyes of personnel.

3. What behavior is projected when employees are underpaid? overpaid?

4. Contrast the four systems of job evaluation with respect to the following: (a) type of scales used, (b) number of scales, (c) type of comparison process, (d) corresponding type of performance appraisal system.

5. John and Walda both worked the following hours this week: Monday, 10; Tuesday, 10; Wednesday, 10; Thursday, 8; Friday, 4. Walda is on contract work and is covered by the Davis-Bacon Act, while John's work is covered only by the Fair Labor Standards Act. The Department of Labor has held hearings and has established $3.60 as the prevailing rate for this job. The firm's not-so-liberal policy is to pay each as little as the laws will permit. How many hours of overtime will there be for each person? How much total pay will there be for each person?

6. Compare and contrast ''equal pay for equal work'' with ''equal pay for comparable value.''

7. Though male and female master of business administration graduates start out after graduation with the same salary, explain why 10 years later the male is making considerably more money.

8. Explain how the factor-comparison systems can be construed as a refinement of grading.

9. Explain the process of translating points into dollars under a point system.

10. If a cardinal principle of job evaluation is not to reduce anyone's pay, through what processes can we eliminate all red-circle rates?

SUPPLEMENTARY READING

GREENE, ROBERT J.: ''Which Pay Delivery System is Best for Your Organization?'' *Personnel,* vol. 58, no. 3, May-June 1981, pp. 51–58.

NEWMAN, WINN: ''Pay Equity Emerges as a Top Labor Issue in the 1980s,'' *Monthly Labor Review,* vol. 105, no. 4, April 1982, pp. 49–51.

PFEFFER, JEFFREY and JERRY ROSS: ''The Effects of Marriage and a Working Wife on Occupational and Wage Attainment,'' *Administrative Science Quarterly,* vol. 27, no. 1, March 1982, pp. 66–80.

RYTINA, NANCY F.: ''Tenure as a Factor in the Male-Female Earnings Gap,'' *Monthly Labor Review,* vol. 105, no. 4, April 1982, pp. 32–34.

SCHNEBLY, JOHN R.: ''Comparable Worth: A Legal Overview,'' *The Personnel Administrator,* vol. 27, no. 4, April 1982, pp. 43–48.

SCHONBERGER, RICHARD J. and HARRY W. HENNESSEY, Jr.: ''Is Equal Pay for Comparable Work Fair?'' *Personnel Journal,* vol. 60, no. 12, December 1981, pp. 964–968.

chapter 13

Variable Compensation— Individual and Group

The establishment of equitable and competitive base pay will assist in attracting personnel to an organization. To achieve the second objective of motivation, the organization can hold out the possibility of varying compensation, the payment of which is dependent upon specified behavior. These monetary motivation appeals can be made to both individuals and groups.

EXPECTANCY THEORY AND COMPENSATION

If money, or any factor, is to motivate behavior, employees must both desire it and believe that it will be forthcoming if they behave in the manner prescribed. Thus, the actual effect of its influence comes from employee assessment of (1) the value of money in meeting personal needs, and (2) the strength of expectancy that the prescribed behavior will actually result in the obtainment of the proffered reward. Vroom therefore suggests the following formula.[1]

$$\text{Motivational force} = \text{valence} \times \text{expectancy}$$

In determining the degree of valence or value of money to employees, one requires knowledge of current need levels. As will be discussed at greater length in Chapter 15, Maslow suggests that those persons whose survival needs are not reasonably well met are likely to place high value upon money as a means of gratifying physiological requirements. In addition, since people are rarely exclusively economic in their orientation, employees will have to compare positive monetary outcomes with all possible losses, such as social rejection if the incentive plan clashes with primary group norms. Despite

---

[1]Victor H. Vroom, *Work and Motivation*, John Wiley & Sons, Inc., New York, 1964, p. 183.

its lower order of importance in certain groups, there is evidence that money is attractive and has real value for large numbers of organizational employees.

The greatest difficulty in monetary motivation lies in the expectancy portion of the formula. Employees will subjectively assess the likelihood that desired compensation will *actually* be forthcoming. This requires consideration of two major items: (1) personal capacity to perform the prescribed act, and (2) perception that such behavior will actually be rewarded. Obviously, if the person highly desires money and is offered $1 million to high-jump 10 feet, the motivational force is likely to be zero, since this is far beyond the current world's record. Supervisors can assist in increasing abilities through training, increasing confidence in capacities by encouragement and removing organizational obstacles to employee performance.

Perhaps the greatest difficulty in regard to expectancy is convincing the employee that management can be trusted to pay off when the prescribed behavior is forthcoming. If the incentive scheme is so complicated that accountants have difficulty in understanding, then expectancy is likely to be low. If superior performance has been accorded little or only slightly higher pay increases in the past, then the assessment of instrumentality of monetary rewards is likely to be low. Organizations that use base pay supplemented by merit-rating schemes to determine periodic pay increases are less likely to breed high expectancies than those utilizing individual incentive plans. In a study of varying degrees of expectancy achieved in a firm of 2,000 employees, Schwab discovered that the perceived individual linkage of money with behavior was highest among those on individual incentive plans, next highest for those on group incentive, and lowest for those on hourly pay plans.[2] Supporting the thesis that objectives have higher valence when attached to performance that requires effort, those on incentive systems tended to place higher values on money.

Research in this same organization revealed that though employees on incentive plans were more highly motivated than those on hourly pay, the latter were *more* satisfied with the pay actually received.[3] Productivity was highest under the individual piece-rate system and lowest under the hourly. In separate measures of satisfaction, hourly paid personnel reported the highest satisfaction with pay received, individual-incentive employees next highest, and those on group plans reported the greatest dissatisfaction. Thus, it is suggested that one may have to choose between developing motivated employees or satisfied employees.

VARIABLE COMPENSATION— INDIVIDUAL

Since the days of scientific management and Frederick Taylor, business organizations have emphasized the use of incentives on an individual, rather than group, basis. This certainly fitted into the traditional American value of individualism where each person looks after his or her own best interests. The following four schemes of administering

---

[2]Donald P. Schwab, "Impact of Alternative Compensation Systems on Pay Valence and Instrumentality Perceptions," *Journal of Applied Psychology*, vol. 58, no. 3, December 1973, pp. 308–312.
[3]Donald P. Schwab and Marc J. Wallace, Jr., "Correlates of Employee Satisfaction with Pay," *Industrial Relations*, vol. 13, no. 2, February 1974, pp. 78–89.

variable pay will be discussed: (1) general merit and/or seniority progression, (2) incentive plans for operatives, (3) incentive plans for managers, and (4) suggestion systems.

Merit/Seniority Progression

As indicated in the preceding chapter, the location of the rate range is controlled by job requirements and wage survey results. Progression through the rate range is dependent on the person. The firm has a choice of controlling this progression by specifying that it be based on merit, seniority, or some combination of the two.

Though the primary use of performance appraisal should be in promoting employee development, many firms also tie the results directly into variable compensation. Organized labor generally prefers either a single rate for all personnel or a rate range operated solely on a seniority basis. Various compromises have been proposed as shown in Figure 13-1a. The first compromise would involve a splitting of each range into two parts with seniority controlling the lower half, and merit the upper half. In this manner, each employee is assured of receiving the middle rate, which is often the going rate, merely by serving the required amount of time on the job. If one expects to receive more than the going rate, he or she must be a better-than-average employee as demonstrated by performance ratings.

A second type of compromise is depicted in Figure 13-1b. Seniority governs completely the progression through the rate range in the lower job classes, and merit governs completely in the higher job classes. In the lower jobs, the employee has less freedom and the job content controls; in the higher jobs, the person can exert a stronger influence on the manner in which the job is performed. This philosophy is also demonstrated in the gradually increasing sizes of rate ranges, which permit a greater percentage of variable pay in the higher jobs.

A few firms have been experimenting with providing employees with the option of receiving pay increases in one lump sum. If allotted an increase of $1,200, the employee

FIGURE 13-1 Employee progression through the rate range.

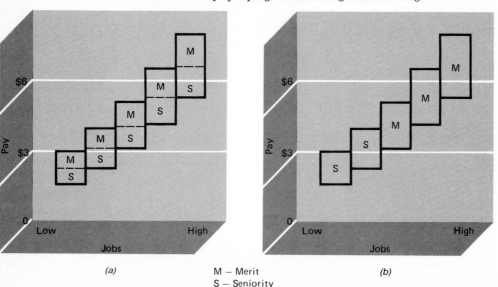

(a)   M — Merit   (b)
          S — Seniority

can choose to receive it all at once, or at the rate of an extra $100 per month. The purpose of the lump sum is to dramatize the size of the increase in the hope of stimulating greater motivation. The usual approach is to treat the lump sum increase as a loan or salary advance, a portion of which must be returned if the employee leaves the organization before the year is up. When the lump sum option is offered, approximately half of all employees elect it. The option has been offered in such firms as Aetna, American Can, B. F. Goodrich, Timex, and Westinghouse.[4]

Incentive Plans for Operatives

In theory there is no ceiling of compensation under an incentive plan for operative employees; the worker can earn as much as he or she is physically and mentally capable of doing. In practice, there are often managerial and fellow employee expectations that serve to put a lid on additional earnings.

In order to establish an incentive pay plan for operatives, two basic items of data are essential: (1) the average amount of output that is necessary for adequate job performance and (2) the fair and equitable amount of money deserved for this average amount of work. We have already discussed the task of determining base pay for the job. We now add the task of measuring work performance. In production jobs, time study is the management technique that typically supplies the answer, for example, 50 units of product to be produced each hour. Portions of the time study process can be characterized as scientific, but much of it is simply systematic. One must select an average worker to study, select a representative sample of his or her work, estimate the speed or pace of work being observed, allow for interruptions and delays, and add in a percentage of time to adjust for accumulating fatigue. Many firms report that three-fourths of their grievances issue from this process of setting a work standard for the individual. In operative jobs in the sales area, one can use time and duty analyses as well as past experience in establishing sales quotas for commission purposes.

It should be noted that nonincentive compensation, that is, payment on the basis of time expended, is the most commonly used arrangement for operative personnel. The percentage of factory workers on incentive plans has steadily declined from 30 percent in 1947 to 18 percent in 1980.[5] As indicated in Figure 13-2, the use of time-payment plans is quite common in industries using automatic and semiautomatic machinery where the worker does not have control of the process, such as cigarettes, paint, refining, automobiles, chemicals, and so on. On the other hand, incentive plans cover from 60 to 80 percent of employees in clothing, shoes, and steel. In clothing and shoe manufacturing the output is identifiable, measurable, and under the control of the worker. Basic steel is unique in that it is highly mechanized but pays incentives to 80 percent of the workers. This is caused by the tradition of including maintenance and service workers in the system. For example, a furnace operator is given the opportunity to earn 35 percent above base, indirect employees such as maintenance personnel may earn up to 23 percent, and secondary indirect personnel such as general labor can earn up to 12 percent. The system recognizes that the individual machine operator could not possibly perform above standard if not provided consistent support help by other personnel.

[4]Charles A. Smith, ''Lump Sum Increases—A Creditable Change Strategy,'' *Personnel,* vol. 56, no. 4, July-August 1979, p. 59.

[5]Norma W. Carlson, ''Time Rates Tighten Their Grip on Manufacturing Industries,'' *Monthly Labor Review,* vol. 105, no. 5, May 1982, p. 15.

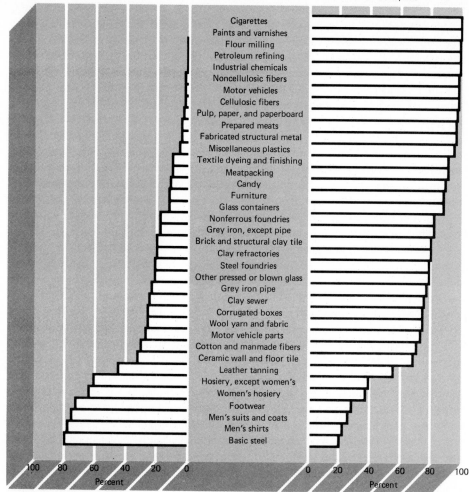

Incentive wage plans   Time-rated plans

Cigarettes
Paints and varnishes
Flour milling
Petroleum refining
Industrial chemicals
Noncellulosic fibers
Motor vehicles
Cellulosic fibers
Pulp, paper, and paperboard
Prepared meats
Fabricated structural metal
Miscellaneous plastics
Textile dyeing and finishing
Meatpacking
Candy
Furniture
Glass containers
Nonferrous foundries
Grey iron, except pipe
Brick and structural clay tile
Clay refractories
Steel foundries
Other pressed or blown glass
Grey iron pipe
Clay sewer
Corrugated boxes
Wool yarn and fabric
Motor vehicle parts
Cotton and manmade fibers
Ceramic wall and floor tile
Leather tanning
Hosiery, except women's
Women's hosiery
Footwear
Men's suits and coats
Men's shirts
Basic steel

100 80 60 40 20 0   0 20 40 60 80 100
Percent   Percent

FIGURE 13-2   Percent of factory workers on time or incentives, 1973–80. (*Source: Norma Carlson, "Time Rates Tighten Their Grip on Manufacturing Industries,"* Monthly Labor Review, *vol. 105, no. 5, May 1982, p. 18.*)

With respect to other personnel, one of a continuing series of surveys indicates that almost all office employees are paid on the basis of time.[6] On the other hand, variable compensation is much more widely used for managerial personnel.

Types of plans   Because of the ease with which one can manipulate the two variables, pay and output, there are a multitude of incentive plans that have been developed. In general, they can be classified into two categories: piece rates and time bonuses. The most commonly used operative incentive plan is straight piece work. Thus, if the standard is 50 units per hour, the base rate is $5 per hour, and the employee produces 600 units in an 8-hour day, then the piece rate is 10 cents each and the total earnings are $60. If

---

[6]John Howell Cox, "Time and Incentive Pay Practices in Urban Areas," *Monthly Labor Review,* vol. 94, no. 12, December 1971, pp. 53–56.

hourly earnings have been guaranteed regardless of output ($40), incentive earnings in this illustration would account for the extra $20.

Payment plans based on time bonuses are more complicated because there are three types of time involved: (1) time worked, (2) time saved, and (3) standard time. For example, if during an 8-hour day, one does a series of assignments that add up to a standard total time value of 12 hours, then time worked equals 8 hours, time saved equals 4 hours, and standard time produced equals 12 hours. We can award the employee a bonus based on any one of the three types of time. One illustration of each will be given.

When standards are poorly set, often based on past experience, the firm may choose to give a bonus that does not fully compensate for all output. The Halsey Plan awards a bonus based on the amount of *time saved,* but only a fraction is awarded since the standards are loose. Thus if 12 hours' standard work is accomplished in 8 hours, the employee receives pay for the hours worked (8 × $5 = $40) plus only 50 percent of the hours saved (4 × $5 × 50% = $10) for a total of $50. If we should later set accurate standards, the bonus percentage should be moved up to 100 percent, which is identical in effect to a straight piecework plan.

If standards are not only poorly set but management has great fear that employees may double or triple total earnings, then the Rowan Plan can be used to insure that this does not happen. An efficiency index is computed by dividing the time saved by the standard time; for example, 4 hours saved divided by 12 standard hours equals 33.33 percent. This bonus percentage is then multiplied by the value of *time worked.* Thus the employee receives pay for hours worked (8 × $5 = 40) plus 33.33 percent of the value of hours worked (33.33% × $40 = $13.33) for a total of $53.33. There is no way for an employee to double the pay.

The most liberal incentive plan was designed by Henry L. Gantt, one of the pioneers of scientific management. The Gantt Task and Bonus Plan pays a fixed bonus percentage multiplied by the total value of *standard time* produced should the employee meet or exceed standard. Thus, if 12 standard hours have been produced during an 8-hour day, the employee receives not only the value of those hours (12 × $5 = $60) but also a bonus of 10 percent, for example, of standard time value (10% × $60 = $6) for a total of $66. If 8 standard hours are not produced, there is no bonus. This plan is used when standards are demanding and management needs a strong incentive. Figure 13-3 portrays the earnings curves for all four types of plans in the examples just described.

The choice of incentive pay plans for operatives is very large, particularly when firms can devise their own custom plans using the basic elements of output, time saved, time worked, and standard time. All such plans should be understandable by the employee and guaranteed against change except in the case of major alterations in equipment or methods. If possible, standards for all jobs should be of uniform difficulty, and the spread between normal hourly earnings and average incentive pay should be sufficient to stimulate above-average effort. Some managements estimate that incentive earnings should be from 30 to 40 percent above straight hourly earnings.

Because of the difficulties of adhering to these characteristics, some firms have abandoned individual incentives for what is termed "measured day work." Standards of performance are retained but employees are paid on a time basis. Comparisons of performance output with these standards are made for the worker, and pressure, supervision, challenge, and praise are substituted for money as the incentive. In most instances, if an employee is definitely and exactly told what is expected, he or she will make every effort to comply.

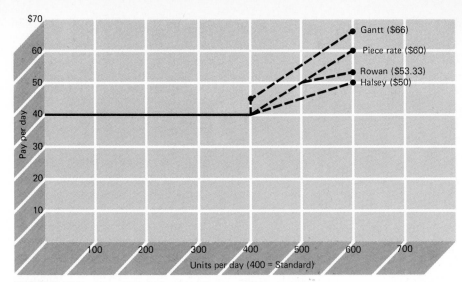

FIGURE 13-3 Compensation under four incentive systems.

Human problems of incentive plans The traditional, official posture of organized labor is one of opposition to individual incentive pay plans. The union desires solidarity among members and uniform compensation on the same job is often deemed prerequisite to this cooperation. At the least, the union will stand guard over the processes of establishing and administering work standards, ready at any moment to process a grievance protesting a decision which leads to less pay for its members. In addition to this more formal problem, there are a number of human relations problems growing out of incentive systems. Among these are (1) the ratebuster, (2) the reaction to changes in methods, equipment, and materials, (3) the reaction to lack of uniformity in tightness of standards, and (4) informal restriction of output. All these problems resolve around employee fear of management and a desire for security.

A *ratebuster* is an employee who produces far in excess of standard, and consequently in excess of the production of most of the members of a work group. There is a feeling among most employees that management will stand for paying only so much bonus, and that if one or more employees make excessive bonuses, the rates will be cut. There is great informal pressure upon all employees to conform to the production level of most of the group. It therefore follows that the employee who does not conform has to have a strong personality, and often a strong physique, in order to resist these pressures.

The ratebuster is usually ostracized by other workers and operates as if isolated. The values of additional money have been balanced against the values of group acceptance, with the decision going to the former. In theory, management should look with favor upon the ratebuster and pay double and triple wages when they are earned. In practice, management often prefers *not* to have a ratebuster, feeling that she or he is a disruptive influence in the shop; and indeed there have been times when the ratebuster has been transferred to other jobs in order to smooth relations. But if the standards are properly established, there is little justification for not paying the production genius all that is earned.

Related to group pressures on the ratebuster is the general pressure on management to abandon pay programs that reward a minority of the entire group. A midwest paper mill recently abandoned an incentive pay plan that gave some hourly workers twice-yearly bonuses.[7] Allocations were based on supervisors' monthly appraisals, and these were attacked by both employees and their union on the basis of subjective measurement. After dropping the plan, the plant productivity dropped 20 percent, the turnover rate of top producers doubled, and their level of job satisfaction decreased. On the other hand, the poorer producers liked their jobs much better. To increase productivity, supervisors turned to the use of reprimands and threatened job layoffs.

No firm is ever static and unchanging. Small and large changes in method, equipment, and materials will be constantly introduced. The worker's desire for security and distrust of management call for an explicit policy to the effect that management will not cut the rate unless there is a substantial change in methods, equipment, and/or materials. If a change is substantial (and there is difficulty in defining this word "substantial"), there should be clear agreement between labor and management that the work standard can be revised. This revision usually means an increase in total pay for the employee even though the unit rate is reduced. This compensation can be construed as a sharing with labor of gains in productivity and a purchase of the employee's cooperation.

Sometimes a mistake has been made in a time-studied standard. This mistake can be one of two types, the creation of an excessively loose standard or an excessively tight one. The former error may be discovered if the greater bulk of employees make bonuses of over 50 percent of regular earnings when only the usual 25 to 30 percent was intended. The error is frequently undiscovered, however, because of restriction of output by the employees. Such errors can occur just as often as mistakes of the other type, an excessively tight standard. In the latter situation, the employee and the union usually demand a restudy in the hope of loosening the standard.

An even more difficult problem lies in the many small and seemingly insignificant changes in method, equipment, and materials that occur in most firms. These changes are initiated by both management and labor, through informal and formal means. No one change appears to justify a change in the rate, but the cumulative effect of many changes can be disastrous. Often there is only one remedy: complete restudy of all jobs under the incentive plan. The accuracy of work standards has a tendency to deteriorate with the passage of time from the very first day of installation.

A third human problem issues from inconsistencies in the accuracy of standards. The supervisor has the additional problem of awarding easy and tough jobs on an equitable basis. If awarded on a systematic basis, such as seniority or taking turns, one must predict in advance the classification of each job. This often means a balance of its easiness in relation to how long it will last.

Various factors have been identified as contributing to lack of uniformity in work standards. Newly studied jobs are likely to have tighter rates while older ones have been affected by many small changes. Rates set during times of prosperity tend to be looser than those established during recessions; time study personnel are psychologically affected by their environment. The smaller the profit margin on an item, the tighter the rate is likely to be. Jobs that involve higher levels of skill tend to have looser rates since they cannot be as closely studied as low-skilled tasks. In departments where there is greater group cohesiveness, which leads to sanctions on the ratebuster and greater cooperation in informally sharing work and falsifying timecards, standards are likely to be looser. In departments with higher percentages of union membership the rates are likely

---

[7]"Labor Letter," *The Wall Street Journal,* November 24, 1981, p. 1.

to be looser in recognition of that threat. Strategic, isolated, and dangerous jobs tend to be favored with looser rates. Thus, the causes are limitless and the possibilities for trouble and problems of administration are great.

In all the above discussion, the concept of restriction of output has been involved. This is the major defense of employees in the informal battle with management that takes place through the incentive wage device. A tabulating of the average incentive earnings of the group can also show this restriction. Instead of a normal distribution of individual outputs, there is a rapid rise to the informally agreed-upon amount, whatever the employees feel management will ''put up with''; and after that point few, if any, operatives make bonuses in excess of this level. Those who make above the allowed amount are ratebusters.

Restriction of output is tangible evidence of the power of social over monetary desires, but it does not eliminate the value of monetary motivation. The entire group is producing at a level in excess of the amount produced under the formerly adminstered time rates. For example, in one corrugated container company, a stable firm operating in a stable industry, the conversion to incentive pay resulted in increased output for 16 of 18 operations.[8] In comparing the average plant efficiency in the 10 months prior to incentive-plan installation (a process consuming 26 months) with that achieved in a 10-month period afterward, it was calculated that an overall increase of 58 percent was effected along with an increase in employee earnings of 25 percent. In more dynamic and uncertain environments, the development of effective incentive schemes is extremely difficult and often impossible.

Incentive Plans for Managers

Because of the complex and variable nature of most managerial jobs, there is much room for different levels and qualities of human performance. A study of 84 firms revealed that 60 percent provide for some type of incentive pay for managers.[9]

The place to begin the design of an executive incentive compensation system is with the types of behavior desired by the organization. Various business firms are having difficulties in properly targeting the behavior desired. It has been noted that two of the most common problems in designing executive incentives are: (1) decoupling the system from overall industry performance and (2) developing one-dimensional systems.[10] In regard to the former, executives have been rewarded for increasing firm growth 15 percent within an industry whose average growth is 20 percent. On a relative basis, the executive is doing less well than others in the same category. With respect to the latter problem, many plans are excessively narrow. If the reward is based on improving return on assets, for example, the executive is tempted to lease equipment rather than buy, and to eliminate investments critical to long-term growth. As emphasized by many critics, one of the basic difficulties with the American business system is its excessive emphasis upon short-term results. In recognition of the values of the long-term orientation of the Japanese reward system, various companies are seeking to develop multiyear systems emphasizing long-range goals.

[8]Donald L. McManis and William G. Dick, ''Monetary Incentives in Today's Industrial Setting.'' *Personnel Journal,* vol. 52, no. 5, May 1973, pp. 387–392.

[9]American Society for Personnel Administration–The Bureau of National Affairs, Inc., ''The Status of Today's Executive,'' *Bulletin to Management No. 1327,* July 17, 1975, p. 2.

[10]Ray Stata and Modesto A. Maidique, ''Bonus System for Balanced Strategy,'' *Harvard Business Review,* vol. 58, no. 6, November-December 1980, p. 157.

In targeting the desired behavior, criteria will vary according to levels of responsibility. For the top executive, the emphasis should be on entrepreneurial behavior emphasizing risk taking, with additional compensation being based on profits, degree of market penetration, and new-product development. For lower-level executives, the emphasis is often on smooth administration and cooperative relationships with others; bonuses may be based on unit ratings of performance with a fixed percentage of base salary constituting the incentive.

There are a multitude of incentive pay schemes for executives, many of which are designed in relation to income tax regulations. A few of these are the following:

1. Cash bonuses based on profits or individual performance evaluations are perhaps the most common type of incentive for executives.

2. The use of stock options where the manager is given the option to purchase company stock at current prices at some future date have been discouraged by the Tax Reform Act of 1976. The increases in value through stock appreciation are now taxed as ordinary income rather than capital gains.

3. Stock appreciation rights are similar to stock options, but the manager can ignore the option to purchase and take a cash bonus equal to the value of the stock's appreciation over a span of time.

4. Performance objectives can be set for the executive and rewards allocated according to degree of achievement. For example, if company earnings grow by an average of 10 percent over a 5-year period, one might be awarded 500 free shares of stock or the equivalent in cash. For a 9 percent average, the award might be 400 shares, and so on.

Each of the above plans is geared to stimulate more effective managerial behavior for the long-run benefit of the organization. With inflation and high individual tax rates, the popularity of various "perks" or perquisites has increased. Among these are use of company automobiles, club memberships, personal financial planning services, use of company airplanes, annual physicals at plush health resorts, and major medical insurance with no deductibles. Many of these are not taxable as income received.

The total amount of compensation for different levels and types of executives will vary by industry and company size. In a survey of 3,157 manufacturing companies conducted by the Executive Compensation Service of the American Management Associations, the chief executive officer typically receives the top money.[11] With this designated as 100 percent, the corresponding percentages for varying executive jobs in smaller firms ($2 million to $5 million in sales) were as follows: chief operating officer, 90 percent; executive vice president, 62 percent; top marketing executive, 60 percent; top manufacturing executive, 54 percent; top financial executive, 51 percent; and top personnel executive, 34 percent. For larger firms ($200 million to $500 million in sales), they were: chief operating officer, 81 percent; executive vice president, 60 percent; top marketing executive, 40 percent; top manufacturing executive, 45 percent; top financial executive, 48 percent; and top personnel executive, 32 percent. According to one 1978 survey, average compensation for the chief executive officer of a hypothetical $4 billion company would have included (1) $480,000 in salary and bonus, (2) $120,000 in pension,

[11]Jay Engle, "Top Management: Hot Topic in Corporate Compensation," *The Personnel Administrator*, vol. 19, no. 1, January-February 1974, p. 35.

insurance, and other benefits, and (3) $85,000 in long-term stock-related capital accumulations, for a grand total of $685,000.[12]

Suggestion Systems

The basic purpose of suggestion systems is to stimulate creative thinking among employees. Rather than working harder to obtain higher incentive earnings, the employee is encouraged to think of ways to do the job more effectively, reduce waste, and improve equipment, materials, and procedures. In one survey of 228 companies, slightly over half used suggestion systems on an intermittent or continuous basis.[13] The larger the enterprise, the more likely that such a system would be undertaken.

The incentive payoff for a usable suggestion is usually about 15 to 20 percent of the calculated first year's savings through its installation. A survey for 1 year by the National Association of Suggestion Systems revealed that the number of suggestions submitted per 100 employees was 40, that 31 percent of these were adopted by management with a consequent average savings of $499.14 each, and the average award given to the employee was $86.85.[14] In that same year, the highest award was $46,165.

As in the case of all variable compensation plans, there are a number of administrative problems. Supervisors sometimes resent subordinates making formal suggestions that might make them look deficient in the eyes of upper management. Fellow employees may resent the award to a single individual if they feel that the primary impact of the suggestion is to cause more work to be done by fewer personnel. Staff specialists are often not excited when the suggestion falls into their particular areas of expertise. There are also routine problems of administration in setting up suggestion boxes and establishing the properly staffed review committees to determine the suggestion's dollar value. As will be noted later, some firms have abandoned the concept of individual suggestion systems and have moved to an arrangement where all employees share in the savings as a group.

VARIABLE COMPENSATION—GROUP

Though more accelerated in other countries such as Japan, there is a slow steady movement toward emphasis upon the group in American management. Cooperation and collaboration are regarded as additional sources of effective action. We shall survey the following systems of variable compensation for groups, proceeding from narrow to broad groupings: (1) group piece rate, (2) production-sharing plans, (3) profit-sharing plans, and (4) employee stock ownership.

Group Piece Rates

In many production operations, the efforts of a single individual cannot be differentiated from the group, such as in a soap-flake packaging line of four operatives or a

---

[12]David Kraus, "Executive Pay: Ripe for Reform?" *Harvard Business Review,* vol. 58, no. 5, September-October 1980, p. 38.

[13]Vincent G. Reuter, "Suggestion Systems," *California Management Review,* vol. 19, no. 3, Spring 1977, p. 83.

[14]National Association of Suggestion Systems, *Suggestion Newsletter,* July 1975, p. 5.

fuel-pump assembly line requiring three employees to complete one pump. Cooperation to meet or exceed set standards can be stimulated through a group bonus.

As an illustration, let us assume that three employees are working as a team to assemble an appliance. Guaranteed hourly rates are set through job evaluation at $8 for person A, $6 for person B, and $4 for person C. For each unit of output, the entire team is allocated $6, and the standard set by time study is 3 units per hour. If the team produces 30 units in an 8-hour day, it has generated $180 ($6 $\times$ 30). From this amount, the guaranteed wages are subtracted ($180 $-$ $144), resulting in a bonus of $36.

There are two philosophies in regard to dividing up the bonus. If one emphasizes cooperation and the essentiality of each person in making the bonus, the $36 can be divided equally—$12 per person. If one follows the philosophy of job evaluation and divides according to hourly base rates, A would receive $8/18$ of the bonus ($16), B would get $6/18$ ($12), leaving C with $4/18$ of the extra money ($8).

Production-Sharing Plans

Expectancy theory would suggest that motivational force will be greatest on individual incentive plans, somewhat weaker on group piecework, and weaker still if the group is so large that it includes the entire production unit. The connection between one's individual efforts and the total group output is more difficult to perceive. Nevertheless, there have been a number of successful systems designed to effect large group cooperation in reducing waste and promoting collaboration. In essence, these plans constitute an attempt to share in productivity gains.

Perhaps the most famous production-sharing plan is that known as the Scanlon Plan. This approach requires the compensation of a normal labor cost per unit of product produced. If through more cooperation and greater efficiency labor costs can be reduced, the entire amount saved, or some fraction, is distributed among the workers in the form of a bonus. For example it may be determined from past records that labor costs constitute 30 percent of sales. If through cooperative efforts these costs can be reduced to 28 percent, then 2 percent of sales is divided among employees on the basis of seniority and/or salary levels. Lesieur, the heir-apparent to Scanlon, recommends that three-fourths of all savings be distributed with the remaining one-quarter retained by management.[15] One of the earliest successful installations of this plan was made by Scanlon, a United Steel Workers official, in the Lapointe Machine Tool Company of Hudson, Massachusetts. Individual incentives were scrapped in favor of the group incentive of the production-sharing plan. Scanlon claimed that individual incentive plans stimulated cutthroat competition to the detriment of the group, whereas group incentives effected constructive cooperation.

The Scanlon Plan is more than a form of monetary compensation. Many authors classify it as a type of union-management relationship rather than a form of remuneration. Essential features of the plan are an attitude of labor-management cooperation and a system of processing suggestions. The processing of suggestions under the Scanlon Plan involves the establishment of departmental production committees composed of the supervisor and a union representative. The supervisor and the union representative meet periodically to discuss individual suggestions and develop general production plans for the department. Suggestions that are either disapproved or outside the province of the

[15]Fred G. Lesieur and Elbridge S. Puckett, "The Scanlon Plan Has Proved Itself," *Harvard Business Review*, vol. 47, no. 5, September-October 1969, p. 112.

department are submitted to a plant-wide screening committee that includes the top leadership of both union and management. There are *no* individual rewards for accepted suggestions. The group prospers through the production-savings bonus. The union is highly involved and encourages suggestions. A contrast of managerial attitudes in eight firms that had abandoned a Scanlon Plan with attitudes in ten firms that had retained their plans revealed a significant difference.[16] Those abandoning the plan had significantly lower estimates of employee judgment, dependability, initiative, and alertness. They were also more suspicious of policies encouraging employee participation in decision making.

At the Parker Pen Company, a unionized firm of 1,000 employees, bonuses have been paid in 142 months out of 168, and range from 5½ percent to 20 percent of payroll.[17] At the Atwood Vacuum Machine Company, a unionized firm of 2,000 employees, bonuses have been paid in 163 periods out of 187, and range from 5 to 20 percent of payroll. Over 25,000 suggestions have been turned in by employees of the latter company. In both instances, the Scanlon Plan replaced an individual incentive system. Under the new arrangement, workers appeared to take a broader interest in company well-being and tended to accept changes and improvements more readily. The number of written grievances dropped because of management's greater willingness to listen. Management was able to stress quality and efficiency in the interests of improving the return to all workers. General sharing led to improved cooperation from indirect workers such as toolroom employees, maintenance personnel, and materials handlers.

Employee Profit Sharing

A still broader group of employees would include everyone who works for the firm. Some claim that relating a top executive's performance to the firm's profits makes sense, but a connection between the efforts of a single rank-and-file employee and company profits is difficult to fathom. Though there are some very large profit-sharing companies, such as Sears, Roebuck and Company, statistics show that the smaller the enterprise the more likely the concept will be adopted.

Employee profit-sharing plans constitute one of the more glamorous forms of monetary compensation used in business. The definition of the employee profit sharing was formulated quite well by the International Cooperative Congress in 1897, as follows: "An agreement freely entered into, by which the employees receive a share, fixed in advance, of the profits." Though the term "profit sharing" is not used precisely by many, a true plan generally involves a definite commitment on the part of management to pay, over and above a fair wage, extra compensation that bears a definite percentage relationship to company profits or declared dividends.

There are two main types of employee profit-sharing plans: (1) cash or current distribution and (2) trust or deferred distribution. Under the current arrangement, benefits are distributed among participants in cash at least once each year. The deferred type involves a trust fund, the benefits from which are distributed in the event of death, retirement, or disability. Some managements prefer to place part of the profit share in trust and to distribute the remainder in cash each year.

---

[16]Robert A. Ruh, Roger L. Wallace, and Carl F. Frost, "Management Attitudes and the Scanlon Plan," *Industrial Relations*, vol. 12, no. 3, October 1973, pp. 282–288.

[17]Ibid., p. 113.

There are varying estimates of the number of profit-sharing plans actually in existence. The major source of information is the Internal Revenue Service, which qualifies deferred-sharing trusts for tax exemption purposes. The Service requires that a qualified plan (1) cover a majority of plant and office employees, (2) stipulate a management commitment of periodic contributions to the fund based on profits, (3) be communicated to all covered employees, (4) contain a formula for allocating shares to employees, and (5) establish a definite method of distribution. A survey of 513 companies utilizing profit sharing revealed that the average company contribution to the fund amounted to 10 percent of total payroll.[18] Half provided for additional employee contributions, while almost a fifth permitted some employee involvement in determining how the fund would be invested.

Profit sharing has received a considerable boost in recent years as various companies have sought means of promoting greater productivity to meet world competition. The most recent General Motors—United Auto Workers contract stipulates that employees will get 10 percent of GM's United States pretax profit in excess of a sum of 10 percent of net worth and 5 percent of other assets. Had the plan been in existence for the past 6 years, each worker would have received $2,231. Ford also adopted a profit-sharing plan. In dealing with similar problems in the tire industry, contracts have been signed to establish profit sharing at Uniroyal and Goodrich. One estimate places the number of profit-sharing plans in the United States at 200,000.[19]

Objectives of and Objections to Employee Profit Sharing

Employee profit sharing is a highly controversial form of employee remuneration. Its ardent advocates are found in the Council of Profit Sharing Industries, an association of employers founded in the 1940s. Among the values claimed for profit sharing are that it (1) effects an increase in productive efficiency through reducing costs and increasing output, (2) improves employee morale and reduces labor-management strife, (3) provides for employee security in the event of death, retirement, or disability, (4) constitutes a mechanism of employee economic education, (5) reduces turnover, and (6) improves public relations. A few managements also view profit sharing as a means of drawing labor and managment closer together, thus inhibiting the development of a labor union. Other specific objectives can be tied into the mechanics of a plan. For example, one firm distributes profit shares solely on the basis of attendance, and its absenteeism rate is far below the industry average. Another distributes shares on the basis of employee savings, thereby contributing to employee security.

The opponents of employee profit sharing are equally vehement in their objections. Profit sharing is a type of compensation about which there is much emotion. One major objection is that such compensation is often a poor incentive to efficiency in production. In the first place, the extra income bears little relation to individual employee effort, for many factors besides labor affect profits. It is also difficult to gauge the varying contributions of individuals. Most plans do not attempt to distinguish among individuals on the basis of effort and contribution. Thus the incentive value is reduced. In the second place, the extra compensation is not paid soon after the employee effort is made. Cash

---

[18]"Editor to Reader," *Personnel Journal*, vol. 59, no. 12, December 1980, p. 964.
[19]"Employee Wrath Hits Profit-Sharing Plan," *Business Week*, July 18, 1977, p. 25.

plans usually pay yearly, and companies utilizing deferred distribution can only issue reports of account balances. Employee profit sharing, therefore, hardly qualifies as an incentive wage plan. A second major objection is that such plans often prove to be a morale depressant rather than stimulant. Employees often regard a reasonably steady profit share as a part of their regular income. When there is no profit share to be paid, they are greatly upset and frequently ask for abolition of the system accompanied by a raise in base pay. If employees cannot or do not distinguish between the regular wage and the profit share, the company is assuming great risk and receiving little or no return.

Concerning the value of increasing employee security, opponents of profit sharing maintain that a properly constituted pension plan will more adequately meet the security objective of employees. Under a pension plan, the benefit is a known amount and the company contributes enough money to produce this amount of pension. Under a deferred-profit-sharing trust, the contribution is variable, depending on profits, and the resulting retirement benefit is also variable. These funds are invested in securities, and recent declines in stock and bond markets have sharply reduced the value of participants' accounts. Sears, which has been using only deferred profit sharing for retirement income, has recently added a noncontributory pension plan for its 230,000 hourly employees. Burlington Industries has also added a new pension program and has guaranteed that all profit-sharing accounts will earn at least as much as a passbook savings account.[20] Polaroid Corporation allows employees to make their own decisions as to how their accounts are to be invested.

Probably the most telling argument against employee profit sharing is its high discontinuance rate. These discontinuances are caused by such factors as employee apathy to the profit-sharing appeal, lack of profits, insufficient shares, union opposition, and unintelligent plan administration. Employee profit sharing *can* work, but it is an extremely difficult form of remuneration to administer effectively, and therefore often constitutes a greater incentive to management than it does to the employees.

The Framework of Employee Profit Sharing

One of the first items to be established under a profit-sharing plan is that of specifying the nature and amount of the company contribution to the profit-sharing fund. It must be decided (1) whether the share shall be a percentage of profits or a wage dividend based on the stock dividend declared by the board of directors; (2) whether the percentage shall be fixed or on a sliding scale based on the amount of profits; (3) whether the percentage shall be computed before or after dividends to stockholders, taxes, and amounts to be reinvested in the firm; and (4) what shall be the amount of profits to be shared. One study showed that profits contributed under current-distribution plans constituted 16 to 25 percent of profits before taxes and that under deferred-distribution arrangements they amounted to 7 to 15 percent.[21] Most firms establish a set percentage to be applied to profits. A few, such as Eastman Kodak, authorize the board of directors to declare a wage dividend each time a stock dividend is paid. A percentage is applied to the employee's total yearly income to determine his or her wage dividend.

---

[20]Ibid., p. 28.

[21]Edwin B. Flippo, *Profit Sharing in American Business,* Ohio State University Bureau of Business Research, Columbus, Ohio, 1954, p. 38.

A second part of the framework of profit sharing is the determination of the personnel eligible for participation in the plan. The usual stipulation is a certain amount of seniority. Current-distribution plans usually specify a period of 1 year or less, while deferred plans ordinarily require from 2 to 5 years of service. Current-distribution plans tend to emphasize the objective of production incentive while plans of the deferred type stress security. Also of importance is deciding how these participating employees shall share in the profit-sharing fund. Two bases are widely used, earnings and service. Often they are used in conjunction with each other, as is shown in the example in Figure 13-4.

FIGURE 13-4 Profit-sharing plan bases of distribution, Champion Paper and Fibre Company.

How your share of the profit is figured

The part of the profit that goes into your account is based on your "Time Service Units." These units are based on your pay and your years in the Plan. It works like this:

During your first 9 years in the Plan
    . . . you get *1* unit for each $100 of total annual pay
During your 10th through 19th years in the Plan
    . . . you get *2* units for each $100 of total annual pay
During your 20th year and all years after that
    . . . you get *3* units for each $100 of total annual pay
("Pay" means your total earnings, except that there is a limit of $10,000 on the amount of salary that may be included.)

years in plan

1	2	3	4	5	6	7	8	9	10	11	12	13	14	15	16	17	18	19	20	21	22	or more
1	1	1	1	1	1	1	1	1	2	2	2	2	2	2	2	2	2	2	3	3	3	3

time service units per $100 of pay

WHAT TIME SERVICE UNITS ARE WORTH

The value of a time service unit in any year depends on two things:
1. The amount of profit going into the profit sharing fund that year.
2. The total number of units of all members.
    You divide the money by the number of units to get the unit value *for example:*

If the profit for the fund is $\dfrac{\$1,700,000}{425,000 \text{ units}}$ = Unit value, $4

. . . and all members have

Then, if your pay for the year was $4,800, you would have 48 units ($4,800 divided by $100) and your share of the profit that year would be

$$
\begin{array}{r}
\$ \;\; 4.00 \\
\underline{48} \\
3200 \\
\underline{1600} \\
\$192.00
\end{array}
$$

Note: In 1955, at the end of the first profit sharing year, the unit value was slightly over $4.18.

Another common approach is to credit each employee with one point for a certain amount of salary, and with another point for each year of service. Thus, one employee may have 30 points from salary and 20 points from service for a total of 50. The total number of points of all employees is divided into the profit-sharing amount. The individual's share is then determined by multiplying the value of one point by the total of 50. Other bases of distribution that are sometimes used are merit rating, attendance, savings, and an equal sharing.

A very few plans have provided for loss sharing as well as profit sharing. The few companies that have provided for scheduled cuts in wages geared to losses have never enforced these provisions. It is significant to note that all these companies have abandoned the practice of employee profit sharing. Employee profit sharing is so difficult to administer effectively that it is safe to say that the firm that entertains the thought of loss sharing might just as well forget about this type of compensation.

Administration of Employee Profit-Sharing Plans

The successful operation of employee profit sharing is difficult to effect. By successful operation is meant a situation in which profits are shared and the company derives a known return in production, cooperation, turnover, morale, or the like. Many firms go through the mechanics of computing and distributing profit shares, but receive little return. Proper administration is essentially a problem of *employee education*. A person must be convinced that the base wage is fair in relation to the going rate, and that any profit shares paid are over and above this rate. One must see the relation between efforts and the success of the enterprise, and must learn to accept profits as variable and the absence of profits as a challenge to increased effort. At the least, one should learn not to be shocked or disgruntled by variations.

In general, successful administration of employee profit-sharing plans encompasses the following activities and policies:

1. The sharing of profits should be accompanied by a feeling of employee-employer partnership. Tangible evidences of this feeling can be given by such activities as the joint administration of the plan, joint labor-management shop committees which consult on operating problems, the distribution of meaningful and understandable financial information, the establishment of an employee stock-ownership plan, the permitting of employee inspection of company books, and the distribution of information concerning production, shipments, receipts, etc.

2. An effective employee educational plan concerning the nature of profits and the profit-sharing plan is necessary if any cooperation is to be expected. This involves some teaching of basic economics. It also involves continuous education concerning the significant events affecting profits and profit sharing. All types of media of communication should be utilized, such as individual status reports, group meetings, letters from the company president, social occasions to dramatize the plan, and supervisory contacts.

3. The nonprofit year should be provided for in advance. Management should not allow itself or its employees to be surprised by the sudden decline or absence of profits and the profit share. The following is presented not as a formula for

avoiding trouble during the nonprofit year but rather as a series of suggestions that have been found helpful in minimizing trouble at this time:[22]

    a. If a company is especially fearful of possible adverse effects during nonprofit periods, it should adopt the deferred-distribution type of plan.

    b. The conditioning of employees to the possibility of profitless years in advance, by education concerning the nature and functioning of profits under the economic system, tends to result in more desirable employee reactions.

    c. If a company is desirous of stimulating employee cooperation and performance during the profitless period it should adopt the current-distribution type. Whereas the deferred type seems to stimulate little reaction during the nonprofit period, the current type usually effects some result. It should be recognized, however, that the chances for loss are almost as great as the opportunities for gain.

    d. The larger the average individual profit share paid to the employee during profitable periods, the more favorable will be the reaction of employees during the nonprofit periods.

    e. It is essential to keep the profit share and the regular wage distinctly separate in the eyes of the employees.

    f. The more education of employees that is undertaken on a continuous basis, the less trouble there is during a nonprofit period.

    g. The adoption of some type of partnership attitude and program tends to induce more favorable employee reactions during nonprofit periods.

4. It should be recognized that labor organizations and employee profit-sharing plans are not necessarily incompatible. Though the traditional attitude of organized labor has been antagonistic, apparently this approach is currently being modified. Thus far, there is no legal requirement that management must bargain over a profit-sharing plan as there is in the cases of pensions and employee stock-ownership plans.

One study suggests that employee profit-sharing plans may be used by companies to forestall organization of employees by labor unions. In a study of a 5-year period, one-half of the representation elections held were sampled.[23] In these it was found that 759 elections were held in plants having profit-sharing plans. Unions won 336 and lost 423, for a winning ratio of 44.3 percent. This compares with a 59.8 percent victory ratio for unions in all other elections held during this 5-year period. After adjustment for such variables as size of company, geographic location, industry, and the particular unions involved, the difference in wins was determined to be statistically significant.

    The primary conclusion of the above discussion is that management should not fall for the glamorous appeal of employee profit sharing and embark upon such a venture thoughtlessly. Profit sharing should not even be considered unless present relationships between labor and management are reasonably good. It can make something better out of something good, but it is quite ineffective in situations of poor labor-management relations.

Employee Stock Ownership

    Perhaps the weakest connection between employee efforts and anticipated monetary returns is found in stock-ownership plans. Whether a stock increases in value or not is

---

[22]Ibid., p. 129.

[23]Edgar R. Czarnecki, "Profit Sharing and Union Organizing," *Monthly Labor Review*, vol. 92, no. 12, December 1969, p. 61.

dependent not only on the company's efforts but the vagaries of the stock market as well. Employee stock-ownership plans had their beginning in this country around the turn of the century. By the 1920s the movement was well established. The Depression of the 1930s dealt these plans a severe blow, and most companies discontinued the practice. Approximately 20 percent of the firms listed on the New York Stock Exchange have some type of stock purchase plan. Such plans are more common among major insurance companies, commercial banks, gas and electric companies, and those with over one-half billion dollars in sales.[24]

The typical employee ownership plan provides a mechanism through which certain eligible employees may purchase the stock of the company at a reduced rate. Eligibility is usually determined by wage level or years of service or both. Though a few firms offer the stock at the market rate, most cut the price 10 to 20 percent. A second typical feature is that provision is made for installment buying. The employee authorizes a payroll deduction, and stock is periodically purchased for her or him in the market by the company. A less-widespread feature of these plans is the issuance of special nonvoting stock for employees at special prices. Most companies prefer to deal in their regular issues. A fourth feature of some plans is the granting of a stock option—a right to purchase a certain amount of stock in the future at a stated price. The stock-option feature is more widely used in executive compensation plans than it is with the rank and file.

The most recent innovation in this field is the Employee Stock Ownership Plan (ESOP) developed by Louis Kelso. With the approval and encouragement of the federal government, firms are allowed to set up an ESOP trust through which they can obtain capital at roughly half the usual cost. The trust borrows money from a bank or insurance company in order to purchase the company's newly issued stock. It pledges the stock as collateral and the firm guarantees the loan. Each year, the firm makes tax-deductible contributions to the qualified ESOP trust which the trustees use to pay off the loan. As the stock is paid for, it is released and allocated to employee accounts. The plan is noncontributory on the part of the employee. Though many view the ESOP as a low-cost capital formation device, it is promoted by the government as a means of broadening corporate ownership among employees.[25]

Whereas Ford and General Motors utilized profit sharing as a means of stimulating greater cooperation, the federal government pressured Chrysler to set up an ESOP as a part of the process of keeping the firm in existence. Chrysler employees gave up $162 million in future wages and benefits and accepted new stock contributed to an ESOP that will eventually amount to a 15 percent interest in the firm. Other firms undertaking this program on a voluntary basis include Exxon, American Telephone and Telegraph Corporation, Atlantic Richfield, and Mobil Oil.

What does the company hope to gain from the creation of an employee stock-ownership plan? One of the commonly cited objectives is to promote a mutuality of interests. The employee is encouraged to consider the viewpoint of the company as a stockholder. He or she is also led to read company literature received as a part owner, which would probably be ignored as an employee. Other possible values are the promotion of thrift and security, the creation of an added incentive to work productively and cooperatively, and the creation of an additional source of investment capital. The

[24]Surendra S. Singhvi, "Motivation through Employee Stock Option Plans," *Personnel Administration/Public Personnel Review,* vol. 1, no. 3, November–December 1973, p. 61.

[25]Wallace F. Forbes and Donald P. Partland, "Pros and Cons of Employee Stock Ownership Plan," *Business Horizons,* vol. 19, no. 3, June 1976, pp. 5–12.

employees of Armco Steel Corporation, for example, own 5 percent of that firm's out-standing stock. It was acquired through employee contributions of from 5 to 8 percent of salary or wages received, supplemented by a company contribution of 50 cents on the dollar saved. Stocks are held in trust until employees choose to withdraw from the plan or terminate with the company. Over 80 percent of Armco personnel participate in this thrift-stock purchase arrangment.

The high discontinuance rate of these plans during periods of economic difficulty has led many to be highly suspicious of the values of employee stock ownership. The objection of placing too many eggs in one basket is often cited. The employee is asked to invest savings as well as talent in one company, with a consequent lack of investment diversification. Instead of promoting organizational morale, these plans at times seem to contribute to its deterioration. Stock prices fluctuate, and the employee can see nothing in the daily operation of the company to justify such fluctuations. As long as the stock prices go up, morale is good; when they go down, the employee is likely to blame the company—the intermediary who produced the stock for her or him. There seems to be an implied obligation for protection. For this reason, some firms have a plan feature that guarantees a certain repurchase price. The unhappy situation of the 1930s, when many employees were still paying for stock purchased at inflated prices prior to the stock-market crash, is one to be avoided. For firms with ESOPs whose stocks are not listed there is a danger that they will not be in sufficiently strong financial condition to guarantee purchase of the stock at the employee's retirement. Some have moved to list on the stock exchange just because of their repurchase liability.

Employee ownership of stock also resembles profit sharing in that the key to effective administration is education of the employee participant. One must understand the nature of stock, dividends, and the stock market. This education requisite is both a duty and an opportunity for the company. Stock ownership, like profit sharing, provides a basis for approaching the employee with company information.

SUMMARY

Variable compensation programs are designed to elicit from individuals and groups speci-fied types of behavior that are regarded as contributing to organizational effectiveness. Money can be a powerful motivator, but the design of such motivational programs is fraught with difficulties.

In general, motivation force will equal the value of money to the person multiplied by the degree of expectancy that it will be forthcoming if the desired act is performed. Assessment of expectancy is affected by self-determination of capacity to perform and by degree of trust in management that the money will actually be allocated.

Linkages between effort and performance, and performance and payoff, must exist if the variable pay plan is to be effective. Linkages are best perceived when plans apply to individuals, such as salary adjustments based on individual merit or seniority, incentive pay based on output, bonuses for individual managers based on profits or specified company goals, and individual suggestion systems. Each of these has managerial prob-lems, such as the subjective nature of performance measurement, social pressures on high performers, and the precise alignment of payoff with desired behavior.

Increasingly, managements are accepting the idea that groups as well as individuals can be motivated to work more effectively. In general, the smaller the group, the clearer the linkage between effort and performance. The group piece rate is an incentive system with better perceived linkage than production-sharing, profit-sharing, or employee stock-ownership plans. The accent in group plans is primarily upon cooperation toward a mutual objective. In production sharing, cost savings are shared. In profit sharing, the employee prospers if the entire firm does well. An even more indirect effect is exemplified by employee stock ownership. If the enterprise prospers, its stock values are likely to increase, provided something else does not happen to affect the stock market or the economy as a whole. Both individual competition and group cooperation are potential sources of organizational effectiveness.

BRIEF CASE

In the steel industry, a group of employees was assigned to the task of strapping several thin sheets of steel to form packages for shipment. Though the average performance of the group under a time-payment system had been at an index of 70, a time study by management had placed normal performance at an index of 90. An incentive pay system was established on the basis of 90 equaling standard performance. Weeks went by, but the employees continued to receive time wages since their performance still averaged 70. As a result, management took the following steps:

1. They checked with other steel companies and found that an index of 90 was prevalent.
2. They did an all-day time study, reanalyzed the figures, and concluded that 90 was fair.
3. On the assumption that poor work methods were being followed, they hired special instructors to teach the employees proper methods.
4. They took pictures of correct motions, enlarged them, and posted them on the walls in the work area.

Despite the above, the employees continued to produce at a rate of 70. As another step, management sent a newly hired time study engineer to the work area. Though dressed in suit and tie, he proceeded to get on hands and knees measuring the dimensions of the work area. When one of the employees could contain his curiosity no longer, he asked the stranger what he was doing. The time study engineer replied, "Oh, I'm measuring to see if we can locate an automatic steel strapping machine in this area."

Questions

1. What do you think the probable reaction of the employees will be to the act of the new time study engineer?
2. What other alternatives would you suggest for management to implement?

DISCUSSION QUESTIONS

1. Define and distinguish between equity and expectancy with respect to the subject of compensation.

2. Arrange the following in terms of strength of expectancy: (1) employee stock ownership, (2) individual piecework plan, (3) employee profit-sharing plan, (4) individual suggestion system, (5) production-sharing plan.

3. Billie produced 1,000 units of product in an 8-hour day. The work output standard established by time study is 100 units per hour. If the base hourly rate is $5, how much income would she receive under (1) straight piece work, (2) the Halsey Plan paying 50 percent, (3) the Rowan Plan, and (4) the Gantt Plan paying 10 percent?

4. Georgia, Carla, and Roger work as a team on a group piecework system. The hourly rates are $6, $5, and $4, respectively. For each unit of output, the entire team is allocated $5. If today, in their usual 8-hour day, the team produced 30 units, what would be each person's total pay if the bonus is divided equally? If it is divided according to base pay?

5. Discuss the major human problems issuing from the administration of incentive payment plans.

6. In effecting merit-seniority compromises in pay increases, (1) what is the rationale for dividing each pay range into two parts? and (2) what is the rationale for dividing the total job structure into two parts?

7. Compare and contrast the traditional suggestion system with the manner in which suggestions are administered under a Scanlon Plan.

8. What is an ESOP and what impact will it have upon employees?

9. Identify some of the major decisions necessary in designing and administering an employee profit-sharing plan.

10. What are some variable compensation plans that can be used to motivate top-level executives?

SUPPLEMENTARY READING

AGARWAL, NARESH C.: "Determinants of Executive Compensation," *Industrial Relations*, vol. 20, no. 1, Winter 1981, pp. 36–47.

CARLSON, NORMA W.: "Time Rates Tighten Their Grip on Manufacturing Industries," *Monthly Labor Review*, vol. 105, no. 5, May 1982, pp. 15–22.

COLLINS, SAMUEL R.: "Incentive Programs: Pros and Cons," *Personnel Journal*, vol. 60, no. 7, July 1981, pp. 571–575.

FOSTER, KENNETH E.: "Does Executive Pay Make Sense?" *Business Horizons*, vol. 24, no. 5, September-October 1981, pp. 47–51.

GOLDSTEIN, S. G.: "Employee Share-Ownership and Motivation," *Journal of Industrial Relations*, vol. 20, no. 3, September 1978, pp. 311–330.

OLSEN, MARIE: "Implementing a Successful Suggestion Program," *The Personnel Administrator*, vol. 27, no. 5, May 1982, pp. 75–80.

chapter **14**

Supplementary Compensation— Fringe Benefits

The primary effect of fringe-benefit type of compensation is to retain the employee in the organization on a long-term basis. There is little or no evidence that the tremendous variety of supplementary pay plans, often termed "fringe benefits," serve to motivate employees to higher productivity.

In a study of 550 white-collar employees, it was concluded that the average employee was aware of about one-half of the supplementary pay program features—this despite an unusually comprehensive and active program of communication with respect to employee benefits available.[1] One of this firm's most costly and widely publicized benefits, a disability wage plan, was essentially unheard of by 60 percent of those responding to the questionnaire. When asked if they felt that they knew enough about these programs, over three-quarters replied that they did. In a second study in another company, 249 new hires were queried concerning their knowledge of benefits explained during a comprehensive induction program.[2] A correlation between knowledge and attitudes toward the company's fringe-benefit program proved to be quite low. The conclusion of the researchers was that an attempt to motivate employees through a fringe-benefit program is probably futile.

Despite the absence of motivational effects, employee benefit programs make up a significant portion of most personnel department budgets. Currently, they amount to over one-third as much money as payroll earnings. According to a series of surveys by the U.S. Chamber of Commerce, total benefit costs have doubled in the last 30 years.[3] Practical operational value to the employing organization include maintenance of work force in competition with other organizations, preservation of some degree of labor-management peace in collective bargaining arrangements, and maintenance of acceptable levels of general morale. Many observers are highly concerned with the markedly in-

---

[1]Arthur A. Sloane and Edward W. Hodges, "What Workers Don't Know about Employee Benefits," *Personnel,* vol. 45, no. 6, November-December 1968, p. 32.

[2]James L. Sheard, "Relationship between Attitude and Knowledge in Employee Fringe Benefit Orientation," *Personnel Journal,* vol. 45, no. 10. November 1966, p. 616.

[3]Fred D. Lindsey, "Employee Benefits, Then and Now," *Nation's Business,* August 1981, p. 62.

creased demands for hygiene and pain-avoidance measures as compared with a lesser concern for attitudes dealing with employee motivation to contribute to productivity.

NATURE OF SUPPLEMENTARY COMPENSATION

Different forms of supplementary compensation have a variety of titles in industry. Some refer to them as "service programs"; others characterize them as "nonwage payments," or "employee benefits"; still others emphasize the costs and label them "hidden payroll." Typically, they have been most often referred to as fringe benefits. In the broadest sense, such "fringes" can be construed to include all expenditures designed to benefit employees over and above regular base pay and direct variable compensation related to output. As major categories, such benefits can include the following:

1. *Payment for time not worked.* Examples in this area would include paid rest periods, paid lunch periods, wash-up time, clothes-change time, get-ready time, vacations, holidays, sick leave, personal leave, voting time, and jury duty. There is seemingly no end to the innovative determination of new reasons for not working for pay. Perhaps the ultimate is a newly negotiated "to-hell-with-it" benefit: a certain number of days are provided for the occasion when the employee simply doesn't *feel* like going to work.

2. *Hazard protection.* There are a certain number of hazards that must be commonly faced by all. Income maintenance during these periods is the purpose of fringes designed to protect against the hazards of illness, injury, debt, unemployment, permanent disability, old age, and death.

3. *Employee services.* All people must have certain services available on a continuing basis, such as housing, food, advice, recreation, and so on. The trend toward the organization's providing such routine and ordinary services is exemplified by such fringe-benefit programs as cafeterias, paid legal services, career counseling, educational tuition, aid in housing, medical services, low-cost loans, use of organization vehicles for personal reasons, day-care centers for children, and paid memberships in certain private organizations.

4. *Legally required payments.* Our society, through its government, has decreed that certain minimum levels of company expenditures will be made in the area of protecting employees against the major hazards of life. Thus, regardless of company policy, organizations covered by federal and state laws must pay for unemployment compensation, workers' compensation insurance, old-age and survivors' insurance under social security, and Medicare.

In view of the above listings, it is little wonder that the term "fringe" is deemed no longer appropriate. As shown in Figure 14-1, total employee benefits as a percent of payroll have moved from 18.7 percent in 1951 to 36.6 percent in 1979. The figure continues to move upward, with a reported 37.1 percent in 1980.[4] During this period, wages and salaries have increased only half as fast. The most expensive categories are

[4]"Labor Letter," *The Wall Street Journal,* January 6, 1981, p. 1.

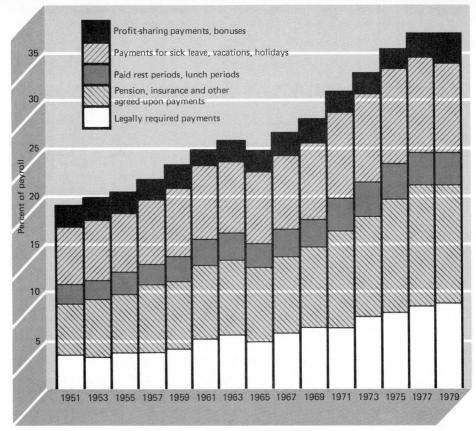

FIGURE 14-1 Benefits as a percent of payroll, 1951–1979. *(Source: Fred D. Lindsey, "Employee Benefits, Then and Now." Reprinted by permission from* Nation's Business, *August 1981. Copyright 1981 by* Nation's Business, *Chamber of Commerce of the United States.)*

public and private pensions, insurance programs of all types, and paid vacations. Fringe benefits have also exceeded the rise in the cost of living. During the 20-year period 1955–1975, benefit costs per employee rose by 387 percent as compared with a 98.6 percent rise in the Consumer Price Index.[5] Currently, the average dollar expenditure per employee is somewhat in excess of $4,000 per year. Predictions for the future indicate greater expenditures and efforts in such fields as group purchasing of all types (for example, group automobile insurance and legal services), longer vacations, no employee expense for major medical coverage, increased dental coverage, increased coverage for psychiatric difficulties, pension portability, cost-of-living adjustments of pension after retirement, annual physical examinations, earlier retirement ages, and possible retraining when severed from the organization.[6] We appear to be limited only by our ingenuity; one firm provides a free jet flight anywhere in the world on the tenth anniversary of service with the firm. Unusual benefits have been noted such as facelifts for executives

[5]John B. Hanna, "Can the Challenge of Escalating Benefit Costs Be Met?" *The Personnel Administrator,* vol. 22, no. 9, November 1977, p. 51.
[6]T. J. Gordon and R. E. LeBleu, "Employee Benefits, 1970–1985," *Harvard Business Review,* vol. 48, no. 1, January-February 1970, pp. 96–101.

and spouses, off-track-betting breaks, adoption fees, no-smoking pay, paternity leave, well pay, weight-loss pay, and self-defense training. When provided for executives, benefits are usually referred to as perquisites or ''perks.'' Among such ''perks'' are found such benefits as the following: chauffeured limousines, home security systems, corporate aircraft and yachts, tax assistance, financial counseling, company apartment or hotel room near the office, club memberships, company credit card, home entertainment expenses, kidnap and ransom insurance, and no-interest loans.

After establishing a managerial philosophy and approach to the offering of fringe benefits, we shall examine in more detail certain optional benefit programs. The legally required fringes are covered elsewhere in this text: workers' compensation in the chapter dealing with safety and health (Chapter 22) and pensions and unemployment compensation in the chapter concerned with retirement and layoff (Chapter 23). We will emphasize payment for time not worked, economic programs designed to protect against major hazards of life, and facilitative services designed to improve the quality of life.

Particular employee benefits will produce varying values. Paid vacations are presumed to provide a mental and physical respite that generates increased interest and activity on the job. Life insurance reduces worry about one's family security and thus leads to greater concentration upon work. Company cafeterias promote the eating of balanced meals, thus reducing fatigue in the late afternoon. Medical services help to keep the employee in good health, thereby reducing absenteeism. All of these are logical, but cost/benefit analyses of fringe benefits are rare indeed.

A PHILOSOPHY OF EMPLOYEE BENEFITS

The growth of employee benefits has been rampant, particularly since World War II, and apparently no end is in sight. It will be recalled that the period of the 1920s, labeled the ''era of paternalism,'' saw a widespread adoption of such benefits as company housing and company stores. The paternalistic approach fell into disrepute, supposedly as a result of the employee's desire for ''industrial adulthood.'' The Depression of the 1930s also served to eliminate many employer-financed services. Since World War II, we have entered the era of the ''new paternalism.'' The services of the 1920s pale into insignificance when compared with those of the present. The attitudes of both employees and the general public toward service programs have changed considerably. The tremendous amount of social legislation of the 1930s, particularly the Social Security Act, has led many to believe that the private firm is morally responsible for the lives of its employees. It is no longer a service initiated by a fatherly, benevolent employer, but a requirement imposed by government, competition, or the labor union.

In summary, the rapid growth of such programs can be traced to such sources as: (1) a changed employee attitude, (2) labor union demands, (3) governmental requirements, (4) competition that forces other employers to match benefits to attract and keep labor, and (5) periodic wage controls that freeze wages but permit the offering of services as a substitute for wage increases. High company income tax rates have also stimulated the offering of services, since they can be brought with cheap dollars.

What should be the philosophy of the manager in the realm of employee services? In a private-enterprise economy, the basic guiding principle should be that no employee benefit should be undertaken unless there is some return to the organization that is at least equal to its cost. This is not to say that government should not have the right and the obligation to impose employee services upon a private company if society feels that it is for the general interest and welfare. The manager must, however, make decisions in the area of freedom that is left, and the basic guide must be a comparison of costs of service with possible tangible and intangible returns to the company.

The returns of employee benefits to the company can take various forms, many of which are not subject to quantification. Among the values often cited are:

1. More effective recruitment
2. Improved morale and loyalty
3. Lower turnover and absenteeism
4. Good public relations
5. Reduced influence of unions, either present or potential
6. Reduced threat of further government intervention

The dollar return from employee benefits is almost impossible to measure. It is safe to state that the overwhelming majority of all employee benefits are taken on faith, rather than justified in dollars and cents. The correct management philosophy should have an economic orientation, modified by the influences of government and labor unions. We should prefer to be able to prove a positive return to the organization; but we cannot deny that fear of present or potential unions and of possible governmental interference has led many managers further into the area of employee benefit programs.

PRINCIPLES OF EMPLOYEE BENEFIT PROGRAMS

The cardinal principle of employee benefit programs has been set forth above; that is, the benefit must make a contribution to the organization at least equal in amount to its cost. In addition to this basic guide, there are several other generalizations that are applicable. Among these principles are the following:

1. The employee benefit should satisfy a real need.
2. Benefits should be confined to activities in which the group is more efficient than the individual.
3. The benefit program should be characterized by sufficient flexibility to enable adaptation to varying employee needs.
4. If the firm is to receive values from providing employee services, it must undertake an extensive and well-planned communication program.
5. The cost of the benefit should be calculable, and provision should be made for sound financing.

The first principle, that of satisfying a real need, would appear to be too obvious to need statement. However, many times benefits have been installed, only to be met with employee apathy or outright resistance. The ego in some managers has led them to believe that they know what is best for their employees. In one case, a company manager who felt that employees needed a sports program budgeted money, purchased facilities, and hired a company athletic director. When the whistle was blown to play ball, nobody wanted to play. Employee apathy sometimes turns into a demand that monies spent for employee benefits be given to them in their paycheck.

The manager takes a step forward when realizing that one must go to the employee to determine the latter's real needs. Even here, there is danger. When questioned about certain proposed services, employees almost always show a favorable reaction. Managers have interpreted this as evidence of real need, when often the employee meant only that it would be "nice" to have such a service. Extreme care and serious research should go into the decision of whether or not to offer a particular employee service.

The benefits selected should be those that can be best handled by a group approach. For example, life insurance purchased as a group can be obtained at a significantly lower price than the same insurance purchased by the individual. Thus, group life insurance meets the requirements of principle 2. On the other hand, there is a serious question as to whether the needs of employees in the recreational field could not better be left to the individuals. This is particularly true if the firm is located in a metropolitan area where numerous private facilities are available. The philosophy behind this principle is a desire to preserve some of the individualism and freedom of our society.

The third concept listed above suggests that not all employees are alike in terms of age, family status, and financial requirements. Whereas the typical benefit offering assumes that it is for a male employee who has a family with a nonworking wife, the continuing changes in our society make this concept obsolete. Today, fewer males are the sole support of their families, and more couples are remaining childless. In 1970, 70 percent of all households were maintained by married couples; today the figure is just about 60 percent.[7] Rather than one standard benefit program, it has been suggested that at least five are needed: (1) single workers, (2) married workers with no children, (3) married with young dependents, (4) married with dependents in college, and (5) "empty nesters."

One technique that can be utilized to inject this needed flexibility is the "cafeteria" style program. Though relatively few firms have undertaken this new approach, Box 14-1 describes the efforts of a few leaders such as TRW Inc. and Educational Testing Service. The system adheres to the principle of individual differences in that it allows the employee to choose from a varied offering those benefits that are the most valuable to her or him. In the Systems Group of Thompson Ramo Wooldridge, minimum coverage is assured each employee in all the major benefit categories. However, the employee is given a choice of three levels of each. If she or he choose more life insurance, for example, the extra cost is charged to the employee. If less-than-average coverage is chosen, paper credit is provided to be spent on some other benefit such as health. For example, a 32-year-old man, married with no children, chose the lowest medical plan and used the credit to buy extra accidental death insurance at no extra cost.[8] In the American Can Company program, the benefit program was reduced to a core, with the difference in costs between the old plan and the new core being given to the employees in the form of dollars or flexible benefits. Thus the employees may have the option of choosing cash as well. The company has found that older employees with working

[7]"New Benefits for New Lifestyles," *Business Week,* February 11, 1980, p. 111.
[8]Berwyn N. Fragner, "Employees' 'Cafeteria' Offers Insurance Options," *Harvard Business Review,* vol. 53, no. 6, November-December 1975, pp. 7–9.

BOX 14-1
More Workers Are Getting a Chance to Choose Benefits Cafeteria-Style
by Deborah Randolph

James Bechtel, a 34-year-old senior associate at Morgan Stanley & Co., figures his wife's employer is covering the family's doctor bills so he skips extra medical coverage and loads up on life insurance.

Jean Choffe, an American Can Co. marketing manager, skimps on medical and life insurance to increase company contribution to a capital accumulation plan for employees. Last month, by borrowing against the fund, she was able to buy a house in Fairfield County, Conn.

Both employees are taking advantage of a trend toward dishing out fringe benefits cafeteria-style. Workers are given a package of benefits that includes "basic" and "operational" items. Basics might include modest medical coverage, life insurance equal to a year's salary, vacation time based on length of service and some retirement pay. But then employees can use credits to choose among such additional benefits as full medical coverage, dental and eye care, more vacation time, additional disability income and higher company payments to the retirement fund.

Among the first to offer its employees flexible benefits was Educational Testing Service, Princeton, N.J., in 1974. TRW Inc., American Can and the city of Batavia, N.Y., followed. Within the past year, PepsiCo Inc., Northern States Power Co., Morgan Stanley and the Kingsport Press division of Arcata Corp. have started similar programs.

And "that's just the tip of the iceberg," says Thomas Paine, a senior partner at Hewitt Associates, a Lincolnshire, Ill., benefits consulting company. He believes many more will start the programs in the next three years. Sixty to 70 large companies

are considering a switch, he says, including Girard Co., a Philadelphia bank-holding company, and Loews Corp., which makes cigarettes and watches, owns theaters, and operates hotels.

There are problems, though.

Under most of the plans, employees can readjust their benefit package once a year, which requires a lot of extra bookkeeping. In addition, to create a pool of flexible benefits without increasing costs, employers have to scale back existing benefit programs, which may alienate employees.

Unions say they are studying the plans. So far, according to John Zalusky, an AFL–CIO economist, most of the people receiving flexible benefits are nonunionized, salaried people, not hourly wage workers. If an employer offered flexible benefits at the bargaining table, the union would insist on finding out the value of the package. "We are going to be looking far more closely at the employers' cost than ever before," Mr. Zalusky says. "Under the NLRB guidelines, we would want to know what each and every benefit costs."

Employers say the plans have a lot of bonuses for them. Educational Testing Service says its employee turnover has been "minimal" since the plan went into effect. Mary Jane Klansky, director of employee benefits, says flexible benefits are also "a great recruitment tool." And she says the plan makes employees more aware of their total benefit package.

Changes in the tax laws have made the plans even more attractive. A 1974 law required taxation of all benefits chosen by employees. Its effect was to freeze "the growth of the plan, be-

cause employers want to offer benefits that will be attractive to their employees," says Theresa Thompson, a principal of Towers, Perrin, Forster & Crosby, benefit consultants. Since the revisions, she says, "companies think it's clear to go ahead with the plans."

The plans also have the advantage of allowing companies to give the illusion of providing employees with more benefits without increasing costs. "When companies can't afford to keep pace with inflation, offering raises, they can give other forms of compensation" through the plans, says Ronald C. Palinzo, president of the American Society of Personnel Administrators.

Some insurers worry that employees will load up on medical options they can make claims against, running up costs for the carrier. "You lose the notion of sharing costs among a lot of people" in cafeteria plans, says David Klein, senior vice president, marketing, for Blue Cross Association.

But Prudential Life Insurance Co. isn't worried. Late last year it formed a flexible compensation services unit to design and consult on the plans. "It's a natural extension for us. We've got the experience of administering insurance systems," says David Balak, vice president of the unit.

As part of its marketing campaign, the unit holds seminars on the plans for businessmen. A recent session in Philadelphia attracted 60 people. Mr. Balak showed charts of suggested plans and gave advice. He urged companies to start the plans gradually, with a few options, and add more when possible. "You need to learn about the concept," he said, "and get the word out to employees."

spouses who have medical coverage elsewhere will take the medical credit and place it in a savings plan for retirement. Younger employees in a similar situation are more inclined to buy extra vacation days.

It is not unusual for a fringe-benefit program costing hundreds of thousands of dollars to be accompanied by an educational publicity program costing only a few thousand dollars. If the employee is unaware of a benefit, there is little or no return to the organization. One survey of 354 organizations revealed that two-thirds spent less than $10 per employee in benefit communication.[9] Among the techniques utilized were booklets and brochures, manuals, word of mouth, pay-envelope inserts, computerized statements, posters, bulletin-board notices, and annual reports.

The last principle is that the costs of the employee benefit must be calculable and its financing be established on a sound basis. This is particularly important in the matter of employee pensions. Sound actuarial estimates must be made, and adequate provisions for financing must be established before conceding the service over the collective bargaining table. These services are not cheap to administer, as is revealed by surveys of personnel management budgets. This is one of the highest single costs of the entire budget of expenditures.

PAYMENT FOR TIME NOT WORKED

The two most costly types of payment for time not worked are vacations and holidays. There has been a constant trend toward lengthening the annual vacation in most organizations. A typical schedule would be as follows:

- One week after 6 months to 1 year of service
- Two weeks after 1 to 5 years of service
- Three weeks after 5 to 15 years of service
- Four weeks after 15 years of service
- Five weeks after 25 years of service

Some firms give as much as 6 weeks of vacation for certain groups. Just as some universities provide for a sabbatical leave for their faculties, Xerox has established a year's paid leave of absence for employees with an approved project that will contribute in some manner to improving society.

Most organizations provide 7 to 12 holidays with pay for their employees. The most commonly observed holidays are New Year's Day, Good Friday, Washington's Birthday, Memorial Day, Independence Day, Labor Day, Veterans' Day, Thanksgiving, and Christmas. A few permit the employee to take a paid holiday on her or his birthday. Many firms now grant "floating" holidays taken either at the employee's option or designated for all employees by management, such as an extra day at Christmas time to make a longer "weekend." In most firms, eligibility for holiday pay for those working is contingent on having worked scheduled days before and after the holiday. Most pay time and a half for holiday work, though a few will award double time.

There are also a number of miscellaneous types of nonworking times that companies sometimes underwrite. These would include jury duty, death in family, civic duty, military obligations, and marriage. It is quite common to pay for a minimum of 4 hours if the employee reports in and finds no work available. Employees engaged in grievance

[9]Richard C. Huseman, John D. Hatfield, and Russell W. Driver, "Getting Your Benefit Programs Understood and Appreciated," *Personnel Journal,* vol. 57, no. 10, October 1978, p. 563.

processing are also paid their usual salaries for the time so spent. There are also paid rest periods, lunch periods, and wash-up time.

It is customary in governmental jobs and white-collar jobs in industry to provide 10 or 12 days a year of sick leave. A few organizations have started "sick-leave banks" where each employee contributes 1 day per year to the bank. If one has used up the authorized amount, a loan or a grant can be awarded from the bank. To avoid conscientious workers' supporting sick-leave spendthrifts, a committee typically passes on each request. In one bank, no future loan will be made until the old one has been paid up.

A few firms have begun to experiment with the concept of extending sick leave to blue-collar employees as well. The Gillette, Polaroid, Kinetic Dispersion, Avon Products, and Black and Decker companies provide for 10 to 15 days of sick leave per year for all employees.[10] In each case, the absence rate went up immediately after inauguration of the plan, but in time decreased to a level slightly higher than under the previous system. The major reasons for the change were to minimize the differences among employee groups and to encourage greater identification with the company and its management.

Returning to Figure 14-1, it should be noted that time off with pay amounts to well over one-third of the total cost of employee benefits. And the trend is toward granting longer vacations, more regular holidays, more personal holidays, and expanding the kinds of employee groups entitled to sick leave.

ECONOMIC PROTECTION AGAINST HAZARDS

In addition to old age and survivors' insurance and unemployment compensation required by the Social Security Act, and workers' compensation required by 50 state laws, most organizations voluntarily provide a number of other programs designed to help employees when faced with adversity. Among these are (1) guaranteed annual wage, (2) life insurance, (3) health insurance, (4) medical services, and (5) credit unions.

Guaranteed Annual Wage

Some progressive managements have long been aware of the value of stable operations and steady employee earnings. The number of managements that have been willing and able to create and administer a private plan to stabilize employment and/or earnings is relatively few. Perhaps the three best-known plans of this type are the systems of the Procter and Gamble Company, George A. Hormel Company, and the Nunn-Bush Shoe Company. It will be noted that all three companies are engaged in producing a consumer good.

Most of the private annual wage plans have three basic characteristics: (1) they guarantee a certain number of weeks of employment and/or wages, (2) they restrict the number of employees who are covered, and (3) they suspend the operation of the plan under conditions of extreme emergency, such as fire, flood, explosion, and strikes. The Procter and Gamble plan, for example, guarantees employment for 48 weeks each year

[10]Robert D. Hulme and Richard V. Bevan, "The Blue-Collar Worker Goes on Salary," *Harvard Business Review*, vol. 53, no. 2, March-April 1975, p. 104.

to employees who have 2 or more years of service. There is no guarantee that the wage rate will not be lowered in the event that an employee must be transferred to another job. Stability of operations and employment has been effected by educating the consumer to buy more steadily, producing to stock during slack sales periods, and transferring personnel from job to job as operations fluctuate. The Hormel plan guarantees a certain amount of wages rather than employment. Fifty-two paychecks a year will be paid to eligible employees, with a minimum weekly pay for 38 hours. Total wages for the year are established on the basis of the sales forecast. This total pay is divided into 52 equal amounts. Actual working hours frequently vary from week to week, but the pay received does not. Overages and underages of time worked relative to pay received are balanced periodically. The Nunn-Bush plan is similar to that of Hormel, providing for a guarantee of 52 paychecks. The guarantee to employees is based on the concept that labor will receive 20 percent of the value of products sold. Thus, the percentage of sales is guaranteed to labor but the dollar amount is not.

Two organizations are well known for a policy commitment to no layoff. The IBM corporation has had no layoffs in 35 years, and the Lincoln Electric Company, manufacturer of arc welding machines and electrodes, formally guaranteed that no employees with a minimum of 2 years of service would be laid off. Though the Lincoln commitment is practically devoid of loopholes and can only be changed on 6 months' notice, no covered employee has been laid off since 1958. The returns to the company are flexibility in job assignments, employee acceptance of technological changes, a monthly turnover rate at one-sixth the competitive level, and compounded annual increases in productivity of 7.73 percent.[11] The company also utilizes individual incentive pay plans, employee stock ownership, and employee profit sharing with shares based on merit. Total annual compensation per employee is typically double that of competitors.

Life Insurance

Life insurance is probably the oldest form of company-sponsored employee benefit. Group life premiums are considerably smaller than those of insurance purchased by the individual. The return to the company of this particular economic service comes from relieving the employee of worry about the security of his or her dependents. Relief from worry should enable a person to devote greater attention to the job and the company. Most life insurance plans include all employees regardless of physical condition and provide for conversion to individual policies without physical examination when leaving the organization.

Health Insurance

Accidents and industrial diseases growing out of the job are compensable under state workers' compensation laws to be discussed in Chapter 22. Illnesses and accidents that are not industrially caused are a source of worry and financial strain upon the employee. Various forms of health and accident insurance are provided, some completely financed, and others whose costs are shared with the employee. Showing again the tremendous variety of fringe benefits, the following types of insurance are provided by various firms.

[11]Robert Zager, "Managing Guaranteed Employment," *Harvard Business Review*, vol. 56, no. 3, May-June 1978, p. 107.

1. Hospitalization
2. Surgical expense
3. Accident and sickness insurance to cover periods beyond regular sick leave
4. Maternity benefits
5. Vision care
6. Dental care
7. Psychiatric care, including alcohol and drug addiction
8. Chiropractic coverage
9. Major medical

The last item is of increasing importance since ordinary medical insurance adequately covers illnesses and injuries whose costs run under $1,000. Major medical plans are designed to cover illnesses whose costs can be as catastrophic as the illness itself.

Though health benefits insurance used to be viewed as an inexpensive fringe, such is no longer the case. In 1980, private businesses paid 27 percent of the nation's personal health costs of $217 million.[12] Health care costs have moved from 5.9 percent of the Gross National Product in 1965 to a projected 10 percent by 1990. General Motors spends more on medical benefits than it does for the steel to make automobiles.

Because of this acceleration of costs, benefit managers are taking an increasing interest in monitoring insurance claims. Inaugurating a hospitalization review program by a third party resulted in a drop in Kennecott Copper's hospital bill of 12 percent, in hospital surgery of 11 percent, and in the use of assistant surgeons of 22 percent.[13] Other attempts to contain costs have included publication of several hundred procedures that can be accomplished on an outpatient basis, paying a higher percentage of outpatient costs than hospital costs, paying higher coverage when second opinions are secured, and reimbursement for health services provided in the home. Private companies can no longer afford to play the passive role of merely providing financing.

Medical Services

Another approach used by some companies to deal with mounting health costs is to provide some of the services directly rather than just financing their provision by others. One vehicle that has been used is the "health maintenance organization" (HMO).

Whether or not a company sponsors one itself, the Health Maintenance Organization Act of 1973 requires employers covered by the Fair Labor Standards Act to offer an HMO as an alternative option to health insurance if one is available in the community. The HMO provides clinical and hospital services for a fixed monthly fee. Henry J. Kaiser pioneered the HMO concept during the 1940s when he established prepaid comprehensive health care for employees in his shipbuilding firm.

It is estimated that there are now approximately 180 HMOs in the nation, covering some 6 million people. The Kaiser plan alone accounts for almost half of the membership. In one comparative analysis, it was determined that for HMO members the number of hospital days each year was 450 per 1,000 people; the rate for nonmembers was 1,100

---

[12]Michael Waldholz, "Businesses Are Forming Coalitions to Curb Rise in Health-Care Costs," *The Wall Street Journal,* June 17, 1982, p. 31.

[13]"The Corporate Attack on Rising Medical Costs," *Business Week,* August 6, 1979, p. 56.

to 1,200 hospital days per 1,000. The accent is on preventive medicine; one is free to go to the clinic at any time at little or no charge per visit.

As a second approach, over 50,000 firms have provided a physical fitness program for their employees.[14] These can vary from simply organizing after-hours athletic teams to the $2.5 million physical fitness center of Kimberly Clark, which has gymnasiums, weight-lifting rooms, swimming pool, sauna, and racquetball and handball courts. Though little concrete evidence exists concerning proved values to the firm, the reasoning followed is presented in Figure 14-2. The ultimate hopes are for lower medical costs, greater productivity, and reduced absenteeism.

Credit Union

A credit union is an organized group of people who pool their money and agree to make loans to one another. Thus one value of fostering a credit union is the relief from

[14]John Kondrasuk, "Company Physical Fitness Programs: Salvation or Fad?" *The Personnel Administrator*, vol. 25, no. 11, November 1980, p. 47.

FIGURE 14-2 A system of relationships of assumptions about physical fitness programs. *(Source: John Kondrasuk, "Company Physical Fitness Programs: Salvation or Fad?" Reprinted from the November 1980 issue of* Personnel Administrator, *copyright 1980, The American Society for Personnel Administration, 30 Park Drive, Berea, Ohio 44017, $30 per year.)*

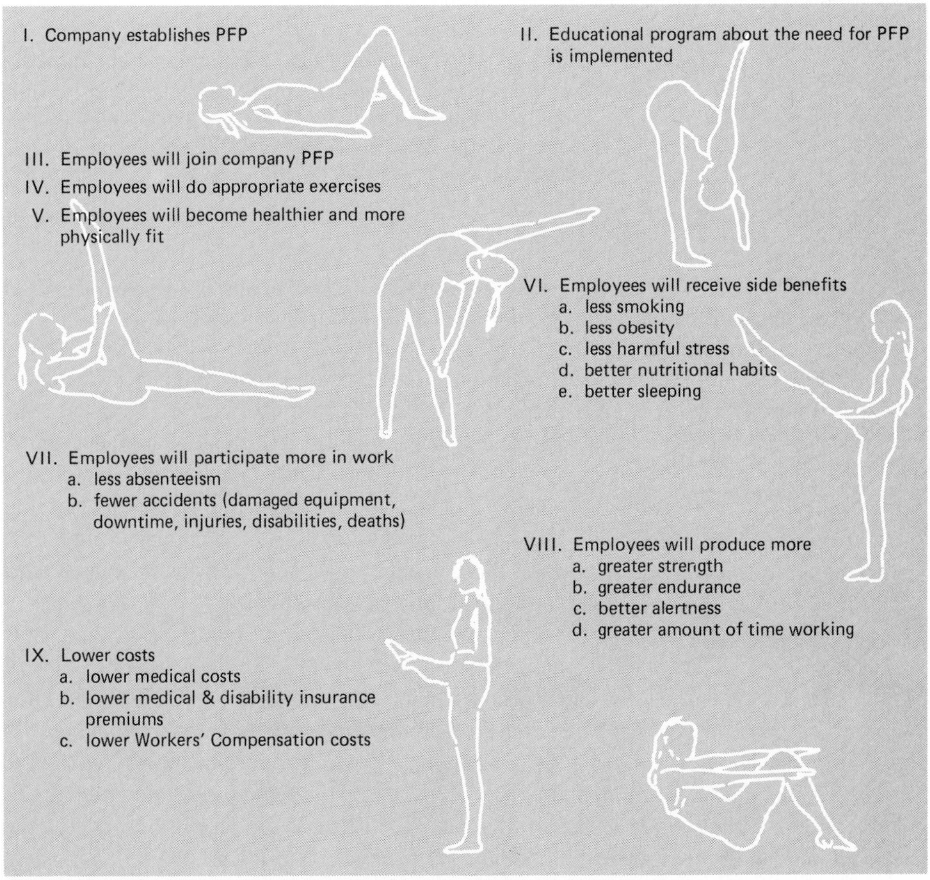

I. Company establishes PFP

II. Educational program about the need for PFP is implemented

III. Employees will join company PFP

IV. Employees will do appropriate exercises

V. Employees will become healthier and more physically fit

VI. Employees will receive side benefits
   a. less smoking
   b. less obesity
   c. less harmful stress
   d. better nutritional habits
   e. better sleeping

VII. Employees will participate more in work
   a. less absenteeism
   b. fewer accidents (damaged equipment, downtime, injuries, disabilities, deaths)

VIII. Employees will produce more
   a. greater strength
   b. greater endurance
   c. better alertness
   d. greater amount of time working

IX. Lower costs
   a. lower medical costs
   b. lower medical & disability insurance premiums
   c. lower Workers' Compensation costs

worry over short-term financial insecurity. A second value is the reduction in employee compensation garnishments by loan agencies when the employee fails to meet loan obligations. Garnishment proceedings are always objectionable to the employer and in some companies constitute grounds for discharge. However, federal legislation enacted in 1970 prohibits discharge because of garnishment for any *one* indebtedness; some states prohibit discharge for reasons of garnishment regardless of number. In addition, the federal law stipulates that the portion of wages available for garnishment must not exceed 25 percent or an amount related to current minimum-wage levels, whichever is less.

This type of employee service illustrates well the principle cited earlier, that employee services should be offered only when they can best be executed by a group rather than an individual. If an individual sought a short-term unsecured loan, he or she would pay interest rates in excess of 30 percent. If that same individual joined a credit union and sought a short-term unsecured loan from this union, the annual interest rate would be no more than 18 percent. Thus, in this instance, the group is more effective than the individual.

FACILITATIVE EMPLOYEE SERVICES

Facilitative services are activities that employees must normally take care of themselves in everyday living. Just as executives have certain perquisites, the trend is in the direction of providing regular employees with special assistance in some of the routine portions of life. Each facilitative service proposes to meet some continuing need. The justifications for the services will be given briefly below.

Recreational Programs

Recreational programs may be divided into two types, (1) sports and (2) social events. In the sports category, activities can be further classified into ''varsity'' and ''intramural'' sports. Varsity sports are those in which a team is selected to represent the firm in competition with other institutions. This type of activity violates the principle of establishing a broad base of participation, but it may return values in improved public relations and in employee pride, particularly if the team is successful. Intramural sports, participated in by a greater number of employees, is the more desirable activity to undertake. Various firms have provided facilities and/or organization for golf, bowling, softball, tennis, swimming, and the like. It is not unusual to see a company purchase a recreational area, complete with golf course, swimming pools, and tennis courts. Such recreational facilities are of great value in employee recruitment.

What values are derived from company picnics, employee country clubs, and sports programs? The first intangible value is that of improved morale. On occasions, however, a company has studied the personnel who participate most in the company sport program and, in one case, discovered a relationship between productivity and participation. The only difficulty, however, was that the relationship was inverse: the most enthusiastic sports participants were among the poorer producers. This served to create grave doubts of the organizational value of such programs. Recreational services do however, serve as excellent recruiting devices, particulary for certain classes of employees. Some employers have attempted to rationalize sports on the basis of their contribution to employee health and consequent indirect benefit to productivity. However, a case can be made for the opposite, particularly when excessive injuries to employees result from participation in company sports activities. The values of recreational services are largely intangible and are extremely difficult to quantify. Many feel that such activities are essential to making the company a ''good place to work'' and let the analysis drop at that point.

Cafeterias

Although morale always enters into the analysis, the most important result in the provision of company cafeterias is improved nutrition. Too often, industrial employees settle for a hot dog and a soft drink if cafeteria service is not available. Improper eating, particularly on heavy jobs, will be reflected in greater fatigue and reduced productivity during the late afternoon. Some firms will practically give away certain foods deemed to be highly nutritious. One should also note that the cafeteria can also be the cause for numerous employee complaints; food quality and variety are subjects dear to the hearts of most workers.

Relocation Assistance

The home life of the employee has a considerable effect upon performance at work. In addition, employers wish to retain the flexibility of moving key employees to new job assignments to enhance the effectiveness of both the individual and the organization. The provision of various relocation services will advance both objectives. Among the various services that may be provided are: (1) help in sale of present home, including its possible purchase for resale by the company, (2) shipping household goods, (3) temporary living and traveling expenses, (4) job-finding assistance for the employee's spouse, (5) information and advice concerning the new area, such as medical facilities, schools, routes to work, and so on, and (6) help in finding and purchasing a new home. With regard to the last item, the acceleration of mortgage financing rates has led to more refusals to relocate. In some instances, the employer will provide a mortgage interest differential for a period of three years to enable the employee to adjust to the new higher mortgage rate. Estimates of the costs to the employer of relocating one employee range from $30,000 to $60,000.[15]

Vanpooling

The rising costs of gasoline have led some 600 companies to organize and finance vanpooling programs.[16] It is estimated that some 150,000 persons are active in this form of ride sharing. Prudential Insurance Company has 435 vans in use in some 30 cities, transporting approximately half of their total employees.

The company derives some investment tax credits in purchasing vans that seat at least 8 adults. The van driver drives free and also has the use of the van for personal use for a small mileage charge. Vanpoolers typically pay $2 per day and also benefit

[15]John M. Moore, ''Employee Relocation: Expanded Responsibilities for the Personnel Department,'' *Personnel*, vol. 58, no. 5, September-October 1981, p. 62.

[16]Scott Dever, ''Vanpooling: How It's Done at Several Companies,'' *The Personnel Administrator*, vol. 26, no. 6, June 1981, p. 33.

from preferred parking places at work. Extensive use of such a program will require the provision of less parking space by the company.

Child Care

Approximately half of all women with children under the age of six are in the work force. For families with both parents working, it is estimated that day care expenses for children average 10 percent of gross income, ranking behind only housing, food, and taxes. In addition, the old family support networks of relatives and neighbors caring for children are rapidly dissolving. Families move about and the woman next door who used to care for children now has a career of her own.

It has been projected that employer provision of some form of child care will be the benefit of the future. As stated by one executive, "by 1990, you'll see the child care benefit as often as you see group medical insurance today."[17] The child care benefit can vary from the provision of counseling services to the actual provision of the service. Steelcase, Inc., provides counselors who discuss work schedules and the types and costs of available care facilities. These counselors also act as middlemen between the families and day care centers in working out various problems. One snag in the program is resentment on the part of other employees who do not have children. This problem could be solved through the cafeteria benefit program, permitting parents to choose the child care benefit while the remaining employees can spend their portion on other selected services. In some instances, voucher allowances are issued, which enables the employee to pay a portion of child care expenses. The Ford Foundation pays 50 percent of the costs for employees earning less than $25,000 per year.[18]

Employee Purchase

The old company store, where the employee redeemed the scrip paid for work, had a very poor reputation in the past. The old type of store is justifiable only when no private stores are available or when the few stores that do exist take advantage of a monopoly situation. Many firms do, however, make available to their employees their own products at discount prices. This provides returns in morale and also stimulates the employee to use and "identify with" the products on which he or she works.

A serious question arises concerning the desirability of a company's opening its purchasing department to miscellaneous employee purchases. When a company purchases consumer goods from other firms, it can obtain them at discount prices for its employees. The anticipated return to the company is that of improved morale, but the potential dangers often outweigh this value. Among these dangers are the following: (1) the employee holds the company responsible for any deficiency or malfunction in the product purchased; (2) he or she requests installment financing of the purchase; (3) the company incurs the ill will of the community retailers who sell the same products bought through the purchasing agent; and (4) the purchasing agent looks upon the scheme with disfavor, since the agent is forced to purchase unfamiliar goods from unfamiliar sources.

---

[17]"Child Care Grows as a Benefit," *Business Week,* December 21, 1981, p. 60.

[18]Joann S. Lublin, "The New Interest in Corporate Day-Care," *The Wall Street Journal,* April 20, 1981, p. 19.

Educational Tuition

Perhaps the most widely offered and least utilized fringe benefit is employee educational assistance through tuition refunds. A survey of 283 firms indicated that over 90 percent of the larger enterprises offer educational assistance.[19] Less than 10 percent of the employees, however, take advantage of these plans. Half of the companies set dollar maximums of $500 or less, and about one-fourth graduate the amounts awarded on the basis of grade received, such as 100 percent for A or B, 50 percent for C, 25 percent for D, and nothing for a failing grade. The most common stipulations for approval of educational assistance are (1) the course taken should be related to the job, (2) the course should be applicable toward a degree, and (3) the worker must still be in the company's employ at the time of the refund.

Educational tuition is a fringe benefit that rests on a sound foundation of mutual interests. The employee gains additional knowledge and skills that contribute to personal development; the organization gains when these skills are put to use on the job. Such plans will also contribute to improved morale and reduced turnover.

Employee Assistance Programs

As the final "catch-all" type of service, various firms are providing advice and assistance for a wide variety of personal troubles. Responses from some 500 firms indicated that 20 percent had some form of an employee assistance program. As indicated in Figure 14-3, the problems most frequently mentioned included alcohol rehabilitation, marital and family counseling, emotional counseling, and drug abuse programs.

Less widely offered assistance programs are in the areas of financial and legal counseling. If employees become involved in financial trouble, they may have access to the credit union, employee savings and loan association, or some other similar service

[19]Charles E. Watson and Alexis L. Grzybowski, "What Your Company Should Know about Tuition Aid Plans," *Business Horizons*, vol. 19, no. 5, October 1975, pp. 75–80.

FIGURE 14-3
Frequency and Effectiveness of Employee Assistance Program Activities

EAP Activity	Percent* Offering	Percent* Perceived Effectiveness
Alcohol rehabilitation	86%	85%
Marital and family counseling	80	65
Emotional counseling	78	67
Drug abuse programs	81	68
Career counseling	55	59
Financial counseling	55	58
Legal counseling	51	47

*Based on 106 respondents.
Source: Robert C. Ford and Frank S. McLaughlin, "Employee Assistance Programs: A Descriptive Survey of ASPA Members." Reprinted from the September 1981 issue of *Personnel Administrator*, copyright 1980, The American Society for Personnel Administration, 30 Park Drive, Berea, Ohio 44017, $30 per year.

offered in the firm. Not infrequently the trouble is more deeply rooted—a chronic inability to handle money. The employee is in need of advice as well as financial assistance. Some predict that prepaid legal insurance will become the "fringe of the future" since its tax status was clarified by the Tax Reform Act of 1976. Group legal service usually includes some degree of coverage for consultation, office work, judicial proceedings, and major expenses above maximums provided in the preceding areas. For example, a plan could provide up to $25 for each visit with an attorney with a maximum of $100 per year, office work up to $250, judicial proceedings up to $665, and 80 percent of the next $2,500 above these maximums.[20] Most legal claims have been in the areas of domestic relations and automobiles.

SUMMARY

Employee fringe benefits can be compared to the mythological animal that immediately grew two heads when one was chopped off. There seems to be no end to the number, variety, and adaptations of such service programs. As an example, one local union demanded that when a retired company employee dies, a representative of the department be given time off with pay to attend the funeral. The limit on this arrangement is 4 hours' time off, unless the representative is asked to act as a pallbearer, in which case one may get the whole day off with pay.

One could reason that the forces governing the determination of wages and other compensation will result in a certain size of compensation package. If the employee desires to take 30 percent of this package in the form of guaranteed annual wages, pensions, insurance, and the like, that is her or his privilege. This presumes that the compensation package can be scientifically determined and that the employee is actually substituting a fringe for a portion of the base wage. Such a precision of measurement is, of course, impossible.

The typical approach to the problem of *what* employee benefits to offer is to attempt to prove or deduce specific and general values to the organization as well as to the employee participant. In general, all such plans should conform to such principles as the following: the benefit should provide organizational value at least equal in amount to its cost; it should meet a real need; group effort should be more efficient than individual; maximum employee participation should be engendered; special efforts should be made to communicate the value and content of the fringe-benefit package; the costs of the benefit should be calculable and provision made for sound financing.

Nonwage payments take a variety of forms, including pay for time not worked, economic benefits to protect against major life hazards, and facilitative services to improve the quality of life. Society through government appears to be most concerned about protecting against major economic hazards issuing from interruptions or stoppages of employment, as judged by passage of such laws as the Social Security Act and the Employee Retirement Income Security Act. There is obvious great concern with employee health, as exemplified by workers' compensation laws, the Occupational Safety and Health Act, and the Health Maintenance Organization Act. Perhaps the greatest

---

[20]Philip M. Alden, Jr., "The Tax Reform Act of 1976 and Prepaid Legal Insurance," *Personnel,* vol. 54, no. 4, July-August 1977, p. 62.

degree of employer-initiated benefits lies in the facilitative services area, such as child care, vanpooling, housing, recreation, counseling, tuition, and so on. Labor unions have been most prominent in steadily increasing the amount of pay for time not worked, such as holidays, vacations, rest periods, and so on. In sum, the average employee working in a firm engaged in interstate commerce and organized by a labor union is likely to be on the receiving end of a multitude of benefits, many of which she or he becomes aware of only when the need arises. Professional personnel managers should be concerned with enhancing organizational returns for this major investment in employee attitudes.

BRIEF CASE

Eastman Kodak is a nonunionized firm with approximately 60,000 employees. With more leisure activities than in the rest of Rochester, New York, it has the largest company-sponsored recreation program in the United States. About 35,000 employees pay $1 per year for membership in Kodak Camera Clubs, which makes available free use of 40 dark rooms, discount purchase of film, and free loan of photographic equipment. In one building, 300,000 square feet of space is allocated to recreation, including movie theaters, bowling alleys, and meeting places. First-run films are shown at lunch time. Employees can shop at a company general store and do their banking at Eastman Savings and Loan. There are free eye examinations, 11 softball fields, amateur vaudeville shows, square dancing, ice fishing, and table tennis tournaments. Kodak has paid annual bonuses to all employees through the form of a ''wage dividend'' profit sharing plan. Many Kodak production areas are decorated with hand-lettered signs that show pride in work groups. For most of the past 100 years, Kodak had dominated the U.S. market with 90 percent of the sales for conventional color film.

Questions

1. Do you think that Kodak has a large benefit program because it is rich or because it pays an economic return to the company?

2. What specific values can issue from a recreational program?

DISCUSSION QUESTIONS

1. Should fringe benefits be called ''fringes''? Why or why not?

2. What are the values and problems of establishing a ''cafeteria'' fringe-benefit program?

3. Identify the more extensive ''time-off-with-pay programs.'' Are companies or labor unions more likely to support this type of fringe?

4. What is a guaranteed annual wage or employment program? What can a company gain from such a program? Cite examples.

5. What is a health maintenance organization? What are its values in comparison with health insurance?

6. What are the rationalized returns to an organization of a cafeteria? a recreational program? educational tuition assistance? housing assistance? child care? vanpooling?

7. Discuss the role of fringe benefits as motivators versus their role as merely stimulating long-term employment.

8. What specific principle of administering fringe benefits best applies to the company purchase of employee life insurance?

9. Identify the major economic hazards of employee life, and cite specific programs that relate to each hazard.

10. Contrast the growth of fringe benefits with increases in wages and cost of living. What additional fringes are envisioned for the future?

SUPPLEMENTARY READING

COCKRUM, ROBERT B.: "Has the Time Come for Employee Cafeteria Plans?" *The Personnel Administrator,* vol. 27, no. 7, July 1982, pp. 66–72.

DEBATS, KAREN E.: "The Current State of Corporate Relocation," *Personnel Journal,* vol. 61, no. 9, September 1982, pp. 664–670.

FOEGEN, J. H.: "The Creative Flowering of Employee Benefits," *Business Horizons,* vol. 25, no. 3, May-June 1982, pp., 9–13.

HAMMER, EDSON G., MOHAMMAD AHMADI and LAWRENCE P. ETTKIN: "Long-term Forecasting of Employee Benefits: An Impossible Task?" *The Personnel Administrator,* vol. 26, no. 12, December 1981, pp. 30–34.

HARRISON, DEBORAH H. and JOHN R. KIMBERLY: "HMOs Don't Have to Fail," *Harvard Business Review,* vol. 60, no. 4, July-August 1982, pp. 115–124.

MOORE, JOHN M.: "Employee Relocation: Expanded Responsibilities for the Personnel Department," *Personnel,* vol. 58, no. 5, September-October 1981, pp. 62–69.

EXERCISES AND CASES FOR PART FOUR

Exercise: Job Evaluation

In experimenting with different ways of producing floral arrangements, the Asbury Florist Corporation divided the job of floral designer into five jobs: (1) a stock man, who controls the order slip and assembles the flowers, (2) the assembler, who prepares the flowers by wiring and wrapping with paraffilm strips, (3) the ribbon tier, who prepares bows and maline backing, (4) the floral designer, who quickly arranges the corsage flowers and attaches the ribbon and maline, and (5) the boxer, who places the corsage in a bag and box. These five persons would work in sequence along a table.

The organizational structure of the firm is as indicated in the accompanying chart. On the following pages are short job descriptions of the 14 separate jobs. Job descriptions were not made for commission sales personnel. The wage rates of these jobs are as follows:

Position	Dollars Per Hour
Administrative officer	$7.00
Assembler	3.40
Boxer	3.40
Delivery chief	3.90
Driver	3.90
Floral designer	7.00
General manager	7.00
Industrial sales officer	Commission
Production supervisor	6.00
Ribbon tier	3.35
Sales control manager	Commission
Sales manager	7.00
Stock man	3.90
Wedding consultant	7.00

A wage survey was undertaken in the local market area for 3 of the 14 jobs. It was discovered that the current competitive rate for floral designers was $7, for drivers, $4.50, and for boxers, $3.50. With the following job descriptions and this wage survey information, the firm is in a position to develop a job evaluation program.

I **Job title:** General manager   **II** Job code: A

III Number employed: One   **IV** Date: June 30, 1982

V Location: Central Office, Asbury Florist, Inc.

VI Job summary: Plans, organizes, controls, and coordinates the activities of the entire firm within limits established by the board of directors.

VII Duties
  A Daily
    1 Plans progress of business, new enterprises, business procedures, policies, and designs many of the necessary forms.
    2 Advises the administrative officer and wedding consultant on the preparation of sales promotional booklets and pamphlets.
    3 Organizes the entire company, assigns duties, and delegates authority.
    4 Recruits, selects, and trains the managerial force.
    5 Reviews all recommendations for dismissal of employees.
    6 Approves or disapproves all buying expenditures of sales manager and the expenditures of the production supervisor for flowers in excess of $100.
    7 Possesses final authority over expenditures under $1,000.
    8 Handles personally selling accounts in excess of $200.
    9 Supervises generally and consults daily with administrative officer and production supervisor.
    10 Spot-checks quality of production.
    11 Prepares retail price lists with the assistance of the production supervisor and administrative officer.
  B Periodical: Prepares weekly report of progress of business to stockholders.
  C Occasional: None.

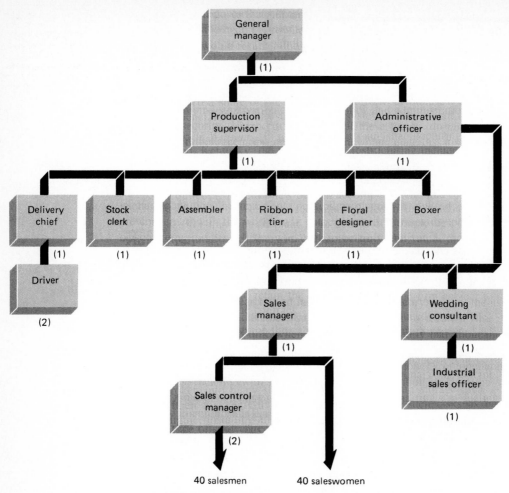

Asbury Florist Corporation.

VIII Job-knowledge requirements: Order procedure, flower code, wholesale and retail prices, characteristics of floral trade, and characteristics of most of the available floral arrangements.

IX Supervision given: Generally supervises administrative officer and production supervisor.

X Working conditions: Vary. Office, production room, and travels.

I **Job title:** Sales control manager   **II** Job code: B

III Number employed: Two   **IV** Date: June 30, 1982

V Location: Administrative and sales department

VI Job summary: Selects, trains, supervises, and compensates a force of 15 to 20 part-time commission salespersons.

VII Duties
    A Daily
80 percent   **1** Selects and trains salespersons in own district.
        2 Contacts salespersons regarding impending social affairs which they are to cover.
        3 Transmits information to salespersons about price, product changes, and delivery.
        4 Holds individual conferences with salespersons to train, orient, and inspire them to greater sales efforts.
        5 Encourages salespersons to collect delinquent accounts.
5 percent   **6** Maintains a work sheet showing schedule and plans for all impending social affairs within district.

    B Periodical
15 percent   **1** Obtains settlement sheet of district sales and receipts from sales manager weekly, and discusses past week's activities.
        2 Informs salespersons of delinquent accounts.
        3 Receives commission weekly from administrative officer, from which the salespersons are paid the commission due them.

    C Occasional: None.

VIII Job-knowledge requirements: Retail prices, flower code, flower characteristics, and delivery schedule.

IX Supervision given: Supervises generally 15 to 20 part-time commission salespersons.
Supervision received: Very general from sales manager.

X Working conditions: Vary.

I **Job title:** Floral designer   **II** Job code: C

III Number employed: One   **IV** Date: June 30, 1982

V Location: Production department

VI Job summary: Designs and fashions bouquets, corsages, sprays, wreaths, and fancy floral designs, determining what flowers to use or using flowers requested by customer.

VII Duties
    A Daily
5 percent   **1** Receives order slip from stock man and reads code to determine flower combination desired.
70 percent   **2** Receives flowers from assembler and arranges specified flower combination into a design which varies at the discretion of the designer.*
15 percent   **3** Selects ribbon and attaches maline backing.
5 percent   **4** Clips wire ends and passes order with order slip to boxer.
1 percent   **5** Advises and consults with sales manager, wedding consultant, and

*Examples of flower combinations are sprays, vases, wedding bouquets, fans, special and standard corsages, baskets, boutonnieres, wreaths, blankets, artificial trees, floats, coronet crowns, candelabras, and centerpieces.

industrial sales officer concerning characteristics of various flower combinations.

B Periodical: None.

C Occasional

1 percent   **1**   Decorates church interiors for wedding.

2 percent   **2**   Makes short talks about floral design before various public groups.

1 percent   **3**   Dyes flowers for special purposes.

VIII   Tools and materials used: Table, wire cutters, flowers, maline, ribbon, wire, dye, baskets, vases, arborvitae, picks, moss, pots, water vials, and floral tape.

IX   Supervision given: None.
Supervision received: General from production supervisor.
Work received from: Assembler and stock clerk.
Work delivered to: Boxer.

X   Working conditions: Inside, artificial light, concrete floor, damp.

I   **Job Title:**   Production supervisor   **II**   Job code: D

III   Number employed: One   **IV**   Date: June 30, 1982

V   Location: Production department

VI   Job summary: Plans, organizes, and controls the activities of the production department, purchases flowers, and maintains the stock records.

VII   Duties

A   Daily

80 percent   **1**   Receives order slips and route sheet from wedding consultant and gives route sheet to delivery chief.

     2   Separates orders by date, delivery hour, type of flower, color, and combination, and places on control board.

     3   Supervises and checks production operation and delivery for effectiveness and idleness and adjusts working hours to the work load.

     4   Consults with general manager on plans for immediate future and reports progress.

     5   Inspects for proper "housekeeping" and examines product for quality from time to time.

     6   Records, selects, and trains production department personnel and records their working time each day.

     7   Supervises all maintenance work in the company.

5 percent   **8**   Determines proper stock level for 50 varieties of flowers and calls personally or by telephone to one of several wholesalers to replenish stocks.

     9   Purchases all production room supplies; is final authority on flower and supply orders not to exceed $200.

    10   Checks stock received from vendor against invoices and turns over invoices to administrative officer.

5 percent   **11**   Maintains stock record daily, showing amount received, amounts on hand, amount utilized, and scrappage.

B   Periodical: None.

C Occasional

5 percent   **1**   Plans layout of production room and arrangement of work places.

5 percent   **2**   Performs various types of maintenance work, such as painting, construction of tables, etc.

VIII   Job-knowledge requirements: Current market prices of flowers, quality of flowers, flower characteristics of floral combinations, order procedure, production method, and flower code.

IX   Supervision given: Supervises closely stock clerk, assembler, ribbon tier, and boxer.
       Medium—delivery chief.
       General—floral designer.
   Supervision received: Rather general from general manager.

X   Working conditions: Inside, concrete floor, artificial light, damp.

I   **Job title:**   Boxer   **II**   Job code: E

III   Number employed: One   **IV**   Date: June 30, 1982

V   Location: Production department

VI   Job summary: Receives flower combination from floral designer, sprays with water, and boxes, attaching order slip and cards.

VII   Duties

   A   Daily

10 percent   **1**   Makes up boxes from flattened-out cardboard.

20 percent   **2**   Lines interior of box with florist green wrapping papers.

20 percent   **3**   Receives flowers from designer, and sprays with water using cotton squares if necessary.

10 percent   **4**   Places flower combination into cellophane bag and/or box.

20 percent   **5**   Places artificial green grass, personal card, and corsage pin in box.

19 percent   **6**   Attaches address label, company label, and c.o.d. slip, if any, to box and passes to delivery chief with order slip.

1 percent   **7**   Assists in cleanup of production room.

   B   Periodical: None.

   C   Occasional: None.

VIII   Tools and materials used: Table, water spray, boxes, paper, flowers, corsage pins, artificial grass, cellophane bags, cotton, personal cards, address labels, and company labels.

IX   Supervision given: None.
   Supervision received: Rather close from production supervisor.
   Work received from: Floral designer.
   Work delivered to: Delivery chief.

X   Working conditions: Inside, concrete floor, damp, artificial light.

I   **Job title:**   Wedding consultant   **II**   Job code: F

III   Number employed: One   **IV**   Date: June 30, 1982

V   Location: Administrative and sales department

VI   Job summary: Collects information of approaching weddings, makes contacts, and handles flower arrangements and procedure for entire wedding. Also performs general office work.

VII   Duties

     A   Daily

65 percent   **1**   Gleans information concerning future weddings from newspapers, salespersons, etc., and files.

     2   Telephones brides and informs them of services offered and makes an appointment if possible.

     3   Calls at home of bride to discuss wedding details.

     4   Prepares a personal data card for each wedding.

     5   Advises as to wedding gowns, colors, floral decorations, wedding procedure, etiquette, etc.

     6   Attends wedding to supervise arrangements.

25 percent   **7**   Receives flower orders from customers by telephone and from sales manager.

     8   Prepares c.o.d. slips, address labels, personal cards, and attaches to original copy of order, giving c.o.d. list to administrative officer.

     9   Delivers original copies to production supervisor and files duplicates.

     10   Receives original copies from production supervisor after delivery and checks against duplicates to guard against loss.

     11   Files duplicates in permanent file and sends originals to sales manager.

10 percent   **12**   Answers telephone.

     13   Performs general office work, such as typing letters and filing.

     B   Periodical: None.

     C   Occasional: None.

VIII   Job-knowledge requirements: Order procedure, flower code, flower prices, wedding procedures, and flower characteristics of wedding work.

IX   Supervision given: General to industrial sales officer.

     Supervision received: Rather general from administrative officer.

X   Working conditions: Inside, office, agreeable.

I   **Job title:**   Assembler   **II**   Job code: G

III   Number employed: One   **IV**   Date: June 30, 1982

V   Location: Production department

VI   Job summary: Cuts, strips, wires, and paraffilms* individual flowers before passing to floral designer.

VII   Duties

     A   Daily

1 percent   **1**   Receives flowers from stock clerk.

*¼-in. strips lightly coated with paraffin.

20 percent	**2**	Breaks stems to 1 inch and strips leaves and outer petals.
5 percent	**3**	Attaches one green leaf to roses only.
35 percent	**4**	Wires flower by inserting wire through the calix, and bending to form substitute stem.
35 percent	**5**	Wraps paraffilm strips around calix and down around wire.
1 percent	**6**	Passes flower on floral designer.
1 percent	**7**	Makes up boxes of cut flowers lined with arborvitae or ferns.
1 percent	**8**	Assists in cleanup and production room.

    B Periodical: None.

    C Occasional

1 percent	**1**	Makes up maline backing by bunching an 8- by 6-inch piece of maline in the center and wiring.

VIII Tools and materials used: Table, wire cutters, scissors, flowers, green leaves, paraffilm strips, wire, and maline.

IX Supervision given: None.
Supervision received: Rather close from production supervisor.
Work received from: Stock clerk.
Work delivered to: Floral designer.

X Working conditions: Inside, concrete floor, damp, artificial light.

I **Job title:** Driver   **II** Job code: H

III Number employed: Two   **IV** Date: June 30, 1982

V Location: Production department

VI Job summary: Delivers flower orders to all parts of the city and collects money for c.o.d.s.

VII Duties

    A Daily

5 percent	**1**	Receives load of orders and district assignment from delivery chief.
10 percent	**2**	Maps out a route from delivery addresses of load.
70 percent	**3**	Delivers orders and collects money for c.o.d.s.
5 percent	**4**	Checks in with delivery chief and turns over c.o.d. money or c.o.d. slip, depending upon whether or not the money was collected.

    B Periodical: None.

    C Occasional

10 percent	**1**	Performs various types of maintenance work, such as painting, constructing tables and shelves, making flower gardens, etc., under the supervision of the production supervisor.

VIII Tools and materials used: Automobile or truck, simple maintenance tools, flower order, and money.

IX Supervision given: None.
Supervision received: Medium from delivery chief and production supervisor.
Work received from: Delivery chief.
Work delivered to: Customers.

X Working conditions: Outside, vary.

I **Job title:** Stock clerk   **II** Job code: I

III Number employed: One   **IV** Date: June 30, 1982

V Location: Production department

VI Job summary: Prepares workplace for operation, takes order slips from control board, assembles specified flowers, and passes on to assembler.

VII Duties
   A Daily

10 percent **1** Sets out wire, paraffilm, scissors, wire cutters, etc., on production line in preparation for work.

5 percent **2** Tasks order slips from control board and thereby regulates the flow of production.

70 percent **3** Reads flower code and assembles flowers specified by obtaining them from icebox.

5 percent **4** Delivers flowers to assembler.

5 percent **5** Gives order slip with personal card, address label, and c.o.d. slip attached to floral designer.

5 percent **6** Takes inventory of flowers in icebox daily and reports to production supervisor.

   B Periodical: None.
   C Occasional: None.

VIII Tools and materials used: Table, control board, scissors, cutters, paraffilm, wire, order slip with cards and labels, flowers.

IX Supervision given: None.
   Supervisor received: Rather close from production supervisor.
   Work received from: Production supervisor.
   Work delivered to: Assembler and floral designer.

X Working conditions: Inside, concrete floor, artificial light, damp, and coldness in the icebox

---

I **Job title:** Sales manager   **II** Job code: J

III Number employed: One   **IV** Date: June 30, 1982

V Location: Administrative and sales department

VI Job summary: Selects, trains, and supervises part-time commission salespersons, handles the sales records, bills customers, receives cash in payment of orders, and manages the retail florist shop.

VII Duties
   A Daily

38 percent **1** Receives flower orders from salespersons and customers by telephone or in person.

   2 Prepares orders in duplicate, personal card, address label, and c.o.d. slip, and sends to wedding consultant.

   3 Receives original copy of order from wedding consultant after delivery, and posts in daily sales journal.

4 Files cash order originals in permanent file and charge copies in temporary files pending payment.

5 Receives cash for orders in person or by mail, records in daily sales journal and accounts receivable ledger, and turns over amount daily to administrative officer; varies up to $250.

10 percent 6 Supplies information about current flower offerings and prices to sales control managers and commission salespersons.

2 percent 7 Receives and refers complaints of customers to administrative officer.

3 percent 8 Assists commission to salespersons in solving small sales problems.

15 percent 9 Arranges retail store displays and waits on walk-in trade.

5 percent 10 Receives and files in tickler file information in regard to "remembrance service" and sends out reminder letters on proper dates.

    B Periodical

4 percent 1 Posts unpaid orders to accounts receivable ledger weekly.

1 percent 2 Prepares summary sheet of week's sales and receipts for each of two sales control managers.

5 percent 3 Prepares and sends out bills to unpaid accounts three times monthly.

3 percent 4 Prepares delinquent accounts list and sends to collection agency monthly.

1 percent 5 Prepares monthly report of industrial sales and sends to industrial sales officer.

2 percent 6 Prepares summary sheet of month's sales and receipts for each of 40 salespersons.

    C Occasional

9 percent 1 Recruits, selects, and trains part-time commission salespersons.

1 percent 2 Buys office supplies for entire firm upon authorization of general manager.

1 percent 3 Receives information from convention bureau about future conventions coming to town and contacts convention organizer concerning floral arrangements.

VIII Job-knowledge requirements: Salesperson-account numbers, flower code, flower prices, order procedure, flower characteristics.

  IX Supervision given: Supervises generally two sales control managers and 40 part-time commission salespersons.
Supervision received: Rather general from administrative officer.

   X Working conditions: Inside, office, agreeable.

  I **Job title:**   Ribbon tier   **II** Job code: K

III Number employed: One   **IV** Date: June 30, 1982

  V Location: Production department

 VI Job summary: Ties different-colored ribbon into a standardized bow.

VII Duties
    A Daily

1 percent 1 Receives instructions from production supervisor as to amount and colors of ribbon bows needed for stock.

70 percent 2 Doubles ribbon into 7 or 8 loops and wires in the center to form a bow.

5 percent 3 Places bows into boxes by color and stacks on ribbon table in the production room.

20 percent 4 Makes up maline backing by bunching an 8- by 6-inch piece of maline in the center and wiring.

1 percent 5 Assists in cleanup of production room.

      B Periodical: None.

      C Occasional

3 percent 1 Paints floral baskets.

VIII Tools and materials used: Scissors, table, ribbon, maline, wire, and boxes.

IX Supervision given: None.
Supervision received: Rather close from production supervisor.
Work received from: Production supervisor.
Work delivered to: Floral designer via production ribbon table.

X Working conditions: Inside, artificial light, concrete floor, damp.

I **Job title:** Industrial sales officer   **II** Job code: L

III Number employed: One   **IV** Date: June 30, 1982

V Location: Administrative and sales department

VI Job summary: Telephones officials of industrial firms and party organizers, solicits flower orders, and follows up with a form letter.

VII Duties

      A Daily

85 percent 1 Obtains names of industrial firms from telephone directory.

         2 Telephones officials of firms, introduces self and company, and informs them of special flower offers for industrial accounts.

         3 Follows up first call with a form letter summarizing information given over the telephone.

         4 Adds new firms as work load permits.

         5 Telephones each firm on growing list once each month.

         6 Maintains a file of calls made recording name, time, and type of response.

         7 Drops firms from call list only upon instructions of wedding consultant.

14 percent 8 Gleans information concerning parties, club meetings, and other social functions from daily newspapers.

         9 Telephones organizers of social functions and solicits orders.

      B Periodical

1 percent 1 Recieves and analyzes monthly report from sales manager on amount of sales to industrial accounts.

      C Occasional: None.

VIII Job-knowledge requirements: Flower prices, discounts to industrial concerns, and flower characteristics.

IX Supervision given: None.
    Supervision received: Rather general from wedding consultant.

X Working conditions: Inside, office, agreeable.

I   **Job title:**   Delivery chief   **II** Job code: M

III Number employed: One   **IV** Date: June 30, 1982

V   Location: Production department

VI   Job summary: Separates flower orders by location and time, assigns loads to drivers, supervises delivery, and checks collection of c.o.d.s.

VII Duties
    A Daily

85 percent   **1**   Receives orders from boxer and files order slip temporarily.
          2   Separates orders by district and delivery time and enters order number on route sheet by district of city with driver's name.
          3   Assigns drivers to districts and dispatches with loads at the proper times.
          4   Checks deliveries made against order slips with driver upon his return and collects money for c.o.d.s.
          5   Turns over money order slips to administrative officer.
          6   Returns orders not deliverable to production supervisor.
    B Periodical: None.
    C Occasional

5 percent   **1**   Instructs drivers as to delivery procedure.
5 percent   **2**   Delivers orders.
1 percent   **3**   Assists boxer in making up carboard boxes.
4 percent   **4**   Performs general maintenance work under production supervisor.

VIII Tools and materials used: Order file, route sheet, automobile, flower orders, money, and general-maintenance tools.

IX Supervision given: Rather general supervision of two drivers.
    Supervision received: Medium from production supervisor.
    Work delivered to: Drivers, administrative officer, and production supervisor.

X   Working conditions: Inside, concrete floor, damp, artificial light.

I   **Job title:**   Administrative officer   **II** Job code: N

III Number employed: One   **IV** Date: June 30, 1982

V   Location: Administrative and sales department

VI   Job summary: Handles all advertising, complaints of customers, office management, company payroll, all receipts and disbursals of cash, and special administrative tasks.

VII Duties
    A Daily

30 percent   **1**   Prepares advertising copy for local newspapers.

		2	Selects the advertising media.
30 percent		3	Supervises the office force.
		4	Receives c.o.d. list from wedding consultant and checks against cash or c.o.d. slips received from delivery chief.
		5	Assists wedding consultant in order writing and checking against deliveries.
20 percent		6	Adjusts customer complaints.
		7	Performs miscellaneous administrative duties such as dealing with company attorney about corporate matters, handling leases, creditor adjustments, etc.
		8	Administers the $25 petty cash fund.
10 percent		9	Receives all cash from customers, directly or through sales manager, deposits in bank, and files deposit slips.
		10	Pays all company obligations with general manager's approval.

B Periodical

7 percent   **1** Receives time slips from production supervisor and prepares and pays company payroll bimonthly.

3 percent   **2** Computes and pays, with assistance of sales manager, the commissions of the sales control managers weekly, and the salespersons monthly.

C Occasional: None.

VIII Job-knowledge requirements: Order procedure, flower code, flower characteristics, income tax provisions, social security tax, workers' compensation tax.

IX Supervision given: Generally supervises sales manager and wedding consultant.
Supervision received: Rather general from general manager.

X Working conditions: Inside, office, agreeable.

Instructions:

1 Using simple ranking techniques, rank the 14 jobs in order of worth.

2 Obtain the *class* ranking by averaging all individual student rankings.

3 Compute the correlation coefficient between your rank and the class rank.

$$1 - \frac{6 \times \Sigma D^2}{N(N^2 - 1)} \qquad \begin{array}{l} N = 14 \\ D = \text{differences for each job} \end{array}$$

4 Prepare a wage diagram with jobs arranged along the abscissa and dollars on the ordinate. Use the class ranking of jobs.

     a Use equal spacing of jobs on the abscissa.

     b Plot all present rates leaving out the two commission rates.

     c Plot the three wage-surveyed rates.

     d Draw freehand a straight line that comes closest to all three of the rates plotted in *c*. You can now compare the present rate structure with the competitive trend line.

5 Prepare a second wage diagram, using the class ranking of jobs.

     a Use variable spacing of jobs on abscissa (see Figure 12-5). One can use the fractional averages for each job obtained during the class averaging process as guides in spacing.

b   Plot the three wage-surveyed rates.

c   Draw freehand a straight line that comes closest to all three of the rates plotted in *c*.

d   Interpolate new wage rates for all jobs (including the commission jobs), by reading up from location on abscissa to the wage trend line.

e   Prepare list of new job rates for all 14 jobs.

Case: George Gridley*

George Gridley secured his college training at a large state university. For his first 2 years, he followed a mechanical engineering curriculum; he then switched to commerce. His major course work centered on motion and time study.

Upon graduation he was hired by Wellington corporation, a large Chicago firm employing 2,500 workers, to work in its standards department. In Gridley's words:

> I was really in a good spot when I graduated. You see, I'm both an engineering and commerce major. You can't beat that combination. I'm just a natural for a standards department because I have the business know-how together with my engineering. Wellington had the best spot for me so I took the job because I could get ahead fastest there. Their interviewer told me when he came over to school to interview us that I had a rare combination his company was glad to find. I went up to Chicago for some additional interviews. I liked them and they liked me, so I took the job.

Gridley reported for work 2 weeks after graduation, having arrived in Chicago 3 days before starting work in order to find a place to live. After the usual processing in the personnel department, he was taken up to the standards department to the office of its chief, Mr. McGuire, who had interviewed George before he was hired. McGuire kept George waiting for 10 minutes and then turned to him. George described this meeting.

> I just sat there in McGuire's office watching him work on some papers, not knowing quite what to expect. Finally, he turned to me and said, "Well, Mr. Gridley, are you all set to go to work?" He never did call any of us younger fellows in the department anything but "mister." He told me that there would be a department staff meeting that morning when he would introduce me to everyone. Meantime he gave me the company standards manual and told me I ought to spend several days getting familiar with it. He called his secretary and told her to take me to my desk and get me all the supplies I needed; that ended the interview. He certainly was a cold fish and all the time I worked for him I never could warm up to him. I didn't get any assignment at all the first week but just sat at my desk and worked over the manual. I got to know several of the fellows around me and we went to lunch together.

Gridley was finally assigned to work up the time study on a simple assembly of refrigerator door handles being assembled in a department in which Mason was foreman. When McGuire gave him the assignment, George was so glad to be working he failed to respond with any questions when given the opening by McGuire's query, "Any questions?"

*Robert Dubin, *Human Relations in Administration*, 2d ed., Prentice-Hall, Inc., Englewood Cliffs, N.J., 1961, pp. 475–478. Used with permission.

I felt so glad at getting a real job at last that I just said, "I think I can handle this easily, Sir," and left his office. I went and got the drawings for the assembly and studied them for a few hours. Then I went down to Mason's department and told him Mr. McGuire had given me the assignment of working up the refrigerator door handle job. He said that was all right with him. Mason was a crusty old guy who didn't seem to have much education at all. Nobody could remember when he started with the company and he'd been a foreman a long time. I got out the drawings and wanted to talk to him about the job but he sort of brushed them aside and started asking personal questions about me. I figured maybe he couldn't read drawings too easily, so I didn't try that approach again. After I told him about myself and my education he said, "Well, this ought to be easy for you. Let's go over and look at the job."

There were ten workers assembling the door handles, working for the second day on this job. The first thing that struck George about the job was the casual attitude that seemed to be evident, and the pronounced talking and minor horseplay that continued after Mason and Gridley came over to observe. Mason left almost immediately, saying to the group, "This is Gridley from standards on this new job. He's new with the company."

In talking about it later, Gridley recalled the subsequent developments of that day with some discomfort. He knew that under the union contract, work on a new job was paid for at a guaranteed rate, until the standards and price were set. Then the work went on an incentive basis. But he was scarcely prepared for the complete irreverence with which he was greeted.

Almost the first remark I heard from the group was, "Well, here is the genius who is going to show us how to bust this job wide open without any work at all." You can imagine how the others laughed and what a spot that put me in. I made some comment about "just doing a job" and began observing the assembly work. It seemed to me there was pretty poor discipline in a company where the workers made remarks like that. It got me so that I just automatically reached for a cigarette and started to light it. That same worker saw me and said, "Say, haven't they told you that only fireproof cigarettes are permitted here?" Then I remembered the no-smoking rule. I was so mad by then I just went off to the washroom and smoked. Those damned ignorant workers sure take a lot of pleasure in making life miserable for their betters.

That afternoon George went back to the department and began observing the operation, and made arrangements with Mason and the union steward to time the job on the following morning. Gridley made no suggestions for any assembly procedures changes, figuring he would time the job "as is" rather than force himself to discuss with Mason and the workers some changes he thought might be useful. The principal saving he could see was in proper flow of materials to each work station and he planned to take this into account in working out some standard procedures and estimated prices based upon them. The time study was made the next day as planned.

Gridley immediately took the data back to his desk and spent that day and the following preparing his report. After waiting still another day getting it typed up, he submitted it to McGuire. The figures showed a price of 60 cents a dozen for assembly. McGuire sat down immediately with the report and read it over. It took him only about 10 minutes to go over it, saying not a word to Gridley, who had been asked to wait. Then as Gridley reported:

He finally looked up at me and said, "Mr. Gridley, this is a good job. From your report I feel your operating scheme is good and your time data shows consistent results. I have Mason's estimate on the job some place. Let me get it." He got out a file and found a memo sheet that had some handwriting on it. "Yes," he said, "here is his estimate. You know in this company we often have foremen estimate prices on simple jobs, just in case we can't handle them up here because of a work load. Then we let the foreman's estimate ride. Mason says 62 cents on that job. You never know how these foremen figure those things out. Mason has done a lot of these refrigerator handle assemblies in his department in the past. Since our study is so close to his figure, I think I'll let his stand. There is only a little better than 3 per cent difference. This is no reflection on you, understand that, Mr. Gridley. I just feel in this instance it would be valuable to the company and to our operations in the standards department to let Mason think his estimate and our study agree."

Can you imagine anything like that? Here I really put out to give them a job and then McGuire goes ahead and uses some off-the-cuff estimate of a foreman who can't even read prints. That doesn't seem to me to be very good management. Does management really want brains around here or are they just going to run the company by-guess-by-gosh all the time?

Questions

1. How scientific is time study? Is George justified in his views of the technique?

2. Assuming that George is correct, what does McGuire get in return for the extra 2¢? Is his decision beneficial to the company?

Case: The Ineffective Incentive

George Morales had worked at the Adams Company for 8 years in the extrusion press department. He had progressed from his break-in job of laborer to sawyer, leadout, and the top job of heater and press operator. The functions of the press operator are to operate the press, act as leadman of the crew, and arrange his work into an orderly sequence. George had spent most of his time on a press of 2,500-ton capacity, although presses of larger capacities were available.

An incentive system had been installed in the press area and was based on the load and extrusion cycles to determine the standard minutes. The actual time to perform the job was divided into the standard minutes to determine the efficiency of the crew.

George had performed satisfactorily for a long period of time in all classifications, particularly in that of operator. He was considered as having a pleasing personality and being an efficient operator with an average efficiency of 116 percent, an excellent co-ordinator of his four-man crew, and highly concerned with the quality of the work he and his crew turned out. He was in good health, and his attendance record was considered perfect.

The firm's profits have been decreasing the past 18 months owing to the effects of stringent competition. Management decided to investigate the methods of performing the work in each department, the objective being to improve methods wherever possible to decrease costs. Some layouts in the press area were modified to the extent that crew sizes could be reduced. George's crew was reduced by one crew member.

About this time, George's attitude and performance changed markedly for the worse. His immediate supervisor found it necessary to caution him several times, first on the quality of his work, then his grouchy attitude which verged on insubordination, and finally his attendance. His supervisor could not determine any satisfactory reason for this situation. It appeared to him that George was just not trying or that he was not paying attention to what he was doing. The supervisor was also unable to determine the reason for the grouchy attitude, except George saying he "didn't feel good."

The supervisor didn't have much time to let the situation ride because the poor quality of George's work was beginning to show up in other process centers. This caused his own superior to get into the act. When the poor quality began reaching the final inspection department, "the roof fell in." The plant superintendent, the general superintendent, and the department supervisor were now on the supervisor's neck. An immediate meeting was held with the supervisor by the plant's top management where he unfolded his meager story. Since this was not an adequate explanation, it was decided to bring George into the meeting. While waiting for him to appear, the general superintendent convincingly advanced his theory that George was offering resistance to the change in methods. The department supervisor objected to his theory since no trouble had been experienced in prior similar situations. When George arrived, he was asked to state why his production had worsened, but he declined to offer any more information than that he had given to his supervisor. He was informed that he would have to improve immediately or be dismissed. He was told he would be given 1 week to make the transition in recognition of his long period of satisfactory service. The proper union officials were informed of all the facts and the proposition. The union officers were perplexed about the change in George but, being aware of his poor performance, reluctantly went along with the arrangement.

The department supervisor was the sole individual not in agreement with the rest. He first quizzed the immediate supervisor again and obtained no new information. He felt somewhat disappointed in him for not being closer to the man and having some idea of what had caused the sudden change. The department supervisor then talked to several union leaders and other members of the organization. None had any additional information. George had been part of the gang up to the time his work performance changed; since then he had become a lone wolf. The union and informal group leaders were aware of the seriousness of his situation if he did not change, and felt that they had let the department foreman down in not being able to shed any light on the case.

The first 3 working days of the week-long waiting period went by with no change. On the fourth day the department supervisor ran into George in the restroom. He asked him what he intended to do. George replied that he guessed they would just have to fire him. The department supervisor looked at his worried, strained face—the previously happy youth looked as though he had aged many years in a short time. The department supervisor asked George what he and his wife were doing about this problem. This question caused George to break down completely; he even cried. A private place was found, and he and George talked. His wife had left him. This was the man's problem. He refrained from telling anyone of this because he had bragged so much of the good relationship he and his wife had, and now that she had left him, he was ashamed to mention it. The department head could do little but sympathize with him. Remarkably enough, George's performance improved the next day.

The department supervisor informed his superiors of what had happened. The plant superintendent was elated, but the general superintendent, while saying the department supervisor had done a good job, was very cool. The recovery for George was slow but positive. The general supervisor continued to "ride" both the department foreman and George about the slow recovery. The general supervisor's attitude was that this company was in business to make a profit and was not a psychological correctional institution. The general supervisor persisted in taking some disciplinary action. The department supervisor resisted and won out at the expense of some lowering of status in the eyes of his superior.

The operator fully recovered his composure in another few weeks and approached his jovial former self. He again talked and joked with his fellow workers. His efficiency returned to his prior average and his quality was again high.

Questions

1. Why did the general superintendent believe that George's behavior was caused by resistance to changes in methods?

2. Should George have received some type of discipline for his declining quality of work, grouchy attitude, and poor attendance?

3. What do you think of the behavior of the immediate supervisor? If you were his superintendent, would you have permitted defiance of your wishes in this case?

PART FIVE

INTEGRATION

It is important that the employee not only be *able* to work (development) but be *willing* to work as well. This willingness is based largely on management's ability to integrate the interests and needs of its employees with the objectives of the organization. Therefore, we must first examine the nature of these employee needs (Chapter 15). Secondly, we must examine how these individual needs can be integrated in the climate of a business organization (Chapter 16) as well as tapping the collaborative inclinations of working groups (Chapter 17). One major and powerful group with which many organizations must contend is the labor union (Chapter 18). The fundamental process of integrating the union takes the form of collective bargaining (Chapter 19). Finally, perfect integration would lead to complete agreement and absence of conflict, a state that is highly unlikely. Consequently, we must examine situations, exemplified by grievances and disciplinary action, in which either the organization or the employee is dissatisfied (Chapter 20).

chapter 15

Nature of the Human Resource

In the sequence of operative personnel functions followed in this text, we have thus far procured our employee, developed the skill and ability to do the job assigned, and determined the manner and amount of monetary compensation. To some, our task would appear to be at an end. The employee would naturally perform the job well since she or he has been properly placed, trained, and compensated. In recent years, however, there has been a growing recognition of the need for particular efforts in dealing with the attitude of an employee. It is not enough that one is able to work; one must also be willing to work. This subject is of such importance and difficulty that this chapter and the following five are devoted to a discussion of the philosophies, approaches, and methods of stimulating a will to work productively and cooperatively.

IMPORTANCE OF HUMAN RELATIONS

As suggested by the title "Integration," there must be a reasonable merger of person and organization if effective action is to result. When the needs of human beings meet the needs of organization, conflict often occurs. It is the purpose of the chapters in Part Five to examine the fundamental nature of the human resource, integration of this resource (as individuals or groups) with organizations, and coping with the inevitable conflicts that ensue. Managerial activities in this regard are termed "human relations." The goal is effecting a reasonable integration leading to productive and creative collaboration toward mutual objectives. The manager will therefore require knowledge and skill in such underlying disciplines as psychology, sociology, anthropology, and ethology in attempting to understand and cope with problems in human relations.

As suggested in Figure 15-1, concern for integration of interests would lie in section *B* where activities conducive to both organization and employee interests would be undertaken. Can an organization be managed in such a way that what is good for the employee is also good for the organization? Research and experience indicate that there is a healthy overlapping of interests in such programs as flexitime, job enlargement and enrichment, semiautonomous work groups, participative decision making, job evaluation, variable compensation plans, and so on. The greater the overlap, the more productivity would coincide with employee satisfaction. There are a number of reports from industry con-

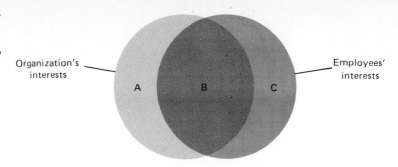

Organization's interests

Employees' interests

A — Advances organization's interests but not employees' interests
B — Advances interests of both organization and employee
C — Advances employees' interests but not organization's interests

FIGURE 15-1 Integration of interests.

cerning an increasing overlap of interests. General Motors has increased the number of social psychologists operating in the field by 2,000 percent.[1] Procter and Gamble has one plant with production costs 50 percent lower than any comparable plant in the company or the industry, a situation that is largely attributed to humanistic practices. Specific evidence of such practices is difficult to come by, for the firms regard their human resources programs as proprietary information just as valuable as new product research. When successful, they tend to decrease accidents, absenteeism, turnover, and operating errors, while simultaneously raising morale, quality, and productivity. At the minimum such programs should prevent undesirable behavior such as sabotage, slow-down, insubordination, strikes, and the use of drugs and alcohol on the job.

Though some theorists suggest there can be a complete overlap of interests, it is more probable that there are situations depicted by sections *A* and *C* in Figure 15-1. Organizations will require things of employees that they would prefer to avoid, such as assignment to narrow and repetitive tasks, meeting high output standards, acceptance of managerial decisions, and so on. For this reason, all organizations have disciplinary action programs as well as some freedom to dispense with the services of particular employees. There are also certain things that employees desire which the organization is reluctant to provide, such as increased wages, totally safe working conditions, time off with pay, insured pension payoffs, shorter work weeks, premium pay for overtime, and so on. If it is concluded that these items will not contribute to greater organizational productivity, then their provision must issue from external pressures.

In general, activities in Section *C* will issue from (1) outside pressures from government, (2) outside pressures from labor unions, and (3) "outside" pressures from the manager's code of ethics. Throughout this text, we have cited the numerous federal and state laws that require private organizations to meet certain employee needs. Their number and content might lead one to believe that Section *C* is larger than Section *B*. In later chapters, we will examine the outside pressures of the organized labor union. These two external pressure points have had much to do with the rise in stature of the key person who must deal with them—the personnel manager.

[1]Ted Mills, "Human Resources—Why the New Concern?" *Harvard Business Review*, vol. 53, no. 2, March-April 1975, p. 125.

Finally, observation of managerial behavior leads one to believe that all decisions are *not* made in the interest of organizational productivity and profits. Employees are often kept on jobs beyond their useful lives simply because of a manager's personal code of ethics. As indicated earlier, hired professional managers are more likely than owner-managers to spend money in the area of social responsibility. Thus, the four major forces that lead managers to become vitally concerned with human relations activities are (1) possible improvements in productivity and effectiveness, (2) governmental intervention, (3) union intervention, and (4) personal codes of ethics.

NATURE OF HUMAN NEEDS

To observe the behavior of a person is one thing; to understand it is another; and to influence that behavior toward a certain direction is still a third problem. Understanding and influencing human behavior require knowledge of human needs. Most psychologists are in agreement that human behavior is not completely disorganized and without motivation. The human personality is composed of multiple elements that are related to effect some degree of apparent balance.

The needs of human beings can be classified into three categories: physiological, social, and egoistic. *Physiological needs,* often termed primary, are those that issue from the necessity to sustain life—food, water, air, rest, sex, shelter, and the like. The "economic man" model assumes that such needs are the sole needs of people. In addition to meeting these basic and fundamental needs, one also must be assured that they will *continue* to be met. Thus, security is a vital need of a high priority to most people. When threatened, as it is by mechanization, automation, and economic recession, it gives rise to much and strongly motivated activity.

The remaining two types of needs are often termed secondary since they are more nebulous and intangible. They vary in intensity from one person to another, much more than do the primary needs. In the *social* category are the needs of (1) physical association and contact, (2) love and affection, and (3) acceptance. Most people are gregarious and desire to live with other people. Physical contact, however, is not enough. People feel a need for love and affection from at least a few other human beings. Thus, we form and maintain ties of family and friendships, relationships that are often vitally affected by policies and practices of the employing organization.

In addition to physical contact and affection, human beings feel a need for acceptance by and affiliation with some group or groups. It has long been noted that modern society has tended toward the formation of more and more groups and that a single individual is usually a member of multiple groups. The need for acceptance and social approval is also reflected in such factors as styles, fashions, traditions, mores, and codes. It is a strong need that provides one of the cornerstones of any organized society.

Egoistic needs are derived from the necessity of viewing one's self or ego in a certain manner. Among the identifiable egoistic needs are the following: (1) recognition, (2) dominance, (3) independence, and (4) achievement. Though a person needs reasonable acceptance by a group, one usually does not wish to merge with it to the point of losing personal identity. We are often caught between two somewhat conflicting needs, one of which requires merger, the other separation. If one accepts a promotion to supervisor, thereby gratifying a need of the ego, one must forgo the association of many old friends, thereby frustrating a social need.

As one matures, a need for dominance often becomes apparent. Dominance may well be a continuation of the need for recognition with the ultimate objective of achieving autonomy and independence. The drive for the formation of labor unions, for example, does not issue solely from physiological needs. In many instances, well-paid employees voted overwhelmingly for a union, which could serve to provide them with the dignity of independence necessary to their self-esteem.

Many psychologists contend that the highest need of the human being is that of achievement or self-actualization. It encompasses not only the ability to accomplish, but the need for actual achievement of something in life. The job or task is the major source of satisfaction for this need.

Conscious or unconscious needs set up in an individual certain tensions that stimulate behavior that will relieve those tensions. The objective of behavioral acts is to gratify these needs. If the person is able to satisfy needs in a manner that is acceptable to both the self and society, one is termed "adjusted." If, on the other hand, the person is unable to satisfy a particular need, or is able to gratify it only in a manner that is unacceptable to society, she or he is termed "maladjusted." Thus, behavior is a process of adjusting to certain human needs. The goal of this adjustment process is satisfaction.

Maladjustment results when human needs are not attained, are attained with great difficulty, or are attained in a manner not approved by society. Typical examples of behavior indicating maladjustment are frequent changes in jobs, withdrawal, daydreaming, jealousy, desire for excessive attention, excessive complaining, bragging, and lying.

Some needs cannot be satisfied in *any* manner by the individual; tensions are not relieved; and the result is termed "frustration." A well-known story will illustrate the essential nature of frustration. While two men were drinking in a bar late one night, they got into an argument over the meaning of the terms "irritation," "aggravation," and "frustration." In order to get his point across, one of the men offered to demonstrate the fundamental distinction among the terms. He walked to a telephone and dialed a number at random. After several rings, a very tired, sleepy voice said, "Hello!" Our man of empirical research said, "Hello! Is Joe there?" The sleepy voice growled that there was no one there by that name, and the connection was broken abruptly. "That," said our man, "is an example of irritation." After waiting a period of thirty to forty minutes, he dialed the same number again, and asked the same question, "Is Joe there?" The response this time was considerably more intensified. After much yelling and shouting, the connection was broken. "That is an example of aggravation." He waited a period of thirty or forty minutes to allow the "guinea pig" to go back to sleep, then dialed the same number, but this time said, "Hello. This is Joe. Any messages for me?" There was complete silence for a long minute before the explosion. That was frustration.

Frustration is often recognized by certain types of behavior such as aggression, regression, fixation, and resignation. *Aggression* usually occurs when the person is attempting to accomplish something that he or she is not capable of achieving. Our guinea pig in the above experiment is unable to get to the man in the bar. Since aggression usually involves an attack upon the obstructing barrier, it is highly likely that the telephone took a beating. A worker in the plant may take out his or her frustration on a machine by abusing it.

Regression is a type of behavior that is exemplified when the person resorts to acts of an immature type. Unreasonable complaining and crying help to relieve some of this frustration, but such behavior has adverse effects upon associates. *Fixation* is an attempt to gratify a need in a manner that has been proved to be worthless. In searching for lost car keys, for example, we tend to look in the same place over and over again, even though we know they were not there the first time. *Resignation* involves complete surrender. Satisfaction of needs is impossible, but there is no unreasonable attack upon obstruction, resorting to tears, or repetition of valueless behavior. Resignation is one of the latter stages of frustration and in an extreme case borders on serious mental illness.

THE NEED TO UNDERSTAND WHY

All managers have a need to explain the behavior of their subordinates in order to provide the basis for such activities as performance evaluation and disciplinary action. Despite its complexity, perhaps the one most useful global generalization is to recognize that there is reason for all behavior. Though a particular act may appear to be "insane" to the manager, she or he should search for the logic behind it. In so doing, the manager acts as a type of naive scientist in drawing conclusions about the behavior of others.

As suggested in Figure 15-2, managers usually attribute behavior to two fundamental sources: (1) the subordinate's basic personality and (2) the characteristics of the situation. Research substantiates the thesis that most managers tend to overestimate the power of personality traits and underestimate the influence of situational characteristics. For example, if the subordinate fails at an assigned task, the manager is prone to blame the subordinate's deficiencies and downgrade the obstacles that exist in the environment. Some portions of the personality are deemed reasonably stable, while the degree of effort expended, for example, is more variable. Similarly, certain characteristics of the situation are fairly stable, while other characteristics are somewhat less predictable. As an example of the latter, managers have been awarded large bonuses for accomplishments that are largely a matter of being lucky enough to be at the right place at the right time.

In research dealing with attribution theory, findings such as the following have been discovered:[2]

1. The greater the empathy of a manager for a subordinate, the more likely that an undesirable result will be attributed to the situation. Experienced supervisors recommend more changes in the environment than do the inexperienced.

2. The more inappropriate the subordinate action, the more likely that it will be attributed to the actor. For example, using drugs while working on an assembly line is more likely to be attributed to a character defect than it is to the possibility that the pressures of the assembly line caused the need for escape.

[2]Jean M. Bartunek, "Why Did You Do That? Attribution Theory in Organizations," *Business Horizons*, vol. 24, no. 5, September-October 1981, pp. 66–71.

FIGURE 15-2 Factors to which managers attribute behavior.

PERSONALITY CHARACTERISTICS		SITUATIONAL CHARACTERISTICS	
Stable	Unstable	Stable	Unstable
1. Ability	1. Effort	1. Task difficulty	1. Luck
2. Temperament	2. Moods	2. Technology	2. Competition
3. Etc.	3. Etc.	3. Etc.	3. Etc.

3. It is easier for the manager to assume that the subordinate is responsible than it is to investigate the total situation. It requires less work to reprimand a subordinate for an undesirable act than to change certain organizational practices that may have led to the act.

4. When subordinate acts result in success, managers are prone to assume the credit as an important influence in the situation. When acts result in failure, the responsibility is more often given to the subordinate.

5. The more serious the failure, the more likely the responsibility is attributed to the subordinate.

6. Successful acts by subordinates who are liked by the manager are typically attributed to the subordinate. Unsuccessful acts by such subordinates are typically attributed to situational obstacles.

7. Managers tend to use their own behavior as a basis for judging the normality of subordinate behavior.

In general, it is contended that people are seen as fundamental causes too frequently, while the situation is allocated too little influence as a cause of behavior. Rather than constantly searching for the "villain" in a problem, concern should be given to the possibility that the villain is in reality a *victim* of the situation.

HUMAN MODELS PROPOSED BY ORGANIZATION PSYCHOLOGISTS

It has often been stated, "Tell me your basic view of what people are, and I'll tell you how you will manage." The statement implies that managers do develop and utilize a basic "human model" in their general approach to subordinates. It also implies that there are multiple models of humanity rather than just one accepted by all. In this section, we shall review the models proposed by four major organization psychologists. In a survey of business firms, one researcher discovered that six psychologists were very well known by many businessmen: Abraham Maslow, Douglas McGregor, Chris Argyris, Frederick Herzberg, Rensis Likert, and Robert Blake.[3] The first four have proposed fundamental conceptions of the nature of human beings, each of which is outlined in Figure 15-3. It will be noted in further discussion that though details differ, there is much in common among the "self-actualized" human of Maslow, the "theory Y" person of McGregor, the "mature" being of Argyris, and the "motivated" person of Herzberg. The last two psychologists, Likert and Blake, have developed specific *leadership styles,* System IV and 9,9 management, that can be utilized if one wishes to manage on the basis of the human models proposed by the first four. These style frameworks will be discussed in the following chapter.

---

[3]Harold M. Rush, "Behavioral Science: Concepts and Management Application," *Studies in Personnel Policy No. 216*, National Industrial Conference Board, New York, 1969.

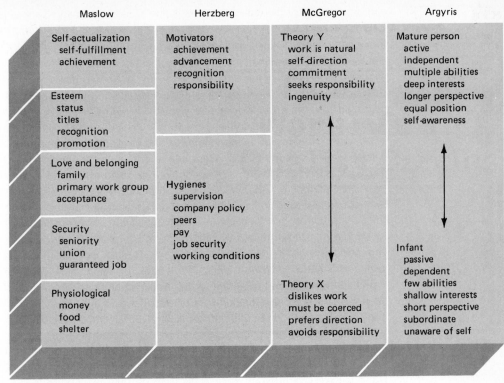

Maslow	Herzberg	McGregor	Argyris

Maslow:
- Self-actualization
  - self-fulfillment
  - achievement
- Esteem
  - status
  - titles
  - recognition
  - promotion
- Love and belonging
  - family
  - primary work group
  - acceptance
- Security
  - seniority
  - union
  - guaranteed job
- Physiological
  - money
  - food
  - shelter

Herzberg:
- Motivators
  - achievement
  - advancement
  - recognition
  - responsibility
- Hygienes
  - supervision
  - company policy
  - peers
  - pay
  - job security
  - working conditions

McGregor:
- Theory Y
  - work is natural
  - self-direction
  - commitment
  - seeks responsibility
  - ingenuity
- Theory X
  - dislikes work
  - must be coerced
  - prefers direction
  - avoids responsibility

Argyris:
- Mature person
  - active
  - independent
  - multiple abilities
  - deep interests
  - longer perspective
  - equal position
  - self-awareness
- Infant
  - passive
  - dependent
  - few abilities
  - shallow interests
  - short perspective
  - subordinate
  - unaware of self

FIGURE 15-3 A comparison of human models.

MASLOW'S NEED HIERARCHY

The need hierarchy proposed by Abraham Maslow is perhaps the most widely accepted model of the human being. He suggests the following order of priority of fundamental needs:[4]

1. Basic physiological needs
2. Safety and security
3. Love
4. Esteem
5. Self-actualization

Since the physiological needs are classified as primary, they are, of course, given first priority. "Man lives by bread alone when there is no bread."[5] If a person is starving,

---

[4]A. H. Maslow, "A Theory of Human Motivation," *Psychological Review*, vol. 50, no. 4, July 1943, pp. 370–396.

[5]Ibid., p. 375.

only food occupies the mind. As soon as one need is reasonably well satisfied, a second need becomes apparent; the person forgets that she or he was starving, and now starts to be concerned about a need that was formerly of less significance. In Maslow's hierarchy, one now becomes aware of the need for *safety and security.* Human beings are motivated by *unsatisfied needs,* not by those that have been gratified. The desire for safety and security is met by such things as an orderly society, job tenure, insurance, religion, and the like. People are never completely satisfied on any need level, but a reasonable amount of gratification of first-priority needs must be forthcoming if they are to perceive a lower-priority need. Maslow suggests that an average citizen might be 85 percent satisfied in physiological needs, 70 percent in safety needs, 50 percent in love needs, 40 percent in the self-esteem category, and 10 percent in self-actualization needs.[6]

Once the necessities for continued existence have been met, the three higher needs of lower priority come into prominence. The need for *love* includes the need for affection and the desire for association with others. The need for *esteem* includes the desire for social approval, self-assertion, and self-esteem. Gratification of the need for esteem contributes to a feeling of self-confidence, worth, and capability. The final need indicated in the list, that of *self-actualization,* refers to the desire for self-fulfillment and achievement. A person desires actualization in that in which he or she has capabilities. This is the highest-level need and has lowest priority. It is not a motivator of behavior until and unless the needs of love, self-esteem, social approval, and self-assertion are fairly well satisfied.

This hierarchy of needs helps to explain certain mistakes of management as well as to justify certain other philosophies. For example, the firm that embarks upon an elaborate personnel services program without the basis of a fair and competitive wage structure is usually wasting its efforts and money. It is also significant to note that company appeals for employee cooperation and loyalty fall on deaf ears when a reasonable degree of security has not been provided.

Some field research has been done that tends to substantiate this hierarchical concept of need perception. In contrasting the levels of need satisfaction of lower- and middle-level managers, it was discovered that the former perceive significantly less need fulfillment in security, esteem, and autonomy.[7] Both groups perceived greater deficiencies in the low-priority categories (autonomy and self-actualization) than in the higher-priority categories (security and social approval). Contrary to expectations, both groups were equally dissatisfied in the self-actualization category. Review of eleven research projects led to the conclusion that "there is a relatively stable pattern of studies that indicate an overall positive association between organizational level and need satisfaction."[8] Admittedly, the level of organization structure is not the only factor affecting need satisfaction, but the differences discovered lend some support to the concept of a hierarchy. It has also been found that top managers in organizations with many levels report greater satisfaction than top managers in flatter organizations. Conversely, middle- and lower-level managers are more satisfied in the flatter structures than are their counterparts in tall structures.

---

[6]Abraham Maslow, *Motivation and Personality,* Harper & Row, Publishers, Incorporated, New York, 1954, chap. 5.

[7]Lyman W. Porter, "Job Attitudes in Management: I. Perceived Deficiencies in Need Fulfillment as a Function of Job Level," *Journal of Applied Psychology,* vol. 46, no. 6, 1962, pp. 375–384.

[8]L. L. Cummings and Chris J. Berger, "Organization Structure: How Does It Influence Attitudes and Performance?" *Organizational Dynamics,* vol. 5, no. 2, Autumn 1976, p. 37.

The Maslow hierarchy of needs, though widely publicized and accepted by theorists and practitioners alike, is basically a theoretical conception issuing from an attempted synthesis of much psychological research. Research in the United States tends to substantiate the existence of the hierarchy. That it may be culturally bounded is suggested by a research project that compared the need hierarchies of American and Mexican employees in plants owned by a common parent company where the jobs, product, and technology were identical.[9] One interesting finding was that although the self-actualization need for the Americans was highly deficient in satisfaction, as hypothesized by the Maslow hierarchy, it was the *second* most satisfied need for the Mexican employees. This difference was attributed to differences in culture and social structure between the two nations.

McGREGOR'S THEORY Y

Philosophers have long been fascinated and puzzled concerning the apparent contradictory and dual nature of human beings. People appear to have a capacity for tenderness, sympathy, and love while at the same time they possess tendencies toward cruelty, callousness, hate, and malicious aggression. If we are basically the former, we need little external regulation. If the latter, we must be controlled for the good of ourselves and society.

Though this philosophical clash is age-old, Douglas McGregor is responsible for introducing the dual theme into management literature. After observing the actual practices of many traditional managers, he proposed that they were operating on a set of assumptions that he labeled "theory X": (1) the average human being has an inherent dislike of work and will avoid it if possible; (2) because of this human characteristic of dislike of work, most people must be coerced, controlled, directed, and threatened with punishment to get them to put forth adequate effort; and (3) the average human being prefers to be directed, wishes to avoid responsibility, has relatively little ambition, and wants security above all.[10]

In disagreement with the assumptions of theory X, McGregor feels that modern management is grossly underestimating the interest and capacities of its organization members. On the basis of psychological and social research results, he submits an opposing theory, called "theory Y," as a more realistic assessment of the capabilities of people.

1. The expenditure of physical and mental effort in work is as natural as play or rest.

2. People will exercise self-direction and self-control in the service of objectives to which they are committed.

[9]John W. Slocum, Jr., Paul M. Topichak, and David G. Kuhn, "A Cross-Cultural Study of Need Satisfaction and Need Importance for Operative Employees," *Personnel Psychology*, vol. 24, no. 3, Autumn 1971, p. 442.

[10]Douglas McGregor, *The Human Side of Enterprise*, McGraw-Hill Book Company, New York, 1960, pp. 33–34, 47–48.

BOX 15-1
Trust: The New Ingredient in Management
Claudia H. Deutsch

Microscopically examining Japanese management practices to discover the secrets of that nation's high productivity has become almost an obsession in U.S. business circles. Treatises on the atmosphere of trust implicit in Japanese management-labor relations are crowding other business books off the shelves. But with all the savants' pronouncements on participatory management, one important element has been almost totally ignored: Japanese managers trust not only their workers but also their peers and superiors.

The existence of that all-encompassing trust leads to a simplified organizational structure that has helped many Japanese companies become low-cost producers. Because Japanese companies assume that personnel at all levels are competent—and, above all, trustworthy enough to have the company's best interests in mind—they do not employ highly paid executives whose only jobs are to review and pass on the work of other highly paid executives. They do not write job descriptions giving managers authority for specific fiefdoms and putting them into conflict with managers of rival fiefdoms. Instead, their operations are lean at the staff level and rich at the line level—where profits are made.

"The Japanese firms may well have more people, but they are in profit-related jobs," notes William H. Newman, a professor at Columbia University's business school. "The Japanese will train their smartest engineers to identify problems, then put them on the shop floor. In the U.S. they'd be sitting at a desk reviewing things."

'Big Brother Syndrome.' Slowly, U.S. business experts are recognizing the bottom-line impact that a preponderance of "reviewers" can have. The addition of layers of highly paid executives to Sears, Roebuck & Co.'s corporate headquarters—rather than to its stores—has helped turn the mammoth retailer into one of the highest-cost merchandisers in the

country. And U.S. auto makers are beginning to see connections between Japanese structural organization and low costs. Japanese foremen, for example, report directly to plant managers, while American foremen must wade through three extra layers of management. Not surprisingly, the Japanese can make a car and ship it here for $1,500 less than it costs a U.S. auto maker to produce and sell a comparable vehicle.

At Ford Motor Co., there are 11 layers of management between the factory worker and the chairman, while Toyota Motor Co. makes do with six. Now Ford's management has come to the uncomfortable conclusion that this excess layering has had two negative results: high overhead and a morass of red tape.

The company recently increased by several million dollars its plant managers' spending authority in order to push decision-making further down the hierarchy. And Ford is starting to disband some of the corporate subcommittees that traditionally had reviewed divisional decisions. "We've had Big Brother syndrome, looking over each others' shoulders, checking and recheck-ing," admits William J. Harahan, Ford's director of technical planning. "I suggest that we can no longer afford these layers of manufacturing management."

Theory Y Management. Clearly, Ford is moving toward what Douglas McGregor would describe as a Theory Y approach to management. McGregor has postulated that a Theory X manager—until recently, a typical American manager—works on the premise that employees cannot be trusted to do their best and thus must be given specific orders and close supervision. A Theory Y manager, by contrast, believes that people want to work hard and respond best to a participatory managerial style. This theory, almost always cited in terms of individual managerial approaches, can easily apply to a corporate cul-

ture. Japanese companies, thus, would be Theory Y companies throughout their hierarchies and would require fewer purely supervisory layers.

Instinctively, the Japanese recognize that a Theory Y approach must be a two-way street. Japanese companies are as conscious of their employees' interests as they expect employees to be of theirs. Work force layoffs are rare, and, similarly, Japanese managers are almost never pushed out. Promotions and raises are based as much on seniority and teamwork as on individual performance. "The Japanese managers do not feel they must constantly cover themselves or be caught up in an individually competitive position to get ahead," maintains Harry Levinson, head of the Levinson Institute, a psychological consulting firm. Adds Junichi Nakamura, general manager for Mitsubishi International Corp. in New York: "There is pride and even sibling rivalry, but there is a family consciousness. Everyone believes that his colleagues and superiors care about his welfare."

It would be unrealistic to expect this atmosphere to exist in an American corporation. Nonetheless, Japanese companies that hire Americans in their U.S. operations manage quite effectively without cadres of supervisors in their executive suites. The presidents of both Quasar Co. and Matsushita Industrial Co. find it comfortable to work with only one vice-president and to have 10 or more managers reporting to them.

Matrix Management. These companies and others like them operate in a manner highly reminiscent of the American concept of matrix management. That concept requires design engineers, production managers, and marketing specialists, for example, to iron out their differences on priorities and scheduling long before their recommendations are passed upward. Implementing a matrix structure has proved to be inordinately difficult in the hierarchy-conscious U.S. business culture, but it is the natural order of things in Japan. Japanese employees learn the intricacies of other departments before they are permitted to specialize. Thus they are sympathetic rather than suspicious of their counterparts by the time they have become managers.

Both Quasar and Matsushita are seeking ways to emulate that approach by educating their American managers in the profit and loss ramifications of operations outside their sphere. "I now have managers all the way down to product-line level who realize the P&L implications of our whole operation and thus (fully understand interrelationships) outside their immediate areas," says Alex Stone, Quasar's president.

No one suggests that the quick fix of a training program can achieve the results garnered from an environment that fosters lifetime security and trust. But it is important for U.S. managers to realize that, at least to a certain extent, it can happen here. There are enough American companies that have tried some small part of the Japanese method to prove that point. Dana Corp., for one, has been existing with only five levels of management between the chief executive and the shop floor, and Chairman Gerald B. Mitchell says his immediate goal "is to reduce this to four." Hewlett-Packard Corp. has been able to dispense with accounting experts who arbitrate transfer prices between divisions supplying goods to each other by establishing a simple formula based on fully loaded factory cost less a percentage negotiated between the departments. Sums up a consultant who has studied the company: "It works because the department heads trust each other."

Still, it will take a while before American business culture moves firmly into the camp of "doers" rather than "reviewers." A recent study of professions in the U.S. and Japan, although not specifically related to business, has some sobering implications for the support-staff mania in this country. It turned up the fact that, on a per capita basis, the U.S. has 20 times as many lawyers as Japan and almost seven times as many accountants. But the study indicates the Japanese have more than five times the number of engineers, per capita. Until the U.S. rethinks the priorities on which professions get the most prestige and the highest pay, its corporations will suffer a superabundance of flab at the top and a shortage of muscle throughout.

3. Commitment to objectives is a function of the rewards associated with achievement.

4. The average human being learns, under proper conditions, not only to accept but to seek responsibility.

5. The capacity to exercise a relatively high degree of imagination, ingenuity, and creativity in the solution of organization problems is widely, not narrowly, distributed in the population.

6. Under conditions of modern industrial life, the intellectual potentialities of the average human being are only partially utilized.

If one accepted the McGregor human model, such managerial practices as the following would be seriously considered: (1) abandonment of timeclocks, (2) flexitime, (3) job enrichment, (4) Management by Objectives with subordinates determining the objectives as well as appraising their own accomplishments, and (5) participative and democratic decision making concerning the general organizational environment. All are based on the concepts of *abilities being widespread* in the population and *trust* in each person to behave in a responsible manner. It is apparent that the person who feels the higher-order needs, such as esteem and self-actualization, is likely to behave in a manner similar to that incorporated into the theory Y model. Thus, management must structure the organizational environment in a manner that will further the release of this tremendous human potential. It is contended in Box 15-1 that Japanese business organizations are modeled after theory Y.

ARGYRIS'S MATURE HUMAN BEING

Though the human being may be "constructed" at birth with all the Maslow needs and "theory Y" potential embedded in embryonic form, Chris Argyris emphasizes that development from that point is naturally in the direction of maturation. He proposes several dimensions of maturation through which the person will develop to achieve good mental health. At the immature-infant end of this continuum are these seven characteristics: (1) being passive, (2) being dependent, (3) being unaware of self, (4) being subordinate, (5) possessing a short time perspective, (6) having casual and shallow interests, and (7) being capable of behaving in only a few ways.[11] On the other hand, natural movement with maturation would be toward behavior characterized by increasing activity, independence, an awareness of and control over self, aspiring to occupy an equal or superior position, having long-term perspectives, developing deeper interests, and being capable of behaving in many ways to satisfy needs.

Organizations need human resources to fill positions necessary to achieve organization objectives. Though one might contend that mature personnel are a prime necessity, Argyris argues that many organizations are structured and managed in such a way that immature, infantlike behavior is required for retention and "success." Employees are asked to submit to orders, plans, policies, procedures, and rules as given. They are asked to work in an environment where they have little control over their lives, are expected to be passive and dependent upon authority, and are asked to use a "few skin-surface shallow abilities."[12]

Faced with the incongruity of organizational demands and mature human needs, it is suggested that the employee will engage in one or more of the following activities: (1) escape, (2) attack, or (3) adapt. One may escape by quitting the job, being absent frequently, or gaining promotion to higher positions where there is more freedom and autonomy. One can attack by practicing malicious obedience, organizing slowdowns, or forming labor unions. The most unhealthy activity, according to Argyris, is to apathetically accept and adapt to infantile situations. This paints a rather gloomy picture of organizational requirements that will lead to widespread psychological failure for organizational members. McGregor tends to agree with this thesis as he poses the theory X and theory Y assumptions. Both he and Argyris suggest that industrial organizations are doing serious harm to human beings through management based on assumptions of employee immaturity and irresponsibility.

On the reverse side is the question of whether *all* employees are mature as defined by Argyris or theory Y types as defined by McGregor. Many have granted the importance of these concepts when dealing with more highly educated professional, technical, and managerial white-collar employees. But Strauss has suggested that the theories advanced by various behaviorists are more indicative of the need structure of highly educated behavioral theorists than they are of rank and file blue-collar employees.[13] Security may mean more to the industrial worker than to the highly educated professional. The former

[11]Chris Argyris, *Personality and Organization,* Harper & Row, Publishers, Incorporated, New York, 1957, p. 50.
[12]Ibid., p. 66.
[13]George Strauss, "The Personality-versus-Organization Theory," in Leonard Sayles, *Individualism and Big Business,* McGraw-Hill Book Company, New York, 1963, p. 70.

often values the freedom of thought permitted by a structured, repetitive, simple task that may be boring to others. Strauss indicates that the need to self-actualize may not be so widely spread in the population as hypothesized by Maslow, Argyris, and McGregor. One study of 83 workers (bench hands, testers, wiremen, machinists, toolmakers, electricians, and so on) in a firm of 8,000 employees revealed a positive correlation between need satisfaction and job structure. The higher the structure, the greater was the need satisfaction in such areas as achievement, affiliation, autonomy, and recognition.[14] Behaviorists would doubtlessly reply that such successful employee adaptation to oppressive and mechanical structures indicates that we have compounded the felony; not only have we forced employees to act in an immature manner, we have also conditioned them to *prefer* that type of behavior.

It should be apparent that most conditions are neither as bad as behaviorists contend nor as good as traditional managers claim. We are always operating in the gray area of optimizing multiple values under conditions of uncertainty. Only a fraction of the jobs in American business are of the highly mechanized, totally controlled type. To the degree that an open job market operates effectively, there will be some matching of varying human needs and organizational demands. One writer points out that 85 percent of American workers indicated that they were satisfied with their jobs, that fewer than 2 percent actually work on an assembly line, and that the typical employee does not even work for a manufacturing organization.[15]

Not all personnel are theory Y types despite arguments concerning how they got that way. Not all organizations demand total obedience on narrowly defined tasks. But, certainly, not all organizations have examined their structures and management approaches to determine where some alterations could produce a better fusion between organizational and human values. In general, it can be contended that most managers in business have tended to underestimate the motivation and capabilities of their personnel. This is confirmed in surveys asking (1) whether managers believe in greater subordinate participation in decision making, and (2) whether managers believe that such participation will increase the quality of operation. The typical result is "yes" to the first question and a "no" to the second. The implication is that greater employee involvement is the price of cooperation, submission, and acceptance, but only managers and other higher types can really make decisions that will improve the quality of the situation.

HERZBERG'S MOTIVATED EMPLOYEE

One of the more stimulating and controversial theories of human nature proposed in recent years is that developed by Frederick Herzberg and his associates.[16] It is consistent with the self-actualization of Maslow, McGregor's "theory Y," and the maturation process of Argyris.

---

[14]William P. Sexton, "Industrial Work: Who Calls It Psychologically Devastating?" *Management of Personnel Quarterly,* vol. 6, no. 4, Winter 1968, pp. 3–8.

[15]Irving Kristol, "Is the American Worker Alienated?" *The Wall Street Journal,* Jan. 18, 1973.

[16]F. Herzberg, B. Mausner, and B. Synderman, *The Motivation to Work,* John Wiley & Sons, Inc., New York, 1959; and F. Herzberg, *Work and the Nature of Man,* The World Publishing Company, Cleveland, 1966.

Herzberg proposes that human beings have two basic needs: the need to avoid pain and survive and the need to grow, develop, and learn. As such, the analysis of employee job satisfaction would result in the formation of two separate continuums rather than the traditional one of satisfaction/dissatisfaction. The first continuum, ranging from dissatisfaction to no dissatisfaction, would be affected by environmental factors over which the employee has limited influence. Typical of these "hygienic factors" are pay, interpersonal relations, supervision, company policy and administration, working conditions, status, and security. Herzberg indicates that these factors do *not* serve to promote job satisfaction; rather, their absence or deficiency can create dissatisfaction. Their presence can only serve to eliminate dissatisfaction.

The second class of factors, referred to as "motivators," makes up a continuum leading from *no job satisfaction* to *satisfaction*. Examples from this class are the work itself, recognition, achievement, possibility of growth, and advancement. All of these are concerned with the work itself, rather than its surrounding physical, administrative, or social environment. If the worker is to be truly motivated, the job itself is the major source of that motivation. All of the other hygienic factors can serve only to "clean up" the environment and prevent dissatisfaction. These two continuums are portrayed in Figure 15-4.

The method of research used in developing this theory was not the usual anonymous objective questionnaire. Rather, subjects were asked to recall a time when they felt exceptionally good or a time when they felt exceptionally bad about their work. These incidents or stories were analyzed to ascertain the particular factors mentioned as contributing to the exceptional satisfaction or dissatisfaction. A preponderance of the motivator factors dealing with the work itself were mentioned when the subject was describing a time of feeling exceptionally good. And the times of feeling very bad were marked by a significantly large number of hygienic factors.

This type of study has been duplicated by other researchers on many occasions. In a summary of twelve investigators encompassing 1,685 employees, incidents describing job satisfaction involved 81 percent motivator factors and only 19 percent hygienic factors.[17] In cases describing job dissatisfaction, 69 percent involved hygienic factors as compared with 31 percent motivator factors.

[17]Frederick Herzberg, "One More Time: How Do You Motivate Employees?" *Harvard Business Review*, vol. 46, no. 1, January-February 1968, p. 57.

FIGURE 15-4 Motivator-hygiene theory.

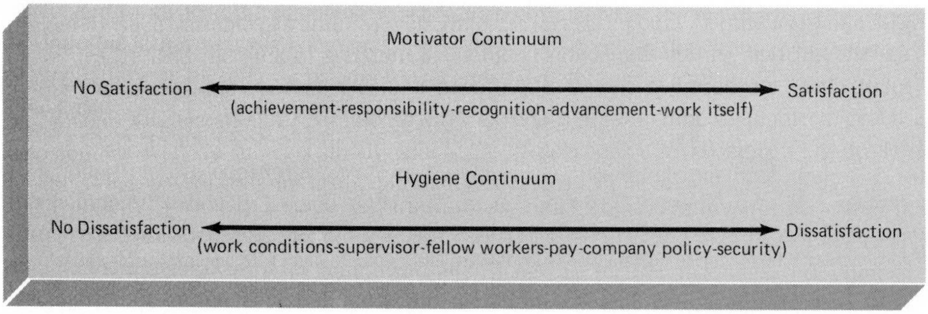

Motivator Continuum

No Satisfaction ⟵————————————————————⟶ Satisfaction
(achievement-responsibility-recognition-advancement-work itself)

Hygiene Continuum

No Dissatisfaction ⟵————————————————————⟶ Dissatisfaction
(work conditions-supervisor-fellow workers-pay-company policy-security)

The Herzberg theory has been criticized by some as being method-bound; that is, individuals tend to blame environmental factors for job failure and consequent dissatisfaction and take credit for any job successes that occur. Thus, subordinates also make attributions about behavior. Those high in self-esteem are more likely to attribute behavior to themselves rather than the situation. A few objective questionnaire studies are in agreement with the Herzberg theory, but most are not. Others have criticized these projective studies as being primarily concerned with higher-level, technical jobs, whose usual occupants are better educated and more interested in their work. However, this method has been used in studies of various types of jobs such as lower-level supervisors, hospital maintenance personnel, nurses, food handlers, agricultural administrators, accountants, Finnish supervisors, Hungarian engineers, and military officers. Herzberg contends that the work itself can be the basic motivating force for lower-level jobs as well as higher and more complex types.

The Herzberg theory is similar to the Maslow hierarchy in that the hygienic factors are related to the higher-priority physiological, security, and social needs, while the motivators correspond to the esteem, ego, and self-actualization needs. The Maslow hierarchy proposes a continuous, rather than disconnected, sequencing of felt needs, whereas the Herzberg theory would not require hygienic factors to be provided as a prerequisite to satisfaction on the job. There is widespread agreement that satisfaction will be higher when both motivational and hygienic factors are well taken care of. There is also evidence that when both are reasonably well met by organizations, the motivators are *more* powerful sources of satisfaction.[18] When they are not well met, hygienic factors are the *more* powerful source, thus tending to substantiate the Maslow hierarchical concept. Other research indicated that older employees as well as the blue-collar tend to value the hygienic factors more highly than do the younger or the white-collar. One study did not find that those individuals with a high level of motivators and a low level of hygienic factors were significantly more satisfied than those who perceived the reverse.[19] In other words, a ''good'' job in a ''bad'' environment will not necessarily result in greater satisfaction than a ''bad'' job in a ''good'' environment. Except for highly unusual instances, employees are likely to be upset by the idea of performing a challenging job for low pay, in a shabby office, under negative leadership styles and inconsistent policies.

Herzberg would certainly not deemphasize the importance of the hygienic factors in successful management. He favors ''good'' environments. The primary impact of his theory is to direct management's attention to the task itself as the primary source of motivation. It rests upon the important human need to self-actualize through doing something interesting, challenging, and important in life.

[18]Hanafi M. Soliman, ''Motivation-Hygiene Theory of Job Attitudes: An Empirical Investigation and an Attempt to Reconcile Both the One- and the Two-Factor Theories of Job Attitudes,'' *Journal of Applied Psychology,* vol. 54, no. 5, October 1970, pp. 452–461; and D. A. Ondrack, ''Defense Mechanisms and the Herzberg Theory: An Alternate Test,'' *Academy of Management Journal,* vol. 17, no. 1, March 1974, pp. 79–89.
[19]Richard Kosmo and Orlando Behling, ''Single Continuum Job Satisfaction vs. Duality: An Empirical Test,'' *Personnel Psychology,* vol. 22, no. 3, Autumn 1969, pp. 327–334.

HUMAN MODELS
OF ETHOLOGISTS

All of the models of the four organizational psychologists have one thing in common: the infinite human capacity to learn, grow, and achieve. It is a human model that is very attractive to the human ego. Humans constitute the greatest resource on this planet, ranking only slightly below the angels. In contrast with this orientation toward human nature, we now turn to the field of ethology, the study of animal behavior. Just as Herzberg cited the dual nature of humans (the need to survive and avoid pain and the need to grow), modern ethologists study humans as animals and humans as humans. They tend, however, to emphasize the first approach as a means of enlarging understanding of the second. Robert Ardrey credits Konrad Z. Lorenz, the Austrian naturalist, with fathering the field of modern ethology.[20] Ethology has been popularized in the last two decades through such writings as Lorenz's *On Aggression,* Ardrey's *Territorial Imperative,* and Desmond Morris's *The Naked Ape* and *The Human Zoo.*

As the titles of the books indicate, the basic thesis is that humans are both animalistic and humanistic. Certain animal characteristics provide a framework that helps to shape the humanizing process. For example, Ardrey's thesis is that humans share with many animals an innate behavioral pattern that leads them to establish a basic area or territory as theirs and to defend it against invaders. This defense leads them to benign aggression, that is, aggressive acts against invaders that are biologically adaptive through contributing to the survival of the species. It ceases when the threat has been removed. Malignant aggression, however, appears to be a learned response that is specific to humans.[21] Humans will kill other humans for reasons that are *not* biologically adaptive.

In lower animals and insects, these innate behavioral patterns that are genetically transmitted are generally referred to as "instincts." Instincts can vary from a completely closed program of behavior, as in the case of ants and bees, to a fairly open one that requires considerable learning after birth. Arguments abound over whether humans inherit any instincts whatsoever. Ashley Montagu, a well-known anthropologist, contends, "It is not human nature, but nurture that is the cause of human aggression."[22] Pioneers in ethology have proposed five possible human instincts that are genetically transmitted: reproduction, hunger, fear, aggression, and grooming. Kefalas and Suojanen suggest that these can be remembered in the form of the five "f's": flirting, feeding, flight, fighting, and feeling.[23] These instincts do not constitute preprogrammed behavior as in the case of lower animals. Rather, they are shapers of learned behavior. Lower animals master their environment through an evolutionary change in genes. Humans master their environment more quickly and effectively through culturally learned behavior. Yet to contend that people are totally human without any genetically transmitted behavioral inclinations would result in an incomplete understanding of the nature of human beings. Both organization psychologists and ethologists can aid in designing a more realistic model of the complex human.

---

[20]Robert Ardrey, *The Territorial Imperative,* Atheneum Publishers, New York, 1966, p. 12.

[21]Erich Fromm, *The Anatomy of Human Destructiveness,* Holt, Rinehart and Winston, New York, 1973. However, recent reports from Jane Goodall in Africa indicate that she has observed some murders among the chimpanzees.

[22]M. F. Ashley Montagu, *Anthropology and Human Nature,* Porter Sargent, Boston, 1957, p. 36.

[23]Asterios G. Kefalas and Waino W. Suojanen, "Organizational Behavior and the New Biology," *Academy of Management Journal,* vol. 17, no. 3, September 1974, p. 523.

To B. F. Skinner, the foremost proponent of behaviorism, there is little need to theorize over the basic nature of the human being. He seeks explanations of human behavior, not from within, but from without. The stimulus to human behavior can be observed and measured. The behavioral response of the human can also be observed and measured. One needs only to establish behavioral objectives and to engineer appropriate responses through a conditioning process. Thus, humans, if anything, are malleable mechanisms. They are without mystery and merit little concern for proposed felt needs of dignity and autonomy. "Operant conditioning shapes behavior as a sculptor shapes a lump of clay."[24]

In his book *Beyond Freedom and Dignity*, Skinner contends that humans can be controlled and shaped while simultaneously feeling free.[25] The basic engineering approach is to *reward* desired behavior while *ignoring* undesirable actions. Over a period of time, the reinforced behavior will tend to be repeated, while the unrewarded will tend to be extinguished and to disappear. Punishment of undesired behavior is to be avoided as contributing to feelings of restraint and to actions of rebellion. Thus, in time, the conditioner can effectively control human behavior without the human becoming aware of being controlled—thus "beyond freedom." Choice has, on the surface, remained with the positively conditioned subject, while the conditioner pulls the strings in an unobjectionable and unnoticed fashion.

At this point, total confusion concerning the fundamental nature of the human resource may have set in. One conclusion is obvious—the human being is a highly complex mechanism not subject to simplistic theories of management. Simultaneous belief in elements of all three approaches is not impossible. Herzberg's hygienic factors and Maslow's physiological and security needs may well be related to the animalistic nature of humans emphasized by ethologists. Ethology does not reject the learning and growth capacity possessed by human beings and so greatly emphasized by the organization psychologists. It merely asks for a broader study to include some of the genetically transmitted shapers of learning. One can also believe and utilize much of the Skinner thesis of shaping behavior without necessarily contending that there is no mystery about the human being. Many Skinner-oriented conditioning devices are totally compatible with participative management recommendations of Argyris and McGregor and the job enrichment programs of Herzberg. Obtaining immediate feedback of results on a newly enriched job is a form of immediate reward connected to job behavior. One major worry is nevertheless attached to the basic Skinner thesis. Who is the conditioner? What are his or her goals in shaping behavior? Skinner's response is that the conditioning technology is ethically neutral; it can be used by both good and evil conditioners.[26] This would not satisfy persons highly concerned with the proposed needs of humans for dignity, autonomy, and self-determination.

---

[24]"Conversation with B. F. Skinner," *Organizational Dynamics*, vol. 1, no. 3, Winter 1973, p. 31.
[25]B. F. Skinner, *Beyond Freedom and Dignity*, Alfred A. Knopf, Inc., New York, 1971.
[26]"Conversation with B. F. Skinner," op. cit., p. 32.

As emphasized in all the preceding human models, the behavior of humans is also heavily influenced by the culture of which they are a part. Culture is composed of the human-created elements of life—customs, beliefs, habits, codes, mores, and laws. Culture arises in part from the need for security, since it is established, conventionalized behavior that changes slowly and possesses great stability. The various types of behavior possible in the pursuit of need satisfaction are restricted by the culture in which this behavior occurs.

The importance of culture in the administration of a business firm can best be exemplified by contrasting one country with another. In Japan, for example, the worker expects advice and guidance from the employer to a degree that would be resented in the United States, with the latter's emphasis upon freedom and equality. A Japanese worker expects to remain a worker and not pass to managerial levels, a situation which *used* to exist in this country. He or she expects to remain an employee of one particular firm for life—incompetency is no justification for dismissal. Promotion is strictly on the basis of seniority, and pay is largely controlled by tenure and family needs.

With respect to managerial practices, it is suggested that the Japanese approach may be more compatible with large, crowded, complex organizations than the American way.[27] American cultural values of individuality and self-sufficiency often lead to competition and rivalry within the organization. Japanese management practices emphasize a cooperative "bottom-up" process of decision making as a fundamental way of management. As stated by one American manager, "Americans will disagree with their boss rarely but violently; the Japanese disagree often but politely."[28] The Japanese manager is a facilitator, communicator, and participant in group decision processes. Americans tend to be independent, entrepreneurial, competitive, decisive, and action-oriented. Obviously, both managerial cultures have their strengths, but cultures will undergo change slowly in response to alterations of the environment.

In identifying varying managerial cultures of the world, the Haire, Ghiselli, and Porter study of 3,641 managers of 14 countries is perhaps the largest single research to identify common values and differences in beliefs and practices.[29] The study identified several significantly different clusters of nations. The United States and England formed one combination with similar views and approaches to subordinate participation, use of authority, and the like. A later separate study found that Australia could also be allied with this group.[30] Other clusters were a Nordic-European group of Denmark, West Germany, Norway, and Sweden; a Latin-European group of Belgium, France, Italy, and Spain; and a developing-nation group composed of Argentina, Chile, and India. Only Japan could not be grouped with any other of the nations included in the study.

Perhaps one of the most commonly cited examples of varying international cultural beliefs is the treatment of time. Most Americans are greatly concerned with the impor-

[27]Richard Tanner Johnson and William G. Ouchi, "Made in America (under Japanese Management)," *Harvard Business Review,* vol. 52, no. 5, September-October 1974, p. 69.

[28]Ibid., p. 63.

[29]Mason Haire, Edwin E. Ghiselli, and Lyman W. Porter, *Managerial Thinking: An International Study,* John Wiley & Sons, Inc., New York, 1966.

[30]Alfred W. Clark and Sue McCabe, "Leadership Beliefs of Australian Managers," *Journal of Applied Psychology,* vol. 54, no. 1, February 1970, pp. 1–6.

tance of time, as witnessed by the widespread availability and use of accurate clocks and watches, the precision of transportation time-schedules, and the pressing necessity to meet scheduled appointments. In various foreign cultures, time does not have this same high value. This does not necessarily mean that these peoples do not value efficiency and coordination. Often, their attitude toward time is a result of poorer transportation and communication facilities, greater degrees of patience, religious philosophies that deemphasize the importance of this day or hour, or a different hierarchical arrangement of values in life. Being 5 minutes late for an appointment in the United States calls for a brief apology; 15 minutes' lateness requires an extended apology for the purpose of communicating great concern and regret; and being 30 or more minutes late is best excused by an act of God. In other countries, being 30 to 45 minutes late for appointments is not an unusual event and is not to be taken as an insult when it passes unmentioned. The symbol of ''lateness'' stands for vastly different things in differing cultures. It has been suggested that the American can adapt by scheduling additional work beyond the appointed hour; considering his or her attitude toward time, the foreign visitor will not be insulted by not being immediately ushered into the executive's office.

Within the United States, there are many subcultures that can affect business operations. There is a subculture for each business organization as well as subcultures cutting across various firms. Engineers and scientists, for example, are hired by many business establishments and bring with them certain beliefs, values, and standards that can conflict with the subculture of the firm. For example, research scientists highly value freedom of investigation and research that meets certain quality standards. The *XYZ* firm may insist that the scientist punch a timeclock and research only those fields that will result in immediate profit for the enterprise. With this clash in cultural values, higher salaries may not serve to keep the scientist from leaving for government or university employment. It is necessary for the manager to study the characteristics, standards, and values of the subcultures whose members one wishes to employ.

SUMMARY

Human relations has been defined as the area of management practice that is concerned with the integration of people into a work situation. It is concerned with motivating personnel to work together cooperatively and productively. In understanding the behavior of human beings, some knowledge of basic needs is necessary. If their satisfaction can be effected in a manner that contributes to organization objectives, then interests have been integrated. They may be classified as physiological, social, and egoistic. The goal of human behavior is adjustment to need-stimulated tensions in a way that will bring satisfaction. When needs are frustrated, employee behavior may be aggressive, regressive, fixated, or resigned.

Various models of human beings have been proposed by separate disciplines. Despite the separate labels of ''self-actualization,'' ''theory Y,'' ''maturation,'' and ''motivators,'' the organization psychologists put forth a highly optimistic view of human beings as possessing an infinite capacity for growth, development, and achievement. Ethologists contend that this capacity for growth rests on a foundation of genetically transmitted behavioral patterns. Behaviorism, proposed by Skinner, eschews interest in what is in the human and confines its attention to stimulus-response. Humans are malleable and behavior can be engineered.

Human behavior cannot be fully understood and accurately predicted apart from a knowledge of the various cultures in which this behavior takes place. The customs, traditions, codes, and laws that make up a culture circumscribe the freedom of management. To a large degree, the problem is one of predicting and adjusting to cultural requirements. But within a single organization, a culture should be developed that will facilitate effective cooperation and fulfillment of quality performance levels. Organization, procedures, and controls must be established by management to ensure coordinated activity. The human desire for stability and security will contribute to greater acceptance of the need for such restrictions.

BRIEF CASE

Joe Harshner was recently hired as a lathe operator in a rough turning department of Atlas Enterprises. He had formerly been the owner of a small machine shop that had gone bankrupt. Despite a tendency to brag about his machine abilities, he was well liked by the work group of fifteen employees. On one occasion when he was bragging about his skill, contending that he was turning out more work than any of the other employees, there were many grins, winks, and raised eyebrows among the listeners. Later that day, Joe was approached by the supervisor. He complimented Joe on his work but asked that he reduce his output to the amount per hour specified. He indicated that he was trying to maintain a steady flow of material while at the same time train new workers as a part of an entry learning program for the plant. There was no room to store materials so the flow must be steady and predictable. Joe was rather shocked at being asked to cut back on his output. The other workers assured Joe that the supervisor was one of the best in the plant and would back up his workers in a bind. The supervisor was also highly respected by management.

Questions

1. Explain Joe's behavior. Why did he behave that way?
2. Explain the supervisor's behavior. Is it consistent with organizational effectiveness?

DISCUSSION QUESTIONS

1. Identify the major forces which lead managements of organizations to improve human relations.
2. When a manager observes an undesirable act of a subordinate, what forces influence his or her attribution of the cause for that act?
3. What types of behavior are likely to be exhibited by a frustrated employee?
4. Compare and contrast the human models of Maslow and Herzberg.
5. Compare and contrast the human models of McGregor and Skinner.
6. What is the basic commonality of the human models proposed by Maslow, McGregor, Herzberg, and Argyris? What are the specific labels of this commonality in each model?

7. If a mature person works as an employee of an organization whose management treats one as an infant, what are the options?

8. What is ethology? What contribution can it make to understanding human beings?

9. Compare and contrast the American and Japanese cultures with respect to managing business organizations.

10. How could the Skinner approach conceivably end up with a human condition of "beyond freedom and dignity?"

SUPPLEMENTARY READING

ADLER, SEYMOUR: "Self-Esteem and Causal Attributions for Job Satisfaction and Dissatisfaction," *Journal of Applied Psychology*, vol. 65, no. 3, June 1980, pp. 327–332.

BARTUNEK, JEAN M.: "'Why Did You Do That? Attribution Theory in Organizations," *Business Horizons*, vol. 24, no. 5, September-October 1981, pp. 66–71.

GOODSTEIN, LEONARD D. and JOHN W. HUNT: "Commentary: Do American Theories Apply Abroad?" *Organizational Dynamics*, vol. 10, no. 1, Summer 1981, pp. 49–62.

JACKSON, LAUREN HITE and MARK G. MINDELL: "Motivating the New Breed," *Personnel*, vol. 57 no. 2, March-April 1980, pp. 53–61.

LEVINSON, HARRY: "What Killed Bob Lyons?" *Harvard Business Review*, vol. 59, no. 2, March-April 1981, pp. 144–162.

MITCHELL, TERENCE R. and LAURA S. KALB: "Effects of Job Experience on Supervisor Attributions for a Subordinate's Poor Performance," *Journal of Applied Psychology*, vol. 67, no. 2, April 1982, pp. 181–188.

chapter 16

Motivation

As indicated in Chapter 1, the organic functions of management are planning, organizing, directing, and controlling. Discussions of the personnel manager's responsibilities for planning, organizing, and controlling the personnel program were presented in Chapter 3. Coverage of the third function of direction was postponed until this point inasmuch as it is a vital component of the operative function of integration. Just as the personnel manager should be more than ordinarily competent in organizing, he or she should be similarly superior in the direction function. This latter function is concerned with *stimulating action to take place*.

The separation and development of the management function of direction is the result of an increasing appreciation of the power of organizational members. We cannot assume that the existence of good plans and excellent organization will result in an automatic undertaking of assigned tasks, thereby leaving the manager with only the responsibility of controlling the activity that develops. Getting organization members to go to work *willingly* and *enthusiastically* is a problem that has been compounded by such factors as the increasing educational level of employees, greater utilization of professional personnel, advancing technology, and the power of labor organizations. It is a task that can be more important than planning, organizing, and controlling.

EMPLOYEE WANTS

The various types of human needs discussed in the preceding chapter will be converted by employees into specific "wants" in the organization. Just as the definition of basic human needs is a highly complex task, it naturally follows that there are no easy assumptions concerning what employees really want from the organization. In various surveys, the following are some of the more typically specified wants:

1. *Pay*. This want helps in satisfying physiological, security, and egoistic needs. As discussed in the preceding section of this text, the design of a monetary compensation system is exceedingly complex since it serves to satisfy multiple needs and cannot alone motivate the whole person.

2. *Security of job*. Because of threats from technological change, this want is high on the list of priorities for many employees and labor unions. The underlying need of general security is also high on the list of priorities in the suggested need hierarchy of Maslow.

3. *Congenial associates*. This want issues from the social need of gregariousness and acceptance. Management can aid the process by carefully planned and executed induction programs, provision of means to socialize through rest periods and recreational programs, and promoting the formation of work teams through proper work-station layouts and human-related work procedures.

4. *Credit for work done*. This want issues from the egoistic classification of needs and can be supplied by management through verbal praise of excellent work, monetary rewards for suggestions, and public recognition through awards, releases in employee newspapers, and the like.

5. *A meaningful job*. This want issues from both the need for recognition and the drive toward self-realization and achievement. This is a very difficult want to supply, particularly in large organizations having minute division of work and mechanically paced assembly lines. But, as discussed in Chapter 5, some research into the possibilities of job enrichment has indicated the possibility of integrating the need of employees for significant work and the need of the organization for productive, coordinated activity.

6. *Opportunity to advance*. Not all employees want to advance. Some feel the social needs more strongly than the egoistic ones. However, most employees like to know that the opportunity is there, should they desire to use it. This feeling is influenced by a cultural tradition of freedom and opportunity.

7. *Comfortable, safe, and attractive working conditions*. The want for good working conditions also rests upon multiple needs. Safe working conditions issue from the security need. The specific attributes, such as desks and rugs, constitute symbols of status denoting a hierarchy of importance. Many managements have discovered that the allocation of such status symbols can be quite as difficult as the allocation of money.

8. *Competent and fair leadership*. The want of good leadership can issue from physiological and security needs. Good leadership helps to assure that the organization and its jobs will continue to exist. In addition, the ego demands that one respect persons from whom orders and directions are to be received. It is very frustrating to be subjected personally to a command from an individual who is deemed unworthy and incompetent.

9. *Reasonable orders and directions*. The order is the official communication of organization requirements. In general, it should be related to the requirements of the situation, capable of being executed, complete but not unnecessarily detailed, clear and concise, and given in a manner that stimulates acceptance. Unreasonable orders incapable of accomplishment serve only to increase insecurity and frustration. Unreasonable orders that work contrary to the best interests of the organization may lead to a form of malicious obedience; the employee takes great delight in following them to the letter in hopes of harming the superior who merits little respect.

10. *A socially relevant organization*. As indicated in Chapter 2, the trend toward greater social expectations of private organizations has impact upon such an organization's employees' expectations. This want issues from human needs of self-esteem, and levies a highly challenging responsibility upon the organization's management.

MOTIVATION

Just as the employee has certain wants that the organization is expected to supply, the organization has certain types of behavior that it wishes to elicit from the employee. The managerial responsibility for eliciting this behavior is usually termed "direction" or "motivation." In essence, it is a skill in aligning employee and organizational interests so that behavior results in achievement of employee wants simultaneously with attainment of organizational objectives.

The motivational force formula proposed by Vroom, briefly introduced in Chapter 13 in relation to monetary incentives, provides the framework for the motivation function. It will be recalled that the formula suggests that the motivational impact upon an employee of an attempted managerial influence is heavily influenced by the employee's assessment of (1) the anticipated *valence* or value of the perceived outcome of the prescribed behavior and (2) the strength of the *expectancy* that the behavior will actually result in a realization of the outcome.[1]

[1]Victor H. Vroom, *Work and Motivation*, John Wiley & Sons, Inc., New York, 1964, chap. 2.

FIGURE 16-1   Expectancy/valence motivation.

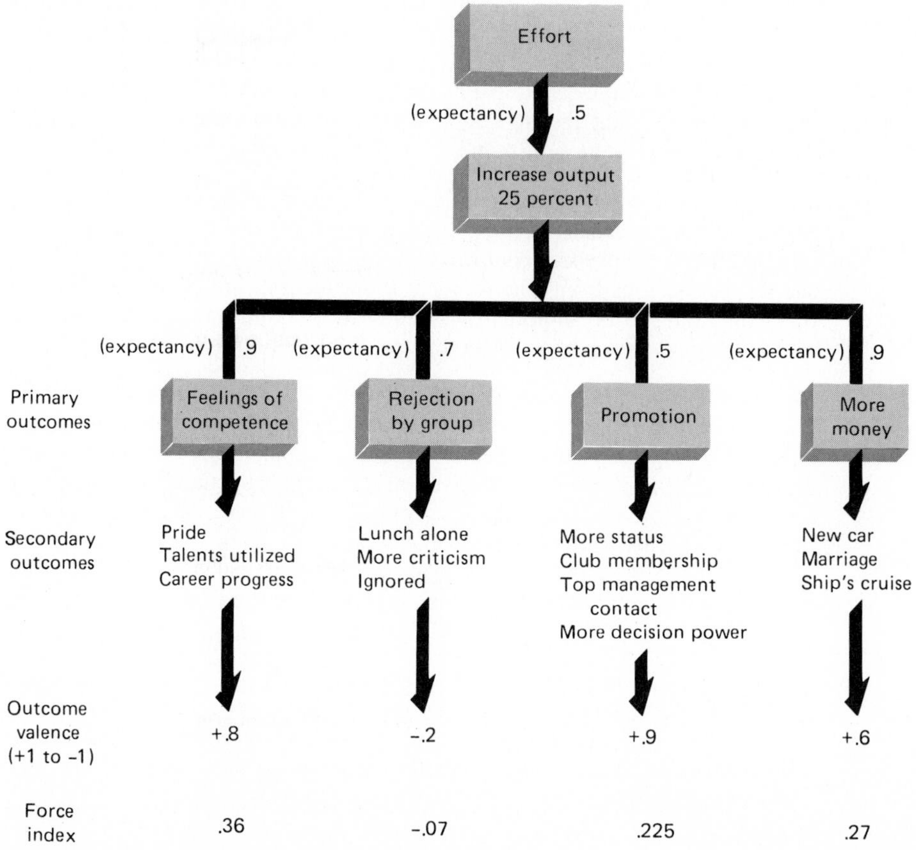

Valence

To ascertain what the employee values are, we must analyze basic human needs and survey current employee wants. As suggested by the simplified model in Figure 16-1, there are two types of outcomes that can be perceived: (1) the immediate or primary outcomes of performing a task, such as money, promotion, rejection by one's peer group, and feelings of competence, and (2) secondary outcomes that can issue from the primary, for example, money will buy a car; promotion will give more status; rejection by one's peers means you will lunch alone; feelings of competence develop pride. These secondary outcomes are most closely related to the needs identified in the Maslow hierarchy. As hypothesized by the hierarchy, a person will not perceive the values of lower priority needs until those of higher priority have been reasonably well satisfied. Among the lower priority needs, the hierarchy can vary according to the job held. Research shows that scientists, engineers, and graduate students feel a stronger need for achievement while managers have a stronger need for power.[2]

There are a number of organizationally controlled incentives that may have value for employees of organizations. We have discussed at length in the preceding section the use of money as a reward. In addition, there are such rewards as: (1) praise, either public, private, or both; (2) promotion to jobs of higher responsibility; (3) leader's personal interest; (4) status symbols; (5) consultation and solicitation of subordinate participation in managerial decision making; (6) feeling of accomplishment; and (7) peer acceptance and approval. Some of the rewards are highly controllable by the leader while others are more under the control of one's self and one's associates. Leaders can encourage peer acceptance but cannot command it. Leaders can construct job assignments and work environments that should permit a feeling of real accomplishment, but they cannot directly effect the feeling. Leaders can, of course, more fully control the payment of money, issuance of praise, allocation of status symbols, solicitation of participation, and demonstration of personal interest in subordinates.

The expectancy theory of motivation is basically a rational model. It assumes that human beings can determine which outcomes they prefer and their relative strength. As indicated in Figure 16-1, the individual can be asked to value outcomes on a scale ranging from plus 1 to minus 1. Though he or she is asked during motivation research projects, it is doubtful if the typical employee is able or willing to assess outcomes with the precisions of $+.6$ or $-.2$.

Expectancy

Though the employee may highly value the proffered reward, its availability will have little impact upon behavior if he or she does not perceive (1) personal capacity to behave in the manner prescribed, and (2) a definite linkage between the behavior desired and the valued payoff. The rationality of the employee is further extended when we ask for probability estimates in both categories. "What are the odds that I can do the task? What are the odds that I'll receive the payoff?"

The first expectancy to be estimated is the relationship between effort and performance. In Figure 16-1, we have assumed that the employee feels a 50 percent chance of

---

[2]Adrian M. Harrell and Michael J. Stahl, "A Behavioral Decision Theory Approach for Measuring McClelland's Trichotomy of Needs," *Journal of Applied Psychology,* vol. 66, no. 2, April 1981, p. 245.

increasing output 25 percent. These expectancies can be improved in various ways. First, research shows that the expectations of significant others, superiors and peers, can influence one's degree of confidence in personal capacity. In one study of low-level office employees, reported views of superiors' estimates of personal abilities correlated .93 with performance evaluations actually accorded.[3] In an experiment where instructors were led to expect more of certain military trainees, the latter performed significantly better on objective examinations.[4] The instructors tended to lavish more attention on those whom they believed to possess significant potential. The researchers concluded that the Pygmalion effect of higher expectations could be deliberately harnessed to improve subordinate effectiveness. Secondly, various programs can lead to higher capacity estimates. Obviously, trained and experienced employees will estimate higher expectancies than new and untrained personnel. A ''Management by Objectives'' program with its emphasis upon participative goal setting should also lead to improved capacity estimates. Research also indicates that one's personality has a major influence. People differ in the degree to which they feel that they control their own destiny. Individuals who view events as dependent on fate or luck (external control) will be less likely to predict higher expectancies than those who regard events as being a result of their own actions (internal control).[5] Those who subscribe to the Protestant ethic are also more responsive.[6] This ethic incorporates agreement with such statements as (1) a distaste for hard work usually shows weakness in character, and (2) anyone who is able and willing to work hard has a good chance for success.

It is believed that expectancy can be more effectively controlled in the early years of experience. Just as the first- and second-grade students are more responsive to teacher expectations than those of upper grades, the beginning employee or manager is more susceptible to the expectations of his or her superior. In one study at American Telephone and Telegraph Company, it was found that what the company expected of recent college graduates was the most critical factor in their subsequent performance.[7]

The second expectancy that the person is asked to estimate is the linkage between performance and primary outcomes. Management can do much to improve these expectancies by the use of formal programs and predictable behavior. A study of 504 managers of a large health care company revealed that the higher the role ambiguity, the lower the estimated expectancies for both effort and performance and performance outcome.[8] In Figure 16-1, we have shown that the employee perceives an almost certain linkage between increasing output and receiving an increase in pay (.9). He or she is not so sure that a promotion will be forthcoming if output is increased 25 percent (.5). There is an excellent chance that the employee will be expelled from the primary work group (.7), and such a performance will almost surely contribute to one's feeling more competent (.9).

---

[3]Abraham K. Korman, ''Expectancies as Determinants of Performance,'' *Journal of Applied Psychology,* vol. 55, no. 3, June 1971, pp. 218–222.

[4]Dov Eden and Abraham B. Shani, ''Pygmalion Goes to Boot Camp: Expectancy, Leadership, and Trainee Performance,'' *Journal of Applied Psychology,* vol. 67, no. 2, April 1982, pp. 194–199.

[5]Henry P. Sims, Jr., Andrew D. Szilagyi, and Dale R. McKemey, ''Antecedents of Work Related Expectancies,'' *Academy of Management Journal,* vol. 19, no. 4, December 1976, p. 556.

[6]Terry R. Lied and Robert D. Pritchard, ''Relationships between Personality Variables and Components of the Expectancy-Valence Model,'' *Journal of Applied Psychology,* vol. 61, no. 4, August 1976, pp. 463–467.

[7]''Some Determinants of Early Managerial Success,'' Massachusetts Institute of Technology, Alfred P. Sloan School of Management Organization, Research Program no. 81–64, 1964, pp. 13–14.

[8]Lawrence R. James, Alan Hartman, Michael W. Stebbins, and Allan P. Jones, ''Relationships between Psychological Climate and a VIE Model for Work Motivation,'' *Personnel Psychology,* vol. 30, no. 2, Summer 1977, p. 250.

The Vroom valence-expectancy model proposes that expectancies should be multiplied by valences to obtain the degree of motivational force. A look at the employee portrayed in Figure 16-1 indicates that the greatest motivational force index is associated with feelings of competence. This is consistent with the high valence placed on promotion, but the latter's force is reduced by the lower expectancy of actually receiving a promotion. This employee is not likely to be held back by group pressures. Overall, perhaps the best way to increase the motivational force indices in this illustration is to improve the employee's estimate of personal capacity (.5).

ORGANIZATIONAL BEHAVIOR MODIFICATION

The Maslow hierarchy may assist management in determining active needs, but the Skinner philosophy and accompanying programs will do much to improve the expected linkages between performance and outcome. After management has defined in specific terms the type of behavior that is desired, behavior in consonance with this standard should be reinforced in positive fashion. Skinner contends that any behavior that is not so rewarded will tend to disappear. Reinforcement through punishment is to be deemphasized or avoided because of its stimulation of subordinate anger, hostility, aggression, and rebellion. It has also been observed that behavior that has been conditioned through punishment not only tends to have relatively short-term effects but encourages innovative behavior to thwart and frustrate the manager, such as providing the absolute minimum required, producing only when supervised, malicious obedience, and so on.

In reinforcing desired behavior in a positive fashion, it is important to allocate that reward *soon* after the behavior is effected so that the subordinate perceives a clear linkage. It has been shown that communication of the desired behavior without feedback concerning level of performance is less effective in establishing linkage.[9] There has been much research concerning the schedule for allocation of rewards. As outlined in Figure 16-2, the basic choice is between a continuous reward schedule and an intermittent one geared to either time or performance. Research indicates that the continuous schedule is

[9]Judith L. Komaki, Robert L. Collins, and Pat Penn, "The Role of Performance Antecedents on Consequences in Work Motivation," *Journal of Applied Psychology,* vol. 67, no. 3, June 1982, p. 334.

FIGURE 16-2
Examples of Reward Schedules

Reward Schedule	Example
1 Continuous	Employee is paid 3¢ a unit for each item produced above standard.
2 Intermittent	
A Time intervals	
1 Fixed	Salary checks are distributed on the last day of the month.
2 Variable	Company president makes random inspections of department that average out to once a week.
B Ratio	
1 Fixed	Employee is paid 30¢ for every tenth unit produced above standard.
2 Variable	Employee who has not been absent or late for a week is eligible for prizes distributed through lottery drawing.

most effective for inexperienced workers and those who are in lower economic brackets.[10] The schedule that has received the greatest amount of attention is the last one listed, the variable-ratio reward schedule. As some have pointed out, pulling the handle of a slot machine for long hours at a time is not intrinsically rewarding. The possibility of a reward on a variable-ratio basis tends to shape the gambler's behavior. This schedule is more interesting to adequately compensated employees, and can sustain behavior over a long period with a minimum of company investment. For example, one organization reduced its absenteeism rate by dealing a single playing card to each worker present on each of the 5 working days of the week. The highest poker hand on Friday received a $10 reward. A lumber specialty firm brought lateness down to zero and reduced absenteeism significantly by awarding "well pay," an extra 8 hours' wages to workers who were neither absent nor late for a full month.[11]

In one well-publicized case of systematic behavior modification, the management of Emery Air Freight used the simple rewards of information feedback and praise to effect significant changes in employee behavior.[12] In responding to customer questions about service and schedules within a 90-minute period, performance moved from 30 percent accomplishment to 90 percent within a few days. Employees were provided feedback charts through which they could monitor their own behavior, and were praised by supervisors on first a fixed- and then a variable-schedule basis. Those who did *not* achieve the desired result were reminded of the goal and then praised for their honesty. This 90 percent achievement remained stable for over 3 years. In a second attempt, the use of large shipping containers by customers at the suggestion of employees moved from 45 percent to 90 percent. Estimated savings to the company were placed at $650,000 per year.

It should also be noted that others in the worker's environment are involved in the allocation of rewards. In an experiment in a large department store, standards were set for the selling function, for example, respond to customer requests in five seconds, be within three feet of displayed merchandise, and so on.[13] For the experimental group, rewards were given in the form of time off with pay, an equivalent value in cash, and a chance to win a paid vacation. During the experimental period, the rewarded group achieved significantly higher levels of effective selling. After the experiment was over and the rewards were withdrawn, the effectiveness of the experimental group remained high. It was concluded that these employees were now being reinforced by smiling and pleasant customers, an inner feeling of pride in doing a good job, and more pleasant relationships with supervisors.

If the manager desires to use organizational behavior modification, the following actions are necessary: (1) identify the desired performance in specific terms, (2) identify the rewards that will interest employees, and (3) make the reward a direct consequence of the behavior. The choice of the particular reward schedule is dependent upon the

[10]Gary P. Latham and Dennis L. Dossett, "Designing Incentive Plans for Unionized Employees: A Comparison of Continuous and Variable Ratio Reinforcement Schedules," *Personnel Psychology*, vol. 31, no. 1, Spring 1978, p. 47.

[11]"How to Earn 'Well Pay,' " *Business Week*, June 12, 1978, p. 143.

[12]"At Emery Air Freight: Positive Reinforcement Boosts Performance," *Organizational Dynamics*, vol. 1, no. 1, 1973, pp. 41–50.

[13]Fred Luthans, Robert Paul, and Douglas Baker, "An Experimental Analysis of the Impact of Contingent Reinforcement on Salespersons' Performance Behavior," *Journal of Applied Psychology*, vol. 66, no. 3, June 1981, pp. 314–343.

reactions of employees. In sum, organizational behavior modification rests upon two fundamental concepts. People act in ways they find most personally rewarding. And by controlling the rewards, people's behavior can be modified in ways that are conducive to organizational effectiveness.

STYLES OF LEADERSHIP

All managers develop a style of leading or motivating subordinates. A leadership style can be defined as a pattern of behavior designed to integrate organizational and personnel interests in pursuit of some objective. As suggested in role analysis, the specific execution of that responsibility can take many forms. As a consequence, there have been developed various frameworks or schemes that depict the types of leadership styles from which a manager may select the one most appropriate to personal, subordinate, and organizational needs.

One of the commonly cited frameworks consists of a simple continuum from total autocracy to almost total democracy. This continuum would consist of the following: (1) coercive autocracy, where the leader *tells* and if necessary threatens; (2) benevolent autocracy, where the leader tells *and* explains, utilizing positive reinforcement if the behavior is forthcoming; (3) manipulative autocracy, where the leader "cons" subordinates into thinking that they are significantly participating as he or she is pulling the strings behind the scenes—in effect, a sophisticated autocrat; (4) consultative leadership, where employees feel and believe that their inputs are truly desired and can have impact upon the decision; and (5) a laissez-faire approach, where the leader wishes to join the group as a fellow participant and do what the group wants to do. Obviously, in the last style, the organization superiors still hold the leader accountable for decision results, thus limiting the degree to which this industrial democracy can be practiced.

The introduction of such a scheme of leadership styles does not require that the leader acquire and develop a single one among the available choices. In a study of 143 British managers, it was found that all but ten used three or more styles, depending upon the nature of the decision.[14] When the decision was important to the organization but not the subordinate, managers tended to be autocratic, with or without explanation. When it was important to subordinates but not to the organization, leaders tended to consult, encourage joint decision making, or actually delegate the decision to them. When the decision was not important to either, leaders tended to save personal time by autocratically deciding or allowing determination by subordinates. When the subject was one of importance to both, the greater majority tended to *consult* with subordinates prior to making the decision themselves. In contrasting style preferences in different portions of organizations, the greatest tendencies toward more subordinate participation were observed within the personnel department and among levels of general management, the least were reported in production and finance units, while sales and purchasing units were in the middle between these two extremes. Reports from industry indicate that the choice of leadership style is also affected by the particular product strategies being pursued. Such firms as Chase Manhattan Bank, Corning Glass, and General Electric have matched basic

---

[14]Frank A. Heller, "Leadership, Decision Making, and Contingency Theory," *Industrial Relations*, vol. 12, no. 2, May 1973, pp. 194–195.

strategies with managerial orientations toward either aggressive growth or cost-containing conservatism.

The implication that leadership style selection should be heavily influenced by forces in the subordinates, leaders, and the situation has led various theorists and consultants to establish situational frameworks of Reddin, Fiedler, Vroom and Yetton, and House. On the other hand, two of the best-known behavioral scientists, Rensis Likert and Robert Blake, propose that there is only one best universal style suitable for all personnel on all occasions. Each of these frameworks will be briefly described below.

Reddin 3-D Theory

Following the research of The Ohio State University, which suggested that two important leadership behaviors were *initiating* and *consideration*, Reddin proposes to identify style mixtures in four basic types of situations.[15] As indicated in Figure 16-3, styles and situations can be placed into a grid format utilizing the dimensions of Task Orientation and Relationships Orientation. Dividing the total area into four cells results in situations where the manager can be (1) separated from both task and human consid-

---

[15]William J. Reddin, *Managerial Effectiveness*, McGraw-Hill Book Company, New York, 1970. For a review of research efforts utilizing the Ohio State factors, see Abraham K. Korman, " 'Consideration,' 'Initiating Structure,' and Organizational Criteria: A Review," *Personnel Psychology*, vol. 19, no. 4, Winter 1966. pp. 361–379.

FIGURE 16-3   Leadership styles framework (Reddin).

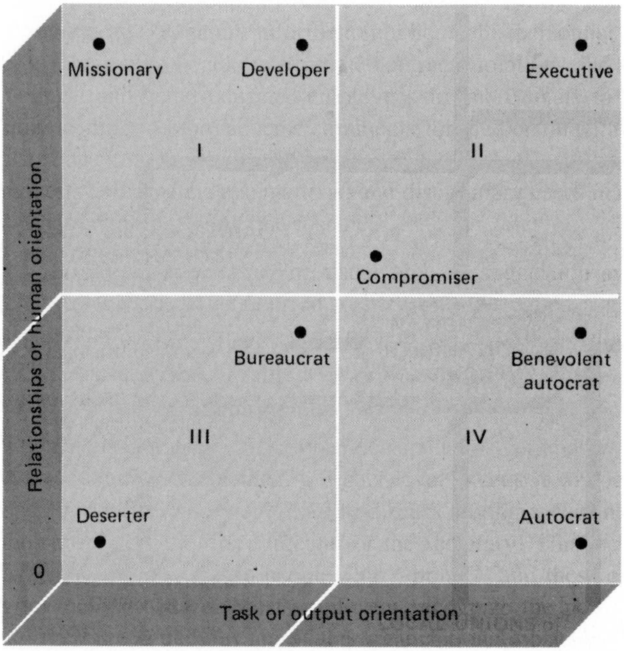

Situation I — Jobs with humanistic orientations, e.g., personnel department
Situation II — Jobs with integrated orientations, e.g., top management
Situation III — Jobs somewhat separated, e.g., data processing, finance
Situation IV — Jobs with heavy task orientation, e.g., production

erations, (2) highly related to the task with limited emphasis upon people, (3) highly concerned with people with limited attention being allocated to the task, and (4) highly concerned with integrating *both* task and human objectives. The scheme is labeled "3-D" inasmuch as in each of these four cells two types of styles are identified—one that is most effective in dealing with a situation and the other less effective. In Situation I, the "missionary" style is too extreme and a more effective style is the "developer" where the orientation is more toward helping people develop skills that will pay off in task accomplishment. Managers working in personnel units tend to have styles located in this area.

Situation II is typical of positions located in upper organizational levels. Here, the long-term accomplishment requires integration of task and human values. The more effective "executive" style attempts to maximize both sets of values while a "compromiser" is willing to work out a political exchange through trade-off and "split-the-difference" approaches. Jobs concerned with enforcement of procedures, data processing, and finance tend to emphasize means more than ends. These are encompassed in Situation III, with the more effective style being termed "bureaucrat" and the less effective "deserter." Situation IV deals with jobs where pressures are great for task accomplishment. The more effective style of "benevolent autocrat" attempts to "purchase" cooperation through persuasion, paternalism, fringe benefits, and executive justice. The more extreme style of "autocrat" tends to engender resistance and insubordination.

Most of the research with respect to the Reddin framework is in the area of associating personal styles with positions held. A forced-choice test is available through which individual scores can be obtained for each of the eight styles.[16] Little has been done in the way of attempting to relate styles to performance and satisfaction outputs.

Fiedler's Contingency Theory

The contingency theory developed by Fred E. Fiedler is also a situational approach.[17] The framework is made up of eight significantly different situations and *two* basic types of leadership styles. In identifying the eight situations, three major elements are analyzed: (1) leader-member relations, (2) task structure, and (3) position power of the leader. Measurement of leader-member relations is done on a group atmosphere scale indicating the degree to which the leader feels accepted by subordinates. The atmosphere may be friendly or unfriendly, relaxed or tense, and threatening or supportive. Task structure is measured by evaluating clarity of goals, verifiability of decisions made, specificity of solutions, and multiplicity of options available for solving problems. The position power of the leader is determined by the degree of influence he or she has over rewards and punishments, as well as by amount of official authority. Through mixing these three elements, eight situations can be identified.

These eight situations vary in accordance with the degree of leader influence and control over the group. There is maximum influence in situation 1 and very little in situation 8. Research evidence indicates that a *task-oriented, controlling leader* will prove most effective when the situations are either very easy (1, 2, and 3) or very difficult (8).

---

[16]"Management Style Diagnosis Test," Organizational Tests Ltd., Fredericton, N.B., Canada.
[17]Fred E. Fiedler, *A Theory of Leadership Effectiveness,* McGraw-Hill Book Company, New York, 1967.

Situation	Leader-Member Relations	Task Structure	Position Power
1	Good	Structured	High
2	Good	Structured	Low
3	Good	Unstructured	High
4	Good	Unstructured	Low
5	Poor	Structured	High
6	Poor	Structured	Low
7	Poor	Unstructured	High
8	Poor	Unstructured	Low

The more *permissive, considerate* leader performs more effectively in the intermediate situations of medium difficulty. In Fiedler's approach, the two leadership styles are measured by asking one to rate her or his Least Preferred Coworker on seventeen bipolar adjective scales, for instance, pleasant to unpleasant. A high-score LPC leader is seen as being personal relations-oriented, and the low-score LPC leader is more task-oriented.

There have been over forty studies dealing with the Fiedler contingency theory, and most seem to be supportive of the concept that leadership styles should be adapted to situational elements. Arguments about specifics of the theory are prevalent in the literature. There has, for example, been little research in situation number 6. In any event, the concept that leadership styles are *contingent* upon situational variables is both highly plausible and consistent with both the continuum and Reddin frameworks.

Vroom and Yetton's Decision Tree

One of the more recent style frameworks is that proposed by Victor Vroom and Philip Yetton.[18] The emphasis here is upon the degree to which the leader should share decision-making power with subordinates. The following five styles are identified:

- AI   The leader makes the decision using information personally possessed.

- AII   The leader obtains necessary information from subordinates and then decides. Subordinates may or may not be told of the nature of the problem.

- CI   The leader shares the problem with relevant subordinates individually, solicits suggestions, and then makes the decision.

- CII   The leader shares the problem with subordinates as a group, obtains collective ideas, and then makes the decision.

- GII   The leader shares the problem with the group, and acts more as a chairperson in generating and evaluating alternatives in search of group consensus.

It is proposed that all five styles are feasible given certain situational conditions. The two key elements in selecting a style of decision making are (1) ensuring that a quality decision is made, and (2) ensuring that the decision receives the acceptance necessary for effective implementation.

[18]Victor H. Vroom and Philip W. Yetton, *Leadership and Decision-Making*, University of Pittsburgh Press, Pittsburgh, 1973.

As indicated in Figure 16-4, these two elements can be protected by asking oneself seven key questions. The first three questions are intended to protect decision quality, and the final four are designed to eliminate styles that would unduly jeopardize subordinate acceptance. When placed in the framework of a decision tree, the leader can come up with a feasible set of styles that will meet both quality and acceptance requirements. Where more than one style is feasible, the leader can choose either a time-efficient approach through selecting the most autocratic, or a human-resources-investment approach through sharing decisions with subordinates.

In checking the model against 181 actual cases of managerial decision making, it was discovered that 117 adhered to model requirements.[19] Of these, 68 percent were deemed to have successful outcomes. Of the 64 that violated model requirements, only 22 percent were regarded as successful. Overall, the more frequently observed successful styles were CII (group consultation) and GII (group decision making). The model is a better predictor of decision acceptance than it is of decision quality.

Path-goal theory of leadership Following the original research from The Ohio State University, R. J. House suggests that the proper mixture of leader consideration and initiation will vary according to the clarity of the path that leads to goal accomplishment.[20] The leader's function consists of clarifying the goals for subordinates, the paths to these goals, and facilitating both intrinsic and extrinsic rewards for proper performance. When the task is varied, complex, and unstructured, it is likely to be intrinsically satisfying and leader behavior in the form of initiating action will help clarify the path. On the other hand, when the task is highly structured and the path is already clear, initiating actions by the leader would be redundant and irritating. The appropriate leader behavior in this situation would emphasize consideration in an attempt to reduce subordinate frustration and help offset the dissatisfying nature of the structured task. Considerable research has supported the path-goal theory in predicting subordinate satisfaction with the leader; the theory has been less predictive in linking leadership style to performance levels.

Management Grid

Moving to the universalists' frameworks, the Management Grid of Robert Blake and Jane Mouton is one of the most widely known style schemes among business managers.[21] If Figure 16-3 were relabeled using "concern for people" for relationships orientation, and "concern for output" for task orientation, we could then number each from 1 to 9. The grid is thus a 9 × 9 checkerboard and a score of 1 denotes low concern and a score of 9 shows high concern. On this basis, five basic styles have been identified as follows:

- 1, 1   The leader whose style exhibits little concern for either people or output. Reddin uses the term "deserter" and agrees that it is typically ineffective.

- 9, 1   The manager who stresses output and operating efficiency with neglect or unconcern for human components. Reddin entitles this "autocrat."

---

[19]Victor H. Vroom and Arthur G. Jago, "On the Validity of the Vroom–Yetton Model," *Journal of Applied Psychology,* vol. 63, no. 2, April 1978, p. 155.

[20]R. J. House, "A Path-Goal Theory of Leader Effectiveness," *Administrative Science Quarterly,* vol. 16, no. 2, June 1971, pp. 321–338.

[21]Robert R. Blake and Jane S. Mouton; Louis B. Barnes and Larry Greiner, "Breakthrough in Organization Development," *Harvard Business Review,* vol. 42, no. 6, November-December 1964, p. 133.

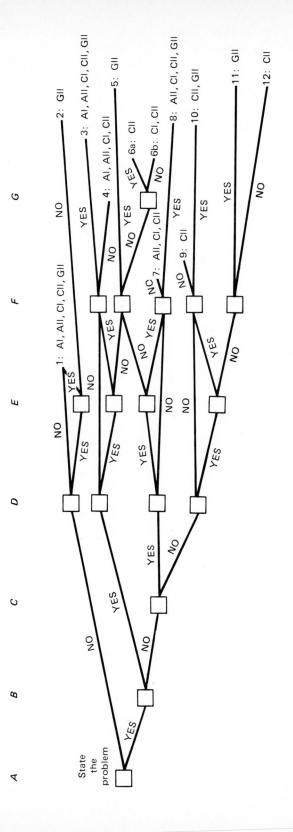

A. Does the problem possess a quality requirement?
B. Do I have sufficient information to make a high-quality decision?
C. Is the problem structured?
D. Is acceptance of the decision by subordinates important for effective implementation?
E. If I were to make the decision by myself, am I reasonably certain that it would be accepted by my subordinates?
F. Do subordinates share the organization goals to be attained in solving this problem?
G. Is conflict among subordinates likely in preferred solutions?

FIGURE 16-4 Decision process flowchart. (Feasible set). (*Reprinted by permission of the publisher from "Can Leaders Learn to Lead?" by Victor H. Vroom, Organizational Dynamics 4 (Winter 1976) © by AMACOM, a division of American Management Association. All Rights Reserved.*)

- 1, 9   The manager who is thoughtful, comfortable, and friendly, and who exhibits little concern for output. Human considerations are placed before organizational requirements. Blake and Mouton have referred to this as "country-club" management, while Reddin uses "missionary." Both agree that it is ineffective.

- 5, 5   The manager who attempts to balance and trade off concern for work in exchange for a satisfactory level of cooperation, a "compromiser."

- 9, 9   The manager who seeks high output through the medium of committed people, a commitment achieved through mutual trust, respect, and a realization of interdependence. Reddin terms this "executive" and agrees that it is more effective than "compromiser" in situations calling for integration.

In the view of Blake and Mouton, *only* the 9,9 style represents a successful integration of organizational and human values in *all* situations. They assume that both values can be maximized simultaneously, and they rest their scheme on the philosophical implications of the human models proposed by Maslow, McGregor, Argyris, and Herzberg, the organizational psychologists.

Blake and Mouton have been successful in converting leadership styles toward the 9,9 corner of the grid. Their total program of organization development encompasses six phases, the first two of which concentrate on altering styles. In one large organization, comparisons were made of managers who had received no Grid training versus those who had been exposed in phases 1 and 2 to both structured insight and team-development training techniques. Among those with no Grid experience, 28 percent described their personal styles in 9,9 terms.[22] For those completing phase 1, the responses rose to 36.4 percent. Almost one-half of those undergoing team development in phase 2 gave a 9,9 response.

Likert's Continuum

The second universalist framework of leadership styles was developed by Rensis Likert, formerly Director of the Institute for Social Research at the University of Michigan.[23] It consists of a classical-behavioral continuum of styles ranging from autocracy to participation in the manner described above. Four basic styles are envisaged: System I—Exploitative Autocracy, System II—Benovolent Autocracy, System III—Consultative Leadership, and System IV—Participative Group Leadership. Only the last style or system is deemed best in the long run for all situations.

System III requires that group members be consulted prior to the decision being reached, but it does not involve them in the actual process. System IV's emphasis is upon a *group* participative role with full involvement in the process of reaching a conclusion. Subordinates feel free to discuss things with their leader, and the leader displays supportive, rather than condescending or threatening, behavior. It is contended that the entire organization should be designed along System IV lines, with work being performed by a series of overlapping groups. The group leader provides a linking pin between his or her group and other units that are higher in the organization. Decision making is

---

[22]Howard A. Hart, "The Grid Appraised—Phases 1 and 2," *Personnel,* vol. 51, no. 5, September-October 1974, p. 52.

[23]Rensis Likert, *The Human Organization,* McGraw-Hill Book Company, New York, 1967.

widespread throughout the enterprise, with the power of knowledge usually taking precedence over the power of authority. If well executed, it is contended that the informal and formal organization can be one and the same—all social forces support efforts to achieve organizational goals.

The frameworks of both Likert and Blake/Mouton rest on the philosophical human models of self-actualization, "theory Y," maturation, and motivator factors. In contrast, the situationalists suggest that organizations, technologies, problems, and personnel will differ, and the successful style is one that adapts to these constraints and contingencies.

SUMMARY

The needs that a human being brings to the organization are made evident in terms of specific wants such as money, security of job, congenial associates, credit and praise, a meaningful job, opportunity to advance, good working conditions, reasonable orders, a relevant organization, and competent and fair leadership. These wants provide an array of motivational tools that managers may utilize to motivate behavior toward desired directions. Motivational force is greatest if the want is highly valued, if the person feels capable of performing as specified, and if he or she perceives that the reward will actually be allocated. Behavior modification suggests that a continuing positive reinforcement schedule is preferred at the beginning of any new program, to be followed by a reward schedule of a variable-ratio type. Ignoring undesirable behavior is preferred to punishment.

Leaders must align and integrate member efforts and interests with the goals of the organization. Style frameworks portraying available choices include those of the situationalists such as Reddin, Fiedler, and Vroom/Yetton, as well as those of the universalists Likert and Blake/Mouton. The latter style schemes propose to implement the human models of the organization psychologists Maslow, McGregor, Argyris, and Herzberg. The total conversion of the organization to this set of values is termed "organization development."

BRIEF CASE

As a consequence of knowing and working with the Division Head, Dick Eisen was hired to supervise a crew of eight employees engaged in field exploration for discovering copper deposits. Techniques used included induced polarization, seismic methods, and electromagnetics. Since the work took place in isolated areas, Eisen's requirements for crew membership included (a) a total absence of pettiness, jealousy, and bigotry, (b) trust in superiors, (c) willingness to work hard, (d) ability to travel anywhere in the world on short notice, and (e) a desire for the highest production rate possible. He particularly emphasized the necessity for the crew members to be congenial with each other.

In comparison with the other exploration crew, Eisen introduced a new motivational system involving the reward of free time. It was found that because of the variance in the earth's natural electrical noise, polarization readings were most accurate during the morning hours. Thus, Eisen awarded bonus free time if the crew could complete a polarization setup by 12:00 noon. Secondly, Eisen assigned time allotments for each exploration area based upon his accumulated experience. If crew members were able to finish ahead of this schedule, the difference in time belonged to them. During a 6-year period, the annual production record for his crew rose from 70 line miles to 300 line miles with improved levels in the quality of the data recorded.

The other exploration crew continued to work under the traditional system. A full 40 hours of work each week was required, and rewards were in the form of annual pay increases depending upon the performance appraisal system. The level of performance was considerably under that of Eisen's crew.

Questions

1. How would you describe the style of leadership exhibited by Eisen?

2. What types of reward schedules are included in the case?

3. What predictions do you have for the future of Eisen in this company? for the relationship between the crews?

DISCUSSION QUESTIONS

1. Briefly outline the valence-expectancy theory of motivation. Relate its component parts to (1) Maslow hierarchy, (2) Management by Objectives, (3) training and experience, and (4) organizational behavior modification.

2. What is the difference between primary and secondary outcomes in the valence-expectancy model? How are these related to the Maslow hierarchy?

3. Describe the personality of an employee who would be most adaptable to valence-expectancy theory analysis.

4. In organizational behavior modification programs, what are the available types of reward schedules? Give an example of each type.

5. Itemize leadership-style frameworks that could be classified as (1) situational, or (2) universal. What is the meaning of this classification?

6. Compare and contrast the style framework of Reddin's 3-D with Blake/Mouton's Management Grid.

7. Apply the Vroom/Yetton Decision Tree model to the following situation: Your boss has ordered you, the engineering supervisor, to designate four of your twelve equally good engineers to go on a rather undesirable 6-month overseas assignment. Answer all questions that apply and follow the tree to the approved style set. Do you agree with the model?

8. What are the philosophical underpinnings of the 9,9 style and System IV?

9. Describe the varying situations that provide the framework for Fiedler's contingency theory.

10. If the department head in a major university wished to motivate young faculty to write and publish more articles, what suggestions could be derived from the formula, motivational force equals valence times expectancy?

SUPPLEMENTARY
READING

BLAKE, ROBERT B. and JANE SRYGLEY MOUTON: "A Comparative Analysis of Situationalism and 9,9 Management by Principle," *Organizational Dynamics*, vol. 10, no. 4, Spring 1982, pp. 20–43.

EDEN, DOV and ABRAHAM B. SHANI: "Pygmalion Goes to Boot Camp: Expectancy, Leadership and Trainee Performance," *Journal of Applied Psychology*, vol. 67, no. 2, April 1982, pp. 194–199.

HAYNES, ROBERT S., RANDALL C. PINE, and H. GORDON FITCH: "Reducing Accident Rates with Organizational Behavior Modification," *Academy of Management Journal*, vol. 25, no. 2, June 1982, pp. 407–416.

KOMAKI, JUDITH L., ROBERT L. COLLINS, and PAT PENN: "The Role of Performance Antecedents and Consequences in Work Motivation," *Journal of Applied Psychology*, vol. 67, no. 3, June 1982, pp. 334–340.

SCOTT, DOW and STEVE MARKHAM: "Absenteeism Control Methods: A Survey of Practices and Results," *The Personnel Administrator*, vol. 27, no. 6, June 1982, pp. 73–84.

WALKER, LAWRENCE R. and KENNETH W. THOMAS: "Beyond Expectancy Theory: An Integrative Motivational Model from Health Care," *Academy of Management Review*, vol. 7, no. 2, April 1982, pp. 187–194.

chapter 17

Quality of Worklife and Quality Circles

The approach to motivating individuals discussed in the preceding chapter is based fundamentally on the concept that people will pursue their own best interests given their understanding of themselves and the situation. Expectancy theory assumes that outcomes, capacities, and behavior-reward linkages can be and are individually calculated. Organizational behavior modification emphasizes reinforcement when the desired behavior is exhibited.

The hierarchy of needs discussed in Chapter 15 portrays the complexity of human beings. Not only do they strive to fulfill egoistic needs, they also derive satisfaction from belonging to a group and working with other people. Collaboration, as much as individualistic competition, is a part of our behavioral repertoire. Managerial interest in the motivation of groups, rather than individuals, is steadily increasing. This increase has been attributed not only to the collaborative models proposed by various behavioralists, but also the model in action exhibited by the Japanese. A major stimulus in this regard is the steadily declining productivity in the American economy. As shown in Figure 17-1, though the United States is still the most productive economy in the world, we are steadily losing our edge. Between 1960 and 1981, our productivity increased only 59 percent as measured in 1981 constant dollars. Only Great Britain, with its 41 percent increase, ranked behind. The most impressive gain was stacked up by the Japanese, who increased their per capita productivity 261 percent. Not all of this can be attributed to the manner in which employees are motivated in Japan. The overall industrial plant of Japan is considerably more modern than that of the United States, having been reconstructed after World War II. In addition, Japanese citizens save more than 15 percent of their income as compared with only 5 or 6 percent for United States citizens. This provides a capital reservoir that will enable the modernization of the Japanese plant to continue. It is estimated that Japan has four times as many industrial robots as any other nation in the world.

Despite the multitude of factors that have contributed to Japan's remarkable level of productivity, credit is given by many to the style of management that emphasizes security, participation, and collaboration, In this chapter, we will discuss one of the major participative techniques contributed by the Japanese—Quality Circles. Many companies in the United States have applied this approach, with some modifications that

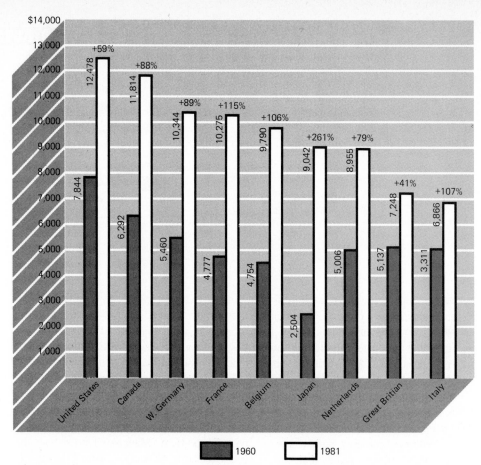

FIGURE 17-1 Output per capita—nine nations (in constant 1981 dollars). (*Source: U.S. Department of Labor.*)

better fit our culture. We shall first undertake a discussion of the basic nature of primary work groups, itemizing various component parts of their anatomy. This will be followed by discussion of a program that, though going under miscellaneous titles, has been most frequently referred to as "Quality of Worklife." This program has also been heavily characterized by participative and collaborative processes. We will end the chapter by outlining the nature and techniques used in Quality Circles. The emphasis throughout the chapter is upon the motivation of groups.

Anatomy of the Group

A group can be defined as two or more people, interacting and interdependent, who have the ability to behave in a unified manner with shared purposes or objectives. Study of the group and group processes was not identified as a separate field of research until the 1930s. Kurt Lewin popularized the term *group dynamics* and aided in the establishment of the Research Center for Group Dynamics, the first organization devoted exclusively to the study of group phenomena.[1] Various disciplines have been involved in group research, including psychology, sociology, anthropology, social psychology, and psychiatry. As a result certain basic components of the group have been identified. Among these are group goals, participants, leaders, norms, cohesiveness, and size.

Group goals Groups usually have two types of goals. First is the task goal, which is the fundamental reason for its formation, for example, process work, reduce costs, develop new concepts, and so on. If the group is to be utilized on a continuing basis, it must always have maintaining itself as a secondary goal. From time to time, attention must be given to group processes, dealing with such issues as the lack of participation by some, the dominance of group processes by others, and interpersonal feelings. One may become impatient with idle chatter, discussion of "irrelevant" issues, or elongation of authorized work breaks, but some of these activities are essential to group self-maintenance. The effective group will recognize and deal with interpersonal conflict instead of hiding or suppressing it. Research indicates that trusting behavior on the part of group members will contribute to increased originality, greater emotional stability, less defensiveness, and improved self-control.[2]

Participants Participants in a group can be volunteers, invited, or assigned. Firms using Quality Circles have emphasized that membership should be strictly voluntary. If the power and status of group members are relatively equal, the amount of participation tends to increase significantly. Democratic leadership will stimulate more member participation than does authoritarian leadership.

Though the formal system may designate an official leader, there will emerge in the group various informal roles. Among these roles can be regulars, deviants, informal leaders, and isolates. A *regular* accepts and conforms to most of the group's expectations regarding behavior. A *deviant* will reject and violate one or more norms, but still retain group membership. He or she will be the recipient of many group interactions to bring behavior back into line, for example, sarcasm, needling, or ostracism. An *informal leader* makes a special contribution in preserving group solidarity, such as helping weaker members, reducing intragroup tensions, and confronting the official leader with group wishes. Organization members who belong to no primary group are *isolates*. This does not mean that they do not feel social needs; rather, they typically are demonstrating psychological allegiance to a reference group apart from the immediate organization. One isolate machinist showed total disdain for group expectations regarding work output inasmuch as he had aspirations for starting up and operating a separate business.

Leaders Although there has been some experimentation with leaderless groups, most researchers have concluded that groups require some central focus. During the initial years, the officially designated group leaders in Quality Circles are usually the unit supervisors. With maturity, the supervisor is willing to step aside and have a subordinate act as official leader for a specific problem. Inasmuch as most groups have the

---

[1]Though founded at the Massachusetts Institute of Technology, the Research Center was moved to the University of Michigan after Lewin's death. Other similar groups are the Social Relations Laboratory at Harvard, the Human Dynamics Laboratory at the University of Chicago, and the Group Dynamics Center at Temple University.

[2]Dale E. Zand, "Trust and Managerial Problem Solving," *Administrative Science Quarterly*, vol. 17, no. 2, June 1972, pp. 229–239.

two basic goals, task and maintenance, it may be necessary to have two leaders—an official task leader and an unofficial social leader. Unusually talented leaders are able to handle both roles simultaneously.

There has been considerable research concerning the appropriate leadership style. As indicated in the preceding chapter, many contend that varying situations call for varying styles. However, if a primary concern is that of stimulating greater employee involvement and participation, the research is clear in substantiating use of the 9,9 style of Blake and Mouton or the System IV of Rensis Likert. When this type of participation is not deemed necessary or desirable, other styles may be more appropriate.

Norms   The formal organization has its standards, and the primary work group has its norms. A norm is behavior that is expected from group members. Those deviants who violate the group's norms are helped to see the errors of their ways. Group norms are usually unwritten rules that new members are gradually taught. For example, a norm might require that one display a lack of concern for the firm. The Japanese emphasize a counterpart norm wherein employees are taught to be loyal through the mechanism of long-term, secure employment. A norm could be to hide mistakes to make oneself look good. Again, the Japanese through their Quality Circles have emphasized the norm of openness so that problems can be solved.

The formal task assigned to the group has an effect upon the establishment of norms. If, for example, the group has been assigned the task of designing a new procedure, behavior norms might include a sense of joint responsibility, central focusing by a leader, and professionalism in discussion processes. If the assigned task is to come up with a new and original creation, norms might include openness, humor, restriction of criticism, support for unusual ideas, and participative leadership. If the assigned task is to negotiate a new contract between management and a labor union, the accompanying norms could include the freedom to disagree openly and the perception of conflict between the two groups as being healthy rather than pathological.[3]

Cohesiveness   Cohesiveness is the degree of attraction that the group has for each of its members. It is exemplified by such attitudes as loyalty to the group, a feeling of responsibility for group efforts, defending against outside attack, friendliness, and congeniality. Cohesive work groups are powerful instruments that can be used for or against the formal organization.

There are various managerial actions that can be taken to promote or preclude primary work group cohesion. Among these are the following:

1. *Stability of membership*. If people are constantly being added or removed from a unit, members will not have time to get to know each other. On the other hand, research shows that groups with high longevity develop such degrees of cohesiveness that communication processes with other groups, both within the firm and in the external environments, are inhibited. In reviewing the efforts of fifty research and development groups, it was found that none of the ten long-tenured groups were classified as high performers.[4] Such groups require considerable contact with others in order to avoid narrowness in outlook and excessive commitment to certain favored approaches.

[3]André L. Delbecq, "The Management of Decision-Making within the Firm: Three Strategies for Three Types of Decision-Making," *Academy of Management Journal*, vol. 10, no. 4, December 1967, pp. 332–338.
[4]Ralph Katz, "The Effects of Group Longevity on Project Communication and Performance," *Administrative Science Quarterly*, vol. 27, no. 1, March 1982, pp. 81–104.

2. *Similar values.* Cohesion is enhanced when members have similar values and prestige levels. Professional and nonprofessional employees often have difficulty in relating to each other. Older and younger employees often have different attitudes and values.

3. *Communication opportunities.* Cohesive work groups are very difficult to form on long assembly lines geared to speedy operation. When management in Volvo wanted such groups to form, they provided for communication opportunities by breaking the long assembly line up into smaller ones, and providing time and space for group meetings to take place.

4. *Physical isolation.* When a group of clerks was located around a corner out of the sight of the supervisor, a very cohesive group formed. Though there was much conversation, shooting of rubber bands, and kidding around, there was also much work being done with members helping each other. When a new layout of the workplace moved this group back into the larger unit, its output dropped immediately to the level of the other groups.

5. *Small size.* It is difficult to generate sufficient opportunities for interpersonal contact in large groups to enable cohesion to be effected. Large groups tend to break up into smaller cohesive groups. Experiences in firms with Quality Circles indicate that such groups should be no larger than nine to twelve members.

Size   There has been considerable research devoted to ascertaining the most effective group size in terms of accomplishing both task and maintenance goals. Distillation of this research leads to the following conclusions: (1) when quality of a complex group decision is paramount, the use of seven to twelve members under a formal leader is most appropriate; (2) when consensus in a conflict situation is important, the use of three to five members with no formal leader will ensure that each member's view will be discussed; and (3) when both quality and consensus are important, five to seven members seem most appropriate.[5] There tends to be a greater group conflict in even-sized groups, and there is more conflict in groups of two and four members than there is in those of six members. In large groups, there is greater member tolerance for autocratic leadership.

Some interesting research concerning the effect of group size on *individual* effort has resulted in the conclusion that "social loafing" exists. When a person feels that his or her contribution to the group cannot be measured with precision, there is a tendency for individual effort to decline. In one research project, measuring the amount of pressure in rope pulling, when only one person was pulling, the pressure was 138.6 pounds; when the group was enlarged to three, the individual pressure fell to 117.3 pounds; when eight were involved, each person exerted an average of 68.2 pounds.[6] To eliminate the possibility that faulty coordination was the source of the decline, the experiment was repeated with the subjects blindfolded and always pulling as individuals. When told that they were members of groups, the same type of decline in effort took place. It has also been observed that in crisis situations, bystanders are less likely to offer help if there are many to share the responsibility.

---

[5]L. L. Cummings, George P. Huber, and Eugene Arendt, "Effects of Size and Spatial Arrangements in Group Decision Making," *Academy of Management Journal,* vol. 17, no. 3, September 1974, p. 473.

[6]Bibb Latane, Kippling Williams, and Stephen Harkins, "Social Loafing," *Psychology Today,* vol. 13, no. 4, October 1979, pp. 104–110.

Quality of Worklife

During the last decade, the term "quality of worklife" (QWL) has appeared in research journals and the press with remarkable regularity. Despite this, there is no general definition of the concept; rather, it has become a catchall phrase encompassing whatever improvement in general organizational climate the practitioner or researcher has observed. In 1977, the staff of the American Center for the Quality of Working Life developed the following definition:[7]

- Quality of work life improvements are defined as any activity which takes place at every level of an organization which seeks greater organizational effectiveness through the enhancement of *human dignity and growth* ... a process through which the stakeholders in the organization—management, unions and employees—learn how to *work together better* ... to *determine for themselves* what actions, changes and improvements are desirable and workable in order to achieve the *twin and simultaneous goals* of an improved quality of life at work for all members of the organization and greater effectiveness for both the company and the unions.

Key elements of the definition are highlighted as being (1) promote human dignity and growth, (2) work together collaboratively, (3) participatively determine work changes, and (4) assume compatibility of people and organizational goals.

It should be noted that "organizations" includes not only the firm but the labor union as well. QWL programs are not be be viewed as union-busting devices since the union is often asked to participate in the program. Nevertheless, some managers are leary of this degree of involvement as exhibited by the statement of one executive, "When you ask a bear to dance, you can't quit just when you get tired."[8] Collaboration on one subject will lead to expectations in other areas.

QWL is fundamentally a philosophy or an approach that can permeate many different activities in the workplace. For example, if the performance appraisal program moves from a scenario where the supervisor plays god, to one of a joint superior-subordinate review and evaluation, it could be characterized as an improvement in QWL. Job enlargement and enrichment, instead of highly specialized job assignments, are also frequently described as QWL programs. Joint union-management programs to reduce accidents and prevent health problems are QWL programs. Merely cleaning up the workplace, improving the lighting, and painting the walls can be construed as an improvement in the quality of working life. Reducing stress on the job and providing counselors are also similarly categorized. In effect, any specific improvement in and around the workplace is often included under the catchall term of QWL. It is estimated that some eighteen to twenty four plants in General Motors have developed QWL programs in cooperation with the United Auto Workers.[9] In its Tarrytown, New York, assembly plant, for example, the grievance load has been cut from 2,000 to 20 as a consequence of an improved labor-management atmosphere issuing from increased worker participation. Teams have a right to vote on matters usually governed by union contracts, such as overtime scheduling and promotions. In another instance, Romac Industries, Inc., a producer of water-

---

[7]Lee M. Ozley and Judith S. Ball, "Quality of Work Life: Initiating Successful Efforts in Labor-Management Organization," *The Personnel Administrator,* vol. 27, no. 5, May 1982, p. 27.

[8]"Quality of Work Life: Catching On," *Business Week,* September 21, 1981, p. 80.

[9]"Hot UAW Issue: 'Quality of Work Life,' " *Business Week,* September 17, 1979, p. 122.

works pipes and fittings in Seattle, handles its pay increases on a peer review basis. In the 84-person firm, new employees are hired as unskilled workers at a plant base rate. After receiving a dollar-per-hour increase 6 months later, any further increases require the employee to "go on the board." She or he fills out a form stating the desired increase, and posts it on the bulletin board along with a picture. After 5 days of observation by other workers, a secret ballot is cast with the majority ruling as to whether the increase is to be granted. Some 90 percent of the raises have been granted, averaging about 16 percent per year. Units produced per person-hour have increased some 44 percent.

Semiautonomous groups   One of the more critical parts of the above cited definition is the concept of subordinate self-determination in work actions. One writer contends that a "not-so-quiet revolution" has occurred in the United States in the last decade with many firms experimenting with the concept of self-managing work groups.[10] Among the prominent features of many such programs are the following:

1. Work group composition that encompasses the full range of necessary skills to do all jobs. Job rotation is practiced and members are expected to learn all jobs.

2. The group sets its own output goals. Instead of individual job enrichment, there is a form of "work group enrichment."

3. Delegating authority or self-assignment of tasks and roles within the group. Usually an effort is made to mix interesting and routine tasks along with opportunities to understudy more complex tasks.

4. Vacancies in the group may be filled by group decision. Instead of merely requisitioning a replacement from the personnel unit, group members may become involved in recruitment and screening processes.

5. Provision for a group monetary reward system. Typically, all members of the group start at the same pay, and pay increases are determined by the number of skills learned. In some cases, fellow members of the group make the decision concerning whether the skill has been mastered.

In some groups, the charter may be enlarged to enable members to do purchasing, inventory, and quality control activities. The group may elect a group leader to communicate with management. The basis for grouping employees is by product rather than specialized function.

Many prominent examples of established semiautonomous work groups have been publicized in recent years. Among these are the following:

1. *General Foods Corporation.* In a dog-food manufacturing plant in Topeka, Kansas, all production tasks were assigned to teams of seven to fourteen members. There are no conventional departments or appointed supervisors. Rather, there are team leaders who work as equals with other team members. Specific techniques utilized are (1) employees are paid for what they know rather than what task they are currently performing, (2) teammates determine pay raises by deciding that the member has mastered a task, (3) the team makes job assignments, and (4) vacancies are filled by team members who interview and hire applicants. Results included a 5 percent lower cost, 40 percent higher productivity, 8 percent

[10]Edward E. Lawler III, "The New Plant Revolution," *Organizational Dynamics*, vol. 6, no. 3, Winter 1978, p. 3.

annual turnover rate, and no lost-time accidents in almost 4 years.[11] Recent reports however, indicate some deterioration of the system. Though the employee groups appear to be handling most problems quite well, various staff managers (personnel, engineering, legal) resent their loss of decision-making power. In addition, some employees find it difficult to pass upon the pay increases of their colleagues. Finally, because the plant is doing so well, employees have demanded a share of the savings in the form of bonuses. Because no other plant in General Foods has such a bonus system, management is resisting the demand.

2. *Sherwin-Williams*. In an automobile paint manufacturing plant located in Richmond, Kentucky, the technological restructuring included the following: (1) development of work teams with a whole task to perform, (2) all members encouraged to learn all jobs, (3) team assignments of jobs, (4) pay for skills acquired, (5) peer review of skill accomplishment, and (6) team building training sessions for all personnel. Results reported include a reduction of the work-force size for this type of plant from 200 to 160 employees. In other contrasts with more traditional Sherwin-Williams plants, this unit's productivity is 30 percent higher and its costs 45 percent lower. It has a 2.5 percent absenteeism rate as compared with the company average of 6.7 percent; ninety four percent of its paint output is rated as "excellent" as compared with 75 percent for other plants.[12]

3. *Volvo*. Though automobiles are typically produced under classical technological conditions, Volvo has built a plant at Kalmar, Sweden, that was designed so that production could be accomplished by teams rather than by continuous assembly lines. The new plant is formed in the shape of four hexagonal blocks to provide bays for team operations. The traditional long assembly line has been broken into many short lines interspersed with storage areas so that teams of fifteen to twenty-five members can perform such tasks as building an entire engine, installing all electrical systems, or installing brakes and wheel systems. Within limits, the teams set their own pace and divide tasks among members. The work cycle for some tasks has been lengthened from 1 to 2 minutes to as much as 20 or 30 minutes. Though the major reason for the new plant was to improve QWL and to reduce the former high rates of absenteeism of 20 percent and of turnover of up to 40 percent, reports indicate that improvements have also been effected in both quality of product and unit costs. Absenteeism and turnover have been drastically reduced.[13]

Degrees of participation   One need not delegate huge amounts of authority as described in the above examples to merit the term QWL. On other topics, if employees are merely informed concerning the reasons for management decisions and action, an improvement in QWL will be noted. The degree of subordinate participation is usually limited by such variables as ability levels, interest levels, amount of time available, skill of the leader, and the area of freedom available. Knowledge, ability, and interest vary among personnel, and the leader cannot transform everyone overnight into the "theory Y" image. Organizational restraints always exist in terms of time available to reach a decision, as well as subjects about which group decisions can be made. Figure 17-2 portrays one way of looking at the alternative degrees available.

[11]"Stonewalling Plant Democracy," *Business Week,* March 28, 1977, pp. 78–82.

[12]Ernesto J. Poza and M. Lynne Markus, "Success Story: The Team Approach to Work Restructuring," *Organizational Dynamics,* vol. 8, no. 3, Winter 1980, pp. 3–25.

[13]Richard B. Peterson, "Swedish Experiments in Job Reform," *Business Horizons,* vol. 19, no. 3, June 1976, p. 16.

Factor	Degrees		
	Low	Moderate	High
Scope of usage	Narrow, minor matters	Selected subjects	Everything of real concern
Frequency of use	Rarely used	Occasional or periodic meetings	Consistently, "way of life"
Persons involved	Select few Top management	Select groups or committees	All supervisors All employees
Part taken	Communication heard	Consulted (consultative management)	Group decision (democratic management)

Source: Robert E. Schwab, "Participative Management: The Solution to the Human Relations Problem?"
Speech before the Cincinnati chapter of the Society for the Advancement of Management, Oct. 2, 1952.

Concerning scope of subject and frequency of use, it was determined in one study that the significance of the subject was a more important factor in producing employee satisfaction than sheer quantity of participative acts.[14] A high quantity of participative interactions on trivial matters is more indicative of manipulative autocracy than of true involvement. In a survey of 3,453 subscribers to *Harvard Business Review*, only one-third of this managerially sophisticated group would agree that employees should be allowed to vote on certain policy issues.[15] If confined solely to subordinate managers ("persons involved" in Figure 17-2), the percentage rose to about half. A second survey taken 6 years later showed movement toward more employee participation in making certain management decisions from 29 percent approval in 1971 to 44 percent in 1977 on mandatory retirement policies, from 29 percent to 43 percent on possible plant relocation, and from 16 percent to 23 percent on whether the company should continue working on controversial defense contracts.[16] Two-thirds of these respondents would not bind management to the results of the vote, thus allocating it to the "consulted" degree for "part taken" in Figure 17-2.

As a final observation, a reading of columns would indicate the extremes of participation. An extremely high position would be that on "everything of real concern" as a "way of life" the leader should allow "all employees" to make a "group decision." Multiple management, a program discussed in Chapter 9, would rank on the moderate degree for scope, moderate on frequency, moderate on persons involved (middle management), and between moderate and high on part taken (95 percent of recommendations were accepted). The Scanlon plan, discussed in Chapter 13, would be moderate on scope, moderate on frequency, high on persons involved, and probably moderate on part taken.

[14]J. B. Ritchie and Raymond E. Miles, "An Analysis of Quantity and Quality of Participation as Mediating Variables in the Participative Decision Making Process," *Personnel Psychology*, vol. 34, no. 3, Autumn 1970, pp. 347–359.

[15]David W. Ewing, "Who Wants Corporate Democracy?" *Harvard Business Review*, vol. 49, no. 5, September-October 1971, pp. 25–28.

[16]David W. Ewing, "What Business Thinks about Employee Rights," *Harvard Business Review*, vol. 55, no. 5, September-October 1977, p. 84.

Quality Circles

The start of Quality Circles (QC) in Japan is generally credited to the Union of Japanese Scientists and Engineers, along with Dr. Kaoru Ishikawa of Tokyo University. In the 1950s Dr. Edward W. Deming of the United States introduced the concept of statistical quality control in a series of lectures in Japan. A decade later, the idea of involving *all* employees, not just staff quality control experts and management, was introduced by the union. With this total effort, Japan has moved from the title of "Junk Merchants of the World" to one of the world's leaders in quality products.

Contrary to popular belief, Japan does not outperform all other countries in all products. They are outperformed by the United States in agriculture, aircraft, nonferrous metals, chemicals, pharmaceuticals, large-scale computers, and large earth-moving equipment. However, Japanese firms have come to excel in the mass production of such products as automobiles, household appliances, steel, word processors, compact computers, and optical equipment. A remarkable degree of collaboration and cooperation has been developed in many firms, and the QC is merely one well-publicized example.

A QC is a self-governing group of workers, with or without their supervisor, who voluntarily meet on a regular basis to identify, analyze, and solve problems in their work field. In the beginning, the key emphasis in Japan was upon the improvement of product quality. Since that time, the province has been broadened to include many other problems such as cost reduction, safety, clerical procedures, and training techniques. A QC is not a task force as outlined in Figure 17-3. Though both are temporary and can be abandoned at any time, the QC has a different framework and orientation.

Objectives Though the original initiation of the QC concept in Japan stemmed from a desire to improve quality, the fundamental objective has been stated as a desire to develop and enhance human resources. Japan viewed human beings as its primary resource, and developed policies and practices that revolved around that attitude. Among specific policies followed were: (1) lifetime employment for a substantial segment of the work force, (2) considerable investment in training inasmuch as the employee will remain in the one organization, (3) broad career paths with the employee working in various occupations within the firm, (4) slow promotion, which reduces the need to cover up mistakes, and (5) collective decision making, which increases the speed of implementation once a decision has been reached.

With the more materialistic emphasis in the United States, it is difficult for managers to adopt the "enhancement of human resources" in place of determining the cost/benefits of the QC. If employees view the QC as another manipulative device whereby their ideas and effort can be exploited by management, then fewer of the values of QC will be

FIGURE 17-3
A Contrast of Quality Circles and Task Forces

	Quality Circle	Task Force
Orientation	People building	Problem solving
Member selection	Voluntary	Appointed
Member source	Same work group	Various functions
Member skill	Does not matter	Most skilled
Group objectives	Selected by members	Selected by management
Implementation of solutions	Largely by QC members	Largely by others

derived. An attempt to downplay the immediate output in preference to human resource enhancement is exhibited by the order of listing objectives in the Hughes Aircraft Company as follows: (1) encourage employee commitment, (2) develop individual skill/morale, (3) build strong problem-solving teams, and (4) generate/implement solutions to work-related problems such as technology, budgets, and schedules.

Circle processes A QC typically consists of four to twelve volunteer members, the average in Japan being about nine per circle. At its first few meetings, instructions in problem-solving approaches are usually given by either the circle leader or a staff specialist. Among the specific techniques often given are:

1. *Brainstorming processes.* The purpose of this technique is to stimulate creativity through free association, unrestricted interaction with others, and the complete restraint of criticism. For a certain time period, any idea that comes to mind is voiced. One idea suggests another. Ridiculous and unrealistic ideas are stimulated and not repressed. No criticism of any idea is permitted and all are recorded faithfully. Some have characterized this process as "cerebral popcorn" but it is a useful initial technique to develop an extended number of ideas.

2. *Cause-and-effect or "fishbone" diagrams.* After a problem is identified, members are asked to suggest various causes for the difficulty. It will be determined that some causes are the results of other causes, and their charting often resembles the bony structure of a fish.

3. *Sampling and charting methods.* Members are taught how to make observations of events in the workplace and chart them in a manner that demonstrates significant relationships. For example, a Pareto diagram orders events in terms of frequency, with the most frequent highlighted for further analysis; for example, basic causes for overshipment of material include vendor attitude (33 percent), duplicate shipments (23 percent), buyer requests (15 percent), and so on.

The working sessions, typically one hour per week, usually follow the sequence outlined in Figure 17-4. The first step in identifying workplace problems can come from listing suggestions from management or other employees, or in utilizing the brainstorming techniques noted above. After discussion, the QC members select a problem to work on. The analysis of the problem can involve any of a number of problem-solving techniques, as well as inviting functional specialists into the meeting to secure additional information. The behavior style of the circle leader promotes a maximum of discussion, participation, and involvement by all group members. This is a major reason for keeping the circle size relatively small. At some point, the group will settle upon a recommended solution to the problem.

The next step in the process can be rather unsettling for employees who have never been asked their opinion about anything in the workplace. Selected members are asked to make a presentation to management discussing what has been found and explaining the nature of the recommended solution. Many managers have been both surprised and greatly impressed with the comprehensiveness and lucidity of these presentations. After hearing the presentation, management must decide whether or not to accept it or any part thereof. Reports indicate that on average about 80 percent of all QC recommendations are accepted.

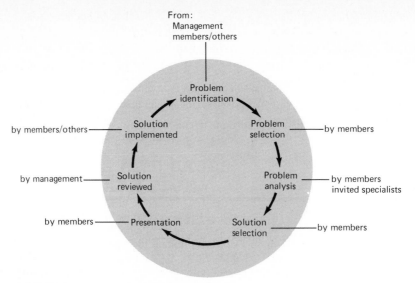

FIGURE 17-4 The quality circle process.

The final step in the process is the actual implementation of the decision. Inasmuch as circle members had a lot to do with the suggested change, the enthusiasm for implementation tends to be high. Implementation often requires cooperation from those not involved in circle processes, and circle members can help here through providing background information to stimulate acceptance and cooperation.

Organization structure for QCs As portrayed in Figure 17-5, the organization structure for a QC program includes four components: (1) a steering committee, (2) facilitators, (3) circle leaders, and (4) circle members. A steering committee usually consists of top-level management representatives from each of the major departments. If

FIGURE 17-5 Organization structure—quality circles.

"The need for specially trained managers to help with quality circles has become increasingly apparent. As participatory management programs became the rage, too many companies simply grouped some workers together, designated a supervisor as team leader, and then gave the leader a one-week course in group dynamics—after which the group was expected to function productively. Instead, the group often addressed the wrong problems or found itself unable to get help from other departments. Meetings frequently degenerated into free-for-alls."

It was rapidly discovered that special personalities were required to get a successful quality circle underway. Facilitators must have good communication skills and the ability to work with both labor and management. When drawn from personnel departments, they get a clearer view of how the production unit operates and how workers relate to their jobs. When taken from line management, they develop improved interpersonal skills and become familiar with how their departments fit into the overall organization. In addition, facilitators develop friendships that they maintain when moving on to other jobs in the firm.

"Recognition of the training benefits of the facilitator role is spreading like wildfire in corporate circles. 'People are just beginning to discover this training aspect, and I point it out whenever I try to convince management in a department to set up a pilot QC program,' notes James R. Widtfeldt, an organizational development specialist at Honeywell Inc. who has helped set up more than 500 quality circles. It is a discovery that is long overdue, says William G. Veltrop, an organizational development adviser for Exxon Enterprises who has been encouraging line managers to fill facilitator and other 'behavioral science' types of roles as part of their development."

"A Serendipitous Training Ground for Managers," *Business Week*, February 15, 1982, p. 52.

a cooperating union is present, union leaders will also be members. This committee sponsors the QC program by setting overall objectives and establishing operational guidelines, particularly in regard to the rate of expansion. A program title is selected and not all are called QCs, for example, "Involvement Teams," "Winning Edge Program." Union Carbide refers to them as PRIDE Circles, standing for *P*roductivity through *R*ecognition, *I*nvolvement, and *D*evelopment of *E*mployees.

The facilitator acts as a consultant to QC leaders and provides feedback to the steering committee concerning circle processes and results. In the beginning, he or she may persuade supervisors to set up QCs and provide training for both QC members and leaders. An essential requirement for such a job is the ability to get along with people at all levels. A facilitator has been described as a coordinator, coach, promoter, teacher, and innovator. As discussed in Box 17-1, companies are finding that the facilitator position is an excellent training ground for future higher managerial positions in the organization. It is a full-time job, particularly when dealing with eight to ten QCs in the startup phases. With more mature QCs, the facilitator can handle more. Though a coordinator for the steering committee, the facilitator usually reports organizationally to either the personnel unit or the director of manufacturing or quality control.

In the initial session of a QC, it is typical for the leader to be the supervisor of the employee members. As the group matures, the leader on future projects may be an employee who has a particular interest or skill in the project selected. After participation in a QC, the supervisor will not ordinarily feel his or her position threatened by turning over the leadership function to a subordinate. The circle leader receives the same type of training as circle members. But in addition, the leader receives special training in group dynamics, participative leadership techniques, and human behavior. If the circle is to be successful, the leader must be skilled in discussion processes that promote the active participation of all members. Such concepts as the following are emphasized:

419

1. Acceptance by all, particularly the leader, that there is more than one way to solve a problem successfully.

2. Encouragement of all members to clarify and build on each other's ideas.

3. Periodic summarizing by the leader or a member to ensure common understanding.

4. Avoidance of heated arguments in favor of one particular position. Vigorous eloquence should not substitute for clarity and logic.

5. Avoidance of such techniques as majority vote and coinflipping to obtain group agreement.

6. Promotion of constructive disagreements in place of dodging arguments in search of an artificial state of harmony.

7. Being suspicious of agreements that come too quickly and easily. A circle leader who is also the supervisor must constantly be aware of the influence of the supervisory position.

Circle members are typically employees of a single official work group. They are volunteers or invited participants. In the initial phases, certain selected employees may be invited by management to participate to ensure the success of early circles. Employees are free to withdraw from participation at any time. Circle meetings usually take place on company time, and if this is not possible, overtime pay is usually given for after-hours meetings.

Circle problems   Impatience and pressures for tangible circle payoffs will quickly lead to circle failures. A theory X type of organizational structure is totally incompatible with the philosophy underlying QCs.

Problems exist in terms of QC payoffs. In the traditional suggestion system, the single individual coming up with the suggestion receives the total award. However, the suggestion coming out of a QC is the result of the efforts of many people. In one company, an improved procedure for training operators on a yarn spinning machine resulted in first-year cost savings of $68,000. In another, reducing the defect rate in roll paper handling produced benefits in excess of $2 million. In Japan, there are typically no allocations of rewards to members of a QC other than the psychological benefits of making a contribution. It is felt that if the firm prospers, then employees with lifetime jobs will also prosper. In the United States, with its emphasis upon individual motivation and financial rewards, some circle members have "wised up" and have asked for a "share of the action" if their participation is to continue. In some organizations, the suggestion from a QC is accorded the same treatment as a suggestion from an individual. The monetary award is divided equally among circle members. In other instances, the award is given to the firm's employee recreation program. If the award is given to circle members, various complicated problems will arise. For example, if outside specialists were used for advice, how much do they get? If a circle member joined the group after the project was begun, or leaves it before completion, what percentage of a full share should be allocated? Managers are usually not allowed to receive monetary rewards for suggestions, so how should the circle leader be compensated?

Perhaps the major underlying problem with QCs in the United States is the one of moving from an individualist, competitive culture to a group-oriented, collaborative one. QCs fit the Japanese culture quite well. All employees come from a common racial origin. They speak the same language and live in a compact geographic region. They have a strong sense of national identity. Even their religious beliefs emphasize the interconnections among humans. On the other hand, the culture of the United States has been more individualistic and materialistic. We admire the John Wayne approach of individually and courageously attacking and overcoming obstacles. We respect and rely upon experts rather than trusting ordinary rank and file employees to deal with a problem. When conflicts among people arise, we utilize an adversary system to solve them. Though the United States has twice the population of Japan, it has 40 times as many lawyers. As we shall discuss in the next two chapters, American unions and managements take an adversary approach in negotiating wages, hours, and working conditions. Japanese unions tend to be company unions, and they exhibit concern for maintaining the health of the employing organization. Quality Circles can be and are being introduced into many American companies. But a total transplant of the concept without change to adapt to different cultural beliefs is not possible. According to the International Association of Quality Circles, there are more than one thousand organizations using QCs in the United States.

SUMMARY

People can be motivated as both individuals and members of groups. As organizations become more complex, managers will increasingly have to stimulate collaboration and cooperation rather than individualism and competition. In the analysis of groups, certain fundamental characteristics must be studied to enable understanding. Among these are task and maintenance goals, the informal roles played by participants, norms, cohesion, size, and leadership. If groups are to be emphasized, management should undertake various activities to promote higher degrees of cohesiveness.

Two group-oriented programs have been introduced into American organizations in recent years. A quality of worklife program is a catchall term that includes any improvement in organizational culture that advances the dignity and growth of employees. A major example of QWL is the semiautonomous groups which have been given powers of self-management. Many of the same concepts employed in individual job enrichment can also be utilized in "work group enrichment," such as group determination of output goals, group assignment of tasks, group-based financial rewards, and so on. The Quality Circle is the most recent group participative program to be introduced in the United States. Rank and file employees volunteer to meet and analyze task problems. Emphasis is given to development of human resources rather than to the development of profitable task problem solutions. Considerable training is required for both circle members and the circle leader. Training is given in such areas as brainstorming, cause-and-effect analysis, data collection, charting, and sampling. A complete program with many circles will require the creation of a steering committee and use of specialized facilitators to train members and coordinate circle efforts. Though most widespread in Japan, there is growing evidence of the use of QCs in this country.

BRIEF CASE

As a result of rapid growth in sales, the Baker Company had to double the size of the central secretarial pool. Many of the current secretaries, ages 35 to 55, had been with the company since its inception. None had more than a high school education. Though the group had previously been given the assignment of hiring new secretaries, it was felt that the doubling of staff required addition of persons with advanced data processing skills. Eight new secretaries were hired by management. Several had education beyond high school, and all were in their 20s. Unexpectedly, the performance level of the pool fell off drastically even though doubled in size. The manager interviewed a few of the old staff and they told him that the new secretaries just didn't fit in. They were hard to work with, wouldn't listen, and would not take direction. When their mistakes were corrected, they got offended. In interviewing a few of the new secretaries, they told him that the older secretaries refused to listen to new and more efficient ideas. They complained they were unable to use their training and the older secretaries would not socialize with them.

Questions

1. Why do you think the productivity of the group has fallen?

2. What would you recommend doing about this problem?

DISCUSSION QUESTIONS

1. If management wants to increase the degree of cohesiveness of a group, what specific activities can be undertaken?

2. Should management favor or oppose increased cohesiveness in work groups? Why or why not?

3. What is the difference between a company standard and a group norm? Cite examples.

4. What is meant by "quality of worklife?" Identify key elements of the definition.

5. What are the key features of a semiautonomous work group? How do these compare with an enriched individual job?

6. What are the objectives of a Quality Circle? In what type of firm can this technique be utilized?

7. Compare and contrast the culture of Japan with that of the United States in determining the appropriateness of using Quality Circles.

8. What types of training are given to Quality Circle members? to Quality Circle leaders?

9. What is a facilitator in a Quality Circle program? Why do occupants of these positions usually advance to higher managerial positions?

10. Describe the process that a Quality Circle will go through after it has completed its initial training.

BUCHAN, P. BRUCE: "Board of Directors: Adversaries or Advisors," *California Management Review,* vol. 24, no. 2, Winter 1981, pp. 31–39.

BUZZO, RICHARD A. and JAMES A. WATERS: "The Expression of Affect and the Performance of Decision-Making Groups," *Journal of Applied Psychology,* vol. 67, no. 1, February 1982, pp. 67–74.

MAHONEY, FRANCIS X.: "Team Development, Part 4: Work Meetings," *Personnel,* vol. 59, no. 2, March-April 1982, pp. 45–55.

OUICHI, WILLIAM G.: "Organizational Paradigms: A Commentary on Japanese Management and Theory Z Organizations," *Organizational Dynamics,* vol. 9, no. 4, Spring 1981, pp. 36–43.

OZLEY, LEE M. and JUDITH S. BALL: "Quality of Work Life: Initiating Successful Efforts in Labor-Management Organizations," *The Personnel Administrator,* vol. 27, no. 5, May 1982, pp. 27–33.

SAMIEE, SAEED: "How Auto Workers Look at Productivity Measures: Lessons from Overseas," *Business Horizons,* vol. 25, no. 3, May-June 1982, pp. 85–91.

chapter 18

The Status of the Labor Union

The nature and significance of the function of integration are well exemplified by the problem of labor-management relations. The successful manager of personnel is one who has effectively integrated the interests of the labor union with the interests of the company. The union represents a set of interests which appear, at least in the immediate sense, to be directly contradictory to the interests of the management and the company. The union proposes, for example, to restrict the freedom of the company in the decision-making process in various areas of personnel management. That this poses some difficulty is revealed in a comparative study of values held by both business managers and labor union leaders. In determining which of several goals are of dominant importance, more than 1,000 business leaders came up with the following rank order: (1) organizational efficiency, (2) high productivity, (3) profit maximization, (4) organizational stability, growth, and leadership, (5) employee welfare, and (6) social welfare. Determining order of priority on the basis of reports from 136 union leaders, the sequence was as follows: (1) employee welfare, (2) organizational efficiency, (3) high productivity, (4) organizational stability, growth, and leadership, (5) social welfare, and (6) profit maximization.[1] It is apparent that though both groups allocate a low relative ranking to social welfare, they disagree markedly on employee welfare and profit maximization. Rank order correlation between the two lists is approximately .22.

Despite these differences, an integration of interests can be and often is effected. It is significant that both sets of leaders view organizational efficiency and high productivity as major avenues to *either* employee welfare or organization profits. Perhaps the major disturbing factor in this research is the relatively low level of importance attached to general societal goals. The complexities of integrating the interests of three parties—employees, the organization, and the union—are demonstrated in Figure 18-1. As suggested in Part A, an employee may have a particular interest that is at odds with both the union and the organization, such as a promotion that is not in accordance with either the union-established seniority system or the management system of performance appraisal. The organization can have an interest with which neither the union nor the employees are happy, such as closing down a plant because of economic difficulties. As depicted in Part C, the union may desire something that neither employees nor the organization favor, such as compulsory union membership in order to obtain a job. More

George W. England, Naresh C. Agarwal, and Robert E. Trerise, "Union Leaders and Managers: A Comparison of Value Systems," *Industrial Relations*, vol. 10, no. 2, May 1971, p. 222.

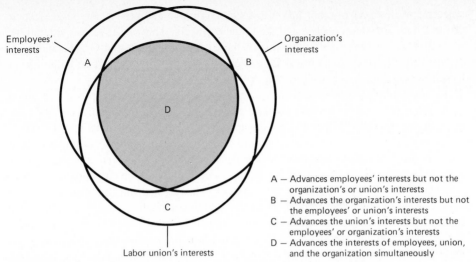

A — Advances employees' interests but not the
organization's or union's interests
B — Advances the organization's interests but not
the employees' or union's interests
C — Advances the union's interests but not the
employees' or organization's interests
D — Advances the interests of employees, union,
and the organization simultaneously

FIGURE 18-1 Integration of interests—employees, union, and organization.

complicated sets of interests can occur when the union and the organization collude
against the employee by setting up a so-called "sweetheart" contract. As in the case of
Figure 15-1 we search for personnel programs that fall into Part D representing an
integration of all interests. The subjects discussed in the preceding chapter, quality of
worklife and quality circles, show great promise of being located in Part D.

In this and the following chapter, we propose to examine the role of the labor union
in the industrial environment, as well as the process in which the role is made effective—
that of collective bargaining. In this chapter, the following subjects will be discussed:
(1) the nature of a labor union, including objectives, types, and current status, (2) the
role of the union as established by law, and (3) the role of the union as established by
the labor contract.

NATURE OF A
LABOR UNION

A *labor union* or *trade union* is an organization of workers formed to promote, protect,
and improve, through collective action, the social, economic, and political interests of
its members. The dominant interest with which the union is concerned is economic. In
this area desires and demands for improved wages, hours, and working conditions are
foremost. Since the early union movement in this country was unduly influenced by
social objectives, it fell to Samuel Gompers and the American Federation of Labor to
emphasize the concepts of business unionism and job consciousness over and above any
interests in brotherhood and social legislation. Business unionism holds to the thesis that
a union's major objective is to protect and improve the economic position of its members.
Certainly, the American Federation of Labor, as formed in 1886, constituted the cornerstone of the American labor movement.

For years, the AFL pursued a policy of nonparticipation in political action. In the
last few decades, this policy has been radically modified. It is now a generally accepted

objective of the modern labor union to seek to improve and protect the political status of the union, the union leader, and the union members. This objective was exemplified by the old Political Action Committee of the Congress of Industrial Organizations and by the Labor League for Political Education of the old AFL. These two organizations have been combined as a result of the AFL–CIO merger of 1956.

A particular employee often has a variety of reasons for wanting to join a union. Frequently, it is the only avenue toward obtaining a job. In three-fourths of the labor contracts of this nation, union membership is compulsory for job retention. A second reason for joining a labor organization is one for which management can find no substitute, a sense of freedom from arbitrary management action. A theoretically perfect management could provide more-than-fair hours, wages, and working conditions, as well as institute a most complete and effective human relations and integration program. But there is no way other than through organized and collective force that an employee can feel independent enough to challenge the actions of formal superiors in management. Perfect management cannot give this desired sense of freedom and importance. The ability to offer freedom from actual or potential arbitrary management decrees and actions concerning the industrial lives of employees is a primary source of strength for the labor union.

TYPES OF UNIONS

In general, there are two types of labor unions, the industrial and the craft. These are often referred to as vertical and horizontal, respectively. The industrial union is vertical in the sense that it includes all workers in a particular company or industry regardless of occupation. It thus constitutes a mixture of skills and lacks the homogeneity of the crafts. Examples of this type of union are the United Automobile Workers and the United Steel Workers.

The horizontal or craft union is an organization that cuts across many companies and industries. Its members belong to one craft or to a closely related group of occupations. Examples of this type are the unions that have organized the carpenters and the machinists. This is the kind of organization emphasized by the AFL from its inception.

The industrial union is not without its craft problems. When unskilled, semiskilled, and highly skilled employees are combined into one organization, internal clashes of interest can and do take place. For example, the industrial union is often prone to negotiate across-the-board increases in pay. If all jobs are raised a certain amount, say 25 cents per hour, the percentage pay differential between top and bottom jobs has been reduced. The skilled worker often feels that if the semiskilled worker obtains 25 cents, he or she should have 30 or 35 cents to maintain established relationships. There have been threats among the skilled in some industrial unions to carve out of the larger industrial union, a craft union of the highly skilled. Yet it is difficult for the industrial union leadership not only to demand a larger increase for the skilled workers but also to back up this demand with the economic force of all, the skilled and the unskilled. The clash of industrial and craft union organizations is not one that is or will be easily solved. The merger in 1956 of the AFL, which emphasized craft unionism, and the CIO, which emphasized industrial unionism, has brought at best only an uneasy peace. There is a built-in conflict between those two types of labor organizations.

The history of the union movement in the United States dates back to the very beginning of this country.[2] Growth was relatively slow until the passage of federal acts in the 1920s and 1930s that gave the protection of law to the organizing process. As of the pre-World War I-period, total union membership stood at approximately 2½ million.[3] The prosperity of the war period, when combined with favorable governmental attitudes, particularly those of the federal government, served to stimulate a rapid and remarkable expansion of union membership to a total of approximately 5 million in 1920.[4] This doubling of the number belonging to labor unions served to stimulate a change in the philosophy of personnel management in many companies, a switch from the mechanical or commodity approach to one that has been labeled "paternalistic."[5] During the 1920s and early 1930s, there was an actual decline in the numerical strength of unions to a level of fewer than 3 million in 1933. With the passage of federal legislation protecting the right to organize without interference from the employer, as exemplified by the Wagner Act of 1935, the union movement started to grow very rapidly. In the 12-year period from 1933 to 1945, the numerical strength of unions increased fivefold, from less than 3 million to approximately 15 million.

The strength of the union movement in terms of membership is difficult to state with precision, though statistics are gathered by the Bureau of Labor Statistics on a biannual basis. The report for the year 1981 indicates that the total membership of national and international unions that had collective bargaining agreements with different employers in more than one state stood at approximately 22 million. As indicated in Figure 18-2, this represents a steadily declining percentage of the nation's total labor force. The high point of unionization was reached in 1953 when 27.1 percent of the total work force was organized. By 1981, this had fallen to 20.5 percent of a total work force of 107 million. As shown in Figure 18-3, unions, during the last decade, have won less than half of all representation elections conducted by the National Labor Relations Board. In 1981, more than 8,000 such elections were federally supervised.

Of the total union membership, slightly less than 70 percent are in unions affiliated with the AFL–CIO, but the largest single union is not affiliated with this national organization—the Teamsters, with almost 2 million members. Though having not been affiliated for many years, the second-largest union, the United Auto Workers, has rejoined the AFL–CIO. Other unions that normally have more than 1 million members are the United Steel Workers, International Brotherhood of Electrical Workers, and the American Federation of State, County, and Municipal Employees.

The steady decline in the proportion of the labor force that is organized is attributed to various causes. Beginning with increased automation in the 1950s, the traditional stronghold of manufacturing has shown steady declines. Currently some 16 percent of the work force is located in manufacturing as compared with 23 percent two decades ago. Forty-six percent are in service industries. The McDonald's hamburger chain, for

[2]See Thomas R. Brooks, *Toil and Trouble: A History of American Labor*, Delacorte Press, New York, 1964.

[3]Harry A. Millis and Royal E. Montgomery, *The Economics of Labor*, vol. III, *Organized Labor*, McGraw-Hill Book Company, New York, p. 132.

[4]Ibid., p. 163.

[5]See Chapter 2.

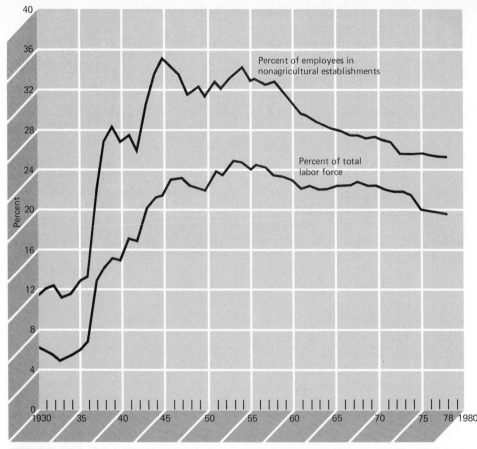

FIGURE 18-2 Union membership as a percent of total labor force and of employees in nonagricultural establishments, 1930–78. (*Source: U.S. Department of Labor*, Directory of National Unions and Employee Associations, 1979, *Bulletin 2079 (1980), p. 60.*)

example, has three times the number of workers as U.S. Steel. Service employees are more difficult to organize inasmuch as they are less concentrated and lack the class-solidarity views of the blue-collar employee.

The proportion of white-collar employees in the work force is now greater than that of blue-collar, and the latter constitute the heart of the union effort. Two-thirds of blue-collar personnel have been organized, as compared with less than 10 percent of such white-collar workers as engineers and technicians. Union leaders are valiantly trying to increase the degree of unionization of the white-collar sector. The number of white-collar workers belonging to unions increased from 7.3 million in 1977 to 8.5 million in 1980.[6] One particular group stands out in this regard: the proportion of government employees unionized has more than doubled in recent years. The three largest unions in this area are the American Federation of State, County, and Municipal Employees, the American Federation of Government Employees, and the American Federation of Teachers. If unions are to halt the steadily decreasing percentage of organized workers, they must concentrate upon winning over the white-collar employee.

[6]"Unions Move into the Office," *Business Week,* January 25, 1982, p. 90.

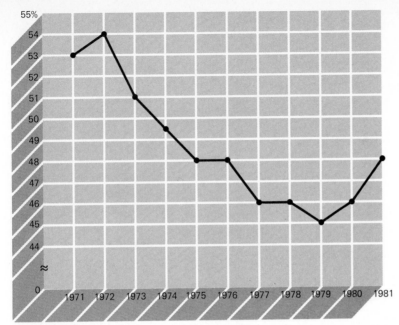

FIGURE 18-3 Percentage of elections won by unions. (*Source: National Labor Relations Board.*)

The AFL–CIO, with approximately 15 million members is obviously the core of the union movement. This organization is not a union; rather, it is a collection or federation of national and international unions. The AFL–CIO is composed of more than 100 national and international unions. The major source of power in the federation lies at the international-union level. The AFL–CIO exercises control over these international unions by establishing criteria for membership and expelling those who do not conform. In 1958, for example, the Teamsters union was expelled from the federation for not complying with certain ethical practices established by the organization. In 1968, the UAW withdrew voluntarily through its refusal to pay dues to the AFL–CIO.

An international union is composed of a number of local unions, the number ranging from 10 to 2,000. As indicated in Figure 18-4, the superstructure of the federation provides for interunion cooperation in such departments as building trades, industrial unions, maritime trades, metal trades, railway employees, and the union label. In addition, cooperation on a geographical basis is encourged by state and local bodies. The president of the federation is usually regarded as one of the major spokesmen for organized labor in America.

Even though total union membership has grown only from 15 to 22 million from 1945 to 1981, as compared with a fivefold growth from 1932 to 1945, it would be inadvisable to conclude that union growth is at an end. It also must be realized that these current union members are located in the most crucial industries in our nation, such as steel, railroads, automobiles, truck transportation, the maritime industries, and construction. One has only to visualize the power that *could* issue from a federation of transportation unions covering trucks, buses, trains, ships, and planes to conclude that the assessment of the strength of the labor union movement cannot be made in numbers alone.

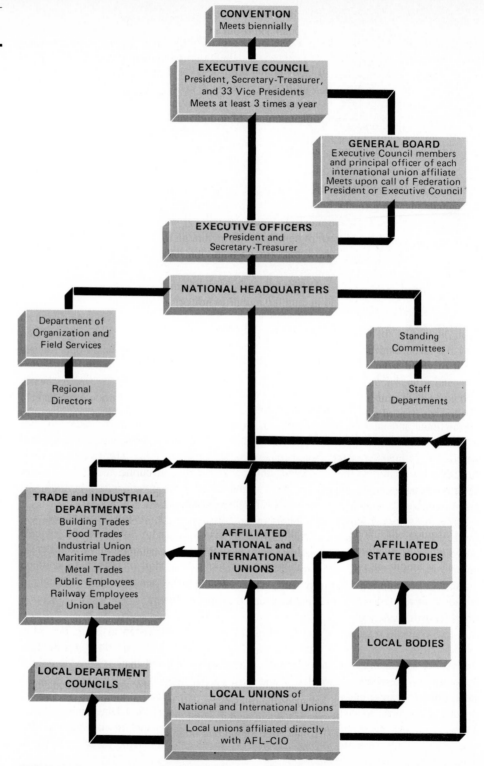

FIGURE 18-4 Structure of the AFL–CIO. (*Source: U.S. Department of Labor*, Directory of National Unions and Employee Associations, 1979, *Bulletin 2079 (1980), p. 2.*)

The power and influence of favorable governmental attitudes have already been indicated in the discussion of the remarkable growth of the union movement during World War I and the late 1930s. Federal legislation cannot be ignored. We shall discuss briefly some of the more significant legislation, emphasizing the following turning points:

1. Early legislation
2. The National Labor Relations Act of 1935 (Wagner Act)
3. The Labor-Management Relations Act of 1947 (Taft-Hartley Act)
4. The Labor-Management Reporting and Disclosure Act of 1959 (Landrum-Griffin Act)

These laws are all federal statutes that apply only to firms engaged in interstate commerce. Other business enterprises, whose activities are exclusively intrastate in nature, are regulated by state labor laws.

Early Labor Legislation

The field of business in which a favorable governmental attitude was first established toward labor organization was that of the railroads. As early as 1898, Congress passed the Erdman Act, which prohibited discrimination against workers by the interstate railroads because of union membership. This constituted an attempt to outlaw the yellow-dog contract, an agreement by which the employee was forbidden to join a labor union while in the employ of the company. This act was declared unconstitutional 10 years later, on the ground that it was an invasion of the right of private property. It was not until 1926, with the passage of the Railway Labor Act, that public policy in favor of labor organization on the railroads was made effective. One of the objectives of this act was to forbid any denial, as a condition of employment, of the right of employees to join a labor organization. This act for the railroad industry was a forerunner of the Wagner Act for the remainder of the business economy.

The Norris-LaGuardia Act of 1932 incorporated the first statement of general public policy concerning labor unionization. This statement of policy attested to the belief that workers should have the right to organize into unions of their own choosing if they desire to do so. This doctrine received relatively limited protection in the act, which provided only for the outlawing of yellow-dog contracts and for a marked restriction upon the employer's freedom to utilize the labor injunction to halt work stoppages. In 1933, the federal government attempted to guarantee this right to organize by means of Section *7(a)* of the National Industrial Recovery Act, which stipulated that every code of fair competition had to incorporate provisions protecting the right to organize. A National Labor Board was established to administer this portion of the act, with Senator Robert Wagner as chairman. This board passed from the scene in 1935, when the NIRA was declared unconstitutional. The provisions of the act pertaining to labor were reintroduced as a separate bill in that same year, and the National Labor Relations Act, or Wagner Act, became the law of the land.

National Labor Relations Act

In essence, the Wagner Act proposed to become the protective tariff of labor. It guaranteed the right of employees to organize by forbidding the employer to (1) interfere or restrain employees in the exercise of this right, (2) dominate or interfere with any labor union, (3) discriminate against anyone for union activity, (4) discriminate against any employee who gave testimony under the act, and (5) refuse to bargain collectively with representatives chosen by the employees. The National Labor Relations Board (NLRB) was established to administer the act. The board had two primary functions: (1) to prevent or correct any of the five unfair labor practices given above, and (2) to establish the appropriate bargaining units and specific representative organizations for the employees. About three-fourths of the cases handled by the board, an average of 45,000 a year, deal with unfair practices committed by management or the union. The other fourth is concerned with conducting representation elections. In effect, this means that the strike of the union to obtain recognition by the employer is now replaced by an orderly process of democratic elections. Workers or their representatives can petition the board for certification of a union as the sole collective bargaining agent. The representative has to demonstrate that there is a substantial number of employees in the company, usually 30 percent of the total eligible, who are interested in joining the labor organization. As a practical matter, no petition to the board is filed until some 60 percent of the employees have exhibited an interest. If a voluntary agreement to recognize a labor union could not be evoked from the employer or if there were doubts as to which of several organizations was to represent the employees, an election would be held to determine the authorized representing organization. A majority of those voting is required to name a bargaining agent.

The Supreme Court of the United States has pointed out in a number of cases that the Wagner Act does not specifically say that an election must be held to select a bargaining representative. Majority status can be established by other means such as showing convincing support on a union-called strike or strike vote, or by union possession of cards from a majority of employees authorizing the union to represent them for collective bargaining purposes. The NLRB has the power to designate the official bargaining representative, and can, with the assistance of court injunctions, compel an employer to bargain in good faith. The commission by the employer of an unfair labor practice can lead to official union designation even when an election is not actually held or, if held, is lost by the union. For example, in 1982 the board ruled that Conair Corporation's "outrageous" violations of federal labor laws justified automatic recognition of the union even though only 32 percent of the workers had voted in the election for representation by the International Ladies' Garment Workers Union.

Through the years, the NLRB has developed many rules of conduct to be followed by both parties in conducting their election campaigns. Examples of these are the following:

1. The company must turn over to the union a list of names and addresses of employees eligible to participate in the representation election, in order that the union may be able to contact all employees.

2. A company may declare its unalterable opposition to unions, but may not term them "enemies" or "communists."

3. A company may tell employees that wage raises, if secured by the union, *might* require a reduction of overtime.

4. A company may say that it believes union dues to be a waste of money.

5. A company may describe experiences of other plants that relocated to avoid union-ization, so long as this is not used as a threat.

6. The company must accept union sound-car broadcast appeals for votes near plant entrances during the 24-hour ban before election time; they are construed merely as a "reminder" to vote.

7. A company may not forbid distribution of union literature in nonworking areas during nonworking time.

8. Information leaflets may be included in pay envelopes even during the 24-hour ban, provided that they do not contain promises or threats. Specifically, part of the wage due can be given separately with a note that this amount (union dues) will be subtracted from the paycheck in the event that the union wins.

9. The company cannot usually prevent employees from wearing campaign buttons. Exceptions are in cases where the buttons will distract or interfere in production process, when they will detract from the dignity of business operations, and when customers have voluntarily complained in writing.

10. Management may *never* wear campaign buttons.

Under the protection of the Wagner Act and the NLRB, the union movement quintupled its strength in a decade.

The Labor-Management Relations Act

During the period of 1935 to 1947, society became alarmed with both the rapidity of union growth and some of the actions of certain union leaders. In the Taft-Hartley Act, labor unions were prohibited from such practices as the following: (1) to restrain or coerce an employee into joining or not joining a labor union; (2) to cause an employer to discriminate against an employee because of nonmembership in the union resulting from any action other than the nonpayment of dues to the union; (3) to refuse to bargain collectively with the employer; (4) to engage in secondary boycotts and jurisdictional strikes; (5) to require workers to pay exorbitant fees; and (6) to require an employer to pay for services not rendered, a practice known as "featherbedding."

Under the Taft-Hartley Act, the strongest degree of union security, the closed shop, was outlawed.[7] The union shop was permitted, but with the stipulation that any state may pass a law, contrary to this act, outlawing the union shop in that state. There are twenty states that now have these so-called "right-to-work" laws. The repeal of this provision of the Taft-Hartley Act has been high on the list of organized labor's political aims for many years.

A number of other provisions of the Taft-Hartley Act served to clarify the roles of unions and union leaders. Supervisors are not permitted to join employees' unions, and the employer may refuse to bargain with a supervisors' union. The employer has freedom of speech and may express an opinion against the desirability of employees' joining labor unions. Management may sue the union in a federal court for breach of contract. They may deduct dues from paychecks (the "checkoff") only when so authorized by the individual employee in writing. The union leader must file union financial reports and

---

[7]This type of union security, as well as several others, will be defined and discussed later in this chapter.

inform members how monies are spent. Any welfare fund, financed in whole or in part by the employer, must be administered by a joint employer-union board. A union leader who had not signed a non-Communist affidavit removes the union from the protection of the National Labor Relations Act.

Just as the union representative has rights of petitioning the NLRB for a representation election, employees may now petition for a similar election to decertify the union if it is felt that it no longer represents the interests of a majority. In recent years, unions have lost three-fourths of all such decertification elections. A new election cannot be held, however, within 12 months of a preceding election. The NLRB retains the right to designate the appropriate bargaining area, industrial or craft, and to certify those employees who are eligible to vote. Unions are most likely to lose decertification elections when the bargaining unit is small. In addition, such petitions for decertification typically occur within 1 to 2 years after initial certification. Once a petition to decertify is filed with the NLRB, the employer is prohibited from bargaining with the union until the question of representation is settled.

One other major provision of the Labor-Management Relations Act of 1947 was that dealing with the handling of national emergency strikes. Excessively long strikes in basic industries, such as steel or coal, could cause great harm to the nation. In such a situation, the President of the United States is empowered to declare a national emergency and to ask for a federal court injunction to terminate the strike for a period of 80 days. If no agreement is arrived at, the injunction is dissolved at the end of 80 days, and the two parties are free to resume the work stoppage. If a national emergency is in fact still present, it is inconceivable that our governmental representatives will allow the nation to be seriously harmed to preserve the principle of free collective bargaining. In such an emergency, it is highly likely that futher and more drastic laws limiting the freedom of both management and union would be passed by Congress.

The Labor-Management Reporting and Disclosure Act of 1959

In the latter part of 1950s, a Senate Select Committee on Improper Activities in the Labor and Management field was set up under the leadership of Senator John McClellan. Its purpose was to investigate and report upon criminal and other improper practices in the field of labor-management relations. In general, this committee concluded that the majority of labor unions were honest and that labor-management relations were conducted upon a sound basis. However, certain objectionable practices were uncovered, which the committee felt should be remedied by law. Among these practices were the following: (1) infiltration of labor organizations by gangster elements, (2) collusion between management and labor leaders in the signing of "sweetheart" contracts to the detriment of the employees, (3) a lack of democratic procedures in the organization and operation of some labor unions, (4) an abuse of the power of the international union to place selected locals under protective custody or trusteeship, (5) widespread misuse of union funds as exemplified by large loans without interest to union officials and poor audits of union accounts, (6) the use of labor spies by management, and (7) union picketing of organizations whose employees have no desire to join the union. The recommendations of this committee resulted in the passage of the Labor-Management Reporting and Disclosure Act of 1959, otherwise known as the Landrum-Griffin Act.

This act is appropriately titled. A large portion of it is devoted to the establishment of a series of reports to be filed with the Secretary of Labor by both unions and management.[8] Among these reports are the following:

1. Report by the union of its constitution and bylaws
2. Submission by the union of an annual financial report covering assets, liabilities, receipts, salaries of officials, and loans to any officer, member, or business enterprise
3. Report by the union of its administrative policies, such as those concerning initiation fees, dues, assessments, qualifications for membership, calling of meetings, ratification of contracts, etc.
4. Reports of officers and employees of a union that disclose any personal financial interest that conflicts with duties in the union
5. Report by the employer concerning any expenditure for the purpose of interfering with, restraining, coercing, or persuading employees in their right to organize
6. Reports by labor relations consultants covering any fees received from employees for the purpose of interfering with, restraining, coercing, or persuading employees in their right to organize

In addition to these reports, the act establishes a bill of rights for union members, which includes freedom of speech and assembly in union meetings, secret ballot on proposed increases in dues and assessments, the right to sue the union, safeguards against improper disciplinary action of members by the union, and equal rights to nominate candidates for union office, to vote, and to have a voice in the conduct of union business. Restriction of the right of the international union to establish trusteeships over any of its locals is provided to safeguard the democratic process. Persons who have been members of the Communist party or have been convicted of certain major crimes are prohibited for 5 years from the termination of membership, or from conviction, from holding office as a union official, labor relations consultant, or officer of an employers' association. The stipulation regarding Communist party membership was declared unconstitutional by the United States Supreme Court in 1965.

The final portion of the law deals with various amendments to the Labor-Management Relations Act of 1947. Among the changes in the Taft-Hartley Act are the following: (1) a repeal of the requirement of a non-Communist affidavit for union officials, (2) the giving to states of jurisdiction over certain types of cases that the NLRB has refused to handle as not significantly affecting interstate commerce, (3) the prohibition of organizational picketing by a union when a rival union has been recognized by the employer or an NLRB election has been held in the last 12 months, (4) the safeguarding for 12 months of the right of an economic striker to vote in union-representation elections held while he is on strike, (5) the prohibition of "hot cargo" agreements in which the employers agreed to stop handling, using, selling, transporting, or dealing in any of the products of another employer against whom the union is exerting economic pressure, and (6) the authorization of union shops in the construction industry, which require membership after the seventh day of employment rather than the usual 30 days.

[8]Public Law 86-257.

In general, labor union leaders were very much opposed to the passing of the Landrum-Griffin Act. It served to limit further authority over the operation of their own organizations. The AFL–CIO leadership felt that they could handle most of such abuses through their ethical-practices committee and through threatened or actual expulsion of the offending union from the AFL–CIO. But the widespread publicity given to the investigations of the McClellan committee for a period of 2 years had seriously weakened the power and prestige of labor unions in the eyes of the public and their elected representatives.

The law is extremely difficult to administer. It is a further inroad by government into the area of labor-management relations. It again emphasizes the fundamental truth that if labor unions and managements do not conduct themselves in a manner approved by society, a diminution of private authority will inevitably follow, with giant strides being taken toward a socialistic state. The public interest is and must be paramount.

TYPES OF UNION SECURITY

One of the foremost objectives of a labor union is to establish and protect the existence and security of the organization. As we have shown above, the law has much to say about union security. Before proceeding with a presentation of a constructive management viewpoint on this matter, let us examine briefly the various types of union security. Discussion of these types will proceed from the least secure position for the union to the most secure.

Restricted shop　This is a situation or attitude rather than a formal type of shop like the union or closed shop. It exists in many firms in one of two types, legal or illegal. The legal restrictive situation exists when the management does what it can to keep a union out without violating the Wagner, Taft-Hartley, or Landrum-Griffin Acts. Such a management may try to buy the employees off by providing more in pay and benefits than could be obtained in competitive unionized firms. Or it may try to manage as perfectly as it knows how in the hope that the employees will not feel a need for organization. The illegal restricted shop would allow activities that are specifically prohibited by law, such as the use of yellow-dog contracts, the searching out and dismissal of persons who show leanings toward unions, the threatening of employees, and the promising of rewards if unionization is voted down.

Open shop　Technically, the restricted shop is an open shop. For our purposes here, however, a true open shop is one in which there is neither a union present nor a management program to promote or keep out a union. The employees are relatively free to decide whether or not they will exercise their legal rights of organization. In the open shop, the employees have not as yet decided to form a union. This does not mean that there are no union members in the company; it merely means that they are not in the majority. This type of shop is fair game for the union organizer.

Simple-recognition shop　The simple-recognition shop is one in which the management has recognized a union as the official and exclusive bargaining agent of all employees in its area of jurisdiction. The act of recognition is the first stage of security for the union. It is usually gained with the assistance of the National Labor Relations

Board and may be derived from a consent election. If a majority of those voting favor the union, there is a legal requirement that the employer recognize and deal with the union. Union security lasts for a minimum of 12 months, inasmuch as the NLRB will not hold recognition elections in any one company more often than this. If 50 percent plus one of those voting favor the *XYZ* union, a simple-recognition shop exists. Though the union may have only 50 percent plus one of the employees as dues-paying members, it is authorized to bargain in behalf of all 100 percent. This is the source of the "free rider" argument of unions, the 49 percent who derive the benefits of organization but do not contribute financially to its support.

Agency shop The agency shop is identical with the simple-recognition shop except for one item: *All* employees pay union dues whether or not they are members of the union. This eliminates the "free rider" argument. In a recent California case, the judge ruled that these dues are only fees for local representation purposes.[9] As such, he ruled that money collected from workers who object to paying dues cannot be used for organizing other workers, holding conventions, or paying per capita dues to the AFL–CIO. These stipulations would require a far more sophisticated cost accounting system than most unions now possess.

Maintenance-of-membership shop This type of shop is a compromise between freedom to join or not to join a union and compulsory unionism. It was a development of World War II, when the government had to arbitrate disputes to prevent work stoppages. There is no requirement that an employee join the union. Once the union is joined, the employee is frozen, or compelled to remain in the union for the life of the contract. Usually, when the contract expires, a short escape period is provided when employees may withdraw their membership. Once this period is ended, the lid goes on again, and the membership is maintained for the life of the contract. The employee is free to join the union at any time. Thus, there is an element of freedom and an element of compulsion.

Modified union shop The union shop is a form of compulsory unionism. The employer may hire whom he or she will, but within a stipulated period the employee must join the union. A modified union shop provides for certain exemptions to this rule. Among the groups that may not be required to join regardless of length of service are those who object to unions on religious grounds, students, and employees who had been hired prior to arrival of the union.

Union shop Under the Taft-Hartley Act, the grace period for a full union shop could be no shorter than 30 days. Thus, assuming no new hires during the past month, all employees will be union members. Under the Labor-Management Disclosure Act, this period can be shortened to 7 days in the construction industry only.

Closed shop The highest degree of union security is the closed shop. It, like some restricted shops, is illegal under the Taft-Hartley Act. Under this arrangement, an employee must be a union member at the time of hiring. The union becomes the *only* source of labor for the employer. Though this arrangement is technically illegal, there are in practice a number of closed shops, particularly in the construction, maritime, and printing industries. The closed-shop clause does not appear in the contract, but it is present in effect through operating rules, customs, a union hiring hall, or management's willingness to use the union as a sole source.

[9]Right-to-Work Gains Shake the Union Shop." *Business Week*, Feb. 16, 1976, p. 25.

If one considers all of the firms in the United States, it is evident that the majority are not organized; that is, they have restricted or open shops. This conclusion is based on the fact that only one-fifth of the total labor force and only one-third of those potentially organizable are now in unions. Of those that are organized, the union shop is by far the most commonly found type of union security. A survey of 400 contracts, constituting a structured sample of 5,000, revealed that 62 percent provided for the union shop, 12 percent permitted a modified union shop, 6 percent had the agency shop as a sole feature, and 4 percent utilized a maintenance-of-membership provision.[10] The agency feature is sometimes added to modified union shops to cover the exempted groups. The remaining 16 percent of the sample had no specific union security provision, thereby relegating them to simple-recognition status. Eighty-six percent of the contracts provided for collection of dues through a "checkoff." In reviewing 221 state and local government union agreements, the following distribution was found: union shop, 23 percent; modified union shop, 10 percent; agency shop, 35 percent; modified agency shop, 2 percent; maintenance-of-membership, 20 percent; maintenance-of-membership plus agency, 3 percent; and simple-recognition, 7 percent.[11]

These figures show that compulsory unionism is a very common phenomenon in the American union movement. Thus, the majority of American employers who deal with unions have accepted, through collective bargaining, the principle of compulsory unionism. The law states that you *must* grant the simple-recognition shop if the union wins a majority of the vote. There is no law requiring an employer to grant the union shop.

A POINT OF VIEW

In viewing the progress of the labor union movement in the United States, a realist must conclude that the unions are a continuing part of our society. There is little or no chance that employers can regain the amount of authority they possessed during the 1800s. Thus, the basic attitudes toward the status of labor unions in general must move from an attempt to undermine and halt the union movement to a desire and attempt to work constructively with the union for the benefit of the entire organization. This does not mean that management must clasp the union to its bosom; such an attitude is not desirable, practical, or legal. It does not mean that a management cannot attempt to determine for itself, with the assistance of the NLRB, that a majority of its employees have chosen the union on a rational and informed basis. If a management is convinced that this is true, and has determined that the particular labor organization concerned is responsible and mature in its objectives and policies, then the employer should accept the union as a major working participant, in spirit as well as in procedure.

In the last decade, the number of recognition elections won by labor unions has been steadily declining. This is due to various reasons, such as the unfavorable publicity received by a few well-known union leaders, the increased militancy of management under the "free speech" provisions of the Taft-Hartley Act, the difficulty of organizing smaller companies, interunion rivalry, and the difficulty of organizing white-collar workers, who now outnumber blue-collar employees. With the legal requirements of Social

---

[10]Bureau of National Affairs, Inc., *Collective Bargaining Negotiations and Contracts 1981*, p. 87.2.

[11]Bernard and Susan Rifkin, *American Labor Sourcebook*, McGraw-Hill Book Company, 1979, pp. 11–48.

Security, minimum wages, unemployment compensation, and workers' compensation, many employees feel that a union is no longer necessary.

Each manager must also determine his or her basic attitude toward the concept of compulsory unionism. Those who are against this concept in principle see it as the abolition of freedom for each individual to choose or join or not to join an organization in order to keep a job. In addition, they contend that a highly secure position for the union may well lead to an abdication of union leadership responsibility. On the other side, compulsory unionism ensures that all shall share equally in the support and financing of the labor organization that is authorized by law to represent all employees. Compulsory unionism ensures that attempts to undermine the union will be ineffective. But more important, it is certain that every union will work and fight as long as it does *not* have the secure status of the union shop. Lacking this degree of security, the union leadership is highly suspicious of every management action and is reluctant to cooperate in programs initiated for the good of the entire organization.

One point of view on this issue involves a compromise with the ideal of complete freedom on the part of the employees to choose to join or not to join a labor organization. If the employer discovers that the vast majority of the employees have voluntarily joined the labor organization, and if the union gives signs of continued fight and a withholding of needed cooperation, and if the management desires to obtain some constructive good from the labor organization, it may well be that the granting of the union shop would be a highly desirable management reaction. If the organization gains substantially from this process in the long run, it may be necessary to sacrifice the freedom of choice of the remaining 10 to 20 percent of the employees.

On the other hand, if through various legal actions the employer is able to develop an environment in which the employee feels no need for the outside protection of a union, freedom of choice is preserved. A study of 26 nonunion companies suggests nine actions that can improve employee relations, aid productivity, and, as a by-product, prevent unionization.[12] These factors are: (1) demonstrate a sense of caring for employees through such actions as using first names, providing identical benefits for all, and use of flexitime; (2) choose rural or suburban plant sites and limit the size of the operation to between 200 and 1,200 employees; (3) maintain close ties between management and ownership, (4) provide employment security, (5) promote from within, (6) give "clout" to the personnel department, (7) provide competitive pay and benefits, (8) listen to employee views, and (9) carefully train all managers and immediate supervisors. These 26 companies made an earnest effort to create a climate of cooperation between employees and management.

SUMMARY

The role of the labor union in our society is a fairly secure one as measured by the degree of its growth and public support. From slightly less than 3 million in 1933, unions grew to some 15 million members in 1945. In the last 30 years, the pace of growth has slackened considerably, and the approximate current total is 22 million members. This figure indicates that unions occupy a strong position in the economy, particularly when we realize that the overwhelming number of our key industries are almost completely

[12]Fred K. Foulkes, "How Top Nonunion Companies Manage Employees," *Harvard Business Review*, vol. 59, no. 5, September-October 1981, pp. 90–96.

organized. On the other hand, the slackening of the pace in the last three decades indicates that all labor is not going to be organized overnight, as some had feared. The majority of the total are found in international unions affiliated with AFL–CIO.

The status of the labor union within the company is largely affected by management attitudes and controlled by the type of union security arrangement that has been agreed upon. These positions can range from an illegal restricted shop to an illegal closed shop, including, according to degree of security, (1) the restricted shop, illegal and legal, (2) the open shop, (3) the simple-recognition shop, (4) the agency shop, (5) the maintenance-of-membership shop, (6) the modified union shop, (7) the union shop, and (8) the closed shop. Approximately three-fourths of all contracts provide for the compulsory unionism of a union shop.

Federal laws have had much to do with creating the current status of organized labor. Passage of the National Labor Relations Act (Wagner) led directly to a fivefold increase in membership. The Labor-Management Relations Act (Taft-Hartley) attempted to redress the balance of power by imposing many restrictions upon union actions. The Labor-Management Reporting and Disclosure Act (Landrum-Griffin) continued the move toward greater labor union regulation. Despite the considerable slackening in the growth pace, it is certain that the labor union will continue to be a major factor affecting the practice of modern personnel management. Most key industries are heavily organized, and slow but steady inroads are being made among white-collar employees.

The solution to the problem of establishing and maintaining equitable relationships among management, employees, and the union involves large elements of subjectivity. In this field there is no exact science. The answer to the problem, as expressed in our national policy, is that of collective bargaining. This process will be examined in the following chapter.

BRIEF CASE

The management of a restaurant chain, unhappy with its relationships with an employees' union in one branch, decided to attempt to prevent unionization in a second unit. As a part of this effort, the following letter was distributed to all employees:

■ As you know, there will be an election on September 9. At that election you will have an opportunity to determine whether or not you want to be represented by the union. You are much luckier than the employees at our east-side restaurant. Some time ago, they were led down the primrose path by union promises of increased wages and benefits and consequently voted for union representation.

After that election, the union negotiated a contract with us that, in my opinion, gave the employees no more than they would have gotten had there been no union—and probably gave them less. In addition, I believe many of those employees will be hurt by the inflexibility of the union contract. For a contract that produces nothing more than you would expect to receive were there no union, you are afforded the privilege of paying union dues.

We do not want a union at this restaurant! Our experience in the east-side unit shows us that the presence of the union results in a tense working relationship with extreme disharmony among the employees. This can result in a loss of customers, and a loss of income to our employees who serve those customers. The union benefits no one but itself.

Questions

1. Do you think that the above letter is legal in the eyes of the NLRB?

2. Are there any promises or threats in the letter?

DISCUSSION QUESTIONS

1. Briefly summarize the current status of the labor union movement in the United States.

2. Trace the major changes in union membership figures that have occurred in this century. What forces have led to these fluctuations?

3. Compare and contrast the values of labor union leaders with those of business managers in the areas of employee, societal, stockholder, and organizational welfare.

4. Compare and contrast the philosophies of the National Labor Relations Act (Wagner) and the Labor-Management Relations Act (Taft-Hartley).

5. Define the agency shop security arrangement. What are its values and problems?

6. What is the status of compulsory unionism in this country? What forms does it take in union security clauses?

7. What is the AFL–CIO? What is its role in society?

8. What is the National Labor Relations Board? What is its role in labor-management relations?

9. How does a union actually obtain recognition from an employer?

10. While preserving true freedom of choice for the employee, what legal actions can a management take to prevent employee unionization?

SUPPLEMENTARY READING

ANDERSON, JOHN C., GLORIA BUSMAN, and CHARLES A. O'REILLY III: ''The Decertification Process: Evidence from California,'' *Industrial Relations*, vol. 21, no. 2, Spring 1982, pp. 178–195.

FULMER, WILLIAM E.: ''Resisting Unionization: How Outsiders Working For You Can Work Against You,'' *Business Horizons*, vol. 25, no. 1, January-February 1982, pp. 19–22.

HARRISON, EDWARD L., DOUGLAS JOHNSON, and FRANK M. RACHEL: ''The Role of the Supervisor in Representation Elections,'' *The Personnel Administrator*, vol. 26, no. 9, September 1981, pp. 67–72.

HOOVER, JOHN J.: ''Union Organization Attempts: Management's Response,'' *Personnel Journal*, vol. 61, no. 3, March 1982, pp. 214–219.

SANDVER, MARCUS H. and HERBERT G. HENEMAN III: ''Union Growth Through the Election Process,'' *Industrial Relations*, vol. 20, no. 1, Winter 1981, pp. 109–116.

SAPPIR, MARK Z.: ''The Employer's Obligation Not to Bargain When the Issue of Decertification is Present,'' *The Personnel Administrator*, vol. 27, no. 2, February 1982, pp. 41–45.

chapter 19

Collective Bargaining

It is the public policy of the United States that the determination of employer-employee relationships in firms engaged in interstate commerce shall take place through collective bargaining. To this end, the right of the employee to join and work through organizations is protected by the various labor statutes. The National Labor Relations Act specifies that it is an unfair labor practice for the employer to refuse to bargain collectively with chosen representatives of a certified labor organization. The Labor-Management Relations Act specifies that it is an unfair practice for the representatives of a labor organization to refuse to bargain in good faith with the employer. Current national policy, therefore, not only states that collective bargaining is the approved answer to the employee-employer relationship problem, but that this policy is to be implemented through the National Labor Relations Board and the federal courts.

TRADITIONAL AND INTEGRATIVE BARGAINING

Collective bargaining is a process in which representatives of two groups meet and attempt to negotiate an agreement that specifies the nature of future relationships between the two. The Wagner Act gives the legally authorized labor representative the right to bargain for all employees in its jurisdiction, whether members of the union or not. On subjects where bargaining is required by law, the employer is no longer free to make and enforce unilateral decisions. And on matters not so legally mandated, the employer is influenced by such risks as strikes, slowdown, and the withholding of cooperative efforts.

There are two basic types of collective bargaining between labor and management: (1) traditional and (2) integrative. Traditional bargaining is concerned with the distribution of benefits, such as wages, working conditions, promotions, layoffs, management rights, and so on. Focus is on such variables as the economic costs of offers made, likelihood and cost of a strike, and the sources of bargaining power. Tactics often include presenting demands, haggling, cajoling, presenting counteroffers, and threatening strikes and lockouts.

Though not as frequent as traditional bargaining, there is an increasing number of instances when an integrative bargaining approach is taken. If this type of bargaining is

"American management may be running roughshod over the unions in the current trend of 'giveback' bargaining, but it is beginning to pay a price that was unthinkable in good times. More and more companies, big and small, are opening their books to unions and divulging information about costs, competition, and investment plans—a trend that could lead ultimately to a sharing of power in making high-level decisions on matters such as investment and plant location."

Examples of the above trend would include:

1. General Motors agreed to allow an independent auditor to study confidential data, thereby convincing employees that the ink was really red.
2. Waterbury Rolling Mills Inc. of Connecticut not only opened its books but also put a union representative on the board of directors.
3. United Airlines Inc. granted "insider status" to a committee named by the Air Line Pilots Association to verify the company's position.
4. Pan American World Airways Inc. agreed to recommend that its board elect a director proposed by four unions that negotiate with the company.
5. The president of the United Auto Workers was given a seat on the board of directors of Chrysler Corporation.

"Union-management relations will not move overnight to the power-sharing stage that exists in some European countries because of co-determination laws there requiring labor representation on supervisory boards. U. S. management and labor by and large have opposed this concept."

"Tasting a New Kind of Power," *Business Week*, February 1, 1982, p. 16.

to be utilized, each group must view the other as cooperative and trustworthy. Both must withhold commitment to a definite position while soliciting information and discussing problems and feelings. The philosophy is to pursue a win-win solution in preference to one where one party wins and the other loses.

Integrative bargaining tends to grow out of stressful situations. As will be discussed later, the pressures placed on companies and unions by international competition have led to the giving back by the union of certain items gained through traditional bargaining. In several instances, the agreement stipulated that the firm would (1) open its books and provide full disclosure of all pertinent information to the union, and (2) develop quality circles wherein employee-union members can engage in decision-making processes governing the workplace. As suggested in Box 19-1, there is a feeling that once this process begins, there will be no turning back. In some cases, this power-sharing approach is supplemented with an employee stock-ownership or profit-sharing plan. In a few instances, a labor union representative is placed on the company's board of directors thereby enabling him or her to receive all types of management information.

With this nation's tradition of utilizing adversarial methods of resolving conflict, there is some doubt about the staying power of the integrative aproach. Born in stressful conditions for both management and labor, there is a likelihood that increasing prosperity will see less use of cooperative integrative approaches, and a greater emphasis upon the traditional approach. A survey of 211 union leaders relegated integrative bargaining to such subjects as allocating work resources and loads, designing interesting jobs, and the general area known as "quality of worklife."[1] Only 23 percent felt integrative bargaining should be used in determining working hours, earnings, fringe benefits, promotion pro-

[1]Lee Dyer, David B. Lipsky, and Thomas A. Kochan, "Union Attitudes toward Management Cooperation," *Industrial Relations*, vol. 16, no. 2, May 1977, p. 165.

cedures, safety, and job security. Another survey of 171 union members tended to agree.[2] They strongly preferred traditional bargaining when dealing with traditional union concerns, and accepted joint integrative efforts when quality-of-worklife issues were involved. It should be noted that specific integrative programs often issue from the traditional bargaining sessions where one program is matched with another; for example, management will establish quality circles in exchange for freezing wages and guaranteeing income for high-seniority employees.

THE PROCESS OF COLLECTIVE BARGAINING

Despite the wide variety of shapes that traditional bargaining can take, there are certain fundamental procedures and stages of action that deserve consideration, among them (1) the prenegotiation phase, (2) the selection of negotiators, (3) the strategy of bargaining, (4) the tactics of bargaining, and (5) the contract.

The Prenegotiation Phase

The labor organization is an institution engaged in the full-time job of protecting and improving the status of the employee. The company, whose major objective is the production and distribution of an economic good, can ill afford to consider collective bargaining as a fringe duty that merits little special attention. Such an attitude may turn the bargaining process into a unilateral determination of relationships by the union.

The prenegotiation phase of the process is vital. When the contract has been signed for one period, the prenegotiation phase begins for the next. Data of all types should be maintained religiously by management, including, of course, facts and figures in the more tangible areas of wages, hours, pensions, vacations, and similar types of remuneration. From sad past experience, firms are lengthening the prenegotiation phase in order to avoid last-minute crises that lead to undesirable contract provisions.

It is also important for the company representatives to study very carefully the labor organization with which they are to bargain. Since most unions do business with many firms, copies of other contracts negotiated by this union should be secured and studied. This analysis will at least show some of the union's thinking as well as indicate its power. If the union is an industrial one, it is very likely that its leadership will have a social philosophy. It is also likely that the union representatives will have less power in the negotiations to commit the union than will the representatives of a craft union. The craft union is usually more interested in wages, hours, and working conditions than in anything else, and its representatives are usually delegated an ample amount of authority to execute an agreement with the company. Not only must the organization be analyzed, but the background and personality of the particular union negotiators must also be studied.

---

[2]William H. Holley, Hubert S. Feild, and James C. Crowley, "Negotiating Quality of Worklife, Productivity and Traditional Issues: Union Members' Preferred Roles of Their Union," *Personnel Psychology,* vol. 34, no. 2, Summer 1981, p. 309.

The Negotiators

On the company side, the particular negotiator may be any one of a number of persons. It may be the industrial relations director, the head of the production area, an executive vice president, or the company lawyer. The team or committee approach is frequently used, thereby broadening the base of participation. The practice of allowing all major division heads to participate and a few supervisors to observe on a rotating basis has great advantages in the area of communication and education.

Lawyers should have a place on the negotiating committee although they should not be the prime or sole negotiators. Lawyers have skills that management can well use, particularly a skill in evaluating the acts and statements of the labor representative so as to separate and identify feelings, facts, bluff, and conviction.

Some consider it sound planning to keep the president of the firm out of the negotiation process. Because of the nature of the bargaining process, delays for the purpose of reevaluation of positions are often desirable. If the president is present on the bargaining team, she or he may be forced to give an instant yes or no on an issue that deserves more careful consideration. In addition, selecting someone other than the president as spokesperson places the two bargaining teams on an equal footing. The union representative must check with rank and file on tentatively accepted offers. The company representative must check with top managment on union demands.

On the union side, the team approach is also customarily used. The team may consist of business agents, some shop stewards, the president of the local, and, when the negotiation is basic and vital, representatives of the international union. Always in the case of industry-wide bargaining, the chief spokesperson is a representative of the international, and often it is the president of that organization. Most of these union bargainers are full-time specialists in the art of bargaining and negotiating with various managements.

Strategy of Bargaining

Because of the considerable importance of the labor agreement, it is essential for management to plan its strategy and tactics carefully in preparation for the bargaining sessions. Strategy is concerned with mapping out the plan and basic policies to be followed in the bargaining process. Tactics are the particular actions that are taken while at the bargaining table. The labor union will also have a similar strategical plan and will execute tactical actions that will promote the accomplishment of union objectives.

Before management ever enters the conference room, certain elements of the basic plan must be worked out. The key personnel must agree on the *maximum concessions* that can be granted to the anticipated demands of the union. Often the union files its demands with the employer in advance of the first bargaining session. The company must know how far it can go before it will seriously risk the possibility of a work stoppage. As illustrated in Figure 19-1, the basic strategical limits of the two parties on pay are illustrated at 10 percent for management and 8 percent for the union. Tactics call for an opening company offer of 4 percent and an opening demand of 16 percent. If these conditions prevail, a settlement in the 8 to 10 percent range is likely.

Other fundamental parts of a firm's strategical plan could include the following:

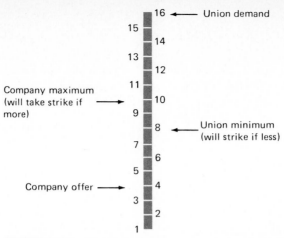

FIGURE 19-1 Bargaining over pay increase percentage.

1. Avoid mutual agreement clauses that would prevent management action. Management should retain the right to manage the firm subject to challenge by the union under the contract.

2. Keep one's eyes on the entire package. A work-procedure concession may eventually cost more than a substantial pay increase.

3. Keep the company personnel informed of the progress of bargaining sessions. Supervisors must be involved, and union members are also employees.

4. Develop agreements where the union leaders can always maintain that they "won." Union leaders have to run for reelection on their record, and management can more frequently afford the appearance of having "lost."

5. Determine the point at which the company is willing for the union to go on strike. The union is fully aware of the fact that the strike is its most potent bargaining weapon, and as such it is frequently used in its "threat" form. Management must adopt a basic attitude of not being afraid of a strike.

Tactics of Bargaining

Although many authors have asked for more objectivity in collective bargaining, the fact is that bargaining, by its very nature, will involve acts and tactics that are calculated to mislead the other party. This does not mean that factual bargaining cannot be introduced nor blue-sky demands toned down. Bargaining does, however, require a shrewd study of the other side and an awareness of the impact of one's actions on all concerned.

A tactic of the General Electric Company has been declared by the National Labor Relations Board to constitute failure to bargain in good faith. It has been the policy of this company, variously labeled as "truth in bargaining" and "Boulwareism" (after the former vice president who developed it), to work out a "firm and fair" set of offers and stick to them regardless of the length and intensity of negotiation meetings. The company also carried on an intensive publicity campaign with its employees to inform them of the benefits offered. The company contends that the NLRB decision requires it to follow tactics of "haggling-for-haggling's sake" and to hold back its maximum concessions until the very last moment in order to give the appearance of bargaining through "bluff and counter-bluff." The decision of the board was appealed to the United States Circuit Courts of Appeals at New York. In 1969, this Court upheld the position of the board, indicating, "We hold that an employer may not so combine 'take-it-or-leave-it' bargaining methods with a widely publicized stance of unbending firmness that he is himself unable to alter a position once taken."[3] It was emphasized, however, that the Court was neither forbidding the "best offer first" bargaining tactic nor requiring "auction bargaining."

A great many tactics of bargaining have been used to advance the strategies of both sides. Unions attempt to obtain management final approval on each clause as the bargaining progresses. Management refuses to give final approval until the entire package is developed. All-night sessions are often used when the contract expiration date draws near, since some unions follow the tactic of "no contract, no work." Certainly, there are many tactical tradings of concessions in one area for a benefit in another. There are also theatrical performances in the forms of shouting, table pounding, walkouts, and the like. In Figure 19-1, if the union's initial demand is for a 9 percent increase, management is likely to follow the tactic of resistance even though this percentage is well within its acceptable range. If one gives in easily on basic issues, this may encourage higher demands in the future.

In the event of a deadlock in the bargaining process, various tactics can be used. A subcommittee, composed of members of both sides, can be appointed to investigate the dispute while the main bargaining committee proceeds to other points. Or the designated point may simply be tabled until other clauses in the agreement have been worked out. In the event that the deadlock is very serious and could well lead to a work stoppage, appropriate governmental mediators should be notified. The mediation process is discussed in a later section in this chapter.

The Contract

The labor-management contract stipulates in formal terms the nature of the relationship between management and labor for the ensuing year or years. The average contract runs for 2 or 3 years. It has been the unique history of the American labor movement to become involved in detailed specifications of union-management relationships. It has not been a class-conscious political movement geared toward changing the economic system, but rather one that has been oriented toward increasing union power in the operation of the business. In response, management attempts to protect its prerogatives by spelling out in unambiguous language those specific areas in which they have agreed to share power with the union. This approach may well be a broader, more fundamental feature in our society. It has been pointed out that, "The United States was the first nation in history to organize its governmental apparatus by written constitution, which fairly quickly came to be regarded as the true source of all authority."[4] It also noted that the United States has four times the population of Great Britain, but twelve times as many lawyers.

---

[3]"Labor Month in Review," *Monthly Labor Review*, vol. 92, no. 12, December 1969, p. 2.
[4]Martin Mayer, "Justice, the Law, and the Lawyer," *Saturday Evening Post*, Feb. 26, 1966, pp. 36–37.

Most labor contracts include clauses covering the following subjects:

1. Union security (see the preceding chapter for the various types of union security)

2. Grievance procedures, including steps, time limitations, and provisions for arbitration (see Chapter 20)

3. Promotion, transfer, and layoff, covering particularly the nature and effect of seniority (see Chapters 11 and 23)

4. Wages, including shift and Sunday premiums, cost of living, and job evaluation (see Chapters 12 to 14)

5. Hours of work, including absenteeism, overtime, holidays, and vacations (see Chapters 1, 14, and 16)

6. Incentive wages and time study (see Chapter 13)

7. Discharge (see Chapter 23)

8. Safety and health (see Chapter 21)

9. Management responsibilities (see Chapters 3 to 5)

10. Miscellaneous clauses covering such subjects as severance allowances, military service, a saving clause which keeps the rest of the agreement valid should a court declare any one part invalid, and termination dates

As can be seen, the labor contract refers to most of the subjects discussed in this text.

UNION BARGAINING PRESSURES

The labor union, as the other bargaining members, has certain strategies and tactics that it utilizes to extract greater concessions from the employer. Union representatives use most of the particular tactics described for the employer above. They haggle, horsetrade, act, demand more in the expectation of getting less, and make tentative agreements subject to ratification by the membership. In addition to these maneuvers there are certain stronger types of pressure that are sometimes used. These are strikes, picketing, and boycotts.

Strikes

A strike is a concerted and temporary withholding of employee services from the employer for the purpose of exacting greater concessions in the employment relationship than the employer is willing to grant at the bargaining table. The possibility of a strike is the ultimate economic force that the union can bring to bear upon the employer. It is the power that offsets the employer's right to manage the firm and lock out the employee. Without the possibility of a strike in the background, there can be no true collective bargaining. When the strike is prohibited by law, some other mechanism, such as arbitration, must be established as a substitute for collective bargaining.

There are various types of strikes. Among them are the following:

1. *Recognition strike.* This is a strike to force the employer to recognize and deal with the union. This type of strike has been largely replaced by the consent elections administered by the National Labor Relations Board.

2. *Economic strike.* This is the typical strike, based on a demand for better wages, hours, and working conditions than the employer is willing to grant.

3. *Jurisdictional strikes.* When two unions argue about which has jurisdiction over a type of work and attempt to exert pressure upon the employer to allocate it to one or the other, a jurisdictional strike may ensue. For example, both carpenters and metal workers wish to hang metal doors. If either group strikes to force the employer to grant the work to its members, this is a jurisdictional strike. The employer is caught in the middle between two warring unions. Under the Taft-Hartley Act such strikes are illegal.

4. *Wildcat strike.* Wildcat strikes are the quick, sudden, and unauthorized types of work stoppages. Such strikes are not approved by union leadership and are contrary to the labor agreement. They are sometimes viewed as a form of "fractional bargaining" by a subgroup of employees who have not achieved satisfaction through regular grievance processing or collective bargaining procedures.

5. *Sit-down strike.* When the employees strike but remain at their jobs in the plant, this is termed a "sit-down strike." Such strikes are illegal since they constitute an invasion of private property. Employees are free to strike for certain objectives, but they must physically withdraw from the company's premises.

6. *Sympathy strike.* If other unions who are not party to the original strike consent to strike in sympathy with the original union, this is termed a "sympathy strike." It is an attempt to exert an indirect pressure upon the employer. This type of strike is also outlawed by the Taft-Hartley Act.

When any type of strike occurs, the employer should have a well-thought-out plan for functioning during the work stoppage. Among other items, he or she must make provision for the following: (1) making sure that the plant is left in good physical condition; (2) explaining the employer's side of the issue to the employees; (3) giving a statement to the press; (4) notifying suppliers and customers; (5) notifying the appropriate mediation services; (6) determining to what extent nonunion personnel will be maintained on the working staff; and (7) paying off striking workers for work completed in the past. There are few, if any, friendly strikes. Employers should do all in their power, short of violating law and public policy, to win the strike. Yet they must be aware of the many costs of a strike. As outlined in Figure 19-2, these include the prestrike costs issuing from the tension between the two parties, the obvious costs accruing during the actual work stoppage, and the poststrike costs, many of which issue from ill feelings generated by actions undertaken during the strike. One study places strike costs at $200 per employee-day for smaller companies with 100 or fewer employees, and approximately $300 per employee-day for companies with 500 to 1,000 employees.[5] However, if collective bargaining is to operate properly, there can be no automatic capitulation to union terms solely in the interest of maintaining harmony after the strike. If harmony and cooperation are the sole objectives, the employer should have given up before the strike stage was ever reached.

[5]Woodruff Imberman, "Strikes Cost More Than You Think," *Harvard Business Review*, vol. 57, no. 3, May-June 1979, p. 137.

FIGURE 19-2
Costs of a Strike

Prestrike costs
   Legal costs
   Executive negotiations
   Productivity slump
   Loss of orders from cautious customers

Strike costs
   Loss of profits from no production
   Legal costs
   Executive negotiation costs
   Inventory carrying charges
   Fringe benefits of strikers
   Extra security guards
   Executive time performing operative tasks
   Overtime in other plants to make up loss
   Continuing salaries of office staff

Poststrike costs
   Hiring and training replacements
   Overtime to catch up on orders
   Loss of customer orders switching to others
   Productivity slump

Picketing

The union desires to keep the plant completely closed during a strike. The patrolling of strikers in front of plant entrances—picketing—is the most effective device for accomplishing this objective. If the employer accepts the shutdown and makes no attempt to reopen the plant, picketing will be routine and peaceful. If the employer attempts to start a back-to-work movement, picketing can turn into violence as nonstrikers are attacked and cars damaged.[6] Peaceful persuasion through picketing is entirely permissible and legal, but violence is not. For this reason, the employer can often obtain court injunctions to limit the number of pickets that can be placed in front of any plant entrance.

Secondary Boycotts

A secondary boycott takes place when a union, which is seeking a concession from employer A, places pressure on employer B to influence employer A to grant the concession. The union may attempt to make employers B, C, D, and so on refuse to deal with employer A until A falls in line with their demands. The "hot cargo" agreement is a particular type of secondary boycott. This is an agreement by which the employer agrees that the union does not have to work on materials that come from employers whose plants have been struck or who have not recognized a union. The Taft-Hartley Act sought to make such secondary pressures illegal and attempted to keep labor-management disputes confined to the primary parties. The Labor-Management Disclosure Act of 1959 strengthens this objective in the case of "hot cargo" clauses. This act did, however, authorize such boycott agreements in the construction and clothing industries.

---

[6]Modern technology has obviated some personal clashes. A few plant managements have used helicopters to avoid patrolling pickets, leading to the suggestion by some that barrage balloons will have to be used to extend picket lines into the sky.

When disagreements between labor and management become serious, a third party often enters the controversy. The third party may be a (1) fact finder, (2) mediator, (3) conventional arbitrator, (4) final offer arbitrator, or (5) mediator-arbitrator. *Fact finders* may be appointed by the government or be selected by the two parties. After investigation of the dispute, a report will be filed and made public. Not only are the two parties likely to modify extreme positions on the basis of additional facts, but the power of public opinion will be brought to bear. The major limitation of this approach is its lack of finality.

Mediation is a process by which the third party attempts to stimulate labor and management to reach some type of agreement. Mediators cannot decide issues; they can only listen, suggest, communicate, explain, and persuade. Among other requirements, effective mediators must (1) establish and maintain themselves as strict neutrals in the dispute, (2) exhibit confident belief that a solution is not only possible but probable, (3) listen, (4) ask intelligent questions, (5) keep the two parties talking, and (6) when asked, propose compromise solutions based on knowledge of the "rock-bottom" positions of both parties. Mediators are most heavily used in new-contract negotiations. They rarely enter the labor-management picture in grievance processing that occurs after the contract is signed. Contracts constitute "new law," and the two parties are generally unwilling to allow third parties to make final decisions. Grievances involve interpretations of existing law, and both labor and management are willing to allow arbitrators to act as industrial judges.[7] Thus there is much contract mediation and grievance arbitration, and little grievance mediation and contract arbitration.

Most mediators are supplied by the state and federal governments. In the interest of preserving the neutrality of the Federal Mediation and Conciliation Service, that organization was removed from the supervision of the Secretary of Labor and now operates as a semi-independent body under the President. Mediators must be accepted and trusted by both parties; they must maintain the same relationship with both parties; they must be equally friendly and equally withdrawn. If one party proposes to drive them away, they must withdraw from the other party in like manner or, perhaps, withdraw from the dispute entirely. Styles vary with mediators, and some prefer to operate as "orchestrators" emphasizing a joint-meeting approach, while still others prefer to be "dealmakers" in going back and forth between separate meetings of the parties. One study of a field office of the FMCS revealed that 30 percent of the meetings were joint, 44 percent were held separately, and 26 percent were party caucuses without the presence of the mediator.[8]

Third parties can do much to promote an agreement. They can at least keep the two parties talking. They can take the initiative in calling conferences and keep ever before the disputants the desirability and inevitability of reaching an agreement at some time or other. If both sides trust as they should, mediators know their basic, immovable positions. They therefore know whether an agreement is possible from these positions, although being careful to reveal neither one. At times, mediators permit themselves to be "used," to save face for one or both parties. The company or union representative may take an

---

[7]See Chap. 20 for a discussion of grievance arbitration.

[8]Deborah M. Kolb, "Roles Mediators Play: State and Federal Practice," *Industrial Relations*, vol. 20, no. 1, Winter 1981, p. 5.

undesirable, yet inevitable, contract clause back to their principals and label it a suggestion of the mediators, when in reality it was not. At times, the mediators are also abused. Through all of this use and/or abuse, the mediator must fill his or her role with stability, maturity, confidence, neutrality, and competence.

Arbitration is a process in which the third party collects the facts from the two primary parties and proceeds to make a decision that is usually binding on labor and management. As indicated in the following chapter, most collective bargaining contracts provide for the arbitration of grievances as a final step. Its use in new-contract negotiation is relatively rare. In the steel industry, most issues not settled must be submitted to an impartial arbitration board. Certain issues are excluded, such as union membership, cost-of-living provisions, management rights, and industry uniformity. Some airlines have recently developed arbitration procedures to prevent work stoppages. The 1978 agreement between Braniff and the Air Line Pilots Association called for 30 days of talks, then 30 days of mediation, then binding arbitration on unresolved issues.[9]

Arbitration of new contracts is more commonplace in public employment where employees are not permitted to strike. It has been suggested that such a procedure creates a ''chilling effect'' upon negotiations since arbitrators are well known for splitting the difference between the two final positions. Since negotiation is preferable to arbitration, a few states and cities have experimented with *final offer arbitration*. The power of the arbitrator is restricted to selecting between the two final offers. It is contended that this will stimulate the two parties to take more reasonable positions since the differences cannot be split. Critics have pointed out that the arbitrator may be forced to choose between two very poor settlements, and that one party may slip ''zingers'' into its generally highly attractive offer in order to obtain concessions that could never be gotten in any other way. Variations on final offer arbitration have been suggested to remedy these problems: (1) repeated final offers when neither of the initial ''final offers'' is accepted with no explanation from the arbitrator; (2) modified final offer where the arbitrator can write his or her own settlement as a third choice and reverts to the usual procedure should either party object; (3) multiple final offers where each party produces two or three final offers, the arbitrator announces the winning party, and the loser gets to choose among the winning party's alternatives; and (4) final offer arbitration on each separate issue rather than the entire package.[10] Studies contrasting final offer and conventional arbitration revealed that the former tended to have a less chilling effect.[11] It was also determined that final offers on an entire package, in comparison with issue-by-issue, resulted in closer agreement between the two offers. In all states and cities, arbitration of any type cannot be undertaken without prior processes of negotiation, fact finding, mediation, and a cooling-off period. The procedure recently adopted in New Jersey provides not only for mediation and fact finding, but several choices among various arbitration approaches. As portrayed in Figure 19-3, the parties together can select either conventional or final offer arbitration, and arbitration on the whole package or issue by issue. As a final choice, ''tri-offer'' arbitration may be selected wherein the arbitrator may choose among the packages or issue positions of management, labor, and the fact finders.

In other public jurisdictions, interest is growing in the possible use of a *mediator-*

[9] An Airline Rejects Stepped-up Bargaining,'' *Business Week*, May 1, 1978, p. 34.

[10] Clifford B. Donn, ''Games Final-Offer Arbitrators Might Play,'' *Industrial Relations*, vol. 16, no. 3, October 1977, pp. 311–312.

[11] Peter Feuille, ''Final Offer Arbitration and the Chilling Effect,'' *Industrial Relations*, vol. 14, no. 3, October 1975, p. 307.

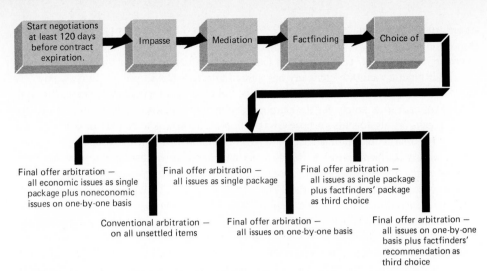

FIGURE 19-3 New Jersey fire and police bargaining and arbitration procedure.

arbitrator. This is "mediation with muscle," since both parties know that if they do not come up with a resolution, their mediator will supply the final answer. Thus they will *not* deal with the mediator at arm's length, nor do they adopt the semilegalistic stance of pure arbitration. In experience thus far, the overwhelming bulk of issues have been resolved through the mediation process, with only a few finally being decided by the mediator-arbitrator. In resolving eighty-nine issues in California nursing negotiations, only one had to be arbitrated. Of thirteen issues submitted for mediation-arbitration from a Pacific longshoremen's dispute, all were settled through mediation.[12]

CURRENT ISSUES
IN BARGAINING

As times change, the dominant issues in collective bargaining tend to change. The issue of union recognition has been replaced by economic issues of wages, hours, and working conditions. With the advent of mechanization and automation, job security and supplementary employee benefits have assumed greater importance. Among the current issues of significance are the following: (1) appropriate subjects for bargaining, (2) concessionary bargaining, (3) productivity bargaining, (4) public employee bargaining, and (5) coalition bargaining.

Bargaining Subjects

In the final analysis, the National Labor Relations Board and the federal courts are the determinants of the subjects that both parties must bargain over in good faith. The basics of wages, hours, and working conditions have rarely been challenged since the passage of the Wagner and Taft-Hartley Acts. There has been, however, continuing controversy over the question of whether the firm must bargain with a union on the

---

[12]Sam Kagel, "Combining Mediation and Arbitration," *Monthly Labor Review,* vol. 96, no. 9, September 1973, pp. 62–63.

subject of going out of business. In 1956, the Deering Milliken Company closed a plant shortly after the Textile Workers Union of America won a representation election. After 24 years of litigation, both the board and the courts held that the company committed an unfair practice and the company has agreed to pay some $5 million in back pay.

The basic position of the NLRB and the courts is that a company cannot close one part of an operation solely for the purpose of avoiding a union. It can, however, go out of business entirely for this purpose. If a portion of the firm is to be closed, the employer must prove that its decision is based solely on economics. In a 1981 case, *First National Maintenance Corporation v. NLRB,* the Supreme Court ruled that an employer need not bargain concerning the closing of part of an operation so long as its decision is related solely to economic considerations. However, it must still bargain with the union concerning the handling of the impact and effects of a decision to close down a plant.

Another current subject is that of discrimination against employees on the basis of race, nationality, religion, sex, or age. Demonstrating that this is a legitimate subject for union activity, the NLRB has ordered Westinghouse to provide to the International Union of Electrical Workers the following: (1) the number of male, female, black, and Spanish-surnamed employees in each labor grade, (2) the number in each classification in each plant who are paid on a daywork basis and incentive basis, (3) the number of employees by race, sex, and Spanish surname who have less than 1 year's seniority, 1 to 2 years', 2 to 4 years', 5 to 9 years', 10 to 19 years', and 20 or more years' seniority, (4) the number of persons hired in each classification during the last year with a breakdown by sex, race, and Spanish surname, and (5) the number of promotions in the last year broken down by category. The data must be provided for union personnel, and the union must demonstrate relevance if nonunion personnel data are requested. Though the collection and provision of such information will be expensive for the firm, the board ruled that such information is necessary for the union to protect itself from charges of violating the duty of fair representation.

Concessionary Bargaining

As indicated earlier, difficult economic positions have led many managements to seek "give-backs" or concessions from organized labor. As an example, the recent General Motors—United Auto Workers contract provided for the following concessions by the union: (1) a freeze on basic wages, (2) giving back 9 personal paid holidays, (3) deferring 3 cost-of-living adjustments for 18 months, (4) penalizing employees with excessive absenteeism, and (5) promoting establishment of new work rules. The last item, if properly implemented, will raise productivity some 10 percent. For example, if an electrician is allowed to use a screwdriver to take the cover off an electrical contact instead of calling a millwright to do this task, both time and money will be saved. Unions have adapted to the Taylor system of narrow, fragmented jobs by specifying strict work rules governing who may legally perform specific tasks.

In return for these concessions, General Motors agreed (1) to keep open 4 of 7 plants that it had planned to close, (2) inaugurate an employee profit-sharing plan, (3) guarantee income protection on layoff to employees with 10 years of seniority, and (4) lay off supervisory personnel in proportion to the layoff of hourly workers. Similar concession arrangements have been made at Ford, Chrysler, and Goodyear among others. The United Steel Workers accepted an 11-year no strike clause to help lure a new Timken Company steel plant to Canton, Ohio.

Productivity Bargaining

The typical approach in labor-management bargaining is that labor makes demands and management makes counteroffers related to those demands, for example, labor demands a 12 percent pay increase and the company offers 6 percent. Productivity bargaining would change the managerial stance to one of volunteering wage increases *provided* the union will accept new work practices that will enhance company efficiency and productivity. Certainly, in the United States we have a very difficult and pressing problem of increasing productivity to cope with general economic problems. There are some signs that particular labor unions are beginning to recognize that *other* matters besides employee benefits must be negotiated to improve general productivity.

In every plant, there are certain existing practices, formal or informal, that serve to inhibit organizational efficiency. In the construction industry, for example, there are a variety of union rules that serve as a drag on productivity. Concerning one extreme instance, a master mechanic, earning $10 per hour, was entitled to pay for the full time that *anyone* was on the job servicing machinery, day or night, regardless of whether he was actually around.[13] In 1 year he collected $94,000 pay for 107 hours a week for 52 weeks, mostly at overtime rates. Leaders of construction unions are beginning to move to reduce, through productivity bargaining, some of the major drags on output. Among these inefficient practices are requiring electrician pay for only plugging in equipment when it is moved, requiring a plumber to attach hoses to faucets, restricting the width of paint brushes, restricting use of rollers in painting except at premium pay rates, barring the use of plastic pipe, and barring the use of prefabricated units or requiring that they be disassembled and reassembled on the job. In one instance, five different crafts were required to install a water fountain. In railroads, the definition of a "day's run" is still heavily influenced by the slower steam-engine travel speeds of decades ago.

In productivity bargaining, the mode has been more traditional than integrative. Employers may be forced to pay a one-time premium for the right to introduce efficiency-enhancing programs; for example, management paid approximately $30 million for the right to eliminate inefficient practices in the loading and unloading of ships by longshoremen. There is now considerable hope that productivity bargaining will assume an integrative mode. The recent Ford agreement requires the establishment of Employee Involvement Teams, a form of quality circles. Savings from a United States Steel agreement are to be used not only to modernize plant but to start a quality circle program. Productivity used to be a word meaning "speed up" and hard work for employees. Today, it is regarded as a way to preserve some jobs in the face of foreign competition.

Public Employee Bargaining

If labor unions and collective bargaining work well for employees of private enterprises, it is logical to suggest that they would be equally advantageous for public employees. A presidential executive order has provided the basis for encouraging union organization among federal employees. Observation of the effectiveness of labor union negotiations with private employers has stimulated widespread interest in such organizations among state and local government personnel. It is estimated that 50 percent of

---

[13]"The Unions Begin to Bend on Work Rules," *Business Week*, Sept. 9, 1972, p. 100.

the employees in the federal government are organized; only 25 to 30 percent of state and local government employees belong to unions.[14]

Under Executive Order No. 11491 of 1969, a form of collective bargaining is provided for employees of the federal government. It provides for exclusive representation by a single union if approved by a majority of those voting. Bargaining units and eligibility for voting are decided by the Assistant Secretary of Labor-Management Relations, with provision for appeal to a Federal Labor Relations Council. The latter is peopled by the Chairperson of the Civil Service Commission, the Secretary of Labor, and members of the Executive Office. Neither the union shop nor the agency shop is permitted; thus "free riders" are possible. Bargaining is restricted to issues not determined by legislation; compensation rates and fringe benefits are thus outside of the union-management relationship. In the event of an impasse in negotiations, arbitration is provided through a Federal Services Impasse Panel. This panel, made up of seven appointed experienced arbitrators, may impose a settlement. The strike is illegal, the penalty being a fine of not more than $1,000 or imprisonment for not more than 1 year and a day, or both.

Some have decried the prohibition of strikes by public employees as effecting a type of second-class citizenship. Others feel that public employment offers unusual degrees of job security, for which the employee should be willing to give up some other economic rights. With reference to state and local governments, it is estimated that only one-third require or permit organized collective bargaining for public employees.[15] Some permit union and agency shops, in contrast to the federal pattern. Bargaining tends to be much broader and includes such issues as salaries, hours of work, and fringe benefits. Binding grievance arbitration is common, as is the provision of third parties to deal with impasses. Strikes are permitted in the following eight states: Alaska, Hawaii, Minnesota, Montana, Oregon, Pennsylvania, Vermont, and Wisconsin. The law in Hawaii, for example, permits such strikes when (1) there is no danger to public health and safety (thus excluding police and fire), (2) both parties have exhausted mediation and fact-finding processes, and (3) the union has issued a 10-day notice of the strike. In a review of 51 settlements made in a 6-year period, 23 required some form of third-party assistance.[16] Mediation and arbitration were most commonly used and only one 2-week strike took place, which was finally settled by arbitration.

Application of the private model to public employment causes problems not only in the right-to-strike area, but also in reference to existing civil service systems. Merit systems operated by independent civil service commissions must also be integrated with collective bargaining processes in the public sector. As yet, it is too soon to determine how these two systems will be acommodated to each other.

Coalition Bargaining

Specific bargaining units are recognized by the National Labor Relations Board upon petition by labor or management for a representation election. As a result, there is often no overall plan for a large company or a major industry that deals with numerous

---

[14]Harry Graham and Virginia Wallace, "Trends in Public Sector Arbitration," *The Personnel Administrator,* vol. 27, no. 4, April 1982, p. 73.

[15]Felix A. Nigro, "Labor Relations in State and Local Governments," *Personnel Administration,* vol. 33, no. 6, November-December 1970, p. 42.

[16]Jack E. Klauser, "Public Sector Impasse Resolution in Hawaii," *Industrial Relations,* vol. 16, no. 3, October 1977, p. 285.

unions. Exceptions to this are the cases of the United Automobile Workers and the United Steel Workers. In the steel industry, there is three-tier bargaining: (1) industry-wide master contract bargaining by a committee of employers and the USW, (2) company-wide master contract bargaining by a single company and the USW, and (3) plant bargaining by plant management and a local of the USW to cover unique problems. There has been less intercompany cooperation in the automobile industry, and negotiations are often confined to the latter two tiers. In any event, there is a single labor organization with which the entire industry or major companies must negotiate. It is no accident that these two unions are among the most powerful in the country and can call strikes affecting the entire nation.

In most other instances, a number of bargaining units and unions have developed under the auspices of the NLRB. General Electric, for example, deals with 150 bargaining units represented by more than 80 unions; American Standard, Inc., negotiates with 5 unions, and Union Carbide must deal with 26 unions. In the copper industry, companies have extended their technology from mining to fabrication, resulting in numerous facilities involving different processes at widely separated locations. As a consequence of this, numerous bargaining units have also developed. The net result of this situation is a diminution of power of the multiple unions in opposition to a coordinated plan from a single, large, national company. In recent years, therefore, there has been a move toward coalition bargaining among cooperating unions, a situation viewed with alarm by management because it enhances union bargaining power. In most instances, the goals of coalition bargaining, and some seek to encourage it in order to reduce the degree and increases, and a common expiration date for all contracts. The last goal is for the purpose of achieving the power of a UAW or USW in calling a national strike. At present, the company can divide and conquer, or negotiate, as each smaller-unit contract expires. Company managements are fearful that such industry-wide bargaining would encourage greater government interference and pressures leading to political decisions in public-interest strikes.

Under the guidance of the Industrial Unions Department of the AFL–CIO, it appears likely that the move toward coalition bargaining will continue. If the actual presence of outside union representatives is prohibited, then the "road show" approach encouraging common agreement by the separate unions is likely to be the tactic adopted. Common expiration dates for multiple contracts is to be continually sought, or at least the time intervals will be steadily shortened. On the other hand, all employers are not against coalition bargaining, and some seek to encourage it in order to reduce the degree and number of inconsistencies and complications in dealing with multiple unions. In most instances, these are employers operating in a single location. The large, integrated employers with widely separated sites and differing technologies still seek the values of flexibility.

A PHILOSOPHY OF LABOR-MANAGEMENT PEACE

Every manager has a philosophy of labor-management relations, a philosophy based on experience and formal and informal education. The importance of the problem to the future of the American economy dictates that considerable and mature thought should be devoted to working out such a philosophy. This philosophy should not only advance the objectives of the particular organization but also be consistent with the continued development of a relatively free, competitive economic system.

The cornerstone of a constructive philosophy of labor-management peace must be that of *acceptance*. Management must accept the labor union as the official representative and watchdog of the employee's interests. The union must accept the management as the primary planners and controllers of the company's operations. The union must not feel that management is working and seeking the opportunity to undermine and eliminate the labor organization. The company must not feel that the union is seeking to control every facet of the company operation, thereby creating a partnership of authority but not of responsibility.

A second basic characteristic of the constructive labor-management philosophy is acceptance by both parties of the principle of *free collective bargaining* and *free enterprise* consistent with the advancement of the public interest. Neither should want to substitute outside force or governmental control for the usual pressure of the marketplace. The objective should be to improve one's lot under the present system rather than to change to another involving greater regulation and a shifting of ownership to the state. Both parties must recognize their obligation to handle this freedom in a manner consistent with the public interest and must realize that abuse by either side in effect calls for a different type of economic system.

A third element of a philosophy should be an emphasis upon a *problem-solving attitude and a deemphasis of the legalistic approach*. Such an approach is not, of course, possible until and unless the preceding two requisites have been established. There will be less interest in finding loopholes in the contract, in pulling "slick" deals to the detriment of the other party, or in relying solely upon the lawyer to develop and preserve the union-management relationship. A problem-solving philosophy would often entail a seeking of union help by the management. It also would require a union respect for management as the primary director of the organization.

Finally, both parties must be cognizant of *obligations to the principals* in the situation. For the union, the principal is obviously the union member, for whom the organization was formed. This obligation requires the adherence to democratic processes in order that the union may be truly responsive to its members. For management, the principal has traditionally been the stockholder. As indicated in Chapter 2 of this text, this philosophy is out of date. Management has many principals, among whom are stockholders, the public, customers, and employees. The modern, mature union should also number among its principals the general public and the customers of the business firm. It is apparent that the employee is a principal of both union and management. This realization does not justify any attempt on the part of management to alienate the worker's allegiance to a responsible union. But it does lead to an awareness that the union member is also a company employee and that a relationship must be established that will further the interests of all parts of the organization and not just those of the stockholder alone, the consumer alone, the employee alone, or the public alone.

SUMMARY

Since collective bargaining has been established in our national policy as the basic method for the solving of labor-management problems, it is important to devote some attention to this process. Collective bargaining has its tactical and strategic implications as well as its national and local aspects. Both labor and management have an obligation to develop a philosophy and approach that will promote labor-management peace while advancing the objectives of a free economy.

Though both traditional and integrative bargaining processes exist, the former is more typical as it seeks to distribute benefits between the two parties. The traditional bargaining procedure has certain fundamental phases: (1) the prenegotiation phase, (2) selection of negotiators, (3) setting strategy, (4) selecting tactics, and (5) writing the contract. Current issues of significance in bargaining would include the closure of plants, concessions from the labor union, productivity, and coalition bargaining.

In the event of no agreement, various pressures are brought to bear upon management by the union, such as strikes, picketing, and boycotts. The basic management pressure is that of waiting until the absence of the payroll makes itself felt on every union member. There are often third-party pressures involved in these disputes, including fact finders, mediators, conventional arbitrators, final offer arbitrators, and mediator-arbitrators. Negotiators in collective bargaining in the private sector generally prefer to use the mediator in new-contract bargaining and the arbitrator in grievance processing. In the public sector, where the strike may be prohibited, there is much more concern for innovation, entailing varied use of fact finders buttressed by public opinion, arbitrators restricted to either-or decisions, and mediator-arbitrators engaged in both processes sequentially.

Both parties have a basic obligation to establish a constructive relationship of working harmony in the advancement of labor-management peace. Such a relationship would include (1) labor union and management acceptance of each other as responsible parties in the collective bargaining process, (2) acceptance by both parties of the free-enterprise system with its concomitant obligations and the authority of private ownership and private operation of business organizations, (3) an emphasis upon a problem-solving approach with a deemphasis upon excessive legalism, and (4) an awareness of basic obligations to principals, who include employees, stockholders, customers, and the public.

BRIEF CASE

In Adler University, there was considerable antagonism between various groups of faculty and university administrators. Faculty leaders felt that administrators were prone to make important decisions with a minimum of faculty consultation. Departments were merged, research programs begun or abandoned, and new deans and vice presidents added. As a result, an organization of faculty members was developed and an election held under the auspices of the NLRB. University management contended that the faculty was not entitled to the collective bargaining rights provided employees under the National Labor Relations Act. They contended that faculty authority in most academic matters was absolute. They decided what courses would be offered, when they would be scheduled, and to whom they would be taught. They debated and determined teaching methods, grading policies, and matriculation standards. They decided which students would be admitted, retained, and graduated. In effect, the faculty determined the product to be produced, the terms upon which it will be offered, and the customers who will be served. In addition, faculty members play a role in faculty hiring, tenure, sabbaticals, termination, and promotion.

In rebuttal, the faculty contended that its role in decision making was not managerial because it involves only the exercise of independent professional judgment in academic governance. Faculty members pursue their own interests and therefore do not represent the interest of the employer. The very fact that a union was voted for indicates that the faculty does not perceive its interests to be aligned with those of university administration. The NLRB contends that faculty members are professional workers whose interests were separate from those of the institution.

Questions

1. Do you think that university faculty members should be allowed to form unions and bargain with university administrators?

2. Are faculty members managers or operatives? Are their interests aligned or opposed to those of university administrators?

DISCUSSION QUESTIONS

1. Define and distinguish between traditional and integrative collective bargaining.

2. Define and distinguish between mediator and arbitrator.

3. Why has the "final offer" form of arbitration developed? What variations have been suggested?

4. What is productivity bargaining? Describe conventional bargaining approach to this subject. Describe an integrative bargaining approach.

5. What is "Boulwareism"? Is it a "fair" tactic of bargaining?

6. Compare and contrast the following methods of conflict resolution: compromise, problem solving, mediation, and arbitration.

7. What is concessionary bargaining? Is it traditional or integrative?

8. Compare and contrast private and public employee collective bargaining.

9. What is coalition bargaining, and why has it been developed?

10. Interrelate the four concepts of grievances, new contracts, mediation, and arbitration.

SUPPLEMENTARY READING

————: **"Concessionary Bargaining:** Will the New Cooperation Last? *Business Week,* June 14, 1982, pp. 66–81.

FREEDMAN, AUDREY and WILLIAM E. FULMER: "Last Rites for Pattern Bargaining," *Harvard Business Review,* vol. 60, no. 2, March-April 1982, pp. 30–48.

GALLAGHER, DANIEL G. and M. D. CHAUBEY: "Impasse Behavior and Tri-Offer Arbitration in Iowa," *Industrial Relations,* vol. 21, no. 2, Spring 1982, pp. 129–148.

GRAHAM, HARRY and VIRGINIA WALLACE: "Trends in Public Sector Arbitration," *The Personnel Administrator,* vol. 27, no. 4, April 1982, pp. 73–77.

HOLLEY, WILLIAM H., HUBERT S. FEILD, and JAMES C. CROWLEY: "Negotiating Quality of Worklife, Productivity and Traditional Issues: Union Members' Preferred Roles of Their Union," *Personnel Psychology,* vol. 34, no. 2, Spring 1981, pp. 309–328.

JOHNSTON, ROBERT W.: "Negotiation Strategies: Different Strokes for Different Folks," *Personnel,* vol. 59, no. 2, March-April 1981, pp. 36–44.

chapter 20

The Management of Conflict

T he process of integrating interests requires both preventive and curative activities. Despite the best of management practices in acting and communicating, conflicts between employees and the organization will occur. A total absence of conflict would be unbelievable, boring, and a strong indication that such conflicts are being suppressed. One of the characteristics of a mature group is its willingness and ability to bring suppressed conflicts to the surface where they may be discussed with a greater opportunity of resolution. It would be naive to insist that all conflicts can be eliminated in some manner or other, but their exposure and discussion will contribute greatly toward their reduction. Conflict per se is neither bad nor contrary to good organization. Disagreements and dissatisfactions can lead to reexamination of basic assumptions and practices, to the end that adjustments can be made to improve overall organizational effectiveness.

Thus, the first step in the resolution of conflicts is their discovery and exposure. There are many upward channels of communication that can be developed for the purpose of bringing dissatisfaction to the surface. After a brief discussion of these channels, greater attention will be given to the grievance procedure, which is perhaps the most significant means of discovering and resolving employee complaints and dissatisfactions. On the other hand, there is the distinct possibility that the organization will become dissatisfied with a particular employee. Though the Skinner approach to operant conditioning of behavior would preclude the use of punishment, typical practice of most organizations includes programs of negative disciplinary action ending up with the maximum penalty of discharge from the organization. Finally, the chapter will conclude with a discussion of the alternative methods of dealing with conflict. Certain basic methods have been used in all types of conflicts, whether they are between individuals, between groups, or between the organization and an individual or group.

THE DISCOVERY OF CONFLICTS OF INTEREST

There has been a trend toward increasing the number of upward channels of communication. Part of the impetus for this trend comes from a growing recognition of the importance of good organization morale. Credit can also be given to the growth of labor unions, which exemplified a need for additional communication channels. In any event, the voice of the employee is much louder today in American business than formerly.

461

Some would view this vociferousness as evidence that the amount of disagreement and trouble has been on the increase. On the other hand, it may be that such trouble has always existed, but that now it can rise to the surface and be observed.

Grievance procedure The most important channel through which to communicate dissatisfaction to management is a properly constituted grievance procedure. Such a channel presumes that the individual has the courage to submit a complaint to the supervisor for discussion. One contribution to communication that the labor union has made is the provision of some of this needed courage. Because of the importance of this means of discovering conflicts of interest, a large portion of this chapter will be devoted to the processing of grievances.

Direct observation Not all conflicts will be voiced to other people. A good supervisor knows the customary behavior of subordinates, and when significant changes in that behavior occur, he or she is concerned with possible motives. Often such motives are apparent, as in the case of an individual who failed to receive an expected promotion. Though nothing was said, the individual's work and work habits deteriorated rapidly. Such a conflict is difficult to resolve, but if productivity is not to be adversely affected, the person's disappointment must be somehow alleviated.

In addition to direct observation of individual human behavior, the study of various records and statistics can often give clues to general areas of trouble. Analysis of the number of formal grievances filed by a department, regardless of their content, may disclose additional unvoiced conflicts. In a study of some 4,000 grievances over a 6-year period in a plant employing 25,000 workers, the person who was most likely to file a grievance was (1) younger, (2) better educated, (3) more likely to be absent or late, and (4) had more derogatory information in her or his personnel file.[1] In sum, this is a picture of a person who is able to perceive contract violations and is willing to actively protest. Younger and better-educated employees are more likely to question the status quo, possibly leading to more adverse comments for the personnel file. Absenteeism and lateness also constitute symbols of protest. Thus, analysis of grievance rates, accident rates, requests for transfer, resignations, and disciplinary cases may reveal general patterns that are not apparent in any one instance.

Suggestions boxes The usual type of suggestion system has been discussed in Chapter 13. The type referred to here may be called a gripe box. The company that establishes an anonymous gripe system is concerned with the problem of bringing *all* conflicts of interest to light. Anonymity may provide the courage to submit a dissatisfaction that will otherwise go unvoiced.

Open-door policy The open-door policy is commonly announced but seldom works. As it is usually established, a higher-level executive announces that the door is always open to anyone who would like to discuss anything with her or him. But try to get past the supervisor, the first sergeant, or the secretary! This technique of discovering dissatisfaction appeals only to people with ''brass,'' and these could well use the established grievance procedure. Most employees recognize the policy for the window dressing it is. They are acutely aware of the organizational obstacles as well as of their own deficiencies in dress, speech, and manner, which make it impossible for them to walk through the door. The policy sounds good and democratic, but it is generally ineffective.

---

[1]John Price, James Dewire, John Nowack, Kenneth Schenkel, and William Ronan, ''Three Studies of Grievances,'' *Personnel Journal,* vol. 55, no. 1, January 1976, p. 35.

Personnel counselors   Some of the larger organizations hire trained psychologists to act as counselors for employees. Ordinarily these counselors are members of a staff personnel department. The rationale for a counseling system is somewhat similar to that for the gripe box. When employees do not wish to go to a superior, they can go to a person outside the chain of command who will protect their identity and confidence. It takes time to build up an atmosphere of impartiality and trust about the personnel counselor, who is often considered a member of management in a staff capacity.

Exit interview   If the conflict or disagreement is so great that the employee resigns, the exit interview provides one last opportunity to discover the nature of the complaint. The exit interview, however, is very difficult to conduct effectively. The nondirective type of interview is usually preferred. If the employee is quitting because of some dissatisfaction with the company, he or she is usually very reluctant to discuss it. There is little to be gained from burning bridges behind one. No matter how you might enjoy "leveling" with the interviewer and saying what you really think of the boss or the organization, references for the next job must come from the present organization. Consequently the exit interviewer must exercise skill in getting to the true reason for the resignation, and often, the interview itself does not reveal the reason. Resignation statistics gathered by departments over a period of time frequently uncover general sources of difficulty.

In a survey of 426 companies in manufacturing, approximately 70 percent required an exit interview upon separation from the firm.[2] The announced objective of the interview included possible improvement of personnel practices, counseling of the employee, attempting to identify weak supervisors within the firm, and general public relations value. A few companies have found that an exit questionnaire mailed after 3 months have passed produces a substantial amount of information. By this time the exemployee usually has another job and no longer fears a poor reference.

The ombudsman or ombudswoman   An organizational "patch" that is attracting increasing interest among management theorists is the ombudsman or ombudswoman. This is a special position in that one acts, not as the right arm of the president of an organization, but rather as an additional set of ears. In effect, one operates a complaint office to which individuals may go when they feel that they have exhausted the more usual means of receiving an acceptable hearing. An ombudsman or ombudswoman has only the right of acceptance or rejection of such complaints. In the event of acceptance, the holder of this unusual position has rights of investigation and recommendation to responsible organization officials. Failing satisfactory resolution of the conflict in this direct manner, a recommendation can then be made to the president of the organization.

Though the concept has existed for about 150 years, only recently have some American business firms set up the post of ombudsman or ombudswoman. Xerox Corporation inaugurated the position in 1972 and reports that 40 percent of the final decisions favored the employee, 30 percent were opposed, and 30 percent represented some type of compromise.[3] In one major unit of General Electric Company, some 300 cases were processed in 1 year with the most complaints centering around salary, performance appraisal, layoff, and fringe benefits.

---

[2]National Industrial Conference Board, *Personnel Practices in Factory and Office: Manufacturing,* Studies in Personnel Policy, no. 194, New York, 1964, p. 20.

[3]"Where Ombudsmen Work Out," *Business Week,* May 3, 1976, pp. 114–116.

Miscellaneous channels   Numerous other channels of upward communication have been utilized at one time or another as a means of bringing conflicts of interest to light. *Group meetings* or gripe sessions are conducted by some supervisors who have the courage and balanced perspective to solicit complaints publicly. An individual acts differently in the company of others than when alone, and a group meeting may stimulate the submission of gripes that otherwise may be repressed. The keystone of teamwork in the Pitney Bowes Company is monthly meetings in all departments involving every employee.[4] *Unsolicited employee letters* sometimes constitute an additional channel. One firm utilized a blackboard in a manner similar to the gripe-box method. The complaint or rumor was written on one side, and the management wrote an answer opposite it on the other. In addition to interviews of the exit type, *scheduled interviews* of present employees can be conducted to attempt to discover the source of difficulty. For example, the morale-survey score may show one department far out of line from the rest. The survey has identified the area, and the interview may be used within the area to pinpoint the trouble further. Of course, *collective bargaining* is a highly formalized method of discovering the discontents of employees. Finally, on rare occasions, *the informer* has been used. The employment of labor spies is not to be recommended, but this technique utilizes a basic principle of communication. In order to understand people, they must be studied where they stand, in their customary social and physical environment. Though an employer may have the best intentions in utilizing an informer, that is, of wanting to know what employees truly believe without thought of reprisal or punishment, the practice is highly objectionable to all concerned. More orthodox techniques will produce more value in the long run.

THE PROCESSING
OF GRIEVANCES

The definition of a grievance often varies from company to company and from author to author. The broadest interpretation of the term would include any discontent or dissatisfaction that affects organizational performance. As such it can be either stated or unvoiced, written or oral, legitimate or ridiculous. The only major restriction in this definition is that the discontent must affect worker performance.

The broad definition of a grievance has its value as far as basic managerial philosophy is concerned. The manager has to be concerned with *all* discontents regardless of a personal opinion of their validity. One has to watch for unexpressed dissatisfactions. Thus it is the basis for a sound approach to the development of good morale.

In the business world, however, the term "grievance" is usually more restricted in its meaning. Many managements distinguish between a "complaint" and a grievance. A *complaint* is a discontent or dissatisfaction that has not, as yet, assumed a great measure of importance to the complainant. Complaints are often submitted in a highly informal fashion. An employee may complain that it is too hot in the shop, that another employee will not cooperate or that one has been assigned a distasteful job. There are many more complaints than there are grievances. A complaint becomes a grievance when the employee feels that an injustice has been committed. If the supervisor ignores the complaint

[4]John M. Roach, "Giving Top Management the Message at Jobholder Meetings," *Personnel,* vol. 52, no. 4, July-August 1974, pp. 26–32.

and the dissatisfaction grows within the employee, it usually assumes the status of a grievance. A grievance, in business organizations, is *always* expressed, either verbally or in writing. It can, of course, be either valid or ridiculous, and must grow out of something connected with company operations or policy. In many instances it must involve an interpretation or application of provisions of the labor contract. Negotiation through the grievance procedure is often considered to be a continuation of the collective bargaining process, which theoretically stopped with the signing of a new contract.

The Grievance Machinery

A grievance machinery or procedure is usually thought of in connection with a company that deals with a labor union. Though the union must be given a considerable amount of credit for stimulating the installation of such procedures, all companies, whether unionized or not, should have established and known methods of processing grievances. This channel of communication is vital to all organizations, and the managements who have waited for the demands of a labor union have been remiss in their obligations. Employees should know where they stand in matters pertaining to the justice or injustice of their treatment. Though they must rely primarily upon executive justice, they should have access to a judicial type of justice when they feel that it is necessary. The mere fact that such a procedure exists is satisfying, even though an employee never has an occasion to use it.

In a survey of 400 labor contracts, 98 percent had provisions detailing formal grievance procedures.[5] The primary value of a grievance procedure is that it can assist in minimizing discontent and dissatisfaction that may have adverse effects upon cooperation and productivity. The procedure also has value in that it serves as a check on arbitrary management action. Being aware of the right of employee appeal should help supervisors to avoid the tendency toward corruption and arbitrariness that power and authority often bring.

The details of a grievance machinery vary with the organization. It may have as few as two steps or as many as ten, depending primarily upon the size of the organization. The first and last steps are almost always the same for all organizations, particularly for those that are unionized. In the discussion that follows, the intermediate steps will be summarized for purposes of concise coverage. Though a labor union is not essential to the establishment and operation of a grievance procedure, one is assumed in the illustration in Figure 20-1. The following four steps of the machinery are presented:

1. Conference among the aggrieved employee, the supervisor, and the union steward

2. Conference between middle management (e.g., superintendent, general supervisor, and plant manager) and middle union leadership (e.g., committee representative, committee of stewards, and business agent)

3. Conference between top management and top union leadership

4. Arbitration

Each of these steps and problems pertaining thereto will be briefly discussed.

[5]Basic Patterns in Union Contracts, 8th ed., Bureau of National Affairs, Inc., May 1975, p. 32.

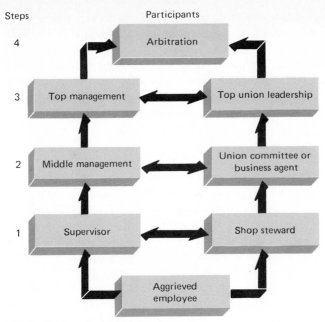

Steps   Participants

4   Arbitration

3   Top management   Top union leadership

2   Middle management   Union committee or
                                business agent

1   Supervisor   Shop steward

                    Aggrieved
                    employee

FIGURE 20-1   A grievance procedure.

Initial step   The greatest opportunity for the settlement of a complaint or grievance lies in the initial step of the procedure. The higher the discontent rises through the organization, the more difficult it is to resolve. The give-and-take of the shop is lost and saving face becomes more important at higher levels.

In the unionized concern, the first step of the procedure usually involves three people: the employee with the unresolved complaint, which has now become a grievance; the supervisor; and a representative of the union. The supervisor, as always, is a key individual and can do much to reduce the number of grievances that get past to higher steps in the machinery. Proper training and the adherence to a basic problem-solving process, to be discussed in the following section, will do much to resolve trouble on the shop level. In one large organization that handles up to 3,000 grievances per year, the percentage settled at this first step was increased from 33 to 54 percent after a training program that included both supervisors and union stewards.[6] In addition, the number of grievances filed per 100 employees was reduced from 17 to 7 during an 8-year period.

The shop steward can also do much to reduce the flow of grievances. He or she is usually an elected representative of the union and a full-time employee of the company. In a survey of 63 stewards representing more than 3,000 employees, it was found that 30 percent *never* try to talk an employee out of filing a grievance.[7] Another one-third very seldom did so. This issues both from activities deemed necessary for getting elected, and from personality traits of the steward. The greater the need for dominance on the part of the steward, the larger the number of grievances filed.

[6]C. Pettefer, ''Effective Grievance Administration,'' California Management Review, vol. 12, no. 1, Winter 1970, p. 18.

[7]Dan R. Dalton and William D. Todor, ''Manifest Needs of Stewards: Propensity to File a Grievance,'' *Journal of Applied Psychology*, vol. 64, no. 6, December 1979, p. 654.

In the past, a common view of union leaders was that the union "owns" the grievance. It may decide not to file a grievance because of the greater importance of other bargaining processes with the company. Or it may "horsetrade" by agreeing to withdraw a number of filed grievances if the employer will voluntarily grant the remainder. In recent years there have been a number of "fair representation" cases involving complaints by workers that their unions inadequately represented them in processing grievances. The NLRB reports that the number of such complaints have tripled over the past 10 years to several thousand annually.[8] In the landmark Supreme Court decision, *Vaca vs. Sipes,* it was ruled that the union breaches its duty for fair representation if it acts arbitrarily, perfunctorily, or in bad faith. Other court cases have held that the processing of grievances in an inept manner is also a violation of the union's duty to properly represent its members. The union is still free to choose to process a particular grievance, but the decision must be made on the merits of the case and not involve "horse trading" or other factors that are not pertinent, such as political interests of present and would-be officers in coming elections, possible effect upon other employees if a precedent is established, or stimulating a tremendous work load of "me, too" grievances by other employees.

Despite the legal obligations, there is a considerable amount of informal byplay between the union steward and members of management, as is illustrated by an incident that occurred in one company. A representative of the personnel department, who was active in the grievance procedure, was walking through a department. Suddenly the shop steward rushed up to him, shouting and waving his arms. When the representative from personnel finally got the gist of the shouting, he realized that the steward was blasting him concerning a grievance that had arisen in this department. The confusing thing was that earlier in the day, this grievance had been settled in the second step in favor of the union, but the settlement had not yet been generally announced. The steward was well aware of these facts. It was apparent that he was doing a little "politicking" for the benefit of his employee constituents, who were watching with great interest. He could not lose since (1) he was telling management what to do in no uncertain terms, and (2) tomorrow management would announce a win for the union in this particular grievance. Not to be outdone by the steward, the personnel representative hurried back to the grievance file and selected another which he felt was going to be conceded to the union. Returning to the department, he threw his arm around the shoulders of the shop steward, and told him that he liked him so much that he was going to concede another grievance. While the personnel specialist was talking, the shop steward was fiercely whispering, "Get away from me! The boys are watching!" Obviously, it is not good union politics to be too closely identified with management.

Lower-management officials are not above utilizing the grievance procedure as a means of convincing superiors of the inappropriateness of particular orders and policies. There are occasions when an unrealistic top-management order causes chaos among the work force, and lower managers are unable to have the order rescinded or altered. In such instances, application of the order as quickly and clumsily as possible will ultimately lead to a decision against management by an outside arbitrator. The record will show that the lower manager did not reject the plan; the arbitrator did.

It is also interesting to note that the union steward has a legal obligation to represent *all* employees in the jurisdiction, regardless of whether they are union members. In

---

[8]"On Trial: A Union's Fairness," *Business Week,* August 13, 1979, p. 76.

accordance with a basic principle of organization, the authority given to a union to represent all employees in the bargaining unit, whether they are members or not, must be equated with a responsibility to properly represent their interests, individually as well as collectively. As a practical matter, the nonunion employee generally does not expect or get individual representation.

If the supervisor, the aggrieved employee, and the steward are unable to work out a settlement of the grievance and thus effect an integration of interests, the dispute is placed on paper and is sent to a higher step in the procedure. Contract limits for the entire procedure run from 1 week to a year, but most stipulate periods shorter than 2 months.[9]

Intermediate step As Figure 20-1 indicates, the next step on the management side of the machinery is to submit the dispute to middle management. In a large organization there are a number of intermediate steps. Superintendents, general supervisors, and plant managers are typical of the management personnel involved. It is important to ensure that the line management assumes prime responsibility for the settlement of a grievance. In many firms, however, the personnel department is injected into the procedure as a decision-making power. This violates a basic principle of line and staff relationship, in giving a personnel representative authority to reverse and overrule a supervisor. The personnel manager can play one of several roles in dealing with grievance processing. In a survey of 80 personnel managers, the more common roles taken were to act as mediator (50 percent) or management's "policeman" (20 percent).[10] The mediator role is particularly difficult since line managers often say, "Whose side are you on anyway?" while union leaders may still regard personnel managers as policemen. Other, less-frequent, roles include acting as the employees' advocate, being a judge with authority to settle a dispute, and staying on the sidelines as an adviser in accordance with the principles of line and staff relationships.

On the union side, intermediate levels are represented by higher personnel in the union hierarchy. In some unions a committee representative supervises several shop stewards and constitutes the second step; in others, a committee of shop stewards may be involved; and in still others the business agent, a full-time negotiations specialist of the union, takes over the intermediate and sometimes the final step. The presence of a business agent may explain why management is often outmaneuvered by the union. Business agents are specialists in union-management negotiations. It is their full-time job. The line manager often considers grievance processing a minor, incidental, and distasteful duty. This lack of specialization and interest on the part of line management has led to the situation in which the staff personnel department is given authority to make decisions about grievances. Specialization of the union is met with specialization of management. In one survey of personnel department rights concerning grievances on discharges, 26 percent of 185 companies required compulsory consultation while 22 percent gave the department the final decision for the company.[11]

Final company-union step The final step to be undertaken by the company and union is a discussion of the grievance between representatives of top management and

[9]Robert W. Fisher, "When Workers Are Discharged—An Overview," Monthly Labor Review, vol. 96, no. 6, June 1973, p. 6.

[10]Jeffrey Gandz, "Resolving Conflict: A Guide for the Industrial Relations Manager," *Personnel,* vol. 56, no. 6, November-December 1979, pp. 22–25.

[11]*Employee Conduct and Discipline,* The Bureau of National Affairs, Inc., Washington, D.C., 1974.

Subject	Number	Positive Outcomes for Union	Positive Outcomes for Company
Suspension	104	30.1%	69.9%
Seniority	52	56.6	43.4
Miscellaneous	43	30.0	70.0
Transfer	37	29.7	70.3
Termination	33	23.5	76.5
Discipline	33	39.4	60.6
Scheduling	32	68.6	31.4
Vacation	29	44.8	55.2
Grievance processing	22	54.6	45.4
Management performing operative work	17	75.0	25.0
Safety	17	52.9	47.1
Discrimination	17	37.6	62.4
Performance evaluation	15	86.3	13.7
Union representation	10	70.0	30.0
Sick benefits denial	10	20.0	80.0
Pay	9	66.6	33.4
Excused time	8	62.5	37.5
Work out of classification	6	33.3	66.7
Training	3	33.3	66.7

Source: Dan R. Dalton, and William D. Todor, "Win, Lose, Draw: The Grievance Process in Practice." Reprinted from the March 1981 issue of *Personnel Administrator,* © 1981, The American Society for Personnel Administration, 30 Park Drive, Berea, Ohio 44017, $30 per year.

top union officials. For management, it may be the president in important grievances, a vice president, or a high-level industrial relations executive. For the union, it may be the president of the local union, the union executive committee, or a representative of the international union. It is very difficult to secure an integration of interests at this high level. The grievance has usually become an issue that has political implications. The types of grievances filed by a single west coast union local during 1979, along with their outcomes, is presented in Figure 20-2.

Arbitration If the grievance has not been settled by top management and top union leadership, three possibilities remain: (1) the union can temporarily or permanently drop the issue; (2) the union can call a strike if the contract permits (sometimes there are unauthorized wildcat strikes over a grievance); or (3) the case may be submitted to an impartial arbitrator. In 96 percent of 400 contracts, arbitration was substituted for the strike as the final step in the grievance procedure.[12] Arbitration is usually handled by either a single individual or a panel of three, consisting of a representative of labor, one of management, and an impartial third person.

An arbitrator is an outside third party who is brought in to settle a dispute. He or she has the authority to make a decision. The arbitrator may be hired for a particular case or may be appointed as a permanent official for the industry or the company and the union. Naturally, the person must be acceptable to both union and management. Salary is usually paid by both, since it is important that no undue influence be brought

[12]*Basic Patterns in Union Contracts,* op. cit. p. 37.

to bear on his or her deliberations. The American Arbitration Association maintains a list of arbitrators for consideration by managements and unions, as do the Federal Mediation and Conciliation Service and the National Mediation Board. Approximately 3,000 people are on these boards, and some 10 percent handle 90 percent of the cases. The boards merely provide a list of arbitrators to the parties; they do not engage in any of the arbitration proceedings. Analysis of arbitrators selected in 1 year revealed the following order of preference: (1) attorneys, (2) prior experience in industry or government, and (3) university faculty.[13]

Even though arbitration rulings tend to favor management in two-thirds of the cases, it is a very costly process. In one study, the average time consumed from the point where an official request for arbitration was filed until handing down of the award was 168 days.[14] When costs of lawyer fees, stenographic records, witnesses, and arbitrator fees are considered, the totals for each party can run from $500 to $1,000 a day during the hearing.[15] Because of the shortage of acceptable arbitrators and the extended periods of time involved, there has been a move toward "expedited arbitration" where no major issues of contract interpretation are involved. In these "mini-arb" cases, it is often a dispute over facts. General Electric confines this approach to employee disciplinary cases only. In expedited hearings, no briefs are filed, stenographic records are not kept, and lawyers are rarely used. In some instances, the arbitrator may hold the hearing at the company site rather than at a neutral location. The total costs involved are half that of the more typical arbitration proceedings. Once the decision has been made, both parties must accept it and abide by it; otherwise the contract has been violated.

Mediation is distinguished from arbitration in that a mediator is a third party who enters a dispute with no power of decision. One can only suggest, coax, recommend, or merely keep the two parties talking to each other. Only 2.6 percent of the contracts surveyed revealed a provision for mediation.[16] It is widely used in the negotiation of new contracts and in the settlement of strikes. In such instances, both labor and management refuse to delegate the authority of decision to an outside party. In the case of a grievance, a dispute arising within the realm of a present contract, such a delegation of authority to decide is much more acceptable to both parties.

Grievance procedures in nonunion firms   One great truth taught managements by unions is that justice is often more important than wages, hours, and working conditions. As a consequence, many companies have voluntarily introduced grievance procedures when there is no union present. Rather than the basic pattern described above, these procedures take a number of forms as described in Box 20-1. The most common model involves a recorded number of steps beginning with the immediate supervisor, and culminating in a final decision by the firm's chief administrative officer. Some buttress it with a major role by an ombudsman, but very few provide for final decision by an outside arbitrator. A survey of 41 nonunionized companies revealed that 24 had established formal grievance procedures, most within the last 10 years.[17]

[13]Walter J. Primeaux, Jr., and Dalton E. Brannen, "Why Few Arbitrators Are Deemed Acceptable," *Monthly Labor Review*, vol. 98, no. 9, September 1975, p. 29.

[14]"The Demand for Arbitrators Outruns Supply," *Business Week*, January 8, 1972, p. 62.

[15]Lawrence Stessin, "Expedited Arbitration: Less Grief over Grievances," *Harvard Business Review*, vol. 55, no. 1, January-February 1977, p. 129.

[16]"Processing of Grievances," *Monthly Labor Review*, vol. 87, no. 11, November 1964, p. 1271.

[17]Thomasine Rendero, "Grievance Procedures for Nonunionized Employees," *Personnel*, vol. 57, no. 1, January-February 1980, p. 4.

BOX 20-1
Grievance Procedures in Nonunion Situations

"Of all the techniques that managements are using in the current campaign to create a 'union-free environment,' probably the most important was originated by the unions. It is the establishment of a system for adjudicating a worker's complaints about his job or his boss. Increasingly, companies are installing grievance procedures, often patterned after union systems, and sometimes even including arbitration as the final determinant, for nonunion employees. But the final irony may be that this antiunion ploy itself contains the seeds of unionism."

The commonly announced "open-door" policy used by many firms promises more than it can deliver. Some specific structure that provides a measure of protection is necessary to reduce the fears of retribution for complaining about one's superior. Examples of these are as follows:

1. Both McDonald's Corporation and Singer Company have appointed ombudsmen to rule on workers' complaints.
2. Northrop Corporation and TransWorld Corporation have agreed to submit unresolved grievances to outside arbitrators.
3. Taktronix Inc. of Oregon provides a five-step procedure culminating with a face-to-face meeting with the President, who has the final say.

"The spread of grievance mechanisms in nonunion situations is partly attributable to employer recognition that today's workers are more independent and better-educated than ever before and partly to a very conscious effort to keep the unions at bay. A workable grievance procedure is 'probably the single most important way to keep a union out of a plant,' says John G. Wayman, a senior partner of the Pittsburgh law firm of Reed Smith Shaw & McClay, which represents employers on labor matters."

"The Antiunion Grievance Ploy," *Business Week*, February 12, 1979, p. 117.

Perhaps the absence of outside power sources, such as labor unions and arbitrators, has led to disuse of these procedures by employees. In a sample of 56 nonunion firms with formal systems, the median number of complaints that went beyond the first step was 5.[18] Only 1 to 2 percent of the employees used the procedure. In unionized firms, the usage rate is closer to 10 to 15 percent.

A Manager's Steps in Handling a Grievance

At any one stage of the grievance machinery, the dispute must be handled by some member of management. In the solution of a problem, the greater burden rests on management. As indicated earlier, the clearest opportunity for settlement is found at the first stage, before the grievance has left the province of the supervisor. For this reason, many firms have specifically trained their supervisors in how to handle a grievance or complaint properly.

One of the most widely adopted grievance-handling procedures is that presented in the Training within Industry Program in its job relations training. The dispute or grievance constitutes a managerial problem, and the scientific method is usually most productive in arriving at a satisfactory solution. As applied to grievances, directions for this procedure could be as follows:

1. *Receive and define the nature of the dissatisfaction.* The manner and attitude with which the supervisor receives the complaint of grievance is very important. As a principle applicable to this step, the supervisor should assume that the employee is fair in presenting the complaint or grievance. Statements should not

[18]Brian P. Heshizer and Harry Graham, "Discipline in the Nonunion Company: Protecting Employer and Employee Rights," *Personnel*, vol. 59, no. 2, March-April 1982, p. 73.

be prejudged on the basis of past experience with this or other employees. The supervisor should not be too busy to listen and should not give an impression of condescension in doing so. Research indicates that the supervisor's basic leadership style can do much to reduce the number of grievances. In one study, the incidence of grievances correlated negatively with supervisory inclination toward "consideration" for people ($-.51$), and correlated positively with a style characterized by "initiating structure" ($.71$).[19] Thus supervisors who were heavily task-oriented, as contrasted with people-oriented, tended to experience a significantly greater number of grievances being filed in their units.

Instead of trying to deal with a vague feeling of discontent, the supervisor should attempt to define the problem properly. Sometimes the wrong complaint is given or received. He or she must listen carefully and with empathy, in order to make sure that the true complaint or grievance is being voiced.

2. *Get the facts.* Facts must be separated from opinion and impressions. In gathering facts, one quickly becomes aware of the importance of keeping proper records, such as performance ratings, job ratings, attendance records, and suggestions. In addition, with the increasingly legalistic bent that is characteristic of modern labor-management relations, the supervisor is wise to keep records on each particular grievance. One may be called upon to testify, in later steps in the procedure, if the grievance is not resolved here. It is equally important that the supervisor possess and exercise some skill in interview, conference, and discussion.

3. *Analyze and decide.* With the problem defined and the facts in hand, the manager must now analyze and evaluate them, and then come to some decision. There is usually more than one possible solution. The manager must also be aware that the decision may constitute a precedent within both the department and the company.

It would be foolish to deny the existence of frequent "horse trading" between shop stewards and supervisors in the handling of these problems. Some grievances are very important to the steward's political position. He or she may trade a favorable decision from the supervisor for unusual cooperation in the future. At times the union leadership may wish to preserve good relations with the company in order to be able to negotiate more important disputes that are coming up. In the meantime, small but legitimate grievances may get little or no attention from the steward. On the other hand, management frequently encourages the establishment of informal agreements and compromises in the first stage of the grievance machinery in order to confine the difficulty to that level. It is not unusual for an immediate supervisor to have to walk a narrow path, hemmed in by union, upper management and staff specialists.

4. *Apply the answer.* Even though the solution decided upon by the superior is adverse to the employee, some answer is better than none. Employees dislike supervisors who will take no stand, good or bad. In the event of an appeal beyond this stage of the machinery, the manager must have the decision and reasons therefore properly recorded. If a decision favorable to the employee is reached at any stage of the machinery, the privilege and responsibility of communicating the answer to the employee should be delegated to the immediate supervisor. There is too often a tendency to let the supervisor communicate all the bad news and to allocate the favorable contacts to some other member of higher management or staff.

[19]E. A. Fleishman and E. F. Harris, "Patterns of Leadership Behavior Related to Employee Grievances and Turnover." *Personnel Psychology*, vol. 15, no. 1, Spring 1962, pp. 43–56.

5. *Follow up*. The objective of the grievance procedure is to resolve a disagreement between an employee and the organization. Discussion and conference are important to this process. The purpose of its follow-up phase is to determine whether the clash of interest has been resolved. If follow up reveals that the case has been handled unsatisfactorily or that the wrong grievance has been processed, then redefinition of the problem, further fact finding, analysis, solution, and follow up are required.

Among the common errors of management encountered in the processing of grievances are (1) stopping too soon in the search of facts, (2) expressing a management opinion prior to the time when all pertinent facts have been discovered, (3) failing to maintain proper records, (4) resorting to executive fiat instead of discussion and conference to change minds, and (5) settling the wrong grievance—a mistake which may in turn produce a second new grievance. Follow up is the step in the procedure that tells us when a mistake in handling has been made.

DISCIPLINARY ACTION

In addition to the confusion over the meaning of a grievance, there is also a certain ambiguity in the term "disciplinary action." A broad interpretation would consider the words to mean any conditioning of future behavior by the application of either rewards or penalties. This approach would include positive motivational activities, such as praise, participation, and incentive pay, as well as negative motivational techniques, such as reprimand, layoff, and fines. Both types of activities seek to condition employee behavior in order to achieve good discipline in the organization.

The more commonly accepted definition of the term, and the one to be used in this text, is that disciplinary action is confined to the application of penalties that lead to an inhibition of undesired behavior. Though the majority of employees do conform to orders, policies, and regulations, a minority still require the stimulus generated by penalties. One of the most difficult tasks of a supervisor is the effective administration of negative disciplinary action. It is our purpose in this portion of this text to discuss a general manner of approaching the problem, before presenting a series of commonly accepted principles of disciplinary action. Our general objective is still that of developing an integration of interests. The approach has shifted, however, to a utilization of *negative* means to achieve that integration.

Basic Elements of the Disciplinary-Action Process

The first element of the disciplinary process must be location of the responsibility for the administration of disciplinary action. There is general agreement that it must be a line responsibility. A staff personnel agency can and should provide advice and assistance, but disciplining subordinates is so close to the essential nature of leadership and command that it should not be taken away from the supervisor. Unfortunately, there has been a trend in recent years to reduce the authority of the supervisor in disciplinary matters, a trend which is due partly to the increasingly legalistic approach to personnel problems as specified by government and labor contracts. Some restriction of the grant of authority to supervisors to discipline must come with the advent of greater and greater government and labor union interference. But it must also be realized that the power to discipline, even though it is rarely used, is essential to the maintenance of a management position.

The second element of a disciplinary-action program must be a clarification of what is expected of an employee in the way of behavior. This requires an establishment of reasonable rules and regulations that contribute to effective operation. A no-smoking rule in a department working with inflammable materials is not made to harass the employee. The objective of disciplinary action is not to inflict punishment. Rather, a certain type of behavior is desired, and the employee is informed of the nature of that behavior and the reason for it. If it requires a penalty to produce that type of behavior, then disciplinary action must be administered. Rules and regulations are established in such areas as attendance, safety, theft, insubordination, intoxication, fighting, dishonesty, solicitations, smoking, and housekeeping. In addition, there are often written or implied rules governing aspects of private life, such as loose morals, destructive criticism of the organization, and garnishment of wages.

In specific cases appealed to the outside arbitrator in grievance processing, the general approach has been a functional rather than a geographical analysis of the act. If the off-the-job act adversely affects the enterprise, management can legally invoke organizational disciplinary action. For example, off-the-job Communist activities are punishable only when the employer can provide tangible proof of damage to the company. In off-the-job fighting, the employer can discipline when supervisory personnel are involved in order to preserve the authority hierarchy. Criminal convictions will be upheld by arbitrators as a cause for discharge if it is determined that they will either jeopardize the company's relations with customers or create substantial doubts about the safety of fellow employees.

It is also interesting to note that employees who are union members are subject to union disciplinary powers. Over 90 percent of 158 union contracts covering more than 16 million workers provide for disciplinary action by union locals. Examples of such union offenses are engaging in work speed contests, buying without the union label, participating in wildcat strikes, working for less than union scale, disclosing union secrets, refusing to parade on Labor Day, and encouraging establishment of piece-rate incentive systems. A court decision upheld the right of the labor union to discipline members for exceeding the union-established quota of production output. Though contrary to the values of economy and efficiency, the court determined that preservation of solidarity to protect the labor organization had higher priority.

A basic problem in all such codes is that of informing employees, so that they have an opportunity to act in the desired manner. Many of the rules should be apparent to most employees, but the unusual ones must be covered in indoctrination sessions given by either the personnel department or the supervisor. In addition, it is important that the rules be enforced fairly consistently over a period of time. If the no-smoking rule has not been enforced for several months, it is unfair and contrary to the labor agreement, according to many arbitrators, suddenly to start picking up violators on some Monday morning.

With reasonable authority possessed by the supervisor, and the employees well apprised of what is expected of the, the basis of disciplinary action has been established. When an offense takes place, it is important to establish and maintain proper records concerning the nature of the event, the participants, and the surrounding circumstances. Record should also be made of any action taken by the supervisor. Such written evidence is highly important, should the event be the basis for a grievance filed by the employee. Thus, in modern management's increasingly legalistic environment, written records constitute a third basic element of a well-organized disciplinary-action program.

In taking disciplinary action, the attitude of the supervisor is extremely important. One should be objective in collecting facts. One should approach the problem, if possible, with a nonjudicial attitude. Making a mistake in the handling of a grievance may mean that the grievance has not been solved and that it is still with us. Making a mistake in disciplining someone who does not deserve it could well mean a permanent destruction of the morale of the employee and a general loss of respect for the supervisor.

Disciplinary-Action Penalties

If the facts and policies warrant the application of a penalty, the supervisor must choose one from the number he or she is authorized to use. It is not unusual for the list of rules to specify also the corresponding penalties for their violation. Ordinarily, there are varying penalties for first, second, and third offenses of the same rule. Among the penalties available in business are:

1. Oral reprimand
2. Written reprimand
3. Loss of privileges
4. Fines
5. Layoff
6. Demotion
7. Discharge

The penalties are listed in the general order of severity, from mild to severe.

For most cases, an oral reprimand is sufficient to achieve the desired result. The supervisor must know her or his personnel in determining how to give a reprimand. For one person, a severe "chewing out" may be necessary in order to get attention and cooperation; another person may require only a casual mention of a deficiency. If the offense is more serious, the reprimand may be put in written form. Since a written reprimand is more permanent than an oral one, it is considered a more severe penalty.

For such offenses as tardiness or leaving work without permission, fines or loss of various privileges can be used. The fines usually have some relationship to the work time actually lost. The loss of privileges includes such items as good job assignments, right to select machine or other equipment, and freedom of movement about the workplace or company.

The more severe penalties of layoff, demotion, and discharge are usually outside the grant of authority to the immediate supervisor. Disciplinary layoffs can vary in severity from 1 to several days' loss of work without pay. The use of demotions as a penalty is highly questionable. If the employee is properly qualified for the present assignment, he or she will be improperly placed on a lower job. Discharge is the most severe penalty that a business organization can give and constitutes "industrial capital punishment." Since this requires exit of the employee from the organization, it will be discussed in a later chapter dealing with several types of employee-employer separations.

Guides to Disciplinary Action

Experience and some research have provided a number of guides to assist the manager in undertaking negative disciplinary action. Some contend that the fundamentals can be summed up in the "hot stove rule." Applying disciplinary action can be compared to touching a hot stove: (1) you have warning—knowing that it is hot you should realize what is likely to happen if you touch it; (2) the burn is immediate—you can see the connection between the two events; (3) the burn is consistent—the stove burns all who touch; and (4) the burn is impersonal—you are burned for touching and not because you are a particular individual. Among the more commonly cited concepts are the following:

Disciplinary action should be taken in private. Perhaps the most commonly cited guide of disciplinary action is that such action should be administered to the person in private. Our purpose is to condition behavior, not to punish. Holding a person up to public ridicule often has the opposite of this desired effect. This is not to say that the grapevine will not be working, passing either correct or incorrect information about the act. But even so, the grapevine cannot take away the penalized person's pride or dignity, for no one knows for sure that a penalty has been given, whereas a public reprimand leaves no doubt. In addition, a public reprimand generally stimulates resentment toward management among the employees not disciplined.

An application of a penalty should always carry with it a constructive element. There is little in the penalty itself that is constructive. The individual should be told clearly and precisely the reasons for the action that is to be taken. The employee should also be told how to avoid such penalties in the future.

Disciplinary action should be applied by the immediate supervisor. Even though an act meriting disciplinary action has been observed by the superior of the immediate supervisor, any action that is taken should be carried out by the supervisor. In this manner we avoid violating the principle of single accountability and in addition we preserve the status of the supervisor.

Promptness is important in the taking of disciplinary action. The desire for promptness should not lead to quick but unfair punishments. Yet, on the other hand, if punishment is delayed too long, the relationship between the penalty and the offensive act becomes hazy. The penalty not only tends to lose its positive effect on behavior but also seems to stimulate greater resentment than if it were applied earlier.

Consistency in the administration of disciplinary action is highly essential. This guide of disciplinary action has in it an interesting contradiction. The characteristic of consistency can be applied to the cause (the penalty) or to the effect (the employee reaction). As applied to the penalty, it would require equal treatment under the code. If two persons are caught smoking in a no-smoking area, both are given identical penalties, assuming that neither has more offenses in the past than the other. The fact that one has a strong personality and the other is somewhat timid would have little to do with it. If consistency is to be applied to the effect, the concept of individual differences tells us that two people react differently to the same action. A reprimand for one may have the same effect as a 2-day layoff for another.

Despite the significance of the individual-differences concept, the practical supervisor must emphasize the consistency of penalty. Not only must one be concerned with the offenders; one must also be aware of the possible reactions of other employees. Charges of favoritism would surely arise if different penalties were awarded based solely on the psychological differences of the recipients. Reports of manager practice indicate that consistency in penalty application is more common than a clinical or judicial approach that could result in varying penalties for similar offenses.[20] This consistency can take the form of a "legalistic" approach where a rule is a rule, or a "humanitarian" approach where the rule is not enforced through disciplinary action. In the latter case, rules are viewed as educational devices, and violations are deemed accidental and unintentional. Encouragement is preferred to punishment as a means of conditioning employee behavior.

In reviewing the "disciplinary styles" of grievance arbitrators, it was found that they tend to use a legalistic, rule-enforcing approach on cases involving dishonesty, illegal strikes, insubordination, and company rule violations.[21] Issuance of awards characterized by a more humanitarian and behavior-correction approach was more prevalent in cases of absenteeism, intoxication on the job, fighting, and job incompetence.

An immediate supervisor should never be disciplined in the presence of his own subordinates. The concept of privacy would forbid the disciplining of anyone in the presence of others. It is doubly important in the case of managers, who must preserve a position of status and power in addition to the formal authority granted by the organization. The importance of this guide should be obvious, but the author has observed more than one occasion when it was violated. The grapevine will be active enough when managers are disciplined, without their status being completely destroyed by public action.

After the disciplinary action has been taken, the manager should attempt to assume a normal attitude toward the employee. This is an important but difficult guide to follow. If the manager continues to regard the employee with great suspicion after the action has been taken, the employee may oblige by providing the trouble expected. It is better to assume that the incident is closed after the penalty has been inflicted, with advice as to how to alter behavior in the future. Certainly the disciplined employee is aware that the supervisor remembers what has happened, and the supervisor will be interested in seeing if the person's behavior has been successfully conditioned. But one should not go about seeming to wait and hope for the next offense.

When management is dissatisfied with the behavior of an employee, its goal is to effect a change more consistent with organization requirements. Penalties or punishments constitute only one means of doing this, and should be used as a last resort. The attitude of the immediate supervisor should be one of counseling and understanding, rather than "police and punish." One company even goes so far as to suspend for 1 day *with full pay* in order that the employee may think through personal problems. After a sincere effort has been made through casual warnings, counseling interviews, and perhaps a short suspension with pay, then unions, arbitrators, management, and sometimes the employee might well agree that discharge is the next logical event.

CONFLICT RESOLUTION

Conflict occurs when two or more people or groups perceive that they have (1) incompatibility of goals, and (2) interdependence of activity. Unless one believes in a utopian world where all interests are additive, overlapping, and compatible, one must admit to

---

[20]Fremont A. Shull, Jr., and L. L. Cummings, "Enforcing the Rules: How Do Managers Differ?" *Personnel,* vol. 43, no. 1, March-April 1966, p. 36.

[21]Hoyt N. Wheeler, "Punishment Theory and Industrial Discipline," *Industrial Relations,* vol. 15, no. 2, May 1976, p. 239.

possible conflicts accompanied by deliberate behavior characterized by interference and blockages. Employees and organizations need each other and are therefore interdependent. Employees and organizations have some values that conflict, for example the ego versus control, self-actualization versus division of labor, and freedom versus efficiency.

The traditional managerial approach to conflict is one of suppression and elimination; conflict is the antithesis of cooperation and organization. Behavioral scientists have recommended a philosophy of acceptance; conflicts should be uncovered and ultimately worked through for the betterment of all. Both appear to agree that the final goal is the elimination of conflict; they merely disagree on means.

In a contingency approach to managing, it is envisioned that conflict can be both good and bad depending upon the situation. The Penn Central Railroad went quietly bankrupt with its board of directors offering no conflictive and challenging questions to management. Small-group research has demonstrated that when study groups are formed in which a "devil's advocate" was placed to challenge dominant positions, more analysis and better decisions resulted. Yet when one member was allowed to be dropped from the group, it was always this conflicting person who "got the axe." Thus, rather than total suppression or total acceptance of conflict, managers should accept the inevitability of conflict, recognize those reactions that are helpful to organizational renewal, and minimize reactions that interfere with and block attainment of legitimate goals.

In Figure 20-3 the reconciliation of conflict between party 1 and party 2 can be approached in seven ways: (1) *win/lose fashion,* where one party *forces* the other to concede; (2) withdrawal and retreat from argument—"Silence is golden"; (3) smoothing or playing down the differences—*"We're one big happy family"*; (4) superordinate goals, where both parties are asked to temporarily suspend the conflict in the interest of cooperation toward a higher and more important value, for instance, no strikes during wartime; (5) compromising, splitting the difference, and bargaining in search of inter-

FIGURE 20-3 Methods of conflict resolution.

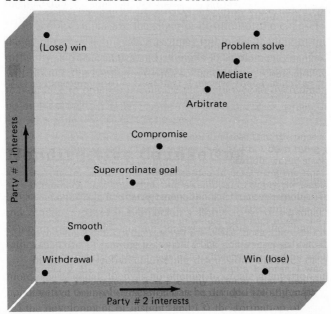

mediate acceptable positions; (6) submission to an outside third party for decision—an arbitrator; (7) inviting an outside third party to mediate and help the two primary parties reach a reconciliation; and (8) problem solving or confrontation through an open exchange of information and working through of the differences so that both can win. It should be apparent that the basic behavioral approach in this regard is the last—the traditional *"win/lose"* or *"lose/lose"* approach should be replaced by the behavioral *"win/win"* philosophy.[22] It is illustrative of the ideal 9,9 leadership-style world, where after the conflict is resolved, both parties are fully satisfied with the results—their values, after all, were overlapping. As usually practiced, confrontation is characterized by such elements as an open and trusting exchange of views and facts and acceptance of the concepts (1) that conflict is caused by relationships among people and is not in the person, (2) that rarely is one completely right and the other completely wrong, and (3) that granting concessions is not a sign of weakness or capitulation.

Even without contending that confrontation and problem solving will always result in solutions that simultaneously maximize both parties' positions, this approach will usually effect better resolutions than the other six. In a study of five methods used in an engineering department of a large corporation, opinions of seventy-four managers were obtained concerning their relative efficacy. Correlations were computed between methods used and resolution effectiveness, with the following results: (1) withdrawal, $-.19$; (2) smoothing, $+.20$; (3) compromising, $-.08$; (4) forcing win/lose, $-.26$; and (5) problem solving, $+.26$. Only the last two were significant statistically.[23] A second study of 53 managers from various organizations was undertaken, where these people were asked to write descriptions of both good and bad conflict resolutions that they had experienced. In coding these narratives by the five methods, 58.5 percent of the effective resolutions utilized the confrontation approach and 24.5 percent used forcing a win/lose decision. Of the ineffective, none used confrontation while 79.2 percent used forcing. Withdrawal was utilized in about 10 percent of the ineffective stories.

Despite the behavioral views of the efficacy of the problem-solving, confrontation approach, the facts of organized life do indicate that we are often unable to achieve the answer that maximizes competing values simultaneously. We can agree that withdrawal or avoidance, as well as smoothing over real conflicts, are not viable methods of handling this type of problem. However, compromise is often the result of collective bargaining processes between two groups of equal power, such as labor and management, or the United States and Russia. Neither may be completely happy, but coordinated activity is allowed to continue. When the two parties are unable to reach a solution, either through problem solving or compromise, third parties may enter the scene. In Figure 20-3, arbitration is placed just above compromise to indicate what often happens in such proceedings: the arbitrator, whose salary is equally shared, will over a period of many cases tend toward a balanced position in his or her awards. The mediator, who has no power of decision, is located closer to the problem-solving position in the figure, indicating the greater possibility of *three* parties being able to discover that elusive position of simultaneous maximization. When time for conflict resolution is limited or when basic values are directly conflicting, methods of resolution that are less than the best are often considered to be the "practical" approach.

[22]Robert R. Blake and Jane Srygley Mouton, "The Fifth Achievement," *Personnel Administration,* vol. 34, no. 3, May–June 1971, pp. 49–57.

[23]Ronald J. Burke, "Methods of Resolving Superior-Subordinate Conflict: The Constructive Use of Subordinate Differences and Disagreements," *Organizational Behavior and Human Performance,* vol. 5, no. 4, July 1970, pp. 400–403.

SUMMARY

Despite the best efforts of all, conflict among people and between people and organizations will occur. It is important to discover these clashes of interest as quickly as possible through such means as gripe boxes, direct observation of behavior, analysis of records, an open-door attitude, personnel counselors, morale surveys, exit interviews, ombudsmen and ombudswomen, and grievance procedures.

A grievance is a complaint that the employee feels is serious enough to justify some type of formal submission and action. It may be ridiculous or justified, but whether or not it is a grievance is up to the employee and not to the management. The usual steps in a grievance procedure are (1) conference among the aggrieved employee, the supervisor, and the union steward, (2) conference between middle management and middle union leadership, (3) conference between top management and top union leadership, and (4) arbitration. The manner of processing the grievance on any one level should follow the sequence of functions found in the scientific method, that is, (1) receive and define the grievance, (2) get the facts, (3) analyze and decide, (4) apply the answer, and (5) follow up. The grievance procedure is the most fundamental method of discovering and resolving disagreements, since it both follows the chain of authority and provides for conference and discussion.

Just as the individual makes certain demands upon the organization, so the organization expects certain things from its members. Codes of behavior are established. For those individuals who do not choose to conform to the codes, negative disciplinary action must be applied. The supervisor should seek to condition behavior and not merely to punish. In the application of penalties, the following guides have been found to be valuable: (1) disciplinary action should be administered in private; (2) an application of a penalty should always carry with it an explanation of what constitutes proper behavior; (3) disciplinary action should be applied by the immediate supervisor; (4) promptness is important in the taking of disciplinary action; (5) consistency in penalty is highly essential; (6) an immediate supervisor should never be disciplined in the presence of his or her own subordinates; and (7) after the disciplinary action has been taken, the manager should attempt to assume a normal attitude toward the employee.

The basic method of conflict resolution advocated by behavioral scientists is problem solving and confrontation, a stance that approaches the 9,9 leadership style in the Managerial Grid. Other commonly used approaches are withdrawal, smoothing, establishing superordinate goals, compromise, mediation, arbitration, and forcing. The conflict must be managed to produce long-term organizational effectiveness.

BRIEF CASE

In a continuous-process operation, employees of a grain-milling company submitted a grievance to their first-line supervisor concerning the company's decision to remove coffee pots from the operating area. The pots were removed because they tended to be gathering spots, and management felt employees were taking advantage of the situation. There were no specific statements in the union contract on the use of coffee pots, nor was there any discussion of this subject during bargaining. The union accepted and processed the grievance on the basis that the contract stipulated that both parties had an obligation to discuss any problems or procedures related to wages, hours, or working conditions. Management pointed to the management rights clause that gave the company the right to manage the operation except as specifically modified by the labor contract. They maintained that they had a right to remove the coffee pots if they deemed it to be a problem. Management decided it was a problem since supervisors had to continually remind employees to return to their work stations. Reaching no agreement, the grievance was finally submitted to an outside arbitrator.

Questions

1. What alternatives did management have other than removing the coffee pots?

2. Who do you think should win this grievance? Why?

DISCUSSION QUESTIONS

1. What are the varying philosophies that one can take toward organizational conflicts?

2. Describe the method of conflict resolution preferred by behavioral scientists. How does it relate to the subject of leadership styles?

3. Ignoring the forced win/lose approach to conflict resolution, define the continuum of methods ranging from avoidance to confrontation.

4. In discovering conflicts of interest, compare and contrast gripe boxes with an open-door policy; ombudsmen or ombudswomen with personnel counselors.

5. Describe the role of the immediate supervisor in processing grievances with respect to the employee, union steward, and the personnel department.

6. Discuss the use of mediation and arbitration in a grievance procedure. Which is more commonly used? Why?

7. Discuss the concepts of ''consistency'' and ''individual differences'' in handling cases of disciplinary action.

8. Identify the major elements of a disciplinary action program.

9. Relate the personnel function of integration to the concepts of grievances, disciplinary action, and conflict resolution methods.

10. Describe the role of the union steward in dealing with employees, supervisor, and higher union officials.

SUPPLEMENTARY READING

BRIGGS, STEVEN: ''The Grievance Procedure and Organizational Health,'' *Personnel Journal,* vol. 60, no. 6, June 1981, pp. 471–474.

DALTON, DAN R. and WILLIAM D. TODOR: ''Antecedents of Grievance Filing Behavior: Attitude/Behavioral Consistency and the Union Steward,'' *Academy of Management Journal,* vol. 25, no. 1, March 1982, pp. 158–169.

HARRISON, EDWARD L.: ''Legal Restrictions on the Employer's Authority to Discipline,'' *Personnel Journal,* vol. 61, no. 2, February 1982, pp. 136–141.

HESHIZER, BRIAN P. and HARRY GRAHAM: "Discipline in the Nonunion Company: Protecting Employer and Employee Rights," *Personnel*, vol. 59, no. 2, March-April 1982, pp. 71–78.

KING, DENNIS: "Three Cheers for Conflict!" *Personnel*, vol. 58, no. 1, January-February 1981, pp. 113–122.

TJOSBOLD, DEAN: "Effects of Approach to Controversy on Superiors' Incorporation of Subordinates' Information in Decision Making," *Journal of Applied Psychology*, vol. 67, no. 2, April 1982, pp. 189–193.

EXERCISE AND CASES
FOR PART FIVE

Exercise: Leadership Style*

Apply the Vroom and Yetton Decision Tree to the following three episodes in order to determine the feasible leadershp style set:

Example 1 You are general foreman in charge of a large gang laying an oil pipeline. It is now necessary to estimate your expected rate of progress in order to schedule material deliveries to the next field site.

You know the nature of the terrain you will be traveling and have the historical data needed to compute the mean and variance in the rate of speed over that type of terrain. Given these two variables it is a simple matter to calculate the earliest and latest times at which materials and support facilities will be needed at the next site. It is important that your estimate be reasonably accurate. Underestimates result in idle foremen and workers, and an overestimate results in tying up materials for a period of time before they are to be used.

Progress has been good and your five foremen and other members of the gang stand to receive substantial bonuses if the project is completed ahead of schedule.

Example 2 You are the head of a staff unit reporting to the vice president of finance. He has asked you to provide a report on the firm's current portfolio including recommendations for changes in the selection criteria currently employed. Doubts have been raised about the efficiency of the existing system in the current market conditions, and there is considerable dissatisfaction with prevailing rates of return.

You plan to write the report, but at the moment you are quite perplexed about the approach to take. Your own specialty is the bond market, and it is clear to you that a detailed knowledge of the equity market, which you lack, would greatly enhance the value of the report. Fortunately, four members of your staff are specialists in different segments of the equity market. Together they possess a vast amount of knowledge about the intricacies of investment. However, they seldom agree on the best way to achieve anything when it comes to the stock market. While they are obviously conscientious as well as knowledgeable, they have major differences when it comes to investment philosophy and strategy.

You have 6 weeks before the report is due. You have already begun to familiarize yourself with the firm's current portfolio and have been provided by management with

---

*Reprinted from *Leadership and Decision-Making* by Victor H. Vroom and Philip W. Yetton, by permission of the University of Pittsburgh Press © 1973, pp. 41–44.

a specific set of constraints that any portfolio must satisfy. Your immediate problem is to come up with some alternatives to the firm's present practices and select the most promising for detailed analysis in your report.

Example 3 You are on the division manager's staff and work on a wide variety of problems of both administrative and technical nature. You have been given the assignment of developing a universal method to be used in each of the five plants in the division for manually reading equipment registers, recording the readings, and transmitting the scorings to a centralized information system. All plants are located in a relatively small geographic region.

Until now there has been a high error rate in the reading and/or transmittal of the data. Some locations have considerably higher error rates than others, and the methods used to record and transmit the data vary between plants. It is probable, therefore, that part of the error variance is a function of specific local conditions rather than anything else, and this will complicate the establishment of any system common to all plants. You have the information on error rates but no information on the local practices that generate these errors or on the local conditions that necessitate the different practices.

Everyone would benefit from an improvement in the quality of the data, as it is used in a number of important decisions. Your contacts with the plants are through the quality-control supervisors who are responsible for collecting the data. They are a conscientious group committed to doing their jobs well, but they are highly sensitive to interference on the part of higher management in their own operations. Any solution that does not receive the active support of the various plant supervisors is unlikely to reduce the error rate significantly.

Case: The Staff Enforcer

Ron Powell, 28 years of age, is a job and wage analyst in the industrial relations department within the transport division of Acme Aircraft. The division produces a line of twin-engined passenger planes for the commercial market, and a militarized version of the same plane for the U.S. Air Force. The production work force was fairly stable at 6,000 employees working 2 shifts in such areas as fabrication, subassembly, final assembly, and support functions. Ron had been in the IR department for 7 months, being the junior person in the unit. However, he had been with Acme for 6 years, serving in the final assembly unit as leadman on the electrical checkout crew, and in the electrical planning unit as a planner. While in the latter position, he heard of the opening in industrial relations.

While working for many years on the night shift in final assembly, he took advantage of the opportunity to return to college and get a degree in Business Administration. He had been looking for a way to utilize this knowledge, and saw the job and wage analyst opening as a golden opportunity to do so. Movement into the position was much easier than he had anticipated. It was a salaried position with a good pay increase. Wage and salary personnel wore a candy-striped badge with a star on it, to which hourly workers, who wore mustard-colored badges, attached a good deal of prestige.

The wage and salary section within IR was composed of 6 analysts and a section head. Two covered jobs in engineering, 3 maintained surveillance over the fabrication and assembly departments, and 1 was assigned to technical and office positions. There were approximately 1,000 employees per analyst. After receiving 6 weeks' training under one of the more experienced analysts, he was assigned to the subassembly and final assembly units.

Jim Hardy, 39 years of age, was the wage and salary section head. He had been with the company for 16 years, and in W&S for 10. Having no formal education beyond high school, he had risen through the ranks from punch press operator to general supervisor. Ten years ago, when Acme suffered a severe cutback, he was saved by transfer to IR. His work in W&S had gained him a great deal of respect from division management.

Hardy laid down a few simple but firm rules for his analysts to follow. The overall thrust was to be fair to all concerned. Among the specific rules were:

1. Every employee must be working under the proper job class and in the proper pay range for that class.

2. The work in each unit is to be evaluated on a regular basis, and classified by labor grade in accordance with the skill and knowledge required.

3. The number of employees in each class is to be kept in line with the available type of work in each unit.

4. All requests for classification changes, lateral or upgrading, are to be personally investigated by the analyst and substantiated on the basis of work actually being performed.

5. All requests for merit increases are to be personally discussed with the department supervisor initiating the request, to verify justification.

6. All job classification changes and merit rate increases require approval of the W&S section.

7. The use of "name dropping" of higher-management authorities by analysts to exercise control will not be condoned.

Until about 6 weeks ago, Ron had enjoyed the independence with which he was allowed to work. Hardy occasionally stopped in his office cubicle for a short chat to inquire if there were any problems, and to remind Ron to keep an eye out for any changes in work patterns in his units. The other analysts said that when he called you to *his* office and closed the door, that's when you really found out what he was like. Though the work had been proceeding at a reasonable rate, recently Ron found himself reluctant to leave the office and spend time out in the units. Employees had begun to approach him, wanting to know when they were going to get an "A" classification. All Ron would say was, "That's a matter between you and your supervisor." His old acquaintants, however, seemed to be avoiding him.

One day Ron was stopped as he was leaving the plant after work by an irate employee who said that his supervisor had told him that he had put him in for a raise, and that W&S had turned it down. He demanded an explanation even though Ron could remember seeing no such request. Ron told him that if he had a "beef," he should see his shop steward. After he said it, he realized that that hadn't been too swift an answer, but he had been caught by surprise. When he told Hardy of the episode the next morning, all the latter said was, "Yeah, there's some real weak supervisors out there. You had better have a serious talk with them."

Ron's current problem is processing six requests for classification changes for personnel. All six were for upgrading to "A" class; all had come in on the same day 2 weeks ago from the same general supervisor—four from the final assembly unit and two from electrical harness assembly. Final assembly presented a special challenge. In other departments where people worked on machines, one could look at the type of parts being manufactured and spot-check to see if they were making their own set-ups. Even in subassembly, when people worked at a regular station or bench, it wasn't too difficult to determine the level of work being performed. However, in final assembly, where people worked in groups all over the aircraft, inside and out, and frequently changed tasks, it was practically impossible to determine who was doing ''A'' work. Watching at close hand for any period of time was out—analysts were supposed to stay in the background. It was forbidden to talk to workers about the work they were doing without an invitation from the supervisor to do so. Even in this case, a shop steward had to be present. In final assembly, the analyst was forced to put his trust in the decisions of the unit supervisor. Ron was especially concerned about these latest change requests since Hardy had recently commented, ''Final assembly is top-heavy; don't let it get out of hand.''

In the electrical assembly unit, most of the employees were female. The change requests were for two women on the second shift. The ''A'' classification called for working from blueprints to make up harness peg boards, or assembly work on certain harnesses where the soldering of plugs was especially difficult or critical. The ''A'' jobs were easy to spot, especially since they tended to be only in one area of the assembly floor. Ron had been keeping an eye on the situation for 2 weeks. The two employees had been moved into the ''A'' area, but it was clear to him that they were still doing ''B'' work. The supervisor had said that they were helping out on some of the ''B'' work in which the unit had fallen behind.

The same time had come to make a decision on all six requests for class upgrading. Ten working days were allowed for investigation by the analyst. Ron decided to go over and talk to Dick Perry, general supervisor of both units.

Ron. Mr. Perry, I'd like to talk to you about these classification changes.

Perry. What's to talk about? I signed them, didn't I?

Ron. Well, if you get too many more "A" classifications than you have "A" work for, some of them are going to be working on "B" work all the time. That could cause some problems. Some of the other "B" people may think they should have the "A" classification too—you know how aggressive the shop stewards are. We could end up with a bunch of grievances. This is especially true for the women in electrical assembly. I'd like to see them put on some "A" work for a few weeks before they are considered for the classification. That's company policy.

Perry. Dammit! Don't quote me company policy! Was there any question in your mind that I was running this department when you used to work for me?

Ron. No.

Perry. Well, I'm *still* running it—not wage and salary. I promote whoever I please, whenever I please. I know my supervisors, and they know their people and what they're doing. I'm not going to stand for your questioning their judgment. I'm not afraid of the union either. I know the head of industrial relations, "Red" Folsom, personally, and I'll just go to see him about this.

Ron. Well, if you know him personally, I sure can't stop you from talking to him. I just hope he realizes that I'm trying to do my job.

Saying that, Ron snatched up the request forms and left Perry's office. At his first opportunity, he went into Hardy's office to explain what had happened. He expected Hardy to close the door. But Hardy just said, ''Well, if that's where you think he was headed, you might start gathering up your personal belongings and putting them in a cardboard box. I hope not. I have a meeting with 'Red' this afternoon and then we'll know.''

Ron heard no more about it that day. When 3 days had passed, he figured that maybe he had passed the crisis. Then, in walked the labor relations specialist who told him that three grievances had been filed from units in Ron's area: one from final assembly, and the two from electrical harness. Ron thought, ''What now?! What kind of support will I get from Perry? Will he help kill them at the first step? If they get further, losing a grievance could only be bad news for a new analyst.''

As matters turned out, Perry was able to kill the final assembly grievance at the first step. Grievances for the two female employees went to a third-step hearing. In this hearing, the labor relations specialist gave one of the women a blueprint to interpret. She started to cry, and the company agreed to keep both employees in the ''A'' area, but they were to be given ''A'' classification only after a 6-weeks' training program.

Ron still had his job. He hadn't received a closed-door session from Hardy, who let him know anyway that he didn't think the situation had been handled very smoothly. Hardy hoped that Ron had learned something from it. Ron guessed he had learned something, but he wasn't sure what. In retrospect, he wondered if he shouldn't have gotten an engineering, rather than a business, degree.

Questions

1. What are the role expectations of the various persons contacted by Ron?

2. How would you suggest that Ron handle the various conflicts encountered on this job? How did he handle each?

Case: The New Engineer*

Frank David, a design engineer working with an electronic business machines group in an eastern city, decided to move to Arizona for a change of scenery. The only company in the area that was hiring at the time was Electronics Inc. (EI). With an introduction from one of the vice presidents of the largest bank in town, he contacted EI and was introduced to the Product Engineering manager and six or seven other managers. Accepting an offer of 25 percent less salary than he had been making in the east, Frank moved his family to Arizona and reported to work in a firm whose products he had no knowledge of, and in an environment which was strange and appeared to be somewhat hostile.

When Frank reported to work the first day, he noticed many things that were quite unusual. All offices were alike—very plain. There were no names on doors or desks, or any place else in the building. The president of the company and the janitor dressed alike—very casually. The manager of his unit, the production engineering department, was a man five feet seven inches tall. Except for the manager, Frank was the shortest man in the department. Frank was six foot one. When the whole department went to a meeting, everyone noticed: ''Here come the giants!'' Frank wondered if he was hired for his technical ability or his size. He was provided with a desk, stapler, paper clips, pens, pencils and paper. Everybody was very busy and Frank was left alone at his desk to ponder his future and his new position.

*Contributed by David T. Wiener

When Frank asked about a company organization chart, he was told that none existed and it was against company policy to make one up. "How is one to know who reports to whom?" he asked. "Nobody reports to anybody; we are flexible," he was told.

No work assignment was given to Frank. A number of days passed and Frank spoke to his manager and asked for an assignment. The manager told him to work with one of the technicians. The technician was building a piece of complex test equipment by copying it from another and making an identical twin. There were no prints available. For 2 days, Frank helped copy this item and when it was finished he didn't know what he had built or how to use it. Again Frank was left alone. The technician told him that one of the production lines was having trouble testing something and that he could help them out. Frank went out to the line and spoke to the tester. He asked to see a circuit diagram, and was provided one that was old, torn, and worn out. He took its number and got another copy from the print room. Armed with the drawing, he located the problem, which was trivial, and was then back looking for work again. Nobody gave him any work so he started to roam around looking for something to do. Most of the time he could find something that needed doing but because of the unorthodox systems which were in use he needed help in locating things. If a particular piece of test equipment were needed, he would have to find it himself. It could be somewhere on a bench or in a cabinet; there was no place for the test equipment to call home.

EI had a second shift that operated from 3:30 P.M. until midnight. Frank thought that if he could work this shift for several months, he would be forced to learn the ropes. The work of the production engineer on this shift was being handled by a technician named Harry. Harry knew everything and everybody. He was an extremely competent person. He had long hair, dressed very shabbily, and ran around making animal noises. Harry taught Frank the routine of the place, and a very fine working relationship developed with a great deal of mutual respect. Frank set up a schedule and organized the work. He then asked Harry to work on jobs in a particular order. On checking on the progress of one assigned job, Harry told him that the job had not even been started since another supervisor had preempted his services. Frank immediately issued a memo that all the jobs were to come to him, and he would assign the work to Harry. Harry did not like this but accepted it. When someone approached Harry with a job, he would loudly proclaim, "You'll have to see Frank. I can't make my own decisions any more." Everyone brought their problems to Frank and everyone gave Frank a hard time about his treatment of Harry. Within 2 weeks, Frank dropped the requirement that all work be scheduled through him.

Frank grew to like the people on the second shift. Their social life revolved around work. They had pot lucks and parties and dressup nights. They were very resourceful since many of the services were closed for the second shift. The second shift produced many marriages and divorces during the time Frank worked it.

Frank had come to EI from a very high production environment. EI, on the other hand, was a low-production, high-quality, specialty house. As the market expanded, EI found itself with many new high-volume orders. Frank observed that the old, informal operation system used by EI was not well suited to volume production. He thought he knew what should be done. He went to see several managers and explained to them that the system for producing had to be changed to suit the business as it now existed. The results of his disclosure to management were opposite to what he had expected. Instead of management showing an appreciation for his insight, they generally ignored him. One manager even went so far as to say, "We are making more money now than ever before.

Our growth is unprecedented. We must be doing something right. Who are you to tell us we are doing things wrong?'' Frank learned that challenging the system only made enemies and did not change anything. There was nothing to do but watch and wait.

Questions

1. Based on the events described in this case, what leadership style is being practiced in this firm?

2. What changes in leadership style is Frank suggesting? Why?

Case: Irwin Manufacturing Company*

In August of 1982, B. A. Warner, personnel director of the Irwin Manufacturing Company, was trying to decide what action he should take with regard to Dan Johnson, an employee of the company. Johnson had submitted an acceptable suggestion but, before submitting the idea, had given it a trial run, thus violating a long-standing rule that no change could be put into effect without the prior approval of the engineering department.

*Garret L. Bergen and William V. Haney, *Organizational Relations and Management Action*, McGraw-Hill Book Company, New York, 1966, pp. 517–522. Used with permission.

EXHIBIT 1 Irwin Manufacturing Company: Partial organization chart.

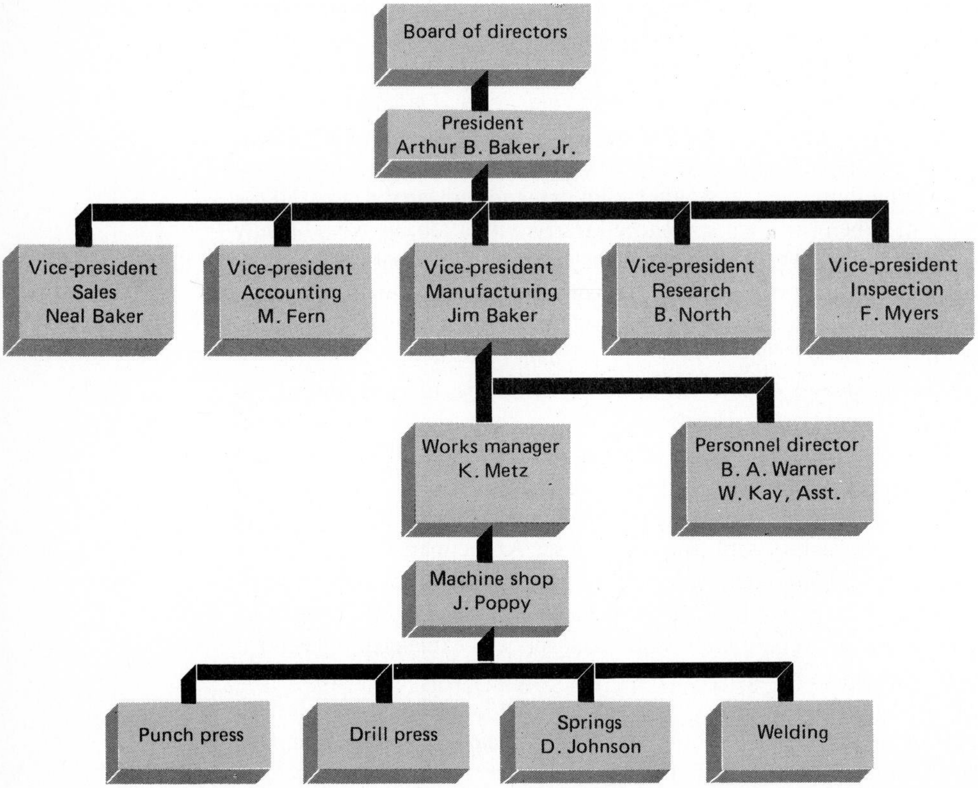

EXHIBIT 2
Irwin Manufacturing Company: Selected Data on Dan Johnson
Personal: 38 years old, married, two children. 1 year high school.

Salary:	Effective Date	Hourly Wage	Effective Date	Hourly Wage
	4/29/71	$4.60	5/1/77	$ 6.35
	8/26/71	4.70	1/3/78	6.85
	11/18/71	4.80	1/18/79	7.55
	6/3/72	4.90	9/30/79	7.95
	12/15/72	5.05	8/12/80	8.95
	9/18/75	5.15	2/10/81	9.95
	3/29/76	5.25	11/1/81	10.25

Irwin Manufacturing Company produced electrical equipment and was located in a large city in the Midwest. It had been formed in 1919 by Mr. A. B. Baker, father of the present president and grandfather of two of the vice presidents. The company organization is shown in Exhibit 1. The company had a reputation for being a ''good place to work.'' Employees were not unionized. Most of the company's products were mass-produced to very close tolerances. They were sold in 48 states by a sales force numbering almost 400. These salesmen worked out of 53 company-owned branches and sold on commission. Home-office employment was in the neighborhood of 1,300.

Dan Johnson had started with Irwin as a drill-press operator in 1971, shortly after arriving in Chicago from his former home and birthplace, Kentucky. Irwin was the first place to which he had applied, and he was offered the job on the spot. During his time with Irwin, he had received frequent pay increases. Exhibit 2 contains a record of Johnson's wage progress. Exhibit 4 provides a history of suggestion rewards.

In 1976, 5 years after Johnson joined Irwin, he was promoted to setup man in the newly formed spring department. This department came about as a result of a large government contract. After the contract expired, the volume of Irwin's regular products had expanded enough to make it unnecessary to transfer Johnson back to his job as drill-press operator. As a setup man, he was responsible for the setting up of the automatic equipment in his department as well as the supervision of the ten spring loopers who also worked in the department. The springs were automatically formed by machine. They were then moved to benches where spring loopers, using special pliers, formed the ends. Johnson also operated a special-purpose engine lathe designed to manufacture heavy-duty springs. This engine lathe was not in constant use. When needed, it was usually scheduled for reasonably long runs.

In reviewing Johnson's personnel folder, Warner noticed that this was the third time he had violated the same rule. Other details concerning Johnson are noted in Exhibit 3. Dan's latest violation was a serious one, according to company engineers. If it had not been detected, serious damage might have resulted.

Johnson's idea concerned the forming operation of a certain heavy-duty spring— performing it in one step rather than two, thus eliminating one complete job element. He designed a special tool bit to accomplish the the form. Before submitting his suggestion, Dan decided to try out his idea. He ran 5,000 of these heavy-duty springs. After inspecting them and seeing nothing wrong with the results, he moved them to the assembly area, where they would eventually become parts of machines which sold for $500.

EXHIBIT 3
Irwin Manufacturing Company: Comments on Back of Personnel Record Card

Date	Comment
6/15/76	Discussed importance of not initiating changes without approval. While walking by, noticed Dan grinding tool bit. Upon inquiring, learned he was trying out a new idea. Carefully explained the function of the suggestion system. *Joe Poppy*
2/9/78	Ran 11,000 defective parts. Failed to use lubricant. Said he was experimenting and couldn't understand why the lubricant was needed. *J. Poppy*
9/15/78	Offered chance to attend foremanship training. Refused. *Karl Metz*
9/16/80	Same comment of 9/15/78. *K. Metz*
10/8/80	Ran 6,000 defective springs. Failed to use specified tool bit for cutoff. His own design resulted in a burr. Warned he would not get another chance. *J. Poppy*
9/18/81	Offered chance to attend foremanship training. Refused. *B. A. Warner*

They remained unnoticed in the assembly area for almost a week, until it came time to use them in final assembly. At this point, an inspector observed the difference and placed a stop order on the parts, pending investigation. Product engineers were called in, and they immediately called for Joe Poppy, Johnson's immediate supervisor. When Poppy expressed ignorance of the situation, Johnson was called in. He readily admitted making the change and commented, ''Why, only yesterday, I mailed in the suggestion form.'' This occurred on the eighteenth of the month. Dan was told to return to his department until disposition of his case had been determined.

Company engineers explained to Warner that they could not be sure at the time if Johnson's idea was a good one. They feared that his form job set up a stress concentration that might fail under repeated loadings. They further explained that if this were so, it was fortunate that the inspector had caught the mistake. Otherwise, the springs would have been assembled into machines, which could develop trouble in the field and require expensive servicing.

On the afternoon of the eighteenth, Warner asked Bill Kay, a personnel assistant, to interview Johnson to learn more about his background. Bill Kay's comments follow:

EXHIBIT 4
Irwin Manufacturing Company:
Suggestion Record—Dan Johnson

Date	Award	Date	Award
6/15/76	$20.00	12/18/80	$30.00
8/11/77	10.00	2/12/81	50.00
9/6/77	30.00	8/2/81	30.00
3/4/78	40.00	1/14/82	20.00
7/21/79	10.00	2/16/82	20.00

Note: No record of the total number of suggestions submitted is available, as the suggestor only identifies himself if he wins an award.

■ A very likable, sincerely motivated worker.... Realizes he did wrong. When reminded that he had previously been warned about trying ideas out without approval, he expressed regrets and could offer no explanation. He said he was only sorry he didn't have more of an education, as he would like to study spring engineering and design. He also related an unhappy experience that happened to him about a month ago. As one of the engineers was walking through the department, Dan had stopped him and inquired if there were any books he could borrow to explain the theory of spring design. The engineer replied, "What would a hillbilly like you want with a book? Stick to your comic books and leave the technical publications alone." Dan said he didn't mention the incident to anyone, but he thought the women in the department had overheard the engineer's remarks. He would not give the name of the engineer. Dan said his home life was fine. He spent two evenings a week in Boy Scout activities and bowled on another night in the company league. When asked why he had refused to attend foremanship training classes, he said he hated to spend another evening away from his family. Dan ended the interview with the hope that he would be given another chance. *Bill Kay*

Late in the next day, Kay interviewed Joe Poppy. Poppy said he was in favor of firing Johnson. He explained that only this morning, his boss, Karl Metz, had "chewed him out" about Johnson. Neal Baker, vice president and sales manager, had heard about the incident and called Metz on the carpet. Mr. Baker had expressed horror at the thought that 5,000 defective machines might have gone out to customers. Poppy also said Johnson did a fairly good job as supervisor but that he could no longer tolerate his constant experimenting.

Warner was reviewing the case after lunch on the nineteenth, in preparation for a meeting with Poppy and Metz to decide Johnson's fate, when the phone rang. It was Ralph Brown, product engineer, who reported that Johnson's idea was thoroughly sound. Based on this evidence, he was recommending a $75 suggestion award.

Warner hung up the phone wondering what effect this should have on his decision. Company policy provided that even if Johnson were discharged, he would still be in line for the award.

Questions

1. Does the company want conformity, creativity, or both? What evidence is there for your conclusion?

2. If one applied the Maslow hierarchy model to Johnson, what need level is operative?

3. What action would you recommend in dealing with Johnson? Describe the type of behavior you would like to see from him in the future.

PART SIX

MAINTENANCE

The fifth function of personnel is to maintain that which has been established, that is, an effective work force with the ability and willingness to perform organizational tasks. Maintenance would naturally encompass a continuation of all operative functions discussed thus far. But special efforts must be made through communication and counseling processes to maintain employee attitudes (Chapter 21). Both complex technologies and governmental legislation have levied a special burden upon employers to maintain the employee-citizen's physical and mental health (Chapter 22).

chapter **21**

Communication and Counseling

Having procured, developed, compensated, and integrated employees for the organization, one must now face the task of maintaining the effective work force that has been assembled. Two major features of this work force must be specifically maintained: (1) attitudes and (2) physical condition. The number of factors affecting the development and maintenance of employee attitudes is limitless, but verbal and nonverbal communication processes are involved in all stages. In this chapter we will examine the nature of communication processes, channels and structures through which they flow, and means through which blockages and filters can be minimized. Specific attention will be given to the maintenance function of counseling to assist in alleviating attitudes detrimental to both the employee and the organization. The second work-force feature, physical condition, will be examined in the following chapter.

NATURE AND IMPORTANCE OF COMMUNICATION

The term "communication" has many and varied meanings. To some it denotes the means or media of passing information, as for example the telephone, telegraph, or television. To others it has to do primarily with the channels of communication in the organization, such as the grapevine, the formal chain of command, the complaint box, and the grievance procedure. The definition to be discussed in this chapter has to do with the *act* of imparting ideas and making oneself understood by others. Communication is the act of inducing others to interpret an idea in the manner intended by the speaker or writer. The term is derived from the Latin word *communis*, which means "common." If we effect a communication of ideas, we have established a common meeting ground for understanding.

Perfect communication between two people has probably never been achieved. The story is told of the old man who strolled along talking to himself, and who, when asked why he did it, gave two reasons: "I like to talk to myself, first, because I like to talk to a smart man, and second, because I like to hear a smart man talk." This is probably as close to perfect communication as one can get; the sender and the receiver are bound up in one person and one mind. Even here, some would say, the fact that the old man is talking to himself is evidence that he is confused and does not actually understand himself.

Communication is a very important subject to any manager. Managing is getting things done through others, a task which requires the manager to communicate with other people. Both traditional and behavioral managers are interested in developing good communication. The former wishes to assure that orders are understood and that the downward channels are open. Behaviorally inclined managers would add the values derived from knowing subordinate attitudes and feelings toward the job, firm, supervisor, and environment. Not only would they emphasize the importance of establishing numerous upward channels of communication, they would attempt to create an ''open'' organization in the interest of developing creativity and self-control among all organization members.

All estimates concerning the percentage of time allocated to communication processes are quite high, ranging from 75 to 90 percent of our working hours. ''Five percent of this communication time is spent in writing, 10 percent in reading, 35 percent in talking, and 50 percent in listening.''[1] We often communicate unknowingly as others observe our actions and facial expressions and derive inferences or conclusions from them. The fact that we all send and receive communication signals constantly leads us to assume that we are experts in the process. However, the lack of understanding and acceptance and the wealth of confusion and disagreement which follows are tangible evidence that the signals being sent are not received in the form intended by the sender. If no one is listening or if no one understands what is being said or written, then there is no communication.

CHANNELS AND STRUCTURE

Within an organization, many communication signals will be sent through formally designated channels. Traditional management is noted for insisting that channels be followed in order that work can be coordinated and unity of command preserved. Behaviorists, such as McGregor and Argyris, would recommend less structuring in communication. All personnel are deemed to be capable and responsible, and greater participation in management decision making should be sought.

In research conducted by Bavelas, Guetzkow, Simon, and others, it has been discovered that structuring communication flow will lead to the efficiency desired by traditional managers.[2] Experiments consisted of the establishment of various communication networks, three examples of which are shown in Figure 21-1. The first network is most similar to the formal structure of a firm (four persons able to communicate with only a central fifth person—the manager). The second network is representative of the behaviorally oriented free-flow concept (everyone can communicate with each other). In the circular network of 21-1c, each person can communicate only with his or her two neighbors, somewhat reminiscent of an assembly line.

---

[1]Aurelius A. Abbatiello and Robert T. Bidstrup, ''Listening and Understanding,'' *Personnel Journal,* vol. 48, no. 8, August 1969, p. 593.

[2]Alex Bavelas, ''Communication Patterns in Task-oriented Groups,'' *Journal of Acoustical Society of America,* vol. 22, pp. 725–730, 1950; and Harold Guetzkow and Herbert A. Simon, ''The Impact of Certain Communication Nets upon Organization and Performance in Task-oriented Groups,'' in Albert H. Rubenstein and Chadwick J. Haberstroh (eds.), *Some Theories of Organization,* The Dorsey Press, Inc., and Richard D. Irwin, Inc., Homewood Ill., 1960, pp. 259–277.

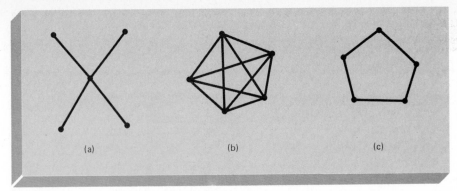

FIGURE 21-1   Communication networks.

In dealing with simple tasks, the highly structured network of Figure 21-1a was not only the most accurate but also the fastest. However, the level of task satisfaction was significantly higher in the free-flow group. Participants using the circular network were considerably slower and made more mistakes. When a complex task was provided, the free-flow network completed the tasks more rapidly than the structured one. In addition, for either type of task, participants in the free-flow network tended to be more innovative. Thus, some control of communication is essential to efficiency through division of work, coordination of effort, and preservation of unity of direction. However, the resulting regimentation is somewhat detrimental to morale and employee satisfaction and also represses a tendency toward innovation.

In an earlier chapter, a number of formal channels of communication were discussed through which subordinates could communicate *upward* to superiors. Provision for such formal channels is deemed necessary in order to discover clashes of interest, reconcile conflicts, and coordinate efforts. A more complete list of such upward channels of communication would include the following: (1) face-to-face contacts, (2) supervisory "cracker-barrel" group meetings, (3) special organization-wide elected councils that meet with top management periodically, (4) "speak up" programs where employees are given a telephone number to call, (5) anonymous complaint boxes, (6) annual employee meetings paralleling annual stockholders' meetings, (7) a grievance procedure, (8) morale questionnaires, (9) exit interviews, (10) open-door policy, (11) the labor union, (12) the grapevine, (13) ombudsmen and ombudswomen, and (14) employee counseling programs. As discussed in Box 21-1, some top managers are beginning to conduct "no-holds-barred" sessions with the rank and file.

On the other hand, management must establish *downward* channels through which information and commands can flow. Among the downward channels would be the following: (1) the chain of command, (2) posters and bulletin boards, (3) company periodicals, (4) letters to employees, (5) employee handbooks, (6) information racks, (7) a loudspeaker system, (8) pay inserts, (9) the grapevine, (10) annual reports, (11) group meetings, and (12) the labor union. Use of these downward channels is highly attractive to managers, but exclusive and excessive use can be potentially damaging to effective communication. In one study, the correlation between manager satisfaction and use of

BOX 21-1
Deep Sensing: A Pipeline to Employee Morale

Item: John J. Byrne, chairman and chief executive officer of Government Employees Insurance Co., embarrassed himself in front of 15 or so GEICO employees when he let slip a word descriptive of equine waste products in response to a question about dental insurance plans.

Item: David T. Kimball Jr., Leeds & Northrup Co.'s CEO, was meeting with a similar employee group when a low-level supervisor raised a plant safety question. Kimball asked how she thought the problem should be handled, and she snapped back, "If I knew the answer to that, I'd have your job!"

No question about it, executives who sit down with employees in no-holds-barred sessions are taking their lumps. But nonetheless, an ever-growing number of them are doing it—so much so that psychologists have given the process a formal, somber-sounding name: deep sensing, defined as the attempt by top managers to find out face to face what is on the minds of the rank and file.

"It's a powerful tool, one of the most powerful ones for top management I've ever observed," maintains Walter Heidt, director of manufacturing at Lockheed Corp., who says that 3 of the 18 division managers reporting to him are holding regular sit-down sessions with groups of 10 or 15 employees at a time. "When you have 25 people in your company, it's easy to communicate, but 2,000 people don't all have lunch together," explains Edward B. Corell, engineering vice-president at Centronics Data Computer Corp., who has been having frequent breakfasts with small groups of secretaries, technicians, and engineers. "And with fast-growing companies," he adds, "new ways are needed to convey corporate goals and objectives."

Hard questions While sensing meetings provide a golden opportunity for airing gripes, most sessions are indeed devoted to discussions of the business. At Northern Natural Gas Co., for one, President Samuel F. Segnar holds monthly luncheons with employees who have hit the five-year service mark. Tressie C. Trogdon, a capital-expenditures specialist, notes that while such things as physical office conditions came up at the meeting she attended, her main question had to do with the company's coal-exploration activities. "The employees ask hard questions, not silly things, and it confirms that most people are genuinely interested in the business," says James M. McClymond, the company's vice-president of personnel and organization.

In fact, some companies have turned to sensing as a direct alternative to gripe sessions. "We became concerned with the confrontation nature [of prior meetings] and wanted to soften that so we could talk together," explains Alan E. Reidel, senior vice-president of administration for Cooper Industries Inc. Reidel says that the company's monthly sensing meetings between labor and top plant management usually stress discussions about work loads and competition rather than gripes.

Such meetings can also "nip gripes in the bud," says Sylvester Laskin, chairman of Minnesota Power & Light Co. Laskin, who just completed a five-month round of 65 sensing meetings with MPL employees, cites one location where a new unit was being built and where employees were concerned that not enough people were being hired to staff it. "It was a communications misunderstanding, and I was able to convince them there would be no problems," Laskin says.

The setup of sensing meetings varies across the lot. Some involve meals, while others are held in conference rooms. Some companies choose attendees randomly—every sixth name on an alphabetized list of all employees, for example—while others group participants by job category, length of service, or the like. Some use consultants or managers from different divisions to run the meetings, while at others the top manager goes it alone with his people.

The method seems immaterial—the bottom line for all of them is, at the least, an across-the-board boost in morale. "I feel I'm heard now, that I'm not just a number," says a clerk at Shell Canada Ltd. Claims Marie Boulton, a Leeds & Northrup secretary: "You can write memos when you want to raise an issue, but verbal contact is always better." And James Jaskowiak, a grinder at TRW Inc.'s J. H. Williams Div., notes that "the meetings really give you the feeling the company wants to help."

Appreciated Of course, morale can plummet quickly if issues raised at sensing meetings do not result in action. But they usually do. For example, L&N began using a productivity measure called PDPE—profit dollars per employee—when Kimball discovered that such conventional productivity measures as return on sales were not fully understood by lower-echelon employees. Special meetings that Kimball held with secretaries also led to a standardized secretaries' manual and to training sessions for managers who did not appear to be using their secretarial help efficiently. TRW started a new house organ and is now posting job openings as a result of comments made at the company's "One-in-Five" meetings—a name derived from TRW's intention to include 20% of all employees.

Even seemingly minor changes are appreciated. Patricia McGillicuddy, a production control clerk at J. H. Williams, notes that the meetings led to the placement of running mats to catch snow and ice at the cafeteria entrance and also to a switch in paydays so that employees can take advantage of longer banking hours on Fridays.

Of course, some managers shy away from sensing. Lasker Meyer, the

Continued on following page

newly named president of Foley's, the big Houston department store chain, shuns the concept because, he says, "there's a danger involved in having people to a meeting like that and being faced with problems that management may not be able to do anything about."

Sensing proponents, however, say that a workable feedback system is enough to let employees know that they were not talking into a vacuum. MPL's Laskin, for one, recorded every question he could not answer and responded to it by memo later on. The questions and answers were bound into volumes for any employee to look at. Similarly, Leeds & Northrup's Kimball has a 1½-in.-thick book of all the issues and ideas that spewed forth at a series of meetings he held a few years ago. This year he called another series of meetings to review the data in the book and discuss what actions had been taken.

Elaborate response TRW probably has the most elaborate feedback system of all. The company's one-in-five meetings are run by two-person teams of managers who, though gleaned from TRW's ranks, hold sessions only in plants other than their own. While one conducts the meeting, the other records everything that is said on a large easel in front of the room. "Literally thousands of comments wind up on that easel," says Harrison Johnson, director of employee communications. "Even if the interviewers know the answer to a question, they won't give it; they simply write the question down." The theory is that the responsibility to act rests with plant management.

The interviewers give the plant managers more than enough to work with. They hold separate meetings for exempt employees, nonexempts, first-line supervisors, and hourly wage earners. After each group of meetings, they go through the long list of comments and identify basic issues that were raised, such as attitudes toward supervision or communications problems. The team then gives plant management a separate report for each of the four employee groups. The report lists the issues in priority order (based both on the number of times something was mentioned and the intensity with which it was brought

up), interprets them, and then lists all the comments related to the issue.

The interpretations are short, but to the point. One recent report, for example, described attitudes toward supervision as: "Hourly employees feel there is a lack of cooperation between foremen, which is causing serious production problems. They also feel that foremen don't really care about employees except for their favorites." The interviewers cap off their reports with a "mood, tone, and feeling" section, which describes the degree of hostility, contentment, or other emotion that seemed to prevail at the meetings.

Empty gestures? Other companies spurn the outside facilitator approach. At General Electric Co., for example, plant managers hold their own meetings because the company wants the leader to be "someone who is in a position right there to do something about the concerns and has an interest in doing it," explains Dan C. Crabtree, corporate manager of employee communications.

Most executives couch their views on sensing in terms of employee concerns. In actuality, though, results often go to the direct benefit of the company. Shell Canada, for one, has been holding meetings to "sense" employee feelings on specific issues such as career planning and cost reduction. Marjorie Blackhurst, employee communications manager, says that the 600 employees involved in the sessions turned up ideas that yielded the company more than $1 million in savings. For example, employee suggestions led to the elimination of 35 jobs (not surprisingly, none of which was held by the suggesters).

Despite such encouraging results, though, the pitfalls of sensing are legion. For one, employees will not always trust the motives behind the meetings. Jack D. Steele, dean of the University of Southern California's business school, recently conducted "FAC-YAK," a semester-long sensing program involving monthly lunches with professors. Steven Kerr, a USC organizational behavior professor who monitors some of the sessions, says: "Most of us generally approved of the dean's motives, but some saw the meetings as an attempt by the dean to manipulate them."

Even if nothing sinister is spotted, sensing participants can still see the meetings as empty gestures. "We're still at their beck and call, performing for them when they want to listen, not when we have something to say," notes a disgruntled magazine employee whose publisher has frequently tried the sensing approach. "It was like a command performance for the queen."

Path-smoothers USC's Kerr cites other problems. "There's the cost of being excluded—it's inevitable that many people down the ranks never get invited," he notes. Middle managers may feel uncomfortable when they see their subordinates going off to lunch with the big boss, he adds. And finally, he says, companies are "naive" about sensing. "It's not that easy for the lion and the lamb to sit down and eat together. It's tough to throw off years of hierarchy for an hour once a month."

The problems are solvable, though. GE, for example, publishes a master list of employees who are going to attend a session so that people who are not invited have ample time to ask the attendees to raise specific questions they want answered. TRW, which, in addition to the one-in-fives, holds special sessions between high-level managers and President Stanley C. Pace, asks each invited executive to get input from three of his peers prior to the meetings.

Breaking through the lion-lamb barrier takes more subtlety, but it, too, is doable. Many executives bring in co-hosts to start a give-and-take going. "John (Byrne) and I usually banter around for 10 minutes between ourselves to help make everyone feel comfortable," says Edward H. Utley, a GEICO senior vice-president. Kaiser Aluminum & Chemical Corp.'s CEO, Cornell C. Maier, places his co-host at his monthly luncheons at the opposite side of the table. "The people are nervous about sitting with the president, and it helps to have someone else there getting everyone involved," says Howard M. Nelson, vice-president and general manager of Kaiser's Refractories Div. and a frequent co-host for Maier.

Continued on following page

downward channels was a significant plus .33. In contrast, the relationship between satisfaction and the use of upward channels was a significant minus .22.[3] Managers must guard against the tendency to overuse downward channels by insuring availability of upward channels.

COMMUNICATION FILTERS

In large firms, some channels are long, running through several levels of organization. This emphasizes a significant problem in communication, the filtering that takes place at each level. As information is sent up to management, the sender is well aware that it can be used for two purposes: (1) to aid in coordinating and controlling the organization toward basic goals and (2) to evaluate him or her and the quality of performance. Usually, the sender does not object to the first purpose. But concerning the second, one will be influenced by selfish motives of wanting to appear well in the eyes of superiors who control the future. This introduces a filtering effect through conscious and unconscious withholding, interpreting, and altering of facts to be transmitted. The higher the management position in an organization, the more uncertainty its holder must deal with.

There have been many managerial attempts to reduce both the number and the thickness of the authority filters that clog organization communication channels. Among these are the following:

1. Decentralization and broadening spans of control will flatten the structure and reduce the number of authority filters.

2. Use of the ombudsman or ombudswoman enables bypassing of organizational levels.

3. Hired consultants can cut through the organization on various levels, thus reducing the number of authority filters.

[3]Karlene H. Roberts and Charles A. O'Reilly III, "Measuring Organizational Communication," *Journal of Applied Psychology*, vol. 59, no. 3, June 1974, p. 325.

4. Regularly constituted staff positions can bypass intervening levels of line organization to obtain information. However, if staff is used for police and surveillance, this will harm its effectiveness in its consulting and advice role.

5. The information technologist's dream of total management information system with an unlimited computer memory would provide direct access to information. Yet even here, controls are typically introduced to deny certain types of information to particular organization levels.

Perhaps the most important approach toward the filter problem is the development of leadership skills among all supervisors. If supervisors can acquire the skills of openness and receptiveness, the thickness of the authority filter can be reduced. That this is a problem in many business organizations is made evident by various surveys conducted by Opinion Research Corporation.[4] Among the various findings were: (1) over half of all employees believe that telling one's supervisor everything one felt about the company would probably get them into a "lot of trouble"; (2) almost three-quarters of all employees feel that management is not interested in employee problems; (3) most employees rate their supervisor as "good" on job knowledge and operating problems, but only one-third say that she or he is "good" on being easy to see with a problem, and one-quarter allocate the supervisor a level of "good" on handling complaints and encouraging suggestions; (4) less than one-quarter feel that management usually takes prompt action in connection with employee complaints; (5) almost three-quarters of the supervisors feel that they need more training in communication practices, particularly in how to listen.

That such training is worth the effort is suggested by a study in six offices of a large public utility.[5] In relating the perceived degree of openness between supervisor and subordinate to employee satisfaction, a clear-cut effect was discovered. The greater the openness of either supervisor or subordinate, or both, the greater the degree of employee satisfaction with the company, the job, and the supervisor. Equal degrees of openness on the part tended to result in greater satisfaction, as contrasted to situations where one or the other was more open. Another study found that those employees who pass on more information to others are rated as better performers by their supervisors.[6]

JOHARI'S WINDOW

In developing supervisory skills to effect openness and interpersonal trust, a conceptual device originated by Joseph Luft and Harry Ingham provides a basis for understanding the basic process involved.[7] As indicated in Figure 21-2, the model consists of portraying the varying degrees of information held in common between two people, as well as methods that can be utilized in increasing the size of one's "window." Cell 1 of the figure denotes the "arena" of communication, that is, information held in common and

[4]Alfred Vogel, "Why Don't Employees Speak Up?" *Personnel Administration,* vol. 30, no. 3, May-June 1967, pp. 20–22.

[5]Ronald J. Burke and Douglas S. Wilcox, "Effects of Different Patterns and Degrees of Openness in Superior-Subordinate Communication on Subordinate Job Satisfaction," *Journal of the Academy of Management,* vol. 12, no. 3, September 1969, p. 326.

[6]Charles A. O'Reilly III and Karlene H. Roberts, "Communication and Performance in Organizations," *Proceedings of the Academy of Management,* 37th Annual Meeting, Orlando, Fl., August 14–17, 1977, p. 376.

[7]Joseph Luft, *Of Human Interaction,* National Press Books, Palo Alto, Calif., 1969.

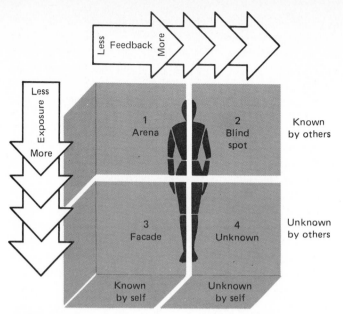

FIGURE 21-2 The Johari window: a model of interpersonal processes. (*Source: Jay Hall, "Communication Revisited,"* California Management Review, *vol. 15, no. 3, Spring 1973, p. 58. Used with permission.*)

known simultaneously by oneself and others. Cell 2, labeled the "blind spot," is information known by others but not by oneself. One of the purposes of sensitivity training is to reduce the size of the "blind spot" through providing increased honest feedback from others about one's personal style. The old phrase, "Even your best friend will not tell you," is indicative of the existence of such a class of information.

Cell 3, termed the "facade," is a class of information known to ourselves but *not* to others. It is the protective front that all people find necessary to some degree in order to defend the self. The final cell is that information which exists but is unknown to all. Hall suggests that this is indicative of a hidden potential, the unconscious, or the "data base of creativity."[8]

Communication will be enhanced if Cell 1, the "arena," is increased in size. This can be effected through two processes: (1) exposure of self to others and (2) soliciting feedback from others. Exposure requires an open, candid, and trusting approach where one "lets it all hang out." Feedback requires an active solicitation of feelings, opinions, and values from others. For these processes to be fully developed, reciprocity is required. An attempt to use one to the exclusion of the other often generates resistance from associates in the long run.

In research conducted by Hall, it was discovered that interpersonal styles of exposure/feedback correlated with types of leadership styles as depicted on the Management Grid.[9] In a study of 200 managers, classified into the 5 leadership styles of deserter

---

[8]Jay Hall, "Communication Revisited," *California Management Review,* vol. 15, no. 3, Spring 1973, p. 58.

[9]Ibid., pp. 64–66. Measurement of "arena" sizes was effected through the *Personnal Relations Survey,* authored by Jay Hall and Martha S. Williams of Teleometrics International, Conroe, Tex.

(1,1), autocrat (9,1), missionary (1,9), compromiser (5,5), and problem-solving integrator (9,9), measurements were taken of the size of their reported "arenas" in Johari's Window. The greater bulk of the 1,1 managers possessed a relatively small "arena," characterized by personal behavior of aloofness, coldness, and indifference. The 9,9 managers had the largest "arena," involving a balanced and heavy use of both exposure and feedback processes. The 5,5 manager also exhibited a balanced utilization (as did the 1,1), but the size of the "arena" was intermediate, lying between the 1,1 and 9,9. Autocratic managers, 9,1, tended to overuse exposure, resulting in the creation of a large blind spot. They did not solicit feedback from subordinates and colleagues as much as they were willing to convey their own opinions, orders, and values. The missionary style, 1,9, tended to emphasize feedback to the detriment of exposure, with the "facade" assuming greater importance.

Attempts have been made to develop a means of auditing a manager's communication style. In one study, six independent dimensions of style were identified: (1) careful transmitter, (2) open, two-way communicator, (3) frank, (4) careful listener, (5) wordy, and (6) informal.[10] When combined with assessment of the manager's credibility, it is contended that these dimensions are related to job satisfaction, role clarity, and effectiveness.

THE COMMUNICATION PROCESS

All people have "arenas" in Johari's Window, whether large or small. The process of exposure and feedback can be further analyzed by the specific skills of sending information to others, as well as by the methods of receiving feedback that facilitate accurate perception. Thus, the communication process can be portrayed as having three basic elements: (1) the sender of the signal, (2) the media by means of which the signal is sent, and (3) the receiver. The sender can be anyone who attempts to transmit some type of meaning or intent to another person. We must encode our intent or meaning into *symbols* and send the symbols to the other person. The major symbols of communication are (1) words, (2) actions, (3) pictures, and (4) numbers. As indicated in Figure 21-3, the communicative skills of sending are speaking, writing, acting, and drawing, while those of receiving are listening, reading, and observing. A person who would improve communicative skills as a manager must develop in these areas.

---

[10]Bernard M. Bass and Rudi Klauss, "Communication Styles, Credibility and Their Consequences," *The Personnel Administrator,* vol. 20, no. 6, October 1975, p. 33.

FIGURE 21-3 The communication process.

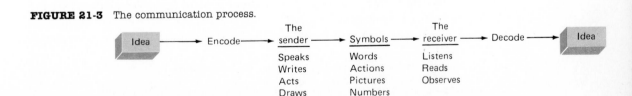

Communication Symbols: Words

As Korzybski has written, language can be compared to a map that purports to represent a certain area or territory.[11] Just as the map is *not* the territory itself, a word is *not* the object or idea it represents. We have less difficulty in effecting a transfer of meaning when the words used represent tangible objects, such as a chair, a building, or a street. But it is much more difficult to transmit the intent of the sender when words representing intangible concepts are used, such as "management," "labor," "liberal," "attitude," or, for that matter, "communication." We do not even have the advantage of using only *one* map to represent the objects and/or ideas. The speaker has her or his own frame of reference and selects words that it is hoped will convey the meaning intended. The listener has a slightly different map, even though both may be referring to a common dictionary. The term "management" may have a favorable connotation to one and a highly objectionable one to another, depending upon background, education, associates, and experience.

The English language further complicates the process of communication by assigning several meanings to one word. The term "team," for example, has several uses and connotations. In one plant, a female employee was insulted because her supervisor had asked her to "pull with the team"; she felt that she was being compared to an animal. In another instance, the plant superintendent opened his talk to a group of supervisors by stating that he wished "to discuss production problems from your level." He was referring to organizational levels, whereas the supervisors chose to interpret the remark as condescending, implying a stepping down to a lower level of status and competency.

Words constitute the most important symbols used in the communication process. They can be transmitted orally and be received by listening, or they may be given in written form and be received by reading. Thus speaking, writing, listening, and reading constitute fundamental communication skills. A manager spends almost all her or his time in using one or the other of these skills.

Though more of a manager's time is spent in oral communication, it is important also to study carefully the nature of effective writing. Sheer size of an organization plus the inevitable phenomenon of turnover compels us to communicate by means of the written word. In oral communiation we can rely upon oral response or observation of the expression on the listener's face to determine whether we have transmitted the meaning intended. In written communication we do not have that advantage and, thus, must redouble our efforts to ensure that the reader will receive, as closely as possible, our original intent.

"Bafflegab" and "gobbledegook" are terms that have been coined to describe unnecessarily complex writing in which a hundred words are used to say what could have been said in thirty. Pompous, vague, and intangible words are used whenever possible, with a heavy sprinkling of five- and six-syllable words. Several mechanical systems have been developed that enable writers to estimate the readability of their material. The Flesch system incorporates an analysis of average sentence length and number of syllables per 100 words.[12] The average sentence length is multiplied by 1.015 and the total number of syllables per 100 words is multiplied by 0.846. The sum of these two figures is then subtracted from 206.835 and the result is a score ranging from 0 to

[11]Alfred Korzybski, *Science and Sanity,* 3d ed., The International Non-Aristotelian Library Publishing Co., Lakeville, Conn., 1948, p. 58.

[12]Bergen Evans, "Our Changing Language," *Machine Design,* July 20, 1967, p. 192.

100. The 90 to 100 range is rated "very easy" and can be handled by those with a fourth-grade education. The range of 60 to 70 is "standard" and is equivalent to seventh- or eighth-grade education. Scores from 0 to 30 are rated "very difficult" and require a college degree for comprehension. That which is rated "very easy" can be read and understood by over 90 percent of our adult population. The "very difficult" can be understood by only 4 percent.

A system similar to that of Flesch is the "fog index" by Robert Gunning.[13] The index is obtained by adding the average number of words in a sentence to the number of words with three or more syllables in a hundred-word passage. Multiplying this figure by 0.4 gives a result that corresponds roughly to the number of years of formal schooling a person would require to read the passage with ease and understanding. With this index, most best-selling books test at seventh- or eighth-grade reading level, the Bible at sixth- or seventh-grade, air force regulations at the sixteenth-grade, and air force numbered letters at the eighteenth-grade level. Most adults prefer to read at least two grade levels below their ability level.

Soon after the appearance of the Flesch scale, Davis analyzed the readability of 71 employee handbooks and discovered that 92 percent of them were too difficult for their intended readers. In a follow-up study of 29 of these same company handbooks 15 years later, little or no improvement was noted.[14] As judged by the scale, 18 of the 29 handbooks were lacking in appeal for those employees who were not college graduates. Consciousness of the importance of the proper use of words should encourage us to seek improvement in the skills of speaking and writing.

Communication Symbols: Actions

The manager must recognize the fact that he or she communicates by actions as well as by words. If the actions belie the words, the former will carry the weight of meaning to the receiver. If a superior suddenly stops beside a worker, pulls out a notebook, and enters a short notation, the employee may think, "What have I done now?" Yet the supervisor may have been only scribbling a list of groceries to bring home that evening. A manager must realize that she or he is a center of attention to subordinates. All observable acts communicate something to the observer whether intended or not by the supervisor. Within the single office, the location of one's desk can communicate formality and dominance, or openness and equality. Body language also communicates; for example, crossing the arms connotes resistance, leaning forward indicates liking, frequent gesticulation suggests liking, nodding of the head shows positive feelings, a head cocked to the side suggests rejection and suspicion. When the pitch of the voice is low and soft and the talk is at a slow rate, such actions typically show liking for the other person.

When unexplained actions by management occur, a vacuum of meaning is thereby created, which is usually filled by the receiver's own interpretation of the actions. For example, the manager who removes various machines from the production floor is communicating, whether realizing it or not. If he or she does not tell the subordinates why

---

[13]Robert Gunning, "How to Improve Your Writing," *Factory Management and Maintenance,* vol. 110, no. 6, June 1952, p. 134.

[14]Keith Davis, "Readability Changes in Employee Handbooks of Identical Companies during a Fifteen-Year Period," *Personnel Psychology,* vol. 21, no. 3, Winter 1968, pp. 413–420.

the machinery is being removed, they will supply the missing signal by creating one of their own. The manager may have no intention or desire to communicate a possible shutdown to the employees, but unexplained actions, coupled with the fear of insecurity, often lead to such a communication of meaning.

Communication Symbols: Pictures

Comic pages, motion pictures, and television have demonstrated the power of pictures in conveying meaning and understanding to other people. Business has also made extensive use of pictures to communicate understanding. Blueprints, posters, charts, motion pictures, and graphs can and do convey more meaning in certain situations than could be transmitted by volumes of words. Some business managers (and textbook writers) have discovered that the people they hope to reach do not like to read long, uninterrupted passages of writing. Important, comprehensive, and accurate reports have been given little attention because of the complexities of reading. The writer did not communicate, not because the signal was not clear and accurate, but because the reader did not avail herself or himself of the signal. The same report, organized in conformance with the exception principle and supplemented by summarizing graphs, charts, and pictures, conveys more meaning in less time.

A chart or graph has the advantage of depicting many relationships of a complex type in one picture. Contrasts can be seen and grasped more clearly. Trends can be more easily recognized. Among the various types of charts and graphs that are used in business are the curve, bar, column, circle, pie, pictorial, map, organization, ranking, and frequency distribution. Pictorial illustration is especially effective in communicating with groups of people.

Communication Symbols: Numbers

It is generally true that people are greatly impressed with data that consist largely of figures and statistics. Words may flow around them and pictures appear interesting, but when a few figures are tossed into a presentation, acceptance and belief tend to rise. There is a pronounced tendency to accept figures as facts. There is a worship of the number.

Darrell Huff has made a contribution in his book, *How to Lie with Statistics,* in demonstrating how people can be purposefully misled by adroitly selected numbers.[15] Unscrupulous persons can profit through the communicative power of the number symbol and transmit meaning in a manner that engenders acceptance. For example, biased samples of a population are easily devised through skillful selecting or influencing of the sample. The arithmetic mean can be used to portray a central tendency when it suits the communicator's purpose in a particular situation. One may shift to the median to make an entirely different point in another problem. If a chart is not impressive enough, the bottom can be cut off and the spacing intervals widened, thus creating in Huff's terms a "Gee Whiz" chart similar to that depicted in Figure 21-4. Correlations between two sets of data can be used to confuse cause and effect without mentioning the possibility

[15]Darrell Huff, *How to Lie with Statistics,* W. W. Norton & Company, Inc., New York, 1954.

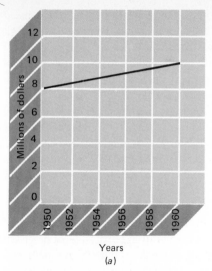

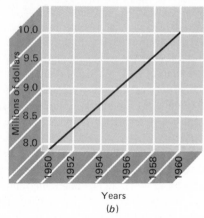

FIGURE 21-4 The creation of a "Gee Whiz" chart for purposes of emphasizing a point. (*Source: Adapted from Darrell Huff,* How to Lie with Statistics, *W. W. Norton & Company, Inc., New York, 1954, chap. 5.*)

that a third factor may be influencing both sets. Undue emphasis can be given to small differences between two figures. For example, one applicant's test score was 84, another's, 83. If the communicator wishes to hire the first person, one makes much of the one-point difference, a difference which is probably insignificant in view of the current quality of testing.

Skillful use of numbers and statistics can be applied to lead or mislead. We are not suggesting that the manager should not use these particular communication symbols in dealings with others. On the contrary, he or she will find them to be one of the most valuable means of communicating. However, it is important to understand how much statistics can be misused, so that one is not fooled by another's attempted communication. It is also important for the communicator to use data properly and admit the deficiency of statistics when necessary. Numbers and statistics are very powerful tools of communication. It is to be hoped that the increasing sophistication of readers and listeners in this area will make it more difficult to "lie with statistics" in the future.

Listening

Sending is only a part of the process of communication. Some attention must be directed to the problem of receiving. Receiving communication signals is effected primarily through listening, inasmuch as most communication is of the oral type. Several firms, however, have undertaken to improve the reading skills of their managers in order to speed up and make more effective the process of communication.

One of the major obstacles to effective oral communication is the discrepancy between the speeds of speaking and of listening. It takes far less time to listen and think than it does to speak. We usually speak to others at a rate of from 120 to 160 words per minute. We can listen and think four times faster than that. It would appear that this speed should make listening all the easier. On the contrary, it presents an obstacle, in that it leads the listener to poor or marginal listening to the speaker, while thinking ahead of what *he* or *she* is going to say in reply. Good listening is not passive; one has to work at it to do it properly. Research indicates that usual listening efficiency will result in 50 percent retention immediately after a 10-minute talk, with a decline to 25 percent retention after 48 hours. "The biggest block to personal communication is man's inability to listen intelligently, understandingly, and skillfully to another person."[16]

Various types of listening have been identified as (1) marginal, (2) evaluative, and (3) projective. Marginal listening is, as the term implies, a process of giving the speaker a small degree of one's attention. This dangerous type of listening can lead to misunderstanding of the speaker and even insult to the person. The manager who pretends to listen to a subordinate while actually worrying about some other problem is asking for trouble.

Evaluative listening is attentive rather than marginal. As we hear what is being said, however, we utilize the time created by the slowness of speech and the rapidity of listening to judge and evaluate the remarks. We approve or disapprove of what he or she says from our own point of view. We often form mental remarks of rebuttal in anticipation of our own opportunity to speak. Instead of ideas being transferred from speaker to listener, we end up with two ideas, the speaker's and listener's, neither of which is really communicated to the other. If we spend our time criticizing, approving, or disapproving the remarks of the speaker, we actually are devoting little time and effort to the task of really understanding what she or he wants to say.

Real communication takes place when the listener truly hears and understands the position and intent of the speaker. This requires a type of listening that is called "projective." While hearing the remarks of the speaker, the listener purposefully avoids any attempt to criticize, approve, or disapprove. We attempt to project ourselves into the mind of the speaker and really try to understand his or her viewpoint *without* evaluation at this time. Evaluation of the content of a speaker's remarks must come in any communication process, but it should not come until the listener has heard, studied, and understood the meaning of the remarks. Carl Rogers suggests a rule to be followed in a discussion, which will facilitate projective listening. "Each person can speak up for himself only *after* he has restated the ideas and feelings of the previous speaker accurately and to that speaker's satisfaction."[17] The quality of empathy is essential to good listening. There is no necessity to agree with the statements of the speaker, but there is every need to try to understand them and the speaker's intent and attitude.

Most training efforts have been directed toward increasing listening efficiency, thereby decreasing marginal listening. In one programmed-learning course, participants listen to a series of tape-recorded statements. The beginning statements are short and easy; later ones become progressively longer and more complex. Often the statements are technical in content, accented with anger, and delivered in a poorly organized fashion against a background of office noise. The student is asked to write a summary of the statement, which can be compared with the summary in an instruction booklet. A study of several hundred supervisors indicated that before training the average retention rate was 25 percent; after training the group average had increased to 90 percent.[18] A retest of the group 1 year later did not show a decline in this level of efficiency.

---

[16]Carl R. Rogers and F. J. Roethlisberger, "Barriers and Gateways to Communication," *Harvard Business Review*, vol. 30, no. 4, July-August 1952, p. 52.

[17]Ibid., p. 75.

[18]Abbatiello and Bidstrup, op. cit., p. 596.

One of the more sophisticated communication forms used in attempting to maintain constructive employee attitudes is counseling. It would appear that a maximum of openness and candor could be effected between counselor and counselee. However, the degree to which this can be done is greatly affected not only by the counseling method utilized, but also by the position and skills of the counselor.

The view that the typical manager is autocratic, tough-minded, and opposed to counseling of any type is an erroneous one. Managers have long been aware of emotional conflicts in the workplace and have attempted in their own way to reduce the impact of such conflicts. They generally wish to know as quickly as possible the nature of the difficulty. From a "superior" knowledge of position and background, he or she immediately "understands" the problem, formulates the "correct" answer, and proceeds to persuade the employee to perceive this answer in the same way. This general approach is usually labeled "directive counseling."

Behavioral scientists, on the other hand, recommend relying more heavily upon the employee to solve his or her own problem. This would be consistent with the human models proposed by organization psychologists. Rather than acting as an initiator and problem solver, the counselor views her or his proper role as one of sympathetic and active listening. This approach is termed "nondirective counseling," and often requires skills and environments that are beyond those possessed by line managers.

Counseling for Stress

In recent years, there has been a considerable amount of attention given to the impact of stress on the human body. When any external force threatens the body, the pituitary gland signals the alarm and sends hormones to the endocrine glands, which in turn secrete adrenalin and nonadrenalin hormones into the bloodstream. As a result, the body gets ready to adapt through neutralizing or minimizing the damage on the human as a whole. Professional counseling can aid the person in understanding the nature and impact of stress upon one's psychological and physiological well-being. Stress is any experience that creates a physiological or psychological imbalance within the individual.

In correlating levels of stress with job performance, there is no clear-cut conclusion on its effects. Life would certainly be boring if there were no demands placed on the human being. Experiments with rats show that when placed in a "rat heaven," where there is unlimited desirable living room, food, and water, after a time they become listless and stop multiplying. Stress researchers, however, contend that each person has a fixed and finite reservoir of adaptation energy to feed the endocrine system. "Getting used to" the threats so that they are no longer stressful is still costly, and the tab mounts up. The sources of stress are seemingly limitless; a few are itemized in Figure 21-5. In one adaptation rating scale, the following "costs" were proposed: 100 units for the death of one's spouse; 73 for a divorce, 63 for a jail term; 50 for marriage; 47 for losing one's job; 45 for retirement; 36 for a change in line of work; 28 for an outstanding personal achievement; 20 for trouble with the boss; 20 for changes in working hours and conditions; and 11 for minor violations of the law.[19] It is also suggested that if in a single year one accumulates 200 or more units, there is a 50–50 chance of experiencing a serious breakdown in health.[20]

[19]L. O. Ruch and T. H. Holmes, "Scaling of Life Change: Comparison of Direct and Indirect Methods," *Journal of Psychosomatic Research*, June 1971, p. 224.
[20]Dennis W. Organ, "The Meanings of Stress," *Business Horizons*, vol. 22, no. 3, June 1979, p. 38.

FIGURE 21-5
Sources of Stress

On-the-Job	Off-the-Job
Role ambiguity	Unemployment
Role conflict	Marital problems
Role overload	Children problems
Time pressures	Physical difficulties
Coercive supervision	Financial concerns
Inadequate performance feedback	Change in residence
Changes of any type	Political uncertainties
Career-goal discrepancy	Economic uncertainties
Interpersonal/group difficulties	
Spatial crowding	
Job hazards	
Responsbility for people/things	

Directive Counseling

After a preliminary statement of the nature of the difficulty by either the directive counselor or the employee, the former controls the discussion. He or she may seemingly permit the latter to volunteer solutions by directing a series of leading questions to the employee. For example, the employee's difficulty may be one of chronic tardiness. The directive counselor, after condemning the behavior, may ask why the employee has this difficulty. This will often result in a noncommittal response. The counselor then fires a rapid series of leading questions: Did you oversleep? Were you ill? Did you have car trouble? Is it the children? Are you overworking? and so on. Not only does the process usually *not* lead to discovery of the source of the trouble, it suggests to the employee possible excuses the manager-counselor might find acceptable.

The major tools of correction used by the directive counselor, upon discovering the nature of the difficulty, are advice, warning, exhortation, praise, and reassurance. All these actions emphasize the superior position of the counselor and the dependent one of the employee. The manager assumes full understanding of the fundamental nature of the difficulty and determines and attempts to implement changes in attitudes or actions that will resolve the conflict. At times, the directive counselor will make use of praise and reassurance in order to encourage the employee to overcome problems, or to realize that no problem really exists.

Nondirective Counseling

The philosophical framework of nondirective counseling is consistent with the behavioral approach to management theory. It rests upon a fundamental respect for the individual—a belief in the person's ability to solve personal problems with the aid of a sympathetic listener—and emphasizes the role of the counselor as one of understanding rather than one of passing judgment. The goal is to facilitate development of self-insight.

In the nondirective counseling discussion, the roles of counselor and employee are more nearly equal; there is no attempt to create a superior-subordinate relationship. The nondirective counseling session can be divided into three parts: (1) the release of tension; (2) the development of insight; and (3) the formation of new plans and choices.

The nondirective counselor assumes that the employee is in the best position to know and understand the problem. This requires a permissive, friendly atmosphere, with actions and statements that exhibit continuing interest but *not* judgment. Silence is also an invitation for the employee to speak further. At times the counselor may make a summary statement, being ever careful that it is truly reflective and not altered in any essential manner. Probing questions are more directive but are often helpful in obtaining a fuller statement—such questions as, "Could you tell me more about . . . ?" or "I'm a stranger to this situation; could you fill me in on . . . ?" The counselor should learn to listen for feelings as well as for words. The hope is that, as the employee verbalizes the problem, the situation will clarify itself and both will have a truer awareness of what lies behind the difficulty.

A difficult task for the counselor, particularly if a manager, is the handling of *negative* feelings. The employee may attack the organization, other employees, or the counselor. The natural tendency is to refute these accusations and demonstrate logically, or with the use of authority, that the employee is in error. If this should occur, the counselor has become directive. Though it is difficult for many managers to accept, having to listen to negative expressions is *not* evidence of refused managerial authority. If he or she but continues to listen, it is almost certain that these hostile expressions will diminish and the discussion will turn to more fruitful areas.

As a result of the new insight gained by the employee, he or she can develop new plans, actions, or attitudes. At this point the counselor may be of assistance by making sure that the employee has considered as many alternatives as possible. One may ask, "What would happen if you did what you suggest?" or "Have you considered such and such?" The expression of these probes must not, of course, reveal a bias toward any of the alternatives. There are occasions, however, when the counselor becomes convinced that resolution of the problem will require action by the *organization* rather than re-orientation by the individual. In this event, it is helpful if the counselor has the authority to inaugurate such organizational changes. There is still a third possibility, that of arriving at no acceptable solution. In this event, the use of nondirective counseling might be condemned as worthless. But at least it can be said that listening does little actual harm and has the possibilities of doing considerable good.

Organization for Counseling

In selecting the appropriate person to execute the counseling function, the two most apparent choices are either the immediate supervisor or a staff personnel counselor. In addition, there is a certain amount of counseling done by friends and acquaintances, as well by outside professional personnel such as psychiatrists, psychologists, and representatives of religious organizations.

We have noted that nondirective counseling has many advantages over directive counseling. To achieve the necessary permissive, confidential, and nonjudgmental atmosphere, many have concluded that specialized staff personnel constitute the best organizational arrangement. A staff psychologist can set up a zone of neutrality, while the immediate supervisor must work within the framework of formal authority. On the other hand, the staff personnel counselor has little or no authority to institute organizational changes, a fact which is also apparent to the employee. In effect, then, communications are going up one channel—employee to personnel counselor—and possible action is taking place down another—supervisor to employee. For these reasons, the immediate supervisor is viewed by some as the most effective counselor.

When supervisors accept a counseling obligation, the temptation is to assume a directive role, for it is difficult to be directive on the plant floor and nondirective in the office. The supervisor protests that nondirective counseling is fine in theory but impractical in operation inasmuch as he or she is lacking in both skill and time. With the authority allocated to the position, one could never hope to create a truly free and permissive atmosphere.

Keith Davis has proposed as one answer to this dilemma a third type of counseling, which he has termed ''cooperative counseling,'' lying somewhere between directive and nondirective counseling.[21] Cooperative counseling begins with exclusive emphasis upon the nondirective approach. The employee is encouraged to voice difficulties, and the supervisor accepts as a first role that of listening actively, interestedly, and intelligently.

After the supervisor is certain that she or he has heard as much as the counselee will provide, a more directive role in counseling is assumed. One may reassure the employee that the problem is not really insoluble, or one may provide more information about the broader situation. If some action is necessary, he or she will take this as the employee's supervisor rather than as counselor. The supervisor must demonstrate a willingness to listen and a desire to come to some conclusion that helps the employee as is consistent with the needs of the organization. If the problem is a sensitive one, whose causes are outside the organization, such as trouble with family, the supervisor's role should be one of sympathetic listening *only*. Providing advice in this area is to be avoided. If the problem seems to require a major reorientation of values, the supervisor should recognize his or her lack of ability as a nondirective counselor and refer the employee to skilled help either within or without the organization.

Thus, the type of counseling that is appropriate to the immediate supervisor should be neither completely directive nor completely nondirective in nature. *It is employee-centered in the beginning and supervisor-organization-centered in the end*. It may not be as effective as the purely nondirective approach, but it will do less harm than the purely directive approach. At least the supervisor will have more information than he or she had before and will acquire a greater understanding of the needs of subordinates.

SUMMARY

The subject of communication is one of the broadest in the field of personnel management. It encompasses a consideration of the subjects to be communicated, media, channels, communicators, and the symbols of communication. In this chapter we have been primarily concerned with the *communication process,* that is, the transfer of meaning and understanding from one human being to another. This process breaks down fundamentally into three elements: the sender of the signal, the means by which the signal is sent, and the receiver.

No true communication is established unless the receiver actually understands the original meaning and intent of the speaker or writer. If you have been confused by this chapter, the author has written rather than communicated.

[21]Keith Davis, *Human Relations at Work,* 5th ed., McGraw-Hill Book Company, New York, 1977, p. 427.

Since meaning and understanding cannot be physically transferred from one mind to another, we must rely upon symbols, which are substitutes for the actual idea, concept, or thing about which we propose to communicate. They constitute a map of the meaning we wish to convey. When the symbols are received, they constitute a second map for the receiver. Thus we not only must deal in symbols, but must realize that the same symbols often have slightly different meanings for sender and receiver.

The symbols of communication are four in number, namely, (1) words, (2) actions, (3) pictures, and (4) numbers. An understanding of both phonetics and semantics is essential for the modern manager. The receiver of these symbols is charged with the responsibility of listening or reading attentively. There are various types of listening, such as (1) marginal, (2) evaluative, and (3) projection. The chances of real communication between two persons are greatly enhanced when both realize the empathic values of projective listening. They are also increased when both parties are willing to utilize the processes of exposure and feedback in creating a larger "arena" in Johari's Window, thereby effecting greater degrees of openness, candor, and trust.

Counseling is one of the more effective approaches toward reducing conflict and integrating interests. Directive counseling, widely practiced by most managers, rests on the philosophy that the manager can best understand both the situation and the individual problems arising therefrom. Nondirective counseling rests on the belief that the individual can best understand his or her own emotional problems and work out an effective solution to them. This is done with the aid of a nondirective counselor whose major contribution is that of active and empathic listening. If the supervisor is to attain any of the values of the nondirective approach, she or he should attempt to use it in the early portions of the counseling interview. Given the limited possession of highly sophisticated counseling skills, as well as the contamination of the atmosphere by one's formal authority, the supervisor can only hope to improve a basically directive approach with greater initial attempts to listen, to display openness, and to encourage feedback.

BRIEF CASE

Joe Roscoe, a product manager, needed the signature of a plant manager, Bill Macy, on a new product that the latter did not like. Having had several arguments with Macy over the merits of the product, Roscoe felt that he didn't have the time to force a signature through the formal structure. So Roscoe undertook the following actions: (1) he had another person who Macy respected send him a memo favorable to the product; (2) he got a customer to casually praise the new product in conjunction with a phone call on another subject; (3) he arranged for two engineers to conduct a conversation in Macy's hearing about favorable test results on the new product; and (4) he arranged a meeting to discuss the product where those invited were both favorable toward the product and were respected by Macy.

Questions

1. Do you think that Macy signed off on the new product? Why or why not?

2. Do you think that Roscoe's actions were manipulative? ethical? legitimate?

DISCUSSION QUESTIONS

1. Can all personnel problems be solved by effective communication? Why or why not?

2. What communication skills will increase the size of one's arena in Johari's Window?

3. Which cells in Johari's Window are usually associated with which leadership styles on the Management Grid?

4. What organizational approaches have been used to reduce the number of authority filters that reduce communication effectiveness?

5. If one cannot eliminate a particular authority filter, how can its thickness or density be reduced?

6. Outline the fundamental process of person *A* communicating with person *B*. When the process is effective, what state exists?

7. What are the Flesch and "fog" indexes, and how can a manager make use of them in improving communication processes?

8. What are the respective roles of counselor and counselee in both directive and nondirective counseling?

9. Contrast the roles of supervisor and professional staff counselor in executing the counseling function.

10. Why is projective listening recommended for improved communication? What are the other alternatives in listening style?

SUPPLEMENTARY READING

BENSON, HERBERT and ROBERT L. ALLEN: "How Much Stress is Too Much?" *Harvard Business Review,* vol. 58, no. 5, September-October 1980, pp. 86–92.

DiGAETANI, JOHN L.: "The Business of Listening," *Business Horizons,* vol. 23, no. 5, October 1980, pp. 40–46.

GLICKEN, MORLEY D. and KATHERINE JANKA: "Executives under Fire: The Burnout Syndrome," *California Management Review,* vol. 24, no. 3, Spring 1982, pp. 67–72.

KIKOSKI, JOHN F.: "Communication: Understanding It, Improving It," *Personnel Journal,* vol. 59, no. 2, February 1980, pp. 126–131.

SAMARAS, JOHN T.: "Two-Way Communication Practices for Managers," *Personnel Journal,* vol. 59, no. 8, August 1980, pp. 645–648.

SCHULER, R. S.: "Definition and Conceptualization of Stress in Organizations," *Organizational Behavior and Human Performance,* vol. 25, April 1980, pp. 184–215.

chapter 22

Safety and Health

Having developed an effective work force, it is necessary that this work force be available and ready for work on a continuing basis. Though the bulk of this chapter will concentrate upon maintaining the physical and mental well-being of the employee, attention will also be given to the continuing problem of assuring reasonable daily attendance, that is, the reduction of excessive absenteeism.

In this chapter, we will review the legislative setting for health and safety. What the Civil Rights Act is to fair employment practices, the Occupational Safety and Health Act is to employee health and safety. We will also discuss the content of programs that will contribute to reducing the incidence of industrially caused accidents and diseases. If we are to use this nation's citizens as organizational employees, we have a definite obligation to maintain and preserve their physical condition.

BACKGROUND OF SAFETY AND HEALTH PROGRAMS

The modern safety movement is believed to have started around 1912 with the First Cooperative Safety Congress and the organization of the National Safety Council. Just prior to this time, in 1906, the Massachusetts Board of Health had started the industrial health movement by appointing health officers to inspect factories, workshops, schools, and tenements. The early movement was interested primarily in acquainting the general public with the fact that there existed in business a high incidence of industrially caused accidents and diseases. In 1980, the National Safety Council reported that the number of work injuries totaled 2,200,000, down 100,000 from the 1979 figure.[1] The industrial death toll was placed at 13,000, a decrease of 300 from 1979. As indicated in Figure 22-1, the number of deaths per 100,000 workers has steadily decreased. The National Institute for Occupational Health and Safety has estimated the impact of various industrial and chemical work hazards, examples of which are indicated in Figure 22-2. For asbestos

---

[1]National Safety Council, *Accident Facts*, 1981, p. 23.

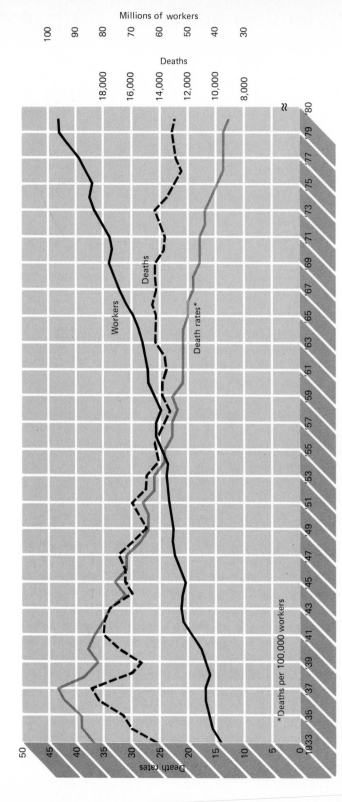

FIGURE 22-1 Trend of workers, deaths, and death rates (per 100,000). (*Source: National Safety Council, Accident Facts, 1981, p. 23.*)

FIGURE 22-2
Industrial Hazards Identified by the National Institute
for Occupational Safety and Health

517
Safety and Health

Hazard	Estimated Number Workers Exposed	Human Impact
Acrylonitrite	125,000	Lung and colon cancer, tumors
Asbestos	8 to 11 million since 1940s	Lung cancer, asbestosis, mesothelioma, gastrointestinal cancer
Asphalt fumes	500,000	Tonsilitis, bronchitis, emphysema
Benzene	2 million	Leukemia
Chloroprene	2,500	Adverse effects on central nervous system, liver, kidneys
Coal tar products	145,000	Lung and skin cancer, liver and kidney damage
Cresol	11,000	Necrosis of the liver and kidneys
Dibromochloropropane (DBCP)	2,900	Sterility and cancer
Ethylene dibromide	650,000	Cancer, mutations in reproduction
Inorganic arsenic	660,000	Lung and lymphatic cancer
Kerosene	100,000	Acute nervous system depression
Trichloroethylene	100,000	Cancer

Assembled from *Occupational Safety and Health Review*, Quarterly Report to Members of American Society for Personnel Administration, 1977 and 1978.

alone, over 10 million employees have been exposed to this hazard which can cause cancer or asbestosis 15 to 35 years later. We are just lately becoming more fully aware of the potential impact of modern technology upon the health of our work force. A 1977 survey indicated that 20 to 25 percent of all workers are exposed to serious safety or health hazards, and some 16 percent had experienced an injury or industrial illness in the past 3 years.[2]

There were various reasons for the increased attention being devoted to health and safety. Workers' compensation laws, to be discussed later, levied a financial burden on the employer by requiring that the work force be insured against injuries and diseases. More sophisticated managements discovered that safety programs were cost effective. The hidden costs of accidents are typically four times the direct and obvious costs. And federal legislation and accompanying court decisions have added a "police and punish" approach in the form of surprise inspections and fines. The personnel manager is vitally concerned since people-caused accidents typically outnumber those technically caused 4 to 1.

OCCUPATIONAL SAFETY
AND HEALTH ACT

Because of the increasing complexity and hazardous nature of modern industrial operations, in 1970 the Occupational Safety and Health Act was passed. Basically, the approach in OSHA is one of the setting comprehensive and specific standards, govern-

[2]R. Quinn and G. Staines, *Quality of Employment Survey*, Survey Research Center, University of Michigan, Ann Arbor, Mich., 1977.

mental policing of company practices and workplaces, and enforcement through citations, fines, and other penalties.

The act applies to firms engaged in interstate commerce having one or more employees; approximately 74 million employees are covered. The enforcement agency is the Occupational Safety and Health Administration in the Department of Labor. The research agency with respect to industrial hazards is the National Institute for Occupational Safety and Health located in the Department of Health and Human Services. States that submit qualified programs can take over administration of them, receiving a federal grant equal to 50 percent of their costs; slightly over half have done so.

Safety Procedures

Thus far, the greater bulk of time and money under OSHA has been spent in the area of safety. For example, during one 12-month period, OSHA conducted more than 100,000 safety inspections and fewer than 7,000 health inspections. Though it has established more than 5,000 safety standards, it has issued fewer than 20 new regulations dealing with dangerous chemicals.

There are four fundamental types of inspections that OSHA personnel will make: (1) general "surprise" inspections, constituting 71 percent of the 1975 construction industry total; (2) follow-up inspections to check on corrections, 19 percent; (3) inspections in response to specific employee complaints, 8 percent; and (4) inspections of major accidents that have occurred, 2 percent.[3] In the typical general inspection, inspectors are not allowed to give advance notice of arrival on company premises. In a recent Supreme Court decision, the court ruled 5 to 3 that OSHA inspectors must produce a search warrant if an employer refuses to consent to a workplace inspection. This ruling was softened by not requiring "probable cause to believe that conditions in violation of OSHA exist," but rather demonstration that the inspection was a part of a general administrative plan. The ruling would not preclude an inspector from trying to obtain a search warrant without the employer's knowledge prior to arriving at the workplace. In 1979, OSHA was told to get a warrant in only 2.5 percent of 35,000 inspections, a figure that nevertheless caused procedural difficulties in 850 instances.[4]

The inspector is authorized to select a worker to accompany him or her on the "walk-around" inspection. Employer discrimination against this employee is prohibited, though OSHA no longer has a rule that he or she must be paid for the time expended. It was concluded that the vast majority were voluntarily compensated by the employer, particularly in unionized establishments. In nonunion workplaces, the inspection is often conducted without an accompanying employee. If a violation is discovered, a citation can be issued on the spot. If the employer disagrees, the citation may be appealed to a review commission and ultimately to the U.S. Circuit Court of Appeals. Three types of violations are possible: (1) "nonserious" ones, which have a direct effect on health or safety but will not generally result in death or serious physical harm; (2) "serious violations," which are likely to result in death or serious harm; and (3) "willful violations," where the employer deliberately and knowingly violates the law and makes no reasonable

---

[3]Chao Ling Wang and Harvey J. Hilaski, "The Safety and Health Record in the Construction Industry," *Monthly Labor Review,* vol. 101, no. 3, March 1978, p. 8.

[4]Urban C. Lehner, "OSHA Resisters May Suffer from Bad Advice," *The Wall Street Journal,* Oct. 18, 1979, p. 22.

effort to eliminate hazardous conditions. The penalties can range from zero to $1,000 for nonserious violations, $1,000 for each serious violation (inspectors can reduce this up to 50 percent), and up to $10,000 for willful violations. In review of one 30-month period, the average fine for nonserious violations was $14.99, for serious violations $618.66, and for willful violations $866.44. Inasmuch as 98.5 percent of all violations are nonserious and most companies have a less than 10 percent chance of being inspected in any given year, "a decision-theory approach based on historic inspection and citation data yields an expected fine of $1.82."[5] Many labor union leaders are quite critical of these small amounts.

Federal court interpretations have held that the employer is fully responsible for employee violations of OSHA standards. Though in one case the employer had educated, threatened, and cajoled employees to wear protective hard hats, their refusal to do so led to fines being levied upon the employer. Several lower-court decisions had denied the right to an employee to refuse what she or he considers to be a hazardous work task. However, the 1981 *Whirlpool Corporation v. Marshall* Supreme Court decision upheld an OSHA regulation that forbids employers from taking reprisals against workers who, lacking any reasonable alternative, refuse in good faith to carry out dangerous work assignments. Two workers had refused to step out on a wire-mesh screen 20 feet above the factory floor to retrieve fallen objects. Earlier task assignments had resulted in two men's falling through the screen, one to his death. The court held that the law did not convey any general right to walk off the job because of unsafe conditions. Rather, workers must use the procedures of OSHA, including requesting an OSHA inspection. Workers must (1) feel that there is a real danger of death or serious injury, (2) request the employer to eliminate the hazard, (3) conclude that there is no time to eliminate the hazard, and (4) run the risk that a review of the decision to refuse will be ruled as having been made in bad faith.

A recent OSHA rule gives to employees, or their designated representative, the right to examine their on-the-job medical records. These records follow the employee from job to job and must be kept for the duration of employment plus 30 years. Those exposed to toxic substances or harmful physical agents must be so informed at least once a year. Records must also be given to OSHA when requested in order that various analyses can be made. Release of this information to the employee can be refused only if a medical doctor feels that such information would be detrimental to the employee's mental health.

Many employers have accused OSHA of needless and nitpicking harassment. Standards governing physical conditions and work practices are published in a voluminous *Federal Register*. Many were taken from existing private organizations, such as the National Fire Protection Association, and immediately given the force of law. Recently, the director of OSHA abolished more than 1,000 small and inconsequential standards in a single directive; for example, round toilet seats had been deemed hazardous. And a U.S. Court of Appeals has ruled that OSHA must weigh economic impact before requiring a company to install costly engineering controls to meet its noise standard. The company argued that it had met the 90-decibel noise standard by requiring workers to wear earplugs. The court returned the case to the OSHA Review Commission to determine if health benefits for employees equipped with earplugs are worth the $30,000 cost.[6]

In response to numerous criticisms of the agency, OSHA under the Reagan admin-

[5]Darold T. Barnum and John M. Gleason, "A Penalty System to Discourage OSHA Violations," *Monthly Labor Review,* vol. 99, no. 4, April 1976, p. 30.
[6]"A Court Orders OSHA to Consider Economics," *Business Week,* October 1977, p. 45.

istration has announced a number of changes in its inspection procedures. Among these are the following:

1. Reduce safety reporting requirements for one-half million establishments, over 90 percent of which have fewer than 2 injuries each year.

2. Reduce inspections for firms having fewer than 10 employees or an injury rate less than the national average for manufacturing.

3. Perform no inspection when a complete inspection turned up no serious violation in the previous year.

4. Provide for on-site consultation to improve safety and health practices.

5. Exempt firms from most inspections if labor-management committees are established to advise and monitor the firm's safety practices. For the first few years, OSHA will assign a resource liaison to answer questions, attend meetings, and take part in walk-around consultative inspections.

Health

Though accidents are extremely costly in both economic and human terms, perhaps the greatest potential danger lies in the many health hazards that often are hidden in our complex technological environment. It is estimated that there are approximately 2 million chemical compounds in existence, but scientists have developed information of the toxicity of only about 100,000.[7] Of these, some 13,000 are known to be toxic and 1,500 are suspected of causing cancer. Figure 22-2 lists only a fraction of these hazards, which have endangered millions of workers. It is the task of the National Institute for Occupational Safety and Health (NIOSH) to recommend minimum standards of exposure to OSHA for its approval and enforcement. For example, OSHA recently lowered the permissible amounts of benzene from 10 parts to 1 part per million parts of air for an 8-hour average. The maximum permissible amount during any 15-minute period can be only 5 parts per million.

There is much controversy with respect to the trade-off between economics and health. The cleaning of the environment is quite costly and employers contend that the perfectly safe environment is not possible. Rather than the piecemeal investigation of each hazard with numerical specification of permissible allowances, OSHA has proposed a policy of "lowest feasible" exposure on any chemical shown to be a carcinogen by a confirmed study on either humans or two mammalian species of test animals. The need for some type of effective cancer policy was underscored in an epidemiological study showing that in 39 United States counties having a heavy concentration of petroleum refineries, there were "significantly higher rates for cancer of the lung, the nasal cavity and sinuses and the skin."[8]

A number of Supreme Court decisions in recent years have dealt with the issue of costs versus safety. The general conclusion has been that the law as written places benefits to worker health above all other considerations save those of technological feasibility, or endangering an entire industry's financial viability. In the benzene case, *Industrial*

---

[7]"Stressing Health over Safety—A Switch in On-the-Job Rules," *U.S. News and World Report,* July 11, 1977, p. 66.

[8]"Using Cancer's Rates to Track Its Cause," *Business Week,* Nov. 14, 1977, p. 69.

Union Department AFL–CIO v. American Petroleum Institute, the Court ruled that OSHA must prove that a significant risk is present at the original level of benzene (10 parts to 1 part of air). Since OSHA had not linked its new proposed standard (1 part per million) to specific estimates of lives saved, the change in standard was denied. However, in a later, cotton-dust case, the Court ruled that the law does not require a cost/benefit analysis, and OSHA's proof that health was threatened and protection was technologically feasible without endangering the industry's financial foundation, justified the changed standard for cotton dust. Thus the Court has endorsed the concept of some type of risk analysis, without requiring the cost/benefit approach preferred by the Reagan administration.

There are also dilemmas posed in adhering to both the Civil Rights Act and OSHA. Tolerance to lead is lower in children than in adults, and it is lower still in the fetus. Research shows that a 30-milligram level of lead in the blood of expectant mothers can cause miscarriages or birth defects. As a result, some companies deny job opportunities to females in environments where there is exposure to lead; many such jobs are higher-paying ones. If the Equal Employment Opportunity Commission orders these jobs open to females on an equal basis, the company can be assailed by OSHA. OSHA contends that there is no dilemma—that male employees in lead environments show excessive amounts of lead in their sperm, which can also cause reproductive problems. The problem is one of establishing the proper exposure limits for all.

Despite the confusion and controversies, it is certain that occupational health is the one area in which OSHA can be most productive. Though the Society of Toxicology has only 800 members, the demand from both government and industry has driven annual salaries for toxicologists to over $75,000.[9]

WORKERS' COMPENSATION LAWS

Prior to OSHA, the major legal influences on health and safety were the 50 state workers' compensation laws. Under these laws, the employer is financially liable for all accidents arising out of, and in the course of, employment, regardless of whether the employee was specifically at fault. In most states, certain groups are exempt from coverage, particularly farmers, domestics, casual labor, athletes, and employers with fewer than 5 employees. The employer insures against accident liability with either a private or a state insurance agency. Approximately 80 percent of all firms are insured with private insurance companies. Large employers may have the option of insuring themselves. Many states provide for some incentive to reduce accidents through schedule and experience rating. *Schedule rating* is a means of obtaining reduced premiums through the establishment and maintenance of a safe physical plant. *Experience rating* is a means of obtaining reduced premises through having a low accident record.

The benefits to injured employees are of two types, substitute compensation for regular pay and medical benefits. Most laws specify that only one-half to two-thirds of the average wage will be paid as a substitute for regular compensation. However, many

---

[9]Douglas Martin, "Search for Toxic Chemicals in Environment Gets a Slow Start, Is Proving Difficult and Expensive," *Wall Street Journal,* May 9, 1978, p. 40.

states have maximum limitations that result in employees' receiving less than one-half of the average wage normally received. The National Commission on State Workers' Compensation Laws recommends establishment of 100 percent of the state's average weekly wage for those on temporary disabilities and 66⅔ percent for those on permanent total disabilities. Only a few states have met these high standards. In 1981 the maximum weekly benefit ranged from $98 in Mississippi to $859 in Alaska.

Payments in the various states also vary according to the duration of the disability. There are four main types of injuries. *Temporary total* disabilities, which constitute approximately 95 percent of all injuries, occur when employees are totally off the job for a restricted number of days. Usually they are compensated for this full time, less the one-week waiting period. A *permanent total* disability occurs when the employee lives but will never work again. Many states provide compensation in this instance for life, but some restrict duration to 300 to 700 weeks. A *permanent partial* disability occurs when the employee is permanently disabled but can return to work. Examples of such injuries are loss of an eye, arm, leg, or toe, Most of the laws establish a specific schedule of benefits for each specific injury without respect to occupation. There is little consistency among the states in this regard. The loss of an arm at the shoulder is worth $43,525 in Arizona, $6,750 in Massachusetts, and $107,420 in Pennsylvania; loss of a hand is worth $36,437 in Arizona, $8,736 in Colorado, and $111,323 in Washington, D.C.; and loss of an eye is valued at $21,862 in Arizona, $6,000 in North Dakota, and $66,975 in Connecticut. The final type of injury is *death*. Permanent partial injuries constitute about 4 percent of injuries, permanent totals less than ⅒ of 1 percent, and deaths about ⁹⁄₁₀ of 1 percent.

The workers' compensation law is usually administered by a state industrial commission, which investigates and makes the injury award. An injured employee typically waives his or her right to sue after receiving workers' compensation. But in some instances the employee still sues, claiming that employment was "coincidental" with other roles. In one instance where the employer had manufactured the truck in which the employee was injured, the employee not only received workers' compensation benefits, he also sued the employer for faulty manufacture of the truck.[10]

The philosophy of these laws has thus far been to compensate personnel for loss of wages sustained as a result of an industrially caused injury. Recent cases concerning loss of hearing have altered this philosophy to some extent. Some employees have received compensation for injury to hearing even though their earning capacity was never impaired and no wages were lost. Another type of injury with which we must be concerned in the future is an injury resulting from exposure to radiation hazards. Bone tumors, skin cancers, and lung cancers may arise years after exposure and years after the worker has left the job and the company.

Finally, the largest cloud on the workers' compensation horizon is the increasing likelihood that industry will be asked to underwrite the costs of emotional breakdowns issuing from job stresses. Since these injuries are not covered by existing legislation, employees turn to state courts to ask for compensation. At least six states have ruled that emotionally ill employees are covered by workers' compensation even though no specific major event caused the illness. It appears that the trend is in the direction of making an employer responsible for any and all human ills that may arise out of employment.

[10]"On-the-Job Injuries: Now, Suits against the Boss," *Business Week,* Jan. 25, 1982, p. 114.

Effective action in any field calls for advance planning. Once management's interest in safety has been stimulated, there remains the task of mapping out a program. Any particular safety program could be composed of one or more of the following elements:

1. Support by top management
2. Appointing a safety director
3. Engineering a safe plant and operation
4. Educating all employees to act safely
5. Record keeping
6. Accident analysis
7. Safety contests
8. Enforcing rules

Support by Top Management

As in every other area, top management must lend a safety program its active support in order for it to survive and be effective. Management must give more than just lip service. Supervisors and superintendents are the first to know, however, whether top management really means what it says. Research in twenty-two firms revealed a strong relationship between top management support and reduced worker injuries.[11] Management support was characterized by personal attendance at safety meetings, periodic personal inspections, insistence on regular safety reports, and inclusion of safety figures and achievements on the agenda of the company's board of directors' meetings. A report by the National Institute of Occupational Safety and Health produced the profile of the safe workplace portrayed in Figure 22-3.

FIGURE 22-3
Profile of the Typical Low-Injury Workplace

Formal safety training courses including refresher training
Cash awards for safety performance
Stable work force with low turnover
Low absenteeism rates
Workers on first-name basis with supervisors
Management concern for worker problems
Less heat and noise, better lighting and ventilation
Safety unit has authority to approve changes in design of work facilities
Encouragement of employee identification of work hazards
Supervisors, rather than lead workers, train new employees

Source: Study of the National Institute for Occupational Safety and Health, 1980.

[11]Rollin H. Simonds, "OSHA Compliance: 'Safety Is Good Business,' " *Personnel*, vol. 50, no. 4, July-August 1973.

A Safety Director

To get any program off the ground, some one person must be given primary responsibility for its installation and maintenance. If the company is too small to justify staff differentiation of the function from the line, it is still important to assign some one person the additional duty of promoting the safety effort.

In the larger firm, a staff safety director, often entitled a "safety engineer," is usually appointed. Such a person should be as much inclined toward the personnel approach as toward engineering. In some firms the relationship between safety director and line employees is functionalized; that is, the director has the authority to issue and enforce orders in the functional field of safety. On the other hand, there is strong evidence that the greatest potential for progress in safety lies in the area of education. Consequently, many safety directors prefer *not* to have functional authority so that they will not be tempted to use it. They view their job as largely one of education and positive motivation, and are inclined toward a deemphasis of its involvement with negative enforcement. A survey of 116 firms revealed that the impact of OSHA resulted in a substantial number (one-third) creating a new safety officer position; in two instances, they were allocated vice presidential status.[12]

Engineering

Sound and forward-looking engineering must certainly be an essential requirement of any safety effort. Recognition of this fact is indicated through the schedule rating established by many state workers' compensation laws. Workplaces should be clean, well lighted, and properly ventilated. Mechanical devices for material handling should be provided. All dangerous equipment should be safeguarded insofar as possible. But, to illustrate again the inevitability of the human factor in engineering a safe plant, there is probably no engineered safeguard that some employee cannot alter or circumvent if he or she gives sufficient thought to it. On punch presses, for example, two buttons are often provided, both of which must be hit simultaneously to permit the press to descend. This supposedly ensures that the worker will not get a hand caught by the press. It is not unusual to find that the employee has taped one button down so that she or he can work the press with one hand instead of two. Safety glasses are often required in departments involving metal working, but lenses have been removed from these glasses so that the employee appears to be wearing them but does not have to look through sweaty lenses. Safety precautions usually entail some delay or extra effort, and people are often prone to shortcut the engineered device.

Education

A large part of the safety program must be devoted to the process of educating the employee to act, think, and work safely. There are many avenues that this education can take, among which are the following:

1. Induction of new employees

---

[12]Bureau of National Affairs, "Impact of OSHA on Personnel Management," *Bulletin to Management No. 1204,* American Society for Personnel Administration, Mar. 8, 1973, p. 1.

2. Emphasis of safety points during training sessions, particularly in on-the-job training

3. Special efforts made by the first-level supervisor

4. Establishment of employee safety committees

5. Holding of special employee safety meetings

6. The use of the company periodical

7. Charts, posters, and displays emphasizing the need to act safely

Any or all of the above approaches can be used effectively. If safety is a major goal in an organization, the time to begin safety education is in the hiring process. Part of the induction procedure can be devoted to the safety policies and rules of the company. Certainly all training should be accompanied by warnings concerning dangerous points of job operations. Leadership is often by example, and the first-level supervisor must make concern for safety apparent through both word and deed.

The use of safety committees is highly effective in employee education because of the emphasis upon participation and responsibility. Such committees have, of course, operational objectives, which may include accident investigation and periodic safety inspections of the various company departments. It is significant to note, however, that personnel placed on such committees usually demonstrate a marked reduction in their own accident records. In addition, the committee member can exert a salutary influence on other employees. Receiving suggestions, aid, or advice from a colleague is often more effective than receiving them from a supervisor. The holding of regular safety meetings provides the basis for a reduction in workers' compensation insurance premiums in some states. It has been observed that companies holding such periodic educational sessions usually experience a reduction in their accident rate.

Record Keeping

One of the requirements of OSHA is that the employer keep accurate records with respect to number of accidents, occupational illnesses, and lost workdays. These must be shown to inspectors on request and filed with OSHA annually. Injuries and illnesses to be reported include (1) fatalities, (2) cases involving lost workdays, and (3) cases involving no lost workdays but necessitating action beyond immediate first aid. The measurement base that permits comparison with other employers is as follows:

$$\frac{N}{H} \times 200,000$$

N stands for the number of injuries and illnesses; H for the total hours worked by all employees during the year; and 200,000 for the hours that 100 employees will work during the year, assuming a 40-hour week and 50 weeks. As shown in Figure 22-4, the national industrial average in 1980 was 7.81. Considering only those cases involving lost workdays, the average was 2.70. The average total lost workdays was 61. The National Safety Council would refer to the two rates as measuring both frequency (number) and severity (days lost).

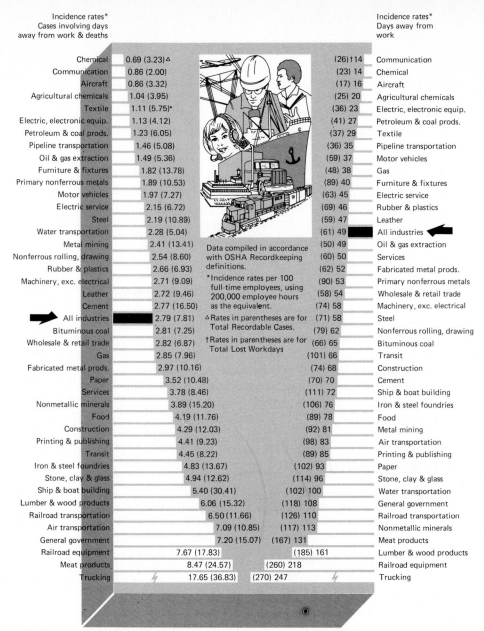

Incidence rates* — Cases involving days away from work & deaths

Chemical	0.69 (3.23)△
Communication	0.86 (2.00)
Aircraft	0.86 (3.32)
Agricultural chemicals	1.04 (3.95)
Textile	1.11 (5.75)*
Electric, electronic equip.	1.13 (4.12)
Petroleum & coal prods.	1.23 (6.05)
Pipeline transportation	1.46 (5.08)
Oil & gas extraction	1.49 (5.36)
Furniture & fixtures	1.82 (13.78)
Primary nonferrous metals	1.89 (10.53)
Motor vehicles	1.97 (7.27)
Electric service	2.15 (6.72)
Steel	2.19 (10.89)
Water transportation	2.28 (5.04)
Metal mining	2.41 (13.41)
Nonferrous rolling, drawing	2.54 (8.60)
Rubber & plastics	2.66 (6.93)
Machinery, exc. electrical	2.71 (9.09)
Leather	2.72 (9.46)
Cement	2.77 (16.50)
All industries	2.79 (7.81)
Bituminous coal	2.81 (7.25)
Wholesale & retail trade	2.82 (6.87)
Gas	2.85 (7.96)
Fabricated metal prods.	2.97 (10.16)
Paper	3.52 (10.48)
Services	3.78 (8.46)
Nonmetallic minerals	3.89 (15.20)
Food	4.19 (11.76)
Construction	4.29 (12.03)
Printing & publishing	4.41 (9.23)
Transit	4.45 (8.22)
Iron & steel foundries	4.83 (13.67)
Stone, clay & glass	4.94 (12.62)
Ship & boat building	5.40 (30.41)
Lumber & wood products	6.06 (15.32)
Railroad transportation	6.50 (11.66)
Air transportation	7.09 (10.85)
General government	7.20 (15.07)
Railroad equipment	7.67 (17.83)
Meat products	8.47 (24.57)
Trucking	17.65 (36.83)

Incidence rates* — Days away from work

(26)†14	Communication
(23) 14	Chemical
(17) 16	Aircraft
(25) 20	Agricultural chemicals
(36) 23	Electric, electronic equip.
(41) 27	Petroleum & coal prods.
(37) 29	Textile
(36) 35	Pipeline transportation
(59) 37	Motor vehicles
(48) 38	Gas
(89) 40	Furniture & fixtures
(63) 45	Electric service
(69) 46	Rubber & plastics
(59) 47	Leather
(61) 49	All industries
(50) 49	Oil & gas extraction
(60) 50	Services
(62) 52	Fabricated metal prods.
(90) 53	Primary nonferrous metals
(58) 54	Wholesale & retail trade
(74) 58	Machinery, exc. electrical
(71) 58	Steel
(79) 62	Nonferrous rolling, drawing
(66) 65	Bituminous coal
(101) 66	Transit
(74) 68	Construction
(70) 70	Cement
(111) 72	Ship & boat building
(106) 76	Iron & steel foundries
(89) 78	Food
(92) 81	Metal mining
(98) 83	Air transportation
(89) 85	Printing & publishing
(102) 93	Paper
(114) 96	Stone, clay & glass
(102) 100	Water transportation
(118) 108	General government
(126) 110	Railroad transportation
(117) 113	Nonmetallic minerals
(167) 131	Meat products
(185) 161	Lumber & wood products
(260) 218	Railroad equipment
(270) 247	Trucking

Data compiled in accordance with OSHA Recordkeeping definitions.

*Incidence rates per 100 full-time employees, using 200,000 employee hours as the equivalent.

△Rates in parentheses are for Total Recordable Cases.

†Rates in parentheses are for Total Lost Workdays

FIGURE 22-4   1980 incidence rates* of principal industries (reporters to the National Safety Council). (*Source: National Safety Council*, Accident Facts, *1981, p. 32.*)

Accident Analysis

An accident is an unplanned incident and should be analyzed in terms of both costs and causes. In one year, it was determined that work injury costs as a percent of wages amounted to 2.3 percent in the chemical industry, 3.8 percent in the paper industry, and 10.6 percent in wood products firms.[13] If insurance premiums under workers' compensation laws can be termed a direct cost, it is estimated that the indirect costs of an accident are four times as great. Among these indirect costs are the following:

1. Cost of damage to equipment, materials, and plant
2. Cost of wages paid for time lost by workers not injured
3. Costs of wages paid to injured workers over and above compensation required by law
4. Costs of supervisors and staff in investigating, recording, and reporting
5. Costs of replacing the injured employee
6. Miscellaneous costs including any overtime caused by the accident, loss of income due to missed delivery dates, and the costs of maintaining a first-aid dispensary for accidents that do not technically result in lost work time

As employers become fully educated in regard to the true costs of an accident, they become more highly concerned with accident analysis and prevention. The causes of accidents can be separated into two categories, technical and human. Technical causes are connected with deficiencies in plant, equipment, tools, materials, and the general work environment. The elimination of these causes is effected largely through engineering. Human causes are connected with deficiencies in the individual, such as improper attitudes, carelessness, recklessness, inability to perform the job, daydreaming, alcoholism, and the use of drugs on the job. It is estimated that there are four accidents caused by human deficiencies to every one that is caused by technical or mechanical defects. Thus a safety program must concentrate more on the personnel aspects than it does on the technical.

There is an increasing appreciation in industry of the importance of the human factor in accidents. Accident-prone individuals are the cause of a large proportion of the total number of accidents. Others attribute accident proneness to physiological deficiencies, such as poor reaction times and inadequate muscular coordination.

In recent years it has been observed that some people are accident-prone for a time and then seem to get over it, with a consequent radical reduction in the accident rate. It has been noted that although a few accident-prone people are responsible for a large share of the accidents in a short period of time, the membership of this group will change.[14] The solution to this problem is not one of dismissing the accident-prone individual, though the effect on the total accident rate of the company makes this action very attractive to many managers. The obvious answer of transferring to safer jobs is sometimes successful. The exclusion of an accident-prone person from the organization

---

[13]Foster C. Rinefort, "A New Look at Occupational Safety," *The Personnel Administrator*, vol. 22, no. 9, November 1977, p. 35.

[14]Wayne K. Kirchner, "The Fallacy of Accident Proneness," *Personnel*, November-December 1961, pp. 34–37.

FIGURE 22-5
Injury Experience by Duration of Employment, 1977

Employment Duration	Percentage of Injury and Illness Cases	Percentage of All Workers	Incidence Ratio
1 to 3 months	20.8	14.0	1.49
4 to 12 months	22.9	18.1	1.27
2 to 3 years	20.4	21.8	.94
4 to 5 years	11.0	12.0	.92
6 to 10 years	12.8	15.8	.81
11 or more years	12.0	18.2	.66

Source: Fred Siskind, "Another Look at the Link between Work Injuries and Job Experience," *Monthly Labor Review*, vol. 105, no. 2, February 1982, p. 38.

through an effective selection procedure is also a possibility. It must be noted, however, that no valid test of accident proneness has yet been developed.

The accident-prone individual is only one human cause of accidents. Some managements have discovered a direct relationship between accident frequency and seniority, the longer-service personnel having the fewer accidents. As indicated in Figure 22-5, though workers with less than a year's experience constitute 32 percent of the work force, they account for 43.7 percent of the number of injuries and illnesses. Those with 6 or more years of experience make up 34 percent of the workforce, but account for only 25 percent of the accidents. Other employers have discovered a relation between the type of motivation employed by management and the frequency of accidents; the tension caused by driving, negative supervisors tends to increase the likelihood of accidents. Certainly there are many accidents caused by horseplay, carelessness, exhibitionism, alcoholism, boredom, and fatigue. Thus, statistics should be accumulated over a period of time so that accidents can be classified by such factors as person, seniority, department, supervisor, equipment involved, unsafe acts, and job. Analysis of this record may show underlying causes that are not apparent in any one accident.

Safety Contests

Safety contests could be considered as one form of employee education, but they are sufficiently different in approach to merit separate discussion. There is a good deal of controversy over the merits of the safety contest. It usually happens that the accident level drops during the period of the contest, only to rise again after it has ended. This result is to be expected, since the contest prizes serve to stimulate great effort in the direction of accident prevention. It is to be hoped, however, that the habit of acting safely, gained during the contest period, will remain to some degree. Furthermore, it is to be hoped that the new accident level, though higher than during the contest, will be lower than in the precontest period.

There are various bases that can be established for a safety contest. Frequency and severity rates are indexes around which a departmental contest can be arranged. It is necessary, however, to handicap certain departments whose physical working conditions are not in line with the rest of the plant. Other bases that can be used are the number of hours worked without a lost-time accident, attendance at safety meetings, good housekeeping, safety essays, and safety suggestions. In one case, each worker who went accident-free for a week was permitted to draw a playing card from a deck and attach the corresponding decal to her or his hardhat. At the end of 5 weeks, prizes were awarded to team members with the best poker hand. During a 6-month period when "safety poker" was played, the number of injuries decreased some 37 percent.

The incentive provided by some safety contests has led to abuses. Serious accidents have *not* been reported, and as a result inadequate medical attention has been received by the injured. The accident record becomes all-important, temporarily, and actual events are misrepresented in order that they may show up favorably on the record. Any minor injuries will certainly receive scant attention during the competition period. All incentive arrangements, from the profit system to safety contests, have in them the stimulus to undesirable as well as desirable action. But if, on balance, the good that is stimulated outweighs the ills accompanying the system, then the use of incentive arrangements is justified.

Enforcement

Undoubtedly the fundamental approach to a safety program must be positive in nature; but it is naive to argue that disciplinary action has no place. Individuals differ, and for some only the negative approach will stimulate the desired behavior. Reprimands, fines, layoffs, and discharge have their proper place in an effective safety program. With the heavy responsibility levied upon employers by OSHA, many managements are becoming more hard-nosed in using discipline to enforce safety regulations.

THE HEALTH PROGRAM

The prevention of accidents is a major part of the function of employee maintenance, but constitutes only one segment of a comprehensive program. The employee's physical condition can be harmed through disease, stress, and strain as well as through accidents. It is important for the firm to be concerned with the general health, both physical and mental, of its employees for both economic and humanitarian reasons. Many state workers' compensation laws provide for compensation for specific occupational diseases. A major part of the OSHA effort is being directed toward prevention of illnesses issuing from the workplace environment. Moreover, poor employee health leads to a high level of absenteeism and a low level of productivity.

Physical Health

There is considerably more industrial activity in the field of safety than there is in the field of health. When health and medical programs are provided, it has been customary in too many firms to attach this function to the safety unit, as indicated in Figure 22-6. Too often the health portion of the program consists solely of a group of medical personnel, who administer physical examinations in the hiring process. The Occupational Health Institute would add to the placement physical examination the following requirements for a properly organized health program:

1. A stated health and medical policy

FIGURE 22-6   Organization of health and safety, 1.

2. The performance of periodic physical examinations on all employees exposed to health hazards

3. The availability of facilities for voluntary periodic physical examinations for all employees

4. A competent medical consulting staff

5. Systematic attention to sanitation, safety precautions, and industrial hygiene

6. A chief medical officer who reports to a responsible member of management

7. A well-equipped dispensary for emergency cases and physical examinations

8. Properly qualified medical and nursing personnel

It is apparent from the list of specifications laid down that only the larger firms would qualify as having properly organized health programs. DuPont, for example, at one time employed 90 full-time physicians, 150 nurses, 1 psychiatrist, and 50 industrial hygienists to service 110,000 employees.[15] A survey of 4,636 plants by the National Institute for Occupational Safety and Health indicated that only 3.1 percent of all workplaces provide industrial hygiene services.[16] This figure rises to 42 percent if confined to plants with more than 500 employees. However, approximately two-thirds of the nation's labor force is employed in smaller organizations.

In line with both an economic motivation and a social responsiblity, the larger companies are undertaking a broader ''whole person'' approach toward industrial health. Some are studying the chronic diseases, such as cancer and heart trouble, and approaching them as a total complex or system involving both industrial and nonindustrial sources. In one company, it is estimated that nonoccupational illnesses account for more than 70 percent of its absenteeism. Payments in the form of sick leave or health fringe benefits may run ten times the amount expended under workers' compensation laws. It is maintained that environmental health must stem from *inside* industry, inasmuch as outside doctors cannot possibly know what goes on inside the plant.

With respect to the field of industrial hygiene referred to previously in item 5, some firms have made an effort to elevate the hygienist to an organization position superior to that of the safety director. As indicated by Figure 22-7, he or she may be placed in a

---

[15]''Industry Doctors Try New Approach,'' *Business Week*, May 13, 1967, p. 82.
[16]American Society for Personnel Administration, *Occupational Safety and Health Review*, December 1977, p. 8.

position coordinating safety and medical services. The reasons for this move are several. First, as actually practiced, safety is often backward-looking. The safety engineer learns through mistakes—accidents or diseases. It is quite typical for a serious accident to generate a tremendous amount of activity *after* the fact. The industrial hygienist is trained to adopt the preventive approach, to spot obvious and incipient dangers, and to request the appropriate specialty to eliminate those dangers. Secondly, a well-qualified industrial hygienist must undergo 1 or 2 years of college training in such subjects as physiology, psychology, air analysis, toxicology, and the radiological aspects of industrial health. He or she thus has the background that stimulates analysis and prevention of health and accident hazards.

The industrial hygienist usually analyzes health problems in terms of stress and strains. The sources of occupational stress are four in number: chemical, physical, biological, and social. Occupational stresses result in certain strains being placed upon the human body and mind. The total strain is often greater than the sum of the individual stresses. When the stress is too great, the human body or mind breaks down. Thus, the emphasis is upon the elimination or control of the sources of occupational stress.

Measures for the prevention and control of occupational stress can be applied to the following: (1) the *source* of the stress, (2) the *media* of stress transmission, and (3) the *individual* subjected to the stress. In most health problems, research and correction should be applied in the order given. For example, the industrial hygienist has discovered a machining process that is throwing off a large volume of dustlike particles in the air. The first problem is to discover whether the process constitutes a health hazard. One must analyze the size of the particles to determine whether they are small enough to be breathed into the lungs or are large enough to cause them to be coughed out of the throat. One must analyze the rate of fallout of such particles in the various parts of the room. Assuming that a health hazard is found to exist, the first approach is to tackle the source. If the source of the stress can be eliminated, there is no need to restrict the movements and actions of the employee. It may be possible for the process to be changed or for people to be completely eliminated from the offending area.

Failing the elimination of the source of stress, the next approach is to analyze the transmitting media. Can a baffle, screen, or some other type of protection be established to keep the particles away from the person? Can the air be washed and cleaned? The final step is that of protecting the worker. If neither the source nor the media can be corrected, the human being must be safeguarded. One may be forced to breathe through an oxygen mask.

FIGURE 22-7 Organization of health and safety, 2.

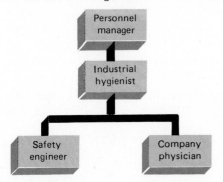

Mental Health

In recent years, an increasing amount of attention has been devoted to industrial mental health. It is difficult to determine how far a business firm should go in such matters as this. As indicated previously, various state court decisions are assigning liability to employers for emotional stresses engendered by employment.

The rationale for a company mental health program is the same as for programs designed to maintain physical health. In the first place, American business is responsible for creating many of the tensions and pressures of modern life, which in turn often lead to mental breakdowns. Secondly, mental difficulties of various types are reflected in the firm's productivity and profit records. Mental illness takes its toll through alcoholism, high accident rates, high tardiness rates, high labor turnover, and poor human relationships. Studies have shown that the emotionally ill have more accidents and safety violations, file more grievances, and are discharged more often than healthy workers.

Despite the logic of the above, mental health ranks third behind safety and physical health as an area in which private industrial managements expend resources. It will be recalled that the outstanding pioneering effort of DuPont included 90 physicians but only 1 psychiatrist. When efforts have been made, as they have in DuPont, Eastman Kodak, and Metropolitan Life Insurance Company, significant improvements have resulted. The fact that a company psychiatrist is on the premises will often result in visits, when a referral to someone across the street will often be ignored.

The rehabilitation of the alcoholic employee is perhaps the best example of what private firms can do in regard to mental health programs. It is estimated that 5 to 10 percent of the national work force at all levels is affected by a drinking problem. One study indicates that the alcoholic employee was absent 19.4 days annually, as compared with 5.8 days for the nonalcoholic.[17] Because of this cost, plus those issuing from increased accidents and reduced efficiency, more than 50 major corporations conduct rehabilitation programs in this field. Because of the alcoholic's overriding concern for job security, such programs are usually more effective than pleas of family and friends; some studies have shown recovery rates of between 65 and 85 percent, as compared with a general public recovery rate of 30 percent or less.[18]

The recommended procedure for dealing with the alcoholic employee is as follows:

1. The supervisor maintains accurate records on employee performance, such as productivity, absenteeism, lateness, leaving the workplace, warnings, innovative excuses, and so on.

2. Though suspecting an alcoholic source, the supervisor talks with the employee only about his or her objective record of performance.

3. If performance does not change, it is suggested that the employee join the supervisor in meeting with a counselor in the personnel unit.

4. During the initial phases of this meeting, the supervisor presents the objective performance record and then withdraws.

5. The counselor "lays it on the line" and suggests that a discharge is imminent if performance is not improved.

---

[17]Merrill T. Eaton, "Alcohol, Drugs, and Personnel Practices," *Personnel Journal,* vol. 50, no. 10, October 1971, p. 755.

[18]Wilbur J. Cohen, "Revolution in Mental Health," *Personnel Administration,* vol. 32, no. 2, March–April 1969, p. 7.

6. If the employee indicates that alcohol is the source of the performance difficulties, she or he is retained on the payroll and referred to an appropriate outside agency, such as Alcoholics Anonymous, a psychologist, or a hospital specializing in alcoholism treatment.

7. The counselor follows the case for 1 year after referral to determine the extent of rehabilitation.

Implementation of the above procedure in the Hughes Aircraft Company resulted in a success rate of 75 percent.[19]

A related, but newer, problem is that of employee use of drugs on the job. In a study of 95 subjects in a drug rehabilitation center, 91 reported use of drugs while on the job, 48 reported they had sold drugs to other employees, and 68 indicated forms of criminal behavior, including stealing materials, payroll forgery, and so on.[20] That the problem does involve a significant portion of the work force is indicated by a survey of more than 7 million workers in the state of New York. Use of heroin was reported by 1.3 percent, of LSD by 2.6 percent, of methedrine by 2 percent, and of marijuana by 12 percent.

Though it would appear that the same approach could be taken to drug use as to alcoholism, fewer firms are willing to put forth a significant rehabilitation effort. Some claim that alcoholics do not proselytize for alcoholism; they can be helped while keeping them on the job. The drug user often wants to share his or her discovered escape route from the world with other workers. In addition, users may have to sell drugs to finance their personal habit. It is also suspected that the management does not understand the "drug culture" as well as the "alcohol culture." The typical alcoholic is older and has had longer service. The typical drug user is younger and has not built up a service record in the firm. Finally, the illegality of drug usage combined with changing public attitudes toward certain drugs makes management uncertain about reporting requirements to various government agencies. A not unusual reaction to discovery of a drug user is immediate discharge or an immediate leave of absence without pay.

ABSENTEEISM

One of the most common reasons given for being absent from work is physical illness, and thus a sound health and safety program should contribute to reduced absenteeism. There are, however, many other reasons for missing work, and their analysis and correction will help to maintain the work force.

"Absenteeism" is the title given to a condition that exists when a person fails to come to work when properly scheduled to work. The most common measure is the percentage of scheduled time lost as was presented in Chapter 6. There is probably some irreducible overall minimum of absenteeism; some project 3 percent as this figure. It is also contended that for some jobs a reasonable amount of absenteeism serves as a maintenance function. When a job is either too demanding or not demanding enough, periodic "unauthorized vacations" enable the employee to deal with feelings issuing from difficulties in coping. A study of 348 employees in 32 different jobs revealed that higher

---

[19]"Business Dries Up Its Alcoholics," *Business Week*, Nov. 11, 1972, p. 169.

[20]Jerome Siegel and Eric H. Schaaf, "Corporate Responsiveness to the Drug Abuse Problem," *Personnel*, vol. 50, no. 6, November-December 1973, p. 9.

FIGURE 22-8
Absenteeism by Occupation, 1977—1979

Occupation	Total Percent Time Lost	Percent Time Lost	
		Illness	Other
Professional/technical	2.5	1.4	1.1
Managers	2.0	1.2	.8
Sales workers	2.7	1.7	1.0
Clerical workers	3.3	2.1	1.2
Craft workers	3.3	2.3	1.0
Operatives	5.7	4.0	1.7
Transport operatives	4.2	2.9	1.3
Nonfarm laborers	4.2	2.9	1.3
Service workers	4.5	3.0	1.5
ALL OCCUPATIONS	3.5	2.3	1.2

Source: Daniel E. Taylor, "Absences from Work among Full-time Employees," *Monthly Labor Review*, vol. 105, no. 3, March 1981, p. 70.

performers in frustrating situations (high growth needs in low-level job) had higher absence rates.[21]

As indicated in Figure 22-8, absenteeism rates tend to vary according to occupations held. During the period 1977–1979, the lowest rate of absenteeism was among managers (2 percent) while the highest was among operatives (5.7 percent). The overall rate for all occupations was 3.5 percent, with two-thirds of this being caused by illness. Rates also vary by industry with such reported percentages in 1980 as: retail stores—6.7 percent, government agencies—5.2 percent, manufacturing—4.3 percent, banks—3.7 percent, and hospitals—3.6 percent.[22] Size of firm is a factor, with firms having more than 2,500 employees reporting significantly higher rates.

Excessive absenteeism constitutes a considerable cost to the firm even when the absent employee receives no pay. Work schedules are upset and delayed, quality of product tends to deteriorate, overtime may be required to make up work, and many fringe benefits are still paid regardless of attendance. When sick pay is authorized, the costs mount up even more rapidly. It was estimated in one instance that for a plant of 1,000 employees, an increase in the absentee rate 1 percent costs approximately $150,000 per year.[23] It is therefore desirable that management should attempt to reduce the rate and, in any event, include the known rate in their decision concerning human resources requirements.

As outlined in Figure 22-9, the causes of absenteeism can be categorized by elements of the job situation, personal characteristics, and ability to attend. Attendance motivation is affected not only by the general economic environment but by specific programs developed by management to reduce absenteeism. Both negative disciplinary action and positive reinforcement programs based on organizational behavior modification have been

[21]Barry M. Staw and Greg R. Oldham, "Reconsidering Our Dependent Variables: A Critique and Empirical Study," *Academy of Management Journal*, vol. 21, no. 4, December 1978, p. 539.

[22]Prentice-Hall Editorial Staff, *Absenteeism and Lateness*, Prentice-Hall, Inc., Englewood Cliffs, N.J., 1981, p. 11.

[23]John C. Kearns, "Controlling Absenteeism for Profit," *Personnel Journal*, vol. 50, no. 1, January 1970, p. 50.

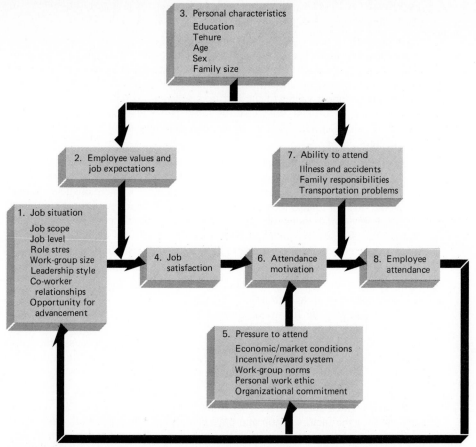

FIGURE 22-9 The major influences on employee attendance. (*Source: Richard M. Steers and Susan R. Rhodes, "A New Look at Absenteeism,"* Personnel, *vol. 57, no. 6, November-December 1980, p. 62. With permission of the publisher, © 1980 by AMACOM, a division of American Management Associations. All rights reserved.*)

used with success.[24] Insight into the problem can be provided by classifying each absence as to basic characteristics. Such characteristics and emerging patterns as the following have been discovered:

1. *Name of the employee.* It is often found that there are absence-prone persons in an organization. But like the accident-prone, the membership of this group changes. One study revealed that on the average 17 percent of the employees were responsible for 90 percent of the paid absences during one 3-month period.[25] But when the analysis was extended to a 21-month period, the membership of the group accounting for 90 percent of the absences encompassed one-half of the

[24]Loretta M. Schmitz and Herbert G. Heneman III, "Do Positive Reinforcement Programs Reduce Employee Absenteeism?" *The Personnel Administrator,* vol. 25, no. 9, September 1980, pp. 87–93.

[25]Kathleen R. Garrison and Paul M. Muchinsky, "Evaluating the Concept of Absentee-Proneness with Two Measures of Absence," *Personnel Psychology,* vol. 30, no. 3, Autumn 1977, p. 392.

work force. A "core" of employees does account for a disproprotionate share of the absence, but the core makeup changes from time to time.

2. *Reasons given.* Illness is doubtlessly the number one reason given for an absence, accounting for well over half of the cases. Correction of this involves a combination of private and organizational health programs. Other reasons given are frequent transportation difficulties, personal requirements, and care of children. One of the foremost values of the flexitime schedule, discussed in Chapter 1, is the reduction of official time lost for these personal requirements. Problems related to care of children could also be alleviated by employer-sponsored childcare centers.

3. *Projected reasons.* Many employers contend that the real reason for high absenteeism is a lack of an employee sense of responsibility. Though some will blame the gradual switch from a work ethic to one of a more existentialistic character, we would do well to also look at the environment in which we expect employees to live daily. Monotonous and demeaning jobs, relatively poor pay, oppressive and pressureful supervision, and poor working conditions do not inspire daily loyalty. Correlations of absenteeism rates by general desirability of the job serve to support this contention.

4. *Age.* In 1972, the part-week unscheduled absence rate for teenage employees was the highest of all age groups.[26] The rate for the 55- to 64-year category was lowest. However, the full-week absence rate was just the reverse. The young employee tends to be absent for short periods more frequently, suggesting placement in low-entry jobs or personally compensating for the business practice of according longer vacations to senior employees. Older employees tend to be out for longer periods, suggesting problems related to health.

5. *Sex.* Many studies show a higher rate of absenteeism for females as compared with males. Such statistics are very misleading inasmuch as they are often not analyzed for the factors of job and pay. Females as a group tend to have higher absence rates because they have been improperly allocated to lower-paid, less-desirable jobs. When corrected for job type, compensation levels, and formal education, the difference between the sexes tends to disappear.

6. *Date.* Tabulating absences by date often shows such interesting patterns as high rates on Mondays and Fridays, after paydays, before and after holidays, and on opening days for various seasons such as hunting and baseball. A top manager in one automobile firm stated that the rate sometimes amounted to 13 to 15 percent on Monday and Friday. The 4-day, 40-hour week has been proposed to provide an officially approved 3-day time-off period.

SUMMARY

Laws, economics, and morals lead to organizational programs designed to promote employee safety and health. The Occupational Safety and Health Administration has utilized a police-and-punish approach. Lately it has emphasized improvement of the industrial environment with a view toward preventing disease. Workers' compensation laws make

---

[26]Janice Neipert Hedges, "Absence from Work: A Look at Some National Data," *Monthly Labor Review,* vol. 96, no. 7, July 1973, p. 28.

the employer fully liable and use the stimulus of insurance premiums to reduce accidents and diseases. Full information about the costs of industrial accidents and diseases puts the force of productivity and profits behind health and safety efforts.

Full realization of the economic and human costs of inadequate health and safety programs has led many organizations to undertake a more systematic approach to the effecting of personnel maintenance. Such programs can include one or more of the following elements:

I   Safety
    A   Top management support of special safety effort
    B   Appointing a safety director
    C   Engineering a safe plant and operation
    D   Educating all employees to act safely
    E   Maintaining accurate records of costs and causes of accidents
    F   Accident analysis
    G   Safety contests
    H   Enforcing safety rules through disciplinary action

II   Health
    A   Physical
        1   Preplacement physical examinations
        2   Periodic physical examination for all key personnel
        3   Voluntary periodic physical examination for all personnel
        4   A well-equipped and staffed medical dispensary
        5   Availability of trained industrial hygienists and medical personnel
        6   Systematic and preventive attention devoted to industrial stresses and strains
        7   Periodic and systematic inspections of provisions for proper sanitation
    B   Mental
        1   Availability of psychiatric counseling
        2   Cooperation with outside psychiatric specialists and institutions
        3   Education of company personnel concerning the nature and importance of the mental health problem
        4   Development and maintenance of a proper human relations program

Over and above any economic costs, evading the maintenance responsibility will inevitably lead to increasing governmental interference and control of private company operations. The preservation of the physical and mental status of the nation's citizens is a social objective that transcends any company objective of producing economic goods, profits, wages, salaries, and the like.

BRIEF CASE

The Jones Corporation was recently visited by an inspector from OSHA. This being their first inspection, they requested permission from the inspector for a member of the personnel department to accompany him on the walk-around. The inspector requested a worker representative to go along as well. As a result of the inspection, Jones was issued the following citations:

1. Two workers in a group of 12 were not wearing their hard hats in a dangerous area.

2. The noise level in one department was measured at 100 decibels, some 10 units above OSHA's standard.

3. Jones Corporation has refused to show one worker his medical record even though this has been requested by both the worker and the union.

4. Jones Corporation laid off one worker for 1 day without pay for refusing to go into an empty 25-foot-deep vat in order to clean it.

The company protested all four citations contending that (1) they do their best to enforce the hard-hat rule and have evidence to prove that disciplinary action has been taken, (2) they require all employees in the noisy department to wear earplugs, (3) the company doctor felt that this particular worker's mental health would be threatened if shown his medical record, and (4) the cleaning of the vat had been done many times in the past with no injury to workers.

Questions

1. If you were the review commissioner, how would you rule on the four citations?

2. What is the reasoning behind each of your rulings?

DISCUSSION QUESTIONS

1. An OSHA inspector suddenly shows up on your firm's doorstep. What is likely to happen now?

2. Compare and contrast the philosophies of workers' compensation laws and the Occupational Safety and Health Act.

3. Can a worker refuse a supervisor's order to perform a dangerous task? What requirements are involved?

4. Discuss the issue of worker health versus the economics of creating a perfectly safe workplace. How has the Supreme Court approached this issue?

5. You have been designated to investigate an excessively high injury frequency rate in one department of the firm. Indicate how you would go about this task.

6. What are the various costs associated with an industrial accident?

7. Compare and contrast the typical programs of dealing with the alcoholic with those for dealing with the user of illegal drugs.

8. Rank the following in the order of private-industry concern and activity, indicating reasons therefor: (1) mental health, (2) safety, (3) physical health.

9. What is the relation between workers' compensation laws and mental health?

10. Outline the elements of a comprehensive educational program in the field of safety.

COOKE, WILLIAM N. and FREDERICK H. GAUTSCHI III: "OSHA, Plant Safety Programs, and Injury Reduction," *Industrial Relations,* vol. 20, no. 3, Fall 1981, pp. 245–257.

GILDEA, JOYCE ASHER: "Safety and Privacy: Are They Compatible?" *The Personnel Administrator,* vol. 27, no. 2, February 1982, pp. 80–83.

HAYES, MARY: "OSHA Final Rule Gives Employees the Right to See Their Exposure and Medical Records," *The Personnel Administrator,* vol. 27, no. 3, March 1982, pp. 71–75.

IVANCEVICH, JOHN M. and MICHAEL T. MATTESON: "Optimizing Human Resources: A Case for Preventive Health and Stress Management," *Organizational Dynamics,* vol. 9, no. 2, Autumn 1980, pp. 5–25.

PATI, GOPAL C. and GLENN MORRISON: "Enabling the Disabled," *Harvard Business Review,* vol. 60, no. 4, July-August 1982, pp. 152–168.

SISKIND, FRED: "Another Look at the Link between Work Injuries and Job Experience," *Monthly Labor Review,* vol. 105, no. 2, February 1982, pp. 38–40.

EXERCISE AND CASES
FOR PART SIX

Exercise: Communication

1. One person will prepare a diagram such as the following. Any arrangement other than this example will suffice.

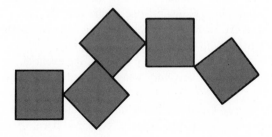

2. The person stands with his or her back to the class and proceeds to give oral directions concerning the above series of squares. Class members are not allowed to ask questions nor give audible responses. Their goal is to duplicate the person's design as closely as possible. The time that the person takes to complete the instructions is recorded.

3. The person prepares a second but similar diagram. He or she stands facing the class and replies to questions asked by class members. The time taken is again recorded.

4. Both diagrams, 1 and 2, are shown to the class and each member determines the number of accurate placements; for example, all, four, three, two, or one.

5. A comparison of the time taken and degree of accuracy under one-way and two-way communication is made by the instructor. A median accuracy score can be determined for each diagram.

6. A discussion can be held concerning time, accuracy, and level of confidence developed through both types of communication. Class members can be asked for personal examples that illustrate one-way and two-way communication.

Case: The Misguided Missile

The Jones Paper Products Company is a firm of approximately 2,200 employees. Its employees are organized by a national papermakers union that is affiliated with the AFL–CIO. Relations between company management and union have been reasonably good and peaceful. The Jones Company attempts to take a modern, enlightened approach to personnel management, and its personnel department has subsections in employment, training, compensation, labor relations, employee services, and safety. Total personnel in the department is twenty-one.

Joe Roscoe has been employed by the Jones Company for 2 years. He joined the organization immediately after being discharged from the service. His job consists of removing various paper products from a machine, weighing these products, and transporting them to a storage area. At present, Joe works on the shift that begins around midnight and ends at 7:30 A.M. A skeleton crew works this shift, and Joe's supervisor is responsible for a very large area. Joe is on his own a good deal of the time, which is one of the attractive things about the job. In addition, an individual incentive bonus system has been set up, based on the tonnage of paper moved. He has found that he can make bonus and still have time to rest and read magazines occasionally. Sleeping is too risky.

One morning at about 3 o'clock, Joe was struggling with a load of paper, attempting to get it to the weighing scale. For some reason, the load simply would not move. He pushed, shoved, sweated, and swore. Suddenly he discovered that one of the metal weights of the scale had jammed against one of the wheels. This irritated him considerably, and he grabbed the metal weight and flung it without looking. It fractured the skull of a fellow employee, who was immediately rushed to a hospital, where he remained for several weeks. Joe, of course, was very upset by the event and went to the hospital with the injured employee. He was very much relieved when the doctors pronounced him out of danger.

As we said, the Jones Company has a safety section. This section consists of the safety director and two assistants. The safety director had been offered a functional type of authority over all personnel in matters affecting safety. He had refused this authority, preferring to work only in a staff capacity. His main thesis was that a man could not be *made* to act safely; he had to be persuaded, shown, and educated. The safety director did not want the temptation of organizational authority.

Joe's night supervisor filed disciplinary charges against him for the incident described above and recommended discharge. A committee hearing was held, at which the supervisor and Joe both testified. After all the facts were revealed, the safety director was asked for his recommendation. He argued that Joe should not be discharged. He felt that the Jones Paper Products Company was largely at fault in this incident. In the first place, Jones was remiss in not providing adequate supervision on the night shift. Had a supervisor been in the area, Joe would probably have been more restrained in his actions. Secondly, the Jones management should be fully aware of the effects of an incentive wage plan. The purpose of this plan is to stimulate an increase in employee output. The company wants its employees to respond, and Joe did respond. Naturally he was upset when he found that his progress was hindered by the scale weight. Thus the company incentive wage program was a contributing factor in the accident. Thirdly, Joe has a plant reputation of being a hothead. He is a good, steady employee, but he has been known to have a low boiling point. Plant management was aware of this side of his personality as were most of his associates. Management was therefore at fault in coupling a temperamental employee with adverse working conditions. The safety director recommended that some lighter penalty should be given to Joe, that discharge was too severe.

The disciplinary committee listened attentively to the advice of the safety director. They concluded that the seriousness of the incident more than offset any of the extenuating circumstances offered by him. Joe was fired. The union immediately filed a grievance.

Questions

1. Do you agree with the safety director's position on the amount of authority he should have? Why or why not?

2. What is the validity of each of the charges made by the safety director? Where does the fault lie in this accident? Why does the director take this particular position?

Case: The Unfettered Employee

Dan Walton was hired for a summer job as a carpenter's helper by a home-building firm. On reporting to his supervisor, the verbal assignment given was, "Just stay busy. I can't be concerned with everything you do. Just don't let any superintendents catch you standing around." The following is the sequence of events as related by Dan.

I was primarily engaged in supplying the framing crew of carpenters with adequate material to allow them to proceed from one structure to the next without any delays. I was relatively naive concerning union procedures that designated what I would be allowed to perform, as well as the basic work responsibilities that my employer would expect me to fulfill. My supervisor, who was in charge of fifteen carpenters and three laborers, was not concerned with individual performances as long as the completion schedule was met, and therefore offered little guidance in assigning tasks to be performed.

Our crew, the framing division, arrived at the residential site after the foundation had been poured. At the time of our arrival the bricklayers would also have the walls up on the houses. The first task of our crew was to have an individual chalk out the location of the walls from a blueprint. The laborers would then supply the dwelling with "studs" and "longs," which were the types of lumber used to build the internal frame for the walls of the house. The laborers would at this time stand planks around the outside brick walls which would be attached to the top of the brick walls to seal the walls. The roofing segment would then attach sheets of plywood to complete our division's tasks. The laborers would then sweep out the dwelling and gather all the scraps of lumber into piles, which would be dumped by the cleaning crew.

At first I relied on the other two laborers to teach me the basic procedures of our operations, but they had specific duties that they did not want infringed upon and at times resented my encroachment on their standard tasks.

The carpenters also offered little help. As certain duties had to be completed I was randomly instructed by various carpenters to either assist or perform a particular task related to the general responsibilities of the crew. Meanwhile my supervisor as the occasion arouse would similarly instruct me in the operation of some type of machinery or the desired performance of some necessary operation.

Upon arriving at work one morning my supervisor, Herb, informed me that I would have to remove all the unused lumber and various other supplies that had not been used from the streets. Herb stated that a paving company would be arriving the next day to grade the streets and could not be delayed by the obstruction of our materials. He then told me to stack the leftover "studs" in 3-foot-by-3-foot stacks, which I should then bind together with a binding instrument. He then instructed me to take the forklift, since the usual operator was on vacation, and pick up the bound stacks of studs, and place them on the flatbed truck. He also stated that I should then drive the truck to the main yard and unload the truck, using the forklift to remove the stacks of lumber.

As my initial reaction I told Herb that I didn't know what a binding tool was, let alone how to operate it. He assured me that the instructions on the case would be self-explanatory. I then proceeded to stack the lumber into the 3-foot-by-3-foot stacks as had been suggested. I soon realized that the reason many of these studs had not been used was because they were severely warped. After the stack was about 2 feet high the stack would then, because of the warped material, tumble to the ground. I soon became very discouraged and frustrated and the continual collapsing of the stacks of studs. A carpenter named Bob, who had been watching me and sensing my frustration, came over to where I was working and told me that after the stack had reached about a foot and a half, to place pieces of wood crossways on the top of the stack so the next tier of the stack would have a foundation. The idea sounded very logical and I wondered why I had not thought of it.

My next duties would be to load the stacks onto the truck with the forklift. I was apprehensive about running the forklift, even if the operator was on vacation. I had seen previously even the most experienced operators drop loads before, and I could only imagine the difficulties a novice would have. I decided to tell Herb that I did not really think I should operate the forklift. Herb's reaction was, "If you can drive a truck, you can drive the fork; just go play around with it before you move anything."

I walked down to the yard where the forklift was kept and climbed up on the machine. I finally got it started, but with all the various levers, it was confusing as to which sequence they were to be used in operating the machine. A carpenter named Al came into the yard at the same time to pick up a supply of nails. He then offered to demonstrate the operation of the machine. He suggested bits of advice that he thought were pertinent to the machine's operation. Al stated that first of all, the rear wheels turned on a forklift, which is different from most vehicles, and that this was important to remember when operating the machine. He also stated that it was important to keep the lift slightly tilted toward the machine when moving the stacks to counterbalance any sway in the load that might cause the load to shift and fall off the lift. He then explained the sequence in which the levers had to be operated to properly maneuver the machine. As I drove the forklift out of the yard I was confident that I would be able to operate the machine, thanks to Al's help.

After loading the stacks of lumber onto the truck it was about time to go home. Most of the other members of the crew had already started cleaning up for the day, and although I had not yet unloaded the stacks of lumber from the flatbed truck, I did feel I had accomplished a great deal. I decided that I might as well drive the forklift back to the yard. As I started toward the yard, Herb came over and said he would drive the forklift back, and that I could drive the boom truck, which the beam crew had been using to set the trestles on the houses.

As I walked over to the boom truck, I noticed that the telescopic boom was fully extended and holding up one of the trestles that had not been hung yet. I started up the engine of the truck and tried to figure out which handle would slacken the line so I could detach it from the beam. I finally succeeded in detaching the line. I then brought the line and boom back onto the truck and attempted to apply the safety brace that keeps the boom from bouncing and being bent when the truck is moving. It was difficult to set the brace because it required someone holding the brace while the boom was lowered on top of it. I decided to lower the boom and wedge the brace under the boom. As I drove back to the yard I hit a bump which jarred the brace loose and it fell from under the boom. At this same time a car drove up to the truck and a man got out and introduced himself as the business agent of the operating engineers. He said he would help me put the brace in properly. He also stated that since I was a laborer, I was not allowed to operate machinery. He suggested that I tell my foreman that I had been instructed by the business agent of the operating engineers to not operate any machinery.

I thanked the business agent for his help and drove the truck to the yard. When I arrived I saw Herb, but I decided that it was not my duty to tell my supervisor what to do, since he rarely helped me perform my assigned tasks. So I jumped in my car and headed home.

Questions

1. If Dan had injured himself or others while operating the forklift truck and the boom, who would be responsible?

2. How do you explain Herb's behavior as a supervisor? Is the business agent safety conscious?

PART SEVEN

SEPARATION

The final operative function of personnel is separation of the employee from the organization in order to return him or her to society. Prominent among the separation processes are retirement, layoff, discharge, and outplacement (Chapter 23). And finally, personnel research is essential to improved performance in all of personnel management (Chapter 24).

Separation
Processes

With the first function of personnel management being that of procuring employees from society for use in the organization, it is logical that the final function should be the return of those employees to that same society. The function of separation can be as complex and challenging as any of the preceding five functions, which served to select and merge the employee with the organization. After an introductory discussion of the costs of turnover, we shall review three processes of separation: (1) the retirement of older employees; (2) the layoff or release of qualified younger employees no longer needed by the organization; and (3) the discharge of employees who do not meet the organization's expectations. All of these are important and sometimes traumatic events for both the employee and the organization's management.

TURNOVER

In the broad sense, "turnover" refers to the movement into and out of an organization by the work force. This movement is an index of the stability of that force. An excessive movement is undesirable and expensive. When an employee leaves the firm, such costs as the following are usually involved:

1. Hiring costs, involving time and facilities for recruitment, interviewing, and examining a replacement.
2. Training costs, involving the time of the supervisor, personnel department, and trainee.
3. The pay of a learner is in excess of what is produced.
4. Accident rates of new employees are often higher.
5. Loss of production in the interval between separation of the old employee and the replacement by the new.

6. Production equipment is not being fully utilized during the hiring interval and the training period.

7. Scrap and waste rates climb when new employees are involved.

8. Overtime pay may result from an excessive number of separations, causing trouble in meeting contract delivery dates.

Greater appreciation of the significance of these costs has stimulated considerable managerial interest in the problem of labor turnover. In a survey of twenty-four California firms, the greatest turnover costs issued from lost production while the position was vacant and the substandard production of the replacement while learning.[1] These were estimated to be 70 percent of the total. Next in order of significance were costs of supervision, employment, formal training, taxes, and exit procedure.

Separations can be classified by department, reasons for leaving, length of service, and personal characteristics, such as age, sex, marital status, home ownership, and amount of insurance. High turnover from certain departments suggests a need for improvements in working conditions and/or supervision. Reasons given for leaving must be analyzed carefully to ascertain their truth. Because of the difficulty of getting real answers in exit interviews, a few firms try to elicit them by questionnaire after the exiting employee has had time to procure another position. In a comparison of reasons given at the exit interview with those obtained through follow-up questionnaires, one firm discovered agreement between the two sources in only 11 out of 116 cases.[2]

Analysis of length of service often indicates that a large percentage of voluntary quits occur in the first 6 months of employment, a fact that suggests errors in placement and orientation. In a statistical study of quits and stays in a relatively routine clothing-manufacturing job, one firm discovered that stable employees (in relation to turnover) were over the age of 29 at hiring, owned their own homes, had prior work experience, and had no more than 9 years of formal schooling.[3] Each of these characteristics could be credited with point values on the application blank. Other things being equal, the stable employee is favored during the hiring process.

In dealing with separations from the firm, the objective is *not* their total elimination. Some losses are functional to the firm in that employees leaving can be replaced with higher-quality types. In one instance, a high—32 percent—annual turnover was further analyzed to discover that only 18 percent was undesirable to the firm.[4] When this 18 percent was analyzed to determine if any were unavoidable, the figure was further reduced to 9 percent. Unavoidable losses were attributed to summer employees, those leaving for education purposes, and employees with health and family problems. Separations can produce values to the organization in the forms of new ideas entering the enterprise, possible higher quality of personnel being added, and lowering of salaries paid when older, high-seniority persons are replaced by lower-paid entrants. Nevertheless, any movement in or out of the organization produces the many costs listed above.

[1]Joseph C. Ullman, "Using Turnover Data to Improve Wage Surveys," *Personnel Journal,* vol. 45, no. 9. October 1966, p. 529.

[2]Jerry Levine, "Labor Turnover," *Personnel Administration,* vol. 33, no. 6, November-December 1970, p. 35.

[3]Gordon D. Inskeep, "Statistically Guided Employee Selection: An Approach to the Labor Turnover Problem," *Personnel Journal,* vol. 49, no. 1, January 1970, p. 21.

[4]Dan R. Dalton, David M. Krackhardt, and Lyman W. Porter, "Functional Turnover: An Empirical Assessment," *Journal of Applied Psychology,* vol. 66, no. 6, December 1981, p. 718.

Around the beginning of this century, the average life expectancy of a citizen of the United States was 49 years. By 1981, this had risen to 70.3 years for males and 77.9 years for females. On the basis of these figures, it is apparent that large numbers of employees will live beyond the usual working age, thereby requiring an event known as "retirement."

Retirement has been characterized by some as a "roleless role." With a society built on a work ethic, the move from a recognizable productive work role on one day to a roleless role on the next has stimulated the belief that retirement leads to mental and physical illness and sometimes premature death. To many, work is life and idleness is a living death. In a *Time* magazine article it was stated "there is a disproportionate death rate among those forced to retire, and 25 percent of all known suicides are committed by people over 65."[5]

Other researchers have concluded that this drastic impact on health is largely a myth. In a longitudinal study of 2,000 participants both before and after retirement, it was concluded that health declines are associated with age, but *not* retirement.[6] In fact, unskilled workers demonstrate a slight improvement in health after retirement. A second study of over 11,000 people ended with the conclusion that no support had been found that retirement is detrimental to the health of older persons.[7] Other research has emphasized the extent to which poor health actually induces workers to retire, thus making health the cause of retirement instead of an effect. Over one-half of the men retiring before age 65 and claiming reduced Social Security benefits listed failing health as the primary reason for stopping work. Less than one-fourth gave this reason when retiring at the more usual age of 65.[8]

Whether cause or effect, it is evident that retirement is a major event in one's life cycle, and the organization has a major responsibility in facilitating the transition from one stage to the other. People must become able to accept the idea that one can successfully live in dignity as an adult without having a job. Rather than a roleless role, retirement forces an increase in the scope of decision making about one's personal life. If these decisions are made well, the individual, the organization, and society in general stand to gain.

Mandatory vs. Voluntary Retirement

One of the key issues of modern times is whether the decision to retire should be made by the organization or be left to the employee concerned. Of some 460,000 workers retired in a 2-year period, 30 percent indicated that a compulsory retirement age had been established in their organizations.[9] The most common age set was 65, a practice that dates from the 1880s when the German Chancellor Otto von Bismarck initiated a social security system and arbitrarily picked that particular age. Of course, in those days

---

[5]"Now, the Revolt of the Old," *Time*, Oct. 10, 1977, p. 18.

[6]Gordon F. Streib and Clement J. Schneider, *Retirement in American Society*, Cornell University Press, Ithaca, N.Y., 1972, p. 66.

[7]Dena K. Motley, "Health in the Years before Retirement," *Social Security Bulletin*, December 1972.

[8]U.S. Department of Health, Education, and Welfare, *Reaching Retirement Age: Findings from a Survey of Newly Entitled Workers 1968–1970*, Research Report No. 47, Social Security Administration, Office of Research and Statistics, 1976, p. 43.

[9]Ibid, p. 54.

few workers lived long enough to hit the retirement age. It will be recalled from Chapter 4 that the Age Discrimination Act of 1968 prohibits discrimination against employees between the ages of 40 and 65 for reasons of age. The 1978 amendment to this act raised the limit to 70 years. Thus, it is currently illegal to require an employee to retire solely for reasons of chronological age prior to reaching 70 years. About two-thirds of private firms require retirement at age 70, while the remaining third have not stipulated any age. Approximately 20 percent of the nation's work force is 65 years or older.

Many organizational managers have maintained that compulsory retirement at a fixed age for all is beneficial. Among the reasons cited are: (1) it is simple to administer with no complications to prove that the older employee no longer meets job requirements; (2) openings are created to which younger employees can advance; (3) human resources planning is facilitated when retirement schedules are known; (4) graceful exits are provided for employees who are no longer qualified, inasmuch as the firm often will wait out the final few years of declining productivity, and (5) it stimulates employees to make plans for retirement in advance of a known date. The new legal age of 70 years has led some to suggest that managements will deal more harshly with marginal workers above the age of 60, and the health care costs of employees will mount since there will be more older employees on the work force. There is some evidence that this new-found freedom to delay retirement until age 70 will not lead large numbers of persons to do so. In General Motors, the mandatory blue-collar age for retirement stood at 68 for many years; the average retirement age, however, was 58. Only 20 percent of Exxon's employees wait until 65 to retire, whereas only 33 percent wait at General Foods Corporation.

The arguments against any fixed compulsory retirement age revolve largely around individual freedom and utilization of all available talents. People age at different rates in terms of productivity, energy, and creativity. Forced retirements would result in significant losses of real talent; consider the contributions after age 65 of such persons as Winston Churchill, Averill Harriman, Margaret Mead, and Arthur Fiedler. A fixed retirement age will often lead to employee antagonism and resentment, as well as a "short-timer" attitude in the years just prior to retirement. "Short-timers" tend to be less interested and committed to the organization's challenges and problems, and may even "retire" on the job. If there is no fixed age, the organization is forced to do a more effective job of appraising employee performance. Some people should be retired at the age of 60 while others can still make a valuable contribution beyond the age of 70. Rather than relying on the crutch of a fixed age for all, management must deal more with individual differences. And finally, if more workers do continue on the job beyond age 65, it will lessen the strain on our Social Security System. Twenty years ago, the ratio of employees working to those collecting benefits was 5 to 1. It is currently down to 3 to 1.

The Retirement Cycle

Sociologists have identified several phases through which an employee may go in experiencing the retirement event. As indicated in Figure 23-1, the first phase begins many years prior to the actual retirement date. Very few people expect to die before reaching retirement age, and similarly, very few expect to keep working until they die. At some point, awareness of approaching retirement hopefully has some effect in providing for the two most essential elements of successful retirement—financial security

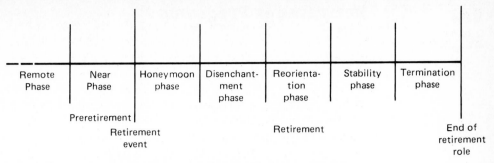

| Remote Phase | Near Phase | Honeymoon phase | Disenchant-ment phase | Reorienta-tion phase | Stability phase | Termination phase |

Preretirement

Retirement event

Retirement

End of retirement role

FIGURE 23-1 Phases of retirement. (*Source: Robert C. Atchley*, The Sociology of Retirement, *Schenkman Publishing Company, Inc., Cambridge, Mass., 1976, p. 64. Used with permission.*)

and leisure skills. This awareness should occur in the remote phase of preretirement inasmuch as neither of these two essentials can be developed overnight. The second phase occurs just prior to the event and makes the fact of imminent retirement highly explicit. One begins to perceive that fellow employees view him or her in short-term perspectives. Involvement in major programs tends to lessen. One may be asked to train a replacement. And in many instances, certain rites of passage in the form of retirement ceremonies and receptions are held.

For many people, the third phase of the cycle is termed the "honeymoon" stage. One wallows in the new-found freedom and lives out fantasies that finances will permit—traveling, fishing, golfing, visiting, seeing the grandchildren, and so on. When asked how the retirement is going, the reply is often, "Why I've never been so busy!"

Not everyone goes through the fourth phase, but when life finally slows down, the honeymoon is over and a certain acmount of disenchantment sets in. The highly desired constant travel and visiting become boring. Those who have not developed a variety of interests and skills in preparation for retirement are likely to experience this stage more severely. It may be particularly difficult if one has moved to a different community after retirement.

Hopefully, the disenchantment phase will be followed by one of reorientation. One attempts to structure a life-style that can run for many years. Help can be obtained from many community agencies and churches that have various programs designed to help retirees determine their level and quality of involvement. It requires exploring new opportunities and making realistic choices in the light of personal interests and skills.

In the stability stage of the cycle, the retiree has developed a philosophy and pattern of decision making resulting in a reasonably busy, predictable, and satisfying life. The retirement role has been mastered. The individual is able to cope and adapt to declines in physical capacity that inevitably come with advancing age. He or she is a self-sufficient adult who has translated the roleless role into a dignified, responsible, and meaningful position in society.

One may, of course, die suddenly while experiencing any of the preceding six phases of the retirement cycle. If life continues, one could enter the termination phase, where the retiree is longer self-sufficient. Loss of able-bodied status or loss of financial support may mark the end of retirement as defined. The person ceases to be retired, becomes dependent upon others or societal institutions, and thereby loses some of the dignity associated with the role of retirement.

551

Retirement Programs

A survey of 267 organizations revealed that 36 percent had preretirement counseling programs, two-thirds of which include spouses.[10] Most provided the minimum of informing employees of company and government retirement benefits. Only about half offered programs designed to actively facilitate an effective transition from the working to the retirement role. Given the fact that retirement can no longer be automatically enforced, it would appear that more effective programs would make retirement more attractive to many employees. Research indicates that prospective retirees predict far more dissatisfaction with the retirement role than they actually experience after leaving the organization. Properly designed programs can do much to lessen these anxieties.

Retirement programs can also provide considerable values for the organization and society at large. Successful retirees are walking ambassadors of good will for the organization. They reduce the burden on the firm's personnel department after retirement inasmuch as most of their questions have been answered. It is also possible that their productivity in the few years prior to retirement has been enhanced because of the lessening of anxiety about the future. Society in general also profits from successful programs. Retirees possess a valuable societal resource—a daily supply of free time. Programs that inform prospective retirees of places where they can continue to serve in voluntary organizations enhance society's wealth. Programs that enable greater self-sufficiency in financial planning can do much to reduce the burden of society for taking care of its aged citizens.

The two key elements of most effective retirement programs are (1) voluntary attendance and (2) information to assist in self-planning. Most firms attempt to avoid the stigma of paternalism by not forcing this type of program on their employees. To some extent, this is unfortunate inasmuch as those who would profit most, the semiskilled, are least likely to show up. Employees in upper-status jobs are also unlikely to attend; they are among the most reluctant to retire and are accustomed to manipulating their own environments. Thus, most programs are geared for the literate, middle-income group.

The emphasis should be on the provision of information required for planning one's life after retirement. Research indicates that the individual outlook on future finances is the most important single factor affecting one's attitude toward the retirement event. The most popular topics are itemized in Figure 23-2, and can be grouped into four major categories: (1) financial matters, (2) housing, (3) use of leisure time, and (4) physiological and psychological health.

Particular instructional devices are many and varied. Perhaps the basic one is the group meeting where expert speakers are invited: a lawyer to speak on estate taxes and wills; a physician to speak on health problems of senior citizens; a state employment service representative to speak on the availability of part-time jobs, and a federal administrator to speak on Social Security procedures. At times, meetings are held with former retirees for an informal exchange on the problems of switching roles. Work sessions are conducted where each potential retiree is asked to fill out a personal affairs check list so that retirement income can be estimated. In relation to that income, prospective budgets can be worked out. Some organizations provide access to a library of materials on retirement as well as giving subscriptions to such publications as *Retirement Planning*. In a large organization, specialized counselors may be available for individual

---

[10]Bureau of National Affairs, Inc., *ASPA–BNA Survey No. 39, Retirement Policies and Programs, Bulletin 1559,* Jan. 24, 1980, p. 1.

FIGURE 23-2
Topics Covered in Preretirement Counseling

Topic	Percentage of Companies with Program
Social Security benefits	92
Company pension benefits	92
Other company benefits/services	82
Financial planning	60
Wills and inheritance provisions	55
Earning money after retirement	52
Recreation and hobbies	52
Health problems	51
Organizations for retirees	50
Mental/emotional aspects	48
Where to live	43
Volunteer activities	42
Safety precautions for older persons	24

Source: Bureau of National Affairs, Inc., *Retirement Policies and Programs,* Bulletin 1559, January 24, 1980, p. 4. Reprinted by permission from ASPA–BNA Survey No. 39, © 1980 by the Bureau of National Affairs, Inc., Washington, D. C.

problems of adjustment. Some companies in the Los Angeles area have contracted with nonprofit agency called Second Careers to help place retirees in part-time jobs, meaningful volunteer roles, or training for small businesses.

The introduction of the above information can occur at different ages for the older worker. One company begins at the age of 55 so that the employee can have a decade to make extra financial arrangements, pretest hobbies, and try out other communities while on annual vacation. At age 61, specific financial information is covered so that the employee can determine if he or she wishes to seek early retirement at 62 under the Social Security System.

There have been various suggestions for softening the shock from a company-managed work life to a self-managed retirement life. The length of the annual vacation can be gradually extended to force employees to deal with large blocks of free time. It has even been suggested that pay be reduced for a part of these longer vacations to force income budgeting. One company provides for sabbatical leaves, similar to those given by universities, where a year's time can be self-managed on an acceptable project. Others provide part-time employment in the years just prior to retirement should the employee desire it. IBM provides potential retirees and spouses with $2,500 each in tuition aid to be used during 3 years prior to retirement and 2 years afterward. Pitney Bowes allots $300 per year for tuition and books for employees 50 years old and older.

Research indicates that the more experience that people have with retirement, the more they see it as a good thing. In one study of 3,500 retirees, 83 percent reported liking retirement, and of these about a fifth reported anticipating that they would not like it.[11]

Effective retirement programs will reduce employee uncertainty, minimize worries about health, reduce the tendency to miss one's old job, enable a more satisfactory

[11]Robert C. Atchley, *The Sociology of Retirement,* Schenkman Publishing Company, Inc., Cambridge, Mass., 1976, p. 89.

arrangement of retirement income, and increase the amount of social participation on the part of the retiree.

Public and Private Retirement Income Plans

The major breakthrough on retirement income came with the Social Security Act of 1935, when compulsory retirement insurance was introduced to American society. The limited amounts of benefits provided in this manner stimulated many organizations to develop supplementary private plans to enable a reasonable level of total retirement income to be effected. As indicated in Figure 23-3, benefits now paid amount to almost 30 percent of total federal spending. Since it is basically a pay-as-we-go system, the steady dropping of the ratio of payers to benefit recipients poses serious financial problems for the nation. Changes have been proposed such as increasing the retirement age to 67, reducing cost-of-living adjustments, and reducing some benefits paid.

Public plan   The benefits provided under the Social Security program are financed by both employer and employee in equal amounts. These benefits are four in nature: (1) retirement income for those 62 years of age and older who are not working; (2) survivors' benefits paid to the family of a deceased covered person; (3) disability benefits to workers who are physically unable to continue, provided they have worked under the program for at least 5 of the past 10 years; and (4) "medicare" for hospitalization of covered persons over the age of 65. Medical insurance for doctor's fees and laboratory services is also available for a small additional monthly fee. Full retirement benefits are available only to those who retire no earlier than at age 65.

Though the initial tax on both employers and employees was a small 1 percent of the first $3,000 of covered earnings, the financial health of the public system has required increasingly larger and larger amounts of contributions. In 1983, the tax rate for both employer and employee stood at 6.7 percent on a wage base of $35,700. It is anticipated that during this decade, the tax rate will rise to 7.65 percent on a wage base approaching $60,000. The self-employed currently pay at the rate of 9.35 percent.

Benefits are paid to a retiree, his or her dependents, or survivors if insured under

FIGURE 23-3
Social Security—Payers and Recipients

Year	Ratio of Payers to Recipients	Percentage of Federal Spending for Social Security
1950	16 to 1	1.8
1960	5 to 1	12.0
1970	4 to 1	18.8
1980	3 to 1	26.4
1982	3 to 1	28.2 (estimated)
1984	3 to 1	31.5 (estimated)
2030	2 to 1	(unavailable)

Source: Social Security Administration, U.S. Office of Management and Budget.

the law. One is *currently* insured if having worked in covered employment during $1\frac{1}{2}$ years out of the last 3. One is *fully* insured if having worked in such employment for 10 years. No retirement payments are made if the employee is not fully insured. Some survivors' payments are made if the employee was only currently insured. Thus, if the employee hopes to retire and collect Social Security benefits, he or she must be *fully* insured.

Retirement, disability, and survivors' benefits are calculated on the basis of one's average monthly earnings up to the taxable amount. The taxable base has been increased on a sporadic basis since 1935, and thus no one can retire and receive the currently specified legal maximum because of past years of lower wage bases. Retirement benefits can be adjusted automatically upward when rises in the Consumer Price Index exceed 3 percent. Benefits are reduced if the retiree continues to work in covered employment and receives money in excess of $6,000 in 1982 for those 65 and older. There is currently no such limit for those 70 years of age.

Private plans   The retirement benefits provided by Social Security are insufficient for most retirees. As a result, both employers and labor unions have moved to establish private plans to supplement the public benefit. A National Labor Relations Board decision in 1948 forced employers to bargain over the subject of pensions with organized labor unions. As of 1972, approximately 63 percent of employees in the nonfarm private economy were covered by some type of private retirement plan.[12] Unions continued to be more successful than nonunion groups in obtaining retirement benefits for their members. Only 9 percent of the employees in unionized groups, were in firms that had no retirement plans; this compared with 48 percent for those belonging to no union. There are more retirement plans in manufacturing firms than there are in nonmanufacturing; less than half of the employees in trade and services are covered by such plans.

Unlike the 50–50 sharing of costs in Social Security, the employer completely finances approximately 75 percent of private retirement plans. Where employee contributions are required, the Supreme Court has recently ruled that larger contributions cannot be required for female retirees even though actuarial tables prove that they live longer than men.[13] Such differential pricing was deemed to be in violation of the Civil Rights Act. The Court maintained that even a true generalization about a protected class is insufficient reason for disqualifying an individual to whom that generalization did not apply. For example, in a group of 65-year-old males, some 80 percent will live as long as the average female. As one way out, the company could set aside equal amounts of contributions for both males and females, and turn the accumulated totals over at retirement for individual purchase of annuities. Such differential purchasing at retail is not in violation of the act.

Society has seen fit not to trust the private firm in its administration of private retirement plans. Many plans have gone bankrupt, leaving retirees with only their inadequate Social Security benefits. In 1974, the Employee Retirement Income Security Act was passed to ensure that employees covered by private plans will actually receive something at retirement. The act does not compel an employer to initiate a plan; rather, if one is initiated, it must comply with provisions assuring proper administration.

One of the fundamental provisions of ERISA is the establishment of the Pension

[12]Donald R. Bell, "Prevalence of Private Retirement Plans," *Monthly Labor Review*, vol. 98, no. 10, October 1975, p. 17.
[13]"The Sex-Bias Threat to Pension Funding," *Business Week*, May 8, 1978, p. 40.

Benefit Guaranty Corporation in the Department of Labor.[14] Employers with pension plans are required to pay a premium of $2.60 per participant to guard against plan bankruptcy. In the event of plan failure, employees will receive benefits from the Guaranty Corporation of their vested (owned) portion of the fund, up to $750 a month or 100 percent of average wages during the highest-paid 5 years of employment, whichever is less. The employer is still liable for any insurance benefits paid upon plan failure up to 30 percent of the company's net worth. This is a revolutionary requirement that subjects the entire firm to a possible pension fund liability; some feel it may be an unlawful confiscation of shareholder's property. Some accountants are now stipulating that the total amount of unfunded pension liabilities for present employees should be highlighted in financial reports.[15]

A second major feature of the act requires that employee vesting or ownership of pension amounts be provided. For many years, employers used pension fund accumulations as "golden handcuffs"; the employee could not afford to quit since he or she would lose the pension. Under ERISA, vesting must be provided but the employer has a choice of three options: (1) 100 percent vesting after 10 years of service, (2) 25 percent vesting after 5 years, grading up to 100 percent after 15 years of service, or (3) 50 percent vesting when age and service equals 45, grading up to 100 percent 5 years later. Surveys indicate that most employers are choosing the first option of delaying all vesting until after 10 years' service.[16]

Other provisions of this revolutionary act include the following: (1) prohibits eligibility requirements of more than 1 year of service or an age greater than 25 years, (2) requires annual funding of the full cost of current benefit accruals plus amortization of past benefit liabilities, (3) restricts investment of pension funds in company securities to no more than 10 percent, (4) permits transferability of vested amounts from the company to other companies or private individual retirement funds, and (5) permits all employees to set up their own Individual Retirement Accounts, whether or not they are members of a private employer system. The limit on income tax deductions for such private accounts is 15 percent of employee compensation up to $2,000; $2,250 if married and the spouse is unemployed.

Where does the personnel manager fit into the requirements of ERISA?[17] The first duty is to fulfill the act's requirement that every employee be given a Summary Plan Description of the private system that is accurate, comprehensive, and written in layman's language. Some consider the concepts of accuracy and layman's language to be contradictory. The employee must also be given an annual statement of how the entire fund was administered, including receipts, investments, and benefit payouts. Each employee is entitled, on request, to one annual statement concerning his or her particular vested amount.

A second major responsibility may fall on the shoulders of the personnel manager. The fund must be administered by trustees appointed either within or without the firm. Should the personnel manager be one of the trustees, he or she has unlimited liability for breaches of administrative responsibility and portfolio mismanagement. ERISA re-

---

[14]Those opposed to the act as an excessively complicated and unwarranted intervention into the affairs of the firm refer to ERISA as "Every Ridiculous Idea Since Adam."

[15]"Paper Gains in Covering Pension Liabilities," *Business Week*, Aug. 9, 1982, pp. 70–74.

[16]American Society of Personnel Administrators–Bureau of National Affairs, Inc., "Impact of the Pension Reform Law," *Bulletin to Management* No. 1365, Apr. 8, 1976, p. 3.

[17]Some personnel managers report that two-thirds of their time is devoted to fulfilling the requirements of three laws—Civil Rights Act, Occupational Safety and Health Act, and ERISA.

quires that the "prudent-man" rule of administration be applied and subjects the administrators to possible suits. As a consequence, many funds are becoming quite conservative, favoring diversification of investments with a preference for fixed-income types. Liability insurance would seem to become increasingly necessary, as it is for doctors, lawyers, nurses, and other professionals in our society.

LAYOFF

In the free enterprise system, there are many occasions when a qualified employee will be released from employment (layoff) because the organization no longer requires her or his services. Layoffs can be temporary as the firm adjusts to variations in market demand for its products. They can also be permanent as the firm goes out of business or transfers to a distant location. When the company lays off older blue-collar employees, the event can be quite shocking. Employees have refused to accept the fact of a plant closedown, and in one case the company had to send personnel technicians to knock on doors to pull people out of their houses to begin searches for new jobs. Blue-collar employees may receive offers to transfer to another plant of the firm but this is not usually accompanied by moving expenses. Older employees are typically reluctant to move from a community in which they have lived for most of their lives. As industry moves from the Northeastern portion of the United States to the West, South, and Southwest, serious problems have been created in the communities left behind. Some states have proposed laws requiring a 2-year notice of a plant closing plus company contributions to a state fund to assist in local redevelopment.

Layoff is a very difficult problem not only for the employee but for the company and the labor union as well. Since layoff involves the loss of income, the employee and the union are prone to restrict the company's freedom of decision. The company typically wishes to take advantage of the layoff to retain its most able employees, and let the more marginal ones go. On the other hand, the employee and union try to regulate layoff decisions through seniority systems. It is generally found in practice that seniority is a stronger factor in layoff than it is in promotion decisions. In one survey of union-management contracts, seniority was the *sole* factor controlling layoff decisions in 25 percent of the contracts, a primary factor in one-half (seniority controlled if the more senior employee could meet minimum performance requirements), and a secondary factor in the remainder (seniority controlled only if the more senior employee was relatively equal in ability to the person to be replaced).[18]

Unemployment Compensation

A major element of the Social Security Act of 1935 was to provide financial assistance for employees who are laid off from work due to no fault of their own. This portion of the act also levied a tax of 3 percent of the first $3,000 of pay, but unlike retirement the tax applied only to employers. Amendments to this part of the act have also occurred over the years, with the requirement in 1978 calling for a 3.4 percent tax on the first $6,000 of pay. This federal law provides an incentive to states to pass suitable

[18]Winston L. Tillery, "Layoff and Recall Provisions in Major Agreements," *Monthly Labor Review,* vol. 94, no. 7, July 1971, p.44.

unemployment compensation. If state laws and administrations meet certain federal standards, most of the tax monies (2.7 percent) can be retained by the state. The remaining 0.7 percent is also usually returned under special conditions, such as extended benefits for employees when the unemployment rate is unusually high, and benefits paid that cannot be charged to the employer's account. Needless to say, all 50 states have passed suitable legislation so that the funds raised may remain within the state. Present laws cover over 90 percent of the work force. Because of the many layoffs during the recent recession, an increase in the tax rate has been made to 3.5 percent of the first $7,000 of pay, effective 1983.

In the states, reserve accounts are established for each employer and the applicable tax rate may increase or decrease, depending upon the firm's experience. In Minnesota and Vermont, for example, the tax rate can rise to 5 percent for employers with unusually bad experiences. Overall, the average tax collection throughout the nation has been less than 1 percent of total wages in covered employment.

If a person is laid off by the firm, she or he is eligible for unemployment compensation for a 26-week period. If the nation's unemployment rate is above 4.5 percent, an additional 13 weeks of compensation is provided, the monies for which are not charged to the employer's reserve account. In general, the employer's fund is not charged if the person quits, is discharged for cause, is on strike, or refuses suitable employment in other firms. The states of New York and Rhode Island specifically authorize payments when employees are on strike. The Employment Security Amendment of 1970 provides, however, that total refusal of the state to pay unemployment compensation can be based on only two reasons: (1) discharge for misconduct in connection with work and (2) fraud in connection with filing a claim. Thus, the employee who merely quits or refuses suitable work cannot be denied *some* compensation. Most states provide for a penalty in these cases, for example, a 5-week waiting period instead of the usual 1, or a 25 percent reduction in maximum benefits. Though the employer's fund is not charged in these instances, the fact that the government will still pay compensation from other tax monies indicates that this is becoming a form of welfare payment.

It is estimated that unemployment benefits actually received amount to only one-fourth to one-third of wages lost during the payment period. Though the federal government has established a goal for the states of a minimum payment of two-thirds of the average weekly wage, only 5 of the 52 states and territories have met this standard. Thirty-seven, however, have maximum benefits amounting to over 50 percent of the average weekly wage.[19] In 1982, the weekly pay ranged from $90 in Alabama to $222 in Alaska. Specific rules and administrations vary from state to state, and some labor unions have established a classification of state administrations ranging from "tough" to "easy."

Supplemental Unemployment Compensation

Though unemployment compensation benefits below a certain amount are not taxed as income, the relatively low amount has led unions and employees to demand some supplementation in the form of a fringe benefit. In the vanguard of this movement have

---

[19]Joseph A Hickey, "State Unemployment Insurance Laws: Status Report," *Monthly Labor Review,* vol. 96, no. 1, January 1973, p. 37.

been three labor unions: the United Auto Workers, the United Steel Workers, and the Ladies' Garment Workers. Though these plans are frequently referred to as "guaranteed annual wage" plans, their makeup is more accurately described by the terms "supplemental unemployment compensation" or "supplemental unemployment benefits."

In all cases the plan is financed solely by the company, usually at the rate of 10 cents per hour worked. A trust fund is established into which these monies are paid, and the size of this fund is a major factor in determining the amount of benefits to be paid. Employers earn credits at the average rate of one-half per week worked, and these are cashed in upon layoff at the rate of one credit for 1 week of compensation. In most cases, an employee can accumulate a maximum of only 52 weeks of credit. If the trust fund is low in funds, more than one credit may be required for each week of benefits.

In most plans, the unemployed individual must qualify for state unemployment compensation. Payments from both sources usually amount to 50 to 80 percent of weekly wages, but the United Auto Workers Union has negotiated an arrangement that pays 95 percent of normal wages less a small charge ($7.50) for job-related expenses that would not be incurred by the laid-off employee. An automobile worker with 7 years of seniority is entitled to this 95 percent of normal pay for up to a year. A worker with 1 year of seniority is eligible for 95 percent for 31 weeks.

Many people have claimed that instead of being a true guaranteed annual wage plan, these arrangements merely constitute an additional fringe benefit of a dime an hour, which the employees have chosen to receive in this form rather than as a part of the wage. Certainly many of the high-seniority employees, who are unlikely to receive any benefit from this fund, are not enthusiastic about such arrangements.

There is one final problem that worries many managements. If the total benefits are raised from 60 percent to 80, 90, or 100 percent of straight-time earnings, what happens to the incentive to seek work? Many would claim that the unemployed person would attempt to *avoid* return to work if 39 to 52 weeks of regular earnings are assured while *not* working. Doubtlessly some individuals would be thus affected; some even lose their desire for work under a less than 40 percent average payment of state unemployment compensation. Though the trend in this country is to provide some minimum compensation for all, the difference between that and average income does not make the guarantees highly attractive. Those influenced by the work ethic would still find work attractive regardless of financial benefits. If the movement of the young toward an existentialist ethic continues and if the *lack* of movement by most organizations toward job enrichment is unchanged, then perhaps we will become increasingly concerned about the impact upon behavior of larger financial guarantees.

The California Plan

In 1978, the state of California adopted a Work-Sharing Unemployment Insurance program, which authorizes the receipt of both wages and unemployment compensation. If an employer is forced to cut production during a downturn, the workweek is cut for all employees an equal amount. For example, if an employee is paid $200 for a 5-day workweek and is cut back to 4 days, she or he receives $160 in pay from the employer. However, the employee is now authorized to receive 20 percent of the state unemployment benefit. Assuming that the weekly benefit is $100, the employee will receive $20 from the state, $160 from the employer, for total compensation of $180. In addition, the unemployment benefit is not taxable.

The work-sharing program avoids many of the social and economic problems normally resulting from layoff of personnel. Employees lose less income, retain such benefits as health insurance, and do not lose social status in their community. The employer avoids the costs of labor turnover, avoids losing valuable trained employees, and maintains any progress that might have been made on an affirmative action program. Again, older employees least likely to be laid off during a cutback are often not among the enthusiastic supporters of such a plan.

OUT-PLACEMENT

Though the typical rank and file employee is governed by the layoff provisions of the contract, there is growing evidence of organizational concern for personnel displacements not covered by such contracts. A 1981 survey of 2,000 firms revealed that four out of ten provided out-placement assistance to departing employees, up from two out of ten 5 years ago.[20] Many programs are contracted out to specialized consulting firms as described in Box 23-1.

When firms required to make substantial cutbacks in personnel, there are very difficult decisions to make concerning which activities should be retained and which personnel within the firm should be let go. In general, most firms utilize a cutback situation to remove poorer-performing personnel, those whose salaries have grown to exceed their foreseeable value, and those who, though not incompetent, have no identifiable real strengths on which to build in the future. A personal out-placement activity is based on the ideas that these personnel have salable skills usable to other firms, and that the extent of the market for these types of skills is largely hidden.

When the firm has identified the particular people to be dismissed, after presumably conducting an internal search for possible transfers, the next and most difficult steps are to prepare the termination letter and conduct the termination interview. Though general knowledge of a cutback has helped to prepare the way to some degree, the individual is never fully prepared for the shock of the axe on his or her employment neck. Thus, it is strongly recommended that termination notice should be given early in the workweek, and never on Friday. Immediate activity, rather than solitary brooding, is the avenue to positive action to overcome the current difficulty.

In a well-developed out-placement function, the displaced person will be assigned to a counselor. The immediate major problem is to rebuild the confidence and self-esteem of the rejected employee. The employee is quickly removed from his or her regular work environment to reduce loss of "face" and to permit full-time efforts to be devoted to job search. Firms are also generous in providing severance pay to finance the job search and in allowing dismissed employees to retain an office base from which the search can be conducted. Daily conversations and exchange of job tips among the total group of displaced personnel help to maintain morale.

The second task of the counselor is to develop a data base for each individual. This will contain job experience, salary history, educational background, and career objectives. Depth interviews and psychological tests may be administered to assist in identifying personal strengths.

Third, the actual process of job search will be undertaken. The counselor will make

---

[20]"Outplacement Assistance," *Personnel Journal,* vol. 60, no. 4, April 1981, p. 250.

BOX 23-1
Concerns Offer Counseling to Executives, Lower-Level Workers Who Are Laid Off
Deborah A. Randolph

Back in the 1960s, some companies started euphemistically "outplacing" their executives instead of "firing" them. And the more conscience-ridden companies began offering "outplacement counseling" to ease executives into the big, bad world of unemployment.

In the 1970s, a few companies, notably Corning Glass Works during the 1973–1975 recession, used counseling experts to help their white-collar workers as well as executives, who were being laid off.

Now, with another recession at hand, some employers are hiring counseling firms to console and advise secretaries, clerks, foremen and even factory hands when layoffs become necessary. In some cases, the counselors are directly involved in placing the workers in new jobs.

Among the companies leading the way are Sears, Roebuck & Co., Goodyear Tire & Rubber Co., Firestone Tire & Rubber Co., Jones & Laughlin Steel Corp. and Colonial Penn Group Inc. With layoffs spreading in the long-predicted economic downturn, other employers are expected to join the trend. A notable exception so far is the auto industry which isn't planning any counseling programs for blue-collar workers who are undergoing large-scale layoffs.

Less Paternalism

Declining paternalism among large companies, personnel executives say, points to quicker layoffs of less-productive employees as business slows down. But the counseling programs can help to ease the blow.

"Outplacement counseling is likely to grow tenfold during the 1980s as businesses realize they can't carry unproductive employees for an extended period," says James Gallagher, Chairman of Career Management Associates, a New York counseling firm.

Fired executives usually get individual help from a consultant. Laid-off wage earners usually are counseled in groups, receiving advice on interviewing, resume writing and the like. The counselors also try to give workers a much-needed morale boost, sometimes by such methods as having a roomful of workers stand up and shout, "I'm terrific." Some counselors organize job fairs for laid-off workers to meet prospective employers.

The employers' motives aren't entirely matters of conscience or altruism. The faster a laid-off worker finds a job, the faster he stops collecting unemployment compensation, which comes out of the former employer's pocket.

Good Investment

Goodyear, for instance, believes it can save as much as $3 million by giving job-seeking advice to most of the 1,450 employees who were laid off in the February closings of its Los Angeles and Conshohocken, Pa., plants. So Goodyear considers the $300,000 it spent for counseling sessions a good investment.

Thomas Jackson, President of Career Development Team Inc., the New York-based firm that conducted the Goodyear sessions, calls such programs "pragmatic humanism." By offering more than a perfunctory handshake and an escort to the door, he suggests, managers can soothe their consciences about making tough, unpleasant decisions. And the programs are considered good community relations.

Although there isn't any solid proof that the workshops, job fairs and morale boosting actually help workers find jobs faster, advocates offer evidence that they do. They cite a study of laid-off aerospace workers in Southern California during 1969 and 1970, when the state sponsored workshops to aid the unemployed. Those who attended were subsequently out of work for an average of about two months, while those who didn't attend averaged seven or eight months of unemployment. But the workshops may have attracted the better-motivated people to begin with.

Job fairs sometimes yield instant results, however, When Colonial Penn Group, a Philadelphia-based insurance company, laid off 300 employees a few months ago, it called in Fox-Morris Associates, which organized a job fair of 27 local employers for data-processing workers. Two Colonial Penn workers got job offers on the spot; another 12 took jobs shortly afterward.

Transferable Skills

Most of the Colonial Penn employees were office workers. Experts say they stand a better chance than blue-collar workers of finding another job right away because they more easily can transfer their skills from one job to another. Shelley Kramer had handled customer accounts at Colonial Penn for 18 months when she lost her job. She attended the job-search seminar and landed a job six days later as a claims adjuster at Hancock-Gross Inc., a Philadelphia plumbing-supply firm.

Job offers usually don't come quite so easily for blue-collar workers. Beverly Blair, president of Blair Associates, a Peoria, Ill. employment agency, says factory workers trained for a specific job in a specific industry can have problems finding work, especially if they don't want to relocate.

"Building tires is all I'm trained for," says Paul Slifer ruefully. He built bias-ply tires for 14 years at the Conshohocken plant, which was operated by Goodyear's Lee Tire unit. Radial tires have proved a tough competitor to the bias-ply products built there, and last August Mr. Slifer learned that the plant would close within six months. He was shocked. "What other kind of job could I do?" he recalls asking himself.

He was skeptical of the counseling offered to him at the plant. "I thought it was a rip-off. If they (the counselors) weren't going to offer me a job, who cares? But I was curious. Anyway, it was on company time, so I went," he recalls.

Still Looking

Mr. Slifer still hasn't found a job, but he says the counseling work-

Continued following page

shops made him realize that life goes on, and another job is a must. He would like to repair typewriters or do construction work. "I'm thinking about what I want to do, and that's a start," he says.

William Simon was more fortunate, partly because his skill was more transferable. He was an electrician at Lee Tire for more than 10 years. Three months before the plant closed in mid-February, he took a counseling workshop and began looking for jobs. By the time of the closing, Mr. Simon had already lined up a job at Johnson & Johnson's McNeil Laboratories division. He attributes his speedy success to the counseling. "I'm just surprised it happened this quickly," he says.

Some counselors consciously put the laid-off workers in stressful situations. Mr. Jackson, the New York consultant who handled the Goodyear layoff, took some flak about having the workers shout, "I'm terrific." Many Goodyear employees said they felt absurd.

"We want them to be emotional," Mr. Jackson retorts. For one thing, he says, the exercises help workers project their voices, especially in nerve-racking circumstances—such as job interviews.

Interview Techniques

He also uses videotape to help workers practice interview techniques. Stan Sachaczenski, a mechanical engineer at Goodyear, learned in one such session that he didn't speak dynamically enough to impress interviewers. Dynamism "isn't a creative person's nature," Mr. Sachaczenski says, but he realized the effort could help him land a job. Within a week after the Conshohocken plant closing, Mr. Sachaczenski got a job at United Technologies' Teledynamics unit in Fort Washington, Pa.

At Colonial Penn, about 220 of the 300 people laid off went to a seminar the next day. "Where do you go from here? It's up to you," Warren Nuessle, vice president of Fox-Morris, told the crowd. He gave the workers tips about how to prepare themselves for hard interview questions and how to write resumes. Later, their resumes were distributed among Fox-Morris counselors, and within a week over 100 of them had been interviewed for jobs.

Labor unions generally seem to be withholding judgment about the counseling. A United Rubber Workers official says the union "hasn't had enough experience" to decide whether outplacement counseling is worthwhile. However, John Davis, president of the rubber workers' Local 785 at Lee Tire, says the counseling is helpful. He helped plan the workshops.

Some practices are criticized, though. Mr. Gallagher, whose New York company specializes in individual counseling sessions with executives, questions whether employment agencies such as Fox-Morris should be directly involved in placing laid-off workers in new jobs. He says the agencies get paid for trying to get people into jobs as quickly as possible, and for an employee "it isn't always best to take the first thing that comes along."

Conflict Is Denied

Sanford Fox, president of Fox-Morris Associates, denies any conflict of interest. He says, for instance, that his firm is paid by Colonial Penn to provide both counseling and placement, and that the companies accepting the workers aren't paying the firm. Counseling alone is "handholding" that falls short of placing someone in a job, he says.

Sometimes the whole process flops. In 1978 Goodyear planned its own one-hour informal "outplacement" session for white-collar workers faced with layoffs at its Akron plant. A job fair followed, where only 40 workers showed up to talk with 23 companies, and it resulted in only 10 jobs, say Thomas Bailey, manager of salaried personnel. The main problems were the short counseling session and the loyalty of the workers to the company that was laying them off. "They expected that the plant would eventually reopen, and they came only because Goodyear was sponsoring" the fair, he explains.

This time, with a broader program and more-extended sessions, Goodyear hopes that its failure won't be repeated, Mr. Bailey says.

available knowledge of typical job sources and provide specific assistance in preparing resumes and introductory correspondence. Practice in interviewing techniques will often be conducted with particular attention being devoted to applicant attitudes. Many jobs have been lost because of applicant approaches and attitudes that "turn off" the prospective employer. Help will be provided in evaluating particular job offers through providing information on salary ranges and examining all facets of the potential job, such as advancement potential, indirect benefits, similar positions in other companies, and so on.

In one firm, the special out-placement unit formed in the personnel department was successful in placing 90 to 95 percent of all displaced personnel on new jobs of comparable salaries within a 4-month period.[21] A survey conducted by Business Careers,

[21]Basil Robert Cuddihy, "How to Give Phased-out Managers a New Start." *Harvard Business Review,* vol. 52, no. 4, July-August 1974, pp. 66–69.

Inc. showed that 88 percent of 250 terminated executives were placed in higher-paying jobs.[22] Such special efforts and counseling reduced the average time to find new jobs by one-third.

DISCHARGE

Perhaps the most stressful and distasteful method of separation is that of discharge. The employee is deemed to be fundamentally unsatisfactory in terms of performance and/or attitude. One-fifth of the nation's labor force is protected by organized labor unions whose contracts typically provide for grievance processing. Should a discharged employee and the union feel that the forced separation is unjust, most grievance procedures provide for the intervention of a third party, an outside arbitrator. Arbitration records reveal that cases involving discharge and discipline constitute the most prevalent types of grievances appealed. In approximately one-half of these cases, the company's decision to discharge is reversed or softened.

In an analysis of 391 such instances, the major reasons for reversal were (1) the desire of the arbitrator to give the grievant a second chance because the offense was an isolated incident in a generally satisfactory work record (27 percent), (2) inconsistency of the company in enforcement of rules (19 percent), and (3) determination that the punishment was too harsh in terms of industrial practice generally (14 percent).[23] Other, less-frequent reasons were the commission of procedural faults by the company in processing, management being partly at fault in the incident, retroactive application of a new rule, and discipline of union officials for actions in connection with their official union business. In addition to union restrictions on the right of discharge, there are, as outlined in Figure 23-4, other major sources that reduce employer freedom to discharge. The employer cannot base a discharge on union activity, race, religion, nationality, age, sex, or the reporting of safety violations to OSHA. Both state and federal courts are moving in the direction of protecting employees from arbitrary and unjust discharges. It is estimated that an average of 1 million employees are discharged each year without receiving a "fair hearing."[24]

FIGURE 23-4
Restrictions on the Employer's Right to Discharge

Source	Nature of Restriction
National Labor Relations Act	Union activity
Civil Rights Act	Minority races, religions, nationalities, sex
Age Discrimination Act	Ages 40 to 70
Occupational Safety and Health Act	Reporting safety violations
Labor union contract/arbitration	Discharge for not just cause
Various courts	Discharges contrary to public good or in violation of oral or written agreements

[22]"Personnel Roundup," *Personnel*, vol. 55, no. 1, January-February 1978, p. 45.

[23]Morris Stone, "Why Arbitrators Reinstate Discharged Employees," *Monthly Labor Review*, vol. 92, no. 10, October 1969, p. 48.

[24]"The Growing Costs of Firing Nonunion Workers," *Business Week*, April 6, 1981, p. 95.

Discharge for cause makes the exemployee ineligible for unemployment compensation in most states. It should be used only for serious or habitual infractions of company standards and rules. In a survey of 185 companies, immediate discharge without warning was reported as the penalty by the following percentages of firms: 90 percent for theft, 88 percent for falsifying the application blank, 70 percent for possession of narcotics, 63 percent for possession of firearms, 62 percent for willful damage to company property, 58 percent for falsifying work records, and 54 percent for fighting on the job.[25]

Discharge of Nonunion Personnel

A basic characteristic of the free enterprise system is to allow the private employer to hire and fire at will in the interest of obtaining the most productive and efficient employees. As indicated above, one-fifth of the nation's workers have a protector in the form of a labor union. The remaining four-fifths can rely only upon the law and our courts in making sure that the employer's decision is best for the nation's economy. There is increasing evidence that society is moving to restrict the freedom of the employer on the subject of discharge. Since more than 90 percent of the nation's workers are employees, "governmental and public concern has shifted away from protection for the producer and the capitalist philosophy to a new concern for the consumer and the welfare state."[26] The job has a substantial effect on the employee's social, cultural, and recreational life, and its loss has far more devastating consequences than just the temporary loss of income. In the case of *Monge v. Beebe Rubber Co.,* the New Hampshire Supreme Court overruled a discharge of a female employee who refused to be "nice" to a foreman.[27] The court stated, "A termination by the employer of a contract of employment at will which is motivated by bad faith or malice, or based on retaliation is not in the best interest of the economic system, or the public good and constitutes a breach of the employment contract."

Termination of Key Personnel

Of all the types of separations, perhaps the most difficult for the organization is the dismissal of a key person, typically a higher-level manager. Though there is no question of unionization, there are several factors that will give the management pause. The key person often has political support either within the organization or from major forces in the community. Dismissal of such a figure is always disruptive for the unit that he or she heads. All of this is compounded if more than one key person is to be let go at any particular time.

The sole justification of the release of a key person is a serious need for organizational improvement. Helpful to this process is the use of an outside consultant who can force the manager to examine both the reasons for the proposed release as well as processes that should be followed. If a type of due process is not followed faithfully, high-ranking key people are often prone to file suit in court.

The first stage in the termination process should be a frank conversation with the person whose performance is seriously deficient. He or she should be counseled as to

[25]*Employee Conduct and Discipline,* The Bureau of National Affairs, Inc., Washington, D.C., 1974.

[26]Tony McAdams, "Dismissal: A Decline in Employer Autonomy?" *Business Horizons,* vol. 21, no. 1, February 1978, p. 70.

[27]114 N.H. 130, 316 A 2d 549, 551 (1974).

the nature of the organization's expectations, and these should be documented. This should be followed by steady supervision to ascertain if changes are forthcoming. In the event that the behavior is still unsatisfactory, specific notice should be given that the relationship will be terminated by a certain date if changes specified are not effected. At this point, if not before, considerable tension will exist and communications will undoubtedly be adversely affected. When the notice date arrives, the person's resignation should be specifically requested. The manager must be prepared for a verbally explosive reaction, and remain calm and cool throughout the session. It has been suggested that the terminated person typically goes through the following stages: (1) shock and disbelief, (2) rage and anger, (3) defensive reactions such as denial, displacement, or repression, (4) despair and depression, (5) reflective grief, and (6) positive behavior.[28] Understanding this, the manager is better able to help the terminated person move on to the last stage of initiating a new job search.

To contain possible adverse repercussions among the remaining personnel, the resignation should be communicated to them as soon as possible. Their own insecurities should be assuaged by assurances that this is not a wholesale change in staff. The specific reasons for the dismissal should not be divulged in the interest of protecting the rights of the released party, this despite the great temptation to present the organization's side of the story. Following such procedures will do much to deter legal action on the part of the dismissed person.

Dismissing a key individual is such a distasteful process that many organizations have let bad situations drag on for as long as 2 to 3 years before a deserved discharge was given. Some managers have developed unusual means of eliminating a person without an outright discharge. The flow of work may be altered so that it goes around the particular person; thus, the employee may become bored or take the hint and submit a resignation. Or the job may be abolished and the duties scattered about among other employees; then after the person has left, the duties can be reassembled and a new employee hired to fill the job. In some cases, the undesired person may be "kicked upstairs" and promoted out of the way; he or she may be made a special consultant and never be consulted. One smooth-talking manager invited the person to be dismissed to lunch at a plush restaurant. After eating and drinking, a genial and skillful discussion was held concerning the person's performance. When he got home that night, he very proudly and excitedly told his wife about having lunch with the "big boss." After hearing a blow-by-blow account of the conversation she turned to him and said, "Why Henry, you haven't been promoted. You've been fired!" And so he had been.

SUMMARY

The final function of personnel is the opposite of the first. Employees at some time or another will be separated from the organization. It is to the advantage of employee, organization, and society that such separations be carried out with skill and compassion.

With the increasing age level of our population, retirements will constitute the most common type of separation. Moving from a productive role to one deemed by some as "roleless" calls for years of preparation. The trend is in the direction of voluntary

---

[28]Dennis J. Kravetz, "Counseling Strategies for Involuntary Terminations," *Personnel Journal*, vol. 23, no. 10, October 1978, pp. 51–52.

retirement and voluntary attendance to informational programs that will facilitate this transition. Financial status is a key element that makes for successful retirements. Public retirement income is required under the Social Security Act and private retirement income plans are controlled by the Employment Retirement Income Security Act. The second key element is in providing assistance in helping the employee utilize her or his leisure time.

Separation of employees through layoff also requires controls and financial assistance. Unemployment compensation is required in all 50 states under the general guidance of the federal government. Some firms supplement these monies with extra benefits of their own. Release of highly skilled professional employees no longer required can be facilitated by planned out-placement processes.

Perhaps discharge of persons is the most distasteful form of separation. Such discharges for unionized employees are under general review of a grievance procedure ending up in arbitration. For nonunionized personnel, only laws and courts can serve to restrict the power of the private employer in discharging personnel. The tendency in modern times is to gradually restrict the employer in this major decision process. Discharges because of union activity, sex, age, color, religion, race, and nationality are legally prohibited. Discharges because of disloyalty, insubordination, and the like are still legal until challenged in court in specific cases.

BRIEF CASE

A salesman who had worked for a large steel corporation was discharged. The reason, he contended, was because he had questioned whether the steel tubes he was selling had been adequately tested. He maintained that the tubes, designed to be used under high pressure in the oil and gas industry, constituted a serious danger to anyone around them. His boss told him to just follow orders and sell the tubes as before. The salesman expressed his doubts to a vice president in the firm who he knew personally. As a consequence, the firm retested the tubes and withdrew them from the market. The salesman was discharged by his boss.

Questions

1. If the salesman should sue the company, what argument could he use to overcome the discharge?

2. What restrictions are there on the right to hire and fire at will?

DISCUSSION QUESTIONS

1. If a firm has a separation rate of 30 percent per year, indicate the various ways in which this can be analyzed to better understand the problem.

2. Describe the retirement cycle, indicating what the employee and employer can do in each of its phases to ease the transition.

3. What types of information should be emphasized in an organized retirement educational program?

4. Compare and contrast the taxing provisions of the retirement and unemployment compensation portions of the Social Security Act.

5. What types of financial benefits are provided for by the Social Security Act?

6. Discuss the philosophy and major provisions of the Employee Retirement Income Security Act.

7. If a firm's management should feel a responsibility for out-placement of professionals and other key personnel, what would be the nature of such a program?

8. Compare and contrast unemployment compensation with supplemental unemployment compensation.

9. What protections do union and nonunion personnel have in guarding against unjust discharges?

10. Describe the process of discharging a key high-level management official in an organization.

SUPPLEMENTARY READING

BLUEDORN, ALLEN C.: "Managing Turnover Strategically," *Business Horizons,* vol. 25, no. 2, March-April 1982, pp. 6–12.

BUCALO, JOHN P., Jr.: "Administering a Salaried Reduction-in-Force . . . Effectively," *The Personnel Administrator,* vol. 27, no. 4, April 1982, pp. 79–89.

DREHER, GEORGE F.: "The Role of Performance in the Turnover Process," *Academy of Management Journal,* vol. 25, no. 1, March 1982, pp. 137–147.

MONTANA, PATRICK J.: "Pre-Retirement Counseling: Three Corporate Case Studies," *The Personnel Administrator,* vol. 27, no. 6, June 1982, pp. 51–63.

SHKOP, YITZCHAK M. and ESTHER M. SHKOP: "Job Modification as an Alternative to Retirement," *Personnel Journal,* vol. 61, no. 7, July 1982, pp. 513–516.

STYBEL, LAURENCE J.: "Negotiating Your Own Severance Arrangements," *Business Horizons,* vol. 25, no. 1, January-February 1982, pp. 77–80.

chapter 24

Personnel Research, Change, and the Future

There is no field of management that will not benefit from systematic and purposeful research. Certainly the field of personnel management is in great need of more systematized knowledge and sound principles. There should be less "by guess and by gosh" and more accurate prediction of human behavior in an industrial environment. There should be less taking on faith and more proof of operating results. If personnel management is to obtain and retain the status of a legitimate management field and profession, research must provide the foundation.

Research can be defined as systematic and purposive investigation of facts with the object of determining cause-and-effect relationships among such facts. From research we hope to establish principles that define the relationship between two or more phenomena. The manager then attempts to use these principles in her or his philosophy, approach, attitude, and specific practices as a manager.

Research by itself is sterile if nothing is done with its results other than to publish them in journals and books. The personnel manager has an obligation, not only to assist in implementing research, but, more important, to see that usable results are actually implemented in his or her organization. This chapter will conclude with the basic change process, as well as fundamental humanistic challenges that must be faced in the future.

NATURE OF PERSONNEL RESEARCH

Personnel research is more difficult and frustrating than many of the types of research in the physical sciences. It is unlikely, and probably undesirable, that human beings will ever be completely predictable in their behavior. Yet every event need not be a complete surprise to the observer. Known relationships usually exist between a particular causal act of management and a resulting reaction or act from an employee.

Personnel research finds its roots in a number of disciplines. Various types of psychological research can be applied in the personnel field, particularly those dealing with what is known as industrial psychology. The products of sociological research are also useful to the personnel manager, as are the findings of the economist, particularly in the function of compensation. The psychologist, however, dominates in numbers. Of the 65 personnel researchers with doctorates employed by 50 major business firms, 61 possessed a degree in psychology, 3 had degrees in sociology, and 1 was unspecified.[1] Of the 62 researchers with master's degrees, 27 were in psychology, 6 in sociology, 5 in business, 1 in economics, and 23 were unspecified. The median size of the personnel research unit was 7. Berry estimates that these 50 firms constitute 60 percent of the business organizations that have research departments. Outstanding in this regard are General Electric, International Business Machines, Texas Instruments, and DuPont.

Turning to the public sector, a survey of 39 state governments revealed that 54 percent had separate personnel research units.[2] Again, the degree held by most specialized researchers was in the field of psychology—73 percent of the doctorates and 55 percent of the masters. The next most prevalent majors were in the fields of statistics and public administration. The emphasis upon psychology and statistics is consistent with the more frequently reported research areas—test validation, test construction, item analysis, and criterion development.

In classifying personnel research as a function of personnel management, it is apparent that there should be research in all six operative functions. The fundamental purpose is to improve the philosophy and practice of personnel management in general. It is eclectic in approach inasmuch as it typically involves multiple fields of knowledge, including psychology, sociology, economics, statistics, engineering, and management.

Types of Personnel Research

Two general types of research are usually identified as (1) basic or exploratory and (2) operational or applied. Exploratory research is concerned with the discovery of knowledge for its own sake. The scientist builds conceptual models and tests various hypotheses against them. Many of the published results of such research would appear highly theoretical and of little practical applicability to the business manager. Yet these are the generalizations that mark advances in the field, both in theory and in practice. Much of the pure research in personnel is accomplished by governmental institutions and colleges or universities.

Operational or applied research is directed toward the solution of particular business problems. The payoff of such research is immediate, observable, and tangible. The extent of such operational research can vary from the very elaborate, lengthy, and expensive studies of the Western Electric Company in the 1920s to a fairly quick analysis of company records to find the cause, for example, of excessive absenteeism. This type of research is based on the products of pure research. The pure scientist indicates the possibility of certain fundamental generalizations governing relationships among various factors. The individual company manager may take the scientist's idea and test it in a particular situation. The operational environment is never identical with that under which the exploratory research was conducted. The findings of such research are not therefore invalidated; they are applicable under the conditions specified and must consequently be

---

[1]Dean F. Berry, *The Politics of Personnel Research*, University of Michigan Bureau of Industrial Relations, Ann Arbor, Mich., 1967, p. 55.

[2]Frank A. Malinowski and Sheldon R. Hurovitz, "Personnel Research in State Government," *Public Personnel Management*, vol. 6, no. 4, July-August 1977, p. 261.

adapted to the situation in which the particular manager is located. Operational research can be elaborate, expensive, and carefully controlled. It can be conducted by the business manager, social engineer, or research scientist. Such research can also be performed every day by every manager in a somewhat less rigidly controlled manner.

In the terms of Byham, both of the above-described types of research would be classified as "behavioral science based."[3] The researcher seeks to discover basic relationships that can lead to improved personnel decision making in such areas as increasing job satisfaction, assessing managerial potential, and increasing organizational effectiveness. Byham indicates, however, that most companies perform "descriptive" personnel research when they collect statistics to keep management informed about the existing personnel situation, such as turnover data, wage surveys, absenteeism rates, and so on. A survey of 91 organizations showed that the number regularly collecting data in named subjects stood as follows: (1) separations—83, (2) accidents—80, (3) absences—73, (4) merit increases—49, (5) productivity—44, (6) grievances—41, and (7) disciplinary actions—33.[4] Only one-half reported conducting personnel research studies, with the most popular areas being training effectiveness, recruitment resources, performance appraisal evaluations, and validation of selection devices.

The Researchers

A wide variety of people and institutions engage in either pure or applied research. Among these researchers are (1) colleges and universities, (2) governmental agencies, (3) private research organizations, (4) company personnel departments, and (5) the line manager. In one study, it was found that personnel research being conducted was divided among the following agencies: 39 percent by private research organizations, 34 percent by colleges and universities, 22 percent by the federal government, and 5 percent by business.[5]

Colleges and universities are set up to operate in both the pure and the applied phases of personnel research. It is common to see bureaus of business research that engage in personnel projects as well as in investigations in the other fields of business management. Among the outstanding university centers of personnel research are the Institute for Social Research of the University of Michigan, the Personnel Research Board of the Ohio State University, the Institute of Industrial Relations of the University of California, and the Behavioral Sciences Group of Carnegie Institute of Technology. The funds for such research agencies come from the university, business firms, and foundations of various types. The bureau often undertakes a great variety of applied and operational research projects for individual firms. A portion of the income from such projects may be set aside to finance pure or basic research to be conducted by various faculty members. Basic research is also financed through grants made by various foundations, such as the Ford Foundation.

Various *governmental agencies* conduct basic and applied research. Units in the

[3]William C. Byham, *The Uses of Personnel Research*, American Management Associations Research Study 91, New York, 1968, p. 9.

[4]Bureau of National Affairs, Inc., *ASPA–BNA Survey No. 37, Personnel Policies: Research and Evaluation*, Bulletin No. 1516, March 22, 1979, p. 2.

[5]Cecil E. Goode, *Personnel Research Frontiers*, Public Personnel Association, Chicago, 1958, pp. 18–21.

Department of Labor are particularly interested in research dealing with personnel management. For example, the *Dictionary of Occupational Titles* and various occupational descriptions were prepared by the United States Employment Service for the general use of industry. Particular departments, such as the Department of Defense, do basic and applied research appropriate to their particular problems. For example, the findings of Air Force research in studying human reactions to various types of environmental stimuli have their uses in business situations.

Private research organizations take a number of different forms. Some are employers' associations that accomplish particular projects of special interest to an industry. For example, industry wage and salary surveys may be conducted by an employers' association on a continuing basis. In addition, there are the larger employer groups like the National Association of Manufacturers and the Chamber of Commerce of the United States. Other associations are established strictly for the purpose of conducting business research—such organizations as the National Industrial Conference Board, The Brookings Institution, RAND Corporation, and the Stanford Research Institute. And finally, there is the management consultant. He or she is doing and selling operational research of a type, particularly when *not* attempting to sell a ready-made system that proposes to solve the same problem in any firm with which the consultant comes into contact.

Individual companies also do personnel research, particularly of the operational or applied type. One of a series of surveys showed that 3 percent of the total expenditures made by personnel departments were applied to research. A later survey by the same group indicated that manufacturing firms, having a total personnel department manpower ratio of 0.77, allotted 0.02 to research activities.[6] For banking, finance, and insurance companies, the ratios were 0.95 and 0.04, respectively.

Just as the *individual manager* finds all functions of personnel inescapable to some degree, one must also consider research to be a part of the professional manager's job. He or she is in a key position to observe ongoing events and develop hypotheses concerning the causes of personnel problems. And when the specialized personnel research unit of the firm undertakes specific research projects, the understanding cooperation of the operating manager is critical to the success of the projects.

Sources of Information

It is important in all research to be aware of the possible sources of information concerning any particular subject. There is a danger, in operational research, that the manager will conclude that all information must come from the environment of one's particular department and firm. In effect we close our eyes to all work done by others.

The professional manager must learn to read and to make reading a part of his or her everyday operation. It is impossible to list all the books available in personnel management, or even a small fraction thereof. It would be equally impossible for the manager to read or even skim them all. Some services provided by such organizations as the American Management Associations will condense, summarize, and recommend publications to be read in the field of personnel. These should suggest the sources that the manager will find interesting and useful in the job of manager.

[6]Roberta J. Nelson, George W. England, and Dale Yoder, "Personnel Ratios, 1960: An Analytical Look." *Personnel*, November-December 1960, pp. 18–28.

Periodicals and magazines are an excellent source of research information and ideas. The following are some of the periodicals that are of general value in the personnel field:

Academy of Management Journal

Academy of Management Review

Across the Board

Administrative Science Quarterly

Advanced Management Journal

American Journal of Sociology

Arbitration Journal

Business Horizons

California Management Review

Compensation Review

Employment Service Review

Fortune

Harvard Business Review

Human Organization

Human Resource Management

Industrial and Labor Relations Review

Industrial Management Review

Industrial Psychology

Industrial Relations

Journal of Applied Behavioral Science

Journal of Applied Psychology

Journal of Industrial Psychology

Labor Law Journal

Management Review

Monthly Labor Review

Organizational Behavior and Human Per-
  formance

Organizational Dynamics

Personnel

Personnel Administrator

Personnel Journal

Personnel Management Abstracts

Personnel Psychology

Psychological Abstracts

Public Personnel Management

Supervision

Training and Development Journal

Research Methods

All research involves the application, in some manner, of the scientific method. There are various specific forms that individual research projects can take, among them (1) controlled experiments, (2) surveys, (3) historical studies, (4) case studies, and (5) simulations.

Controlled experiments   The controlled experiment is relatively rare as conducted by private concerns. Perhaps the most famous experiment of this type was the Hawthorne study of the Western Electric Company, begun in 1927. This study, conducted by Elton Mayo and his associates, was and is a classic in the field of personnel research. An earlier study, begun in 1924, was designed to isolate and discover the effect of lighting and other physical factors on employee output. Regardless of the level of lighting, output improved. These confusing results led to introduction of behavioral scientists from Harvard, and the study of the five ''girls'' in the relay assembly test room began. In this group there was an attempt to keep all variables constant and then to introduce one variation into the situation. The ensuing output result could, they thought, be attributed to the single variant factor. In this manner, changes that sought to introduce rest periods, new pay systems, different work schedules, and the like, led to immediate and significant improvements in group output. To validate further the discovered relationships between these variables and output, conditions were returned to their original status, in the expectation that productivity would drop. To everyone's surprise, output did *not* drop but continued to improve. Obviously, all the conditions of the experiment had not been rigidly controlled. What was not controlled were the minds and attitudes of the participant workers. They liked working in the experimental room with an observer rather than a supervisor; they felt rather important as a result of the special attention allocated and the involvement in decision making. Regardless of what was introduced, they attempted to produce more.

One of the continuing elements of this project that is reflected in all experiments is the so-called "Hawthorne effect." In analyzing results from the controlled introduction of a variable, one must be cautious in determining what degree of the result can be attributed to the experimenter or to the insertion of *anything new* into the environment. One must be careful in reaching conclusions about results from short-term studies where the "Hawthorne effect" may still be in operation. Other observers maintain that though this effect may have been present in the Hawthorne studies, the true cause of output improvement was the significant and real participation of the employees in making decisions about their work lives. Despite the contention of recent writers that the researchers departed from the scientific method and twisted their findings to favor the human component, these landmark experiments led to the development of a second school of management thought, the humanistic or behavioral approach.[7]

In setting up a controlled experiment, the simplest design would include (1) selection of an experimental group, (2) selection of an equivalent control group, (3) measurement of both groups prior to the experiment, and (4) measurement of both groups immediately after the experiment. If significant differences are discovered, these are attributed to the experimental variable. To determine the degree of contamination arising from the measurement process, additional experimental and control groups can be selected with only postexperiment measures being applied. A constant and major problem in all such efforts is the obtainment of equivalent groups whose membership is not significantly reduced from quits and transfers during the process of the experiment. This problem is particularly acute when the researcher wishes to introduce a "post-post" measurement some months later.

Surveys   The survey is a commonly used research method. It usually takes the form of a questionnaire or structured interview. Its object is to determine present practices or approaches and to attempt to relate certain results to particular causes. For example, we may wish to know certain things about employee profit sharing. Can such plans survive a profitless year? If so, how many profitless years? What can management do to help ensure survival? Certain hypotheses must be established around which survey questions can be phrased. Perhaps elaborate employee education will help the firm through the profitless years. Perhaps the payment of large regular shares will help do the job in times of crisis. Perhaps the use of the deferred type of plan will result in less employee objection when there are no profits to share. But maybe the deferred arrangement will also result in no additional effort on the part of the employee to ensure a profitable result in the next year.

These are some of the hypotheses that can be formulated concerning the factors that may determine employee reactions in profitless years. Now, what criteria can be established so that we can judge the correctness of such hypotheses? One criterion might be the objective evidence of continued operation of the plan during many profitless periods. Another criterion might be employee attitudes during these periods. A third might be measures of productivity during the profitless periods. At this point, the actual survey is taken. Companies are asked questions concerning the possible causes of, as well as the

---

[7]Alex Carey, "The Hawthorne Studies: A Radical Criticism," *American Sociological Review*, vol. 32, no. 3, 1967, pp. 403–416.

facts that will indicate employee reactions to, the absence of profits. Correlations between possible causes and observed effects are then computed. As a result, certain generalizations deducible from the survey study can be made. Examples of these are: (1) the greater the number of educational efforts, the more favorable the reaction of employees in terms of attitudes and productivity; (2) the larger the regular share paid, the greater the effort made by employees during the nonprofit period; and (3) the use of the deferred-distribution plan tends to result in no employee reaction, good or bad, during the nonprofit period.

Such generalizations can be of value in suggesting to the individual manager what one might do in reference to this particular problem. In effect, we propose to use the efforts of *many* companies that appear to have solved this problem successfully. An alternative approach is to select a smaller set of units or companies that have been matched on the bases of selected characteristics and degree of effectiveness. For example, we can compare the practices of six effective production units with those of six ineffective ones. In some projects it has been determined that effective units often follow a pattern of activities that is distinctly different from that followed by the ineffective units.

Historical studies   There is a wealth of useful information in the files of most firms, including valuable records about personnel. Suppose, for example, a manager wishes to do research on a problem of high labor turnover. He or she can study turnover experience on the basis of such variables as sex, age, department, home ownership, marital status, and stated cause for leaving. One may find, for example, that turnover is high among the very young, employees of department D, employees who rent their homes, and unmarried personnel. Such results may lead to a revision of procurement policies and further investigation, in greater detail, of discovered trouble spots. General Motors, for example, tracked 200 randomly selected new hires over a 6-month period. Results showed that persons with the lowest absenteeism rates were (1) oriented to their new jobs as individuals rather than in groups, and (2) assigned to an above-average operator for training rather than to one rated as average in performance.[8]

Case studies   The case-study approach is considered by many to be a separate method of research. Quite frequently, however, case studies result only in the creation of further hypotheses requiring additional research to validate. This method can be contrasted with the survey method. Surveys are usually extensive, in that a few carefully designed questions are asked of a large number of firms. Case studies are intensive, in that a great number of subjects are investigated in detail in a relatively limited number of firms. Complete case studies often suggest a great many more hypotheses than can be used by a single researcher as he prepares a survey questionnaire or designs a controlled experiment. Any conclusions drawn from a relatively limited number of case studies are, of course, of a highly tentative nature. The experiment in the test relay room at Hawthorne was followed by extensive observation of work behavior in the bank wiring room. From this intensive case study the concept of "informal organization" was developed.

Simulation   In recent years, simulation of performance has become an increasingly popular method of research in many fields. In political science, for example, there is some research through simulation to determine the factors affecting conflicts of interest

[8]Howard C. Carlson, "Organizational Research and Organizational Change: GM's Approach," *Personnel,* vol. 54, no. 4, July-August 1977, p. 15.

and possible means of reconciling and integrating these conflicts. A simulation of the world situation through the formation of nations with varying degrees of power and resources provides the stage for introducing new variables. For example, when power forces were more equally divided among these simulated nations, the ties of alliance began to break down. Similar simulations have been used in business environments for studying problems of production control, inventory control, purchasing, and marketing. Role playing is a specific type of performance simulation which has been used to research human behavior. The advances in computer technology will make possible greater use of business simulations to determine and predict the effect of introduced new variables.

Research Needs
in Personnel Management

There is literally no end to the number of things we need to know about personnel and personnel management. In this text we have attempted to survey the field in a broad fashion. The approach has been taken that *all* managers of necessity direct and manage personnel in addition to directing a particular technical function. The six operative personnel functions are fundamental and inescapable. Among the many items of information needed are the following:

1 Procurement
   a Interviews with higher reliabilities
   b Valid measures of personality
   c Valid measures of leadership potential
   d Better methods of establishing content validity of tests
   e Development of more realistic criteria for validating selection devices

2 Development
   a Valid measures of performance levels of employees
   b Bridging the gap between off-the-job development and on-the-job performance
   c Career development programs
   d Team and organization development
   e Coordinated and effective Management-by-Objective programs

3 Compensation
   a Determining impact of money on employee motivation to work
   b Coping with the effects of inflation
   c Cooperative exchange of wage and salary information
   d Implementing cafeteria-style fringe-benefit programs
   e Deriving more organizational value from fringe-benefit programs

4 Integration
   a Reducing employee alienation
   b Determining causes of declining productivity
   c Adapting to societal changes in customs, habits, and beliefs
   d Introducing constitutionalism into the private firm
   e Developing integrative collective bargaining with unions
   f Implementing and evaluating quality of worklife programs
   g Adapting quality circles to the competitive system

5 Maintenance
   a Setting appropriate environmental standards that protect both the physical and mental health of the employee and the economic health of the organization
   b Determining the human impact of all new technologies and products used in the industrial environment
   c Examining the impact of the workplace upon employee mental health
   d Establishing the role of counseling within a private organization
   e Reducing the number of communication filters in formal organizations

6 Separation
   a Developing more effective retirement counseling programs
   b Determining the full impact of the Employee Retirement Income Security Act upon private pension plans
   c Establishing white-collar security for blue-collar workers
   d Development of out-placement programs
   e Investigating the possibility of gradual phase-out of older workers

With respect to actual practice in personnel research, the survey of 44 companies by Byham revealed the following subjects were being actively researched: 98 percent were conducting research in selection, 75 percent in opinion measurement, 30 percent in training and development, 20 percent in appraisal, 18 percent in motivation, 16 percent in organizational effectiveness, and less than 10 percent in such areas as managerial obsolescence, counseling, and recruitment.[9] Berry's survey of 50 companies is in general agreement, with the 4 dominant subjects being selection, training and development, attitudes and leadership, and measurement devices.[10] In a third survey of 319 personnel administrators, the areas where they see the greatest usefulness of research are employee motivation (60 percent), managerial selection (59 percent), and managerial training (59 percent).[11] The single greatest need was for more useful research in motivation. The single smallest need was in job evaluation. Over three-quarters of these personnel managers believed that an industrial psychologist could increase productivity and satisfaction within their companies.

THE PERSONNEL MANAGER AS CHANGE AGENT

Assuming that research indicates that changes should be made in areas pertaining to personnel, the personnel manager must assume some responsibility for the effective introduction of change. It is one thing to intellectually determine that change is necessary and to lay out its dimensions. It is quite another to translate the plan into action.

In general, two basic approaches can be taken in effecting organizational changes. First, a change in *structure* and/or *technology* can be introduced, which brings consid-

[9]Byham, op. cit., p. 14.
[10]Berry, op. cit., p. 72.
[11]George C. Thornton, III, "Image of Industrial Psychology among Personnel Administrators," *Journal of Applied Psychology,* vol. 53, no. 5, October 1969, p. 437.

erable pressure to bear upon organizational members. If, for example, the content of a job is altered, a new machine purchased for use, or a new form designed for collecting control information, participants must respond in some manner to these objective changes. Second, a *therapeutic approach* can be taken, where organization members are counseled and encouraged to alter their behavior in line with some proposed model. Assuming, for example, that management concludes that the organization culture should be changed to one that is more trusting, supportive, authentic, and participative, change tactics of both types are often used. In the structural area, job enrichment, wider spans of control, and decentralization of authority have all been used to generate more real participation. In the therapeutic area, individual members have been sent to stranger "T-group" or sensitivity training sessions to stimulate more individual openness and supportiveness. Within the firm, organization development sessions with job-family groups have been held to stimulate teamwork and to work on interpersonal problems.

Arguments abound as to the most appropriate approach to effecting change. With the limited formal authority of staff personnel managers, there has been a considerable use of therapy rather than structural changes. It requires relatively little authority to implement training programs designed to affect attitudes. It requires a considerable amount of authority to alter the "guts" of the organization—its jobs, technology, and operating procedures. It is highly probable that structural changes are more lasting; there is less opportunity for backsliding. But certainly structural changes without some accompanying behavioral therapy are often nullified by informal deviations from the prescribed change.

The personnel manager as a change agent must move through the basic stages of change introduction. As outlined by Lewin, they are (1) unfreezing the present status quo, (2) moving to the new level of change, and (3) refreezing the organization at the new level. Each of the stages will be briefly discussed in the following sections.

Unfreezing the Status Quo

If people are not truly involved and committed to a proposed change, the long-term impact upon their behavior is likely to be minimal. Thus, the first stage in effecting changes is to generate self-doubts as to the appropriateness of present practices. Admittedly, a manager with authority can command that a change be effected and enforce its implementation through threats, punishments, close supervision, and the like. Once embarked on this road, the manager finds that continuation of the change demands constant and close surveillance. A more permanent and substantial change can be induced if the person truly wants and feels a need to change.

Generating receptivity to change often calls for pressures, both external and internal. External pressures from the environment are typically most powerful. If the firm is about to go out of business because of stringent competition, organization members are more inclined to receive and implement *any* change that has a chance of contributing to organizational survival. At times, personnel managers bring outside experts into the organization to generate self-doubts about current practice; for instance, assessment and normative evaluation of leadership styles by well-known consultants, such as Robert Blake and Rensis Likert, may lead to greater receptivity to change. Certainly, two of the major external sources of pressure of significance in the personnel field are government and the labor union. Personnel managers often point to legal requirements for changes in all the areas covered in this text—discrimination, safety and health, compensation, and so on. And the steady strong pressures of organized labor have led to a strengthening of the personnel manager as a change agent in the organization.

The personnel manager must also understand the necessity for obtaining top management support for changes proposed in his or her area. It is no accident that the first session of most training programs is attended and supported by significant higher officials. Systematic accumulation of operating and organizational data concerning performance will also help to convince participants of the desirability of change. In one instance, the personnel manager was convinced from such data that a change was necessary—more older females should be hired in the firm. Middle-level supervisors resisted and did not believe. Rather than argue, persuade, or threaten, the manager asked the supervisors to collect their own data, perhaps with the idea that older females should be avoided. When the data were collected, supervisors discovered, to their surprise, the same favorable situation as the personnel manager, and all resistance to the idea faded. Sometimes a "fact" is not a "fact" until one collects it oneself.

Finally, in unfreezing present behavior of people, it has been found that temporary isolation is often conducive to receptivity. Sensitivity training laboratories as well as team development sessions are usually conducted at a site apart from the workplace and at a time when only the one subject is being considered. Religious organizations as well as the military have discovered and utilized isolation as a means of opening up the person to change, as in basic training, monastic orders, and so on.

The Action Plan

If sufficient individual, group, or organization self-doubt has been generated, the personnel manager moves to the next stage—the change itself. Research as well as experience has demonstrated that the impact of change is more social and subjective than it is technical and objective. The first concern of most people is possible alterations in interpersonal and social relationships that the change will require. As a consequence, a significant role must be established for the changee in the creation of action plans. Plans that are technically perfect and not acceptable to those expected to carry them out are not likely to effect long-lasting results.

As outlined in Figure 24-1, the change agent can pursue a number of different strategies with varying advantages and drawbacks. These range from explicit coercion to participative involvement, with intermediate stops at education, facilitation, manipulation, and negotiation. The most effective strategies ususaly involve a reciprocal relationship between change agent and changee. Rather than a one-way flow of suggestions or commands, the change agent does well to observe the norm of reciprocity. The roles of agent and changee should be blurred, rather than sharp. Suggestions should be made on a tentative basis, and changees should be encouraged to contribute and participate in final determinations. In an analysis of eighteen studies of organization change by Greiner, it was discovered that successful changes utilized patterns involving sharing approaches—that is, change agents sought participation of changees in decision making.[12] In the less successful change attempts, the approaches were either highly autocratic or highly democratic.

The personnel manager as change agent can also make use of a number of organizational devices to encourage internal acceptance of the change. Guarantees of security to present personnel are often a requirement for effective acceptance; for example, no one will be laid off as a result of technological innovation, or base pay is guaranteed

---

[12]Larry E. Greiner, "Patterns of Organization Change," *Harvard Business Review,* vol. 45, no. 3, May-June 1967, pp. 120–122.

FIGURE 24-1
Methods for Dealing with Resistance to Change

Approach	Commonly Used in Situations	Advantages	Drawbacks
Education + communication	Where there is a lack of information or inaccurate information and analysis	Once persuaded, people will often help with the implemention of the change.	Can be very time-consuming if lots of people are involved
Participation + involvement	Where the initiators do not have all the information they need to design the change, and where others have considerable power to resist	People who participate will be committed to implementing change, and any relevant information they have will be integrated into the change plan.	Can be very time-consuming if participants design an inappropriate change
Facilitation + support	Where people are resisting because of adjustment problems	No other approach works as well with adjustment problems.	Can be time-consuming, expensive, and still fail
Negotiation + agreement	Where someone or some group will clearly lose out in a change, and where that group has considerable power to resist	Sometimes it is relatively easy way to avoid major resistance.	Can be too expensive in many cases if it alerts others to negotiate for compliance
Manipulation + co-optation	Where other tactics will not work, or are too expensive	It can be a relatively quick and inexpensive solution to resistance problems.	Can lead to future problems if people feel manipulated
Explicit + implicit coercion	Where speed is essential, and the change initiators possess considerable power	It is speedy, and can overcome any kind of resistance.	Can be risky if it leaves people mad at the initiators

Source: John P. Kotter and Leonard A. Schlesinger, "Choosing Strategies for Change," *Harvard Business Review*, vol. 57, no. 2, March-April 1979, p. 111. With permission.

when new incentive plans are introduced. Certainly, the personnel manager will have to work with and through the normal political processes of the organization. Superiors will have to be persuaded, interacting parallel staff units will have to be informed and coordinated, and the labor union cannot be ignored. Welcoming the union as a significant participant in proposed changes will do much to reduce real or pretended political resistance. The personnel manager should consider any resistance to change to be a "red flag" denoting need for investigation and analysis, rather than regarding it as a symbol of immaturity, "theory X," or chronic unenlightenment.

Like all specialists, the personnel manager must be wary of excessive personal ownership of change ideas. The "pet idea" can lead to minds closed to significant, or even minimal, alteration by others. Change introduction becomes one of "managing the personal image" rather than one of managing the process of change implementation. Finally, one must be ever on guard against apparent contradictions in philosophies. There have been various instances where participative management has been introduced in an autocratic manner. In effect, "This company is going to be managed in a democratic and participative manner, and those that don't like it can get out!" or "I order you to be independent!" If one subscribes to the concept that changees must truly want to change, then greater measures of patience and tolerance must be forthcoming.

Refreezing the New Status Quo

One of the early discoveries in sensitivity training was that the impact upon participants lasted only a short while after their return to the organization. The on-going culture of the operating organization was not supportive of the individually induced changes toward openness, empathy, and trust. Thus, attempts toward fundamental changes of this type in attitude and behavior inevitably lead to the conclusion that the total culture must be altered, thereby fostering an organization development approach. In some instances of job-enrichment structural changes, there was too little consideration of the impact of the changed job upon surrounding and interacting personnel and units. In one case, the supervisor felt that his job had been "raped," leaving him with little to do; he therefore reacted by practicing close supervision over the "enriched" incumbent in order to fill his time, thus generating a situation completely contrary to the philosophy of job enrichment. In another, the computer service center was totally unprepared to respond to new requests for information from incumbents on newly enriched jobs. It has been observed that profound and long-lasting changes are most likely to be effected if the total system can be designed from scratch. For example, the new plant built in Sweden by Volvo and at Topeka, Kansas, by General Foods involved total design, startup, and operation in a manner consistent with the behavioral, participative model. In this way, all of the interesting subsystems can be aligned to reflect the model desired; for example, all personnel use a single entrance, all park in the same lot, performance of operations is on a group basis, pay is allocated to groups, and so on. When attempting such changes in an existing plant, they tend to take the form of "paste-ons," which ultimately "fall off" if surrounding personnel and interacting systems are not intelligently attuned and aligned.

Finally, the change will be thoroughly digested only if the rewards system of the organization is geared to the new form of behavior. An employee's job may be substantially enriched in terms of content and self-supervision, but if the change is not accompanied by properly enriched pay, working conditions, and recognition, dissatisfaction is likely to ensue. Individuals and groups who comply with the change in spirit as well as deed must be recognized and rewarded by the organization.

CHALLENGES OF THE FUTURE

Contrary to the feeling of some that the personnel field is "bankrupt," we believe that increasing attention must and will be given to human problems in the years ahead. In a postindustrial society such as ours, human problems tend to take on greater degrees of importance and to occupy the center stage. On the basis of present trends and anticipated developments in the field of personnel management, we anticipate increased attention being allocated to the following:

1. Reducing employee alienation within organizations
2. Increasing human and organizational creativity and productivity
3. Expanded personnel manager roles in helping the private organization to meet its ever-increasing social responsibility
4. Expanded personnel manager roles in designing organizations

As Walton states, "Managers don't need anyone to tell them that employee alienation exists," as evidenced by "blue-collar blues," salaried dropouts, dislike of jobs, resentment of bosses, aggressive acts of sabotage and demonstrations, and escape through tardiness, absenteeism, turnover, and inattention to work.[13] The roots of this alienation lie in a clash between changes in basic social forces and the relatively few responding changes in design and management of organizations. Today's employees are better educated and more affluent; they display less obedience to arbitrary authority and greater concern for self-expression in place of competitive winning. On the other hand, typical organizations emphasize traditional career patterns, task specialization, authoritarian hierarchies, and monetary reward systems. Thus, a major challenge for the future is developing basic methods of reconciling clashes of values, thereby reducing the amount of employee alienation. The injection of constitutional rights of citizenship within the employing organization will help to reduce feelings of *helplessness*. The gradual movement toward job enrichment should assist in reducing feelings of *meaninglessness*. Facilitating the development of viable primary work groups should help reduce feelings of *normlessness*. Personnel managers must continue to seek approaches that will more effectively integrate human and organizational values.

Recent significant declines in the general level of productivity, accompanied by significant increases in the level of inflation, have highlighted an extremely serious need for greater productivity and creativity. Personnel managers have an obligation to help general management tap the vast reservoir of human capability that is present within all organizations. This would include not only moving to productivity bargaining with organized labor, but also promoting multiple and varied programs of real subordinate participation on real issues. Real participation on fake issues, and fake participation on real issues constitute pallid attempts at manipulative autocracy, thereby continuing the situation where the bulk of the burden for productivity rests solely on management. Personnel managers must continue to seek ways to involve the brains as well as the bodies of all organization members in the pursuit of meaningful organizational goals. This will entail serious examination of the quality of worklife within organizations, as well as study of ways in which such cooperative efforts as quality circles can be implemented in our type of society.

As suggested earlier in this text, the personnel manager has a considerable burden placed upon him or her in helping the private organization define and execute its proper social role in total society. Certainly, the unavoidable minimum is to comply with the continuing flow of social legislation designed to protect and promote the interests of society's citizens who happen to be organizational employees. The professional manager

---

[13]Richard E. Walton, "How to Counter Alienation in the Plant," *Harvard Business Review*, vol. 50, no. 6, November-December 1972, p. 70.

must go beyond this and propose programs and policies that meet social obligations that are not as yet defined by law. This is a difficult challenge inasmuch as he or she must do this while still recognizing the necessity of operating within the cost/effectiveness framework of a profit-seeking enterprise. Increased personnel research with respect to various social issues (employment of the culturally disadvantaged, employee freedom of speech, movement of females into responsible managerial positions, and so on) may well demonstrate a considerable overlapping of social interests *and* the economic interests of the firm.

If the above challenges are successfully met, it will undoubtedly have a considerable impact upon the design of organization structures. The personnel manager, who faces both outward to the social environment and inward to the technological environment, has skills and knowledge that can be utilized in creating organizational designs that can be effective on both fronts. The personnel unit already has expert knowledge about jobs through job analysis, and about personnel capabilities through various programs of hiring, training, and appraisal. Though the basic responsibility of organizational design must continue to rest with top managers, the personnel manager has an obligation to place this existing store of knowledge at their disposal, as well as to provide counsel and advice in aligning the basic organizational thrust with major trends in societal values.

With respect to what specific personnel practices are likely to develop further during the 1980s, a survey of 1,500 members of the American Society for Personnel Administration, as shown in Figure 24-2, indicates the views of the practitioner. All of the listed practices received 50 percent or greater agreement, with the greatest consensus being on the greater use of employee surveys, application of organization development to alter company climates, cutbacks in government spending, and a greater emphasis upon an employee ''bill of rights.'' With respect to the last item, the majority predict that mandatory retirement at any age will be made illegal, and that an employee privacy protection program will be required by law.[14]

SUMMARY

Systematic and purposive research is an obvious and continuing necessity in the field of personnel management. Exploratory and operational personnel research is done by such persons and institutions as colleges and universities, governmental agencies, private research organizations, personnel departments of private companies, and individual managers. Since the main variable in personnel research is that of people, it is very difficult to do exacting and lengthy research. Controlled experiments, surveys, historical studies, case studies, and simulations are five possible approaches to personnel research. There is much to be learned about the procurement, development, compensation, integration, maintenance, and separation of personnel. These fundamental functions are universal for all who propose to be managers.

When research develops results capable of utilization by the organization, the personnel manager's task is one of introducing change. All staff personnel must have skills of change introduction, and the personnel manager should again have an unusual expertise because of a basic understanding of people. The status quo must be unfrozen through the generation of doubt about current practices. Moving to the new level should entail

---

[14]Harold L. Schneider, ''Personnel Managers Look to the '80s, *''The Personnel Administrator,* vol. 24, no. 11, November 1979, p. 49.

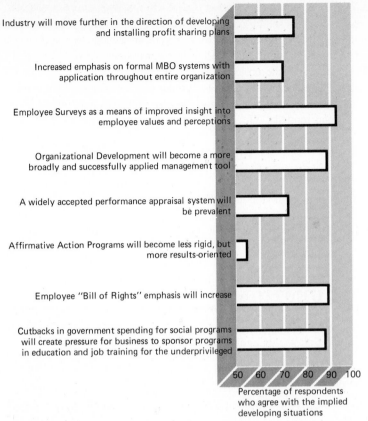

Percentage of respondents
who agree with the implied
developing situations

FIGURE 24-2 Predicted management practices in the 1980s. (*Source: Harold L. Schneider,
"Personnel Managers Look to the '80s." Reprinted from the November 1979 issue of* Personnel
Administrator, © *1979, The American Society for Personnel Administration, 30 Park Drive,
Berea, Ohio 44017, $30 per year.*)

significant changee participation to stimulate improvements, adaptations, and the acceptance necessary for effective implementation. The new level should then be refrozen
through various means, not the least of which is the organization's reward system.

Very serious challenges to the personnel manager exist in the future. There is
widespread concern for increased employee alienation and reduced productivity and creativity. Personnel managers have a special obligation to assist in coping with these essentially human problems. Perhaps the significant pressures issuing from basic social
forces will generate sufficient top management self-doubt to unfreeze the current status
quo and allow constructive changes to be introduced.

BRIEF CASE

A group of four private consultants was retained by the federal government to write a
new regulation governing the management of maintenance on air bases. Kent Clark, a
GS-16 in the Civil Service, heard of this effort and telephoned the group inviting them
to look at a new maintenance setup that he had installed at a Georgia air base. He said
that he had left the base some 4 weeks earlier, but would fly to Georgia from Washington,

D.C. to meet the team. Clark personally escorted the four to the base, and proceeded to outline the procedures involved in setting up a maintenance repair project. After explaining the route sheet, he led them into the next room where an airman was sitting at a desk. Clark gestured toward a huge chart covering the entire side of two walls in the room. He said, "Now, let's take the project listed on the second line. You see that it begins with its identifying number, followed by the proposed scheduled time for starting it. . . . Wait a minute! That doesn't make sense! Airman, what's going on with this control board?" The airman replied: "Oh, Mr. Clark, we stopped using this chart over three weeks ago."

Questions

1. Why did the military personnel stop using the chart immediately after the departure of Mr. Clark?

2. What methods of change introduction could Clark have used to insure that the change will continue to be implemented?

DISCUSSION QUESTIONS

1. If one wanted to be a personnel researcher in a large business or governmental organization, what type of academic preparation would be best? Why?

2. Suppose that you wanted to determine the effects of job enrichment on employee attitudes and output; describe how a controlled experiment could be set up.

3. Indicate how the objective in question 2 could be accomplished using a survey questionnaire.

4. You have been asked to determine why so many new employees quit during their first 6 months of employment. How would you find out?

5. What is the "Hawthorne effect"? How can its impact be reduced?

6. Cite one basic research need for each of the six functions of personnel.

7. In introducing change, contrast the structural with the therapeutic approach. Which is the personnel manager more likely to use?

8. Research in your firm has determined that more considerate supervisors will get better results. How would you go about unfreezing the status quo?

9. When executives who have been sent to sensitivity training return to the organization, how can we assure that what they have learned will be put to use?

10. Of the four major personnel challenges of the future, which do you think is most important? most difficult? Why?

SUPPLEMENTARY READING

ARVEY, RICHARD D. and PAMELA SHINGLEDECKER. "Research Methods in Personnel Management," in *Personnel Management*, Gerald R. Ferris and Kendrith M. Rowland (eds.), Allyn & Bacon, Inc., Boston, 1982, Chap. 2.

LUTHANS, FRED and TERRY L. MARIS: "Evaluating Personnel Programs through the Reversal Technique," *Personnel Journal*, vol. 58, no. 10, October 1979, pp. 692–697.

MEEHAN, ROBERT H.: "The Future Personnel Executive," *The Personnel Administrator*, vol. 26, no. 1, January 1981, pp. 25–28.

PETERS, THOMAS J.: "Management Systems: The Language of Organizational Character and Competence," *Organizational Dynamics*, vol. 9, no. 1, Summer 1980, pp. 3–26.

SHEPPARD, STEWART and DONALD C. CARROLL (eds.): *Working in the Twenty-First Century*, Philip Morris, Inc., New York, 1980.

TOEDTMAN, JAMES C.: "A Decade of Rapid Change: The Outlook for Human Resources Management in the '80s," *Personnel Journal*, vol. 59, no. 1, January 1980, pp. 29–35.

EXERCISE AND CASES FOR PART SEVEN

Exercise: Discharge*

The company: Ransom Meat Packers, Inc.
The union: Meat Workers of America, Local 231

On July 2, Charles Manton was suspended for striking and kicking his foreman. The foreman later recommended that he be discharged. This recommendation was reviewed and approved by the plant superintendent and other company representatives. On July 12, Manton was discharged. The case was appealed by the union to Francis X. Maguire, permanent arbitrator under the contract. The union had never previously protested the discharge of a worker for striking a superior.

Your task: Determine what additional information you require to determine whether or not the discharge is just. Your instructor will volunteer nothing. He will respond only to specific requests for information. This exercise illustrates that fact finding is just as important as fact analysis in making decisions.

Case: On Firing the Boss

Much to his dismay, Captain Joe Grant was transferred from a combat unit to the personnel division of a major U.S. Army Command Headquarters. Despite his disappointment and lack of experience in high-level personnel policy formulation, he worked hard to learn the new job and within 6 months was deemed to be one of the best research technicians in the division. Contributing to his success was his inclination toward and ability in making numerous informal contacts with influential people from other sections in headquarters. These relationships enabled him to get rapid interstaff support for his projects, and his boss, Major George Jones, often used him to get information to assist on other division projects. He was soon recognized by the commanding general as the command authority on his project subjects, and most of the time his recommendations became policy.

In appreciation for this quality performance, Major Jones permitted him several privileges not available to other personnel, such as not being required to sign in and out,

---

*Garret L. Bergen and William V. Haney, *Organizational Relations and Management Action*, McGraw-Hill Book Company, New York, 1966, p. 656. Used with permission.

being allowed to locate his desk where he wanted it, taking breaks and lunch period when desired, and so on. Other personnel in the division sometimes expressed open resentment of this favored treatment.

After Captain Grant had been on the job for 1 year, his boss was notified of an impending transfer to an overseas assignment. Major Jane Clark was transferred in as deputy to understudy Jones before his departure. When she was introduced to the division staff, she said, "Since we'll be working closely together, we can eliminate some of the formalities. Call me Jane. In my present capacity as deputy chief, I'll make some minor changes. Unlike Major Jones, I don't intend to actually work with you on any of your projects. My job is to supervise and I don't like being bothered with nitty-gritty details of problems you're having. I do expect, however, to get information from you before Major Jones or Colonel Johnson do. Do you have any questions?" There were no questions. Grant commented to a fellow worker that his major personnel allocation (PA) project required extensive overtime and much help from Major Jones if the deadline was to be met. He wondered how it would get out if he was to receive no help from Major Clark when she replaced Jones. This was one project that the commanding general always went over piece by piece.

In the days that followed, Major Clark began to clamp down on Captain Grant. She forced him to revise numerous letters with her preferred wording even though Grant and others believed that the fundamental meaning was unchanged. She commented on his special privileges. The next week, the new PA project came through and Major Jones made arrangements for Grant and himself to work overtime to meet the deadline. He also ordered Major Clark to help, but she showed up late and contributed little or nothing to the effort. She said, "I told both of you earlier that this will not be my job when I take over as chief."

On returning from leave 3 weeks later, Captain Grant found that Major Jones had left and Major Clark was in control. She told him, "I'm the chief now and I had better not see any more of your argumentative attitude. All of this unofficial coordination you do in headquarters staff has got to stop. You will sign in and sign out, and provide me with a written record of your conversations with other sections. Your special privileges are at an end." Captain Grant stated that he understood and began signing in and out for every observable movement including trips to the rest room. He still maintained his contacts with other section personnel and recorded them only when absolutely unavoidable.

Major Clark's personal attention to Captain Grant continued in the form of many specific orders. He was ordered to eat lunch on the job so that he might be available for consultation. He was required to take two 10-minute breaks at designated times. When he was absent for 2 days because of illness, all his accumulated work was piled on his desk. Though in the past under Major Jones other employees helped each other, Major Clark prohibited anyone from helping with Captain Grant's backlog. She began to assign many small jobs that normally would have been done by secretaries, such as cleaning out the office files, and getting Major Clark a new nameplate. She appointed him classified documents custodian, a task requiring extensive inventory of six office safes and updating the office publications library. Captain Grant maintained a careful written record of all such assignments including dates and amount of time to execute.

Captain Grant knew that it was time to begin preparing background data for the next PA, scheduled to arrive in 4 weeks. He did not tell Major Clark of this, and kept working diligently, but slowly, on the many small assignments given to him. The PA request arrived and was due to be submitted to the commanding general in 2 weeks. He took the project to Colonel Johnson, Clark's superior, and said, "Sir, it will take me 1 month to be ready for a PA briefing. I have no background data ready to use." Colonel Johnson said, "What in the hell have you been doing that kept you from getting the background? You know how important this is and here you tell me you're not ready!" Grant replied, "Yes, I know how important PA is but I guess Major Clark doesn't. Here's what she's had me doing for the past month and a half." With that, he put on the desk each of the written directions on the secretarial type of work that Major Clark had given him. After several minutes of uninterrupted profanity, Colonel Johnson dismissed Captain Grant with the admonition that he was expected to work nights and weekends to catch up. He then called Major Clark to his office. She was fired the next day.

Questions

1. What are the sources of power of Captain Grant and Major Clark?

2. How do the tactics of Captain Grant compare with those of Major Clark?

3. Should one ever undertake the task of getting a boss fired?

Case: The Disgruntled Researcher

The Hartley Manufacturing Company is a nationwide concern engaged in producing and distributing electrical products of various types. There are several factories scattered throughout the United States. Recently the personnel division of the home office has undertaken the task of analyzing and describing middle-management jobs throughout the company. The information gathered is to be used primarily in selecting and training persons for these crucial positions. It is part of a broader executive inventory and development program designed to provide a continuing and adequate supply of middle-management talent.

George Hoskins, the head of the personnel research section, was given the responsibility of assembling a team of job and organization analysts to undertake this research project. He got together a team of five persons, all possessing master's degrees and showing indications of high general ability. These five persons were given an intensive training program in job analysis, management principles and policies, and the organization structure of Hartley Company. The immediate objective for the team was to prepare job descriptions of managerial jobs. There seemed to be little knowledge available about managerial job analysis, and the group, under the guidance of Hoskins, worked to develop a standard approach and, insofar as possible, a list of standard attributes of middle-management jobs. Each analyst would then utilize this approach and outline as he interviewed job incumbents and prepared written job descriptions. The difficulty of the analysis involved was highly variable, depending upon the nature and complexity of the job being analyzed. It was difficult for Hoskins to control closely the work of these analysts because of the variable, subjective, and inexact nature of the process. This difficulty was compounded because of the necessity for frequent trips to the field by the analysts, separately at times, often as a group under Hoskins' direct supervision. In view of these situations, Hoskins had purposely hired top-notch personnel, who would require little supervision.

The five analysts on the team were Wilma Hansen, Joe Gordon, Howard Finley, Ronald Peters, and George Halton. They all seemed to get along very well, and Hoskins was proud of his work team and its efforts. There seemed to be few human relations problems.

The remainder of this report is in the words of George Halton.

"In general, we seem to have a pretty good group of guys on this job. The work is very interesting and you have a lot of freedom. But there is one thing about it that bothers me—Howard Finley. Howard is a very nice fellow. I like him personally. He has a good sense of humor, but he is—well—he's a 'goof-off.' While the rest of us are slaving away on job descriptions, he is striding up and down the aisle of the office, reading Shakespeare in loud, resonant tones. At times, he evens attempts to improve upon portions of the Bard's works in a humorous way, and we all greatly enjoy his antics. Yet I think all of us—Ron, Wilma, and myself for sure—are irritated with the small amount of work he turns out. He always has a good story for Hoskins, and I know that the work is hard to evaluate. The thing that gripes us most is that he gets the same pay as all the rest of us. I really don't think Hoskins knows what is going on. None of us feel like laying it on the line. We are all just generally disgruntled. Ron and I have deliberately cut down a third or so on the amount of work we are turning out. Even at that we're doing more than Howard is. Yet, I don't want to do anything to jeopardize my future in Hartley. I guess I need some advice."

Questions

1. Why does Hoskins provide so much freedom for this group of researchers? Could he introduce more controls?

2. What alternatives are open to George Halton?

Name Index

Subject Index